T0091593

World Scientific Proceedings Series on
Computer Engineering and Information Science 13

Machine Learning, Multi Agent and Cyber Physical Systems

Proceedings of the 15th International FLINS Conference (FLINS 2022)

World Scientific Proceedings Series on Computer Engineering
and Information Science

Series ISSN: 1793-7868

Founding Editor: Da Ruan *(Belgian Nuclear Research Centre (SCK.CEN) &
Ghent University, Belgium)*
Series Editor: Jie Lu *(University of Technology Sydney, Australia)*

Published:

For the complete list of titles in this series, please visit
http://www.worldscientific.com/series/wspsceis

World Scientific Proceedings Series on
Computer Engineering and Information Science 13

Machine Learning, Multi Agent and Cyber Physical Systems

Proceedings of the 15th International FLINS Conference (FLINS 2022)

Tianjin, China   26–28 August 2022

editors

Qinglin Sun
Nankai University, China

Jie Lu
University of Technology, Sydney, Australia

Xianyi Zeng
ENSAIT, University of Lille Nord de France, France

Etienne E Kerre
University of Ghent, Belgium

Tianrui Li
Southwest Jiaotong University, China

World Scientific

EW JERSEY · LONDON · SINGAPORE · BEIJING · SHANGHAI · HONG KONG · TAIPEI · CHENNAI

Published by

World Scientific Publishing Co. Pte. Ltd.

5 Toh Tuck Link, Singapore 596224

USA office: 27 Warren Street, Suite 401-402, Hackensack, NJ 07601

UK office: 57 Shelton Street, Covent Garden, London WC2H 9HE

British Library Cataloguing-in-Publication Data
A catalogue record for this book is available from the British Library.

**World Scientific Proceedings Series on Computer Engineering and
Information Science — Vol. 13**
MACHINE LEARNING, MULTI AGENT AND CYBER PHYSICAL SYSTEMS
Proceedings of the 15th International FLINS Conference (FLINS 2022)

ISBN 978-981-126-925-7 (hardcover)
ISBN 978-981-126-926-4 (ebook for institutions)
ISBN 978-981-126-927-1 (ebook for individuals)

For any available supplementary material, please visit
https://www.worldscientific.com/worldscibooks/10.1142/13231#t=suppl

Preface

FLINS, an acronym originally for Fuzzy Logic and Intelligent Technologies in Nuclear Science, was launched by Prof. Da Ruan of the Belgian Nuclear Research Center (SCK·CEN) in 1994 in order to give PhD and Postdoc researchers the opportunity to carry out future-oriented research. For more than 28 years FLINS has been extended to include the theoretical and practical development of computational intelligent systems.

FLINS2022 follows a successful conferences series: FLINS1994 and FLINS1996 in Mol, FLINS1998 in Antwerp, FLINS2000 in Bruges, FLINS2002 in Gent, FLINS2004 in Blankenberge, FLINS2006 in Genova, FLINS2008 in Marid, FLINS2010 in Chengdu, FLINS2012 in Istanbul, FLINS2014 in Juan Pesoa, FLINS2016 in Roubaix, FLINS2018 in Belfast and FLINS2020 in Cologne. FLINS2022 is organized by Nankai University, and co-organized by Southwest Jiaotong University, University of Technology Sydney and Ecole Nationale Supérieure des Arts et Industries Textiles, and University of Lille. It offers a unique international research forum to present and discuss newly-developed ideas, theories, techniques and systems for machine learning, multi agent and cyber physical systems.

As an internationally reputed researcher, Prof. Da Ruan founded the FLINS conferences series and, through these conferences, created a worldwide and multidisciplinary consortium of research on computational intelligence. After his pass-away in 2011, his successors, including the organizers of FLINS2012, FLINS2014, FLINS2016, FLINS2018, FLINS2020 and FLINS2022 have followed his spirit of opening, collaboration and innovation, and continued to consolidate and enlarge this research consortium by developing new theories and applications in computational intelligence and extend in its scope.

As previous conferences, FLINS2022 aims at providing an international platform that brings together researchers in mathematics, AI, computer science, information technology and engineering, actively involved in machine learning, intelligent systems, data analysis, knowledge engineering and their applications, to report their latest innovations and developments, summarize the state-of-the-art, and exchange their ideas and progress. Research areas involve industrial microgrids, intelligent wearable systems, sustainable development, logistics, supply chain and production optimization, evaluation systems and performance analysis, as well as risk and security management.

The FLINS2022 Proceedings consists of five invited lectures by distinguished researchers and 78 conference papers from 16 countries, such as Australia, UK, Germany, France and Spain. The five invited lecturers are 1) *Autonomous and Cooperative Decision-Making in Cyber-Physical Systems*, by Olaf Stursberg from University of Kassel; 2) *Coping with Misinformation Online: Open Issues and Challenges*, Gabriella Pasi from University of Milano-Bicocca; 3) *Toward the "all-inclusive" concept for future human-IA systems*, by Frédéric Vanderhaegen from Université Polytechnique Hauts-de-France; 4) *Automatic SCNT and its application in Animal Cloning*, by Prof. Xin Zhao from Nankai University; 5) *Recent Advances in Evolutionary Transfer Optimization*, by Kay Chen Tan from The Hong Kong Polytechnic University.

Moreover, the contributions of the seven special sessions are playing an important role in FLINS2022. These special sessions are 1) Evolving Deep and Transfer Learning Models for Computer Vision and Medical Imaging, 2) Applications, Theories and New Trends for Networked Systems, 3) Intelligent wearable systems and computational techniques, 4) Decision making under uncertainty: emerging topics and applications, 5) Computational Techniques Based Intelligent Manufacturing Systems in Process Industry, 6) Computational Intelligence for Sustainability, and 7) Advances in Reasoning Based Rational Decision Making.

The accepted regular papers of the conference proceedings are organized as follows. The first part of this book deal with the new developments on intelligent methods, including machine learning, intelligent systems, and knowledge engineering. Part 2 presents multi agent systems, neural networks and image processing. Risk analysis and multi-criteria evaluation methods are presented in Part 3. Researches on intelligent wearable systems and advanced computations for sustainable development are given in Part 4. And the last part is about the methods of feature classification and data processing.

We wish to express our special gratitude to all authors, referees, special sessions organizers, all session chairs, and members of the International Committee of FLINS2022 for their kind cooperation and contributions for the success of the Conference.

Editors

Qinglin Sun
Jie Lu
Xianyi Zeng
Etienne E Kerre
Tianrui Li

Contents

Part 1: Intelligent Systems and Knowledge Engineering

Part 2: Multi Agent Systems, Neural Networks and Image Analysis

Part 3: Risk Analysis and Multi-criteria Evaluation

Part 4: Intelligent Wearable Systems and Advanced Computations for Sustainable Development

Part 5: Feature Classification and Data Processing

Part 1

Intelligent Systems and Knowledge Engineering

Prior knowledge modeling for joint intent detection and slot filling

Chunning Hou, Jinpeng Li, Hang Yu*, Xiangfeng Luo and Shaorong Xie

School of Computer Engineering and Science, Shanghai University
Shanghai, China
*yuhang@shu.edu.cn
{houchunning, lijinpeng, luoxf, srxie}@shu.edu.cn
www.shu.edu.cn

Spoken Language Understanding (SLU), which is a crucial part of spoken dialogue systems, includes slot filling (SF) and intent detection (ID) tasks which are a high degree of correlation and influence each other. A joint learning model can share information between SF and ID to effectively improve experimental results. However, most exciting models do not use the information between SF and ID, making the model perform poorly. In this paper, we propose a novel based on the prior knowledge joint learning model for better utilizing the semantic information between SF and ID. The experimental results on three public datasets show that based on prior knowledge joint learning model can better express sentence semantic information and improve the accuracy of the ID and SF tasks.

Keywords: Spoken language understanding; slot filling; intent detection; prior knowledge.

1. Introduction

Intent detection and slot filling are two crucial steps for spoken language understanding, and the results of ID and SF can also affect the overall accuracy of the spoken dialogue system. Take a buying rail ticket utterance as an example, which is shown in Fig. 1. ID works at the sentence level to indicate the task is about purchasing a rail ticket, while the slot filling works at the level of the words to find out where the departure and destination of the ticket are Beijing and Shanghai.

Traditional methods consider ID and SF as two independent tasks. However, there is a high correlation between ID and SF, and not independent of each other, which cannot neglect to share information across the two tasks. The research fronts are to develop a joint model[1,2] which can share information for ID and SF tasks.[3-5]

4

Sentence:	Buy	a	high-speed	rail	ticket	from	Beijing	to	Shanghai
	↓	↓	↓	↓	↓	↓	↓	↓	↓
SF	O	O	O	O	O	O	B-departure	O	B-destination
ID	purchase_rail_ticket								

Fig. 1.   An example utterance with SF sequence labeling in IOB format and ID, B-departure and B-destination represent the departure and destination.

In this study, we propose a based on the prior knowledge joint learning model (PKJL) for better utilizing the semantic information between SF and ID. The main idea is to capture semantic relationships among SF tags and ID labels directly. We find SF tags and ID labels appear together, as shown in Fig. 2. Therefore, the association between SF and ID can improve the results of ID and SF. So, the relationships between ID labels and SF tags make up the prior knowledge introduced into the information integration unit (IIU) to enhance the experimental results.

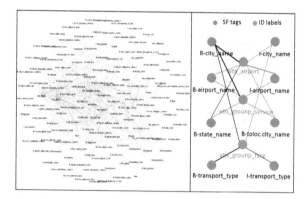

Fig. 2.   The statistical association of SF tags and ID labels (on the left) is the ATIS, where lines of different colors represent the relationships between SF tags and ID labels. The thicknesses of lines indicate the degree to which SF tags and ID labels (on the right) are associated.

We conduct experiments on three benchmarks: SNIPS,[6] ATIS,[7] and CAIS[8] datasets. The results of both experiments show the effectiveness of our framework by outperforming the current state-of-the-art methods by a large margin. Our contributions are summarized as follows:

- Our PKJL-Model show the prior knowledge can be introduced successfully, and the experimental results prove the validity of the model.

- The structure of our model is more accessible than the existing model, indicating that our model can be used in academia and industry areas.
- The experimental results show the PKJL-Model can enhance the overall recognition accuracy of sentences.

2. Related Work

SLU includes intent detection task and slot filling task, which early methods modeled these two tasks independently. However, those methods increase the error propagation in SLU tasks in a pipeline. Recently, more and more studies have been proposed to model the interaction between ID and SF tasks. Li[9] proposed a self-attention and gating mechanism model to utilize intent information as a gate to guide the learning of slot filling. Niu[10] proposed a bi-directional interrelated mechanism for ID and SF to increase the performance. These two studies are similar but with certain limitations. The gate mechanism does not further enhance the experimental effect. Liu[8] proposed a Collaborative Memory Network to build a joint model to address the ID and SF task. However, this method still doesn't capture more semantic features very well. Zhang[11] used a Graph-LSTM model to learn the node represent and deal with the SF and ID. Qin[4] introduced a co-interactive transformer model to build a bi-directional connection to tackle SLU tasks. Compared with SLU in English, Chinese SLU is also a hugely challenging task. Teng[3] introduced a multi-level word adapter to address the Chinese SLU tasks. In contrast with their work, we explore prior knowledge, which is an alternative route, on how to get it and how to use it and build an effective model to tackle the English SLU and Chinese SLU tasks.

3. Method

3.1. Encoder layer

As shown in Fig. 3, the model architecture mainly consists of an encoder layer, an information integration layer, and a decoder layer. The encoder layer mainly comprises two parts, which are word embedding and BiLSTM. Word embedding maps the words in the text to a vector of real numbers, which makes it easy for the computer to perform calculations and speeds up the experiment. For the word sequence $X = \{x_1, x_2, x_3, \ldots, x_t\}$ (t is the length of tokens), the word embedding maps the word sequence to vectors, and then it serves as the input of the BiLSTM neural network. BiLSTM neural network, which can get more information better than LSTM, captures context semantic features hidden states $H = \{h_1, h_2, h_3, \ldots, h_n\}$ (n is

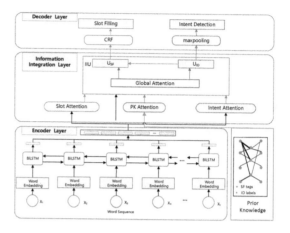

Fig. 3. The architecture of the proposed prior knowledge joint model.

the number of hidden states), $h_i = BiLSTM(emb(x_i, h_{i-1}))(emb(\cdot)$ represents the word embedding function). Hidden states H serve as the input of the Information Integration Layer, which provides basic semantic features.

The prior knowledge part discusses how to get prior knowledge from the dataset. By observing the ATIS dataset and SNIPS dataset, we find that there is a certain correlation between SF tags and ID labels. We propose two hypotheses, one is to calculate the probability of SF_tag when ID_label is given $P_{SF|ID}(SF|ID)$, and the other is to calculate the probability of ID_label when SF_tag is given $P_{ID|SF}(ID|SF)$ as below:

$$P_{SF|ID}(SF|ID) = \frac{res_{SF}^t}{\sum res_{SF}^t} \tag{1}$$

$$P_{ID|SF}(ID|SF) = \frac{res_{ID}^m}{\sum res_{ID}^m} \tag{2}$$

where res_{SF}^t and res_{ID}^m represent the number of times SF_tag and ID_label appear together. t represents one of the SF tags. And m represents one of the ID labels.

3.2. Information integration layer

The information integration layer is mainly the cross-task sharing of knowledge between SF, ID and prior knowledge to improve the accuracy of SF and ID tasks. Attention mechanism[12] allows the model to focus on important information and fully learn and absorb it. There are three attention parts in this part which are ID attention ID_{atten}, SF attention SF_{atten} and prior knowledge attention PK_{atten} as below:

$$Atten(H, W) = \sum H \frac{exp(tanh(W_1H + b_1)^T W_2)}{\sum exp(tanh(W_1H + b_1)^T W_2)} \tag{3}$$

$$ID_{atten} = Atten(H, W_{ID}) \tag{4}$$

$$SF_{atten} = Atten(H, W_{SF}) \tag{5}$$

$$PK_{atten} = Atten((H + P_{SF|ID} + P_{ID|SF}), W) \tag{6}$$

where $Atten(\cdot)$ represents the attention function. W, W_1, W_2, W_{ID}, W_{SF} are the corresponding trainable parameters. H is the hidden states.

The IIU part, which is the core of the PKJL-Model, can realize the information sharing and integration between ID, SF and prior Knowledge. There are three modules, which are global attention, U_{ID} and U_{SF} in the IIU part.

$$Global_{atten} = Atten((H + ID_{atten} + SF_{atten} + PK_{atten}), W) \tag{7}$$

$$U_{ID} = selu(ID_{atten} + matmul(PK_{atten} + Global_{atten}, W)) \tag{8}$$

$$U_{SF} = selu(SF_{atten} + U_{ID} + matmul(PK_{atten} + Global_{atten}, W)) \tag{9}$$

where $selu(\cdot)$ is a kind of activation function, which is used to increase the nonlinear variation. W is the corresponding trainable parameters. $matmul$ is a multiplicative function.

3.3. Decoder layer

To get sufficient interaction between the two tasks, the decoder layer uses different ways to deal with the two tasks. For the intent detection task, which is essentially a text classification problem, the $maxpooling(\cdot)$ is used to generate scores for each intent label. The $max(\cdot)$ is used to select the largest of the scores, and get y_{ID_lable}. For the slot filling task, which is a sequence labeling problem, it needs to consider the relationships between the tags in neighborhoods. Therefore, the $MLP(\cdot)$, which is multilayer perceptron that is used to decode the U_{SF} information, and the conditional random fields $CRF(\cdot)$ are applied to decode the sequence of tags about the sentence utterance.

$$y_{ID\_lable} = max(maxpooling(U_{ID} + H)) \tag{10}$$

$$y_{SF\_tag} = CRF(MLP(U_{SF}) + H) \tag{11}$$

4. Experiments

We choose three public datasets, the ATIS dataset, the SNIPS, and the CAIS which are widely used in the SLU field. Through our observation of these three data sets, we find that there are obvious differences between the three. The comparison between the three datasets can be found in Table 1. We apply three evaluation metrics for ID and SF tasks in the experiments. The accuracy is utilized for the ID task. The F1 score is used for the SF task. The sentence accuracy is used to evaluate the general performance of both tasks in a sentence. Only when the two tasks of SF and ID are accurately predicted the sentence simultaneously is considered correct.

Table 1. Dataset statistics.

Dataset	ATIS	SNIPS	CAIS
Vocab Size	722	11241	2146
Intent	21	7	13
Slot	120	72	76
Training Set Size	4478	13084	7995
Validation Set Size	500	700	994
Test Set Size	893	700	1011
Class distribution	Imbalanced	Balanced	Imbalanced

Experimental results on the single-turn SLU dataset ATIS, SNIPS, and CAIS are shown in Table 2. We have the following observations: (1) Attention mechanism is used to capture semantic information, which allows the PKJL-Model to focus on information from different parts and better comprehend the speech. (2) IIU is used to realize the information sharing and integration between ID, SF, and prior knowledge, which makes the PKJL-Model can improve the results of experiments. (3) The large vocabulary of the SNIP dataset and the broader domain covered caused the experimental results not to achieve more excellent results. However, the model has better performance in other datasets. The ablation study is used to evaluate the effectiveness of the PKJL-Model. Removing different parts proves that each part is indispensable in the model, which shows the effectiveness of our model.

Table 2. Performance comparison on the ATIS, SNIPS and CAIS datasets.

Model	ATIS			SNIPS			CAIS		
	ID (AC)	SF (F1)	Sen. (AC)	ID (AC)	SF (F1)	Sen. (AC)	ID (AC)	SF (F1)	Sen. (AC)
SF-ID[10]	97.1	95.8	86.	97.3	92.2	80.4	-	-	-
CM[8]	96.1	95.6	85.3	98.0	93.4	84.1	94.6	86.2	-
Stack[13]	96.9	95.9	86.5	98.0	94.2	86.9	-	-	-
Graph[11]	97.2	95.9	87.6	98.3	95.3	89.7	-	-	-
Interactive[4]	97.7	95.9	87.4	98.8	95.9	90.3			
Word[3]	-	-	-	-	-	-	95.2	88.6	86.2
PKJL	97.4	97.3	89.8	98.7	94.7	88.4	95.5	89.9	84.5
Ablation Experiments									
GA (w/o)	95.9	94.5	89.5	97.4	93.2	85.3	94.5	85.6	84.7
PK(w/o)	96.4	94.9	89.7	97.4	94.2	87.3	94.2	86.3	85.0
IIU(w/o)	96.9	97.1	89.4	97.3	93.8	85.6	94.9	88.8	83.8
PKJL	97.4	97.3	89.8	98.7	94.7	88.4	95.5	89.9	84.5

5. Conclusion

This study proposes a novel explicit joint modeling PKJL-Model to address SF and ID tasks. We build the prior knowledge that can be understood and calculated by mining the relationship between ID labels and SF tags. Meanwhile, the framework of the model enhances the ability to share and express semantic information. The experimental results prove that prior knowledge and the framework of the PKJL-Model can effectively improve the accuracy of the model.

Acknowledgments

The research reported in this paper was supported in part by the National Natural Science Foundation of China under the grant 91746203 and the Outstanding Academic Leader Project of Shanghai under the grant No. 20XD1401700.

References

1. L. Qin, T. Xie, W. Che and T. Liu, A survey on spoken language understanding: Recent advances and new frontiers, *arXiv preprint arXiv:2103.03095* (2021).
2. Y. Y. Zhao, Z. Y. Wang, P. Wang, T. Yang, R. Zhang and K. Yin, A survey on task-oriented dialogue systems, *Chinese Journal of Computers* **43**, 1862 (2020).

3. D. Teng, L. Qin, W. Che, S. Zhao and T. Liu, Injecting word information with multi-level word adapter for chinese spoken language understanding, in *ICASSP 2021-2021 IEEE International Conference on Acoustics, Speech and Signal Processing (ICASSP)*, 2021.

4. L. Qin, T. Liu, W. Che, B. Kang, S. Zhao and T. Liu, A co-interactive transformer for joint slot filling and intent detection, in *ICASSP 2021-2021 IEEE International Conference on Acoustics, Speech and Signal Processing (ICASSP)*, 2021.

5. C. Zhang, Y. Li, N. Du, W. Fan and P. S. Yu, Joint slot filling and intent detection via capsule neural networks, *arXiv preprint arXiv:1812.09471* (2018).

6. A. Coucke, A. Saade, A. Ball, T. Bluche, A. Caulier, D. Leroy, C. Doumouro, T. Gisselbrecht, F. Caltagirone and T. Lavril, Snips voice platform: an embedded spoken language understanding system for private-by-design voice interfaces, *arXiv preprint arXiv:1805.10190* (2018).

7. G. Tur, D. Hakkani-Tür and L. Heck, What is left to be understood in ATIS?, in *2010 IEEE Spoken Language Technology Workshop*, 2010.

8. Y. Liu, F. Meng, J. Zhang, J. Zhou, Y. Chen and J. Xu, Cm-net: A novel collaborative memory network for spoken language understanding, *arXiv preprint arXiv:1909.06937* (2019).

9. C. Li, L. Li and J. Qi, A self-attentive model with gate mechanism for spoken language understanding, in *Proceedings of the 2018 Conference on Empirical Methods in Natural Language Processing*, 2018.

10. P. Niu, Z. Chen and M. Song, A novel bi-directional interrelated model for joint intent detection and slot filling, *arXiv preprint arXiv:1907.00390* (2019).

11. L. Zhang, D. Ma, X. Zhang, X. Yan and H. Wang, Graph lstm with context-gated mechanism for spoken language understanding, in *Proceedings of the AAAI Conference on Artificial Intelligence*, 2020. Issue: 05.

12. V. Mnih, N. Heess and A. Graves, Recurrent models of visual attention, in *Advances in Neural Information Processing Systems*, 2014.

13. L. Qin, W. Che, Y. Li, H. Wen and T. Liu, A stack-propagation framework with token-level intent detection for spoken language understanding, *arXiv preprint arXiv:1909.02188* (2019).

Distributed adaptive virtual impedance control for power sharing in industrial microgrids with complex impedances*

Peng Zhao, Kai Ma†, Jie Yang and Shiliang Guo

Key Lab of Industrial Computer Control Engineering of Hebei Province
Yanshan University, Qinhuangdao, Hebei 066004, China
†*kma@ysu.edu.cn*
www.ysu.edu.cn

Microgrid technology provides an effective solution for industrial flexible electricity consumption and promotes the utilization of renewable energy. In this paper, to achieve the active and reactive power sharing in industrial microgrids with complex impedances, a distributed adaptive virtual impedance control method is proposed. For the power coupling, an impedance-power droop equation is proposed to generate virtual resistance and inductance, thereby eliminating the effect of mismatches among line impedances. It is highly resilient to power and line changes in industrial scenarios. On this basis, the practical consensus is used to obtain the desired power representing power sharing conditions. Finally, simulations have been carried out in MATLAB/Simulink to illustrate the validity of theoretical results.

Keywords: Power sharing; complex impedance; virtual impedance; practical consensus.

1. Introduction

Industrial microgrids (IMGs) based on distributed generation (DG) have been widely studied for their functional properties of local consumption of renewable energy and flexible power supply in recent years. An IMG is an autonomous system with two operating modes: grid-connected and islanded [1]. The output characteristics of DGs are regulated by inverters, and communication-free droop control is commonly used to achieve plug-and-play and self-regulation of DGs in islanded mode. Droop control requires a single inductive or resistive line impedance to decouple power [2]. However, the resistive and inductive components coexist in line impedances. In fact, complete power decoupling is difficult to achieve. Furthermore, the line impedances corresponding to each DG are

---

*This work was supported in part by the National Key R&D Project of China under Grant 2018YFB1702300; in part by the National Natural Science Foundation of China under Grant 62122065 and Grant 61973264; in part by S&T Program of Hebei under Grant F2020203026, Grant F2021203075, Grant 216Z1601G, Grant 226Z4501G, and Grant 22567612H.

unequal due to the geographical dispersion of DGs. As a result, the load power cannot be shared by DGs proportionally, resulting in a circulating current among DGs and jeopardizing the safety of IMG systems.

To achieve accurate power sharing, [3] and [4] proposed an injection signal method containing power information to eliminate the effects of unequal line impedances. But the injected signal was also a disturbance to microgrid voltage, which reduced the system stability and power quality. A method based on virtual negative resistance and virtual power was proposed in [5] to accomplish power decoupling and sharing. However, it requires knowledge of line physical parameters and cannot dynamically adapt to power changes.

The development of cyber-physical system (CPS) technology provides more possibilities for microgrid control. [6] proposed an adaptive virtual impedance control strategy based on consensus theory. The disadvantage is that it is difficult to adjust control gains, and it is only suitable for inductive lines. For complex line impedance, the authors in [7] and [8] obtain virtual resistance and inductance simultaneously by using the relationship between line impedance and output power to achieve active and reactive power sharing, but it cannot adapt to line changes.

Based on the above works, this paper aims to solve the power sharing problem in islanded IMGs with complex line impedances. To this end, an impedance-power droop equation method is proposed to adaptively adjust the virtual impedance and inductance, further realizing active and reactive power sharing. The proposed method can adapt not only to power changes, but also to line changes, such as microgrid reconfiguration and line faults. In addition, it eliminates the need for knowledge of hard-to-measure line physical parameters. At the same time, the practical consensus is applied to obtain the desired power under the concept of CPS, which does not need to adjust control gains and is easy to apply to practical IMG systems.

The rest of this paper is organized as follows: Section 2 designs a distributed adaptive impedance-power control method. Section 3 shows the simulation verification. Section 4 gives the conclusion.

2. Distributed Adaptive Virtual Impedance Control Method

This section discusses two aspects of local control and distributed coordination.

2.1. *Adaptive impedance-power droop equation*

The parallel DG transmission model is modeled as Fig. 1. The inverters are equivalent to voltage sources and transmit power to common bus through complex line impedances. For the ith DG, U_i and E are the amplitudes of output voltage and bus voltage, respectively, and δ_i is the phase angle between them. $Z_i\angle\theta_i = R_i + jX_i$ is line complex impedance of the ith feeder, and $P_i + jQ_i$ is output power transmitted by DG$_i$.

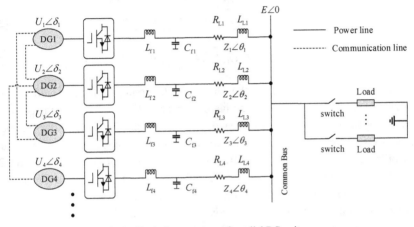

Fig. 1. Single-bus structure of parallel DG units.

With $Z_i\angle\theta_i = R_i + jX_i$,the relationship between power and line resistance and inductive reactance is obtained as Eq. (1).

$$\begin{bmatrix} P_i \\ Q_i \end{bmatrix} = U_i \begin{bmatrix} U_i - E\cos\delta_i & E\sin\delta_i \\ -E\sin\delta_i & U_i - E\cos\delta_i \end{bmatrix} \begin{bmatrix} \dfrac{R_i}{R_i^2 + X_i^2} \\ \dfrac{X_i}{R_i^2 + X_i^2} \end{bmatrix}. \tag{1}$$

$$R_i = \frac{U_i\left(U_i^2 - 2U_iE\cos\delta_i + E^2\right)\left[\left(U_i - E\cos\delta_i\right)P_i - E\sin\delta_i\cdot Q_i\right]}{\left[\left(U_i - E\cos\delta_i\right)P_i - E\sin\delta_i\cdot Q_i\right]^2 + \left[E\sin\delta_i\cdot P_i + \left(U_i - E\cos\delta_i\right)Q_i\right]^2} \tag{2}$$
$$= f\left(P_i, Q_i, E\right),$$

$$X_i = \frac{U_i\left(U_i^2 - 2U_iE\cos\delta_i + E^2\right)\left[E\sin\delta_i\cdot P_i + \left(U_i - E\cos\delta_i\right)Q_i\right]}{\left[\left(U_i - E\cos\delta_i\right)P_i - E\sin\delta_i\cdot Q_i\right]^2 + \left[E\sin\delta_i\cdot P_i + \left(U_i - E\cos\delta_i\right)Q_i\right]^2} \tag{3}$$
$$= g\left(P_i, Q_i, E\right).$$

It can be deduced from Eq. (1) that the line resistance and inductive reactance are expressed by the active and reactive power as Eqs. (2) and (3), where $f(\cdot)$ and $g(\cdot)$ denote different nonlinear representations.

It can be observed that line resistance and inductive reactance are nonlinear expressions of active and reactive power and bus voltage, respectively. Through this expression relationship, we can control the output power by changing the equivalent line impedance. To this end, an adaptive impedance-power droop equation is proposed to adjust the equivalent line impedance as follows

$$R_{vi} = R_{vi}^c - \left(f\left(P_i, Q_i, E_c\right) - f\left(P_{d,i}^{pu} P_i^*, Q_{d,i}^{pu} Q_i^*, E_c\right)\right), \tag{4}$$

$$X_{vi} = X_{vi}^c - \left(g\left(P_i, Q_i, E_c\right) - g\left(P_{d,i}^{pu} P_i^*, Q_{d,i}^{pu} Q_i^*, E_c\right)\right), \tag{5}$$

where the subscript i indicates the ith DG as the control object, P_i^* and Q_i^* are reference values of active and reactive power, and $P_{d,i}^{pu}$ and $Q_{d,i}^{pu}$ are the per-unit values of the desired active and reactive power, respectively. E_c is bus voltage that is set as a constant, so that the required equivalent impedance variation can be obtained by substituting the current power and the desired power into Eq. (2) and (3) respectively and making a difference. R_{vi} and X_{vi} are the desired virtual resistance and inductive reactance, respectively, while R_{vi}^c and X_{vi}^c are the corrected virtual resistance and inductive reactance matching the current line state, obtained from the following equations.

$$R_{vi}^c = f\left(P_i, Q_i, E^c\right) - f\left(P_i, Q_i, E\right), \tag{6}$$

$$X_{vi}^c = g\left(P_i, Q_i, E^c\right) - g\left(P_i, Q_i, E\right). \tag{7}$$

Since Eqs. (6) and (7) are designed based on the current line state, the adaptability of the proposed impedance-power droop equations is not only reflected in power changes, but also in line changes. Even if the line changes, the proposed droop equations can find the desired virtual impedance value matching the current line state according to Eqs. (6) and (7) without knowing the physical parameters of lines, avoiding the misleading effect of line changes on the derived virtual impedance.

2.2. Practical consensus coordinated control

From the above analysis, the desired power needs to be obtained for this method. The active and reactive power sharing requires the following equations to hold:

$$P_{d,1}^{pu} = \cdots = P_{d,i}^{pu} = \cdots P_{d,N}^{pu}, \quad Q_{d,1}^{pu} = \cdots = Q_{d,i}^{pu} = \cdots Q_{d,N}^{pu}. \tag{8}$$

To enhance the stability of IMG systems and coordination among DGs, we adopt a consensus method to accomplish the above equations. Each DG unit only exchanges information with neighboring units, avoiding single point of failure and improving system security. A large variety of consensus controllers have been proposed in recent years to achieve different control objectives. However, in practice, due to the existence of communication delay and the characteristics of physical system itself, it is difficult to achieve the ideal and complete state equivalence. It is feasible to make global state converge to a finite interval, this paper thus adopts the practical consensus to obtain the desired power per-unit values. The dynamic description of active and reactive power per-unit values are given as:

$$\dot{P}_i^{pu}(t) = u_{pi}(t),\ \dot{Q}_i^{pu}(t) = u_{qi}(t). \tag{9}$$

Facing practical scenarios in islanded IMGs, this paper considers the time delay and quantified communication data in a low-bandwidth communication network, and the practical consensus protocols corresponding to active and reactive power are designed as:

$$u_{pi}(t) = \sum_{j \in \Omega_i} a_{ij} \left[\Phi_p \left(P_j^{pu}(t-\tau) \right) - \Phi_p \left(P_i^{pu}(t) \right) \right], \tag{10}$$

$$u_{qi}(t) = \sum_{j \in \Omega_i} a_{ij} \left[\Phi_q \left(Q_j^{pu}(t-\tau) \right) - \Phi_q \left(Q_i^{pu}(t) \right) \right], \tag{11}$$

where a_{ij} is adjacency weight in the undirected connected graph, $a_{ii} = -\sum_{j=1, j \neq i}^{N} a_{ij}$ when $i = j$, Ω_i is the neighbor space of DG$_i$, and τ is transmission delay. $\Phi(z)$ is the quantization function defined as $\Phi(z) = \lfloor (z/\Delta\lambda) + 1/2 \rfloor \lambda$, where Δ and λ are sensitivity and quantization parameter, respectively [9].

Under any finite delay, the active and reactive per-unit values of global DGs converge to a finite set, respectively, and the detailed proof was given in [9]. And the size of the convergent set can be controlled by adjusting Δ and λ. Integrating the above equations, the adaptive impedance-power droop equations are rewritten as:

$$R_{vi} = f \left(P_i^* \int_0^t u_{pi}(t)dt, Q_i^* \int_0^t u_{qi}(t)dt, E_c \right) - f \left(P_i, Q_i, E \right), \tag{12}$$

$$X_{vi} = g \left(P_i^* \int_0^t u_{pi}(t)dt, Q_i^* \int_0^t u_{qi}(t)dt, E_c \right) - g \left(P_i, Q_i, E \right). \tag{13}$$

16

3. Simulations

The effectiveness of the proposed control method is verified by simulating the model in Fig. 1. The model consists of four DGs and several common loads, and the transmission lines are equipped with LC output filters and RL complex impedances. The communication topology is shown by dotted lines in Fig. 1. The main parameters are provided in Table 1.

    The simulation process takes 2 seconds. At $t = 0$s, 100% basal common loads are connected. The waveforms of active and reactive power per-unit values are shown in Fig. 2. Under the action of the proposed control, the per-unit values of active and reactive power converge to a finite interval at $t = 0.3$s, respectively. The 50% basal common loads are increased and decreased at $t = 0.5$s and $t = 1.5$s, respectively. It can be observed that the active and reactive power increases correspondingly by 1.5 times at $t = 0.5$s, respectively. After a brief fluctuation, they each dynamically converge to a new practical consensus set whose size is within 0.1. At $t = 1.5$s, the output power per-unit values are reduced by 0.5 and reach a new limited range after a certain oscillation.

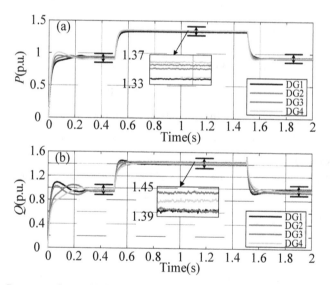

Fig. 2. Power waveforms with the proposed method. (a) Active power. (b) Reactive power.

    Figure 3 shows the changing process of virtual resistance and inductance. The virtual resistance and inductance are synchronized with output power. They vary from zero at $t = 0$s. After 0.3 seconds, the virtual resistance and inductance stabilized at specific values along with the stable convergence of output power.

According to the variation of output power at $t = 0.5$s and $t = 1.5$s, the virtual resistance and inductance are adaptively adjusted by the impedance-power droop equations and reach steady states thereafter. It shows that the proposed control method can reliably achieve both active and reactive power sharing, and the effectiveness is strongly verified.

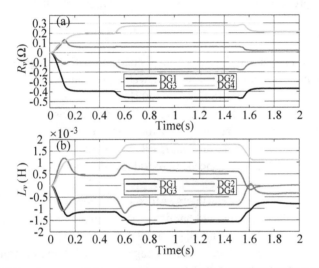

Fig. 3. Virtual impedance waveforms with the proposed method. (a) Virtual resistance. (b) Virtual inductance.

Table 1. Main simulation parameters of IMG model.

Parameter	Value
DC voltage source amplitude	700V
Output filter	$L_f = 3$mH, $C_f = 15\mu$F
Feeder impedance	$R_{L1} = 1.17\Omega, R_{L2} = 0.89\Omega,$ $R_{L3} = 0.76\Omega, R_{L4} = 0.58\Omega,$ $L_{L1} = 3.15$mH, $L_{L2} = 2.7$mH, $L_{L3} = 2.29$mH, $L_{L4} = 1.45$mH
Nominal voltage / frequency	380V/50Hz
Reference power	$P_1^* = P_2^* = P_3^* = P_4^* = 3000$W, $Q_1^* = Q_2^* = Q_3^* = Q_4^* = 750$Var
Basal common loads	12kW + 3kVar
Communication delay	$\tau = 0.06$s

4. Conclusion

In this paper, a distributed adaptive virtual impedance control method based on practical consensus was proposed to realize power sharing in islanded IMGs with complex impedances. First, an adaptive impedance-power droop equation was proposed to obtain the desired virtual impedance, which can adapt to both power and line changes without knowing the line parameters. Then, the practical consensus was adopted to obtain the desired power, which avoided the difficulty of gain adjustment and was easy to implement in practice. Finally, the effectiveness of the proposed method was verified in MATLAB/Simulink.

References

1. Z. Fan, B. Fan and W. Liu, Distributed control of DC microgrids for optimal coordination of conventional and renewable generators, *IEEE Trans. Smart Grid*, Vol. 12, no. 6, pp. 4607–4615, (2021).
2. P. Zhao, C. Dou, K. Ma, Z. Zhang and B. Zhang, Distributed cooperative control based on multiagent system for islanded microgrids with switching topology and channel interruption, *IEEE Syst. J.*, (2020).
3. J. He and Y.W. Li, An enhanced microgrid load demand sharing strategy, *IEEE Trans. Power Electron.*, Vol. 27, no. 9, pp. 3984–3995, (2012).
4. J. He, Y. W. Li, and F. Blaabjerg, An enhanced islanding microgrid reactive power, imbalance power, and harmonic power sharing scheme, *IEEE Trans. Power Electron.*, Vol. 30, no. 6, pp. 3389–3401, (2015).
5. C. Dou, Z. Zhang, D. Yue, and M. Song, Improved droop control based on virtual impedance and virtual power source in low-voltage microgrid, *IET Gener. Transm. Distrib.*, Vol. 11, no. 4, pp. 1046–1054, (2017).
6. H. Zhang, S. Kim, Q. Sun and J. Zhou, Distributed adaptive virtual impedance control for accurate reactive power sharing based on consensus control in microgrids, *IEEE Trans. Smart Grid*, Vol. 8, no. 4, pp. 1749–1761, (2017).
7. R. Razi, H. Iman-Eini and M. Hamzeh, An impedance-power droop method for accurate power sharing in islanded resistive microgrids, *IEEE J. Emerg. Sel. Top. Power Electron.*, Vol. 8, no. 4, pp. 3763–3771, (2020).
8. R. Razi, H. Iman-Eini, M. Hamzeh and S. Bacha, A novel extended impedance-power droop for accurate active and reactive power sharing in a multi-bus microgrid with complex impedances, *IEEE Trans. Smart Grid*, Vol. 11, no. 5, pp. 3795–3804, (2020).
9. L. Li, D. W. C. Ho and J. Lu, A unified approach to practical consensus with quantized data and time delay, *IEEE Trans. Circuits Syst. I Reg. Papers*, Vol. 60, no. 10, pp. 2668–2678, (2013).

Unmanned powered parafoil system altitude control via DDPG-optimized linear active disturbance rejection controller

Yuemin Zheng, Jin Tao*, Qinglin Sun†, Hao Sun, Mingwei Sun and Zengqiang Chen

College of Artificial Intelligence, Nankai University
Tianjin, 300350, China
* taoj@nankai.edu.cn
† sunql@nankai.edu.cn

Xianyi Zeng

Department of Textile Management and Product Design
Ecole Nationale Superieure des Arts et Industries Textiles
Roubaix, 59100, France
xianyi.zeng@ensait.fr

Thrust device adds flexibility to parafoil system. Controlling the flight height of the parafoil system through thrust is of great significance for the parafoil to complete the task. This paper applies a linear active disturbance rejection control (LADRC) method based on Deep Deterministic Policy Gradient (DDPG) optimization to the altitude control of the powered parafoil system. DDPG is used to obtain the adaptive parameters of LADRC, thus achieving better control performance. The simulation results verify the effectiveness of the proposed method by comparing it with traditional LADRC with fixed parameters.

Keywords: Powered parafoil system; linear active disturbance rejection control; deep deterministic policy gradient; altitude control.

1. Introduction

A powered parafoil system is an unmanned aerial vehicle that flies with the lift provided by the parafoil and the thrust generated by the propeller. Compared with the parafoil airdrop system, it adds a thrust device to achieve altitude control. When the airdrop height is insufficient, the thrust device can maintain or raise the height to attain longer-distance target delivery.

At present, the height control of the powered parafoil system is mostly concentrated in traditional control methods such as PID,[1] sliding mode control (SMC)[2] and linear active disturbance rejection control (LADRC).[3,4] Although effective control can be achieved, the controller parameters still remain challenging to tune.

In recent years, deep reinforcement learning (DRL) has become a hot spot in artificial intelligence due to its powerful learning ability. Deep Deterministic Policy Gradient (DDPG)[5] is one of the typical algorithms in DRL, which can solve the sequential decision problem very well. Therefore, this paper uses DDPG for the tuning of LADRC controller parameters, which can adaptively select controller parameters according to the observed state of the system.

The rest of this paper is organized as follows. Section 2 presents a dynamic model of powered parafoil. The LADRC controller design process is given in Section 3. Section 4 presents the DDPG-based parameter optimization algorithm. Section 5 provides simulation results to illustrate the effectiveness of the method. Section 6 relates our conclusions.

2. Studied 8-DOF Dynamic Model

The structure diagram of the parafoil system with thrust device and payload is shown in Fig. 1. Three coordinate systems are established to facilitate the model analysis, as specified in the ground coordinate system $O_d x_d y_d z_d$, the parafoil coordinate system $O_s x_s y_s z_s$, and the payload coordinate system $O_w x_w y_w z_w$. Assuming that in the parafoil coordinate system, there is the velocity vector $V_s = [u_s, v_s, w_s]^T$ and angular velocity vector $W_s = [p_s, q_s, r_s]^T$.

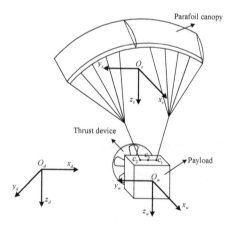

Fig. 1. Schematic diagram of powered parafoil system.

Then there is the following expression:

$$
\begin{bmatrix} \dot{x} \\ \dot{y} \\ \dot{z} \end{bmatrix} = \begin{bmatrix} c\theta c\psi & c\theta s\psi & -s\theta \\ s\phi s\theta c\psi - c\phi s\psi & s\phi s\theta s\psi + c\phi c\psi & s\phi c\theta \\ c\phi s\theta c\psi + s\phi s\psi & c\phi s\theta s\psi - s\phi c\psi & c\phi c\theta \end{bmatrix}^T V_s \tag{1}
$$

where $s\theta$ denotes the $sin\theta$, and $c\theta$ denotes the $cos\theta$. And ϕ, θ, and ψ are three Euler angles consist of roll angle, pitch angle, and yaw angle, respectively. Due to space limitations, this paper will not introduce the model building process in detail, and readers can refer to Ref. 6.

3. LADRC-based Altitude Control

The design of the LADRC controller needs the order of the controlled system, so according to Eq. (1), the following expression can be obtained

$$
\dot{z} = -u_s \sin\theta + v_s \sin\phi \cos\theta + w_s \cos\phi \cos\theta \tag{2}
$$

Its second-order differential form is expressed as:

$$
\ddot{z} = -\dot{u}_s s\theta + \dot{v}_s s\phi c\theta + \dot{w}_s c\phi c\theta - (u_s c\theta + v_s s\phi s\theta + w_s c\phi s\theta)\, \dot{\theta}
$$
$$
- (w_s c\theta s\phi - v_s c\theta c\phi)\, \dot{\phi} \tag{3}
$$

According to Ref. 6, there is:

$$
\begin{cases} \dot{v}_s = f_1 + \frac{\cos\theta_r \sin\psi_r}{m_s + m_{a,11}} T_x \\ \dot{u}_s = f_2 + \frac{\cos\theta_r \cos\psi_r}{m_s + m_{a,22}} T_x \\ \dot{w}_s = f_3 + \frac{-\sin\theta_r}{m_s + m_{a,33}} T_x \end{cases} \tag{4}
$$

where f_1, f_2, f_3 represent omitted items and T_x denotes the value of thrust.

Then combining Eq. (3) and Eq. (4), the relationship between $\ddot{z}$ and T_x can be obtained as:

$$
\ddot{z} = f + bT_x \tag{5}
$$

where f is the sum of terms irrelevant to input and output, regarded as an internal disturbance. And b is expressed as:

$$
b = -\frac{s\theta c\theta_r c\psi_r}{m_s + m_{a,11}} + \frac{s\phi c\theta c\theta_r s\psi_r}{m_s + m_{a,22}} - \frac{c\phi c\theta s\theta_r}{m_s + m_{a,33}} \tag{6}
$$

Generally, we replace b with a tunable parameter b_0:

$$
\ddot{z} = f + (b - b_0)\, T_x + b_0 T_x
$$
$$
= \tilde{f} + b_0 T_x \tag{7}
$$

where $\tilde{f}$ can be regarded as the total disturbance to the system. According to Eq. (7), it can be found that the system order is 2. Then the three-order linear ESO can be designed as

$$\begin{cases} \dot{\hat{x}} = A\hat{x} + Bu + L\left(\dot{\hat{z}} - \hat{z}\right) \\ \hat{z} = C\hat{x} \end{cases} \tag{8}$$

where $\hat{x}$ is the observed state of $x = \begin{bmatrix} z & \dot{z} & \tilde{f} \end{bmatrix}^T$, and $A = \begin{bmatrix} 0 & 1 & 0 \\ 0 & 0 & 1 \\ 0 & 0 & 0 \end{bmatrix}$, $B = \begin{bmatrix} 0 \\ b_0 \\ 0 \end{bmatrix}$, $L = \begin{bmatrix} \beta_{01} \\ \beta_{02} \\ \beta_{03} \end{bmatrix}$, $C = \begin{bmatrix} 1 \\ 0 \\ 0 \end{bmatrix}^T$.

L is the observer gain vector. And when $|A - LC|$ is asymptotically stable, the estimated state can be approximated to the actual state. Generally, the observer gains are configured at $-\omega_o(\omega_o > 0)$ using the pole placement method:[7]

$$|sI - (A - LC)| = s^3 + \beta_{01}s^2 + \beta_{02}s + \beta_{03}$$
$$= (s + \omega_o)^3 \tag{9}$$

In this way, $\beta_{01} = 3\omega_o$, $\beta_{02} = 3\omega_o^2$ and $\beta_{03} = \omega_o^3$. And the disturbance $\tilde{f}$ can be estimated with appropriate ω_o. To eliminate the influence of disturbance on the system, take T_x in Eq. (7) as

$$T_x = \frac{u_0 - \hat{z}_3}{b_0} \tag{10}$$

with $u_0 = k_p\left(z_d - \hat{x}_1\right) - k_d\hat{x}_2$. z_d is the desired altitude. And k_p, k_d are the controller parameters needed to be adjusted.

4. DDPG-optimized LADRC

DDPG is one of the DRL algorithms handling continuous states and continuous actions. And this paper applies DDPG to controller parameters optimization. As seen from the above description, the parameters that need to be adjusted in LADRC are ω_o, b_0, k_p, and k_d. This paper only considers the optimization of k_p and k_d.[8]

Define the state as

$$\begin{cases} s_1(t) = z_d(t) - z(t) \\ s_2(t) = s_1(t) - s_1(t-1) \end{cases} \tag{11}$$

And the reward function based on the state is shown as

$$r = -|s_1| - |s_2| \tag{12}$$

The purpose of DDPG is to select the policy π that maximizes the cumulative reward value $R_c = \sum_{t=0}^{\infty} \gamma^t r_{t+1}$ by observing the state of the environment, where γ is a parameter reflecting the importance of the reward value at the future moment. The process of the DDPG algorithm is shown in Algorithm 4.1.

Algorithm 4.1 DDPG Algorithm

Randomly initialize critic network $Q(s, a | \theta)$ and actor network $Q'(s | \mu)$ with weights θ and μ.

Initialize target network Q_{target} and Q'_{target} with weights $\theta_{target} \leftarrow \theta$, $\mu_{target} \leftarrow \mu$.

Initialize replay buffer $\mathcal{D}$.

if episode $<= M$ **then**

Randomly initialize a process $\mathcal{N}$ for action exploration.

Receive the state $s(1) = [s_1(1); s_2(1)]$.

if t $<= T$ **then**

$a_t = [k_p(t); k_d(t)] = Q'(s(t) | \mu) + \mathcal{N}_t$.

Execute the action a_t to get the reward value r_t and the state value $s(t+1)$.

Store $(s(t), a_t, r_t, s(t+1))$ in $\mathcal{D}$.

Randomly extract m sets of data from $\mathcal{D}$.

Set $y_i = r_i + \gamma Q_{t\,arg\,et}\left(s(i+1), Q'_{t\,arg\,et}(s(i+1) | \mu_{t\,arg\,et}) | \theta_{t\,arg\,et}\right)$.

Update the critic network with the loss function: $J = \frac{1}{m} \sum_i (y_i - Q(s(i), a_i | \theta))^2$.

Update the actor policy using the sampled policy gradient: $\nabla_\mu J \approx \frac{1}{m} \sum_i \nabla_a Q(s, a | \theta) |_{s=s(i), a=\mu(s)} \nabla_\mu Q'(s | \mu) |_{s(i)}$.

Update the target networks with moving average method: $\theta_{t\,arg\,et} \leftarrow \tau\theta + (1 - \tau)\theta_{t\,arg\,et}$, $\mu_{t\,arg\,et} \leftarrow \tau\mu + (1 - \tau)\mu_{t\,arg\,et}$.

end if

end if

---

5. Simulation Results

The parameters of the parafoil system used in this paper are shown in Table 1. The initial velocity and angular velocity of the parafoil are $V_s = [14.9, 0, 2.1]^T$ m/s and $W_s = [0, 0, 0]^T$ rad/s, respectively.

Table 1. Parameters of the parafoil system and DDPG algorithm.

Parameter Description	Value	Parameter Description	Value
Wing span	4.5m	Simulation run time	100 s
Mean aerodynamic chord	1.3 m	Simulation sample step	0.01 s
Mass of the parafoil	1.7 kg	Number of iterations	475
Mass of the payload	20 kg	Learning rate of networks	10^{-4}
Wing area	6.5 m^2	Discount factor	0.99
Rope length	3 m	τ	10^{-3}

In this paper, the action network is a fully connected neural network with three hidden layers, and the number of neurons in each hidden layer is 100. The network's input is the system states, and the output is the action. As for the critic network, the structure is shown in Fig. 2.

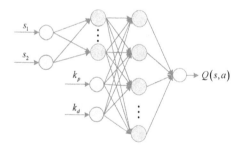

Fig. 2. Structure diagram of critic network.

In this paper, $\omega_o = 12$, $b_0 = 0.5$, and the action space is $\begin{cases} k_p \in [0.01, 0.2] \\ k_d \in [0.5, 1] \end{cases}$. Assuming that the initial height of the parafoil is 1050m, and the planned height is 1000m, then the simulation results are as follows.

Figure 3 shows the results of altitude control with DDPG-optimized parameters. To demonstrate the effectiveness of the proposed method, we compare the effect of the LADRC controller with boundary values of k_p and k_d. It can be seen that the height obtained by the proposed method

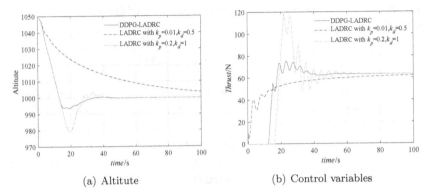

(a) Altitute   (b) Control variables

Fig. 3.   Altitute control results and control variables of parafoil system.

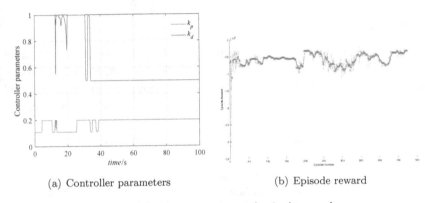

(a) Controller parameters   (b) Episode reward

Fig. 4.   Adaptive parameters and episode reward.

has a minor overshoot and settling time than that of LADRCs with fixed parameters. The adaptive parameters are given in Fig. 4(a). Figure 4(b) reflects the episode reward during the training process, where the blue represents the cumulative reward value of each episode, and the red is the average episode reward.

6. Conclusion

This paper applies a DDPG-optimized LADRC controller to the altitude control of a powered parafoil system. Firstly, the 8-DOF model of the powered parafoil system is established. Then based on the order between height and thrust, the LADRC controller is designed. Furthermore, the DDPG algorithm is used to get the adaptive controller parameters to achieve better control performance. At last, the effectiveness of the proposed method is verified by simulation.

Acknowledgments

This work was supported by the National Natural Science Foundation of China (Grant No. 61973172, 61973175, 62003175 and 62003177), the National Key Research and Development Project (Grant No. 2019YFC1510900), the key Technologies Research and Development Program of Tianjin (Grant No. 19JCZDJC32800), this project also funded by China Postdoctoral Science Foundation (Grant No. 2020M670633), Tianjin Postgraduate Research and Innovation Project (Grant No. 2021YJSB084) and China Scholarship Council Fund.

References

1. Y. Li, M. Zhao and M. Yao, 6-dof modeling and 3d trajectory tracking control of a powered parafoil system, *IEEE Access* **8**, 151087 (2020).
2. Q. Sun, L. Yu and Y. Zheng, Trajectory tracking control of powered parafoil system based on sliding mode control in a complex environment, *Aerosp Sci Technol*, p. 107406 (2022).
3. J. Tao, Q. Sun and Z. Chen, Linear active disturbance rejection altitude control for parawing unmanned aerial vehicle, *Journal of National University of Desense Technology* **39**, 103 (2020).
4. E. Zhu and H. Gao, Guidance-based path following control of the powered parafoil, *Control Engineering and Applied Informatics* **22**, 42 (2020).
5. Y. Hou, L. Liu and Q. Wei, A novel ddpg method with prioritized experience replay, in *Proc. IEEE Int. Conf. Syst. Man Cybern.*, (Banff, Canada, 2007).
6. E. Zhu, Q. Sun and P. Tan, Modeling of powered parafoil based on kirchhoff motion equation, *Nonlinear Dyn.* **79**, 617 (2014).
7. Z. Gao, Active disturbance rejection control: A paradigm shift in feedback control system design, in *2006 American Control Conference*, (Minneapolis, USA, 2006).
8. H. Qin, P. Tan and Z. Chen, Deep reinforcement learning based active disturbance rejection control for ship course control, *Neurocomputing* **484**, 99 (2022).

Acoustic manipulation simulation based on the method of Deep Reinforcement Learning*

Xiaodong Jiao, Hao Sun† and Qinglin Sun‡

College of Artificial Intelligence, Nankai University
Tianjin, Haihe Education Park, China
†*sunh@nankai.edu.cn*
‡*sunql@nankai.edu.cn*

Jin Tao

Silo AI, Helsinki, Finland
taoj@nankai.edu.cn

Research on the acoustic micro-nano manipulation starts from the discovery of Chladni effect. Acoustic manipulation is expected to be applied to the culture of biological tissue and cell, micro nano element assembling, allocation of chemical raw materials and other micro nano scale fields. Meanwhile, acoustic manipulation shows the characteristic of contactless, biocompatibility, environmental compatibility and functional diversity. Whereas, the accuracy and intelligence of acoustic manipulation still have a big gap to be crossed. Very recently, the method of the deep reinforcement learning is hotly discussed, which provides a new idea for micro nano manipulation. In this paper, the Deep Q Network(DQN) algorithm is considered to improve the efficiency and intelligence in the process of acoustic manipulation. As a demonstration, linear motion tasks based on acoustic wave are trained and displayed. Consequently, the accurate acoustic frequency sequence can be obtained to direct the actual process of acoustic manipulation.

Keywords: DQN; Chladni effect; acoustic; micro-manipulation, deep reinforcement learning.

1. Introduction

Traditionally, the processing and assembling of the industrial components can be carried out by directly applying external mechanical force through the large-scale equipment [1]. On the contrary, the manipulation requirements of micro components and targets are hard to be satisfied in the previous way. In recent years, some effective micro nano manipulation methods are put forward one after another. Typically, the methods of optical tweezers [2-5], electromagnetic control

---

*Work partially supported by grant No. 62003177, 61973172, 61973175, and 62073177 of the National Natural Science Foundation of China, and Grant No. 19JCZDJC32800 of the key Technologies Research and Development Program of Tianjin.

mode [6-7] and acoustic manipulation [8-10] have gained a great deal of concern. Additionally, each method has its own advantages and disadvantages, such optical tweezers technique have high precision, but haven't biological compatibility, electromagnetic control mode is limited to the micro targets with electromagnetic and characteristics. In comparison, the method of acoustic manipulation not only has high control accuracy, but also with manipulation target diversity and environmental compatibility. Consequently, the method of acoustic manipulation should be put into a lot of research, especially the intellectualization, functionality and accuracy of acoustic manipulation.

The principle of the acoustic manipulation is the Chladni effect [11], which is discovered by Chladni, Ernst Florens Friedrich in 1787 and described as a wide sheet of metal is placed on a violin and sprinkled sand evenly on it, then played the violin with the bow, as a result, these sands were automatically arranged into different beautiful patterns. With the different tunes and increasing frequency of the strings, the patterns became more and more complex. As a result, making full use of the influence of specific frequency on the motion of micro nano targets on the thin plates, the acoustic manipulation of micro nano targets can be realized. And some meaningful research findings have testified the value and prospect of micro nano fabrication and manipulation based on the method of acoustic wave. For instance, in [12], the motion of multiple micro objects are controlled based on the Chladni effect, in [13], by using the bulk acoustic waves and machine learning, the controlled manipulation and active sorting of particles inside microfluidic chips are realized, in [14], rotational manipulation of single cells and organisms using acoustic waves are reported.

On the other hand, the intellectualization of the acoustic manipulation process is a very important and meaningful direction. In the last few years, the intelligent algorithms have developed unprecedentedly. Such as, deep learning algorithm, reinforce learning algorithm and deep reinforce learning algorithm [15-17]. Each algorithm is suitable for different applications. In the deep reinforce learning algorithm category, it can be divided into DQN, DDQN, DDPG, PPO and so on according to the continuous and discrete characteristics of states and actions in the targeted problems. In this work, DQN algorithm is applied to solve the problem of frequency selection in the acoustic manipulation process.

The rest of this paper is organized as follows: In Section 2, the problem of frequency selection in acoustic manipulation and its principle are demonstrated, and introduce the mechanism of DQN algorithm. Section 3 designs the DQN algorithm for acoustic manipulation process. In Section 4, the simulation experiment and test are performed, which verify the effectiveness of the DQN algorithm. Conclusions and future work are given in the final section.

2. Problem Formulation

In the field of micro nano robot assembling, microchip processing, microbial cultivation and allocation of micro materials, by the mean of traditionally exerting external mechanical force is difficult to complete the corresponding tasks. The reason is that the equipment has the problems of large volume and low control accuracy. Urgently, some technologies of micro nano manipulation needs to be proposed and developed. Typically, with the help of physical principles, the methods of optical tweezers, electric and magnetic manipulation, acoustic vibration technology and microfluidic technology. Compared with other control technologies, acoustic manipulation has the unique advantages. Such as miniaturization of control equipment, contactless manipulation, diversity of manipulation targets and manipulation environment compatibility and so on. Hence, a lot of attention should be paid to the acoustic manipulation.

Equipment of acoustic manipulation is consist of a centrally fixed metal plate pasted with a piezoelectric actuator, a control computer, camera suspended perpendicular to the thin plate, data acquisition card and amplifier, as is shown in Fig. 1. Usefully, the hardware experimental platform based on Chladni effect can be used to realize micro nano manipulation. Meanwhile, the corresponding acoustic frequency library has been established and studied in the [12]. Additionally, the accurate frequency selection is the most critical step before the actual manipulation.

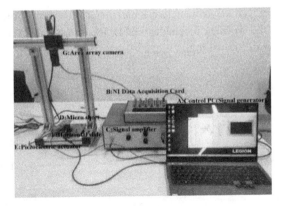

Fig. 1. Hardware device platform.

The method of deep reinforcement learning has attracted much attention. Advantageously, deep reinforcement learning has the applicability of potential problem areas, combining the perception ability of deep learning (DL) with the decision-making ability of reinforcement learning (RL), it can be controlled directly according to the input information, and it is an artificial intelligence method closer to human thinking mode. In this work, we try to perform the frequency selection with DQN algorithm. So that the required frequency sequence can be obtained to complete the given trajectory task.

The workflow of the DQN is depicted by the variables $\{s,a,r,\gamma\}$, in which s is the set of states, a is the set of actions, r is the reward function, γ represents the discount factor. DQN uses a MainNet to generate the current Q value and another target to generate Target Q value. Q-Target is a kind of mechanism to disrupt correlation, and there are two networks with exactly the same structure but different parameters in DQN. The network MainNet for predicting Q estimation uses the latest parameters, while the neural network Target Net for predicting Q reality uses the parameters of a long time ago. In our work, the particle coordinate position on the plate is the states s, and a is the actions referring to the acoustic waves with specific frequencies. The update method of DQN is the same as that of Q-learning, with detailed value function

$$Q(s,a,\theta) \leftarrow Q(s,a,\theta) + \alpha[r + \gamma \max_{a'} Q(s',a',\theta') - Q(s,a,\theta)] \tag{1}$$

The loss function is defined as follows

$$L(\theta) = E[(Target\ Q - Q(s,a;\theta))^2] \tag{2}$$

$$Target\ Q = r + \gamma \max_{a'} Q(s',a';\theta') \tag{3}$$

in which, θ indicates that the network parameter is the loss of mean square error.

Succinctly, the working mechanism of DQN algorithm can be summarized as the frame diagram shown in the Fig. 2.

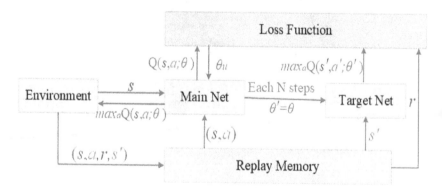

Fig. 2. Flowchart of DQN algorithm.

By training the network, the optimal policy is obtained to give the best action *a* fort he arbitrary state *s*. And then, the optimal policy is used to direct the particle move towards the target point.

3. Design of Deep Q Network Algorithm

In this section, the Deep Q Network algorithm are designed for the purpose of improving the acoustic manipulation process. Consequently, the constructed network algorithm are used to conduct training according to the target requirements.

Algorithm: DQN algorithm

Build the multi-layer neural network
estimation network(QNet_Eval) and target network (QNet_Target)
  Parameter definition and initialization:
  Learning rate 0.05; Discount factor 0.9; Greedy 0.9; Experience pool 1000;
  Replace 200; MaxIte 20; MaxStep 400; Batch 64;
for Ite = 1: MaxIte **do**
    Set initial point and environment initialization
    for Step = 1, MaxStep **do**
    With the probability of greedy 0.9 choose the action a_i by QNet_Eval
    otherwise the action a_i is chosen arbitrarily.
    Execute the action a_i, calculate the reward r_i and judge the termination
      conditions.
    Set $s_{i+1} = s_i$,
    Replay memory $(s_i, a_i, r_i,)$
    Calculate the Q_eval, Q_next, Q_target.
    Correct the Q_target according to Q_update = r + 0.9*max (Q_next),
    Network training.
    Judge whether the cycle ends according to the boundary conditions and
    update the current position.
    Update QNet_Target: QNet_Target = QNet_Eval.
    end for
  end for

Algorithm shows the execution process of the Deep Q Network designed for the acoustic manipulation. The state(position of particles on thin plate) and action(specific excitation frequency) are regarded as the input of neural network, and then the Q value of action can be obtained after neural network analysis. The underlying idea of the parameter update is the max function, which is performed off-line using the set of experiences.

4. Simulation Experiment and Test

In Section 3, the DQN algorithm are designed for the frequency selection of acoustic manipulation process. Then, we used the DQN algorithm to perform network training. Considering a simple acoustic manipulation case, linear motion of particle from start point **S** to the target point **T**, and the geometric principle is shown in Fig. 3, in which the vector a is the target vector, the vector b is resulted by a specific selected frequency. The included angle α can be regarded as a control factor of the reward function. Consequently, the reward mechanism is considered as below

$$D = norm(a) \tag{4}$$

$$reward\_sign = sign(dot(a,b)) \tag{5}$$

$$\alpha = \frac{a\cos(dot(a,b))}{norm(a) * norm(b)} \tag{6}$$

If $reward\_sign = 1$, $reward = -|\alpha| - D$, else $reward = 0$.

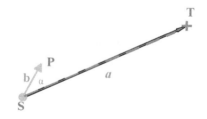

Fig. 3. Geometric principle of linear motion.

The acoustic manipulation simulation data in [12], [18] is used to perform the neural network training. The database is obtained by using the experimental equipment shown in the Fig. 1, which conducted a large number of repeated experiments and fitted experimental data including about 60 acoustic frequencies and about 390000 data points. The database contains the displacement field of micro target on the horizontal and vertical directions of the thin plate under the action excitation of an acoustic frequency.

Finally, we perform the simulation experiment to verify the effectiveness and accuracy of the designed Deep Q Network algorithm in the last section. Figure 4 shows two of the test results, the starting point and the ending point of two groups of linear motion are set as $S_1(0.1, 0.21)$, $T_1(0.19, 0.45)$, and $S_2(0.25, 0.20)$, $T_2(0.16, 0.38)$ respectively. From the test results, the target straight-line task can

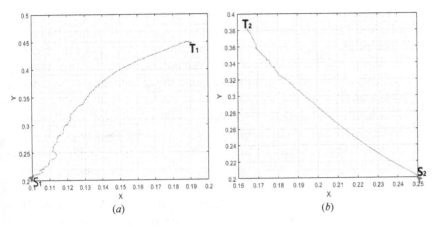

(a)   (b)

Fig. 4. Test results based on the DQN algorithm.

be accurately arrived, in other words, the DQN algorithm can be used to help improving the acoustic manipulation process.

5. Conclusions and Future Work

In this paper, the problem of frequency selection in acoustic manipulation process is transformed to be solved by the method of neural network. Firstly, the actual problem background and Deep Q Network workflow are introduced in detail. And then, the DQN network is designed for specific problem. Lastly, the reward mechanism is explained, and simulation experiments and tests are performed, which verify the validity of the DQN algorithm. In the future work, the improved deep reinforcement learning algorithm should be excavated to improve the accuracy of frequency selection in acoustic manipulation. On the other hand, the diverse manipulation functions needs to be further studied exploringly.

Acknowledgments

This work was supported by the National Natural Science Foundation of China (Grant No. 62003177, 61973172, 61973175, and 62073177), the key Technologies Research and Development Program of Tianjin (Grant No. 19JCZDJC32800).

References

1. C. Xia, Z. Pan, Y. Li, et al. Vision-based melt pool monitoring for wire-arc additive manufacturing using deep learning method. (The International

Journal of Advanced Manufacturing Technology, 2022).

2. M. Sroczyńska, A. Dawid, M. Tomza, et al. Controlling the dynamics of ultracold polar molecules in optical tweezers. (New Journal of Physics, 2022).

3. F. Bazouband, E. Bazouband, T. Golestanizade, et al. Efficient arbitrary polarized light focusing by silicon cross-shaped metaatoms. (Journal of Physics D: Applied Physics, 2022).

4. A. Yang, S. D. Moore, B. S. Schmidt. Optical manipulation of nanoparticles and biomolecules in sub-wavelength slot waveguides. (Nature, 2009).

5. X. Zhu, N. Li, J. Yang, X. Chen. Revolution of trapped particle in counter-propagating dual-beams optical tweezers under low pressure. (Optics Express, 2021).

6. A. Zhukov, M. Ipatov, M. Churyukanova, S. Kaloshkin, V. Zhukova. Giant magnetoimpedance in thin amorphous wires: From manipulation of magnetic field dependence to industrial applications. (Journal of Alloys & Compounds, 2014).

7. A. Snezhko, I. S. Aranson. Magnetic manipulation of self-assembled colloidal asters. (Nature Materials, 2011).

8. C. Devendran, D. J. Collins, A. Neild. The role of channel height and actuation method on particle manipulation in surface acoustic wave (SAW)-driven microfluidic devices. (Microfluidics and Nanofluidics, 2022).

9. A. Wixforth, C. Strobl, C. Gauer, et al. Acoustic manipulation of small droplets. (Analytical and Bioanalytical Chemistry, 2004).

10. T. Staff. Correction: Three-Dimensional Mid-Air Acoustic Manipulation by Ultrasonic Phased Arrays. (Plos One, 2014).

11. Y. Luo, R. Feng, X. Li, D. Liu. A simple approach to determine the mode shapes of Chladni plates based on the optical lever method. European Journal of Physics, 2019).

12. Q. Zhou, V. Sariola, K. Latifi, V. Liimatainen, Controlling the motion of multiple objects on a Chladni plate. (Nature Communications, 2016).

13. K. Yiannacou, V. Sariola, Controlled Manipulation and Active Sorting of Particles Inside Microfluidic Chips Using Bulk Acoustic Waves and Machine Learning. (Langmuir, 2021).

14. D. Ahmed, A. Ozcelik, N. Bojanala, et al. Rotational manipulation of single cells and organisms using acoustic waves. (Nature Communications, 2016).

15. Y. Wang, Z. Chen, M. Sun, Q. Sun. Load frequency active disturbance rejection control for an interconnected power system via deep reinforcement learning. (2021 IEEE 10th Data Driven Control and Learning Systems Conference).

16. Y. Zheng, Z. Liu, J. Tao, et al. Double Deep Q Network Optimized Linear

Active Disturbance Rejection Control for Ship Course Keeping. (2021 Chinese Intelligent Systems Conference).

17. Y. Zheng, J. Tao, Q. Sun, et al. An intelligent course keeping active disturbance rejection controller based on double deep Q - network for towing system of unpowered cylindrical drilling platform. (International Journal of Robust and Nonlinear Control, 2021).

18. X. Jiao, J. Tao, H. Sun, Q. Sun. Acoustic Manipulation Simulations of Single Target Particle Based on the Local Optimal Controller. (6th International Conference on Robotics and Automation Engineering, 2021).

A hierarchical reconciliation least square method for linear regression

Cong Zhang[1,*], Tianrui Li[2,†] and Chongshou Li[1,2,‡]

[1] *SWJTU-Leeds Joint School, Southwest Jiaotong University*
Chengdu 611756, China
[2] *School of Computing and Artificial Intelligence, Southwest Jiaotong University*
Chengdu 611756, China
[*] *sc18cz@leeds.ac.uk*
[†] *trli@swjtu.edu.cn*
[‡] *lics@swjtu.edu.cn*

Data is usually hierarchically structured and can be aggregated at various levels in three dimensions of object, time and location. Different aggregations result in data of different granularities, and their relationships can be used for improving the learning ability of models. In this paper, we utilize one of them and establish a simple yet effective consistency constraint (CC) for the learning process: **the sum of fine-grained forecasts should be equal to the corresponding coarse-grained forecast**. Based on it, we propose a hierarchical reconciliation least square (HRLS) method for a group of linear regression problems. In order to evaluate the consistency, a new performance indicator is designed. Moreover, our method has been tested on both real-world and synthetic datasets, and compared with existing hierarchical and non-hierarchical methods. The experimental results demonstrate its superiority in terms of both forecast accuracy and hierarchy consistency. Finally, we note that the proposed HRLS can be explained as a new way of regularization, and the source code and data of this paper is online accessible at `https://github.com/charlescc2019/HRLS`.

Keywords: Hierarchical learning; linear regression; consistent constraint.

1. Introduction

In this paper, a 2-level hierarchy is built for the n problems, which is displayed by Fig. 1. Each linear regression problem P_i $(1 \leq i \leq n)$ is represented by a leaf node, and the root node, which is noted as problem P_0, is constructed by consolidating all the n leaf nodes (problems); specifically, the explanatory variables/features/predictors are built by concatenating

---

[‡] Corresponding author.

that of the n leaf nodes, while the response Y is computed by summing up that of all the leaf nodes. Here we remark that the root node corresponds to a coarse-grained problem while the leaf nodes represent n fine-grained problems. In this structure, the CC is: the sum of all forecasts of leaf node models $(P_1, P_2, \ldots, P_n)$ should be equal to the forecast of the root node model P_0, namely, $\hat{Y}^0 = \sum_{i=1}^{n} \hat{Y}^i$. Based on this structure, conventional hierarchical forecasting (HF) methods are widely studied and two popular of them are: (1) top-down (TD) and (2) bottom-up (BU).[1,3,4,8] The TD method only solves the root node (aggregate, coarse-grained) problem and generates its forecast; then forecasts of leaf node (un-aggregate, fine-grained) problems are got by decomposing the aggregate forecast based on proportions of the training data. The reverse process is the BU method. These two methods are simple and widely used in practice.[1] But they fail to incorporate this hierarchical structure into learning process, and only perform simple operations of aggregation and decomposition. They can only be viewed as simple post-processing techniques. In order to fulfill this gap, here we propose **the hierarchical reconciliation least square (HRLS)** method, and solves all the $n+1$ linear regression problems $P_0, P_1, \ldots, P_n$ simultaneously. It not only minimizes the gap between forecasts and ground-truths but also maximizes the consistency between forecast of the root node and sum of leaf nodes'. It reconciliates the forecasts by balancing the forecast accuracy and consistency.

Having said that the forecast results should satisfy the consistency constraint (CC), namely, $\hat{Y}^0 = \sum_{i=1}^{n} \hat{Y}^i$. In order to qualify the consistency degree for a group of forecasts, we propose a new evaluation method, Mean Consistency Error (MCE), for it. The relationship between consistency measurement and the forecast accuracy measurement is provided empirically. Insights are useful for designing algorithms to new hierarchical learning problems. The contributions of this paper are given as follows.

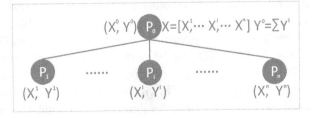

Fig. 1. A 2-level hierarchy for linear regression.

(1) Based on the CC, we propose the HRLS method with an adaptive gradient descent (AGD) algorithm to the hierarchical learning (HL) problem. To the best of our knowledge, it is the first work to apply HL for linear regression problems.

(2) In order to measure forecast consistency over the hierarchy, a new evaluation metric, Mean Consistency Error (MCE), is established.

(3) The proposed HRLS is evaluated on both real-world and synthetic datasets, and compared with the state-of-the-art hierarchical methods (like TD, BU) and non-hierarchical method (e.g., Sep). The results show that HRLS performs better than others in terms of both forecast accuracy and consistency. The relevant source code and data has been released publicly at `https://github.com/charlescc2019/HRLS`.

2. Related Work

Our work is highly related to hierarchical forecasting (HF), which is widely studied in the existing literature.[1,4] The HF leverages the natural hierarchical structure of data and forecast problem in three dimensions of time, location and object; it uses the relationship among different angularities to improve the forecasting accuracy. The first HF can be traced back to Orcutt et al.[7] Depending on the dimensions that the HF relies on, the HF can be divided into two categories: (1) cross-sectional hierarchical forecasting (CHF) and (2) temporal hierarchical forecasting (THF).[2] According to the way how the hierarchy is used, the HF can be roughly classified into three groups: (1) top-down (TD), (2) bottom-up (BU), and (3) middle-out (MO).[3,8]

The TD approach decomposes the aggregate forecast into disaggregate forecasts. The decomposition is usually based on historical proportions,[5] while the BU approach sums forecasts of the lowest aggregation level to generate forecasts for all aggregation levels in the hierarchy. Besides the TD and BU, Hyndman and Athanasopoulos[6] introduce the middle-out approach combining the BU and TD. The TD and BU have been compared with each other and each approach has its own advantages and disadvantages.[3,8,9] The BU and TD can be performed in every dimension of a forecast problem. Having said that, if they are applied in time dimension, the forecasting process is the THF;[2] if implemented in the object or location dimension, it is the CHF. The limitation of extant HF methods is that they fail to incorporate the hierarchy and relationship of different aggregation levels into the learning process; current HF methods are simple pre-processing or post-processing techniques for forecasting. The proposed HRLS is expected to fulfill this gap.

3. The Hierarchical Learning Problem

In this section, we present the 2-level hierarchy model for linear regression models. Figure 1 provides a visualization illustration for this structure. Having said that, there are n linear regression problems with ground-truth models: $Y^i = X^i \beta^i + E^i$ ($1 \leq i \leq n$). For each problem P_i, there is an affiliated dataset $\mathcal{D}_i$. Here in order to formulate learning (training) process, for each problem P_i, we divided the affiliated dataset $\mathcal{D}_i$ into training set $\mathcal{D}_i^T$ and test set $\mathcal{D}_i^E$. Note that $\mathcal{D}_i^T = \{(X^i, Y^i) | X^i \in \mathbb{R}^{m_t \times p}, Y^i \in \mathbb{R}^{m_t}\}$, $\mathcal{D}_i^E = \{(X^i, Y^i) | X^i \in \mathbb{R}^{m_e \times p}, Y^i \in \mathbb{R}^{m_e}\}$, $\mathcal{D}^i = \mathcal{D}_i^T \cup \mathcal{D}_i^E$, $\mathcal{D}_i^T \cap \mathcal{D}_i^E = \emptyset$, and $m = m_t + m_e$. The learning objective of the HRLS is the following minimization problem.

$$\min_{\hat{\beta}_k^i, \hat{\beta}_{ik}^0 \in \mathbb{R}, 1 \leq i \leq n, 1 \leq k \leq p} \underbrace{\sum_{i=1}^{n} \sum_{j=1}^{m_t} (\hat{y}_j^i - y_j^i)^2}_{\text{Least square for } n \text{ leaf node models}} + \underbrace{\sum_{j=1}^{m_t} (\hat{y}_j^0 - y_j^0)^2}_{\text{Least square for root node model}}$$

$$+ \underbrace{\sum_{j=1}^{m_t} (\hat{y}_j^0 - \sum_{i=1}^{n} \hat{y}_j^i)^2}_{\text{Consistent constraint}} \tag{1}$$

$$= \sum_{i=1}^{n} \sum_{j=1}^{m_t} (\sum_{k=1}^{p} x_{jk}^i \hat{\beta}_k^i - y_j^i)^2 + \sum_{j=1}^{m_t} (\sum_{i=1}^{m_t} \sum_{k=1}^{p} x_{jk}^i \hat{\beta}_{ik}^0 - y_j^0)^2$$

$$+ \sum_{j=1}^{m_t} (\sum_{i=1}^{n} \sum_{k=1}^{p} x_{jk}^i \hat{\beta}_{ik}^0 - \sum_{i=1}^{n} \sum_{k=1}^{p} x_{jk}^i \hat{\beta}_k^i)^2 \tag{2}$$

Below are additional notations of the above model.

- $\hat{\beta}_k^i, \hat{\beta}_{ik}^0$, parameters to be estimated, $1 \leq i \leq n, 1 \leq k \leq p$; they are coefficients of the forecast models of leaf nodes and root node, respectively.
- y_j^i, ground-truth value of the response variable of the leaf node models, and the jth element of column vector Y^i, $1 \leq i \leq n, 1 \leq j \leq m_t$, $Y^i = [y_1^i, \ldots, y_j^i, \ldots, y_{m_t}^i]^T$.
- $\hat{y}_j^i$, the predicted value of y_j^i, $1 \leq i \leq n$, $1 \leq j \leq m_t$, and generated by a linear regression model, $\hat{y}_j^i = x_{j1}^i \hat{\beta}_1^i + \cdots + x_{jk}^i \hat{\beta}_k^i + \cdots + x_{jp}^i \hat{\beta}_p^i = \sum_{k=1}^{p} x_{jk}^i \hat{\beta}_k^i$.

– y_j^0, ground-truth value of the response variable of the root node/aggregated/coarse-grained model, and the $j$the element of column vector Y^0, $1 \leq j \leq m_t$, $Y^0 = [y_1^0, \ldots, y_j^0, \ldots, y_{m_t}^0]^T$; $y_j^0 = \sum_{i=1}^{n} y_j^i$.

– $\hat{y}_j^0$, the predicted value of y_j^0, $1 \leq i \leq n$, $1 \leq j \leq m_t$, and generated by a linear regression model, $\hat{y}_j^0 = \sum_{i=1}^{n}(x_{j1}^i \hat{\beta}_{i1}^0 + \cdots + x_{jk}^i \hat{\beta}_{ik}^0 + \cdots + x_{jk}^i \hat{\beta}_{ip}^0) = \sum_{i=1}^{n} \sum_{k=1}^{p} x_{jk}^i \hat{\beta}_{ik}^0$.

For the consistency measurement, we propose a Mean Consistency Error (MCE) to qualify the consistency degree that the hierarchical modeling violates. Its definition over test datasets $\{\mathcal{D}_i^E | 0 \leq i \leq n\}$ is provided as follows.

$$\text{MCE}(\{\mathcal{D}_i^E | 0 \leq i \leq n\}) = \frac{1}{m_e} \sum_{j=1}^{m_e} \left| \hat{y}_j^0 - \sum_{i=1}^{n} \hat{y}_j^i \right| \tag{3}$$

For forecasting accuracy measurement, the indicator we employed in this study is the popular Mean Absolute Error (MAE), and below is the definition over test dataset $\mathcal{D}_i^E$ ($0 \leq i \leq n$).

$$\text{MAE}(\mathcal{D}_i^E) = \frac{1}{m_e} \sum_{j=1}^{m_e} |\hat{y}_j^i - y_j^i| \tag{4}$$

4. Learning Algorithm

In this section, we develop the AGD algorithm to solve the optimization problem in Section 3. We first introduce new notations for the learning algorithm development, parameters set $\hat{\boldsymbol{\beta}} = \{\hat{\beta}_k^i, \hat{\beta}_{ik}^0 | 1 \leq i \leq n, 1 \leq k \leq p\}$, and the optimization objective can be alternatively noted as the loss function of parameters set $L(\hat{\boldsymbol{\beta}})$.

$$
\begin{aligned}
L(\hat{\boldsymbol{\beta}}) &= L(\{\hat{\beta}_k^i, \hat{\beta}_{ik}^0 | 1 \leq i \leq n, 1 \leq k \leq p\}) \\
&= \frac{1}{2} \left\{ \sum_{i=1}^{n} \sum_{j=1}^{m_t} \left(\sum_{k=1}^{p} x_{jk}^i \hat{\beta}_k^i - y_j^i \right)^2 + \sum_{j=1}^{m_t} \left(\sum_{i=1}^{m_t} \sum_{k=1}^{p} x_{jk}^i \hat{\beta}_{ik}^0 - y_j^0 \right)^2 \right. \\
&\left. + \sum_{j=1}^{m_t} \left(\sum_{i=1}^{n} \sum_{k=1}^{p} x_{jk}^i \hat{\beta}_{ik}^0 - \sum_{i=1}^{n} \sum_{k=1}^{p} x_{jk}^i \hat{\beta}_k^i \right)^2 \right\}
\end{aligned} \tag{5}
$$

Here $\frac{1}{2}$ eases the solution development. AGD algorithm calculates the optimal parameters iteratively. At each iteration, it computes the gradient over all training data and then updates the parameter. Each $\hat{\beta} \in \hat{\boldsymbol{\beta}}$ is updated by the following rule.

$$\hat{\beta}^{\text{new}} \leftarrow \hat{\beta}^{\text{old}} - \eta \frac{\partial(L(\hat{\beta}))}{\partial(\hat{\beta})} \tag{6}$$

Here η is the learning rate. The AGD changes learning rate η if two requirements are satisfied: (1) the loss is very small and close to the optimal, $L^{\text{itr}+1} \leq \epsilon$. (The ϵ is set to be 1.0.); (2) the training loss is increased, $L^{\text{itr}+1} > L^{\text{itr}}$. The first requirement is required. This is because, at initial iterations, the gradient is not stable and jumps; it is likely that the training loss increases. The second requirement is to confirm that current learning rate is too large to reduce the training loss when the solutions is close to the optimal. The AGD algorithm stops once the number of iterations reaches maxInteractions. It is a hyper-parameter and computed by the grid search.

5. Experimental Studies

Both real-world and synthetic datasets are used for experiments, and the following methods are used as baselines for comparison analysis.

- Bottom-Up (BU) method:[3] forecasts of root node (aggregate) model is computed by summing up forecasts of the leaf node models.
- Top-Down (TD) method:[5] first trains the root node model and produces the aggregate forecast. Forecasts of leaf node models are decomposed proportionally from the aggregate forecast; proportions are based on available training data.
- Separate (Sep) method: this method solves the $n + 1$ linear regression problems individually and does not take the hierarchical relationship into account.

5.1. *Salary prediction problem*

In this subsection, we provide a simple but illustrative example to demonstrate the effectiveness of the proposed HRLS method. The database we used here is from an automobile manufacturing company. The aim is to build a linear regression model and predict the employee's salary based on his/her working years. The settings of parameters are: (1) the number of explanatory variables is 2, $p = 2$, including the provided "*working years*" and the fixed "1" for intercept; (2) there are 100 samples/instances, and we consider two leaf node models only, $n = 2$. For each leaf node, there are 50 samples/data instances, namely, $m = 50$. Because of the limited size, we employ 5-fold cross-validation (CV) to comprehensively evaluate the proposed approach; validation results are provided by the following Table 1.

Table 1. Forecasting results of Average MAE of 5-fold CV.

Regression	Method			
Problem ID	BU	TD	Sep	**HRLS (proposed)**
P_0 (Root)	1061.88	1059.41	1059.41	**1054.07**
P_1 (Leaf node 1)	690.07	1988.12	690.07	**680.09**
P_2 (Leaf node 2)	730.53	1857.26	730.53	**728.99**

By Table 1, we can get the following observations: (1) Overall the Sep method and the proposed HRLS perform better than the BU and TD. This indicates that either BU or TD loses information and predictive power in the process of aggregation or decomposition. (2) In terms of average MAE over five runs, the proposed HRLS performance is the best among all methods. (3) The MAE of TD for the root problem, P_0, is the same as that of Sep; similarly, the MAEs of BU for leaf node problems P_1 and P_2 are equal to that of Sep, respectively. This is guaranteed by the definition of BU and TD.

Now we proceed to the consistency analysis. We first note that MCE of both BU and TD is zero because they are defined based on the CC, and Fig. 2 displays the MCE of Sep and the proposed HRLS. From it, we can conclude that Sep produces highly inconsistent foresting results.

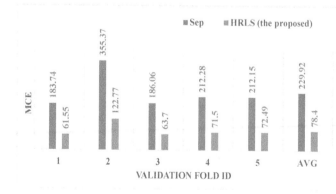

Fig. 2. Results of MCE for Sep and HRLS methods over validation sets of 5-fold CV.

5.2. Synthetic datasets with different ground-truth models and distributions

In this subsection, we manually generate datasets for leaf node problem P_1 and P_2 with different ground-truth models and data distributions. Specifically, 500 samples for leaf node problem P_1 and P_2, $m = 500$ are produced. Below are the detail settings.

- For leaf node P_1, the ground-truth model is $y_j^1 = 1 + 10x_{j2}^1 + \epsilon_j^1$ ($x_{j1}^1 = 1$) for each $1 \leq j \leq m$; the noise term ϵ_j^1 follows a normal distribution with zero mean and standard deviation of 80, $\epsilon_j^1 \sim \mathcal{N}(0, 80)$; the feature x_{j2}^1 is got by randomly sampling from a uniform distribution $[0, 200]$.
- For leaf node P_2, the ground-truth model is $y_j^2 = -2 - 5x_{j2}^2 + \epsilon_j^2$ ($x_{j1}^2 = 1$) for $1 \leq j \leq m$; setting of the noise item is $\epsilon_j^2 \sim \mathcal{N}(0, 50)$; feature x_{j2}^2 is uniformly sampled on $[-200, 0]$.
- For the root node P_0, the ground-truth data is produced by aggregating leaf nodes P_1 and P_2. For each $1 \leq j \leq m$, $y_j^0 = y_j^1 + y_j^2$, and features are x_{j2}^1 and x_{j2}^2.

We randomly sample 80% data points as training dataset ($m_t = 400$) and the rest 20% data points as test set ($m_e = 100$). Table 2 displays the results of MAE and MCE over the test set, by which we can see that the proposed HRLS dominates the other three methods in terms of either forecasting accuracy measurement MAE or consistency measurement MCE. These results further support the superiority of HRLS.

Table 2. Forecasting results of MAE and MCE over test set of the synthetic dataset.

Method	MAE			MCE
	P_0 (Root)	P_1 (Leaf node 1)	P_2 (Leaf node 2)	
BU	77.95	68.48	39.17	0
TD	78.44	245.96	251.62	0
Sep	78.44	68.48	39.17	2.27
HRLS (the proposed)	**77.45**	**68.34**	**37.97**	**0.24**

6. Conclusion

This paper studies how to learn a group of linear regression problems which are hierarchically structured. A natural, simple yet important relationship, CC (**the sum of fine-grained forecasts should be equal to the corresponding coarse-grained forecast**), is considered in the learning process for problems of different levels in the hierarchy. Experimental studies confirm its significance, and indicate that it plays a role of *"reconciliation"* and looks for the optimal balance between the forecast accuracy and consistency; it can also be explained as a new approach of regularization for a group of linear regression problems. The limitation of current work is lack of theoretical analysis which is the future work.

Acknowledgments

This research is partially supported by the Fundamental Research Funds for the Central Universities (Grant No. 2682022CX067), the Natural Science Foundation of Sichuan Province (Grant No. 2022NSFSC0930), the Summer Research Inspiration Internships and Youth Talent Startup Grant from SWJTU-Leeds Joint School.

References

1. Athanasopoulos, G., Gamakumara, P., Panagiotelis, A., Hyndman, R.J., Affan, M.: Hierarchical forecasting. In: Macroeconomic Forecasting in the Era of Big Data, pp. 689–719. Springer (2020)
2. Athanasopoulos, G., Hyndman, R.J., Kourentzes, N., Petropoulos, F.: Forecasting with temporal hierarchies. European Journal of Operational Research **262**(1), 60–74 (2017)
3. Dangerfield, B.J., Morris, J.S.: Top-down or bottom-up: Aggregate versus disaggregate extrapolations. International journal of forecasting **8**(2), 233–241 (1992)
4. Fliedner, G.: Hierarchical forecasting: issues and use guidelines. Industrial Management & Data Systems (2001)
5. Gross, C.W., Sohl, J.E.: Disaggregation methods to expedite product line forecasting. Journal of Forecasting **9**(3), 233–254 (1990)
6. Hyndman, R.J., Athanasopoulos, G.: Forecasting: principles and practice, Chapter 10. OTexts (2018)
7. Orcutt, G.H., Watts, H.W., Edwards, J.B.: Data aggregation and information loss. The American Economic Review **58**(4), 773–787 (1968)
8. Schwarzkopf, A.B., Tersine, R.J., Morris, J.S.: Top-down versus bottom-up forecasting strategies. The International Journal of Production Research **26**(11), 1833–1843 (1988)
9. Wanke, P., Saliby, E.: Top-down or bottom-up forecasting? Pesquisa Operacional **27**(3), 591–605 (2007)

An improved contradiction separation dynamic deduction method based on complementary ratio

Guoyan Zeng[*], Yang Xu[†] and Shuwei Chen[‡]

School of Mathematics, Southwest Jiaotong University, Chengdu 611756, China
National-Local Joint Engineering Laboratory of System Credibility Automatic
Verification, Southwest Jiaotong University, Chengdu 611756, China
[*]guoyanzeng_math@163.com
[†]xuyang@home.swjtu.edu.cn
[‡]swchen@home.swjtu.edu.cn

Automated Theorem Proving (ATP) is hard research of automated reasoning. The inference mechanism of most state-of-the-art first-order theorem provers is essentially a binary resolution method. The resolution method involves two clauses, and generates a clause with many literals in every deduction step, the search space will explode very quickly. Multi-clause standard contradiction separation (S-CS) calculus for first-order logic as a breakthrough of automated reasoning can restrict limitations. Based on S-CS rule, we propose a novel method called complementary ratio in this paper. Complementary ratio then is integrated into the leading ATP system Vampire, and we test the CASC-28 competition theorems (FOF division). The results show that complementary ratio can improve the performance of CS-based prover and Vampire.

Keywords: Theorem proving; multi-clause dynamic synergized deduction; binary resolution; clause selection.

1. Introduction

Automated Theorem Proving (ATP) is a very interesting research area. ATP is used in many domains [1, 2], including mathematics, software creation, software verification, hardware verification, etc. In 1965, resolution principle was proposed by Robinson [3]. It is one of the important tools for ATP. The resolution principle has been successfully used in state-of-the-art first-order theorem provers, for example, Vampire [4, 5], Eprover [6, 7], Prover9 [8], etc.

The core of the resolution principle is binary resolution. Binary resolution requires that only two clauses participate in each deduction, and the two clauses involve a complementary pair. So that only two literals are deleted in every deduction step. For binary resolution, there are usually a lot of literals remaining in the search space, and the proof space will grow rapidly. In order to break through the limitation of binary resolution, a standard contradiction separation (S-CS) rule was proposed in [9, 10]. S-CS rule is an extension based on binary resolution, binary resolution is a special kind of S-CS rule. In each deduction, S-CS rule can involve multiple (two or more) clauses and delete at least a complementary pair. S-CS rule has a stronger ability to delete complementary pair than binary resolution.

Currently, some literal and clause selection strategies are proposed, which can improve the capability of the CS-based prover. For example, the stability of term [11, 12], decision literal strategy [13], literal selection strategy and clause selection strategy [14, 15]. However, few strategies study complementary pair during S-CS deduction process. In fact, there exists at least a complementary pair in each S-CS deduction, so we noticed that the number of the complementary pair in every deduction is a key feature. A new idea is that we evaluate the feature based on S-CS rule. We propose a weight evaluation method (called comple-mentary ratio method), where the method primarily refers to reflecting the complementary level of a given clause in a clause set. The method has a guidance effect on the selection of subsequent input clauses. Complementary ratio method can be used for a clause set with unit clause. There are many clause sets that have unit clause, such as Horn sets [16].

On the other hand, some combinational ATP systems (e.g., SDDA_V, SDDA_E, and CoProver) were proposed in [11, 17]. CoProver could solve some hard problems with rating=1, and SDDA_V (SDDA_E) could improve the performance of Vampire (E). In this paper, a novel combinational ATP system is proposed, CS_V 4.5, which combines the advantages of S-CS rule using complementary ratio and binary resolution.

The rest of the paper is structured as follows. In Section 2, we present basic concepts of S-CS rule. Complementary degree and complementary ratio are proposed based on S-CS rule, then some examples are used to illustrate how these proposed definitions work in Section 3. We provide experimental evaluation in Section 4. In the last section, we show the results obtained and possible future work.

2. Overview of Standard Contradiction Separation Rule

We make some necessary preliminaries and basic concepts of S-CS rule.

Definition 2.1. [18] A literal is either an atom A or a negated atom $\sim A$. Two literals are said to be a complementary pair if one is the negation of the other, denoted as $\{A, \sim A\}$. An atom is an n-ary predicate (denoted P or Q) applied to n

terms. A term is either a variable, a constant or an n-ary function (denoted f or g) applied to n terms. A substitution is a mapping from variables to terms.

Definition 2.2. [19] A clause is a disjunction of literals, i.e., either a literal, called a unit clause, or a string of the form $L_1 \lor ... \lor L_n$ where the L_i are literals.

Definition 2.3. [19] An expression that is true in all interpretations is said to be valid, or a tautology.

Definition 2.4. [9, 10] Suppose a clause set $S = \{C_1, C_2, ..., C_m\}$ in first-order logic. Without loss of generality, assume that there does not exist the same variables among $C_1, C_2, ..., C_m$ (if there exists the same variables, there exists a rename substitution can then be applied to make them different). The following inference rule that produces a new clause from S is called a *standard contradiction separation rule*, in short, an S-CS rule:

For each clause C_i ($i = 1, 2, ..., m$), firstly apply a substitution σ_i to C_i (σ_i could be an empty substitution but not necessary the most general unifier), denoted as $C_i^{\sigma_i}$; then separate $C_i^{\sigma_i}$ into two sub-clauses $C_i^{\sigma_i-}$ and $C_i^{\sigma_i+}$ such that:

(1) $C_i^{\sigma_i} = C_i^{\sigma_i-} \lor C_i^{\sigma_i+}$, where $C_i^{\sigma_i-}$ and $C_i^{\sigma_i+}$ have no common literal;

(2) $C_i^{\sigma_i+}$ can be an empty clause itself, but $C_i^{\sigma_i-}$ cannot be an empty clause;

(3) $\bigwedge_{i=1}^{m} C_i^{\sigma_i-}$ is a standard contradiction, that is $\forall (x_1, ..., x_m) \in \prod_{i=1}^{m} C_i^{\sigma_i-}$, there exists at least one complementary pair among $\{x_1, ..., x_m\}$.

The resulting clause $\bigvee_{i=1}^{m} C_i^{\sigma_i+}$, denoted as $C_m^{s\sigma}(C_1, C_2, ..., C_m)$ (here "s" means "standard", $\sigma = \bigcup_{i=1}^{m} \sigma_i, \sigma_i$ is a substitution to $C_i, i = 1, 2, ..., m$), is called a *standard contradiction separation clause* (S-CSC) of $C_1, C_2, ..., C_m$, and $\bigwedge_{i=1}^{m} C_i^{\sigma_i-}$ is called a *separated standard contradiction* (S-SC).

Definition 2.5. [9, 10] Suppose a clause set $S = \{C_1, C_2, ..., C_m\}$ in first-order logic. $\Phi_1, \Phi_2, ..., \Phi_t$ is called a *standard contradiction separation based dynamic deduction sequence* from S to a clause Φ_t, denoted as D^s, if

(1) $\Phi_i \in S, i \in \{1, 2, ..., t\}$; or

(2) there exist $r_1, r_2, ..., r_{k_i} < i$, $\Phi_i = C_{r_{k_i}}^{s\theta_i}(\Phi_{r_1}, \Phi_{r_2}, ..., \Phi_{r_{k_i}})$, where $\theta_i = \bigcup_{j=1}^{k_i} \sigma_j, \sigma_j$ is a substitution to $\Phi_{r_j}, j = 1, 2, ..., k_i$.

3. Clause Complementary Ratio Based on S-CS Rule

In this section, not only does there exist a complementary relationship between the two literals, but we can also define a new complementary relation between clauses. We then give a complementary ratio function of a clause in first-order logic.

Definition 3.1. (Clause complementary condition) Suppose two clauses $C_1 = x_1 \lor \ldots \lor x_m$ and $C_2 = y_1 \lor \ldots \lor y_n$, where x_i ($i = 1,\ldots,m$) and y_j ($j = 1,\ldots,n$) are literals of C_1 and C_2 respectively, and neither C_1 nor C_2 is tautology. Without loss of generality, assume that there do not exist the same variables between C_1 and C_2 (if there exist the same variables, a rename substitution can be applied to make them different). If there exists a substitution θ of C_1 and C_2 such that, there exists at least one complementary pair among $\{x_1^\theta, \ldots, x_m^\theta, y_1^\theta, \ldots, y_n^\theta\}$. Then it is said C_1^θ and C_2^θ satisfy the clause complementary condition.

Definition 3.2. (Clause complementary degree) Suppose two clauses $C_1 = x_1 \lor \ldots \lor x_m$ and $C_2 = y_1 \lor \ldots \lor y_n$, wh ere x_i ($i = 1,\ldots,m$) and y_j ($j = 1,\ldots,n$) are literals of C_1 and C_2 respectively. If C_1 and C_2 satisfy the clause complementary condition, the number of all complementary pairs is called clause complementary degree (CCD) between C_1 and C_2, denoted as

$$CCD(C_1, C_2) = \sum_{j=1,\ldots,n} \sum_{i=1,\ldots,m} \left|\{x_i^\theta, y_j^\theta\}\right|, (x_i^\theta \in C_1^\theta, y_j^\theta \in C_2^\theta, y_j^\theta = \sim x_i^\theta),$$

where $\left|\{x_i^\theta, y_j^\theta\}\right|$ is the number of complementary pair $\{x_i^\theta, y_j^\theta\}$.

Remark 3.1. The complementary pair $\{x_i^\theta, y_j^\theta\}$ (where $x_i^\theta \in C_1^\theta, y_j^\theta \in C_2^\theta, y_j^\theta = \sim x_i^\theta$) is also denoted as $\{y_j^\theta, x_i^\theta\}$ (where $y_j^\theta \in C_2^\theta, x_i^\theta \in C_1^\theta, x_i^\theta = \sim y_j^\theta$), therefore clause complementary degree between C_1 and C_2 satisfies symmetry.

The following example illustrates how the proposed complementary degree of two clauses work.

Example 3.1. Let two clauses $C_1 = P_1(x_{11}) \lor \sim P_2(x_{12}) \lor \sim P_3(f(x_{13}))$, $C_2 = \sim P_1(x_{21}) \lor P_3(x_{21})$. Here $x_{11}, x_{12}, x_{13}, x_{21}$ are variables, f is a function symbol, P_1, P_2, P_3 are predicate symbols.

According to Definition 3.2, there are 2 complementary pairs: $\{P_1(f(x_{13})/x_{11}), \sim P_1(f(x_{13})/x_{21})\}$ and $\left\{\sim P_3(f(x_{13})), P_3\left(\frac{f(x_{13})}{x_{21}}\right)\right\}$. Clause complementary degree of C_1 and C_2 is two, where $\theta = \{f(x_{13})/x_{11}, f(x_{13})/x_{21}\}$.

A clause is usually defined to be a finite set (or multiset) of literals [19], so we also define a method to reflect the complementary level of a clause according to a finite literal set. In fact, there exist many unit clauses during S-CS deduction process. Based on unit clauses, a novel clause selection method is proposed, which includes two aspects: the clause complementary degree and the number of literals of clause.

Definition 3.3. (Complementary ratio) Suppose a literal set $D_{l_m} = \{l_{d1}, \dots, l_{dm}\}$ and a clause $C = l_1 \vee l_2 \vee \dots \vee l_n$, where each $l_{di} \in D_{l_m}$ is a literal of a unit clause. If C^θ and $D_{l_m}^\theta$ satisfy the clause complementary condition, where θ is a substitution to C and D_{l_m}. Then the complementary ratio (CR) of clause C in D_{l_m} is the $CCD(C^\theta, D_{l_m}^\theta)\,/\,n$, denoted as

$$CR(C^\theta, D_{l_m}^\theta) = \frac{1}{n} * \sum_{j=1,\dots,n} \sum_{i=1,\dots,m} \left| \{ l_j^\theta, l_{di}^\theta | l_j^\theta \in C^\theta, l_{di}^\theta \in D_{l_m}^\theta, l_{di}^\theta = \sim l_j^\theta \} \right|.$$

Remark 3.2. We suppose all the literals in D_{l_m} have no complementary pair. The larger the clause complementary ratio, the higher priority of clause selection. From Definition 3.3, we can see that if $CR(C^\theta, D_{l_m}^\theta) = 0$, it means that all literals of C^θ have no complementary pair in $D_{l_m}^\theta$. If $CR(C^\theta, D_{l_m}^\theta) = 1$, it means that all the literals of C^θ have complementary pairs in $D_{l_m}^\theta$, and the original clause set is unsatisfiable.

The following example illustrates how the proposed complementary ratio work.

Example 3.2. Let $C_1 = P_3(a_1)$, $C_2 = P_2(a_1, a_3)$, $C_3 = P_1(a_1, f_1(a_1), f_1(a_3))$, $C_4 = P_1(a_3, a_3, f_1(a_3))$, $C_5 = P_2(x_{11}, x_{14}) \vee \sim P_3(x_{11}) \vee \sim P_1(x_{12}, x_{15}, x_{14}) \vee \sim P_2(x_{11}, x_{12}) \vee \sim P_2(x_{11}, x_{13})$. Here $x_{11}, x_{12}, x_{13}, x_{14}, x_{15}$ are variables, f_1 is a function symbol, P_1, P_2, P_3 are predicate symbols.

According to Definition 3.3, we have the literal set $D_{l_4} = \{P_3(a_1), P_2(a_1, a_3),$ $P_1(a_1, f_1(a_1), f_1(a_3)), P_1(a_3, a_3, f_1(a_3))\}$. There are 4 complementary pairs: $\{\sim P_3(a_1/x_{11}), P_3(a_1)\}$, $\{\sim P_2(a_1/x_{11}, a_3/x_{13}), P_2(a_1, a_3)\}$, $\{\sim P_1(a_3/x_{12}, a_3/x_{15}, f_1(a_3)/x_{14}), P_1(a_3, a_3, f_1(a_3))\}$, $\{\sim P_2(a_1/x_{11}, a_3/x_{12}), P_2(a_1, a_3)\}$, therefore complementary ratio $CR(C_5^\theta, D_{l_m}^\theta) = 4/5$, where $\theta = \{a_1/x_{11}, a_3/x_{12}, a_3/x_{13}, f_1(a_3)/x_{14}, a_3/x_{15}\}$.

4. Experimental and Performance Analysis

4.1. Experimental setup

Two novel combinational ATP systems CS_V 4.5 and CSN_V 4.5 are constructed by CS-based prover and Vampire 4.5, which combine the advantages of S-CS rule and binary resolution. CS_V 4.5 uses complementary ratio and CSN_V 4.5 does not use complementary ratio.

In the same hardware environment, ATP systems CS_V 4.5, CSN_V 4.5, and Vampire 4.5 test 500 problems from First-Order Form division of CASC competition (CASC-28) [20]. Experiments are carried out on a PC with 3.4 GHz Inter(R) Core (TM) i7-6700 processor and 11.1GB of RAM, OS Ubuntu15.04 64-bit, with the default CPU time limit of 300 s.

4.2. *Experimental results and analysis*

Rating is a number ranging from 0.0 to 1.0 that shows the difficulty of TPTP problems. A problem with rating 0.0 means that it can be solved by all state-of-the-art ATP systems, and a problem cannot be solved by all state-of-the-art ATP systems with rating 1.0.

The performance of CS_V 4.5, CSN_V 4.5 and Vampire 4.5 are shown in Fig. 1. From Fig. 1, Vampire 4.5 can solve 453 problems, CSN_V 4.5 can solve 455 problems, and CS_V 4.5 can solve 460 problems. The problem-solving ability of CS_V 4.5 is stronger than Vampire 4.5 and CSN_V 4.5. The average time for Vampire 4.5 to solve 453 problems is 16.77 seconds, and the average time for CSN_V4.5 to solve 455 problems is 17.25 seconds, the average time for CS_V4.5 to solve 460 problems is 18.06 seconds.

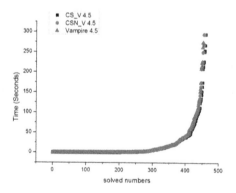

Fig. 1. Comparison on solved problems by CS_V 4.5, CSN_V 4.5 and Vampire 4.5.

Table 1 shows the comparison on solved problems by CS_V 4.5 and Vampire 4.5. From Table 1, we can see that 12 problems with a rating almost greater than 0.8. These problems are solved by CS_V 4.5 but unsolved by Vampire 4.5, and they all have unit clause.

Table 1. List of problems solved by CS_V 4.5 but unsolved by Vampire 4.5.

No	Problem	Rating	Number of Unit	Time (Seconds)
1	GEO310+1	**0.86**	37	29.208
2	GEO316+1	**0.86**	44	44.478
3	GEO319+1	**0.86**	20	32.814
4	GEO323+1	**0.86**	37	36.526
5	GEO495+1	0.69	14	220.647
6	NUM695+4	**0.94**	209	70.157
7	SET948+1	**0.94**	8	26.823
8	CSR036+3	0.5	3281	0.366
9	ITP011+1	**0.92**	20	123.837
10	ITP020+5	**0.97**	1793	7.422
11	SEU157+2	0.72	36	18.966
12	LCL888+1	0.78	6	54.24

Table 2 shows the comparison on solved problems by CSN_V 4.5 and Vampire 4.5. From Table 2, we can see that 5 problems are solved by CSN_V 4.5 but unsolved by Vampire 4.5. In particular, Table 1 and Table 2 show that CS_V 4.5 can solve some GEO problems (GEO310+1, GEO316+1, GEO319+1, GEO323+1, and GEO495+1), but these problems are unsolved by CSN_V 4.5 and Vampire 4.5. So, complementary ratio method can effectively improve the ability of Vampire 4.5.

Table 2. List of problems solved by CSN_V 4.5 but unsolved by Vampire 4.5.

No	Problem	Rating	Number of Unit	Time (Seconds)
1	CSR036+3	0.5	3281	0.372
2	ITP011+1	0.92	20	123.98
3	ITP020+5	0.97	1793	7.58
4	SEU157+2	0.72	36	18.917
5	LCL888+1	0.78	6	54.256

5. Conclusions and Future Work

In this paper, we have proposed a novel complementary ratio method, which can select clause during deduction. This method has a guidance effect on the selection of subsequent input clauses and literals. It is applied to a clause set with unit clause. Complementary ratio method is beneficial to finding the proof path. Experiments show that the performance of CS_V 4.5 is better than Vampire 4.5. Complementary ratio can effectively improve the ability of Vampire.

For future work, we will continue to study complementary degree and complementary ratio, and try to improve the method based on S-CS rule.

Acknowledgments

This work has been partially supported by the National Natural Science Foundation of China (Grant No. 61976130).

References

1. G. Burel, G. Bury, R. Cauderlier, D. Delahaye, P. Halmagrand, O. Hermant, First-order automated reasoning with theories: when deduction Modulo Theory meets practice[J], J. Autom. Reason, 64(6): 1001-1050, 2020.
2. V. Pavlov, A. Schukin, T. Cherkasova, Exploring automated reasoning in first-order logic: tools, techniques and application areas[C]//International Conference on Knowledge   Engineering and the Semantic Web, Berlin, Springer-Verlag, 102-116, 2013.
3. J. A. Robinson, A machine oriented logic based on the resolution principle, J. ACM, 12(1): 23-41, 1965.
4. A. Azanov and A. Voronkov, The design and implementation of vampire [J], AI Communications, 15(2-3): 91-110, 2002.
5. L Kovács, A. Voronkov, First-order theorem proving and vampire[C]// International Conference on Computer Aided Verification, Berlin, Springer-Verlag, 1-35, 2013.
6. S. Schulz, E-a brainiac theorem prover [J], Ai Communications, 15(2-3): 111-126, 2002.
7. S. Schulz, System description: E 1.8[C]// International Conference on Logic for Programming, Artificial Intelligence and Reasoning, Berlin, Springer-Verlag, 735-743, 2013.
8. W. MCCUNE, Release of prover9[C]//Mile High Conference on Quasigroups, Loops and Nonassociative Systems, Denver, Colorado. 2005.
9. Y. Xu, J. Liu, S. W. Chen, and X. M. Zhong, A novel generalization of resolution principle for automated deduction, The 12th International FLINS Conference on Uncertainty Modelling in Knowledge Engineering and Decision Making (FLINS2016), ENSAIT, Roubaix, France, August 24-26, 483-488, 2016.
10. Y. Xu, J. Liu, S. W. Chen, X. M. Zhong, X. X. He, Contradiction separation based dynamic multi-clause synergized automated deduction, Information Sciences, 462, 93-113, 2018.

11. J. Zhong, Y. Xu, F. Cao, A novel combinational ATP based on contradiction separation for first-order logic, International Journal of Computational Intelligence Systems, 13(1): 672-680, 2020.

12. J. Zhong, Y. Xu, S. W. Chen, et al., Stability-based term evaluation method in first-order logic, Computer Engineering, 45(11): 183-190, 197, 2019. (In Chinese)

13. S.W. Chen, Y. Xu, Y. Jiang, et al., Some synergized clause selection strategies for contradiction separation based automated deduction, 2017 12th International Conference on Intelligent Systems and Knowledge Engineering (ISKE), IEEE, 1-6, 2017.

14. F. Cao, Y. Xu, S. W. Chen, et al., A contradiction separation dynamic deduction algorithm based on optimized proof search, International Journal of Computational Intelligence Systems, 12(2): 1245-1254, 2019.

15. F. Cao, Study on a first-order logic automated theorem prover based on contradiction separation deduction [D], Southwest Jiaotong University, 2020. (In Chinese)

16. L. Henschen, L. Wos, Unit refutations and horn sets [J], Journal of the ACM, 21(4): 590-605, 1974.

17. F. Cao, Y. Xu, J. Liu, S. W. Chen, J. B. Yi, A multi-clause dynamic deduction algorithm based on standard contradiction separation rule, Information Sciences, 566, 281-299, 2021.

18. X. H. Liu, Automatic reasoning based on resolution method, Science Press, 1994. (In Chinese)

19. J. A. Robinson, A. Voronkov, eds, Handbook of automated reasoning, Elsevier, 2001.

20. G. Sutcliffe, M. Desharnais, The CADE-28 automated theorem proving system competition–CASC-28, AI Communications, 2021, 34(4): 259-276.

54

ADRC path following control
based on double deep Q-network for parafoil system

Hong Zhu, Qinglin Sun*, Feng Duan[†] and Zengqiang Chen

College of Artificial Intelligence, Nankai University
Tianjin, 300350, China
* sunql@nankai.edu.cn
† duanf@nankai.edu.cn

Xianyi Zeng

Gemtex Lab, University of Lille, ENSAIT
Roubaix, 59056, France

To achieve optimal path following performance of the parafoil system, we propose a real-time control method based on double deep Q-network (DQN) optimized active disturbance rejection control (ADRC). This method can choose the best parameters for ADRC of the system at different states using double DQN. The tracking performance of the parafoil system is evaluated under environment disturbances. The results show that the ADRC with adaptive parameters optimized by double DQN performs well under external interference and inherent uncertainty. Moreover, compared with the traditional ADRC, the proposed method has better control effects.

Keywords: Deep Q-network (DQN); active disturbance rejection control (ADRC); adaptive parameters; path following control.

1. Introduction

In the past decades, parafoil system navigation has become a critical technology in many fields such as agriculture, military, and aerospace.[1] The increasing demand for high efficiency and reliability is of great engineering necessity to be solved. Accurate path-tracking performance is vital in applications with predefined trajectories, such as aerospace recovery and precision delivery of payloads.[2]

In terms of homing control of the parafoil system, many researchers used ADRC to achieve linear path tracking control, and simulation results proved its advantages of anti-disturbance and model-free.[3,4] However, adjustment of parameters dramatically influences the controller's performance, which usually depends on the experience of experts and is accompanied by redundant and high-cost. Besides, fixed parameters have great limitations for sudden environment disturbances. In order to solve the above deficiencies, the reinforcement learning method is used in this paper.

Reinforcement learning (RL) uses the interaction information between the agent and environment to improve its model and takes the calculated reward of each action as feedback to improve the strategy. Many scholars have used Q learning of RL to optimize the controller parameters of ADRC.[5,6] Deep Q-Network (DQN) is developed based on Q learning, which uses a neural network to deal with high dimensional state space and action space. To improve the stability of training, double DQN is further proposed using another target Q-network to provide Q-value estimates.[7]

In this paper, to avoid parameter tuning process, double DQN is first applied to optimize the controller parameters for path following of the parafoil system. This adaptive ADRC controller based on double DQN shows better anti-disturbance and control performance than constant parameter controller.

2. ADRC Controller Design for Parafoil Path Following

2.1. Tracking error method

In the path following control of parafoil system, the position error between its current position and the reference path is used as a feedback. The parafoil conducts trajectory manipulations through the current error until it reaches the target path. This error is calculated by combining lateral trajectory error and parallax method, as shown in Fig. 1. ℓ is the horizontal distance between the parafoil and the reference path, and parallax ψ_e is the angle between the actual flight direction of the parafoil ψ and the reference direction or tangent direction ψ_r. The calculation of tracking

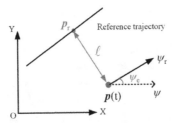

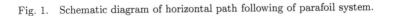

Fig. 1.   Schematic diagram of horizontal path following of parafoil system.

error in horizontal plane is represented as:

$$\epsilon = \psi_e + \kappa \ell. \tag{1}$$

where κ is an adjustable parameter. Thus, the problem of path following can be transformed into heading tracking by the lateral trajectory error method.

2.2. ADRC controller

The linear ADRC is used to design the controller of the parafoil system, which has strong feasibility in practical application.[8] The actual heading angle of the system can be expressed in the second-order differential form:

$$\ddot{\psi} = f + b_0 u, y = \psi \tag{2}$$

where $f = f(\psi, \dot{\psi}) + \omega_d$ represents the total disturbance function of the system, ω_d is the external disturbance, u is the control input, and b_0 denotes the gain of input.

Let ζ be the first derivative of f, and the state variables of the system are expressed as

$$\dot{x}_1 = x_2, \dot{x}_2 = x_3 + b_0 u, \dot{x}_3 = \zeta, y = x_1, f = x_3 \tag{3}$$

An extended state observer (ESO) is constructed to observe the total disturbance f of the system:

$$\dot{z}_1 = z_2 + \lambda_1(y - \hat{y}), \dot{z}_2 = z_3 + b_0 u + \lambda_2(y - \hat{y}), \dot{z}_3 = \lambda_3(y - \hat{y}) \tag{4}$$

where $\hat{y}$ is the estimated output for y, $[\lambda_1 \ \lambda_2 \ \lambda_3] = [3\omega_o \ 3\omega_o^2 \ \omega_o^3]$ is the gain vector of the observer, and ω_o is the observer bandwidth that affects the estimation ability of the observer.

Based on the ESO, the controller is designed as:

$$u = \frac{(u_0 - z_3)}{b_0} \tag{5}$$

where $u_0 = k_p(\psi_d - z_1) + k_d(\dot{\psi}_d - z_2)$ is the output of the state error feedback, ψ_d denotes the given reference heading angle, $k_p = \omega_c^2$ and $k_d = 2\omega_c$ are the control gains, and ω_c is the controller bandwidth.

The output of the system is the heading angle ψ, which can be obtained from the real-time position $\boldsymbol{p}(t) = (x(t), y(t))$ of the parafoil as

$$\psi = \tan^{-1}\left(\frac{\dot{y}}{\dot{x}}\right) \tag{6}$$

where the derivative forms represent the horizontal velocity of the parafoil system. Similarly, the reference heading angle can be obtained by combining the position of the target point $p_d = (x_d, y_d)$:

$$\psi_d = \tan^{-1}\left(\frac{y_d - y(t)}{x_d - x(t)}\right) \tag{7}$$

Substituting Eq. (5) into Eq. (2), we can obtain

$$\ddot{\psi} = f + b_0 u \approx u_0 \tag{8}$$

From the above descriptions, the controller parameters that need to be optimized are ω_o, ω_c and b_0. This paper uses the DQN method to obtain the optimal controller performance. Studies in Ref. 9 have shown that when b_0 is within a certain range, the stability and convergence of ESO can be guaranteed. Hence ω_o and ω_c are primarily adjusted by DQN in this paper.

3. Double DQN based ADRC Controller Parameter Adjustment

DQN combines deep neural networks and reinforcement learning, which avoids the dimensional disaster and non-convergence problem of Q-learning. In addition, to avoid overfitting, this paper uses a double DQN algorithm to optimize the controller parameters. Generally, the reward value r designed in Eq. (12) is used to evaluate the current state-action pair, and the cumulative reward value is used as a reference to take action A in state S with a policy π. The relationship is as follows:

$$Q_\pi(s, a) = E_\pi\left[\sum_{t=0}^{\infty} \gamma^t r_{t+1} | S_t = s, A_t = a\right] \tag{9}$$

where $Q_\pi(s, a)$ is the state-action value function, γ is the discount factor, reflecting the weight of reward value over time. In this work, the selection of action a in the current state s is based on the ε-greedy policy.

Each state-action pair corresponds to a Q value in Q-learning. However, the Q value is replaced by a deep neural network in this work. The larger the Q value, the closer the corresponding action a is to the optimal value. The input of the neural network is the state variables of the system, and the output is $Q(s_i, a_j)$ value of each group of actions corresponding to the input of state:

$$F(s_i, a_j; \theta) \approx Q(s_i, a_j) \tag{10}$$

where θ is the neural network weights.

The ultimate goal of DQN is to train a deep neural network to fit the Q values and finally obtain the optimal solutions. The two neural networks are named as Q_1 and Q_2, respectively, and they have the same structure but different weights. Q_1 network updates the weights θ through training, while Q_2 network is not for training but for obtaining the Q value at the next time step. And the Q2 network is assigned by Q1 network every T time steps. A well-trained neural network can output the Q values corresponding to each group of actions taken in the current state. The action value with the largest Q value is the optimal selection in the current state. In the training process of the neural network, the weights are updated by the gradient descent method:

$$
\theta \leftarrow \theta + \alpha \left[r + \gamma \hat{F} \left(s', \operatorname*{argmax}_{a'} F(s', a'; \theta); \theta' \right) - F(s, a; \theta) \right] \\
\cdot \nabla F(s, a; \theta)
\tag{11}
$$

where r is the instant reward for every selected action, $\alpha \in (0, 1]$ and $\gamma \in (0, 1]$ represent the learning rate and discounting factor, respectively.

Section 2.1 introduced the path following method of the parafoil system and obtained the tracking error described by Eq. (1). All training data comes from a dynamic model of parafoil system built on Ref. 10. In this section, the tracking error and its deviation are defined as state variables $S = [\epsilon, \dot{\epsilon}]$. They are used to calculate the reward r of each action given the states S during the training period.

$$
r = \begin{cases} 100, & (-5 < \epsilon \leq 0 \,\&\, \dot{\epsilon} \geq 0) \| (0 \leq \epsilon < 5 \,\&\, \dot{\epsilon} \leq 0) \\ -100, & (-5 \leq \epsilon \leq 0 \,\&\, \dot{\epsilon} < 0) \| (0 < \epsilon \leq 5 \,\&\, \dot{\epsilon} > 0) \\ -\infty, & otherwise \end{cases}
\tag{12}
$$

The controller parameters are discretized to generate the action space.

$$
\omega_o \in \{\omega_{o1}, \omega_{o2}, \ldots, \omega_{on}\}, \quad \omega_c \in \{\omega_{c1}, \omega_{c2}, \ldots, \omega_{cm}\}
\tag{13}
$$

where $\omega_{oi} = \omega_{o1} + (i-1)\nu_1$, $i \in (1, 2, \ldots, n)$, $\omega_{cj} = \omega_{c1} + (j-1)\nu_2$, $j \in (1, 2, \ldots, m)$, n and m are element numbers of ω_o and ω_c with intervals of ν_1 and ν_2, respectively, that constitute the action space. Here we choose $\omega_{o1} = \omega_{c1} = 0.1$, $\omega_{on} = \omega_{cm} = 1.5$, $\nu_1 = \nu_2 = 0.01$.

4. Simulation Analysis

In order to prove the effectiveness of the proposed method, this section compares the control effect of ADRC with constant parameters and adaptive parameters optimized by double DQN. The desired trajectory is a straight line in the horizontal plane with starting point $(0, 100)$ m and ending point $(1500, 1500)$ m. The wind disturbance is set as 5 m/s along negative Y direction at $t = 85$ s $\sim$ 95 s. And the constant parameters of ADRC are tuned as $w_0 = 0.5, w_c = 0.4, b_0 = 0.2$. The specific simulation conditions are given in Table 1. And the simulation results are shown in Figs. 2 and 3. To measure the path following performance quantitatively, we define the energy consumption τ, the maximum error ℓ_{max}, and the average error

Table 1. Controller parameters.

Simulation time	Time step	α	γ	Training period	Hidden layer neurons
180 s	0.02 s	0.001	0.9	300	$(20, 15, 8)$

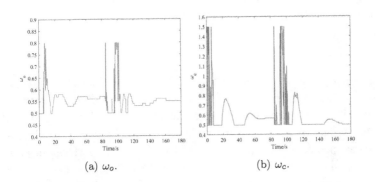

(a) Horizontal path following. (b) Control quantity.

Fig. 2. Horizontal path following results of parafoil system with wind disturbances.

(a) ω_o. (b) ω_c.

Fig. 3. Adaptive parameters of controller under wind disturbances.

ℓ_{ave} as follows

$$\tau = \sum_{i=1}^{N}|u(i) - u(i-1)|, \ell_{ave} = \frac{1}{N}\sum_{i=1}^{N}|\ell(i)|, \ell_{max} = \max_i|\ell(i)| \quad (14)$$

As shown in Fig. 2, both ADRC and double DQN-ADRC controllers can track the reference line well without wind disturbance, but the latter has a higher tracking accuracy. The double DQN-ADRC controls the parafoil system following the target path with better response rates and minor overshoot. As for the wind disturbance, the tracking effect of ADRC is also more difficult to converge to a steady state. The parameter variation curves during the simulation are given in Fig. 3. It can be seen that the frequency of parameters adjustment also increases when the environment changes. The position errors of both controllers are listed in Table 2. From the comparison, the double DQN-ADRC can tackle the influence of wind disturbance more efficiently with less energy consumption by about 10%, and tracking errors are smaller. These guarantees the accuracy of horizontal path following.

Table 2.   Performance indexes of controllers with wind disturbance.

Controllers	τ(dimensionless)	ℓ_{ave}(m)	ℓ_{max}(m)
Double DQN-ADRC	67.6	2.3	7.4
ADRC	75.4	4.6	8.0

The above analysis proved that the proposed double DQN-ADRC outperforms the ADRC controller as it can adjust the optimal parameters automatically. The results show that controller parameters optimized by double DQN can resist atmospheric disturbances quickly and make the system converge to a stable state with smaller steady-state error.

5. Conclusion

This paper proposes a double DQN-based real-time ADRC method for horizontal path following control of the parafoil system. The simulation results show that the proposed method can control the parafoil system to track the target path more accurately and tackle the wind disturbances well. Besides, the developed controller achieves considerable control performance than the fixed parameters ADRC. The double DQN-ADRC control method proposed in this paper can provide a new idea and reference for the path following of the parafoil system.

Acknowledgments

This work was supported by the National Natural Science Foundation of China (Grant Nos. 61973172, 61973175, 62003175 and 62003177), the key Technologies Research and Development Program of Tianjin (Grant No. 19JCZDJC32800), this project also funded by Tianjin Research Innovation Project for Postgraduate Students (Grant No. 2021YJSO2B02) and the China Scholarship Council.

References

1. C. Dek, J.-L. Overkamp, A. Toeter, T. Hoppenbrouwer, J. Slimmens, J. van Zijl, P. A. Rossi, R. Machado, S. Hereijgers, V. Kilic *et al.*, A recovery system for the key components of the first stage of a heavy launch vehicle, *Aerosp. Sci. Technol.* **100**, p. 105778 (2020).
2. Y. Guo, J. Yan, C. Wu, X. Wu, M. Chen and X. Xing, Autonomous homing design and following for parafoil/rocket system with high-altitude, *J. Intell. Robot. Syst.* **101**, 1 (2021).
3. J. Tao, Q. L. Sun, H. Sun, Z. Q. Chen, M. Dehmer and M. W. Sun, Dynamic modeling and trajectory tracking control of parafoil system in wind environments, *IEEE/ASME Trans. Mechatronics* **22**, 2736 (2017).
4. H. Sun, Q. Sun, J. Tao, P. Tan and Z. Chen, Accurate homing control of parafoil delivery system based on active disturbance rejection control, in *2021 IEEE 10th Data Driven Control and Learning Systems Conference (DDCLS)*, 2021.
5. Z. Chen, B. Qin, M. Sun and Q. Sun, Q-learning-based parameters adaptive algorithm for active disturbance rejection control and its application to ship course control, *Neurocomputing* **408**, 51 (2020).
6. Y. Zheng, J. Tao, Q. Sun, H. Sun, M. Sun and Z. Chen, An intelligent course keeping active disturbance rejection controller based on double deep Q-network for towing system of unpowered cylindrical drilling platform, *Int. J. Robust. Nonlin.* **31**, 8463 (2021).
7. J. Pan, X. Wang, Y. Cheng and Q. Yu, Multisource transfer double DQN based on actor learning, *IEEE T. Neur. Net. Lear.* **29**, 2227 (2018).
8. Z. Hong, S. Qinglin and W. Wannan, Accurate modeling and control for parawing unmanned aerial vehicle, *Acta Aeronaut. Astronaut. Sin.* **40**, p. 122593 (2019).
9. W. Xue and Y. Huang, Performance analysis of active disturbance

rejection tracking control for a class of uncertain LTI systems, *ISA Trans.* **58**, 133 (2015).

10. H. Zhu, Q. Sun, X. Liu, J. Liu, H. Sun, W. Wu, P. Tan and Z. Chen, Fluid–structure interaction-based aerodynamic modeling for flight dynamics simulation of parafoil system, *Nonlinear Dyn.* **104**, 3445 (2021).

A transmission line icing prediction method based on informer attention learning

Jinqiang He[1], Ruihai Li[1,*], Bo Gong[1], Hourong Zhang[1], Dengjie Zhu[1],
Zenghao Huang[1], Yi Wen[2,3], Jianrong Wu[2,3] and Huan Huang[2,3]

[1] *Electric Power Research Institute, CSG, Guangzhou 510663, China*
[2] *Electrical Science Institute of Guizhou Power Grid Co., Ltd*
CSG, Guiyang 550000, China
[3] *Key Laboratory of Ice Prevention & Disaster Reducing of*
China Southern Power Grid Co. Ltd., Guiyang 550002, China
* 124478700@qq.com

Transmission line icing prediction can effectively reduce the loss of large-area power grid paralysis caused by icing. The recently proposed model called Informer can be used for transmission line icing prediction. Informer improves self-attention mechanism, reduces memory usage, and speeds up prediction. However, its accuracy is not high in practical application. For the purpose of increasing the accuracy of transmission line icing prediction, we extend the informer model and improve its self-attention distillation mechanism, so that after the encoder module extracts deeper features, the dominant features in the main features are given higher weights. The experiments results on real dataset provided by China Southern Power Grid Corporation show that the proposed method can achieve smaller error and higher accuracy in the field of transmission line icing prediction compared with the traditional SVR and LSTM.

Keywords: Transmission line icing prediction; deep learning; informer; attention mechanism.

1. Introduction

In recent years, with the rapid development of China's power system and power grid construction, the distribution of power grids has gradually developed in a large-scale and intelligent direction, and the reliability requirements of power grids have become higher. As one of the most common disasters affecting the power system, icing often leads to an increase in the load of transmission lines, resulting in line disconnection, ice flash tripping, and damage to transmission line components. The icing disaster has seriously threatened the stable and reliable operation of China's power grid system, which brought huge economic losses to our country, and severely restricted the construction and development of China's power grid system. Predicting the future icing condition of transmission lines, taking immediate and effective ice-melting measures can effectively reduce the losses caused by the large-scale paralysis of the power grid caused by icing. Therefore, transmission line icing prediction is of great significance to the development of China's power system.

Generally speaking, transmission line icing prediction can be described as a multivariate time series forecasting problem or spatial-temporal prediction problem, which includes many aspects.[1] In the past few decades, many scholars have conducted a lot of research on transmission line icing prediction, which mainly used multivariate time series forecasting (MTSF) or spatial-temporal prediction model, such as ARIMA,[2] SVM,[3] Gaussian Mixture Models,[4] ANN.[5] Compared with Transformer,[6] Informer[7] has three major improvements, it propose a ProbSparse self-attention mechanism to reduce the time complexity and use a self-attention distillation mechanism to shorten the length of the input sequence of each layer. Although Informer performs well in wide range of Time Series Forecasting problems, it has low accuracy of the calculation have always been the primary problems faced by transmission line icing prediction. To address the above problems, in this paper, a novel transmission line icing prediction model based on informer attention learning has been proposed. We extend the informer model and improve its self-attention distillation mechanism, so that after the encoder module extracts deeper features, it assigns higher weights to the dominant features with the main features. This paper has two main contribution, we improve self-attentional distilling to reduce the input sequence length of each layer and the memory usage of multiple stacked layers, the other is that, to our best of knowledge, we first use Informer in transmission line icing prediction.

2. Related Works

The existing power grid icing prediction models can be divided into two categories: the model based on physical processes and the model based on data driven.

The former is based on the formation process and generation mechanism of ice coating, which combines with thermodynamics, kinetics and other related disciplines to construct the ice coating prediction model. For example, Ref. 8 proposed a prediction model of icing thickness based on icing growth process. However, it is not universal. We calculate the basic static parameters of the line in the vertical plane without icing. However, the above methods often fail to achieve ideal performance due to the lack of consideration of all possible factors.

For the other hand, the data-driven icing prediction model is mainly based on historical icing data and take advantage of deep neural network model, machine learning algorithm as well as other methods. For instance, an icing alarm system for short-term icing load of overhead power line is constructed[9] by adopting support vector regression (SVR), utilizing historical icing data, online meteorological data and combine with wavelets data preprocessing method and phase space reconstruction theory. This system can predict the real-time icing value of overhead power line for 5 hours. A time series model prediction method based on the combination of meteorological factors and conductor icing is proposed, in which the long short-term memory network algorithm (LSTM) is used to train the prediction model and the actual operation data of the line is used to adjust and optimize the model. In practical application, it is often necessary to predict the icing condition in the next 1-2 days, so the predicted sequence length is large.Aiming at the above key problems, this paper designs a transmission line icing prediction model based on informer attention learning.

3. Problem Formulation

We consider the micro-meteorological and micro-topographic factors like date, temperature, humidity and tension value as the characteristic input. We let the input history sequence length be L_X, the forward prediction length is p, and the number of related influencing variables such as icing is i. Next, we build a tension-related multivariate sequence dataset $X^t = \{x_1^t, ..., x_{L_x}^t | x_i^t \in R^{d_x}\}$.

4. Framework of Improved Informer

4.1. *Model architecture*

We first describe the general framework of our proposed model. As illustrated in Fig. 1, the model consists of an Embedding component, a multihead sparse self-attention mechanism component, a self-attention distillation component, a 1-D convolution component, and an encoder-decoder component. The remainder of this subsection details the rationale and composition of the important components in the model.

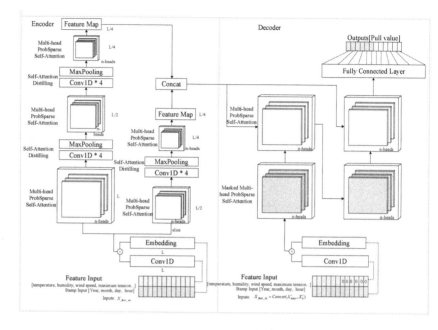

Fig. 1. The framework of improved informer model.

4.2. *Probsparse self-attention*

Vaswani et al.[6] define an attention mechanism, which performs the scaled dot-product as $A(Q, K, V) = softmax(\frac{QK^T}{\sqrt{d}})V$, where $Q \in R^{L_Q \times d_{model}}$, $K \in R^{L_K \times d_{model}}$, $V \in R^{L_V \times d_{model}}$, d_{model} is the input dimension, and L_Q, L_K, L_V represent the lengths of Q, K, V, respectively. ProbSparse self-attention allows us only need to calculate $O(\ln L_Q)$ dot-product for each query-key look up and have the low memory usage. Besides, add a sampling factor (hyperparameter) c, set $u = c * \ln L_Q$. First, randomly sample $u = c * \ln L_Q$ keys for each query, and calculate the sparsity score $\overline{M}(q_i, K)$ of each query, the approximate calculation formula of the sparse metric $\overline{M}(q_i, K)$ is:

$$\overline{M}(q_i, K) = max_j \left(\frac{q_i k_j^T}{\sqrt{d}} \right) - \frac{1}{L_K} \sum_{j=1}^{L_K} \frac{q_i k_j^T}{\sqrt{d}} \tag{1}$$

4.3. *Encoder*

The Encoder is more suitable to tackle long sequence dependency. Hence, we first embedding the input X^t at the time stamp t to a matrix $X_{en}^t \in$

$R^{L_x \times d_{model}}$, where d_{model} is the embedding dimension usually set as 512. Moreover, we have another embedding to keep the time series sequence unchanged after encoding called positional embedding, which defined in Informer.[7] Then, we connect the two embedding vector go to self-attention distilling, the input to Encoder consists of three parts as follow:

$$X^t_{feed[i]} = \alpha \mu^t_i + PE_{(L_x*(t-1)+i)} + \sum_p [SE_{(L_x*(t-1)+i)}]_p \qquad (2)$$

where $i \in \{1, ..., L_x\}$, α is a factor that balances the size between the scalar map and the local or global embedding.

Next, the distilling operation is required to give higher weights to the dominant features with the main features, and generate a focused self-attention feature map in the next layer. Specifically, it is implemented by four Conv1d convolutional layers and a Max-pooling layer.

4.4. Decoder

The Decoder used by the Informer is similar to the traditional Decoder. In order to generate the output of a long sequence, the Decoder needs the following inputs:

$$X^t_{feed_{de}} = Conct(X^t_{token}, X^t_0) \qquad (3)$$

where X^t_{token} is sequence of *starttoken*, X^t_0 is the sequence that needs to be predicted (padded with 0 s), the sequence is then passed through a Masked ProbSparse Self-Attention layer, which prevents each position from focusing on future positions, thus avoiding autoregression. After passing the output of this layer to a Multi-head ProbSparse Self-Attention layer, then pass its output to another combination of Masked ProbSparse Self-Attention + Multi-head ProbSparse Self-Attention. By stacking the Decoder in this way, the mapping relationship between the input and output can be better obtained, so as to improve the prediction accuracy, finally pass through a fully connected layer to get the final output.

5. Experimental Studies

5.1. Datasets and evaluation metrics

We use the icing datasets provided by China Southern Power Grid Corporation. This datasets take the hour as the sampling point from December 1, 2020 to January 31, 2021, which contains four icing related features namely temperature, wind speed, humidity and tension value. Moreover, we utilize Mean Square Error (MSE), Mean Absolute Error (MAE) and Mean Absolute Percentage Error (MAPE) to evaluate the predictive results.

5.2. *Main results*

We make a comparison with the Informer after five times experiments. From the results, our model has a better performance among the three evaluation metrics of MAE, MSE and MAPE, no matter in signal experiment or average results, which shown in Table 1. Figure 2(a) shows that the trend of loss during the training.

Besides, we compare our model with baseline methods. We use the icing datasets provided by China Southern Power Grid Corporation in different models to predict the maximum tension value in the next 24 hours. As illustrated in Table 2, the result shows that our model have a better performance than LSTM and SVR whether in multivariate forecasting or auto-regressive forecasting. As illustrated in Fig. 2(b), after 50 iterations, the value of MAE, MSE and MAPE become pretty low, the decrease of the following iterations is not obvious oscillations.

Table 1. Comparison between our model and Informer.

times	before improvement			after improvement		
	MSE	MAE	MAPE	MSE	MAE	MAPE
1	0.034	0.120	0.108	0.016	0.092	0.089
2	0.037	0.116	0.103	0.021	0.101	0.092
3	0.031	0.114	0.104	0.024	0.119	0.108
4	0.032	0.115	0.102	0.018	0.098	0.093
5	0.034	0.125	0.112	0.028	0.114	0.102
Average	0.0336	0.118	0.1058	**0.0214**	**0.1048**	**0.0968**

Table 2. Comparison in our model and different baselines.

Model	multivariate forecasting			autoregressive forecast		
	MSE	MAE	RMSE	MSE	MAE	RMSE
SVR	0.0570	0.169	0.239	0.130	0.200	0.361
LSTM	0.0234	0.117	0.153	0.054	0.183	0.232
Ours	**0.0174**	**0.089**	**0.132**	**0.024**	**0.120**	**0.154**

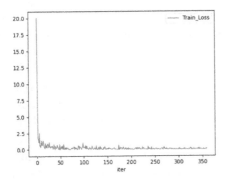

(a) The training loss of the proposed method.

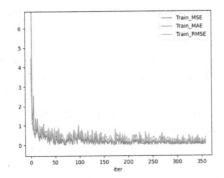

(b) The convergence curve of each evaluation index.

Fig. 2.   The loss convergence curve of the proposed method.

6. Conclusions

In this paper, we proposed a novel transmission line icing prediction model based on Informer attention learning. Due to the Informer cannot extract deep features, we improve its self attention distilling mechanism to alleviate the problem and obtain better prediction accuracy. Besides,the experiments mentioned above show that, our model is more effective than some existing methods in long sequence time forecasting.

Acknowledgments

This work was supported by the big data analytics and artificial intelligence application of power transmission line icing in southern China (Technology Project No. 066600KK52190063).

References

1. X.-B. Huang, H.-B. Li, Y.-C. Zhu, Y.-X. Wang, X.-X. Zheng and Y.-G. Wang, Transmission line icing short-term forecasting based on improved time series analysis by fireworks algorithm, in *2016 International Conference on Condition Monitoring and Diagnosis (CMD)*, 2016.

2. L. Chen and X. Lai, Comparison between arima and ann models used in short-term wind speed forecasting, in *2011 Asia-Pacific Power and Energy Engineering Conference*, 2011.

3. G. Lin, B. Wang and Z. Yang, Identification of icing thickness of transmission line based on strongly generalized convolutional neural network, in *2018 IEEE Innovative Smart Grid Technologies-Asia (ISGT Asia)*, 2018.

4. F. Pernkopf and D. Bouchaffra, Genetic-based em algorithm for learning gaussian mixture models, *IEEE Transactions on Pattern Analysis and Machine Intelligence* **27**, 1344 (2005).

5. J. Wang, X. Xiong, N. Zhou, Z. Li and W. Wang, Early warning method for transmission line galloping based on svm and adaboost bi-level classifiers, *IET Generation, Transmission & Distribution* **10**, 3499 (2016).

6. A. Vaswani, N. Shazeer, N. Parmar, J. Uszkoreit, L. Jones, A. N. Gomez, L. Kaiser and I. Polosukhin, Attention is all you need, *Advances in Neural Information Processing Systems* **30** (2017).

7. H. Zhou, S. Zhang, J. Peng, S. Zhang, J. Li, H. Xiong and W. Zhang, Informer: Beyond efficient transformer for long sequence time-series forecasting, in *Proceedings of AAAI*, 2021.

8. C. Yao, L. Zhang, C. Li, Y. Li and Z. Zuo, Measurement method of conductor ice covered thickness based on analysis of mechanical and sag measurement [j], *High Voltage Engineering* **5** (2013).

9. J. Li, P. Li, A. Miao, Y. Chen, M. Cao and X. Shen, Online prediction method of icing of overhead power lines based on support vector regression, *International Transactions on Electrical Energy Systems* **28**, p. e2500 (2018).

Prediction of crowdfunding project success: An interpretable deep learning model enhanced with persuasion effect[*]

Haoyu Yuan[1], Qiang Wei and Guoqing Chen

School of Economics and Management, Tsinghua University
Beijing 100084, China
[1]*yhy18@mails.tsinghua.edu.cn*

Crowdfunding has become one of the hottest fields in internet finance in recent years, where the success rate of crowdfunding projects is as low as just 39.07%. Though various factors that may impact the success of a crowdfunding project have been investigated, the persuasion effect in the semantically rich project description, i.e., shaping the donors' attitudes and ultimately influencing their donation decisions, has seldom been explored. Due to the intangibility and weak measurability of disclosed project information as well as the small-capital donors' cognitive subjectivity and non-professionalism, the persuasion effect of project description information may play a significant role in impacting donors' decisions. Yet current state-of-art studies have not identified the persuasion effect coupling with deep learning techniques. This paper proposes a hierarchical model to identify key persuasion dimensions and explore the learning of persuasive effect on crowdfunding. Specifically, the bottom-level model, i.e., PSM (persuasion score model), is proposed to identify persuasion dimensions to well unify and represent information from a comprehensive and hybrid perspective. The top-level model, i.e., PEM (persuasion effect model), is composed of a recurrent neural network to capture the complex persuasion inference in the description text. The proposed hierarchical model is evaluated with Indiegogo datasets along with baseline methods for comparison, i.e., demonstrating its outperformance. Moreover, by modeling the persuasion effect into a deep learning framework, the derived results imply good interpretability, showing its merit in supporting managerial practice.

Keywords: Persuasion; crowdfunding; deep learning; interpretability.

1. Introduction

Online crowdfunding has become one of the hottest platforms in Internet finance. In 2020, the crowdfunding market reached $17.2 billion with a growth rate of 33.7%, and the capital per donor is usually small, e.g., 81 dollars on Kickstarter.[†] However, e.g., on Kickstarter, only 39.07% of the candidate projects are finally

---

[*]This work is supported by the National Key R&D Program of China (Grant No. 2020AAA0103801) and the National Natural Science Foundation of China (72172070).
[†]https://www.fundera.com/resources/crowdfunding-statistics

successfully funded, while \$537 million's funds fail in investment.[‡] Therefore, it is crucial to capture the key factors impacting donors from the disclosed project information and make an accurate prediction for both donors and initiators.

Many factors have been explored to predict the success of crowdfunding, e.g., project feature, social media feature, time-series feature, etc. Greenberg et al. (2013) extracted project features from Kickstarter and obtained some high-performance machine learning classifiers, including DT (decision tree), RF (random forest), and SVM (support vector machine). Cheng et al. (2019) designed a neural network scheme that combines information from textual, visual, and metadata to study the influence on project success prediction and obtain 75% recall and 76% precision. Though, by taking multi-modal data and constructing complex model structures, these models may achieve decent accuracy. However, the practical advice of these prediction models is usually weak on managerial interpretability, especially for the "black-box" deep learning ones. For example, an extracted pattern in the category of hi-tech projects might be, e.g., *projects with reward settings greater than 5, the emotions described in the project tend to be extreme, the number of logical connection words is greater than 20 and official social media fans greater than 10000, will highly possibly succeed*, which is not only too trivial and ad-hoc but more critically lack managerial implication and credibility. It contributes little in helping both donors capture insights and make trustable decisions and initiators substantially improve the projects. Therefore, it is valuable to investigate the underlying mechanism driving the donor's decision and well couple the mechanism into a deep learning solution to, i.e., not only retain high accuracy but achieve some good interpretability.

The fundraising and donation in crowdfunding platforms show some specialty. First, the majority of crowdfunding projects are generally in the early stage of information disclosure like new product design or just a novel idea, i.e., with little tangible information and measurable facts. Second, due to the limited capacity of small companies, many crowdfunding projects are usually small extensions or incremental innovations based on some common existing products, e.g., the basic information of these projects might be similar, leading to the high homogeneity in the basic information of these projects. Third, due to the small-capital financial threshold of crowdfunding projects and the non-professionalism of donors (Agrawal et al. 2014), a donor typically makes a relatively quick decision highly depending on the vague and subjective information in the project description. Previous studies have proved that when the basic facts are similar, the written expression of the content may have a significant impact on the donors' decision

---

[‡]https://www.kickstarter.com/help/stats

(Allison et al. 2017). In this context, differently from e-commerce platforms with more measurable and tangible information, the persuasion effect of the project description, i.e., how the description information may influence a donor's attitude or behavior towards the donation purpose, significantly dominates his/her crowd-funding donation decision. Existing studies on crowdfunding have identified that some sub-dimensions of persuasion, such as authority, commitment, and reciprocity, are considered to have various impacts on donors' decisions (Jones and Moncur 2020). More importantly, with the incorporation of the detected persuasion dimensions, an interpretable pattern could be articulated to some extent, e.g., *high authority (evident with some successful experience), together with sufficient reciprocity (reflected by the rewards offered), conveyed in the project description, indeed impact a donor's decision.* Therefore, with the persuasion lens, this derived pattern is enhanced with more insightful semantics, which could help better support managerial decisions. However, the dimensions have not yet been comprehensively explored in prediction modeling, let alone devising a deep learning solution. Hence, we believe that coupling the persuasion effect into deep learning can not only help benefit the crowdfunding project success prediction but output results in a more managerially interpretable manner.

There still exist some major challenges in modeling and coupling the persuasion effect with deep learning techniques. First, as an abstract concept, the dimensions of persuasion need to be carefully and accurately identified. Robert and Nathalie (1987) regard persuasion as an influence with six aspects: reciprocity, commitment, social identity, preference, authority, and scarcity. Besides, evidentiality and gratitude have also been proved to be considerable dimensions of persuasion, which can influence the attitude of the information receiver (Dwyer 2015). The various persuasion dimensions make it difficult to distinguish. Second, persuasion dimensions are essentially hybrid, e.g., a linguistic description sentence may simultaneously cover multiple dimensions in a mixed manner. In a sentence, the overall persuasion effect depends on the mix-up of multi-dimensional latent information. Therefore it is challenging to devise a mix-up dimensions detection and training strategy and embed it into a deep learning solution.

Targeting the above challenges, this paper proposes a hierarchical model, which adopts a label-based attention mechanism and a mix-up training strategy, to achieve persuasion scoring and success prediction. The major contribution of the paper is reflected in three aspects. First, the persuasion effect is subtly captured and recognized in crowdfunding project success prediction. Second, a hierarchical deep learning model enhanced with persuasion effect is proposed, showing satisfactory prediction performance. Third, the proposed model shows some good interpretability.

2. A Hierarchical Model

To predict the crowdfunding project success enhanced with the persuasion effect in the project description, a hierarchical model is built with two parts, i.e., PSM (persuasion score model) and PEM (persuasion effect model). PSM is to score persuasion for each sentence, and PEM uses the sentence score together with the project profile information to predict the success of crowdfunding. Figure 1 presents the framework of the hierarchical model.

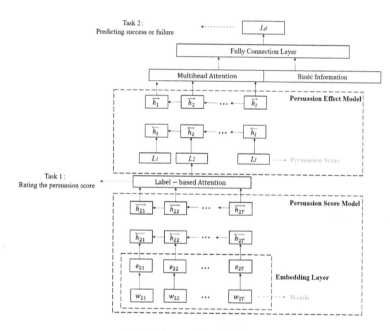

Fig. 1. An overview of the model.

2.1. PSM

Given a sentence with words $w_{it}, t \in [1, T]$, The words can be converted to vectors, i.e., e_{it}, through an embedding matrix W_{embed}.

$$e_{it} = W_{embed} w_{it}, t \epsilon [1, T] \tag{1}$$

Then, a GRU (Gated Recurrent Unit) is deployed, due to its effectiveness in processing texts (Chung et al. 2014), to transfer e_{it} to an integrated vector h_{it} for a given word w_{it} by concatenating the forward hidden state and backward hidden state, which includes the whole contextual information about w_{it}.

$$h_{it} = [\overrightarrow{GRU}(e_{it}, \overrightarrow{h}_{i(t-1)}), \overleftarrow{GRU}(e_{it}, \overleftarrow{h}_{i(t+1)})], t \in [1, T] \tag{2}$$

The attention mechanism has received increasing attention in natural language processing and is believed to help the task achieve good performance (Bahdanau et al. 2015). Typically, a single attention mechanism can be used to help understand which words have an important impact on the final classification task. However, as multiple dimensions in persuasion need to be recognized and identified, we design a label-based attention mechanism instead of one global context vector to vividly grasp the relationship between persuasion dimensions and words. This mechanism is designed as follows:

$$K_{it} = Tanh(h_{it} \cdot W_K)$$

$$Atte_{itl} = Softmax\left(K_{it} \cdot \frac{W_L}{\sqrt{d_{label}}}\right) \tag{3}$$

$$s_{il} = \sum_{t=1}^{T}[Atte_{itl} \cdot h_{it}]$$

where the projections are parameter matrices $W_K \in \mathbb{R}^{(2*hidden_{size})*(2*hidden_{size})}$, $W_L \in \mathbb{R}^{(2*hidden_{size})*label_{size}}$.

By word encoder and label-based attention mechanism, the representation of one sentence can then be obtained to determine the persuasion dimension L_i. Finally, L_i can be derived by conducting linear transformation on s_{il}.

$$L_i = W_s \cdot [s_{i1}, s_{i2}, \ldots, s_{il}] \tag{4}$$

Moreover, due to the hybridity of multiple dimensions, a data augmentation strategy is adopted, namely Mixup (Zhang et al. 2017). Concretely, the text information could be mixed up in the embedding layer, with the specific implementation as follows:

$$\tilde{x} = mix(x_i, x_j) = \lambda(g(x_i; \theta)) + (1 - \lambda)(g(x_j; \theta)) \tag{5}$$

where $g(:; \theta)$ is an encoder model and $\lambda \sim Beta(\alpha, \alpha)$. And α is a hyperparameter to determine prior possibility of weight. Finally, the KL (Kullback-Leibler) divergence loss is chosen to train the model:

$$Loss_{kl} = \mathbb{E}_{x_i \in X_L} KL(y_i || \hat{y}_i) \tag{6}$$

Then, with KL divergence loss, PSM can output the persuasion dimension score.

2.2. PEM

With the persuasion dimension score of each sentence L_i derived from PSM as input, a bidirectional GRU is deployed to encode sentences.

$$h_i = [\overrightarrow{GRU}(L_i, \vec{h}_{i-1}), \overleftarrow{GRU}(L_i, \overleftarrow{h}_{i+1})], t \in [1, L] \qquad (7)$$

Similarly, h_i is the document vector including information in sentence i. In order to measure the impacting strength between each sentence and the target L_d, a multi-head attention mechanism is designed as follows (Vaswani et al. 2017).

$$MultiHead(h, K) = [head_1, \dots, head_n] \qquad (8)$$

$$where\ head_h = \text{Atte}_i\left(\left[h_1, h_2, \dots, h_L\right]_h, K_Q^h\right), K_Q^h = Q_h \cdot W_K^h$$

With the basic information of a project, the representation of a crowdfunding project L_d can be obtained:

$$L_d = softmax([MultiHead(h, K), X_{basic}] \cdot W_d) \qquad (9)$$

The loss function of PEM is designed as follow:

$$\text{Loss}_{bce} = \sum_{d \in D} -g_d \log(L_d) \qquad (10)$$

Here, D denotes the set of all crowdfunding projects, L_d represents the output of the document layer, and g_d refers to the true label of a project. Therefore, with the hierarchical PSM-PEM design, the predicted label of a crowdfunding project can be obtained.

3. Experiments

The dataset *Indiegogo* is used for the experimental analysis, containing the project profile attributes, i.e., project name, project category, project label, currency, raised amount, and the number of comments it receives. In addition to the basic information, the project description is collected as well. This dataset is gathered from September 2016 to April 2020, including about 17,334 records and 540,524 sentences. Moreover, in order to derive the ground truth of persuasion effects, a subset of project descriptions of 100 projects are sampled, and two experts are invited to annotate, i.e., each sentence is annotated with a corresponding persuasion dimension for further training.

For data preprocessing, the crowdfunding descriptions are split into sentences, each of which is tokenized by a natural language toolkit in Python. Words with frequency more than 5 are retained. The word2vec model is used to obtain the embedding matrix W_{embed} of words and the word embedding dimension is set to be 200. The dataset is split into the training, validation, and testing datasets.

Stochastic gradient descent and a mini-batch size of 128 are used to train the model with Adam. The dropout rate of the full connection layer is set to 0.2 to prevent overfitting. The early stop strategy is adopted in learning. The learning process terminates when the loss of the validation dataset no longer decreases after 30 consecutive epochs.

Table 1. Performance of PSM-PEM on *Indiegogo*.

Model		Accuracy	Precision	Recall	F1
Classical models	SVM	0.678	0.619	0.241	0.333
	KNN	0.121	0.093	0.117	0.099
	SGD	0.664	0.621	0.004	0.007
	LR	0.664	0.617	0.004	0.006
	DT	0.641	0.503	0.488	0.488
	RF	0.678	0.560	0.422	0.473
Deep learning models	BiLSTM	0.748	0.335	0.794	0.455
	HAN	0.717	0.437	0.631	0.517
The proposed model	PSM-PEM	**0.836**	**0.682**	**0.797**	**0.726**

For performance comparison, 6 classical models and 2 deep learning models are chosen as baselines. Both the basic information and the persuasion information (i.e., the average scores on nine persuasion dimensions) are used as the input of baselines. Moreover, for deep learning ones, the basic information is concatenated with the output of the last layer of our model and passes through a layer of full connection layer to get the prediction results. The above treatment is to guarantee comparison fairness. The performance results are shown in Table 1. Specifically, because of the weakness in dealing with linguistic texts, the performance of the classical models is not that satisfactory. Due to the suitable NLP capability, both RNN and HAN (hierarchical attention network) achieve relatively better performance than the classical ones. However, the proposed PSM-PEM model shows its significant outperformance, since it could well capture the variety and hybridity in persuasion effect, i.e., with the hierarchical solution.

4. A Case Study on Interpretability

The model is able to provide project initiators with actionable advice thanks to the incorporation of persuasion knowledge. To briefly validate the model's effectiveness on interpretability, a case study is discussed. Specifically, two similar projects, i.e., the successful "Natural Beer Shampoo" (namely NBS) and the failed "Shampoo Station" (namely SS), are chosen. Both of them are about new shampoo products and are quite similar in category, fundraising target, and other basic facts, but their project descriptions are different. This evidently shows the key success impact role of project description rather than other features, which could be appropriately used for conducting a case study. Concretely, by calculating the difference in persuasion score, the proposed model detects that NBS achieves a higher score in the dimension of authority, impact, and commitment than another. Moreover, the model also outputs the highlighted keywords or sentences in each dimension of NBS, i.e., providing detailed insights. For instance, the mapping of Authority to *"We've been in the shampoo bar business for over 4 years now. You see, (name) is founder of the (company name) Brewery and (name) is founder of the (company name) Ltd"* shows the NBS founders' authority with evident on some successful start-up experiences. Moreover, on the Impact dimension, i.e., persuading people to act by emphasizing the positive impact of doing something, the sentence *"Your help in this campaign will create employment"* in NBS shows a positive impact. On the Commitment dimension, NBS emphasizes *"Our shampoo is a bar! That means no plastic bottles are needed, which absolutely reduces waste . . . score one for the Earth :-)"*, i.e., conveying a strong signal on the commitment to environmental friendliness. On the contrary, project SS performs badly on the above dimensions with quite insipid content, i.e., poor persuasion, in the project description. Considering the high homogeneity of the two projects on basic facts, the difference in persuasion effect on the highlighted dimensions in their descriptions indeed plays a dominant role. This case study vividly shows that the proposed model can help detect the key success factors on persuasion and further provide insightful explanations, i.e., showing good interpretability.

5. Conclusion

In this paper, we investigate the important persuasion effect in the description in impacting the success of crowdfunding projects. Considering the variety and hybridity of the persuasion effect, a hierarchical model is built, i.e., with PSM for persuasion dimensions scoring and PEM for predicting project success. The hierarchical model shows its merit on not only satisfactory prediction, but good interpretability, which is validated by the experiments.

References

1. Greenberg, Michael, et al. Crowdfunding Support Tools: Predicting Success and Failure. *Extended Abstracts on Human Factors in Computing Systems*, 2013, 1815–1820.

2. Cheng, C., et al. Success Prediction on Crowdfunding with Multimodal Deep Learning. *Twenty-Eighth International Joint Conference on Artificial Intelligence*, 2019, 2158–2164.
3. Agrawal, A., Catalini, C. and Goldfarb, A. Some Simple Economics of Crowdfunding. *Innovation Policy and the Economy*, 2014, 14(1), 63–97.
4. Jones Helen, and Wendy Moncur. A Mixed-Methods Approach to Understanding Funder Trust and Due Diligence Processes in Online Crowdfunding Investment. *ACM Transactions on Social Computing*, 2020, 3(1), 1–29.
5. Robert B Cialdini and Nathalie Garde. Influence: the psychology of persuasion, New York: Collins, 2007.
6. Dwyer, P. Gratitude as Persuasion: Understanding When and Why Gratitude Expressions Facilitate and Inhibit Compliance. *Dissertations & Theses – Gradworks*, 2015.
7. Allison, T. H., et al. Persuasion in crowdfunding: An elaboration likelihood model of crowdfunding performance. *Journal of Business Venturing*, 2017, 32(6), 707–725.
8. Bahdanau D, Cho K, and Bengio Y. Neural Machine Translation by Jointly Learning to Align and Translate. *In 3rd International Conference on Learning Representations, ICLR*, 2015.
9. Chung J, Gulcehre C, Cho K, Bengio Y. Empirical evaluation of gated recurrent neural networks on sequence modeling. *In NIPS*, 2014.

Fuzzy Lattice Reasoning (FLR) for decision-making on an ontology of constraints toward agricultural robot harvest

Vassilis Kaburlasos, Chris Lytridis, George Siavalas and Theodore Pachidis

HUman-MAchines INteraction (HUMAIN) Lab, Department of Computer Science
School of Science and Technology, International Hellenic University (IHU)
Kavala, 65404, Greece
{vgkabs, lytridic, nesiava, pated}@cs.ihu.gr
http://humain-lab.cs.ihu.gr

Serafeim Theocharis

Viticulture Laboratory, Department of Horticulture and Viticulture
School of Agriculture, Aristotle University of Thessaloniki (AUTh)
Thessaloniki, 54124, Greece
sertheo@agro.auth.gr

A sustainable production of high-quality agricultural products calls for personalized-rather than for massive- operations. The aforementioned (personalized) operations can be pursued by human-like reasoning applicable per case. The interest here is in agricultural grape robot harvest where a binary decision needs to be taken, given a set of ambiguous constraints represented by a Boolean lattice ontology of inequalities. Fuzzy lattice reasoning (FLR) is employed for decision making. Preliminary experimental results on expert data demonstrate the advantages of the proposed method including parametrically tunable, rule-based decision-making involving, in principle, either crisp or ambiguous measurements also beyond rule support; combinatorial decision-making is also feasible.

Keywords: Agricultural robot harvest; fuzzy lattice reasoning (FLR); ontology.

1. Introduction

To meet an ever-increasing demand for food worldwide, especially under human labor shortages as well as ever-increasing production costs, the automation of agricultural production seems inevitable. To the latter end, the practices of "Industry 4.0" are promising toward extending them to agriculture; the latter extension has been named "Agriculture 4.0" [1].

Agriculture 4.0 is often pursued by transferring established industrial practices from a structured factory environment to an agricultural field. Never-theless, an agricultural field is not structured. Moreover, an agricultural field is part of the natural environment; hence, special attention should be taken toward sustaining both food production and life quality as explained below.

For the above reasons, the expected automation of agricultural production, including harvest, needs to be skillfully personalized. That is, instead of carrying out harvest massively (per plant), harvest should be carried out individually (per fruit) such that plants remain intact for the next season.

In the aforementioned context, agricultural robots, or agrobots for short, are being developed including agrobots for grape harvest [2]. In particular, note that "grape harvest" is defined as the collection of uniformly ripen grape bunches. However, the decision regarding grape ripeness is sophisticated *ad hoc* since it considers a desired concentration of: sugars and acids in the must as well as anthocyanins and tannins in the berry skins and seeds; it also involves aromatic maturity; in addition, measurements of temperature, pH and soluble content are considered supportively [3].

To date, grape harvest engages humans to a great extent; nevertheless, it seems to have reached its limits as young people keep abandoning viticulture. There is a need to automate grape harvest [4]. Hence, vine harvester combines have been developed toward massive grape harvest [5], however, at the expense of harvested grape quality. To retain grape quality, harvest should be carried out attentively, (grape) bunch by (grape) bunch.

To meet the needs of personalized grape harvest, the ARG agrobot [6] has been designed as a Cyber-Physical System (CPS) [7] that combines both sensing and reasoning abilities including a varying degree of autonomous behavior. Mathematical models, implemented in software, drive ARG. Among other ARG skills, decision-making is critical. For instance, the binary decision "to harvest (a grape) or not to harvest" is taken, in practice, by considering certain constraints regarding grape maturity indices.

The interest of this work is in logic-based, tunable decision-making for grape harvest by considering certain inequalities regarding grape maturity indices. In particular, the binary degree of satisfaction of certain inequalities gives rise to a crisp Boolean lattice. The latter is fuzzified by a parametrically optimizable *inclusion measure* function $\sigma(.,.)$. In conclusion, fuzzy lattice reasoning (FLR) [8] is applied.

Rigorous mathematical analysis is carried out in the context of the Lattice Computing (LC) information processing paradigm [8], [9] for modeling toward computing with semantics [8], [10]. Recall that LC has been defined as "an evolving collection of tools and methodologies that process lattice ordered data per se including logic values, numbers, sets, symbols, graphs, etc.".

The assumed crisp lattice of inequalities is interpreted here as an ontology. Note that, from a data processing point of view, ontologies have already been engaged in Industry 4.0 as well as in agricultural applications [11]. The novelties of this work include, first, the introduction of the tunable FLRule machine learning method, including combinatorial decision-making, to a lattice-ordered ontology and, second, the implementation of FLRule as an intelligent software agent toward robot harvesting in an agricultural application.

The layout of this work is as follows. Section 2 outlines the mathematical background. Section 3 introduces the FLRule method. Section 4 presents computational experiments and results. Finally, Section 5 concludes by summarizing this work's contribution as well as future work plans.

2. Mathematical Background

Let $(L,\sqsubseteq)$ be a mathematical lattice. An *inclusion measure* function σ: $L \times L \rightarrow [0,1]$ is defined by the following two conditions:

$$
\begin{aligned}
&1. \quad u \sqsubseteq w \Leftrightarrow \sigma(u,w) = 1 \\
&2. \quad u \sqsubseteq w \Leftrightarrow \sigma(x,u) \leq \sigma(x,w)
\end{aligned}
\tag{1}
$$

An inclusion measure σ: $L \times L \rightarrow [0,1]$ can be interpreted as a *fuzzy order* relation; hence, the notations $\sigma(u,w)$ and $\sigma(u \sqsubseteq w)$ are used interchangeably. Any use of an inclusion measure $\sigma(.,.)$ is called *Fuzzy Lattice Reasoning*, or *FLR* for short. FLR supports two modes of reasoning, namely *generalized modus ponens* and *reasoning by analogy*.

There are at least two different functions for defining an inclusion measure; both are based on a positive valuation function v: $L \rightarrow R$ in $(L,\sqsubseteq)$ as follows.

$$
\begin{aligned}
&sigma - meet: \quad \sigma_{\cap}(x,u) = v(x \sqcap u)/v(x) \tag{2} \\
&sigma - join: \quad \sigma_{\sqcup}(x,u) = v(u)/v(x \sqcup u) \tag{3}
\end{aligned}
$$

In a (non-void) complete lattice with least element o and greatest element i, two "reasonable constraints" are assumed: first, $\sigma_{\sqcup}(x,o) = 0 = \sigma_{\cap}(x,o)$ for all $x \sqsupset o$ and, second, $d(x,i) < +\infty$ for all x, where d: $L \times L \rightarrow R_0^+$ is a metric distance. The former constraint implies $v(o) = 0$, whereas the latter one implies $v(i) < +\infty$. Inclusion measures are extended to Cartesian products of lattices, next.

Theorem 2.1. *Let function σ_i: $L_i \times L_i \rightarrow [0,1]$ be an inclusion measure in a constituent lattice $(L_i, \sqsubseteq_i)$, $i \in \{1,...,M\}$. Consider the Cartesian product lattice $(L, \sqsubseteq) = (L_1, \sqsubseteq_1) \times ... \times (L_M, \sqsubseteq_M)$, where $L = L_1 \times L_2 \times ... \times L_M$ and $\sqsubseteq = \sqsubseteq_1 \times \sqsubseteq_2 \times ... \times \sqsubseteq_M$. Given $u = (u_1,...,u_M)$, $w = (w_1,...,w_M)$ in $(L, \sqsubseteq)$ and $k_i \geq 0$ such that $\sum_{i=1}^{M} k_i = 1$, an inclusion measure function σ: $L \times L \rightarrow [0,1]$ can be defined as either*

(A1) $\sigma_{\Sigma}(u,w) = \sum_{i=1}^{M} k_i \sigma_i(u_i, w_i)$, or

(A2) $\sigma_{\Pi}(u,w) = \prod_{i=1}^{M} \sigma_i(u_i, w_i)$.

The proof of Theorem 2.1 will be presented elsewhere.

In the following, the interest shifts to the totally-ordered lattice $(R,\leq)$ of real numbers. For N-tuples of conventional intervals $u = (u_1,...,u_M) = ([a_1,b_1],..., [a_M,b_M])$ and $w = (w_1,...,w_M) = ([c_1,e_1],...,[c_M,e_M])$, a function $\sigma_i(u_i, w_i)$, $i \in \{1,...,M\}$ in Theorem 2.1 can be calculated as follows

$$\sigma_i(u_i, w_i) = \frac{v_i(\theta_i(c_i))+v_i(e_i)}{v_i(\theta_i(a_i \wedge c_i))+v_i(b_i \vee e_i)} \tag{4}$$

where function $\theta_i : R \to R$ is strictly decreasing and function $v_i : R \to R_0^+$ is strictly increasing, $i \in \{1,...,M\}$.

3. Tunable Fuzzy Lattice Reasoning (FLR) for Grape Harvest

In this work, inclusion measure $\sigma_\Sigma(.,.)$ was employed exclusively. Furthermore, the sum of three sigmoid functions $v_i(x) = \sum_{j=1}^{3} A_{i,j}/\left[1 + e^{-\lambda_{i,j}(x-\mu_{i,j})}\right]$ was the positive valuation used per data dimension $i \in \{1,2,3\}$; whereas, the corresponding function θ_i always was $\theta_i(x) = -x$.

The employed data here were pairs $(\bar{x}_i, r_i)$, $i \in \{1,...,N\}$, where $\bar{x}_i \in R^M$ is a vector of M grape maturity indices; whereas, $r_i \in [0,1]$ is the corresponding degree of grape maturity supplied by an expert. The data were partitioned in a training data set and a testing data set including n_{trn} and n_{tst} data, respectively, where $n_{trn}+n_{tst} = N$. The objective, during training, was to estimate optimally the parameters of function $\sigma_\Sigma(.,.)$; then, during testing, the objective was to compute the degree $r_i \in [0,1]$ of grape maturity given a vector $\bar{x}_i \in R^M$.

Algorithm 1 describes "FLRule for training" toward optimizing the 29 parameters k_1, k_2, $A_{i,j}$, $\lambda_{i,j}$, $\mu_{i,j}$, $i,j \in \{1,2,3\}$ that minimize the predictive error Q, whereas Algorithm 2 describes "FLRule for testing". The testing data were applied once in order to predict the grape maturity index $r_i \in [0,1]$ of each testing datum $\bar{x}_i \in R^M$, $i \in \{1,...,n_{tst}\}$. Prediction Accuracy (PA) for Algorithms 1 and 2 was computed as PA= $(n_{trn}-Q)/n_{trn}$ and PA= $(n_{tst}-Q)/n_{tst}$, respectively.

4. Experiments and Results

This section describes expert knowledge as well as data issues followed by computational experiments and results; it concludes with a discussion.

4.1. Knowledge and data

A grape is 100% mature when indices TSS [°Bx] and TA [g/L] values are within their corresponding ripeness ranges [min,MAX] shown in Table 1; the latter is an updated version of Table 2 in [4]. If, in addition, index pH values are in

[3.2,3.6] then a grape is of high quality; otherwise, a grape is of lower quality. However, a grape may be less than 100% mature, as explained below.

Algorithm 1   FLRule training

0. Let n_{tm} be the number of the training data $(\bar{x}_i, r_i)$, $i \in \{1,...,n_{tm}\}$, where $\bar{x}_i \in R^M$, $r_i \in [0,1]$; let Q_{thres} be a user-defined threshold for the predictive error (i.e., fitness function) Q; let n_G be the maximum number of generations of the GENETIC algorithm; let R_0 be a single decision-making rule regarding grape harvest;

1. m = 1; Q $\leftarrow$ Q_{thres} + 1;

2. **while** $(m < n_G)$.and.$(Q > Q_{thres})$ **do**

3. Q $\leftarrow$ 0;
    for i = 1 to n_{tm} **do**

4. Q $\leftarrow$ Q + $|\sigma(\bar{x}_i \sqsubseteq R_0) - r_i|$;

5. **end for**

6. GENETIC optimization of k_1, k_2, $A_{i,j}$, $\lambda_{i,j}$, $\mu_{i,j}$, $i,j \in \{1,2,3\}$;

7. m $\leftarrow$ m + 1;

8. **end while**

Algorithm 2   FLRule testing

0. Let n_{tst} be the number of the testing data $(\bar{x}_i, r_i)$, $i \in \{1,...,n_{tst}\}$, where $\bar{x}_i \in R^M$, $r_i \in [0,1]$; let R_0 be a single decision-making rule regarding grape harvest;

1. Q $\leftarrow$ 0;

2. **for** i = 1 to n_{tst} **do**

3. Q $\leftarrow$ Q + $|\sigma(\bar{x}_i \sqsubseteq R_0) - r_i|$;

5. **end for**

Table 1. Grape maturity indices.

Index name	Acronym	Units	Ripeness [min,MAX] range
Total Soluble Solids	TSS	Degrees Brix (°Bx)	[21, 27]
Titratable Acidity	TA	g/L	[4, 7]
pH	pH	-	[3.2, 3.6]

The following three inequality constraints: *a*. $TSS_{min} < TSS < TSS_{MAX}$, *b*. $TA_{min} < TA < TA_{MAX}$, and *c*. $pH_{min} < pH < pH_{MAX}$ had been considered in the following rule R_0: If $(TSS \in [TSS_{min} = 21, TSS_{MAX} = 27]).and.(TA \in [TA_{min} = 4, TA_{MAX} = 7]).and.(pH \in [pH_{min} = 3.2, pH_{MAX} = 3.6])$ then (grape maturity is 1.00). The powerset $2^{\{a,b,c\}}$ is a crisp Boolean lattice ontology that includes all the combinations of the constraints *a*, *b* and *c*. A subset in $2^{\{a,b,c\}}$ is interpreted as a conjunction of inequalities, e.g. the set $\{a,b,c\}$ is interpreted as $a \wedge b \wedge c$, etc.

A dataset DT was generated by considering, first, 13 values for the index TSS from 18 °Bx to 30 °Bx with step 1 °Bx; second, 15 values for the index TA from 2 g/L to 9 g/L with step 0.5 g/L; third, 11 values for the index pH from 2.8 to 3.8 with step 0.1, resulting in N = 13×15×11 = 2,145 triplets of index values. For each triplet, an expert defined the corresponding degree of grape maturity by a number between numbers 0 and 1 included. In conclusion, DT included pairs $(\bar{x}_i, r_i)$, where $\bar{x}_i = (TSS_i, TA_i, pH_i)$, $r_i \in [0,1]$ for $i \in \{1,...,N\}$.

4.2. Computational experiments and results

A number of experiments was carried out. A datum (TSS_i, TA_i, pH_i) was represented by the trivial interval $([TSS_i, TSS_i], [TA_i, TA_i], [pH_i, pH_i])$.

First, the dataset DT was partitioned randomly in one dataset for training (including 80% of DT) and another dataset for testing (including the remaining 20% of DT). The 29 parameters in Algorithm 1 (FLRule for training) were optimized genetically assuming initial values in the intervals $k_1 \in [0, 1]$, $k_2 \in [0, 1]$, $A_{i,j} \in [0, 1]$, $\lambda_{i,j} \in [0, 1]$, $\mu_{1,j} \in [18, 30]$, $\mu_{2,j} \in [2, 9]$, $\mu_{3,j} \in [2.8, 3.8]$, where $i,j \in \{1,2,3\}$. Then, Algorithm 2 (FLRule for testing) was applied once; a testing datum (TSS_i, TA_i, pH_i) has produced a response $r_i \in [0,1]$, $i \in \{1,...,N\}$.

Second, triplets of non-trivial intervals $([TSS_i-1, TSS_i+1], [TA_i-0.5, TA_i+0.5], [pH_i-0.1, pH_i+0.1])$, $i \in \{1,...,N\}$ were considered as inputs to the FLRule to represent the uncertainty of indices TSS_i, TA_i and pH_i from a random sample of 200 grapes. Table 2 displays all the recorded results.

4.3. Discussion

Table 2 shows that FLRule performed clearly better than a kNN classifier with k=1, nearly as well as a 3×250×250×1 backpropagation neural network (NN) and much better than a 3×5×5×1 NN, all with rectified linear unit activation functions. The latter NN uses nearly as many parameters as the FLRrule, whereas the former NN uses orders of magnitude more parameters. Therefore, the FLRrule has demonstrated here a remarkable capacity for generalization. Advantages of FLRule are: tunable, rule-based (explainable) decision-making even for ambiguous (i.e., interval) measurements, also beyond rule support.

Table 2. Results: Training and Testing prediction accuracy (PA); average and standard deviation (std) for 10 random permutations of the 2,145 data in dataset DT.

Method	Trivial intervals (points)				Non-trivial intervals			
	Training		Testing		Training		Testing	
	average	std	average	std	average	std	average	std
kNN (with k=1)	0	0	0.054	0.005	-	-	-	-
3×5×5×1 NN	0.180	0.021	0.178	0.019	-	-	-	-
3×250×250×1 NN	0.035	0.008	0.038	0.008	-	-	-	-
FLRule	0.039	0.008	0.039	0.009	0.070	0.005	0.070	0.005

The proposed FLRule method for machine learning runs as a software agent on a robotic CPS. In practice, a grape harvest decision is triggered when the FLRule outputs $r > r_{th}$, where threshold $r_{th} = 0.70$ is user-defined.

This work enabled combinatorial decision-making when $\sigma(x,o) = 0$ in a constituent complete lattice with least element o; in particular, grape maturity was decided based on indices TSS and TA exclusively. Another novelty is the employment of FLR on a Boolean lattice ontology. Note that ontologies have been analyzed in the context of formal concept analysis (FCA) [12] without engaging positive valuation functions. Lately, positive valuation functions have been engaged with special ontologies, namely tree data structures [13].

5. Conclusion

This preliminary application work has demonstrated the engagement of the parametric FLRule machine learning method in a sophisticated decision-making problem regarding grape harvest. The proposed FLRule has demonstrated good performance comparatively to two backpropagation neural nets as well as to a kNN classifier. In addition, the FLRule proposes a rule to explain its answers.

This work has used three (grape maturity index) variables. Scaling up to more variables is straightforward. The FLRule here was based on intervals. Future work will engage the FLRule based on distributions of samples [10] also toward an estimation of grape maturity indices visually, from images.

Acknowledgments

We acknowledge support of this work by the project "Technology for Skillful Viniculture (SVtech)" (MIS 5046047) which is implemented under the Action "Reinforcement of the Research and Innovation Infrastructure" funded by the Operational Program "Competitiveness, Entrepreneurship and Innovation" (NSRF 2014-2020) and co-financed by Greece and the European Union (European Regional Development Fund).

References

1. M. De Clercq, A. Vats, and A. Biel, "Agriculture 4.0: The future of farming technology," in The World Government Summit, Dubai, 2018, pp. 11–13.
2. https://roboticsbiz.com/top-14-agricultural-robots-for-harvesting-and-nursery/
3. A. Rabot, "Using of a combined approach by biochemical and image analysis to develop a new method to estimate seed maturity stage for Bordeaux area grapevine," OENO One, vol. 51, no. 1, Mar. 2017.
4. E. Vrochidou, C. Bazinas, M. Manios, G. A. Papakostas, T. P. Pachidis, and V. G. Kaburlasos, Machine Vision for Ripeness Estimation in Viticulture Automation, Horticulturae, 2021, 7, 282.
5. C. W. Bac, E. J. van Henten, J. Hemming, and Y. Edan, "Harvesting Robots for High-value Crops: State-of-the-art Review and Challenges Ahead," J. F. Robot., vol. 31, no. 6, pp. 888–911, Nov. 2014
6. E. Vrochidou, K. Tziridis, A. Nikolaou, T. Kalampokas, G. A. Papakostas, T. P. Pachidis, S. Mamalis, S. Koundouras, and V. G. Kaburlasos, An Autonomous Grape-Harvester Robot: Integrated System Architecture, Electronics, 2021, 10, 1056.
7. V. G. Kaburlasos (Guest Editor), Special Issue on Lattice Computing: A Mathematical Modelling Paradigm for Cyber-Physical System Applications, Mathematics, vol. 10, no. 2, 271, 2022.
8. V. G. Kaburlasos, The lattice computing (LC) paradigm, in Proc. 15th Intl. Conf. on Concept Lattices and their Applications (CLA 2020), eds. F. J. Valverde-Albacete and M. Trnecka, (Tallinn, Estonia, 2020).
9. Sussner, P.; Caro Contreras, D.E. Generalized morphological components based on interval descriptors and n-ary aggregation functions. Inf. Sci. (Ny). 2022, 583, 14–32, doi:10.1016/j.ins.2021.10.012.
10. V. G. Kaburlasos and G. A. Papakostas, "Learning Distributions of Image Features by Interactive Fuzzy Lattice Reasoning in Pattern Recognition Applications," IEEE Comput. Intell. Mag., 10(3) 42–51, 2015.
11. V. R. Sampath Kumar et al., "Ontologies for Industry 4.0," Knowl. Eng. Rev., vol. 34, p. e17, Nov. 2019.
12. G. Fu, "FCA based ontology development for data integration," Inf. Process. Manag., vol. 52, no. 5, pp. 765–782, Sep. 2016.
13. V. G. Kaburlasos, C. Lytridis, E. Vrochidou, C. Bazinas, G. A. Papakostas, A. Lekova, O. Bouattane, M. Youssfi, T. Hashimoto, "Granule-based-classifier (GbC): a lattice computing scheme applied on tree data structures", Mathematics, vol. 9, no. 22, 2889, 2021.

88

New rules for combining classifiers using fuzzy majority and plurality voting

Thiago Batista* and Benjamin Bedregal†

Federal University of Rio Grande do Norte (UFRN)
Natal, Rio Grande do Norte, Brazil
* thiagovvb@gmail.com
† bedregal@dimap.ufrn.br
www.ufrn.br

Ronei M. Moraes

Federal University of Paraíba (UFPB)
João Pessoa, Paraíba, Brazil
ronei@de.ufpb.br

In classification and decision making, combining classifiers is a common approach, forming what is known as a classifier ensemble. The idea behind this approach is to, through diversity, improve classification accuracy. In these systems, perhaps the most important part is combining the different outputs presented by each classifier. However, most approaches found in literature use simple methods like majority voting or weighted means as the combination method. In this paper, we will present new approaches to combine the outputs of classifiers in a classifier ensemble: Fuzzy Majority Voting and Fuzzy Plurality voting, which are fuzzy approaches to the classical majority and plurality voting. Results obtained show that both are promising methods to be used in these systems.

Keywords: Combining classifiers; fuzzy majority voting; fuzzy plurality voting; data classification.

1. Introduction

In the area of classification, a common strategy is to combine a number of classifiers, forming what is known as an ensemble of classifiers. The idea behind this approach is to take advantage of the diversity of the methods to improve the overall classification accuracy. In this approach, the goal is to have different enough classifiers such that when there is a type of data or element which a classifier is underperforming, the other will compensate.[1] Due to its advantages, they have been applied to different areas, such as in analysis of medical images,[2] financial market[3] and water quality control.[4]

The base architecture of a classifier ensemble consists of two layers: the classification layer and the combination layer. In the first, each classifier processes an element and provides an output regarding the classification of such element. In the second, their outputs are combined in one single answer. The classification layer has received much attention in recent years, with many methods proposing improvements and new techniques to improve its diversity and performance. The combination layer, in contrast, doesn't receive the same amount of attention and most algorithms use simple approaches such as majority voting and weighted mean.

One of the most used approaches in the combination layer is voting. Majority voting, for example, is a simple but frequently used technique in classifier ensembles. This approach has as main advantages having almost no computational cost involved and the fact that it often presents decent results. For example, the work of Atallah et al.[5] created and heterogeneous ensemble of classifiers and obtained good results with majority voting. Another type of voting is the plurality voting, where unlike majority voting, the "winner" is only required to receive the most number of votes, instead of having more than 50% of the votes.

Sá et al.[6] proposed Fuzzy Majority Voting and Fuzzy Plurality Voting for combining spatial clustering methods in a geospatial context. In this paper we proposed a new mathematical version of them in order to allow apply them as combining rule for data and image classification. Both methods were tested against well established approaches in literature and verify if there was a significant gain in performance when using Fuzzy Plurality Voting.

2. Combining Fuzzy Rules

This section presents types some well known combinatorial rules based on voting and defines Fuzzy Plurality and Majority voting, with the first being used in experiments in posterior sections. We will define these functions from the point of view of classifier ensembles, in contrast to what was done by Sá et al.,[6] which defined them in the context of geo-objects.

2.1. *Combining rules*

For the following sections, assume the context of a classifier ensemble, consisting of a set of v classifiers $\mathbf{C} = \{c_1, \ldots, c_n\}$, $v = \{1, 2, \ldots, v\}$ and k possible classes ($\Omega = \{x_1, \ldots, x_r\}$), $r = \{1, 2, \ldots, k\}$ for an element a_i being classified. Also, we will define a decision function $\Delta_{rv}(a_i)$ as follows:

$$\Delta_{rv}(a_i) = \begin{cases} 1 & \text{if classifier } c_v \text{ decision for element } a_i \text{ is } r, \\ 0 & \text{otherwise} \end{cases}$$

2.1.1. Majority voting

Let k be the number of decisions in decision space Ω for data from an element a_i, and n is the number of classifiers in the ensemble. Also, let Δ_{rv} the decision function. The majority voting with rejection option[7] in binary case is given by:

$$H(a_i) = decision(r) \ if \ \sum_{v=1}^{n} \Delta_{rv}(a_i) > \frac{1}{2} \sum_{s=1}^{k} \sum_{v=1}^{n} \Delta_{sv}(a_i), \tag{1}$$

i.e. the result is valid if the total number of votes obtained by $decision(r)$ is greater than 50% of the total number of votes. Note that is possible to not obtain a decision if no class has more than 50% of the votes. In this case, a rule must be created to deal with this situation. One possible solution is assigning a "default" classifier which takes the decision in the case of a lack of consensus. Another possible solution is simply assigning the class with the highest number of votes.

2.1.2. Plurality voting

Plurality voting does not require at least 50% of votes for the winner decision. In fact, the largest number of votes is enough without rejection option.[8]

$$H(a_i) = decision(r) \ if \ \sum_{v=1}^{n} \Delta_{rv}(a_i) = \max_{s \in \{1,...,k\}} \sum_{v=1}^{n} \Delta_{sv}(a_i) \tag{2}$$

However, it is also possible to include a rejection option in a plurality voting system. The majority voting and the plurality voting produce the same results in the case of binary (two classes) classification.[7,8]

2.2. Cardinality of fuzzy sets

Zadeh proposed the cardinality for a fuzzy set X, denoted by $\Sigma Count$.[9] It is a real number defined by the sum of membership values for each member of a fuzzy set X:

$$\Sigma Count(X) = \sum_{i=1}^{n} \mu(x_i), i = 1, \ldots, S. \tag{3}$$

3. Fuzzy Voting for Combining Classifiers

As mentioned before, two approaches based on the cardinality of fuzzy sets and they were applied for combining results obtained from manipulations of georeferenced maps.[6] At this moment, we provide new mathematical formulations of them in order to allow apply them as combining rule for data and image classification and they generalized the classical combining rules based on Majority Voting and Plurality Voting, which were presented previously. They are formally presented in the following.

3.1. *Fuzzy majority voting using cardinality of fuzzy sets*

The classical Majority Voting defines the winner decision as that one that obtains more than 50% of votes. Assuming that each classifier v outputs a vector $P_v = [p_{1v}, \ldots, p_{kv}]$, where each element p_{rv} in this vector represents some measure (as for instance, probability or possibility) for the element being classified belongs to class r, according to classifier v. Assuming that the membership function $\mu_{rv}(a_i) = p_{rv}$ for the element a_i, the fuzzy majority voting is given by:

$$H(a_i) = decision(r) \ if \ \sum_{v=1}^{n} \Sigma Count_{rv}(a_i) >$$

$$> \frac{1}{2} \sum_{r=1}^{k} \sum_{v=1}^{n} \Sigma Count_{rv}(a_i) \tag{4}$$

where k is the number of decisions in Ω. The $\Sigma Count_{rv}(a_i)$ is the cardinality of a fuzzy set, as defined by Eq. (3), i.e., it counts the votes for decision r using the classifier v for the element a_i. So, the final decision r is that one which is able to obtain more than the half of all membership values computed by the $\Sigma Count$.

3.2. *Fuzzy plurality voting using cardinality of fuzzy sets*

The classical plurality voting presented by the Eq. (2) defines the winner decision as the one that obtains the greatest number of votes. Using the membership function $\mu_{rv}(a_i) = p_{rv}$, for the element a_i, provided by classifier v, the fuzzy plurality voting is given by:

$$H\left(a_i\right) = decision\left(r\right) \ if \ \sum_{v=1}^{k} \Sigma Count_{rv}\left(a_i\right)$$

$$= \max_{s\in\{1,...,k\}} \sum_{v=1}^{k} \Sigma Count_{rv}\left(a_i\right) \quad (5)$$

According to Zhou[7] in binary cases, the plurality voting and majority voting provide the same results. However, this is not valid for the fuzzy plurality voting and the fuzzy majority voting, proposed here.

4. Results

To test the previously defined model, we applied it in a classifier ensemble system to combine the output of different classifiers. After preliminary tests performed with $5, 10, 15, 20$ and 40 classifiers. We have decided to use an ensemble of 10 classifiers, which presented the best results, consisting of 3 Neural Networks (MLP Algorithm), 3 Decision Trees, 3 K-NNs and 1 Naive Bayes. For the datasets, we have chosen 22 datasets from the UCI Machine Learning repository, and they are described in Table 1.

Consider a problem with p possible classes and n classifiers, in the experiments, we assume that by the end of the classification step, each classifier

Table 1.   Datasets selected to be used in the experiments.

Dataset	Number of Elements	Number of Attributes	Number of Classes
monk's problems 1 (M1)	432	6	2
monk's problems 2 (M2)	432	6	2
monk's problems 3 (M3)	432	6	2
mushroom (MU)	5644	22	2
heart statlog (HS)	270	13	2
winequality-red (WR)	1599	11	6
fertility-diagnosis (FD)	100	9	6
transfusion (TR)	747	4	2
seeds (SE)	210	7	3
bupa (BU)	345	6	2
lymphography (LY)	148	18	4
haberman (HA)	306	3	2
balance scale (BS)	625	4	3
iris (IR)	150	4	3
breast cancer (BC)	683	9	2
glass (GL)	214	10	6
ionosphere(IO)	351	34	2
car evaluation (CE)	1728	21	4
nursery (NU)	12960	26	5
waveform (WA)	5000	21	3
vehicle (VE)	846	18	4
winequality-white (WW)	4898	11	7

will output a vector $P_v = [p_{1v}, \ldots, p_{kv}]$, where each element p_{rv} in this vector represents some measure (as for instance, probability or possibility) for the element being classified belongs to class r, according to classifier v. In this paper, we use these values as estimations for the membership values. For more details on the methodology, refer to Batista et al.[10]

We used a cross-validation approach to perform the tests, which consists of dividing the dataset in m partitions and perform the classification in rounds. Where in each round, one partition is used to test the model and the remaining $m - 1$ partitions are used as a training set. This process is repeated until each partition is used as a test set exactly one time. Here, we adopted a $m = 10$.

The results of the performed tests are in Table 2. We compared Fuzzy Plurality Voting (FPV) and Fuzzy Majority Voting (FMV) against 4 other known methods in literature: Random Forests (RF), AdaBoost (ADA), GradientBoosting (GB) and Bagging (BAG).

From the results, we can verify that FPV and FMV obtained the best result in 13 out of 22 datasets. Moreover, FPV had the highest average

Table 2. Comparison of the results obtained with the Fuzzy Plurality Voting against other ensemble methods.

Base	FPV	FMV	RF	ADA	GB	BAG
M1	**93.03**	83.07	71.52	61.57	61.57	51.15
M2	**64.16**	60.22	61.61	48.07	48.08	60.94
M3	98.38	97.92	98.61	**100.00**	**100.00**	84.74
MU	93.48	93.51	93.28	92.98	93.76	**94.76**
HS	81.85	**82.96**	75.56	77.78	81.11	81.11
WR	**55.91**	45.90	54.22	50.84	52.41	51.60
FD	86.00	**87.00**	86.00	81.00	76.00	86.00
TR	66.44	66.17	65.36	72.30	**72.57**	70.70
SE	**93.33**	91.90	90.48	73.33	87.62	92.38
BU	71.30	**72.46**	64.64	69.28	68.99	64.93
LY	82.44	81.03	**84.46**	66.92	76.90	79.72
HA	68.28	69.60	69.60	64.02	64.02	**71.56**
BS	80.80	74.24	64.48	69.28	**85.60**	76.48
IR	**96.00**	94.67	**96.00**	94.67	95.33	94.67
BC	96.49	96.20	95.18	95.32	94.88	**96.64**
GL	90.60	**91.58**	84.98	73.32	84.93	85.50
IO	89.19	91.46	**92.31**	90.89	90.60	82.91
CE	**80.68**	77.72	73.79	74.12	74.42	72.47
NU	73.18	72.23	64.88	73.80	**73.97**	68.96
WA	84.82	**85.10**	81.96	84.02	84.36	81.50
VE	**77.78**	72.58	75.06	58.63	76.48	69.50
WW	**49.98**	38.02	47.76	39.61	48.49	48.12
Average	80.64	78.43	76.89	73.26	76.91	75.74

from all the compared methods. As we can verify, FPV had a higher average mean accuracy in relation to FMV. However, this difference is not statistically significant. So, since the FPV result was indeed numerically superior, we will use only FPV in further analysis.

In order to verify if the results obtained are statistically significant, we applied the Friedman test by adopting a significance level of 0.05, which resulted in a p-value less than 0.05. It indicates that there are statistically significant differences between the methods. As a post-hoc test, we used the Nemenyi test, which is shown by the CD-Diagram (a visual representation of the Nemenyi test).

On the CD diagram, the top line represents an axis where the mean ranks are plotted. If two methods are connected though a horizontal line, it means that the difference between the methods is not statistically significant. From Fig. 1, we can 1, we can verify that no line crosses FPV, which also had the best result, which shows that FPV was indeed the best approach of the ones that were compared.

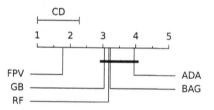

Fig. 1.   CD-Diagram for verifying the statistical difference between the results.

5. Final Remarks

In this paper we provide new mathematical formulations for Fuzzy Majority Voting and Fuzzy Plurality Voting to the context of classifier ensembles. In general, we consider that the proposed approaches had excellent results when compared to other methods in literature, as verified by the statistical tests. Therefore, we consider that this type of fuzzy voting is a promising approach not only to classifier ensembles, but to other types of applications that use some type of voting. As future works, we would like to test this methods against recently proposed techniques for the combination layer. Another possible branching of this work is developing a new approach also for the classification layer to be used with the fuzzy plurality voting.

References

1. M. Mohandes, M. Deriche and S. O. Aliyu, Classifiers combination techniques: A comprehensive review, *IEEE Access* **6**, 19626 (2018).
2. S. Dey, R. Bhattacharya, S. Malakar, S. Mirjalili and R. Sarkar, Choquet fuzzy integral-based classifier ensemble technique for COVID-19 detection, *Computers in Biology and Medicine*, p. 104585 (2021).
3. Y. Cao, Aggregating multiple classification results using Choquet integral for financial distress early warning, *Expert Systems with Applications* **39**, 1830 (2012).
4. H. R. Kadkhodaei, A. M. E. Moghadam and M. Dehghan, Hboost: A heterogeneous ensemble classifier based on the boosting method and entropy measurement, *Expert Systems with Applications* **157**, p. 113482 (2020).
5. R. Atallah and A. Al-Mousa, Heart disease detection using machine learning majority voting ensemble method, in *2019 2nd International Conference on New Trends in Computing Sciences (ICTCS)*, 2019.
6. L. R. de Sá, L. dos Santos Machado, J. de Almeida Nogueira and R. M. de Moraes, New combining rules for spatial clustering methods using sigma-count for spatial epidemiology, in *2020 International Conference on Decision Aid Sciences and Application (DASA)*, 2020.
7. Z.-H. Zhou, *Ensemble methods: foundations and algorithms* (CRC press, 2012).
8. L. I. Kuncheva, *Combining pattern classifiers: methods and algorithms* (John Wiley & Sons, 2014).
9. L. A. Zadeh, A computational approach to fuzzy quantifiers in natural languages, in *Computational linguistics* (Elsevier, 1983) pp. 149–184.
10. T. Batista, B. Bedregal and R. Moraes, Constructing multi-layer classifier ensembles using the choquet integral based on overlap and quasi-overlap functions, *Neurocomputing* **500**, 413 (2022).

Digital twin for energy optimization in the paper drying process based on genetic algorithm and CADSIM Plus

Yishui Zhang, Jiwei Qian, Zhenglei He[†], Yi Man[‡], Jigeng Li and Mengna Hong

State Key Laboratory of Pulp and Paper Engineering
South China University of Technology
Guangzhou, 510640, China
202021028894@mail.scut.edu.cn
[†]hezhenglei@scut.edu.cn
[‡]manyi@scut.edu.cn

Dryer section is the most energy-intensive part of the papermaking process, and the requirements for energy saving and consumption reduction in the dryer section is increasing with the constraints of the environment and energy. In order to reduce energy consumption, this paper proposes a method for constructing a paper dryer model based on digital twin: using the chemical simulation software CADSIM Plus combined with the dryer mechanism model to build a digital twin model. On this basis, the genetic algorithm is used to optimize its energy consumption. The results show that the optimized drying process parameters can achieve the effect of saving energy and reducing consumption.

Keywords: Papermaking process; dryer section; digital twin; genetic algorithm.

1. Introduction

The paper industry is the fourth largest energy-consuming industry in the world. With the increasing energy and environmental constraints, the paper industry has higher and higher requirements for energy conservation and emission reduction. The dryer section is the most energy-intensive in the papermaking process, accounting for about 65% of the total[1,2]. Therefore, reducing the energy consumption of the dryer section in a reasonable way can reduce the cost.

Digital twin is a technology that combines model simulation, real-time data, etc. to construct an interactive mapping relationship between physical space and information space[3,4]. It can realize the monitoring, optimization and prediction of the whole production process. Using digital twin to carry out applied research on dryer section simulation, analysis, optimization and testing can be carried out in the information space before paper production. The model is a bridge connecting the information space and the physical space. However, papermaking is a typical process industry, and the complexity of the process brings great difficulties to the modeling, simulation and optimization of the system. Some papermaking developed countries have developed simulation software specially used for pulping and papermaking[5]. However, it is difficult to apply it to the domestic papermaking industry, and cannot fully adapt to the situation of papermaking industry. There are no simulation software specifically for the pulping and papermaking process and relatively few researches on the simulation of pulping and papermaking in China. Most of the research only involves the modeling and simulation of a specific process or some characteristics of papermaking, and few combine the mechanism model with the simulation model to optimize the key process or the entire process.

To this end, the research group introduced CADSIM Plus chemical simulation process software from abroad. This software has a complete papermaking physical property database and operation unit module library, which is helpful for the simulation of papermaking process flow. This paper is mainly based on the mathematical model of the dryer section established in our previous works[6], and uses CADSIM Plus combined with the mechanism equation to build the simulation process of the dryer section. Through the DDE function, the production data is imported to calculate the model output, which is helpful to more accurately analyze the material consumption and energy consumption of the process, and realize the energy analysis of the process. On the basis of establishing a steady state simulation process, by changing the process conditions, the law and dynamic characteristics of the production process parameters changing with time are studied, and the energy consumption is optimized by using the genetic algorithm. Energy consumption mainly includes electricity consumption and steam consumption. There is little space for optimization of electric energy as it is mainly used for power transmission. So the main optimization target is steam consumption.

2. Construction and Optimization of Dryer Section Model

The traditional multi-cylinder dryer section consists of a paper drying system, a steam-condensate water system, and a ventilation and waste heat recovery system. Combined with the mathematical model of the dryer section established by the research group in the early stage, the dryer process of the paper is divided into the dryer cylinder module and the paper module; the steam-condensed water system is divided into the steam-water separator module, the steam mixing module and the condenser module; the ventilation and waste heat recovery system divided into air mixing module, heat recovery module and air heating module. In this study, each module was built and connected through CADSIM Plus to construct the

98

corresponding energy efficiency optimization module. The subsequent content of this paper will take the paper module as an example to establish a simulation process to verify and optimize the simulation data.

2.1. Construction of paper model

CADSIM Plus has a library of operating unit modules for paper making and provides custom model capabilities. It can also customize the unit operation model. The unit module of the paper module of the dryer section has no corresponding model in the paper library, so we need to customize the unit operation module, Fig. 1 shows the paper module constructed based on the mechanistic model.

When building the paper model, the paper type is selected for the flow type, and the flow components are selected respectively: "WATER", "FIBER", "STEAM", "AIR", "H2O[V]", and temperature and pressure are selected for the flow attribute. Based on the paper mechanism model of the dryer section, a complete paper model was built for it, and the model reached a steady state through testing. At this time, we can use the DDE function of the software to transfer the actual data for it, and study the change law of the process parameters and the dynamic characteristics of the model.

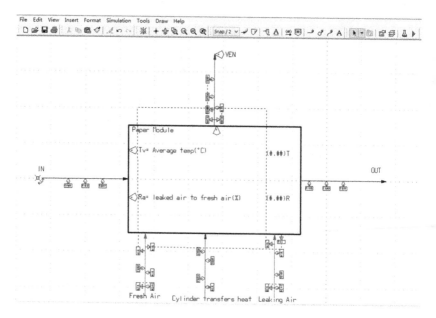

Fig. 1. Paper module.

2.2. *Optimization of paper model*

Genetic algorithm[7] is a random search algorithm, which takes all individuals in a population as the object and guides the fitness function to efficiently search the entire parameter space through crossover and mutation operations. Genetic manipulation mainly includes operations such as selection, crossover and mutation. As is shown in Fig. 2, better offspring can be obtained by selection operation, and excellent individuals can be retained by evaluating individual fitness; crossover operation generates more possible individuals by exchanging genetic loci of individuals, and continuously improves the search ability of genetic algorithm through fitness evaluation; the mutation operation first selects an individual of the population with a certain probability, and then the genetic loci on that individual mutate with a set probability. GA has strong optimization ability, and has the characteristics of high efficiency, parallel and global optimization.

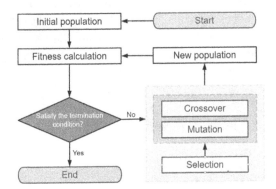

Fig. 2. Flow chart of genetic algorithm.

In this paper, a genetic algorithm is used to minimize the heat (Qsa) of the heated air in the paper module by optimizing the temperature (Tha) of the humid and hot air in the hood, the amount of heated air (Gsa), and the temperature of the heated air (Tsa). The heat required for drying the paper comes from the steam, which condenses and releases heat inside the cylinder. Except for the heating of the cylinder, the steam consumption of the paper module is mainly concentrated in the heating of the fresh air part. When the heat transferred from the cylinder to the model is constant and other parameters are considered reasonable, the heat of the fresh air consumed by drying a certain amount of paper can be optimized to save the steam consumed by heating the fresh air. The objective function is:

$$Qsa = Gsa[Tsa \times (1.01 + 1.88 \times hsa) + 2490 \times hsa]. \qquad (1)$$

Qsa is the heat of the air after heating, and Gsa is the amount of air that enters the hood after heating. Tsa is the temperature of the heated air, which is usually between 85 and 110 degrees when considering safety in production. Hsa is the humidity of the heated air.

$$85 \leq Tsa \leq 110. \tag{2}$$

The incoming air is usually taken from indoor or outdoor air and is mainly affected by the season, changes in air humidity during actual operation can be ignored. The higher the humidity of the hot and humid air in the air hood, the more moisture it will take away under the same conditions, but when the humidity reaches saturation, dew forms and falls on the paper. So the air temperature (Tha) and air humidity (hha) of the hood set constraints for it:

$$Tha \geq 16.964 * ln(1000 * hha) - 15.736. \tag{3}$$

Gv is the amount of evaporated water, Qv is the heat of evaporated water, Gha is the amount of hot and humid air in the hood, Qha is the heat of the hot and humid air in the hood, Gla is the amount of leaked air, Qla is the heat of the leaked air. According to the material balance and energy balance of the paper module, the following equilibrium equation can be obtained:

$$G_v + G_{sa} + G_{la} = G_{ha}. \tag{4}$$

$$Q_v + Q_{sa} + Q_{la} = Q_{ha}. \tag{5}$$

3. Results and Discussion

The wet paper absorbs the heat of the saturated steam in the cylinder, a large amount of water evaporates and needs to be discharged from the hood in time. Otherwise the drying efficiency will be affected. Therefore, it is necessary to pass heated air to remove the water vapor evaporated from the wet paper model. Usually, the air intake and exhaust air volume of the ventilation system in the dryer section is generally adjusted by the operator according to experience, which is highly arbitrary, and it is difficult to choose the appropriate parameters according to the actual situation. The higher the temperature of the heated air, the more water vapor that can be taken away, and the greater the energy consumption of the steam; if the temperature of the heated air is too low, the air temperature in the air hood will drop, when the humidity rises, condensation is easy to occur, and water falling on paper can cause paper disease.

Therefore, by reasonably setting constraints and optimization models, a set of reliable parameters can be provided for the production process to optimize its energy consumption. In this study, 100 sets of actual running data are used to optimize the operation variables by genetic algorithm. The optimization results are as follows:

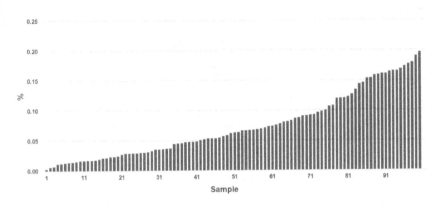

Fig. 3. Comparison of heating air before and after heat optimization.

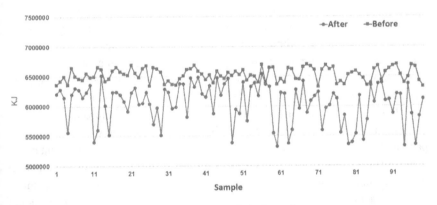

Fig. 4. Percentage of optimized quantity.

Figure 3 shows the comparison between the actual value and the optimized value, and Fig. 4 shows the percentage of the amount of thermal optimization. From Fig. 4, we can see that the amount of optimization less than 10% accounts for about 75%, and that of more than 10% accounts for about 25%. It can be analyzed that the energy saving effect of about 10% can be achieved by using the optimized data under the actual working conditions.

Thus, using genetic algorithm to adjust the process parameters such as the temperature of the humid and hot air of the hood, the amount of heated air, and the temperature of the hot fresh air. It can achieve the purpose of optimization.

The results in the table show the optimization effect of the paper sheet module as an example. With the optimized parameters, the air intake volume of the simulation mode can be reduced by 8% and the heat of the incoming air can be reduced by 10.1%.

Table 1. Process parameters of the optimized paper machine.

parameter	Before	After
Tsa（℃）	102	98.58
hha（kg/kg）	0.05	0.056
Gsa（kg）	38012.22	34859.07
Tha（℃）	80	76.91
Qsa（kJ）	6974207.8	6268486.8

4. Conclusion

In this study, the papermaking module was taken as an example, and a simulation model of the papermaking module in the dryer section based on the digital twin was established. By entering historical data or real-time data, changes in key parameters can be observed from the simulation process, enabling dynamic simulation and process optimization of the sheet module in the dryer section. And use the genetic algorithm to adjust the process parameters of the range hood, such as the temperature of the hot and humid air, the volume of the hot air, and the temperature of the hot fresh air. From the calculation results of the simulation model, it can be concluded that the heat entering the air is optimized by 10.1%.

In the future, this research will be expanded to the whole process of papermaking based on the digital twin technology. Since the establishment of the mechanism model is based on many assumptions, the accuracy is difficult to meet the actual industrial needs. In the subsequent work, on the basis of the mechanism model modeling, more data-driven approach improves model accuracy, and adopt a variety of optimization algorithms to achieve the effect of multi-objective optimization.

References

1. Zheng, Qingying, and Boqiang Lin. "Industrial polices and improved energy efficiency in China's paper industry." *Journal of Cleaner Production* 161 (2017): 200-210.
2. Zhang, Yang, et al. "Energy system optimization model for tissue paper-making process." *Computers & Chemical Engineering* 146 (2021): 107220.
3. Zhang, Hao, et al. "A digital twin-based approach for designing and multi-

objective optimization of hollow glass production line." *IEEE Access* 5 (2017): 26901-26911.

4. Zhuang, Cunbo, et al. "The connotation of digital twin, and the construction and application method of shop-floor digital twin." *Robotics and Computer-Integrated Manufacturing* 68 (2021): 102075.

5. Mălutan, Teodor, and Corina Mălutan. "Simulation of processes in paper-making by WinGEMS software." *Environmental Engineering and Management Journal* 12.8 (2013): 1645-1647.

6. Li, Yu-Gang, et al. "Simultaneous module-based optimization of operation parameters of dryer section in paper machine." *Journal of South China University of Technology* 39.3 (2011): 8-12.

7. Katoch, Sourabh, Sumit Singh Chauhan, and Vijay Kumar. "A review on genetic algorithm: past, present, and future." *Multimedia Tools and Applications* 80.5 (2021): 8091-8126.

A semi-supervised learning method with attention mechanism for pancreas segmentation

Yuhao Mo, Bo Peng*, Caizheng Li and Fei Teng

School of Computer and Artificial Intelligence, Southwest Jiaotong University
Chengdu, 610097, China
Department of General Practice, West China Hospital of Sichuan University
Chengdu, Sichuan, China
*bpeng@swjtu.edu.cn

Computed tomography (CT) is the primary method for the diagnosis of pancreatic cancer. Accurately segmenting the pancreas from abdominal CT images has significant medical value. However, the complex objective characteristics of the pancreas and the high cost of material and human resources in the task of manually labeling medical images make pancreas image segmentation a challenging task. To solve these problems, we propose a nested U-Net network structure with an integrated attention mechanism, which can complete the capture and fusion of global and local information without significantly increasing the computational cost. In addition to this, we propose a semi-supervised learning strategy used to update network parameters. The proposed method is evaluated on the public NIH pancreas dataset. Experimental results show that the DSC value of our proposed network structure is up to 89.13 under the fully supervised learning strategy, which is more promising than other advanced methods. Under the strategy of semi-supervised learning, only a small amount of the training data can achieve the segmentation performance similar to fully supervised learning.

Keywords: Pancreas segmentation; nested U-Net; semi-supervised learning; attention mechanism.

1. Introduction

The pancreas, located in the abdominal cavity behind the stomach, is one of the eight glands in the human body and plays a key role in digestion and glucose metabolism. Pancreatic cancer is one of the most common malignant tumors, and its mortality rate is increasing worldwide. CT is a routine inspection of abdominal organ diseases and an important reference for the diagnosis of pancreatic cancer.

So far, the principal pancreas segmentation methods are divided into conventional pancreas segmentation methods and deep learning methods.

Conventional pancreas segmentation methods include region-based,[1] atlas-based,[2] and level-set-based[3] methods. Deep learning segmentation algorithms include FCN-based,[4] U-Net-based,[5] and GAN-based[6] methods. FCN[7] replaces fully connected layers with convolutional layers to realize pixel-level classification of images on the basis of CNN. The proposal of U-Net[8] has epoch-making significance. Based on FCN, U-Net creatively combines low-resolution and high-resolution information and greatly pushes forward the progression of medical image segmentation. GAN is one of the most popular technologies at present, there are two different neural networks in GAN, namely the generation network and the discriminant network, and the training is realized through a continuous game of them.

Among the current popular CNNs, ResNet and U-Net both use 1×1 and 3×3 convolution filters, the reason why small convolution filters are popular is that they reduce network parameters and speed up the processing speed of convolution operation. However, these convolution networks have problems such as single receptive fields and weak network generalization ability. Our contributions are summarized as follows:

• We propose a network architecture that efficiently captures the local detail and global context information to solve the above problems.

• A semi-supervised learning strategy is proposed to reduce the over-reliance on hand-labeled medical data.

2. Methods

2.1. *BA-RSU module*

Nowadays, the attention mechanism has been widely applied in the computer vision domain.[9] It swiftly scans the whole image, locks the target area, and then pays more attention to this area to strengthen the detailed information of the target area and weaken the useless information of other areas. Given the advantages of the attention mechanism, the Bottleneck Attention Module[10] which can be easily integrated into CNN is chosen.

We propose an RSU structure fused with BAM to reach the above purpose rapidly, as shown in Fig. 1. BA-RSU consists of 5 parts: (a) Double 3×3 convolution operations are performed on the input feature map to convert C_{in} into C_{out} and C_{mid} respectively. (b) The encoding phase includes 2×2 max pooling, during each downsampling process, the number of feature channels is doubled. (c) Regions and contents of interest in the feature map are learned through BAM. (d) The decoding phase consists of bilinear interpolation and concatenation of the corresponding feature maps,

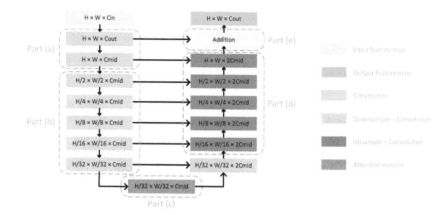

Fig. 1. BA-RSU module.

the number of feature channels is doubled during each upsampling process. (e) Residual connections.

2.2. Network architecture

U-Net, as one of the most successful methods in the field of semantic segmentation, provides novel options and directions for medical image segmentation. Inspired by the nested U-Net,[11] we propose a novel nested U-Net structure based on BA-RSU (**BARU-net**) for CT pancreas image segmentation, as shown in Fig. 2. By comparison with U-Net architecture, BARU-net has made the following improvements: (a) A six-level encoding, five-level decoding structure is adopted. (b) BARU-Net uses the BA-RSU module to replace double convolution in U-Net. (c) During upsampling process, BARU-Net uses unpooling operations to resize feature maps. (d) Saliency map fusion module.

Encoder-decoder is a highly symmetrical structure, the encoding process includes six stages: $S_e = \{S_{e1}, S_{e2}, S_{e3}, S_{e4}, S_{e5}, S_{e6}\}$, and the decoding process consists of five stages in turn: $S_d = \{S_{d1}, S_{d2}, S_{d3}, S_{d4}, S_{d5}\}$. Following the classic skip connection means that the input of the decoder in the current stage is determined by the output of the encoder in the same stage and the output of the decoder in the previous stage:

$$S_{di}^{in} = S_{ei}^{out} \oplus U(S_{e(i+1)}^{out}), \quad i = 1, 2, 3, 4, 5 \tag{1}$$

The fusion module plays an essential role in generating significant probability maps. We select feature maps from S_{e6}, S_{d5}, S_{d4}, S_{d3}, S_{d2}, and S_{d1}

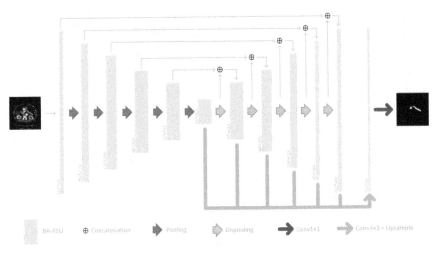

Fig. 2. Network architecture.

outputs. Firstly, we perform a 3 × 3 convolution operation on each feature map and set the output channel to 1, then images are upsampled by using bilinear interpolation to restore their size to the input image size. Finally, six images are connected and a 1 × 1 convolution is used to generate a single-channel saliency map.

In summary, for our proposed BARU-net, a variety of receptive fields with distinctive sizes are mixed. This allows the network to extract both global and local information from different stages and expands the depth of the network architecture without prominently raising the calculation cost.

2.3. Semi-supervised learning

Although deep learning methods have made satisfactory results of medical image segmentation come true, they rely heavily on labeled data. Results will often be unsatisfactory if labeled medical images are insufficient or labeling quality is poor. Pixel-by-pixel labeling of medical images is an extremely time-consuming task with high financial and human costs. Therefore, semi-supervised learning has a place to show prowess.

We propose a pancreas image segmentation method based on semi-supervised learning. The key of the method is the update of the dataset, that is, how to convert unlabeled data into labeled data. The dataset updating strategy is implemented to do it.

Suppose that the given dataset is: $D = \{X_i, Y_i, X_j^* | i \in \{1, 2, ..., n\}, j \in \{1, 2, ..., m\}\}$. Here, D represents the dataset, X and X^* represent labeled and unlabeled original images respectively, and Y represents ground-truth labels corresponding to X. Firstly, the network model (F) is trained by using original images and ground-truth labels, then its parameter (p) is updated as:

$$Y_i = F_p(X_i) \tag{2}$$

Assuming that the updated network parameter is $p1$, we obtain pseudo-labeled images (Y^*) corresponding to unlabeled original images by solving equation:

$$Y_j^* = F_{p1}(X_j^*) \tag{3}$$

The original dataset is updated by adding pseudo labels. The new dataset is as follows: $D = \{X_i, Y_i, X_j^*, Y_j^* | i \in \{1, 2, ..., n\}, j \in \{1, 2, ..., m\}\}$. Through the new dataset, we begin to train the network model:

$$\{Y_i, Y_j^*\} = F_{p2}(\{X_i, X_j^*\}) \tag{4}$$

Eventually, the parameter is updated ($p2$) and we get the network that can segment pancreas images.

3. Experiments

3.1. Implementation details

We carry out experiments on the publicly available NIH dataset.[12] In the process of training, we use the Dice loss function to calculate the loss value and the Adam algorithm to optimize network parameters.

Two commonly used indexes of pancreas CT image segmentation are selected to evaluate the performance of our proposed network. The Dice Similarity Coefficient (DSC) is statistical data used to measure the similarity between two images, the calculation formula is as follows:

$$DSC = \frac{2|X \cap Y|}{|X| + |Y|} \tag{5}$$

Intersection Over Union (IOU), the overlap between the ground truth (T) and the prediction output (P) in percent, similar to the DSC, is expressed as follows:

$$IOU = \frac{T \cap P}{T \cup P} \tag{6}$$

3.2. Experimental results

We evaluate the performance of the proposed BARU-Net network on the NIH dataset and compare the proposed model with the most advanced methods at present under fully supervised learning. The performance of different networks is shown in Table 1. It can be seen that our proposed network is superior to others in Dice and IOU.

Table 1. Comparison of proposed method and others.

Method	Dice	IOU
U-Net[8]	88.47	80.06
U^2-Net[11]	88.72	80.41
Unet++	86.49	77.16
Attention U-Net[5]	88.02	79.61
Segnet	88.05	79.35
Res-UNet	85.26	75.66
FCN[7]	86.93	77.93
Proposed	**89.13**	**81.07**

In addition, to explore the effect of the proposed semi-supervised learning strategy on actual pancreatic image segmentation, we design comparative experiments at different proportions (unlabeled/labeled) while remaining the same quantity of images used for semi-supervised training. The results are shown in Table 2. We compare both learning methods, and the comparison results are shown in Fig. 3.

Table 2. Comparison of unlabeled and labeled data in different proportions.

Proportion	Dice	IOU
4	84.07	74.25
6	79.10	68.65
15	74.76	63.17
30	71.36	59.11
60	57.37	45.16
100	45.20	33.44

The results show that when the number of training is constant, the higher the proportion of labeled data, the better the performance of the network. Although the training effect of using pseudo labels is not as good

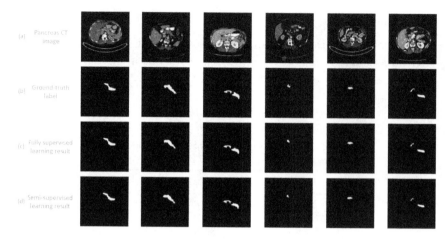

Fig. 3. Comparison of fully supervised and semi-supervised learning methods.

as that of using ground-truth labels actually, the network trained by semi-supervised strategy has certain anti-noise ability and robustness because pseudo labels are not accurate enough and involve some noise.

4. Conclusion

In this paper, we propose a practical network for CT pancreas image segmentation, BARU-Net, which can effectively capture and fuse local and global information without significantly increasing the computational cost. Our model achieves competitive performance compared to other advanced methods. In addition, a method combining deep neural network and semi-supervised learning strategy is proposed, which improves the anti-noise ability of deep neural networks and brings them excellent robustness.

The adaptability of noisy data caused by fuzzy medical images is still a thorny problem to be solved. In the future, our study will be continuously devoted to optimizing semantic segmentation networks and improving semi-supervised learning strategies to achieve superior segmentation results with less manually labeled data.

Acknowledgments

This work was supported by Sichuan Science and Technology Program (No. 2021YFS0014).

References

1. A. Farag, L. Le, H. R. Roth, J. Liu, and R. M. Summers. Automatic pancreas segmentation using coarse-to-fine superpixel labeling. 2017.

2. K. Karasawa, M. Oda, T. Kitasaka, K. Misawa, M. Fujiwara, C. Chu, G. Zheng, D. Rueckert, and K. Mori. Multi-atlas pancreas segmentation: Atlas selection based on vessel structure. *Medical image analysis*, 39:18, 2017.

3. S. Jain, S. Gupta, and A. Gulati. An adaptive hybrid technique for pancreas segmentation using ct image sequences. In *International Conference on Signal Processing*, 2016.

4. D. Zhang, J. Zhang, Q. Zhang, J. Han, and J. Han. Automatic pancreas segmentation based on lightweight dcnn modules and spatial prior propagation. *Pattern Recognition*, 114(6):107762, 2020.

5. O. Oktay, J. Schlemper, L. L. Folgoc, M. Lee, M. Heinrich, K. Misawa, K. Mori, S. Mcdonagh, N. Y. Hammerla, and B. Kainz. Attention u-net: Learning where to look for the pancreas. 2018.

6. Meiyu Li, Fenghui Lian, and Shuxu Guo. An adversarial network embedded with attention mechanism for pancreas segmentation. In *2021 International Conference on Electronic Information Engineering and Computer Science (EIECS)*, pages 631–634. IEEE, 2021.

7. J. Long, E. Shelhamer, and T. Darrell. Fully convolutional networks for semantic segmentation. *IEEE Transactions on Pattern Analysis and Machine Intelligence*, 39(4):640–651, 2015.

8. O. Ronneberger, P. Fischer, and T. Brox. U-net: Convolutional networks for biomedical image segmentation. *Springer International Publishing*, 2015.

9. W. Jin, H. Yu, and H. Yu. Cvt-assd: Convolutional vision-transformer based attentive single shot multibox detector. 2021.

10. J. Park, S. Woo, J. Y. Lee, and I. S. Kweon. Bam: Bottleneck attention module. 2018.

11. X. Qin, Z. Zhang, C. Huang, M. Dehghan, and M. Jagersand. U2-net: Going deeper with nested u-structure for salient object detection. *Pattern Recognition*, 106:107404, 2020.

12. H. R. Roth, L. Lu, A. Farag, H. C. Shin, J. Liu, E. Turkbey, and R. M. Summers. Deeporgan: Multi-level deep convolutional networks for automated pancreas segmentation. *Springer, Cham*, 2015.

112

Rule extraction based on fuzzy linguistic concept knowledge

Qing Guo[1,*], Yifan Lu[2,‡], Kuo Pang[3,||], Xiaosong Cui[2,§] and Li Zou[1,†]

[1]School of Computer Science and Technology, Shandong Jianzhu University
Jinan, 250102, China
*guoqing654321@126.com
†zoulicn@163.com

[2]School of Computer and Information Technology, Liaoning Normal University
Dalian, 116081, China
‡lyfffan@163.com
§cuixiaosong2004@163.com

[3]Information Science and Technology College, Dalian Maritime University
Dalian, 116026, China
||pangkuo_p@dlmu.edu.cn

As an effective tool for analyzing human behavior and decision cognition, rule extraction is one of the important steps of knowledge discovery. In order to make decision with high confidence level and improve the rate of information acquisition in an uncertainty environment, this paper establishes a rule extraction algorithm of fuzzy linguistic concept knowledge under the fuzzy linguistic concept decision formal context. Introduce the weak consistence relationship in the decision context first. And then define the finer relationship between the conditional concept lattice and the decision concept lattice to obtain the consistent relationship between the fuzzy linguistic concept knowledge. Further, mine the implicit rules and their confidence degrees in the decision-making environment. Finally, taking the financial decision-making as an example to illustrate the effectiveness and practicability.

Keywords: Formal concept analysis; linguistic term set; rule extraction.

1. Introduction

Formal Concept Analysis (FCA) is an order theory method for concept analysis and visualization proposed by Wille [1] in the 1980s. FCA can give comprehensive information and knowledge of data. In the classical context, data is the triple composed of a set of objects, a set of attributes and the clear relationship between objects and attributes. However, due to the complexity and uncertainty of human thinking and cognition, it has triggered a lot of research [2-3] on FCA in fuzzy environment.

---

§Corresponding author.

In order to process and characterize the role of linguistic information in concept cognition, some studies [4] have conducted in-depth discussions on the application of linguistic variables in formal concept analysis. Pei et al. [5] provided a new symbolic translation based on fuzzy sets to obtain formal binary linguistic concepts. Zou et al. [6-7] introduced the linguistic concept context and studied the multi granularity linguistic reduction algorithm and reasoning algorithm in incomplete environment, which can improve the accuracy of reasoning results and reduce the loss of information.

Rule extraction [8-9] can extract valuable knowledge from massive information, and it is also an important research direction of FCA. Decision implication is a basic knowledge representation of formal concept analysis in the context of decision-making. Therefore, we represent a rule extraction algorithm of fuzzy linguistic concept knowledge to reduce the loss of information caused by linguistic-valued decisions.

The rest of this paper is organized as follows. Section 2 briefly reviews of linguistic concept and linguistic concept knowledge. Section 3 proposes a rule extraction algorithm based on the fuzzy linguistic concept knowledge. In Section 4, the feasibility and rationality of the algorithm are further verified through the example of financial decision-making. The conclusions and the future works are given in Section 5.

2. Preliminaries

Definition 2.1. [10] Let the linguistic term set $S = \left\{ s_{-\tau}, \ldots, s_{-1}, s_0, s_1, \ldots, s_\tau \right\}$ be a finite ordered set consisting of an odd number of linguistic items, where τ is a positive integer. S satisfies the following conditions:

(1) Reversibility: $Neg(s_{-k}) = s_k$, in particular, $Neg(s_0) = s_0$;

(2) Order: $s_m \le s_n \Leftrightarrow m \le n$;

(3) Boundedness: s_τ and $s_{-\tau}$ are the upper and lower bounds of linguistic items.

Definition 2.2. [6] Let $S = \left\{ s_{-\tau}, \ldots, s_{-1}, s_0, s_1, \ldots, s_\tau \right\}$ be a linguistic term set, $L = \left\{ l^1, l^2, \ldots, l^n \right\}$ be an attribute set, then $l^i_{s_\alpha} \left(1 \le i \le n \right)$ is called linguistic concept.

Definition 2.3. [6] A linguistic concept formal context is a triple $\left(U, L_{s_\alpha}, I \right)$, where $U = \left\{ x_1, x_2, \ldots, x_n \right\}$ is a non-empty finite object set, $L_{s_\alpha} = \left\{ l^1_{s_{-\tau_1}}, \ldots, l^1_{s_0}, \ldots, l^1_{s_{\tau_1}}, l^2_{s_{-\tau_2}}, \ldots, l^2_{s_0}, \ldots, l^2_{s_{\tau_2}}, l^n_{s_{-\tau_n}}, \ldots, l^n_{s_0}, \ldots, l^n_{s_{\tau_n}} \right\}$ is a non-empty finite linguistic concept set, I is a binary relation in U and L_{s_α}, i.e. $I \subseteq U \times L_{s_\alpha}$.

Definition 2.4. [6] Let $\left(U, L_{s_\alpha}, I\right)$ be a linguistic concept context. For any $X \subseteq U$, $B_{s_\alpha} \subseteq L_{s_\alpha}$, define operator " $'$ " as follows:

$$X' = \left\{ l_{s_\alpha} \in L_{s_\alpha} \mid \forall x \in X, \left(x, l_{s_\alpha}^i\right) \in I \right\}$$

$$B_{s_\alpha}{}' = \left\{ x \in U \mid \forall l_{s_\alpha}^i \in B, \left(x, l_{s_\alpha}^i\right) \in I \right\} \tag{1}$$

If $X' = B_{s_\alpha}$ and $B_{s_\alpha}{}' = X$ are satisfied, then $\left(X, B_{s_\alpha}\right)$ is called a linguistic concept knowledge, where X and B_{s_α} are called the extension and intension of the linguistic concept knowledge $\left(X, B_{s_\alpha}\right)$, respectively.

3. Rule Extraction of Fuzzy Linguistic Concept Knowledge

Definition 3.1. A fuzzy linguistic concept formal context is defined as a triple $\left(U, L_{s_\alpha}, \tilde{I}\right)$, where $U = \{u_1, u_2, \ldots, u_n\}$ is a non-empty finite object set $L_{s_\alpha} = \left\{ l_{s_{-\tau_1}}^1, \ldots, l_{s_0}^1, \ldots, l_{s_{\tau_1}}^1, l_{s_{-\tau_2}}^2, \ldots, l_{s_0}^2, \ldots, l_{s_{\tau_2}}^2, l_{s_{-\tau_n}}^n, \ldots, l_{s_0}^n, \ldots, l_{s_{\tau_n}}^n \right\}$ is a non-empty finite linguistic concept set, $\tilde{I}$ is fuzzy relation between U and L_{s_α}, representing the confidence level of objects and linguistic concepts.

For $\forall u \in U$, $\forall l_{s_\alpha}^i \in L_{s_\alpha}$, there exists confidence level $\tilde{I}\left(u, l_{s_\alpha}^i\right) \in [0,1]$. $\left(u, l_{s_\alpha}^i\right) \rightarrow \tilde{I}$ represents that the object u can be described by linguistic concept $l_{s_\alpha}^i$ with a confidence level $\tilde{I}\left(u, l_{s_\alpha}^i\right)$.

Denote $\left(U, L_{s_\alpha}, \tilde{I}_\gamma\right)$ represent the fuzzy linguistic concept formal context under confidence level γ. That is, a threshold of confidence level γ is assigned to the fuzzy linguistic concept formal context $\left(U, L_{s_\alpha}, \tilde{I}\right)$, i.e. $\tilde{I}_\gamma\left(u, l_{s_\alpha}^i\right) \geq \gamma$.

Note: For each linguistic concept in L_{s_α}, the number of linguistic items $\tau_1, \tau_2, \ldots, \tau_n$ can be taken as different values. That is, different attributes can be described with different number of linguistic items.

Definition 3.2. Let $\left(U, L_{s_\alpha}, \tilde{I}_\gamma\right)$ be a fuzzy linguistic concept formal context, and γ be the threshold of confidence level. For $X \in \mathcal{P}(U)$, $B \in \mathcal{P}(L_{s_\alpha})$, $\tilde{B} \in \mathcal{F}(L_{s_\alpha})$, define operator ∇ as follows:

$$\nabla, \mathcal{P}(U) \to \mathcal{F}(L_{s_\alpha})$$

$$X^\nabla = \sum_{\forall l_{s_\alpha}^i \in L_{s_\alpha}} \frac{\lambda_{l_{s_\alpha}}}{l_{s_\alpha}^i} \tag{2}$$

Define operator Δ as follows:

$$\Delta, \mathcal{F}(L_{s_\alpha}) \to \mathcal{P}(U)$$

$$\tilde{B}^\Delta = \left\{ u \in U \mid \forall l_{s_\alpha}^i \in B, \tilde{I}\left(u, l_{s_\alpha}^i\right) \geq \tilde{B}\left(l_{s_\alpha}^i\right) \right\} \tag{3}$$

where X^∇ represents the set of degree of linguistic concepts shared by all objects in X under threshold of confidence level γ, $\tilde{B}^\Delta$ represents the set of objects that can be described by the linguistic concepts in $\tilde{B}$ simultaneously, $\lambda_{l_{s_\alpha}} = \min_{x \in X} \tilde{I}_\gamma\left(x, l_{s_\alpha}^i\right)$ represents the minimum confidence degree that all objects in X share the linguistic concepts $l_{s_\alpha}^i$ under threshold of confidence level γ, $\tilde{B}\left(l_{s_\alpha}^i\right)$ represents the confidence degree corresponding to the linguistic concept $l_{s_\alpha}^i$ in $\tilde{B}$.

Definition 3.3. Let $\left(U, L_{s_\alpha}, \tilde{I}_\gamma\right)$ be a fuzzy linguistic concept formal context, $X \in \mathcal{P}(U)$, $\tilde{B} \in \mathcal{F}(L_{s_\alpha})$. If there are $X^\nabla = \tilde{B}$, $\tilde{B}^\Delta = X$, then the ordered pair $\left(X, \tilde{B}\right)$ is called a fuzzy linguistic concept knowledge, where X and $\tilde{B}$ are called the extension and intension of fuzzy linguistic concept knowledge, respectively.

Definition 3.4. Let $\left(U, L_{s_\alpha}, \tilde{I}_\gamma\right)$ and $\left(U, K_{s_\alpha}, \tilde{J}_\lambda\right)$ be two fuzzy linguistic concept formal contexts, and their fuzzy linguistic concept knowledge sets are $FLCKL\left(U, L_{s_\alpha}, \tilde{I}_\gamma\right)$ and $FLCKL\left(U, K_{s_\alpha}, \tilde{J}_\lambda\right)$, respectively. If for any $\left(Y, \tilde{D}\right) \in FLCKL\left(U, K_{s_\alpha}, \tilde{J}_\lambda\right)$, there always exists $\left(X, \tilde{B}\right) \in FLCKL\left(U, L_{s_\alpha}, \tilde{I}_\gamma\right)$ to make $X \subseteq Y$ and $X \neq \varnothing$ hold, then $FLCKL\left(U, L_{s_\alpha}, \tilde{I}_\gamma\right)$ is said to be weak finer than $FLCKL\left(U, K_{s_\alpha}, \tilde{J}_\lambda\right)$ which can be recorded as:

$$FLCKL\left(U, L_{s_\alpha}, \tilde{I}_\gamma\right) \leq FLCKL\left(U, K_{s_\alpha}, \tilde{J}_\lambda\right) \tag{4}$$

Definition 3.5. Let $\left(U, L_{s_\alpha}, \tilde{I}_\gamma\right)$ and $\left(U, K_{s_\alpha}, \tilde{J}_\lambda\right)$ be two fuzzy linguistic concept formal contexts which have the same universe of discourse, where L_{s_α} is conditional linguistic concept, K_{s_α} is decision linguistic concept and

$L_{s_\alpha} \cap K_{s_\alpha} = \varnothing$, $\tilde{I}_\gamma$ is the fuzzy binary relation between U and L_{s_α}, $\tilde{J}_\lambda$ is the fuzzy binary relation between U and K_{s_α}, then $\left(U, L_{s_\alpha}, \tilde{I}_\gamma, K_{s_\alpha}, \tilde{J}_\lambda\right)$ is called the fuzzy linguistic concept weak consistent decision context under the confidence level γ and the confidence level λ.

Definition 3.6. Let $\left(U, L_{s_\alpha}, \tilde{I}_\gamma, K_{s_\alpha}, \tilde{J}_\lambda\right)$ be a fuzzy linguistic concept weak consistent decision context, and $FLCKL\left(U, L_{s_\alpha}, \tilde{I}_\gamma\right) \leq FLCKL\left(U, K_{s_\alpha}, \tilde{J}_\lambda\right)$. For $Y \neq \varnothing$ and $Y \neq U$, if there exists $(Y, \tilde{D}) \in FLCKL\left(U, K_{s_\alpha}, \tilde{J}_\lambda\right)$, $\left(X, \tilde{B}\right) \in FLCKL\left(U, L_{s_\alpha}, \tilde{I}_\gamma\right)$, and $X \subseteq Y$, then $\tilde{B} \rightarrow \tilde{D}$ is called a fuzzy linguistic concept decision rules, recorded as:

$$\text{if } \tilde{B}, \text{ then } \tilde{D} \tag{5}$$

In the fuzzy linguistic concept decision rules, when the conditional linguistic concept in the antecedent has different confidence degrees, the decision linguistic concepts with different confidence degrees can be deduced. For the same conditional linguistic concept, different confidence degrees will also lead to different decision results.

For a fuzzy linguistic concept weak consistent decision context $\left(U, L_{s_\alpha}, \tilde{I}_\gamma, K_{s_\alpha}, \tilde{J}_\lambda\right)$, the set of all fuzzy linguistic concept rules obtained is denoted as $\tilde{\mathcal{R}}$.

Definition 3.7. Let $\left(U, L_{s_\alpha}, \tilde{I}_\gamma, K_{s_\alpha}, \tilde{J}_\lambda\right)$ be a fuzzy linguistic concept weak consistent decision context. For any two fuzzy linguistic concept rules $\tilde{B}_1 \rightarrow \tilde{D}_1, \tilde{B}_2 \rightarrow \tilde{D}_2 \in \tilde{\mathcal{R}}$, if one of the following conditions is met,
(1) $\tilde{B}_1 \subseteq \tilde{B}_2$ and $\tilde{D}_1 = \tilde{D}_2$;
(2) $\tilde{B}_1 = \tilde{B}_2$ and $\tilde{D}_2 \subseteq \tilde{D}_1$.
then the fuzzy linguistic concept rule $\tilde{B}_1 \rightarrow \tilde{D}_1$ implies $\tilde{B}_2 \rightarrow \tilde{D}_2$, recorded as $\left(\tilde{B}_1 \rightarrow \tilde{D}_1\right) \rightarrow \left(\tilde{B}_2 \rightarrow \tilde{D}_2\right)$, i.e. fuzzy linguistic concept rule $\tilde{B}_2 \rightarrow \tilde{D}_2$ is redundant in rule set $\tilde{\mathcal{R}}$.

Based on the above definitions and properties, this section proposes a rule extraction algorithm of fuzzy linguistic concept knowledge to obtain the implication relationship between conditional knowledge and decision knowledge, as Algorithm 1 shown below.

Algorithm 1: Rule Extraction Algorithm of Fuzzy Linguistic Concept Knowledge

Input: Fuzzy linguistic concept formal decision context $\left(U, L_{s_\alpha}, \tilde{I}_\gamma, K_{s_\alpha}, \tilde{J}_\lambda\right)$

Output: Rules set $\tilde{\mathcal{R}}$

1: *Begin*

2: $\left(U, L_{s_\alpha}, \tilde{I}_\gamma\right) \Rightarrow FLCKL\left(U, L_{s_\alpha}, \tilde{I}_\gamma\right) \Rightarrow \left(X, \tilde{B}\right)$

3: $\left(U, K_{s_\alpha}, \tilde{J}_\lambda\right) \Rightarrow FLCKL\left(U, K_{s_\alpha}, \tilde{J}_\lambda\right) \Rightarrow \left(Y, \tilde{D}\right)$

4:   *If* $\left(FLCKL\left(U, L_{s_\alpha}, \tilde{I}_\gamma\right) \le FLCKL\left(U, K_{s_\alpha}, \tilde{J}_\lambda\right)\right)\{$

5:     *For* $\left(\left(X, \tilde{B}\right), \left(Y, \tilde{D}\right); X \subseteq Y\right)\{$

6:       Get rules $\tilde{B} \to \tilde{D}$;

7:       Add $\tilde{B} \to \tilde{D}$ to $\tilde{\mathcal{R}}^*$;

8:     $\}$ *End For*

9:     Get rules set $\tilde{\mathcal{R}}^*$;

10:     $\forall \tilde{B}_1 \to \tilde{D}_1, \tilde{B}_2 \to \tilde{D}_2 \in \tilde{\mathcal{R}}^*$;

11:     *If* $\left(\left(\tilde{B}_1 \subseteq \tilde{B}_2 \, \&\& \, \tilde{D}_1 = \tilde{D}_2\right) \| \left(\tilde{B}_1 = \tilde{B}_2 \, \&\& \, \tilde{D}_2 \subseteq \tilde{D}_1\right)\right)\{$

12:       Delete redundancy rules $\tilde{B}_2 \to \tilde{D}_2$ from $\tilde{\mathcal{R}}^*$;

13:     $\}$ *End If*

14:     Get all rules set $\tilde{\mathcal{R}}$;

15:   $\}$ *End If*

16: *End*

---

4. An Example of Financial Decision-making

Taking the financial decision-making as an example, assuming that five users' feature choices are collected, the collected information can be converted into a fuzzy linguistic concept formal decision context $\left(U, L_{s_\alpha}, \tilde{I}_\gamma, K_{s_\alpha}, \tilde{J}_\lambda\right)$, as shown in Table 1. Object set $U = \{u_1, u_2, u_3, u_4\}$ corresponds to five users respectively. Conditional linguistic concept set $L_{s_\alpha} = \{a_{s_{-1}}, a_{s_0}, a_{s_1}, b_{s_{-1}}, b_{s_0}, b_{s_1}, c_{s_{-1}}, c_{s_0}, c_{s_1}\}$ corresponds to three characteristics of users, of which a is age, b is net asset

Table 1. Fuzzy linguistic concept formal decision context $\left(U, L_{s_\alpha}, \tilde{I}_\gamma, K_{s_\alpha}, \tilde{J}_\lambda\right)$.

	$a_{s_{-1}}$	a_{s_0}	a_{s_1}	$b_{s_{-1}}$	b_{s_0}	b_{s_1}	$c_{s_{-1}}$	c_{s_0}	c_{s_1}	$e_{s_{-1}}$	e_{s_0}	e_{s_1}
u_1	0.8	0.2	0	0.7	0.3	0	0	0.3	0.7	0	0.4	0.6
u_2	0	0.7	0.3	0.4	0.6	0	0	0.6	0.4	0	0.7	0.3
u_3	0	0.3	0.7	0	0.4	0.6	0.6	0.4	0	0.8	0.2	0
u_4	0.6	0.4	0	0.4	0.6	0	0	0.2	0.8	0	0.3	0.7
u_5	0.4	0.6	0	0.8	0.2	0	0.7	0.3	0	0.9	0.1	0

and c is income ability. Decision linguistic concept set $K_{s_\alpha} = \{e_{s_{-1}}, e_{s_0}, e_{s_1}\}$ corresponds to the risk tolerance. $S = \{s_{-1}, s_0, s_1\}$ corresponds to the linguistic item corresponding to each attribute.

In this example, the trust level threshold is selected as $\gamma = 0.5$. Through the implication mining of the fuzzy linguistic concept knowledge in the conditional part and the decision part, the rules set $\tilde{\mathcal{R}}$ can be obtained as follows:

$$\tilde{\mathcal{R}} = \left\{ \frac{0.6}{a_{s_0}} + \frac{0.8}{b_{s_{-1}}} + \frac{0.7}{c_{s_{-1}}} \rightarrow \frac{0.9}{e_{s_{-1}}}, \frac{0.7}{a_{s_0}} + \frac{0.6}{b_{s_0}} + \frac{0.6}{c_{s_0}} \rightarrow \frac{0.7}{e_{s_0}}, \frac{0.6}{a_{s_{-1}}} + \frac{0.7}{b_{s_0}} + \frac{0.8}{c_{s_1}} \rightarrow \frac{0.8}{e_{s_1}}, \right.$$

$$\left. \frac{0.6}{a_{s_{-1}}} + \frac{0.7}{c_{s_1}} \rightarrow \frac{0.6}{e_{s_1}}, \frac{0.6}{c_{s_{-1}}} \rightarrow \frac{0.8}{e_{s_{-1}}} \right\}$$

Through the acquired rule set $\tilde{\mathcal{R}}$, the hidden information can be mined. When a user's earning ability is low and the confidence level is 0.6, the degree of risk he can take is low and the confidence level is 0.8.

This paper shows an example with partial data, and the proposed method of rule extraction is still applicable when extending to larger data sets.

5. Conclusion

Due to the complexity of human thinking, decision-making problems are often in an uncertain environment. The rule extraction method based on fuzzy linguistic concept weak consistent decision context proposed in this paper can effectively obtain non-redundant rule sets with different confidence levels. By analyzing the implied relationship between conditional knowledge and decision knowledge in the decision-making context with uncertainty linguistic information, the hidden characteristics in the data information are mined to reduce the loss of information.

In the future, the rule set obtained in the context of fuzzy linguistic concept decision-making will be applied to the fields of uncertain linguistic knowledge reasoning, recommendation system, statistical analysis etc., and the superiority of the proposed algorithm will be verified through more applications.

Acknowledgments

This work is partially supported by the National Natural Science Foundation of P.R. China (No. 62176142), Foundation of Liaoning Educational Committee (No. LJ2020007) and Special Foundation for Distinguished Professors of Shandong Jianzhu University.

References

1. Wille R. Restructuring Lattice Theory: An Approach Based on Hierarchies of Concepts[J]. Orderd Sets D Reidel, 1982, 83: 314-339.

2. Benítez-Caballero M J, Medina J, Ramírez-Poussa E, et al. Rough-set-driven approach for attribute reduction in fuzzy formal concept analysis[J]. Fuzzy Sets and Systems, 2020, 391: 117-138.

3. Xin X W, Song J H, Xue Z A, et al. Intuitionistic fuzzy three-way formal concept analysis based attribute correlation degree[J]. Journal of Intelligent & Fuzzy Systems, 2021, 40(1): 1567-1583.

4. Zhang X, Sun B, Chen X, et al. An approach to evaluating sustainable supply chain risk management based on BWM and linguistic value soft set theory[J]. Journal of Intelligent & Fuzzy Systems, 2020, 39(3): 4369-4382.

5. Yan L, Pei Z, Ren F. Constructing and managing multi-granular linguistic values based on linguistic terms and their fuzzy sets[J]. IEEE Access, 2019, 7: 152928-152943.

6. Zou L, Pang K, Song X, et al. A knowledge reduction approach for linguistic concept formal context[J]. Information Sciences, 2020, 524: 165-183.

7. Cui H, Yue G, Zou L, et al. Multiple multidimensional linguistic reasoning algorithm based on property-oriented linguistic concept lattice[J]. International Journal of Approximate Reasoning, 2021, 131: 80-92.

8. Hu Z, Shao M, Liu H, et al. Cognitive Computing and Rule Extraction in Generalized One-sided Formal Contexts[J]. Cognitive Computation, 2021: 1-21.

9. Zhang S, Li D, Zhai Y. Incremental method of generating decision implication canonical basis[J]. Soft Computing, 2022, 26(3): 1067-1083

10. Xu Z. On Generalized Induced Linguistic Aggregation Operators[J]. International Journal of General Systems, 2006, 35(1): 17-28.

Linguistic truth-valued fuzzy negation operator based on lattice implication algebra[*]

Pengsen Liu[1,†], Xinran Yang[2,§], Tie Hou[3,||], Qingkun Liu[2,‡] and Dongqiang Yang[3,¶]

[1]*School of Computer Science, Sichuan University, Chengdu, 610065, China*
†*Liupengsencn@163.com*
[2] *School of Computer and Information Technology, Liaoning Normal University*
Dalian, 116081, China
‡*qing_kun@163.com,* §*yangxinrancn@163.com*
[3] *School of Computer Science and Technology, Shandong Jianzhu University*
Jinan, 250102, China
||*houtie2017@sdjzu.edu.cn,* ¶*ydq@sdjzu.edu.cn*

With the rapid development of artificial intelligence and big data, people's lives are becoming more and more intelligent, thus the utter importance of uncertainty is further recognized and various solutions are proposed successively. Linguistic value is a key tool to obtain information in cognition, decision-making and execution, which can reduce the loss of information in the process of expression. In order to better express the connotation of information, this paper introduces three kinds of linguistic truth-valued fuzzy negation operators and proposes the operation method based on linguistic truth-value logic systems. It can intensify people's understanding of the negative connotation of relationship, so as to better acquire knowledge.

Keywords: Linguistic truth-valued logic system; linguistic truth-valued fuzzy negation operator; lattice implication algebra.

1. Introduction

Artificial intelligence is essentially the simulation and extension of human intelligence. It has a wide range of application in many fields, such as natural language processing, automatic reasoning and so on. In the research of knowledge representation and reasoning, the negative relationship is usually based on classical logic. Wagner [1] puts forward "strong negation" and "weak negation", which are used in computer information processing systems to express the explicit rejection of processed information and the authenticity of linguistic information. Kaneiwa [2] proposes an extensible description logic with classical negation and

---

[*]This work is supported by the National Natural Science Foundation of P.R. China (No. 62176142), Foundation of Liaoning Educational Committee (No. LJ2020007) and Special Foundation for Distinguished Professors of Shandong Jianzhu University.

strong negation. In order to distinguish between denotative negation and connotative negation within the framework of logical concept analysis, Ferré [3] proposes a logic transformation method based on modal logic to expand knowledge. As an attempt to identify different negative relations in knowledge representation, Pan et al. [4-6] propose five kinds of contradictory and opposite negative relations at the conceptual level, and apply them to knowledge representation and reasoning. Wu et al. [7] extend the implication operator of the fuzzy reasoning method CRI, and propose the GFscom closeness with three negations in view of the subjectivity and randomness in the CRI method. Yang et al. [8] propose a multi-attribute decision-making method based on the fuzzy set FScom to optimize the ranking problem of geological disaster risk degree. However, in real-life scenarios, people tend to use linguistic values more often than numerical values. It is imperative to effectively handle linguistic-valued information with negative relations to realistically mimic the different manners of human cogitation. Therefore, this paper aims to provide a novel way to express uncertain linguistic information in terms of linguistic truth-valued fuzzy negation operators.

The remainder of this paper is organized as follows. Section 2 briefly reviews the relevant definitions of lattice implication algebra and linguistic truth-valued propositional logic system. Section 3 proposes the linguistic truth-valued fuzzy negation operator and its average aggregation operator. The conclusion and outline directions for future research are described in Section 4.

2. Preliminary

Definition 2.1. [9] Let $(L, \vee, \wedge, O, I)$ be a bounded lattice with universal boundaries O (the least element) and I (the greatest element) respectively, and "$'$" be an order-reversing involution. For any $x, y, z \in L$, if mapping $\rightarrow: L \times L \rightarrow L$ satisfies:

(1) $x \rightarrow (y \rightarrow z) = y \rightarrow (x \rightarrow z)$;

(2) $x \rightarrow x = I$;

(3) $x \rightarrow y = y' \rightarrow x'$;

(4) $x \rightarrow y = y \rightarrow x = I$ implies $x = y$;

(5) $(x \rightarrow y) \rightarrow y = (y \rightarrow x) \rightarrow x$;

(6) $(x \vee y) \rightarrow z = (x \rightarrow z) \vee (y \rightarrow z)$;

(7) $(x \wedge y) \rightarrow z = (x \rightarrow z) \wedge (y \rightarrow z)$.

Then $(L, \vee, \wedge, ', \rightarrow, O, I)$ is a lattice implication algebra (*LIA* for short).

Definition 2.2. [10] The linguistic truth-valued propositional logic system on $L_{v(2 \times n)}$ consists of the following symbols:

(1) Propositional argument set: $P, Q, R, \dots$;

(2) Constant set: $L_{v(2 \times n)}$;

(3) Logical connectives: $\rightarrow, '$;

(4) Brackets: (,).

3. Linguistic Truth-valued Fuzzy Negation Operator and its Average Aggregation Operation

In the linguistic truth-valued propositional logic system, we introduce fuzzy linguistic concept into the representation of propositions, and formalize the fuzzy linguistic propositional set. Three kinds of linguistic truth-valued fuzzy negation operators and their aggregation operation are also proposed.

Definition 3.1. Let $S = \{s_m \mid m = 1, 2, \dots, \tau\}$ be an odd linguistic term set, where $s_1 < s_2 < \cdots < s_\tau$. For $(h_i, c_n) \in L_{v(2 \times n)}$, we call $P^{(s_m, (h_i, c_n))}$ a fuzzy linguistic proposition.

Definition 3.2. Let U be a fuzzy linguistic propositional set. For $P^{(s_m, (h_i, c_n))} \in U$, the value of $P^{(s_m, (h_i, c_n))}$ can be provided by the assignment function V as follows:

$$V(P^{(s_m, (h_i, c_n))}) = (s_m, (h_i, c_n)) \tag{1}$$

where $(s_m, (h_i, c_n))$ is the fuzzy linguistic value of $P^{(s_m, (h_i, c_n))}$. The function $V : U \rightarrow (S, L_{v(n \times 2)})$ gives the fuzzy linguistic truth values of all propositions on the set U.

Definition 3.3. Let U be a fuzzy linguistic propositional set. For $P^{(s_m, (h_i, c_n))} \in U$, the value of $P^{(s_m, (h_i, c_n))}$ can be provided by the credibility assignment function T as follows:

$$T(P^{(s_m, (h_i, c_n))}) = (h_j, c_t) \tag{2}$$

where (h_j, c_t) is the credibility value of $P^{(s_m, (h_i, c_n))}$.

Definition 3.4. For $P^{(s_m, (h_i, c_n))} \in U$, $T(P^{(s_m, (h_i, c_n))}) = (h_j, c_t)$, the comprehensive linguistic value assignment function V is defined in two cases as follows:

case 1: $c_t = c_n$

(1) When $c_n = c_t = c_1$, $V(P^{(s_m, (h_i, c_n))}) = (s_m, (h_i \wedge h_j, c_1))$.

(2) When $c_n = c_t = c_2$,

if $h_i \le h_j$, $V(P^{(s_m,(h_i,c_n))}) = (s_m,(h_i \wedge h_j,c_1))$,

if $h_i > h_j$, $V(P^{(s_m,(h_i,c_n))}) = (s_m,(h_i \wedge h_j,c_2))$.

case 2: $c_n \ne c_t$

(1) When $c_n = c_2, c_t = c_1$,

if $h_i > h_j$, $V(P^{(s_m,(h_i,c_n))}) = (s_m,(h_{\left[\frac{i+j}{2}\right]},c_2))$,

if $h_i \le h_j$, $V(P^{(s_m,(h_i,c_n))}) = (s_m,(h_{\left[\frac{i+j}{2}\right]},c_1))$.

(2) When $h_i > h_j, c_n = c_1, c_t = c_2$,

if $h_i > h_j$, $V(P^{(s_m,(h_i,c_n))}) = (s_m,(h_{\left[\frac{i+j}{2}\right]},c_1))$,

if $h_i \le h_j$, $V(P^{(s_m,(h_i,c_n))}) = (s_m,(h_{\left[\frac{i+j}{2}\right]},c_2))$.

Definition 3.5. If $\neg_O : (S, L_{v(2\times n)}) \to (S, L_{v(2\times n)})$ satisfies:

$$\neg_O(s_m,(h_i,c_n)) = (s_{\tau-m},(h_i,c_n)) \cup (s_m,(h_i,c_n')) \qquad (3)$$

we call $\neg_O$ the linguistic truth-valued fuzzy opposite negative operator.

Proposition 3.1. For any fuzzy linguistic truth value $(s_m,(h_i,c_n))$, $(s_m,(h_j,c_t))$, $(s_k,(h_i,c_n)) \in L_{v(2\times n)}$, the following holds:

(1) For $(s_m,(h_i,c_n)),(s_m,(h_j,c_t)) \in (S, L_{v(2\times n)})$, if $(h_i,c_n) < (h_j,c_t)$, then $\neg_O(s_m,(h_i,c_n)) > \neg_O(s_m,(h_j,c_t))$;

(2) For $(s_m,(h_i,c_n)),(s_k,(h_i,c_n)) \in (S, L_{v(2\times n)})$, if $s_k < s_m$, then $\neg_O(s_m,(h_i,c_n)) > \neg_O(s_k,(h_i,c_n))$;

(3) $\neg_O\neg_O(s_m,(h_i,c_n)) = (s_m,(h_i,c_n))$.

Definition 3.6. For $P^{(s_m,(h_i,c_n))} \in U$, $T(P^{(s_m,(h_i,c_n))}) = (h_j,c_t)$, the opposite negative assignment function V is defined in two cases as follows:

case 1: $c_t = c_n$

(1) When $c_n = c_t = c_1$, $V(\neg_O P^{(s_m,(h_i,c_n))}) = \neg_O(s_m,(h_i \wedge h_j,c_1))$.

(2) When $c_n = c_t = c_2$,

if $h_i \le h_j$, $V(\neg_O P^{(s_m,(h_i,c_n))}) = \neg_O(s_m,(h_i \wedge h_j,c_1))$;

if $h_i > h_j$, $V(\neg_O P^{(s_m,(h_i,c_n))}) = \neg_O(s_m,(h_i \wedge h_j,c_2))$.

case 2: $c_n \ne c_t$

(1) When $c_n = c_2, c_t = c_1$,

if $h_i > h_j$, $V(\neg_O P^{(s_m,(h_i,c_n))}) = \neg_O(s_m,(h_{\left[\frac{i+j}{2}\right]},c_2))$, if $h_i \leq h_j$, $V(\neg_O P^{(s_m,(h_i,c_n))}) = \neg_O(s_m,(h_{\left[\frac{i+j}{2}\right]},c_1))$.

(2) When $h_i > h_j, c_n = c_1, c_t = c_2$,

if $h_i > h_j$, $V(\neg_O P^{(s_m,(h_i,c_n))}) = \neg_O(s_m,(h_{\left[\frac{i+j}{2}\right]},c_1))$,

if $h_i \leq h_j$, $V(\neg_O P^{(s_m,(h_i,c_n))}) = \neg_O(s_m,(h_{\left[\frac{i+j}{2}\right]},c_2))$.

We call $\neg_O P^{(s_m,(h_i,c_n))}$ the fuzzy linguistic opposite negative truth-valued set of $P^{(s_m,(h_i,c_n))}$.

Definition 3.7. If $\neg_M : (S, L_{v(2 \times n)}) \to (S, L_{v(2 \times n)})$ satisfies:

$$\neg_M (s_m,(h_i,c_n)) = (\mathsf{C}_{L_{v(2 \times n)}} (s_m,(h_i,c_n)) \cap \mathsf{C}_{L_{v(2 \times n)}} (s_m,(h_i,c_n')))$$

$$\cup (\mathsf{C}_S (s_m,(h_i,c_n)) \cap \mathsf{C}_S (s_{\tau-m},(h_i,c_n))) \tag{4}$$

we call $\neg_M$ the linguistic truth-valued fuzzy medium negative operator.

Definition 3.8. For $P^{(s_m,(h_i,c_n))} \in U$, $T(P^{(s_m,(h_i,c_n))}) = (h_j,c_t)$, the medium negative assignment function V is defined in two cases as follows:

case 1: $c_t = c_n$

(1) When $c_n = c_t = c_1$, $V(\neg_M P^{(s_m,(h_i,c_n))}) = \neg_M (s_m,(h_i \wedge h_j,c_1))$.

(2) When $c_n = c_t = c_2$,

if $h_i \leq h_j$, $V(\neg_M P^{(s_m,(h_i,c_n))}) = \neg_M (s_m,(h_i \wedge h_j,c_1))$,

if $h_i > h_j$, $V(\neg_M P^{(s_m,(h_i,c_n))}) = \neg_M (s_m,(h_i \wedge h_j,c_2))$.

case 2: $c_n \neq c_t$

(1) When $c_n = c_2, c_t = c_1$,

if $h_i > h_j$, $V(\neg_M P^{(s_m,(h_i,c_n))}) = \neg_M (s_m,(h_{\left[\frac{i+j}{2}\right]},c_2))$,

if $h_i \leq h_j$, $V(\neg_M P^{(s_m,(h_i,c_n))}) = \neg_M (s_m,(h_{\left[\frac{i+j}{2}\right]},c_1))$.

(2) When $h_i > h_j, c_n = c_1, c_t = c_2$,

if $h_i > h_j$, $V(\neg_M P^{(s_m,(h_i,c_n))}) = \neg_M (s_m,(h_{\left[\frac{i+j}{2}\right]},c_1))$,

if $h_i \leq h_j$, $V(\neg_M P^{(s_m,(h_i,c_n))}) = \neg_M (s_m,(h_{\left[\frac{i+j}{2}\right]},c_2))$.

We call $\neg_M P^{(s_m,(h_i,c_n))}$ the fuzzy linguistic medium negative truth-valued set of $P^{(s_m,(h_i,c_n))}$.

Proposition 3.2. For any fuzzy linguistic truth value $(s_m,(h_i,c_n))$, $(s_m,(h_j,c_t))$ $\in (S,L_{v(2\times n)})$, if $(s_m,(h_i,c_n)) < (s_m,(h_j,c_t))$, then $\neg_M(s_m,(h_i,c_n)) \gtrsim \neg_M(s_m,(h_j,c_t))$.

Theorem 3.1. Let $\neg_M P^{(s_m,(h_i,c_n))}$, $\neg_O P^{(s_m,(h_i,c_n))}$ be two generalized fuzzy linguistic propositional logic formulas, then

(1) $\neg_O(\neg_M P^{(s_m,(h_i,c_n))}) = \neg_M(\neg_O P^{(s_m,(h_i,c_n))})$,

(2) $\neg_M P^{(s_m,(h_i,c_n))} = \neg_M(\neg_O P^{(s_m,(h_i,c_n))})$.

Definition 3.9. If $\neg_C : (S,L_{v(2\times n)}) \to (S,L_{v(2\times n)})$ satisfies:

$$\neg_C(s_m,(h_i,c_n)) = C_{L_{v(2\times n)}}(s_m,(h_i,c_n)) \cup C_S(s_m,(h_i,c_n)) \tag{5}$$

we call $\neg_C$ the linguistic truth-valued fuzzy opposite negative operator.

Definition 3.10. For $P^{(s_m,(h_i,c_n))} \in U$, $T(P^{(s_m,(h_i,c_n))}) = (h_j,c_t)$, the medium negative assignment function V is defined in two cases as follows:

case 1: $c_t = c_n$

(1) When $c_n = c_t = c_1$, $V(\neg_C P^{(s_m,(h_i,c_n))}) = \neg_C(s_m,(h_i \wedge h_j,c_1))$.

(2) When $c_n = c_t = c_2$,

if $h_i \le h_j$, $V(\neg_C P^{(s_m,(h_i,c_n))}) = \neg_C(s_m,(h_i \wedge h_j,c_1))$,

if $h_i > h_j$, $V(\neg_C P^{(s_m,(h_i,c_n))}) = \neg_C(s_m,(h_i \wedge h_j,c_2))$.

case 2: $c_n \ne c_t$

(1) When $c_n = c_2, c_t = c_1$,

if $h_i > h_j$, $V(\neg_C P^{(s_m,(h_i,c_n))}) = \neg_C(s_m,(h_{[\frac{i+j}{2}]},c_2))$,

if $h_i \le h_j$, $V(\neg_C P^{(s_m,(h_i,c_n))}) = \neg_C(s_m,(h_{[\frac{i+j}{2}]},c_1))$.

(2) When $h_i > h_j, c_n = c_1, c_t = c_2$,

if $h_i > h_j$, $V(\neg_C P^{(s_m,(h_i,c_n))}) = \neg_C(s_m,(h_{[\frac{i+j}{2}]},c_1))$,

if $h_i \le h_j$, $V(\neg_C P^{(s_m,(h_i,c_n))}) = \neg_C(s_m,(h_{[\frac{i+j}{2}]},c_2))$.

We call $\neg_C P^{(s_m,(h_i,c_n))}$ the fuzzy linguistic contradictory negative truth-valued set of $P^{(s_m,(h_i,c_n))}$.

Proposition 3.3. For $(s_m,(h_i,c_n)),(s_m,(h_j,c_t)) \in (S, L_{v(2 \times n)})$, if $(s_m,(h_i,c_n)) <$ $(s_m,(h_j,c_t))$, then $\neg_C(s_m,(h_i,c_n)) \not\geq \neg_C(s_m,(h_j,c_t))$.

Theorem 3.2. Let $\neg_O P^{(s_m,(h_i,c_n))}$, $\neg_M P^{(s_m,(h_i,c_n))}$, $\neg_C P^{(s_m,(h_i,c_n))}$ be three fuzzy negation operators, then:

(1) $\neg_M(\neg_C P^{(s_m,(h_i,c_n))}) = \neg_C(\neg_M P^{(s_m,(h_i,c_n))})$,

(2) $\neg_C(\neg_O P^{(s_m,(h_i,c_n))}) = \neg_O(\neg_C P^{(s_m,(h_i,c_n))})$,

(3) $\neg_C(\neg_C P^{(s_m,(h_i,c_n))}) = P^{(s_m,(h_i,c_n))}$.

Definition 3.11. For $P^{(s_m,(h_i,c_n))} \in U$, $T(P^{(s_m,(h_i,c_n))}) = (h_j,c_t)$, three fuzzy negation operators are $\neg_O P^{(s_m,(h_i,c_n))}$, $\neg_M P^{(s_m,(h_i,c_n))}$, $\neg_C P^{(s_m,(h_i,c_n))}$, the generalized fuzzy linguistic proposition negation average aggregation operator (GFLPNA) is defined as:

$$GFLPNA(\neg_O P^{(s_m,(h_i,c_n))}, \neg_M P^{(s_m,(h_i,c_n))}, \neg_C P^{(s_m,(h_i,c_n))})$$
$$= \frac{1}{3}(\frac{\sum \neg_C(s_m,(h_i,c_n))}{|\neg_C(s_m,(h_i,c_n))|} + \frac{\sum \neg_M(s_m,(h_i,c_n))}{|\neg_M(s_m,(h_i,c_n))|} + \frac{\sum \neg_O(s_m,(h_i,c_n))}{|\neg_O(s_m,(h_i,c_n))|}) \tag{6}$$

where $\sum(s_m,(h_i,c_n))$ is the sum of linguistic values s_m and linguistic truth values (h_i,c_n), respectively. $|(s_m,(h_i,c_n))|$ represents the number of fuzzy linguistic truth value $(s_m,(h_i,c_n))$.

Example 3.1. We take 6-element lattice implication algebra as an example. Let $S = \{s_1 = $ "*very low*", $s_2 = $ "*general*", $s_3 = $ "*very high*"$\}$ be the linguistic term set. The linguistic truth-valued set is $L_{v(2 \times 3)}$. For the same paper, different experts will have different review results and credibility performance. If Expert 1 considers the overall evaluation of Paper 1 to be very high, and he/she has very high reviewer's confidence, then Expert 1's review result of Paper 1 is very true. So the fuzzy linguistic proposition can be formally expressed as $P^{(s_3,(h_3,t))}$.

If the credibility value of Expert 1 is "very true", then the comprehensive evaluation result is $(s_3,(h_3 \wedge h_3,t)) = (s_3,(h_3,t))$. It is interpreted as the overall evaluation of Paper 1 is very high and very true. Then the opposite negative linguistic truth value is $V(\neg_O P^{(s_3,(h_3,t))}) = (s_3,(h_3,f))$, which indicates the overall evaluation of a paper is very high and very false. The contradictory negative linguistic truth value is $V(\neg_C P^{(s_3,(h_3,t))}) = \complement_{L_{v(3 \times 2)}}(s_3,(h_3,t)) \cup \complement_S(s_3,(h_3,t))$, which indicates the overall evaluation of a paper is not very high or not very true. The medium negative linguistic truth value is $V(\neg_M P^{(s_3,(h_3,t))}) = (\mathsf{C}_{L_{v(3\times2)}}(s_3,(h_3,t))$

$\cap \mathsf{C}_{L_{v(3\times2)}}(s_3,(h_3,f))) \cup (\mathsf{C}_S(s_3,(h_3,t)) \cap \mathsf{C}_S(s_3,(h_3,f)))$, which indicates the overall evaluation of a paper is general and very true or the overall evaluation of a paper is very high and generally true.

4. Conclusion

The complexity of human thinking gives rise to a series of challenges related to uncertainty due to information deficiency. When reasoning about linguistic values, if we only pay attention to consistency, it will lead to the incompleteness of reasoning results. In addition, we should also consider the negative relationship to improve the accuracy of reasoning. This paper have introduced three kinds of fuzzy negation operators in linguistic truth-valued propositional logic systems, and proposed a negative average aggregation operation method, which can better express the negative relationship.

As future work we intend to investigate the approximate reasoning method based on linguistic truth-valued fuzzy negation operator, and apply it to recommendation systems, statistical analysis and other fields. Furthermore, the superiority of reasoning algorithm will be verified through more applications.

References

1. G. A. Wagner, A database needs two kinds of negation, in Proc. of the 3rd Symposium on Mathematical Fundamentals of Database and Knowledge Base System, (Rostock, Germany, 1991).
2. K. Kaneiwa, Negations in description logic-contraries, contradictories, and subcontraries, in *Proc. of 13th International Conference on Conceptual Structures*, (Kassel Germany 2005).
3. S. Ferré, Negation, opposition, and possibility in logical concept analysis, in Lecture Notes in Computer Science, eds R. Missaoui and J. Schmidt, Vol. 3874 (Springer, 2006), pp.130-145.
4. Z. H. Pan and W. J. Zhu, A new cognition and processing on contradictory know ledge, in *Proc. of the IEEE Int. Conference on Machine Learning and Cybernetics*, (Qingdao, China, 2006).
5. Z. H. Pan and S. L. Zhan, Five kinds of contradictory relations and opposite relations in inconsistent knowledge, in *Proc. of the 4th IEEE Int. Conference on Fuzzy Systems and Knowledge Discovery(FSKD'07)*, (Shanghai, China, 2007).

6. Z. H. Pan, *A logic description on different negation relation in knowledge*, in *Lecture Notes in Computer Science*, eds. D. S. Huang, D. C. Wunsch, D. S. Levine and K. H. Jo, Vol. 5227 (Springer, 2008), pp. 815-823.

7. X. G. Wu, Fuzzy reasoning algorithm with three negations and its application, *Journal of Chongqing University*, 1 (2020). (In Chinese)

8. L. Yang and Z. H. Pan, Multi-attribute decision making method based on fuzzy set FScom with three negations, *Fuzzy Systems and Mathematics* **32**, 174 (2018).

9. Y. Xu, Lattice Implication Algebra, *Journal of Southwest Jiaotong University* **1**, 20 (1993). (In Chinese)

10. L. Zou, J. L. Li, K. J. Xu, and Y. Xu, A Kind of Resolution Method of Linguistic Truth-Valued Propositional Logic Based on LIA, in *Proc. of the Fourth International Conference on Fuzzy Systems and Knowledge Discovery*, (USA, 2007).

TOPSIS decision making method based on linguistic formal context with fuzzy object[*]

Hongliang Zheng[1,†], Chang Qu[1,‡], Meiqiao Sun[1,§] and Li Zou[2,‖]

¹School of Computer and Information Technology, Liaoning Normal University
Dalian, 116081, China
²School of Computer Science and Technology, Shandong Jianzhu University
Jinan, 250102, China
†zheng-hl@263.net
‡quchang123cn@163.com
§5600201@qq.com
‖zoulicn@163.com

Based on linguistic formal context with fuzzy object, this paper describes the relationship between object and linguistic concept, and constructs linguistic concept decision matrix with fuzzy object. At the same time, inspired by the classical TOPSIS decision method and vector operation, the TOPSIS decision method based on linguistic formal context with fuzzy object is proposed. The positive and negative ideal solutions are determined by linguistic concept decision matrix with fuzzy object, and the pseudo-distance and closeness degree between the object and the positive (negative) ideal solutions are calculated to select the most satisfactory alternative object.

Keywords: Formal context; decision matrix; TOPSIS decision method.

1. Introduction

Formal Concept Analysis (FCA) theory is a method of analyzing conceptual hierarchy of Formal context proposed by Wille [1]. In the formal background S=(U, A, I), I(x, A) is usually used to describe the binary relationship between object X and attribute A, but this binary relationship can only be expressed by 1 or 0, which has certain limitations. Zou et al. [2, 3] introduce a reduction algorithm of incomplete linguistic concept formal context based on the basis of granular computing, and the linguistic concept knowledge reduction algorithm is proposed to handle the complexity. Pang [4] proposed a collaborative filtering

---

[*]This work is partially supported by the National Natural Science Foundation of P.R. China (Nos. 61772250, 62176142), Foundation of Liaoning Educational Committee (No. LJ2020007) and Special Foundation for Distinguished Professors of Shandong Jianzhu University.

algorithm based on linguistic concept lattice with fuzzy objects to solve the recommendation fuzzy interpretation problem in recommendation system.

In our daily lives, we are always faced with tasks and activities that require the use of decision-making processes. The TOPSIS decision has attracted a lot of research interest from scholars. Ren et al. [5, 8] proposed a fuzzy linguistic TOPSIS decision making method based on object-linguistic value decision matrix by referring to the classical TOPSIS decision method. Pei et al. [6] proposed a fuzzy linguistic multi-set TOPSIS method for linguistic decision making on the basis of fuzzy multi-set and TOPSIS method. Han et al. [7] proposed the entropy and distance measures of LHPFSs, and improved TOPSIS method through hierarchical thought.

At present, there are few studies on the combination of formal context and TOPSIS method. Linguistic formal context with fuzzy object can be used to construct linguistic concept decision matrix with fuzzy object well. The evaluation information given by decision experts according to decision attributes is no longer the linguistic values of "good", "general" and "poor", but the linguistic values are converted into numerical values, which can more accurately express human thinking. However, in order to avoid a lot of information loss in the process of converting linguistic values into numerical values, this paper introduces the linguistic formal context with fuzzy object into TOPSIS decision method and constructs the linguistic concept decision matrix with fuzzy object to solve the multi-attribute decision problem. Therefore, in order to obtain more accurate decision results, it becomes particularly important to combine the linguistic formal context of fuzzy object with TOPSIS decision method to avoid the loss of evaluation information to the greatest extent.

2. Preliminaries

Definition 2.1. [4] A linguistic formal context with fuzzy object is defined as $(U, L_{s_\alpha}, \tilde{I}, \lambda)$, where $U = \{x_1, x_2, \ldots, x_m\}$ is a nonempty finite set of object, $L_{s_\alpha} = \{l_{s_0}^1, l_{s_1}^1, \ldots, l_{s_g}^1, l_{s_0}^2, l_{s_1}^2, \ldots, l_{s_g}^2, l_{s_0}^r, l_{s_1}^r, \ldots, l_{s_g}^r\}$ is a nonempty finite set of linguistic concepts, is confidence level of objects and linguistic concepts, and $\tilde{I}$ is fuzzy relation between U and L_{s_α}, $\tilde{I} : U \times L_{s_\alpha} \to \lambda$.

For any $\forall x \in U$, $\forall l_{s_\alpha}^i \in L_{s_\alpha}$, there exists a confidence level $\lambda_{\tilde{I}}\left(x, l_{s_\alpha}^j\right) \in [0,1]$. $\left(x, l_{s_\alpha}^j\right) \in \tilde{I}$ represents that the object x can be described by the linguistic concept with the confidence level $\lambda_{\tilde{I}}\left(x, l_{s_\alpha}^j\right)$.

For any $\forall l^j \in L$, the confidence level $\lambda_{\tilde{I}}\left(x, l_{s_\alpha}^j\right)$ often only exists in adjacent linguistic concepts described by the linguistic concept.

Proposition 2.1. In the linguistic formal context with fuzzy object $(U, L_{s_\alpha}, \tilde{I}, \lambda)$,

$\forall l^j \in L$, $\forall x \in U$, $\forall l_{s_\alpha}^j \in L_{s_\alpha}$, there exists $\sum_{v=1}^{g+1} \lambda_{\tilde{I}}\left(x, l_{s_\alpha}^j\right) = 1$, where $g+1$ is the number of items of the linguistic concepts under the same attribute.

Definition 2.2. Let $(U, L_{s_\alpha}, \tilde{I}, \lambda)$ be a linguistic formal context with fuzzy object, for $X \subseteq U$, $B \subseteq L_{s_\alpha}$ the operators "$\rightarrow$" can be defined as follows:

$$\tilde{X}^{\rightarrow} = \cap\left\{l_{s_\alpha}^j \mid l_{s_\alpha}^i \in L_{s_\alpha}, \forall x \in X\right\} \tag{1}$$

and the operators "$\leftarrow$" can be defined as follows:

$$B^{\leftarrow}(x) = \sum_{\forall x \in X} \frac{\lambda_x}{x} \tag{2}$$

Where $\tilde{X}$ represents the set of all objects in X that can be composed of linguistic concepts with a confidence level. $\lambda_x = \min\limits_{x \in X, l_{s_\alpha}^j \in L_{s_\alpha}} \lambda_{\tilde{I}}\left(x, l_{s_\alpha}^j\right)$, $B^{\leftarrow}$ represents the set of objects that can be described by all linguistic concepts with confidence level in B.

For the linguistic formal context with fuzzy object $(U, L_{s_\alpha}, \tilde{I}, \lambda)$, $X \subseteq U$, $B \subseteq L_{s_\alpha}$, if $\tilde{X}^{\rightarrow} = B$, $B^{\leftarrow} = \tilde{X}$, $(\tilde{X}, B)$ is a linguistic concept with fuzzy object, where $\tilde{X}$ is the extent of concept and B is the intent of concept.

3. Constructing Decision Matrix Under Linguistic Formal Context with Fuzzy Object

Based on linguistic formal context with fuzzy object $(U, L_{s_\alpha}, \tilde{I}, \lambda)$, we can transform it into linguistic concept decision matrix with fuzzy object. Then, the construction of linguistic concept decision matrix with fuzzy object is expressed as follows:

$$D_{kj} = \begin{array}{c} \\ x_1 \\ \vdots \\ x_m \end{array} \begin{array}{ccc} l_{s_0}^j & \cdots & l_{s_g}^j \\ \left(\begin{array}{ccc} \lambda_{11}^{kj} & \cdots & \lambda_{1n}^{kj} \\ \vdots & \ddots & \vdots \\ \lambda_{m1}^{kj} & \cdots & \lambda_{mn}^{kj} \end{array}\right) \end{array} \tag{3}$$

where $\forall \lambda_{iy}^{kj} \in [0,1]$, $k = 1,\ldots,t$, $i = 1,\ldots,m$ $j = 1,\ldots,r$ $\alpha = 0,\ldots,g$, $y = 1,\ldots,n$, and $\alpha = y - 1$. Indicate that expert e_k uses the confidence level λ_{iy}^{kj} between object x_i and linguistic concept $l_{s_\alpha}^{j}$ for evaluation under the decision attribute l^{j}. (Where n represents the number of linguistic concept under the same decision attribute)

Example 3.1. An enterprise wants to buy a real estate in Beijing, invited expert e_1 to make a evaluation of the four communities in Chaoyang District of Beijing from two aspects attributes $l = \{l^1, l^2\}$ of property. And expert e_k to use the linguistic term set S={s_0= bad, s_1 = fair, s_2= good} give the following linguistic formal context with fuzzy object.

Table 1. Linguistic formal context with fuzzy object.

U	$l_{s_0}^{1}$	$l_{s_1}^{1}$	$l_{s_2}^{1}$	$l_{s_0}^{2}$	$l_{s_1}^{2}$	$l_{s_2}^{2}$
x_1	0.6	0.4	0	0.4	0.6	0
x_2	0.5	0.5	0	0	0	1
x_3	0	0.3	0.7	0	1	0

The linguistic concept decision matrix with fuzzy object constructed by Table 1 is as follows:

$$
D_{11} = \begin{matrix} & l_{s_0}^1 & l_{s_1}^1 & l_{s_2}^1 \\ x_1 \\ x_2 \\ x_3 \end{matrix} \begin{pmatrix} 0.6 & 0.4 & 0 \\ 0.5 & 0.5 & 0 \\ 0 & 0.3 & 0.7 \end{pmatrix}, \quad D_{12} = \begin{matrix} & l_{s_0}^2 & l_{s_1}^2 & l_{s_2}^2 \\ x_1 \\ x_2 \\ x_3 \end{matrix} \begin{pmatrix} 0.4 & 0.6 & 0 \\ 1 & 0 & 0 \\ 0 & 1 & 0 \end{pmatrix}
$$

4. Construction of TOPSIS Decision Model Under Linguistic Formal Context with Fuzzy Object

The core idea of the classical TOPSIS decision method is that the satisfactory selection object should be closest to the positive ideal solution and farthest from the negative ideal solution. In this section, the method to determine the positive and negative ideal solution of linguistic concept decision matrix with fuzzy object and the method to calculate the pseudo distance and closeness degree between the decision object and the positive (negative) ideal solutions are proposed. The decision objects can be sorted and the satisfactory decision objects can be obtained by the corresponding calculation results.

Definition 4.1. In the linguistic concept decision matrix with fuzzy object, the evaluation results of decision objects x_i provided by expert e_k according to decision attribute l^j are represented by vectors:

$$D_{kj}^i = \left(\lambda_{i1}^{kj}, \lambda_{i1}^{kj}, \ldots, \lambda_{in}^{kj} \right) \tag{4}$$

Definition 4.2. [5] In this paper, the positive and negative ideal solutions of the decision matrix D_{kj} for attribute l^j are:

$$PIS_{kj} = \bigvee_{i=1}^{m} D_{kj}^i = \left(\bigvee_{i=1}^{m} \lambda_{i1}^{kj}, \ldots, \bigvee_{i=1}^{m} \lambda_{ig}^{kj} \right) \tag{5}$$

$$NIS_{kj} = \bigwedge_{i=1}^{m} D_{kj}^i = \left(\bigwedge_{i=1}^{m} \lambda_{i1}^{kj}, \ldots, \bigwedge_{i=1}^{m} \lambda_{ig}^{kj} \right) \tag{6}$$

Therefore, the positive and negative ideal solution of all decision attributes provided by expert e_k is:

$$PIS_k = \left(\bigvee_{i=1}^{m} D_{k1}^i, \ldots, \bigvee_{i=1}^{m} D_{kr}^i \right) \tag{7}$$

$$NIS_k = \left(\bigwedge_{i=1}^{m} D_{k1}^i, \ldots, \bigwedge_{i=1}^{m} D_{kr}^i \right) \tag{8}$$

Definition 4.3. [5] In the decision matrix D_{kj}, the pseudo-distance between objects of decision is defined as follows:

$$h\left(D_{kj}^i, D_{kj}^{i'} \right) = \left\| D_{kj}^i - D_{kj}^{i'} \right\| = \sum_{\alpha=0}^{g} \alpha \times \left| \lambda_{iy}^{kj} - \lambda_{i'y}^{kj} \right| \tag{9}$$

where $k = 1, \ldots, t$, $i = 1, \ldots, m$, $j = 1, \ldots, r$, $\alpha = 0, \ldots, g$, $y = 1, \ldots, n$ and $y = \alpha + 1$.

Definition 4.4. According to the pseudo-distance between each object of decision and positive and negative ideal solutions, the relative closeness $R(x_i)$ between each object of decision and positive (negative) ideal solutions is defined as:

$$h_{\min}^{+} = \min\left\{ h\left(D^1, PIS \right), \ldots, h\left(D^m, PIS \right) \right\} \tag{10}$$

$$h_{\max}^{-} = \max\left\{ h\left(D^1, NIS \right), \ldots, h\left(D^m, NIS \right) \right\} \tag{11}$$

$$R(x_i) = \frac{1}{2} \left(\frac{h\left(D^i, NIS \right)}{h_{\max}^{-}} + \frac{h_{\min}^{+}}{h\left(D^i, PIS \right)} \right) \tag{12}$$

Linguistic concept decision matrix with fuzzy object describes the evaluation information of linguistic concept given by decision experts, which greatly reduces the loss of information. At the same time, this method is further verified and analyzed by an example.

5. An Example Analysis of the Combination of Linguistic Formal Context with Fuzzy Object and TOPSIS Decision Making Method

In order to enrich students' campus life, a university held an online singing contest, and selected a champion from the four students $U=\{x_1, x_2, x_3, x_4\}$ who won the preliminary contest to represent the school in the city's university students singing contest. The school invited a panel of experts to make decision evaluation on the four contestants by using linguistic terms set $S=\{s_0=$ bad, $s_1 =$ fair, $s_2=$ good$\}$ to describe two aspects of l^1: rhythm and l^2: singing technique, attribute weight is $v_1 = 0.3, v_2 = 0.7$. And expert give the following linguistic formal context with fuzzy object:

Table 2. Linguistic formal context with fuzzy object.

U	$l^1_{s_0}$	$l^1_{s_1}$	$l^1_{s_2}$	$l^2_{s_0}$	$l^2_{s_1}$	$l^2_{s_2}$
x_1	0.2	0.8	0	0.4	0.6	0
x_2	0	0.5	0.5	0	0	1
x_3	0	0	1	0	1	0
x_4	0.9	0.1	0	0.2	0.8	0

The linguistic concept decision matrix with fuzzy object constructed

Step 1: Constructing linguistic concept decision matrix with fuzzy object under linguistic formal context with fuzzy object

$$D_1 = \begin{matrix} x_1 \\ x_2 \\ x_3 \\ x_4 \end{matrix} \begin{pmatrix} l^1_{s_0} & l^1_{s_1} & l^1_{s_2} \\ 0.2 & 0.8 & 0 \\ 0 & 0.5 & 0.5 \\ 0 & 0 & 1 \\ 0.9 & 0.1 & 0 \end{pmatrix}, \quad D_2 = \begin{matrix} x_1 \\ x_2 \\ x_3 \\ x_4 \end{matrix} \begin{pmatrix} l^2_{s_0} & l^2_{s_1} & l^2_{s_2} \\ 0 & 0.7 & 0.3 \\ 1 & 0 & 0 \\ 0 & 0.4 & 0.6 \\ 0.2 & 0.8 & 0 \end{pmatrix}$$

Step 2: Identify positive and negative ideal solutions

$$PIS_1 = (0.9, 0.8, 1), \ PIS_2 = (1, 0.8, 0.6), \ NIS_1 = (0, 0, 0), \ NIS_2 = (0, 0, 0)$$

$$PIS = \left((0.9, 0.8, 1), (1, 0.8, 0.6)\right), \ NIS = \left((0, 0, 0), (0, 0, 0)\right)$$

Step 3: The pseudo-distance between object of decision and positive (negative) ideal solution

$$h\left(D_1^1, PIS_1\right) = 0 \times \left|0.2 - 0.9\right| + 1 \times \left|0.8 - 0.8\right| + 2 \times \left|0 - 1\right| = 2, h\left(D_1^2, PIS_1\right) = 1.3,$$

$$h\left(D_1^3, PIS_1\right) = 0.8, h\left(D_1^4, PIS_1\right) = 2.7, h\left(D_1^1, NIS_1\right) = 0.8, h\left(D_1^2, NIS_1\right) = 0.8,$$

$$h\left(D_1^3, NIS_1\right) = 2, h\left(D_1^4, NIS_1\right) = 0.1, h\left(D_2^1, PIS_2\right) = 0.7, h\left(D_2^2, PIS_2\right) = 2,$$

$$h\left(D_2^3, PIS_2\right) = 0.4, h\left(D_2^4, PIS_2\right) = 1.2, h\left(D_2^1, NIS_2\right) = 1.3, h\left(D_2^2, NIS_2\right) = 0,$$

$$h\left(D_2^3, NIS_2\right) = 1.6, h\left(D_2^4, NIS_2\right) = 0.8$$

When attribute weight is $\upsilon_1 = 0.3$, $\upsilon_2 = 0.7$ pseudo distance between each decision object and positive (negative) ideal solution under all attributes

$$h\left(D^1, PIS\right) = 0.3 \times 2 + 0.7 \times 0.7 = 1.09, h\left(D^2, PIS\right) = 1.79, h\left(D^3, PIS\right) = 0.52,$$

$$h\left(D^4, PIS\right) = 1.65, h\left(D^1, NIS\right) = 1.15, h\left(D^2, NIS\right) = 0.45, h\left(D^3, NIS\right) = 1.72,$$

$$h\left(D^4, NIS\right) = 0.59$$

Step 4: The degree of closeness between the object of decision and the positive (negative) ideal solution

$$h_{min}^+ = \left\{1.09, 1.79, 0.52, 1.65\right\} = 0.52, h_{max}^- = \left\{1.15, 045, 1.72, 0.59\right\} = 1.72,$$

$$R\left(x_1\right) = \frac{1}{2}\left(\frac{1.15}{1.72} + \frac{0.52}{1.09}\right) = 0.57, R\left(x_2\right) = 0.28, R\left(x_3\right) = 1, R\left(x_4\right) = 0.33,$$

$$x_3 \succ x_1 \succ x_4 \succ x_2$$

Through the instance analysis can see decision expert according to decision attribute decision-making evaluation on the four contestants get the corresponding linguistic formal context with fuzzy object and constructs the linguistic concept decision matrix with fuzzy object. Rank the four contestants by calculating their relative closeness. Finally, student x_3 won the championship.

6. Conclusions

In this paper, based on the linguistic formal context with fuzzy object, a linguistic concept decision matrix with fuzzy object is constructed, which indicates that decision experts evaluate decision objects by the level of trust described by linguistic concepts under decision attributes. Combined with the classical TOPSIS decision method, the method of obtaining positive (negative) ideal solutions and the calculation method of pseudo distance and closeness degree between the object and positive (negative) ideal solutions are given, and the TOPSIS decision making method based on linguistic formal context with fuzzy object is proposed.

Acknowledgments

This work is partially supported by the National Natural Science Foundation of P.R. China (Nos. 61772250, 62176142), Foundation of Liaoning Educational Committee (No. LJ2020007) and Special Foundation for Distinguished Professors of Shandong Jianzhu University.

References

1. Wille R. Restructuring Lattice Theory: An Approach Based on Hierarchies of Concepts[J]. Orderd Sets D Reidel, 1982, 83: 314-339.
2. Zou L, Pang K, Song X. A knowledge reduction approach for linguistic concept formal context[J]. Information Sciences, 2020, 524: 165-183.
3. Liu P, Diao H, Zou L. Uncertain multi-attribute group decision making based on linguistic-valued intuitionistic fuzzy preference relations[J]. Information Sciences, 2020, 508: 293-308.
4. Pang K, Kang N, Chen S. Collaborative Filtering Recommendation Algorithm Based on Linguistic Concept Lattice with Fuzzy Object[C]// 2019 IEEE 14th International Conference on Intelligent Systems and Knowledge Engineering (ISKE). IEEE, 2019, pp. 57-63.
5. Ren F L, Kong M. A fuzzy linguistic TOPSIS decision making method based on alternatives-linguistic terms decision matrixes[J]. Control and Decision, 2019, 34(03): 602-610.
6. Pei Z, Liu J, Hao F. FLM-TOPSIS: The fuzzy linguistic multiset TOPSIS method and its application in linguistic decision making[J]. Information Fusion, 2019, 45: 266-281.
7. Han Q, Li W, Xu Q. Novel measures for linguistic hesitant Pythagorean fuzzy sets and improved TOPSIS method with application to contributions of system-of-systems [J]. Expert Systems With Applications, 2022, 199, 117088.
8. Ren F L, Kong M. Pei Z. A New Hesitant Fuzzy Linguistic TOPSIS Method for Group Multi-Criteria Linguistic Decision Making[J]. Symmetry, 2017, 9(12), 289.

A transmission line tension prediction model based on auxiliary information

Jinqiang He[1], Ruihai Li[1,*], Bo Gong[1], Hourong Zhang[1], Zenghao Huang[1], Yi Wen[2,3], Jianrong Wu[2,3] and Huan Huang[2,3]

[1] *Electric Power Research Institute, CSG, Guangzhou 510663, China*
[2] *Electrical Science Institute of Guizhou Power Grid Co., Ltd CSG, Guiyang 550000, China*
[3] *Key Laboratory of Ice Prevention & Disaster Reducing of China Southern Power Grid Co. Ltd., Guiyang 550002, China*
* 124478700@qq.com

Transmission line tension prediction in the icing period is essential for developing anti-icing strategies for power grids. Most current time-series-based icing prediction models ignore external factors, such as micro-meteorological information and transmission line element information, In order to better deal with this problem, We propose a novel neural network architecture that uses multi-variance information and other auxiliary information to predict more accurately. The experiments results on real dataset show that our model improves prediction accuracy over existing solutions.

Keywords: Tension prediction; multi-variance time series prediction; information fusion.

1. Introduction

Ice accumulations on transmission line conductors can cause severe damage to the electrical infrastructure and risk its safety.[1] However, the state of ice accumulation on transmission lines is generally difficult to detect due to various external factors. For example, the transmission line is located at a low latitude plateau zone, or the line is near a river. The micro-meteorological environment, such as the temperature, humidity or window speed, also can influence the ice accumulation. Although it is a great deal of effort to estimate the state of ice accumulation,[2] the result is not satisfactory. Hence we frequently utilize the change in conductor tension to represent ice accumulation. Recent studies[3–6] have focused on deploying time series forecasting models to predict ice-covered conditions on the transmission line, ignoring external factors such as micro-meteorological information and transmission line meta-information.

Due to these characteristics, the transmission line prediction issue is a multi-variance prediction problem. This paper proposes a multi-variance time-series prediction model to model the problem. The main contributions of our model are as follows:

(1) We propose a deep learning model based on residual mechanism to model the tension variation in the ice-covered transmission line.

(2) Our model fused the meta information of the transmission line using a gate mechanism to achieve a superior result.

2. Related Work

Ice accumulations on transmission line conductor is a major concern in electric power. Numerous specialists in the domain have provided various models in the past decades. Sun[4] proposed a multilayer perceptron (MLP) model to discriminate ice-covered status on transmission lines using micro-meteorological parameters and then predicted the ice accumulation in the next 24 hours. Han[5] proposed a multivariate fuzzy control technique for transmission line ice-covered state assessment and constructed a set of fuzzy inference rules to predict ice-covered amounts based on multivariate factors accurately. Huang[3] deploys the fuzzy logic theory to construct a prediction model for this problem. Ma[6,7] used the fireworks algorithm to select the input features and then used a weighted least square support vector machine (SVM) to predict ice accumulation. Niu[8] combined the backpropagation neural network and SVM model to optimize the accurate prediction further. Li[9] proposed a model based on multivariate time series to model this question. Transmission line tension prediction can be considered a multivariate time-series prediction problem. The mainstream solutions for this problem use recurrent neural network (RNN),[10–12] temporal convolutional networks (TCN)[13] and transformer.[14] For example, Han[10] uses bi-directional long-short memory networks to sequential model temporal features. Wu[13] uses TCN to model temporal proximity features efficiently. Zhou[14] exploits the property that transformer can capture the long-range dependency between output and input to model the temporal characteristic.

3. Methodology

3.1. *Problem formulation*

Ice tension prediction can be formulated as a multivariate time series problem. Let $x_{i,t} \in \mathbb{R}^D$ donate the value of a multivariate variable of sample i with dimension D at timestamp t. Given a sequence of historical T time steps of observations at time t on multivariate variable, $x_i = [x_{i,t_T}, x_{i,t_{T-1}}, \ldots, x_{i,t_0}] \in \mathbb{R}^{T \times D}$, our goal is to predict the P step away value of $y_i = [x_{t_P}] \in \mathbb{R}^{1 \times D}$, or a sequence of future values $y_i = [x_{t_1}, x_{t_2}, \ldots, x_{t_P}] \in \mathbb{R}^{P \times N}$. More generally, the input signal can be coupled with other auxiliary features such as the model of the tower and the voltage level of the transmission line, which can donate as $e_i \in \mathbb{R}^M$.

3.2. Model architecture

As illustrated in Fig. 1, our model on the highest level consists of several *temporal learning modules* and a *information fusion module*. The temporal learning module sequentially decomposes the time series and learns the critical feature with each iteration to discover hidden associations among multi-variance time series. In order to avoid the problem of gradient van-

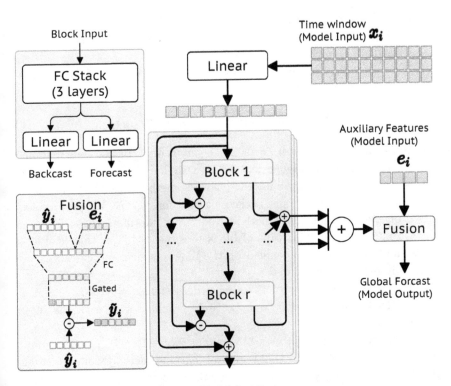

Fig. 1. Model Architecture.

ishing, residual connections have been introduced between the inputs and outputs of the temporal learning module. Skip connections are added after each temporal learning module. The information fusion module incorporates the temporal learning module's output with auxiliary features and projects the hidden feature onto the required output dimension. The components of our model are detailed in further detail below.

3.2.1. *Temporal Learning Module*

Inspired by FC-GAGA,[15] we propose a fully connected residual architecture with a R time feature extraction block. Each Block employ several Fully Connected (FC) layer to extract shared information from input time sequence $\hat{x}_{l-1,r}$, which $\hat{x}_{0,0} \equiv x$. The hidden feature $h_{l,r}$ of the r-the block at module l is described by following equations:

$$h_{l,r} = \text{FC}_{l,r}^3(\text{FC}_{l,r}^2(\text{FC}_{l,r}^1(\hat{x}_{l-1,r}))) \tag{1}$$

The FC layer consist a ReLU activation function to add non-linearity. For instance, $\text{FC}_{l,1}(\hat{x}_{l-1,r}) \equiv \text{ReLU}(\hat{x}_{l-1,r}W_{l,1} + b_{l,1})$, where $W_{l,1}$ and $b_{l,1}$ are learnable parameters.

Then we utilize two residual branches to run backcast and forecast prediction separately. Its operation is described as follows:

$$\theta_{l,r}^b = \text{Linear}_{l,r}^b(h_l), \theta_{l,r}^f = \text{Linear}_{l,r}^f(h_l) \tag{2}$$

Linear here is different from the FC layer. It only contains one mapping matrix to project the hidden feature to a similar dimension of $\hat{x}$ and y. After that operation, we will use the following method to extract the hidden information separately to get backcast $\tilde{x}$ and forecast $\hat{y}$. We propose two kinds of information extract methods to extract information.

Generic Block: This type of block uses one FC layer that is similar to Formula 1. It is not dependent on the time sequence and extracts more common features from hidden vectors.

Trend Block: It constructs a time-ordered tensor $S = [1/t, \ldots, 1/2, 1]$ similar to the input vector and multiplies element-wise with the input vector.

we use $\tilde{x}$ to reconstruct next block input $\hat{x}$ by $\hat{x}_{l,r} = \hat{x}_{l-1,r} - \tilde{x}_{l-1,r}$ and the output of all block in this temporal learning module will sum to get final output $\hat{y}_l = \sum_r y_{l,r}$. And next module input will $\hat{x}_{l,0} = \hat{x}_{l-1,0} + \hat{x}_{l-1,r}$. $\hat{y} = \sum_l \hat{y}_l$.

3.2.2. *Information Fusion Module*

This module will take the auxiliary feature and concatenate it with the output of the temporal learning module $\hat{y}$. The concatenate vector passes through an FC layer to extract information and use a sigmoid function to get the attention weight. The attention weight will be element-wise multiplied by the output of $\hat{y}$ to get the final output $\tilde{y}$.

$$\tilde{y} = \hat{y} \odot \sigma(\mathrm{FC}([\hat{y}, e])) \tag{3}$$

4. Experiment

4.1. *Dataset*

We constructed a real-world ice-covered tension dataset using conductor tensions on transmission lines. To ensure the validity of our model validation, we filtered the set of tension samples from the dataset to include a portion of the icing process (at least from icing-free to icing or icing-off to icing-free state). We also collected meteorological data (temperature, humidity, wind speed) and tower attribute information (voltage level, tower type) for each conductor corresponding to the tower. The dataset period is from December 1, 2020, to January 4, 2021, and the data sampling frequency is hourly. We use the data from December 20, 2020, to December 24, 2020, as the validation data and the data from December 25, 2021, to January 4, 2021, as the test data.

4.2. *Methods for comparison*

In the comparison, we consider the following baselines with various model structures.

- ARIMA:[16] It is a representative method for forecasting time series data.
- Support Vector Regression (SVR):[17] It is a representative method for forecasting time series data.
- Gradient Boosting Regression Tree (GBRT):[18] Gradient boosting regression tree is an iterative and ensemble decision tree algorithm for regression estimation.
- LSTNet:[19] A deep neural network combines convolutional neural networks and recurrent neural networks.

4.3. Hyper-parameter setting

We use the last 48 hours of data for each time point as training data to predict the next 24 hours. The model contains three temporal learning modules, each consisting of 2 generic blocks and a trend block order in each temporal learning module. The hidden state size in Formula 1 in each Block is set to 256.

4.4. Evaluation metrics

To evaluate the prediction performance of our model, we use three metrics to evaluate the difference between the real traffic information Y and the prediction

(1) Root Mean Squared Error (RMSE):

$$\text{RMSE} = \sqrt{\frac{1}{n} \sum_{i=1}^{n} (y_t - \hat{y}_t)^2} \tag{4}$$

(2) Mean Absolute Error (MAE):

$$\text{MAE} = \frac{1}{n} \sum_{i=1}^{n} |y_t - \hat{y}_t| \tag{5}$$

(3) Mean Absolute Percentage Error (MAPE):

$$\text{MAPE} = \frac{100\%}{n} \sum_{i=1}^{n} \left| \frac{y_t - \hat{y}_t}{y_t} \right| \tag{6}$$

Specifically, RMSE and MAE are used to measure the prediction error: the smaller the value is, the better the prediction effect is. MAPE is used to detect the prediction precision: the smaller the value is, the better the prediction effect is.

4.5. Result

Table 1 and Table 2 provide the main experimental results of our model. We observe that our model achieves state-of-the-art results on most of the tasks, and the performance of our model is getting more than 40% LSTNet.

To further assess the effectiveness of each principal component used in our model, we experiment on several model variants on this dataset in Table 2.

Table 1. Baseline comparison.

Methods	MAE	RMSE	MAPE
ARIMA	64.84	102.59	30.84%
SVR	54.96	86.97	16.85%
GBRT	45.4	57.18	13.13%
LSTNet	34.76	45.47	6.37%
FCR-GF	20.54	28.32	5.88%

Table 2. Ablation study.

Methods	MAE	RMSE	MAPE
Remove Trend Block	24.32	34.18	15.32%
Remove Information Module	22.74	31.42	7.01%
FCR-GF	20.54	28.32	5.88%

We remove the Trend Block (using three Generic Block in each temporal learning module) to validate the effectiveness of the Trend Block. We can see that all metrics drop, and spatially MAPE drops a lot. By removing the Trend Block, the model cannot model the time sequence information. We also remove the Information Module, and we can see that Information Fusion Module will provide meaningful information to model this problem.

5. Conclusions

This paper proposes a novel neural network architecture to model tension forecasting problems on transmission lines in ice-covered periods, which can model this multi-variance time series problem and uses multi-variance information and other auxiliary information to predict more accurately. The experiments results on real dataset show that our model improves prediction accuracy over existing solutions. We will further extend the experimental scope of our model by adding more ice-covered transmission line data for evaluation. Then we will further optimize our model by introducing micro-terrain information.

Acknowledgments

This work was supported by the Big Data Analytics and artificial intelligence application of power transmission line icing in southern China (Technology Project No. 066600KK52190063).

References

1. Y. Hao, Z. Yao, J. Wang, H. Li, R. Li, L. Yang and W. Liang, A classification method for transmission line icing process curve based on hierarchical k-means clustering, *Energies* **12**, p. 4786 (2019).
2. L. He, J. Luo and X. Zhou, A novel deep learning model for transmission line icing thickness prediction, *2021 IEEE 5th Advanced Information Technology, Electronic and Automation Control Conference (IAEAC)* **5**, 733 (2021).
3. H. Xin-bo, S. Qin-dong, Z. Guan-jun and M. Jian-guo, Relation of transmission line icing and local meteorology, *High Voltage Apparatus* **44**, 289 (2008).
4. S. Meng, S. Yunhai, L. Wei, Z. Zhenzhen, W. Qi, Z. Hourong, Z. Wuying, Y. Zhaohong, H. Yanpeng and Y. Lin, Prediction of icing risk on transmission lines based on mlp neural network, *Automation and Instumentation*, 165 (2019).
5. H. Yeliang, S. Guofeng, Y. Hongyong and M. Wei, Early-warning model for icing power grid accident based on rough set, *Journal of Tsinghua University* **12** (2010).
6. T. Ma and D. Niu, Icing forecasting of high voltage transmission line using weighted least square support vector machine with fireworks algorithm for feature selection, *Applied Sciences* **6**, p. 438 (2016).
7. T. Ma, D. Niu and M. Fu, Icing forecasting for power transmission lines based on a wavelet support vector machine optimized by a quantum fireworks algorithm, *Applied Sciences* **6**, p. 54 (2016).
8. D. Niu, Y. Liang, H. Wang, M. Wang and W. Hong, Icing forecasting of transmission lines with a modified back propagation neural network-support vector machine-extreme learning machine with kernel (bpnn-svm-kelm) based on the variance-covariance weight determination method, *Energies* **10**, p. 1196 (2017).
9. P. Li, N. Zhao, D. Zhou, M. Cao, J. Li and X. Shi, Multivariable time series prediction for the icing process on overhead power transmission line, *The Scientific World Journal* **2014** (2014).
10. H. Zhao, H. Yang, Y. Wang, D. W. Wang and R. Su, Attention based graph bi-lstm networks for traffic forecasting, *2020 IEEE 23rd International Conference on Intelligent Transportation Systems (ITSC)*, 1 (2020).
11. L. Zhao, Y. Song, C. Zhang, Y. Liu, P. Wang, T. Lin, M. Deng and H. Li, T-gcn: A temporal graph convolutional network for traffic pre-

diction, *IEEE Transactions on Intelligent Transportation Systems* **21**, 3848 (2020).

12. P. Chen, X. Fu and X. Wang, A graph convolutional stacked bidirectional unidirectional-lstm neural network for metro ridership prediction, *IEEE Transactions on Intelligent Transportation Systems* (2021).

13. Z. Wu, S. Pan, G. Long, J. Jiang and C. Zhang, Graph wavenet for deep spatial-temporal graph modeling, *IJCAI International Joint Conference on Artificial Intelligence* **2019-August**, 1907 (2019).

14. H. Zhou, S. Zhang, J. Peng, S. Zhang, J. Li, H. Xiong and W. Zhang, Informer: Beyond efficient transformer for long sequence time-series forecasting, in *Proceedings of AAAI*, 2021.

15. B. N. Oreshkin, A. Amini, L. Coyle and M. Coates, FC-GAGA: Fully Connected Gated Graph Architecture for Spatio-Temporal Traffic Forecasting, *AAAI 2021 - 35th AAAI Conference on Artificial Intelligence*, p. 9 (2021).

16. B. Pan, U. Demiryurek and C. Shahabi, Utilizing real-world transportation data for accurate traffic prediction, in *2012 ieee 12th international conference on data mining*, 2012.

17. C.-C. Chang and C.-J. Lin, Libsvm: a library for support vector machines, *ACM transactions on intelligent systems and technology (TIST)* **2**, 1 (2011).

18. G. Ke, Q. Meng, T. Finley, T. Wang, W. Chen, W. Ma, Q. Ye and T.-Y. Liu, Lightgbm: A highly efficient gradient boosting decision tree, *Advances in neural information processing systems* **30** (2017).

19. G. Lai, W.-C. Chang, Y. Yang and H. Liu, Modeling long-and short-term temporal patterns with deep neural networks, in *The 41st International ACM SIGIR Conference on Research & Development in Information Retrieval*, 2018.

Differential evolution variants for finding D-optimal designs

Lyuyang Tong[1,2], WengKee Wong[3], Bo Du[1], Ye Tian[4] and KayChen Tan[5]

[1] *National Engineering Research Center for Multimedia Software*
Institute of Artificial Intelligence, School of Computer Science, and
Hubei Key Laboratory of Multimedia and Network Communication Engineering
Wuhan University, China
[2] *Department of Computer Science, City University of Hong Kong, Hong Kong*
[3] *Department of Biostatistics, University of California at Los Angeles, USA*
[4] *Institutes of Physical Science and Information Technology, Anhui University, China*
[5] *Department of Computing, The Hong Kong Polytechnic University, Hong Kong*

Finding a D-optimal design to estimate model parameters can be challenging, especially when the model is complex and high-dimensional. Some evolutionary algorithms have been applied to tackle the problem but the design problems are for relatively simple statistical models. We employ several variants of differential evolution to find D-optimal designs for 5 different types of statistical models. Our simulation experiments show that the LSHADE variant outperforms other variants.

Keywords: Approximate design; D-optimal design; differential evolution (DE).

1. Introduction

The statistical design of experiment (DoE) is a valuable tool for sustainability issues. Optimal design is a useful technique to employ the industry application for sustainable energy resources.[1] Model-based optimal experimental regression designs are often constructed under a user-selected optimality criterion and based on the Fisher information matrix.[2] A common criterion is D-optimality for estimating model parameters accurately by maximizing the determinant of the Fisher's information matrix. This matrix measures the worth of the design and is defined below.

Throughout, we supposed we are given a statistical model defined on the compact design space $\mathbf{X}$ and there is a predetermined total number of observations N available for the study. The design problem is to pick N locations from $\mathbf{X}$ to observe the outcome so that the determinant of the information matrix is maximized. The optimization is over all designs from $\mathbf{X}$ and the resulting design is D-optimal. The variables to optimize are the number of points required in the optimal design, their locations $\mathbf{X}$ and the number of replicates at each of the points. These are optimal exact design problems and they are notoriously difficult to solve theoretically. For high-dimensional complex models, optimal exact designs are also also difficult to find numerically.

Metaheuristics is now commonly used to tackle complex optimization problems in engineering and computer science research. Some of the more widely used metaheuristic algorithms are particle swarm optimization and differential evolution. Like most metaheuristic algorithms, each has its own variants and the more popular ones have more variants. Variants are modifications of the original algorithms for enhanced performance. The modifications can be variously motivated and may include a need to solve a class of targeted optimization problems or to ensure the original algorithm converges faster. Clearly, the variants have different capabilities and their performance depends on the problem. In this paper, we consider DE variants: JADE,[3] CoDE,[4] SHADE,[5] and LSHADE[6] and evaluate their relative performance for finding D-optimal designs for five quite different statistical models. Simulation experiments show that the DE variant LSHADE has better performance for finding the D-optimal problems among the comparative algorithms.

2. Background

2.1. Approximate design and the information matrix

All the statistical model have the form

$$Y = \eta\left(\mathbf{x}, \theta\right) + \varepsilon, \quad \mathbf{x} \in \mathbf{X} \tag{1}$$

where Y is a uni-variate response and the continuous response function $\eta\left(\mathbf{x}, \theta\right)$ is known, apart from the $p \times 1$ vector of unknown parameters θ. The given compact design space X contains all possible values of the design factor vector x and the error ε is identically distributed with zero mean and constant variance and independent of one another.

In practice, the design problem is to optimize the number of design points, their values in the design space and the proportions of observations to take at these design points. These are approximate designs and they have the form $\xi = \{(\mathbf{x}_i, \omega_i), i = 1, 2, ..., m\}$ with the support points $x_i \in \mathbf{X}$ and the weight $\omega_i > 0$ and $\sum_{i=1}^{m} \omega_i = 1$. The normalized Fisher information matrix of an approximate design ξ is proportional to

$$M(\xi, \theta) = \sum_{i=1}^{m} \omega_i \frac{\partial \eta(\mathbf{x}_i, \theta)}{\partial \theta} \frac{\partial \eta(\mathbf{x}_i, \theta)}{\partial \theta^{\mathrm{T}}}. \tag{2}$$

2.2. The D-optimal design

Let $\psi\{M(\xi, \theta)\}$ be a optimality criterion. A design that optimizes the criterion is a ψ-optimal and denoted by ξ^*. For D-optimality, we write $\psi\{M(\xi, \theta)\} = -log |M(\xi, \theta)|$ so that it is a convex functional over the space of information matrices. The design that minimizes $\psi\{M(\xi, \theta)\}$ over all design is D-optimal. The convexity of the criterion and the search for approximate designs imply that we have a convex optimization problem and an equivalence theorem is available for finding and checking optimality of a design. The theory comes from convex analysis by considering the direction derivatives of $\psi\{M(\xi, \theta)\}$ in the direction of a degenerate design. Following arguments in Ref. 2, it can be shown a design ξ is D-optimal if and only if for all $\mathbf{x} \in \mathbf{X}$, we have

$$S(x, \xi) = trace(M(x, \theta)M^{-1}(\xi, \theta)) - p$$

$$= trace(f(x)f(x)^T M^{-1}(\xi, \theta)) - p$$

$$= f(x)^T M^{-1}(\xi, \theta)f(x) - p \leq 0, \tag{3}$$

with equality at the support points of ξ. The function $S(x, \xi)$ in the above equivalence theorem for D-optimality is called the sensitivity function of the design ξ. We note that if the dimension of $\mathbf{X}$ is one, a plot of $S(x, \xi)$ over the design space can easily provide a visual appreciate whether the design ξ is D-optimal. Further, from the equivalence theorem, direct calculus shows that a D-efficiency lower bound[7] for a design ξ is

$$D\_Eff(\xi) = \exp\left(-\frac{\max(S(x, \xi_D))}{p}\right) \tag{4}$$

This is a helpful tool to assess the proximity of a design from the optimum, without knowing the optimum. Frequently, for practical purposes, if a design has at least 95% D-efficiency, the design may be considered as close enough to the optimum, without knowing the latter.

3. Repair Operation and DE Variants

3.1. Repair operation

Our experience using DE variants to find the optimal designs is that they frequently were unable to find the optimal designs precisely. In particular, they tend to find designs with several more points with small weights. Sometimes, these points drop out with longer running time but not always. Accordingly, we propose a repair operation that combines nearby support points and their corresponding weights and drops points with very small weights. The points are merged via Euclidean distance clustering and the weights at the design points are adjusted so that they sum to 1. In practice, the repair operation is run just before the results are finalized, but it can also be run periodically during the search for the optimal design.

3.2. DE variants for finding D-optimal designs

Differential Evolution (DE) is a widely used metaheuristic algorithm and is frequently used to search in large spaces filled with candidate solutions. In addition, it does not require gradient information to find the optimum successfully. DE is also one of a couple of metaheuristic algorithm with many variants. We select a few of them to assess their relative performance and test their capability for finding D-optimal designs. The selected variants we investigate are: JADE,[3] CoDE,[4] SHADE,[5] and LSHADE.[6]

4. Experimental Setup and Results

4.1. Experimental setting

In this section, we select 5 different types of statistical model in Ref. 8 to conduct the simulation study. Table 1 displays the models, the nominal values for the parameters in the nonlinear models and the assumed number of support points required in the optimal design for each of the statistical models. The assumed number of support points in the optimal design implies the numbers in the last column, which shows the total number of variables that the algorithms need to optimize. We test SA, SPSO,[9] GA, OFA,[10] CSO[11] and the DE variants, JADE, CoDE, SHADE, and LSHADE, to find the D-optimal design for the 5 statistical models.

In the experimental setup, we used a population size of 50 and the number of function evaluations (FES) for Problem 1-5 is 10000. Each algorithm used default tuning parameters and was run 25 times for each problem.

4.2. Results and discussion

Table 2 displays results from the Wilcoxon rank test for evaluating equality of the criterion values of designs found from different algorithms at the 0.05

significance level. Notations '$-$', '$+$', and '$=$' indicate that the corresponding comparative algorithm in the column of the table is significantly worse than, better than, or similar to the target algorithm listed in the row of the

Table 1. D-optimal design problems for five various statistical models.

Prob-lem	Model	Fac-tors	Param-eters	Assumed number of support points	Vari-ables
1	$Y \sim \theta_1 e^{-\theta_2 x} + \theta_3 e^{-\theta_4 x} + N\left(0, \sigma^2\right), x \in [0,3]$ $g(\theta) = \theta$ nominal values $\theta = (1,1,1,2)^T$	1	4	6	12
2	$Y \sim \theta_1 + \theta_2 x_1 + \theta_3 x_1^2 + \theta_4 x_2 + \theta_5 x_1 x_2 + N\left(0, \sigma^2\right),$ $(x_1, x_2) \in [-1,1] \times [0,1]$ $g(\theta) = \theta$	2	5	10	30
3	$Y \sim \pi_i(\mathbf{x}) = P\left(Y_i = 1 \mid \mathbf{x}\right) = \dfrac{e^{h(\mathbf{x})^T \theta_i}}{1 + e^{h(\mathbf{x})^T \theta_1} + e^{h(\mathbf{x})^T \theta_2}}$ $\mathbf{x} \in [0,6]^3, i = 1,2$ $h(\mathbf{x}) = \left[1, \mathbf{x}^T\right]^T; g(\theta) = \theta$ nominal values $\theta_1 = (1,1,-1,2)^T; \theta_2 = (-1,2,1,-1)^T$	3	8	15	60
4	$Y \sim \theta_1 e^{\theta_2 x} + \theta_3 e^{\theta_4 x} + N\left(0, \sigma^2\right),$ $x \in [0,1]$ $g(\theta) = \theta$ nominal values $\theta = (1, 0.5, 1, 1)^T$	1	4	8	16
5	$Y \sim \dfrac{\theta_1 \theta_3 x_1}{1 + \theta_1 x_1 + \theta_2 x_2} + N\left(0, \sigma^2\right),$ $(x_1, x_2) \in [0,3] \times [0,3]$ $g(\theta) = \theta$ nominal values $\theta = (2.9, 12.2, 0.69)^T$	2	3	10	30

Table 2.   Results of the Wilcoxon rank tests for differences in the D-optimality criterion values of designs generated from various algorithms at the 0.05 significance level.

'$-$'/'$+$'/'$=$'	SA	SPSO	GA	OFA	CSO	JADE	CoDE	SHADE	LSHADE
SA	[0/0/5]	[4/0/1]	[4/1/0]	[3/0/2]	[5/0/0]	[5/0/0]	[5/0/0]	[5/0/0]	[5/0/0]
SPSO	[0/4/1]	[0/0/5]	[1/2/2]	[0/2/3]	[5/0/0]	[5/0/0]	[5/0/0]	[5/0/0]	[5/0/0]
GA	[1/4/0]	[2/1/2]	[0/0/5]	[2/3/0]	[5/0/0]	[5/0/0]	[5/0/0]	[5/0/0]	[5/0/0]
OFA	[0/3/2]	[2/0/3]	[3/2/0]	[0/0/5]	[5/0/0]	[5/0/0]	[5/0/0]	[5/0/0]	[5/0/0]
CSO	[0/5/0]	[0/5/0]	[0/5/0]	[0/5/0]	[0/0/5]	[2/2/1]	[0/5/0]	[1/4/0]	[4/1/0]
JADE	[0/5/0]	[0/5/0]	[0/5/0]	[0/5/0]	[2/2/1]	[0/0/5]	[0/5/0]	[0/4/1]	[4/1/0]
CoDE	[0/5/0]	[0/5/0]	[0/5/0]	[0/5/0]	[5/0/0]	[5/0/0]	[0/0/5]	[5/0/0]	[5/0/0]
SHADE	[0/5/0]	[0/5/0]	[0/5/0]	[0/5/0]	[4/1/0]	[4/0/1]	[0/5/0]	[0/0/5]	[4/0/1]
LSHADE	[0/5/0]	[0/5/0]	[0/5/0]	[0/5/0]	[1/4/0]	[1/4/0]	[0/5/0]	[0/4/1]	[0/0/5]

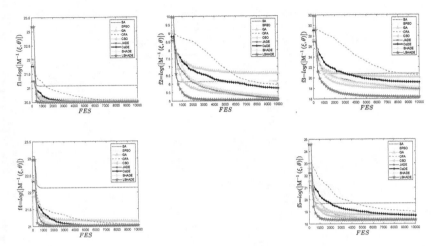

Fig. 1. Relative Mean Performances of the SA, SPSO, GA, OFA, CSO, JADE, CoDE, SHADE, and LSHADE for finding D-optimal designs for Problems 1-5.

table, respectively. We observe from Table 2 that LSHADE outperforms other algorithms in the Wilcoxon rank test.

Figure 1 shows the convergence rates of the various algorithms. The X axis represents the number of the function evaluations and the Y axis is the mean D-optimality criterion values averaged over the 25 runs. It is clear that the LSHADE algorithm shows better convergence performance than the other algorithms for Problems 1-5.

Table 3 shows the designs found by LSHADE under the D-optimality criterion for Problems 1-5. The reported designs are the best among the 25 runs found by LSHADE for each problem. The table shows the number and distribution of the support points and their corresponding weights in the first few columns. We observe that the LSHADE-generated designs have 4, 6, 9, 4, and 3 support points, respectively, for Problems 1-5. The values of the sensitivity function values at the support points are shown in the second to the last column. If the generated design is optimal, the value should be 0 in accordance with the equivalence theorem. The last column displays D-Efficiency Lower bounds of the generated designs by LSHADE. We note that the design found for Problem 3 is not truly optimal because its values at the support points are not all equal to zero and its calculated D-efficiency lower bound is 0.96 and not equal to 1, unlike the other 4 designs. Figure 2 displays the sensitivity plots of the designs found by LSHADE for Problems 1-2, 4-5 are optimal because the figure and results

Table 3. Characteristics of designs generated by LSHADE under the D-optimality criterion for Problems 1-5. The column s displays the values of the sensitivity function evaluated at the support point.

Problem	X			ω	S	D-efficiency lower bound
1	0			0.25	0	1
	0.3141			0.25	0	
	1.1307			0.25	0	
	2.7523			0.25	0	
2	-1	0		0.1875	0	1
	-1	1		0.1875	0	
	0	1		0.125	0	
	0	0		0.125	0	
	1	1		0.1875	0	
	1	0		0.1875	0	
3	0	0	0	0.1973	-0.11	0.97
	0	2.5536	0	0.0376	-0.2664	
	0	2.3873	0	0.1524	-0.2382	
	0	6	3.5812	0.1741	0.1776	
	0.0004	6	3.0119	0.0784	0.2306	
	1.5628	0.5725	0	0.1202	-0.0643	
	1.5915	0.0027	0.0004	0.0918	0.0909	
	6	5.9992	5.352	0.0982	0.063	
	6	0.0021	1.3611	0.05	0.2438	
4	0			0.25	0	1
	0.3305			0.25	0	
	0.7692			0.25	0	
	1			0.25	0	
5	0.2804	0		0.3333	0	1
	3	0		0.3333	0	
	3	0.7951		0.3333	0	

in Table 3 confirm they meet the conditions required in the equivalence theorem for D-optimality. If we had plotted the sensitivity function for the design found by LSHADE for Problem 3, its visual appeal would be compromised because it is difficult to visually appreciate the fine features in a high dimensional plot. For this reason, we omit showing the plot for Problem 3 and note that while the generated design for Problem 3 is not optimal, it is very close to the optimum since it has a D-efficiency of at least 97% relative to the optimum.

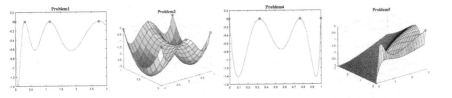

Fig. 2. The sensitivity functions of the LSHADE-generated designs for Problem 1-2 and Problems 4-5 under the D-optimality criterion.

5. Conclusions

Metaheuristic algorithms are general purpose optimization algorithms and so they can be applied to tackle all kinds of optimization problems. While such algorithms have been used to find some optimal designs, this report shows some variants can be more effective than other variants. In particular, we found that for DE, some variant, namely LSHADE, can outperform other DE-variants for finding D-optimal designs for statistical models.

References

1. L. Román-Ramírez and J. Marco, Design of experiments applied to lithium-ion batteries: A literature review, *Applied Energy* **320**, p. 119305 (2022).
2. V. V. Fedorov, *Theory of optimal experiments* (Elsevier, 2013).
3. J. Zhang and A. C. Sanderson, Jade: adaptive differential evolution with optional external archive, *IEEE Transactions on evolutionary computation* **13**, 945 (2009).
4. Y. Wang, Z. Cai and Q. Zhang, Differential evolution with composite trial vector generation strategies and control parameters, *IEEE transactions on evolutionary computation* **15**, 55 (2011).
5. R. Tanabe and A. Fukunaga, Success-history based parameter adaptation for differential evolution, in *2013 IEEE congress on evolutionary computation*, 2013.
6. R. Tanabe and A. S. Fukunaga, Improving the search performance of shade using linear population size reduction, in *2014 IEEE congress on evolutionary computation (CEC)*, 2014.
7. W. Xu, W. K. Wong, K. C. Tan and J.-X. Xu, Finding high-dimensional d-optimal designs for logistic models via differential evolution, *IEEE access* **7**, 7133 (2019).

8. R. García-Ródenas, J. C. García-García, J. López-Fidalgo, J. Á. Martín-Baos and W. K. Wong, A comparison of general-purpose optimization algorithms for finding optimal approximate experimental designs, *Computational Statistics & Data Analysis* **144**, p. 106844 (2020).

9. M. Zambrano-Bigiarini, M. Clerc and R. Rojas, Standard particle swarm optimisation 2011 at cec-2013: A baseline for future pso improvements, in *2013 IEEE Congress on Evolutionary Computation*, 2013.

10. G.-Y. Zhu and W.-B. Zhang, Optimal foraging algorithm for global optimization, *Applied Soft Computing* **51**, 294 (2017).

11. R. Cheng and Y. Jin, A competitive swarm optimizer for large scale optimization, *IEEE transactions on cybernetics* **45**, 191 (2014).

A generalized linguistic variable and a generalized fuzzy set GFScom

Shengli Zhang

School of Information Technology, Minzu Normal University of Xingyi
Xingyi, Guizhou 562400, China
zhangshengli@xynun.edu.cn

Jing Chen

College of Economics and Management, Minzu Normal University of Xingyi
Xingyi, Guizhou 562400, China
chenjing210@163.com

Lei Yang

School of Mathematical Sciences, Minzu Normal University of Xingyi
Xingyi, Guizhou 562400, China
yangleiyl_2010@163.com

This paper presents a generalized linguistic variable which can be viewed as an extension of the (ordinary) linguistic variable proposed by Zadeh. After analyzing the fuzzy sets FScom developed by Pan, we discover that the FScom is at least possessed with several shortcomings: 1) give any fuzzy set A, the medium negative fuzzy set of A is non-normal; 2) in FScom, the parameter λ is non-trivial, namely, the value of λ is not easy to be determined. In order to sketch the essential and intrinsic relationships between fuzzy knowledge and its different negation forms, we define a novel type of generalized fuzzy sets with contradictory, opposite and medium negation GFScom, and further explore several basic algebraic operations, properties and convexity and concavity with respect to GFScom. Moreover, we apply the generalized linguistic variable (or GFScom) to the Mamdani controller and suggest a novel form of fuzzy controller by considering three kinds of negation in a fuzzy system. A simple demonstration in a fuzzy system shows that the generalized linguistic variable (or GFScom) makes the fuzzy reasoning capability of fuzzy system much richer.

Keywords: Negative information; opposite negation; medium negation; generalized linguistic variable; generalized fuzzy sets GFScom; fuzzy controller.

1. Introduction

In the field of knowledge representation and reasoning, negative information (knowledge) plays a very important role [1–7]. In the past years, many scholars suggested that uncertain information(knowledge) processing requires different forms of negations in various fields (see [1-7] for more details and references therein). In a fuzzy system [8-10], fuzzy knowledge(information) is depicted by fuzzy rules. As we know well, it is nontrivial that the membership function of a fuzzy set is constructed in a adequate and effective way. In an applied fuzzy system, however, there exist hundreds of or thousands of different fuzzy subsets, which results in the fuzzy system designer's headache. However, from the negative point of view, many fuzzy subsets are not mutually isolated but in close connection with each other by use of the above-mentioned different kinds of negation. One of the most important aims of this paper is to give out this relevant method.

For convenience, some vital symbols used by this paper are shown in the following Table 1.

Table 1.   List of symbols.

Symbols	Meaning
¬	Contradictory negative operator
⅃	Opposite negative operator
∼	Medium negative operator

2. Generalized Linguistic Variables

Definition 2.1. Given any universal discourse U and finite numerical district D, namely, it has the following forms:$[a, b]$, $(a, b]$, $[a, b)$, (a, b), or $\{a = x_1 < x_2 < \ < x_n = b\}$, where $a, b \in \Re$, called the left and right end of D, respectively, we call the mapping $f : U \to D$ as (one dimensional) finite quantized district mapping.

Definition 2.2. Given any universal discourse U, the mapping f is identical to definition 2.1. A generalized linguistic variable is depicted as a quintuple $(X, T(x), f(U), G, M)$ in which X is the name of the variable; $T(x)$ (or simply T) indicates the term set of X; $f(U)$ is a finite numerical district and is range of X taking on values, where a, b is, respectively, its left and right end; G is a syntactic rule for generating the name of linguistic values of X; and M is a semantic rule for associating with each linguistic atomic word $t \in T(x)$. In addition, $\neg t$, $\dashv t$ and $\sim t$ denote the contradictory, opposite and medium negation w.r.t. t, respectively, and their semantic meanings are defined by Eqs. (1), (2) and (3)

$$M(\neg t)(u) = n(M(t)(u)) \tag{1}$$

$$M(\exists t)(u) = M(t)(a + b - u) \text{ and } M(t)(u) + M(\exists t)(u) \leq 1 \tag{2}$$

$$M(\sim t)(u) = M(\neg t)(u) * M(\neg \exists t)(u) = n(M(t)(u)) * n(M(t)(a+b-u)) \tag{3}$$

where $u \in f(u)$, $*$ is a t-norm [11], and n is a complement [8, 10].

In order to facilitate the symbolism in what follows, some symbols will have two meanings wherever clarity allows this: will denote the name of the variable and the generic name of its values. The same will be true for $t \in T$ and $M(t)$.

By observing FScom [4], we can discover the problems as follows:

1) Given any fuzzy subset A, its medium negative set $A^\sim$ is a non-normal fuzzy subset. In fact, in FScom, one can prove the inequality $1 - \lambda \leq A^\sim(x) \leq \lambda$ (when $\lambda \in [0.5, 1)$) or $\lambda \leq A^\sim(x) \leq 1 - \lambda$ (when $\lambda \in (0, 0.5]$)) follows for any $x \in U$. That means, in whatever cases, there is no object x such that x absolutely belongs to the medium negative set A in U. It is obvious to contradictory to objective minds.

2) The description of the relationship among contradictory negative set $A^\neg$, opposite negative set $A^\exists$ and medium negative set $A^\sim$ with respect to fuzzy subset A is not precise. Since an important result $A^\neg = A^\exists \cup A^\sim$ follows in FScom, we easily see $\forall x \in U, A^\neg(x) = (A^\exists \cup A^\sim)(x) = max(A^\exists(x), A^\sim(x)) \geq A^\sim(x) > 0$ by the above 1).

3) From the applicable point of view, the vigorous definition of three kinds of negation operators restricts range of application. For different fuzzy systems, we often need to check the corresponding operators in order to depict fuzzy knowledge and its negative knowledge appropriately and efficiently.

4) The value of parameter λ is hard to be affirmed in FScom, frequently requires to be given by the domain experts, and entails more subjective thinkings.

Definition 2.3. If a generalized linguistic variable X such that the term set T and semantic rule M can be characterized by some recursive algorithm, we refer to X as a generalized structured linguistic variable.

Definition 2.4. Let X be arbitrary generalized linguistic variable, t_p be a primary(an atomic) term and f be a modified word, then $f(t_p)$ denotes a composition generated by imposing f on t_p. If the term set of X consist of the following elements called a medium expression:

a) Both t_p and $f(t_p)$ are medium expressions;

b) If A, B are medium expressions, then $(A \wedge B), (A \vee B), \lrcorner A, \sim A$ and $\neg A$ are medium expressions;

c) All the medium expressions only are generated recursively by the above steps a) and b)

thus, X is said to be a medium linguistic variable, where $\lrcorner$ (opposite negative operator), $\sim$ (medium negative operator) and $\neg$ (contradictory negative operator) are unary connectives, while $\wedge$ (conjunction) and $\vee$ (disjunction) are binary connectives.

3. Generalized Fuzzy Sets GFScom with Three Kinds of Negation

In [5, 10], the authors proposed the notion of GFScom, and applied it to construct the Mamdani fuzzy system. However,we need to study further a variety of properties of GFScom. In what follows, we will give the basic properties, convexity and concavity of GFScom. In GFScom, the determination of the n contradictory negative set and $\otimes$-n medium negative set of a fuzzy set A is related to complement and t-norm, thereby, in the sequel, to be convenient, it's necessary to point out that we shall consider only the contradictory, opposite and medium negative set of a fuzzy set such that t-norm takes on min-operator and n a linear complement [8, 10]. Moreover, for ease of discussion, the domain U is viewed as a finite numerical district, and $\mathcal{F}(U)$ denotes a set of all the fuzzy subsets in U.

3.1. Basic properties of GFScom

In GFScom, the operations such as containment, equivalency, union and intersection between a pair of arbitrary fuzzy subsets are identical to the counterparts in Zadeh fuzzy sets. Hence, it is not hard to get the following.

Theorem 3.1. *In GFScom, the following hold: commutativity, associativity, distributivity, absorption, idempotency and polarity.*

Proposition 3.1. *Let A, B, C be any GFScom, respectively, then (1) $A^{\neg\neg} = A$; (2) $A^{\lrcorner\lrcorner} = A$; (3) $A^{\sim} = A^{\neg\sim}$.*

Proposition 3.2. *Let* A, B, C *be any GFScom, respectively, then* (1) $(A \cup B)^\neg = A^\neg \cap B^\neg$, $(A \cap B)^\neg = A^\neg \cup B^\neg$; (2) $(A \cup B)^\lrcorner = A^\lrcorner \cup B^\lrcorner$, $(A \cap B)^\lrcorner = A^\lrcorner \cap B^\lrcorner$.

Proposition 3.3. *Let* A, B, C *be any GFScom, respectively, then* (1) $A^\sim = A^\neg \cap A^{\lrcorner\neg}$; (2) $(A \cup B)^\sim = A^\sim \cap B^\sim$.

Proposition 3.4. *Let* A, B, C *be any GFScom, respectively, then* (1) $A \subseteq B \Leftrightarrow A^\neg \subseteq B^\neg$; (2) $A \subseteq B \Leftrightarrow A^\lrcorner \subseteq B^\lrcorner$; (3) $A \subseteq B \Leftrightarrow A^\sim \subseteq B^\sim$.

Proposition 3.5. *Let* A *be any GFScom and* $*, \triangle$ *be any mutually different symbol in* $\{\lrcorner, \sim, \neg\}$, *then the following results cannot hold:*

$$A \cup A^* = U, A^\triangle \cup A^* = U, A \cap A^* = \varnothing, A^\varnothing \cap A^* = \varnothing.$$

3.2. Convexity and concavity of GFScom

In what follows, we suppose for concreteness that X is a n-dimensional Cartesian product D^n, where D is the interval of forms as follows: $[a, b], (a, b], [a, b), (a, b)$ with $a, b \in \Re$.

Definition 3.1. *convexity (up convexity).* A generalized fuzzy set A in X is convex if and only if

$$A(\lambda x_1 + (1 - \lambda)x_2) \geq min\{A(x_1), A(x_2)\}$$

for all x_1 and x_2 in X and all λ in $[0, 1]$.

Contrary to convexity, one can readily get the following notion.

Definition 3.2. *concavity (down convexity).* A generalized fuzzy set A in X is concave if and only if

$$A(\lambda x_1 + (1 - \lambda)x_2) \leq min\{A(x_1), A(x_2)\}$$

for all x_1 and x_2 in X and all λ in $[0, 1]$.

Theorem 3.2. *A generalized fuzzy set* A *in* X *is convex if and only if the sets* Γ_α *defined as*

$$\Gamma_\alpha = \{x | A(x) \geq \alpha\}$$

are convex for all α *in the interval* $(0, 1]$.

Theorem 3.3. (1) *If generalized fuzzy sets* A *and* B *are convex, so is their intersection;* (2) *If generalized fuzzy sets* A *and* B *are concave, so is their intersection.*

Theorem 3.4. (1) *If A is concave, then its contradictory negative set $A^\neg$ is convex;* (2) *If $A^\neg$ is concave, then A is convex.*

Theorem 3.5. *If A is concave, then its medium negative set $A^\sim$ is convex.*

4. Application

In what follows, we shall introduce the generalized linguistic variable in the traditional (ordinary) Mamdani controller [8, 10] so as to obtain a novel type of controller, called Zhang controller.

Consider a simplified pressure system with two inputs labeled and single output. The three variables used are as follows:

(1) PE: Pressure Error, defined as the difference between the present value of the variable and the set point;

(2) CPE: Change of Pressure Error, defined as the difference between present PE and last (corresponding to last sampling instant);

(3) HC: Heat Change(control action variable).

These variables are quantized into a number of points corresponding to the elements of a universe of discourse, and values(terms) to the variables are assigned using seven basic fuzzy subsets: (1) PB: Positive Big; (2) PM: Positive Medium; (3) PS: Positive Small; (4) NO: Nil; (5) NS: Negative Small; (6) NM: Negative Medium; (7) NB: Negative Big. The terms of generalized linguistic variables PE and CPE are quantized into 13 points, ranging from maximum negative error -6 through zero error to maximum positive error $+6$. According to the operating experience, in the generalized linguistic variable PE we can obtain the membership functions of the generalized fuzzy sets PB, PM, PS and NO are, respectively, as follows:

$$PB = \frac{0.1}{+3} + \frac{0.4}{+4} + \frac{0.8}{+5} + \frac{1.0}{+6}; \qquad PM = \frac{0.2}{+2} + \frac{0.7}{+3} + \frac{1.0}{+4} + \frac{0.7}{+5} + \frac{0.2}{+6};$$

$$PS = \frac{0.3}{0} + \frac{0.8}{+1} + \frac{1.0}{+2} + \frac{0.5}{+3} + \frac{0.1}{+4}; \qquad NO = \frac{0.1}{-2} + \frac{0.6}{-1} + \frac{1.0}{0} + \frac{0.6}{+1} + \frac{0.1}{+2}.$$

Meanwhile, for CPE, the membership functions of PB, PM, PS and NO are obtained as follows, respectively :

$$PB = \frac{0.1}{+3} + \frac{0.4}{+4} + \frac{0.8}{+5} + \frac{1.0}{+6}; \quad PM = \frac{0.2}{+2} + \frac{0.7}{+3} + \frac{1.0}{+4} + \frac{0.7}{+5} + \frac{0.2}{+6};$$

$$PS = \frac{0.9}{+1} + \frac{1.0}{+2} + \frac{0.7}{+3} + \frac{0.2}{+4}; \quad NO = \frac{0.5}{-1} + \frac{1.0}{0} + \frac{0.5}{+1}.$$

Similarly, The terms of generalized linguistic variable HC are quantized into 15 points ranging from a change of -7 steps through 0 to $+7$ steps.

To be similar to the above situation, one can get the membership functions of the generalized fuzzy sets NB, NM, NS and NO are as follows, respectively:

$$NB = \frac{0.1}{-4} + \frac{0.4}{-5} + \frac{0.8}{-6} + \frac{1.0}{-7}; \qquad NM = \frac{0.2}{-6} + \frac{0.7}{-5} + \frac{1.0}{-4} + \frac{0.7}{-3} + \frac{0.2}{-2};$$

$$NS = \frac{0.1}{-4} + \frac{0.4}{-3} + \frac{0.8}{-2} + \frac{1.0}{-1} + \frac{0.4}{0}; NO = \frac{0.2}{-1} + \frac{1.0}{0} + \frac{0.2}{+1}.$$

By the definition of the generalized fuzzy sets GFScom, we firstly map the universe of discourse as a finite numerical district. We can take the identity mapping as the finite quantized district mapping f because the domain is $D_{PE} = \{-6, -5, -4, \cdots, +4, +5, +6\}$. On the district D_{PE}, NB can be viewed as the opposite negation of PB, one can easily get NB, NM and NS with the following membership functions by definition of GFScom as follows:

$$NB = \frac{1.0}{-6} + \frac{0.8}{-5} + \frac{0.4}{-4} + \frac{0.1}{-3}; \qquad NM = \frac{0.2}{-2} + \frac{0.7}{-3} + \frac{1.0}{-4} + \frac{0.7}{-5} + \frac{0.2}{-6};$$

$$NS = \frac{0.3}{0} + \frac{0.8}{-1} + \frac{1.0}{-2} + \frac{0.5}{-3} + \frac{0.1}{-4}.$$

So far, we have calculated all the membership functions of fuzzy subsets of generalized linguistic variable PE as shown in Table 2.

Table 2. Relating fuzzy subsets to quantized terms of PE.

	-6	-5	-4	-3	-2	-1	0	+1	+2	+3	+4	+5	+6
PB	0	0	0	0	0	0	0	0	0	0.1	0.4	0.8	1.0
PM	0	0	0	0	0	0	0	0	0.2	0.7	1.0	0.7	0.2
PS	0	0	0	0	0	0	0.3	0.8	1.0	0.5	0.1	0	0
NO	0	0	0	0	0.1	0.6	1.0	0.6	0.1	0	0	0	0
NS	0	0	0.1	0.5	1.0	0.8	0.3	0	0	0	0	0	0
NM	0.2	0.7	1.0	0.7	0.2	0	0	0	0	0	0	0	0
NB	1.0	0.8	0.4	0.1	0	0	0	0	0	0	0	0	0

According to the practical operating experience, we assume a reasonable rule in the above pressure system is as follows:

If $PE = NO$ and $CPE = NS$ then $HC = NM$

Ask: "If $PE = slightly\ NO$ and $CPE = very\ NS$, then what HC is?"

One can do the approximate (plausible) reasoning by using the above Zhang controller and compositional rule of inference (CRI). The computing procedure is the following:

First, for simplicity, we use $\Delta_P, \Delta_C, \Delta_H$ to represent the values of PE, CPE and HC, respectively, where the symbol Δ belongs to $\{PB, PM, PS, NO, NS, NM, NB\}$. Identifying "and" with the intersection, "slightly" with the dilation such that $p = 0.5$, "very" with the concentration with $p = 2$ (see Ref. [8] for the dilation and concentration operator), NS with the "$PS^{\lrcorner}$", we can compute the degrees of match of the above two fuzzy rule as, respectively,

$$\alpha = (NO_p) \cap PS_C^{\lrcorner} = \frac{0.1}{-2} + \frac{0.6}{-1}; \alpha^* = (NO_p)^{0.5} \cap (PS_C^{\lrcorner})^2 = \frac{0.316}{-2} + \frac{0.775}{-1}.$$

Second, the above-given fuzzy rule defines a triple-tuple fuzzy relationship $R(a, b, c) \subseteq D_{PE} \times D_{CPE} \times D_{HC}$, where $D_{PE} = D_{CPE} = \{-6, -5, -4, \cdots, +4, +5, +6\}$ and $D_{HC} = \{-7, -6, -5, \cdots, +5, +6, +7\}$, called also fuzzy implication relationship. In this application, we evaluate the above-given fuzzy implication relationship using the Mamdani implication operator, i.e. minimum operator. By the compositional rule of inference CRI, using the max-min composition we will obtain the result as follows:

$$\beta^* = \frac{0.2}{-6} + \frac{0.6}{-5} + \frac{0.6}{-4} + \frac{0.6}{-3} + \frac{0.2}{-2} \approx fairly\ NM_H.$$

Before an appropriate defuzzification procedure is chosen, the computational core of the control action can be described as a three-steps process consisting of:

1) determination of the degree of membership of the input in the rule-antecedent,

2) computation of the rule consequences by using the compositional rule of inference, and

3) aggregation of rule consequences to the fuzzy set control action

To be similar with the traditional Mamdani controller, the Zhang controller also requires defuzzification methods, such as "extreme value strategies", "center of area", "center of gravity", etc. The reader is referred to Ref. [8] listed below where they are discussed in detail.

5. Conclusion

We present a generalized linguistic variable which is viewed as the extension of the linguistic variable proposed by Zadeh. Subsequently, we have defined a novel type of generalized fuzzy sets with contradictory, opposite and medium negation GFScom, and studied the properties and convexity and concavity of GFScom. A new type of fuzzy controller is proposed by using GFScom to the Mamdani controller. A simple demonstration in the simplified pressure system shows that GFScom not only sketches the relationships between fuzzy knowledge and its three sorts of negation effectively, but also makes the fuzzy reasoning capability of fuzzy system much richer.

Acknowledgments

This work is supported by the Guizhou Provincial Science and Technology Foundation, Grant No. 1458 [2019].

References

[1] G. Wagner, *Web Rules Need Two Kinds of Negation*, in *Principles and Practice of Semantic Web Reasoning*, eds. F. Bry, N. Henze and J. Maluszynski, LNCS, Vol. 2901 (Springer, Berlin, Heidelberg, 2003), pp. 33–55.

[2] S. Ferré, *Negation, Opposition, and Possibility in Logical Concept Analysis*, in *Formal Concept Analysis*, eds. B. Ganter and L. Kwuida, LNAI, Vol. 3874 (Springer Berlin Heidelberg, 2006), pp. 130–145.

[3] K. Kaneiwa, Description logics with contraries, contradictories, and subcontraries, *New Generation Computing* **25**, 443 (2007).

[4] Z.H. Pan, Three kinds of fuzzy knowledge and their base of set, *Chinese Journal of Computers* **35**, 1421 (2012).

[5] S. Zhang and Y. Li, Algebraic representation of negative knowledge and its application to design of fuzzy systems, *Chinese Journal of Computers* **39**, 2527 (2016).

[6] C. Torres-Blanc, S. Cubillo and P. Hernández-Varela, New negations on the membership functions of type-2 fuzzy sets, *IEEE T. Fuzzy Syst.*

[7] J.L. Speranza and L.R. Horn, A brief history of negation, *Journal of Applied Logic* **8**, 277 (2010).

[8] Y.M. Li, *Analysis of Fuzzy System* (Science Press, Beijing, China, 2005).

[9] E. Bas and E. Egrioglu, A fuzzy regression functions approach based on gustafson-kessel clustering algorithm, *Inf. Sci.* **592**, 206 (2022).

[10] S.L. Zhang and Y.M. Li, A novel table look-up scheme based on gfscom and its application, *Soft Comput.* **21**, 6767 (2017).

[11] E.P. Klement, R. Mesiar and E. Pap, *Triangular Norms* (Springer, Dordrecht, Netherlands, 2000).

Part 2

Multi Agent Systems, Neural Networks and Image Analysis

Modeling and analysis of networked discrete event systems by Petri nets[*]

Ke Wu, Zhipeng Zhang[†] and Chengyi Xia[‡]

School of Computer Science and Engineering
Tianjin University of Technology
Tianjin, 300384, China
[†] *zpzhang19@126.com*
[‡] *xialooking@163.com*

With the development of communication technology, modeling and analysis of Petri nets(PN) with network environment have attracted the attention of researchers. This paper investigates the impact of event delay on the modeling and analysis of Petri nets with the help of semi-tensor product(STP). Firstly, Petri nets with fixed-step event delay is expressed by an algebraic form. Subsequently, networked reversibility is proposed for bounded Petri nets with fixed-step event delay, and its necessary and sufficient conditions are given by a matrix condition. Finally, an example is given to verify the validity of the theoretical results.

Keywords: Semi-tensor product; event-delay; reversibility; networked systems.

1. Introduction

Petri nets is a graphical modeling tool with strong mathematical theory support and complete graphical analysis technology, so it is widely used in the field of discrete event systems.[1–3] At the same time, because it can achieve a simple and clear expression for describing and controlling conflicts, synchronization, concurrency, random and uncertain behaviors generated within large and complex systems.[4–7] Therefore, it has received widespread attention from scholars in the field of computer and control. With the development of Petri nets, it is found that the delays[8] factor is unavoidable in the actual production process. The Petri net with time delays defines a mapping from the transition set to a certain time delays

---

[*]This project was partially funded by the National Natural Science Foundation of China under Grant Nos. 62173247 and 62203328, the Tianjin Natural Science Foundation of China Grant No. 21JCQNJC00840, and the Tianjin Research Innovation Project for Postgraduate Students under Grant No. 2021YJSB251.

set, and can be mainly divided into two categories: Time Petir net (TPN)[9] and Timed Petri net (TdPN).[10,11]

Inspired by the temporal Petri nets system, we consider another time factor: event delay, and investigate the impact of event delay on the modeling and analysis of Petri nets. Besides, an accurate mathematical model, semi-tensor product of matrices proposed by Cheng,[12] is introduced. It has been applied to many fields including finite automata,[13,14] Boolean networks,[15] game theory, Petri nets,[16] etc. This paper mainly studies the modeling and analysis of Petri nets with event delay by use of semi-tensor product. Firstly, Petri nets with fixed-step event delay is expressed by an algebraic form by combining the relationship between the adjacency matrix and the event delay. Secondly, networked reversibility is proposed for bounded Petri nets with fixed-step event delay, and the necessary and sufficient condition for determining its reversibility is also given by a matrix approach.

The remaining sections of this work can be arranged as follows. Section 2 briefly introduces the preliminary knowledge to be used in this article, including some key symbols, the semi-tensor product and some basic concepts of Petri nets. Section 3 establishes the algebraic model of Petri nets with fix event delay, and gives the necessary and sufficient condition to verify its reversibility. After that, Section 4 gives an example to demonstrate the effectiveness of the results. Finally, in Section 5, we put forward the conclusion and give the research direction in the future.

2. Preliminaries

2.1. *Notations*

$\mathcal{B}_{m \times n}$ is the set of Boolean matrices. $\mathbb{N}^+$ is the integer set, and $\mathbb{N}^n = \{a | a = (a_1, \ldots, a_n)^T, a_i \in \mathbb{N}, i \in (1, \ldots, n)\}$. $\mathcal{A}_{(i,j)}$ stands for the (i,j)-element of matrix $\mathcal{A}$. $Col_i(\mathcal{A})$ is termed as the i-th column of $\mathcal{A}$. δ_n^k is the k-th column of the identity matrix I_n, where $1 \leq k \leq n$, and $\Delta_n = [\delta_n^1, \delta_n^2, \ldots, \delta_n^n]$.

2.2. *Semi-tensor product of matrices*

This subsection introduces the basics about matrix semi-tensor products briefly.[17]

Definition 1.[17] Given $X_1 \in \mathcal{B}_{m \times n}$ and $X_2 \in \mathcal{B}_{p \times q}$, these Boolean STP can be defined by

$$X_1 \ltimes_\mathcal{B} X_2 = (X_1 \otimes_\mathcal{B} I_{r/n})(X_2 \otimes_\mathcal{B} I_{r/p}), \tag{1}$$

where $r = lcm(n, p)$ denotes the least common multiple, and $\otimes_\mathcal{B}$ is the Boolean Kronecker product.

Definition 2.[17] Denote by $W_{[a,b]} \in \mathcal{B}_{ab \times ab}$ the swap matrix, and it is defined by

$$
\begin{aligned}
W_{[a,b]} = \delta_{ab} \, [&1, a+1, b, (a-1) \, b+1, 2, \\
&a+2, \ldots, (b-1) \, a+2, \ldots, a, 2a, \ldots, ba] \, .
\end{aligned} \tag{2}
$$

2.3. Petri nets

A PN graph can be defined as a four-tuple $N = \{P, T, F, W\}$, where $P = \{p_1, p_2, \ldots, p_n\}$, and p_i is a place; $T = \{t_1, t_2, \ldots, t_m\}$, and t_j is a transitions, and $P \cap T = \phi$, $P \cup T \neq \phi$; $F \subseteq (P \times T) \cup (T \times P)$ represents the set of arc relations; W denotes the corresponding weight function; $M : P \to \mathbb{N}^n$ is a marking vector that assigns a non-negative integer number of tokens to each place. The Petri nets with M_1 (initial state) is called the Petri nets system (PNs).

Without losing generality, the work only discusses ordinary Petri nets. That is, the weight function W on the arc is one, and it can be abbreviated as $N = \{P, T, F\}$.

Definition 3. A net system $PNs = (P, T, F, M)$ is an marking net, and its transition firing rule can be defined as follows.

(1) Denoted by $M[t >$ the transition t which is enabled at the state M,

(2) For the state M, the transition t can fire, and a new state M' is obtained from the transition t (denoted by $M[t > M')$,

$$
M'(p) = \begin{cases} M(p) - 1, \, p \in {}^\bullet t - t^\bullet \\ M(p) + 1, \, p \in t^\bullet - {}^\bullet t \\ \quad M(p), \quad otherwise \end{cases} \tag{3}
$$

The reachability of Petri nets is important in the analysis and control of systems and can be easily represented in an algebraic form. The reachable set $R(N, M_1)$ from the the initial state M_1 can be represented as

$$R(N, M_1) = \{M \in \mathbb{R}^n \mid \exists \lambda \in T^* : M_1[\lambda > M\}, \tag{4}$$

where the $\lambda = t_1 t_2 \cdots t_k \in T^*$ is a transition sequence. In addition, a Petri nets system is said to be bounded if all places in PNs are bounded.

3. Model and Results

This part mainly studies the effect of event delay on bounded Petri nets system, and gives its algebraic expression. At the same time, reversibility of bounded Petri nets are analyzed.

3.1. *Petri nets with fixed-step event delay*

Firstly, a Petri nets with a fixed-step event delay is denoted by $N_{wed} = (P, T, F, ed)$, where ed represents the fixed-step event delay, and its state set Δ_s and transition set Δ_m can be represented as follows, respectively.

$$\Delta_s = \left\{ \delta_s^1, \delta_s^2, \ldots, \delta_s^s \right\}, \tag{5}$$

$$\Delta_m = \left\{ \delta_m^1, \delta_m^2, \ldots, \delta_m^m \right\}. \tag{6}$$

Recall the result in Ref. 16, the authors proposed the state evolution equation for bounded Petri nets without event delay, and it can be expressed as

$$x(k+1) = \mathcal{L} \ltimes_{\mathcal{B}} u(k) \ltimes_{\mathcal{B}} x(k), \tag{7}$$

where $x(k)$ represents the marking states at time t from the initial state $x(1) = M_1$, $u(k)$ denotes the transitions at time t, and $\mathcal{L} \in \mathcal{A}_{s \times sm}$ is the transition state structure matrix. Obviously, the transition state structure matrix $\mathcal{L} \in \mathcal{B}_{n \times mn}$ can be divided into m squares, i.e., $\mathcal{L} = [Blk_1(\mathcal{L}), Blk_2(\mathcal{L}), \ldots, Blk_m(\mathcal{L})]$, where $Blk_i(\mathcal{L})$ is the i-th $n \times n$ square block of $\mathcal{L}$.

Next, the following theorem shows that Petri nets with fixed-step event delay can be expressed by an algebraic form.

Theorem 1. *Given a bounded Petri nets system $PN_{wed}s$ with event delay, such that*

$$x^{ed}(k+1) = D^{ed} \ltimes_{\mathcal{B}} x(k+1), \tag{8}$$

where $D = (B) \sum_{i=1}^{m} Blk_i(\mathcal{L})$ is the transition state adjacency matrix.

Proof. For the convenience to illustrate the proof process, denoted by ∂^d the index of n-dimensional vector. That is, $\varepsilon^d \in \partial^d$ if $Row_{\varepsilon_j^d}(x^d(k+1)) = 1$.
When $d = 0$,

$$x^0(k+1) = x(k+1). \tag{9}$$

It is assumed that when $d = ed - 1$,

$$x^{ed}(k+1) = D^{ed-1} \ltimes_{\mathcal{B}} x(k+1), \tag{10}$$

and the index of $x^{ed-1}(k+1)$ is ∂^{ed-1}. Then, when $d = ed$,

$$D \ltimes_{\mathcal{B}} x^{ed-1}(k+1) = (\mathcal{B}) \sum_{i \in \partial^{ed-1}} Col_i(D) = x^{ed}(k+1). \qquad (11)$$

Next, the formula can be derived as follows.

$$\begin{aligned}
x^{ed}(k+1) &= D \ltimes_{\mathcal{B}} x^{ed-1}(k+1) \\
&= D \ltimes_{\mathcal{B}} D^{ed-1} \ltimes_{\mathcal{B}} x(k+1) \\
&= D^{ed} \ltimes_{\mathcal{B}} x(k+1) \qquad (12)
\end{aligned}$$

The result can be proved. $\qquad\qquad\qquad\qquad\qquad\qquad\qquad\qquad\qquad$ $\square$

We define $R^{ed}(N_{wed}, M_1)$ to be the set of reachable states of PN_{wed} at the fixed ed-step event delay, and naturally, $R_t^{ed}(N_{wed}, M_1)$ can represent the set of reachable states within t steps. Thus, we consider the reversibility of Petri nets with event delay in the next subsection.

3.2. The reversibility of PN_{wed}

In this subsection, we give the definition of networked reversibility, and establish the necessary and sufficient condition for determining the reversibility.

Definition 4. Given a Petri nets system PN_{wed}, $M \in R^{ed}(N_{wed}, M_1)$. If $\forall M' \in R^{ed}(N_{wed}, M)$, satisfy $M \in R^{ed}(N_{wed}, M')$, then M is said to be a returnable identifier or a home state of PN_{wed}; If the initial state M_1 of PN_{wed} is a home state, then PN_{wed} is said to be networked-reversible.

According to the definition of reversibility, we give the necessary and sufficient condition as follows.

Theorem 2. PN_{wed} is networked-reversible if and only if there is $t_{ab} \in \mathbb{N}^+$ exists for any $M_a = \delta_s^a$, $M_b = \delta_s^b$, such that

$$\delta_s^a \in \bigcup_{t_{ab}=1}^{s} \left\{ \bigcup_{\alpha=1}^{m^{t_{ab}}} \Theta(Col_\alpha(D^{ed} \ltimes_{\mathcal{B}} ((\mathcal{L}W_{[s,m]})^{t_{ab}} \delta_s^b))) \right\}. \qquad (13)$$

where for any nonzero Boolean vector $\lambda \in \mathcal{B}_{s \times 1}$, $\Theta(\lambda) = \{\mu \in \Delta_s | \mu \wedge \lambda = \mu\}$.

Proof. According to the state evolution equation, the state M_a is reachable from the state M_b through t_{ab} steps under the event delay of ed-steps $\Leftrightarrow$ $\delta_s^a \in \{\Theta(D^{ed} \ltimes_{\mathcal{B}} ((\mathcal{L}W_{[s,m]})^{t_{ab}} \delta_s^b) \delta_{m^{t_{ab}}}^x)\}$, $\delta_{m^{t_{ab}}}^x$ is the fire sequence, that is

$$\delta_s^a \in \bigcup_{t_{ab}=1}^{s} \left\{ \bigcup_{\alpha=1}^{m^{t_{ab}}} \Theta(Col_\alpha(D^{ed} \ltimes_{\mathcal{B}} ((\mathcal{L}W_{[s,m]})^{t_{ab}} \delta_s^b))) \right\}.$$

And, any two states M_a and M_b in $PN_{wed}s$ are mutually reachable $\Leftrightarrow$ there is $t_{ab} \in \mathbb{N}^+$, so that

$$\delta_s^a \in R^{ed}(N_{wed}, M_b).$$

It can be obtained that any two states in $PN_{wed}s$ are mutually reachable, that is, $PN_{wed}s$ is reversible $\Leftrightarrow$ there is $t_{ab} \in \mathbb{N}^+$, so that

$$\delta_s^a \in \bigcup_{t_{ab}=1}^{s} \left\{ \bigcup_{\alpha=1}^{m^{t_{ab}}} \Theta(Col_\alpha(D^{ed} \ltimes_{\mathcal{B}} ((\mathcal{L}W_{[s,m]})^{t_{ab}} \delta_s^b))) \right\}.$$

$\square$

4. An Illustrative Example

This section takes a simple example to illustrate the proposed results.

Example 4.1. Given a Petri net with event delay $N_{wed} = \{P, T, F, ed\}$, where $P = \{p_1, p_2, p_3, p_4, p_5\}$, $T = \{t_1, t_2, t_3, t_4\}$, $R = \{M_1, M_2, M_3, M_4, M_5\}$. According to the semi-tensor product of matrices, $\Delta_5 = \{\delta_5^1, \delta_5^2, \ldots, \delta_5^5\}$, $\Delta_4 = \{\delta_4^1, \delta_4^2, \ldots, \delta_4^4\}$.

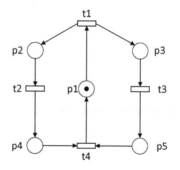

Fig. 1. N_{wed} of Example 1.

By analyzing Fig. 1, Fig. 2 and Table 1, it can be obtained that the transition state structure matrix $\mathcal{L}$ and the transition state adjacency matrix D are calculated in the following.

$$\mathcal{L} = \begin{bmatrix} 0\,0\,0\,0\,0\,0\,0\,0\,0\,0\,0\,0\,0\,0\,0\,0\,0\,0\,0\,1 \\ 1\,0\,0\,0\,0\,0\,0\,0\,0\,0\,0\,0\,0\,0\,0\,0\,0\,0\,0\,0 \\ 0\,0\,0\,0\,0\,0\,1\,0\,0\,0\,0\,0\,0\,0\,0\,0\,0\,0\,0\,0 \\ 0\,0\,0\,0\,0\,0\,0\,0\,0\,0\,0\,1\,0\,0\,0\,0\,0\,0\,0\,0 \\ 0\,0\,0\,0\,0\,0\,0\,0\,1\,0\,0\,0\,1\,0\,0\,0\,0\,0\,0\,0 \end{bmatrix} \tag{14}$$

We assume that the ed-step event delay $D^{ed} = D^2$.

$$D^2 = D \ltimes_{\mathcal{B}} D = \begin{bmatrix} 0\,0\,1\,1\,0 \\ 0\,0\,0\,0\,1 \\ 1\,0\,0\,0\,0 \\ 1\,0\,0\,0\,0 \\ 0\,1\,0\,0\,0 \end{bmatrix} \tag{15}$$

Suppose the initial state $M_1 = \delta_s^1$, we can get the reachable set $R^2(N_{wed}, M_1) = \{M_1, M_2, M_3, M_4, M_5\}$. By observing the calculation results, we know that any state in $R^2(N_{wed}, M_1)$ can reach M1. From the transitivity of reachability, it can be concluded that any two states in the system are mutually reachable.

5. Conclusion

This paper studies the modeling and analysis of a class of bounded Petri nets with fixed-step event delay by using algebraic state space methods. An algebraic representation of bounded Petri nets with fixed-step event delay is established. And based on the algebraic representation method, the necessary and sufficient conditions for networked reversibility is given. Finally, a simple example is given to verify the correctness of the conclusion. In the future, we will continue to analyze other basic properties and try to solve some problems in deadlock.

References

1. Z. Wu, Analysis and implementation of liveness and fairness of bounded petri nets, *Chinese Journal of Computers* 4, p. 003 (1989).
2. Wu Z, Introduction to petri nets, *Beijing, Press of Machinery and Industry*, 15 (2006).

3. C. Yuan, The principle and application of petri net, *Beijing: Publishing house of electronics industry*, 58 (2005).

4. T. Murata, Petri nets: Properties, analysis and applications, *Proceedings of the IEEE* **77**, 541 (1989).

5. R. David and H. Alla, Petri nets for modeling of dynamic systems: A survey, *Automatica* **30**, 175 (1994).

6. C. G. Cassandras, S. Lafortune *et al.*, *Introduction to discrete event systems* (Springer, 2008).

7. F. Wang, S. Shu and F. Lin, Robust networked control of discrete event systems, *IEEE Transactions on Automation Science and Engineering* **13**, 1528 (2016).

8. Z. Zhang, S. Shu and C. Xia, Networked opacity for finite state machine with bounded communication delays, *Information Sciences* **572**, 57 (2021).

9. P. M. Merlin, *A study of the recoverability of computing systems* (University of California, Irvine, 1974).

10. C. Ramchandani, Analysis of asynchronous concurrent systems by timed petri nets (1973).

11. Z. He, Z. Li and A. Giua, Optimization of deterministic timed weighted marked graphs, *IEEE Transactions on Automation Science and Engineering* **14**, 1084 (2015).

12. D. Cheng, H. Qi and Z. Li, *Analysis and control of Boolean networks: a semi-tensor product approach* (Springer Science & Business Media, 2010).

13. Q. Xu, Z. Zhang, Y. Yan and C. Xia, Security and privacy with k-step opacity for finite automata via a novel algebraic approach, *Transactions of the Institute of Measurement and Control* **43**, 3606 (2021).

14. K. Ren, Z. Zhang and C. Xia, I-detectability of networked discrete event systems by matrix approach, *International Journal of Control, Automation and Systems* **20**, 750 (2022).

15. D. Cheng and H. Qi, Controllability and observability of boolean control networks, *Automatica* **45**, 1659 (2009).

16. X. Han, Z. Chen, K. Zhang, Z. Liu and Q. Zhang, Modeling, reachability and controllability of bounded petri nets based on semi-tensor product of matrices, *Asian Journal of Control* **22**, 500 (2020).

17. D. Cheng, H. Qi and A. Xue, A survey on semi-tensor product of matrices, *Journal of Systems Science and Complexity* **20**, 304 (2007).

A model-free synchronization solution for linear discrete-time multi-agent systems based on A3C algorithm

Ye Li, Zhongxin Liu* and Zengqiang Chen

College of Artificial Intelligence, Nankai University, Tianjin 300350, China
* lzhx@nankai.edu.cn

This paper proposes a synchronization solution for model-free discrete-time leader-following systems based on the Asynchronous Advantage Actor-Critic (A3C) algorithm. The optimization object is a value function constructed by the consensus error. Furthermore, the multi-concurrency training method is applied to train the act net and the critic net, which are the nets responsible for generating optimal policies and estimating the value of the error-action pair. In this way, time-related data of the system is turned into independent and identically distributed data, ensuring the feasibility and speed of the algorithm. Finally, a simple simulation is provided to validate the efficiency of the proposed solution.

Keywords: Multi-agent systems; synchronization; reinforcement learning; asynchronous advantage actor-critic algorithm (A3C).

1. Introduction

With the development of computer science, multi-agent systems (MASs) have received more and more attention. Compared to a single agent, the MASs can work jointly and have better environmental awareness, allowing it to complete more complex tasks. In recent years, the MASs technology has been used in various applications such as drone formation,[1] intelligent transportation,[1] and robotics.[2]

Since the synchronization problem is one of the basic problems for MASs technologies, the related issues have been widely studied. It can be divided into leaderless MASs synchronization problem and the leader-following MASs synchronization problem, the former requires the agents eventually reach the same uncertain state, and the latter requires the states of the following agents be the same with the leader. Considering various possible situations in real applications, a lot of work such as fault-tolerant control,[3] synchronization problems for heterogeneous situations, formation control, etc. are also carried out. With the deepening of the research on this problem, more performances indicators need to be satisfied, and this is the optimal synchronization problem. From continuous-time MASs to discrete-time MASs,[4] from leader-following MASs to leaderless MASs,[3] and from homogeneous MASs to heterogeneous MASs,[5] a variety of results have been obtained. However, all the above results are model-based methods, when the models are unknown, we have to estimate the models or design complex observers, and these jobs are complex and time-consuming.

Reinforcement learning (RL) is a kind of methods that can gain experience and achieve optimal control by interacting with the environment. Different from supervised learning methods, the RL methods don't need to prepare datasets with labels in advance, so it is a good way to solve the optimal control problems. In 2009, the RL methods were used to calculate the controllers for continuous-time systems.[6] In 2014, the integral reinforcement learning (IRL) method is proposed to solve optimal control problems for linear or nonlinear systems with partially unknown models.[7] Recently, Li et al. proposed a Q-learning based method to generate the synchronization controller for model-free discrete-time leader-following MASs.[8] However, the above methods can't solve the dimensional explosion problem when the number of agents increases.

In this paper, a novel model-free synchronization solution based on A3C is proposed, and the main contributions are as follows: 1) The dimension extension problem has been solved. The action space and the error-action space are all fitted by neural networks, which avoid high-dimensional matrix calculations and time-consuming policy search processes. 2) The parallel training method is used. In this way, the time-related data generated by MASs are scrambled, and turns into independent and identically distributed data, while speeding up the training process. 3) The proposed method is highly flexible and strongly robust. Many parameters can be adjusted to meet different performances requirements such as control accuracy, synchronization time, etc. Besides, when the system properties change due to temperature, pressure, aging, etc. the controller can adjust the control strategy in real time to achieve optimal control.

The structure of this paper is as follows: In Section 2, some basic knowledge about MASs is introduced, then in Section 3, the A3C based controller is constructed. In Section 4, a simple simulation example is given to show the effectiveness of the proposed solution.

Notations: In this paper, matrix I_n is the $n \times n$ dimensional identity matrix. $\delta_{\min}(\cdot)$ is the function to find the minimum eigenvalue of a matrix. The $L_2 - norm$ of the vector s is defined as $||s||$.

2. Problem Statement

2.1. *Algebraic graph theory*

The topological network for a discrete-time leader-following MASs can be represented as a diagraph $G = (V, E, A)$, where $V = \{v_1, v_2, \ldots, v_n\}$ is the node set with N agents, $E = \{(i, j) \in V \times V\}$ represented the edge set, and $\mathbb{N} = \{1, 2, 3, \ldots, N\}$ is the subscript set. $A = \{a_{ij} \in R^{n \times n} \mid i, j \in \mathbb{N}\}$ is the non-negative adjacency matrix, which contains the communication information between agents. If agent i can receive information from agent j, then $a_{ij} > 0$, otherwise $a_{ij} = 0$. Note that the topologies considered in this paper are simple graphs, so $a_{ii} = 0$, $\forall i, j \in \mathbb{N}$. Then the neighbor information can be represented as $N_i = \{j \mid v_j : (v_j, v_i) \in E, a_{ij} \neq 0\}$. The in-degree of each agent i can be defined as $d_{in}(v_i) = \sum_{j=1}^{n} a_{ij}$, and the in-degree matrix of the system is $D = diag\{d_{in}(v_i) \mid i = 1, 2, 3, \ldots, n\}$. The laplace matrix of the system is defined as $L = D - A$. The connecting matrix between following agents and leader agent is defined as $F = diag\{f_i \mid i = 1, 2, 3, \ldots, n\}$, if the following agent can receive the information from the leader agent i, then $f_i > 0$, otherwise $f_i = 0$.

2.2. *Optimal synchronization problem for leader-following system*

Considering a discrete-time leader-following MASs with $N + 1$ agents, the dynamical equations are as follows:

$$\begin{cases} x_i(k + 1) = Ax_i(k) + Bu_i(k), i \in \mathbb{N} \\ x_0(k + 1) = Ax_0(k) \end{cases}, \tag{1}$$

where $A \in \mathbb{R}^{n \times n}$ and $B \in \mathbb{R}^{n \times m}$ are the coefficient matrices, $u_i \in \mathbb{R}^m$ is the control input, $x_i \in \mathbb{R}^n$ is the states of the following agents, and $x_0 \in \mathbb{R}^n$ is the state of the leader agent. The goal is for all of the agents to have the same state as the leader:

$$\lim_{k \to \infty} ||x_i(k) - x_0(k)|| = 0, \forall i \in \mathbb{N}. \tag{2}$$

And the tracking error is defined as:

$$\eta = x(k) - \bar{x}_0(k), \tag{3}$$

where $x(k) = [x_1^T(k), x_2^T(k), x_3^T(k), \ldots, x_1^T(k)]^T$, and $\bar{x}_0(k) = 1_N \otimes x_0(k)$. However, each agent in distributed MASs can only know the information from surrounding neighbors, so the consensus error is defined as follows:

$$\varepsilon_i(k) = \sum_{J \in N_i} a_{ij}(x_j(k) - x_i(k)) + f_i(x_0(k) - x_i(k)), \forall i \in \mathbb{N}, \tag{4}$$

that is:

$$\varepsilon(k) = -\left((L+F) \otimes I_n\right)x(k) + \left((L+F) \otimes I_n\right)\bar{x}_0(k). \qquad (5)$$

Lemma 2.1. [9] *If matrix $(L+F)$ is non-singular, then the tracking error η is bounded:*

$$\|\eta(k)\| \leq (\delta_{\min}(L+F))\|\varepsilon(k)\|. \qquad (6)$$

Remark 2.1. According to Lemma (2.1), the MASs synchronization can be achieved only by ensuring that the consensus error converges to 0.

If the model is known, the control policies can be designed as:[4]

$$u_i(k) = c(1 + d_i + f_i)^{-1}K\varepsilon_i(k), \qquad (7)$$

where c is the coupling gain, K is the feedback matrix, which can be designed according to model information. However, system modelling is a complex and time-consuming work in engineering, so data-driven model-free methods are urgently needed, and the proposed solution is one of this kind of method.

Assumption 2.1. *The MAS's matrices (A, B) are linear time-invariant and unknown.*

Assumption 2.2. *The topology graph G contains at least a directed spanning tree, and at least a following agent can communicate with the leader.*

Remark 2.2. If Assumption 2.2 is satisfied, the proposed method can achieve the goal of synchronization of the MAS (1). Besides, experiments show that the higher the degree of connectivity between the agents, the faster the synchronization will be achieved.

3. Synchronization Policies based on A3C

Since the state space and action space in MASs are high-dimensional data, BP neural networks are used to fit them to avoid the dimensionality disaster. Figure 1 shows the flowchart of the proposed solution, each part of it will be described separately below. First, a value function $Q(\varepsilon, a, \omega) = \phi(\varepsilon, a)^T \omega$ is designed to evaluate the value of error-action pair, and according to the idea of Temporal Difference Method,[8] the Temporal Difference error (TD error) is defined as follows:

$$\delta = r_{k+1} + \gamma Q(\varepsilon_{k+1}, A_{k+1}) - Q(\varepsilon_k, A_k), \qquad (8)$$

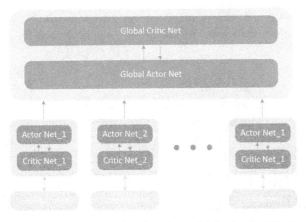

Fig. 1. The A3C based algorithm's flowchart in model-free leader-following MASs synchronization problem.

where $r_{k+1} = \varepsilon_{k+1}^T \cdot \varepsilon_{k+1}$ is the reward at step $k + 1$, γ is the discount factor. And the Mean Square Error (MSE) $L = \frac{1}{N}\delta^2$ is used as the update target for the value net $Q(\varepsilon, a, \omega)$. Thus it can be updated by the following equation:

$$\omega_{k+1} = \omega_k + \beta\delta\phi(\varepsilon_k, a_k), \tag{9}$$

where β is the learning rate.

The update aim of the actor net $\pi(\varepsilon, \theta) = \phi(\varepsilon)^T\theta$, also composed of the BP networks, is to generate policies that can maximize the value function $Q(\varepsilon, a, \omega)$:

$$J_{av}Q(\theta) = \sum_\varepsilon d^{\pi^\theta(\varepsilon)} \sum_a \pi_\theta(s)Q(\varepsilon, a, \omega), \tag{10}$$

where $d^{\pi^\theta(\varepsilon)}$ is the static distribution of the Markov chain generated by the policy π to the state s. Deriving this equation and approximating it with the Law of Large Numbers, we can get the following equation:

$$\nabla J(\theta) = E_{\pi(\theta)}\left[\nabla_\theta \log \pi_\theta(\varepsilon)Q_\pi(\varepsilon, a)\right]. \tag{11}$$

Besides, the Gaussian noise will be added to the output in order to sufficiently explore the action space:

$$a \sim N(\mu(\varepsilon), \sigma^2)$$
$$\nabla_\theta \log \pi_\theta(\varepsilon) = \frac{(a-\mu(\varepsilon))\phi(\varepsilon)}{\sigma^2}, \tag{12}$$

where $\mu(\varepsilon) = \phi(\varepsilon)^T \theta$, the variance can be used as a tunable parameter to control the exploration rate. So the update equation is as follows:

$$\theta_{k+1} = \theta_k + \alpha \nabla_\theta \log \pi_\theta(\varepsilon_k) \left(r_{k+1} + \gamma Q(\varepsilon_{k+1}, A_{k+1}) - Q(\varepsilon_k, A_k) \right), \quad (13)$$

where α is the learning rate.

Since the data in the MASs environment are time-related, direct training may cause nets convergence difficult. DQN uses the Replay Buffer to store data and randomly extracts training to solve it, but excess storage space is not friendly to edge devices. However, the agents in MASs can interact with the environment at the same time, so they will learn and update the controller together. On the one hand, the distributed training approach breaks the data's time-related properties; On the other hand, the training process is substantially accelerated, making it more efficient.

4. Simulation Result

Considering a time-invariant leader-following system with a leader and 5 following agents, the system matrices are as follows:

$$A = \begin{bmatrix} -3 & 1 \\ -2 & 1 \end{bmatrix}, \quad B = \begin{bmatrix} 1 \\ 0 \end{bmatrix}. \quad (14)$$

The communication topology is shown in Fig. 2. The communication matrix between the leader and following agents is $F = diag(1, 0, 0, 0, 0)$, and the Laplace matrix is as follows:

$$L = \begin{bmatrix} 0 & 0 & 0 & 0 & 0 \\ 0 & 1 & -1 & 0 & 0 \\ -1 & 0 & 2 & -1 & 0 \\ -1 & 0 & 0 & 2 & -1 \\ 0 & -1 & 0 & 0 & 1 \end{bmatrix}. \quad (15)$$

The learning curve is shown in Fig. 3. As we can see, the return is initially very low, then gradually increases until it reaches 0 after around 20 iterations. The system's returns fluctuated over that due to distributed learning, and eventually stabilized. The tracking error and consensus error are shown in Fig. 4 and Fig. 5, respectively, the error swings a lot in the first 20 steps, but gradually decreases, indicating that the policy can synchronize MASs over time. Then the states of each agent are shown in Fig. 6. After 20 steps, the following agents can oscillate synchronously with the leader, just like the tracking error and the consensus error. Finally, the energy

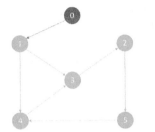

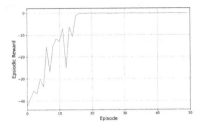

Fig. 2. The communication topology diagram of leader-following MASs.

Fig. 3. The learning curve of leader-following MASs.

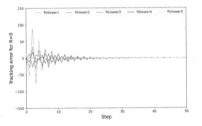

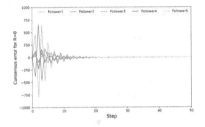

Fig. 4. The tracking error of leader-following MASs.

Fig. 5. The consensus error of leader-following MASs.

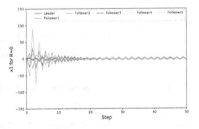

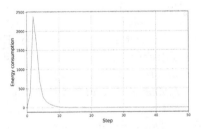

Fig. 6. The states of each agent in MASs.

Fig. 7. The energy consumption of leader-following MASs.

consumption is shown in Fig. 7. In the first 10 steps, the controller needs to consume more energy to synchronize the system. After that, the energy usage is drastically reduced.

5. Conclusion

In this paper, a data-driven model-free synchronization solution is proposed for leader-following MASs. Concurrent training is used, which significantly improves the training speed. Furthermore, while achieving synchronization, the proposed method can also minimize the energy consumption. Finally, a simple simulation is given to show the efficiency of this method. In the future, the model-free synchronization solution for continuous-time leader-following MASs will be considered based on reinforcement methods.

Acknowledgments

This work is supported by the Tianjin Natural Science Foundation of China (20JCYBJC01060), the National Natural Science Foundation of China (62103203, 61973175), and the Fundamental Research Funds for the Central Universities, Nankai University (63221218).

References

1. Y. Lai, R. Li, J. Shi and L. He, On the study of a multi-quadrotor formation control with triangular structure based on graph theory, *Control Theory Appl* **35**, 1530 (2018).
2. G. Dudek, M. R. Jenkin, E. Milios and D. Wilkes, A taxonomy for multi-agent robotics, *Autonomous Robots* **3**, 375 (1996).
3. M. Sader, Z. Liu, F. Wang and Z. Chen, Distributed robust fault-tolerant consensus tracking control for multi-agent systems with exogenous disturbances under switching topologies, *International Journal of Robust and Nonlinear Control* **32**, 1618 (2022).
4. K. Hengster-Movric, K. You, F. L. Lewis and L. Xie, Synchronization of discrete-time multi-agent systems on graphs using riccati design, *Automatica* **49**, 414 (2013).
5. Y. Zheng, Y. Zhu and L. Wang, Consensus of heterogeneous multi-agent systems, *IET Control Theory & Applications* **5**, 1881 (2011).
6. K. Doya, Reinforcement learning in continuous time and space, *Neural computation* **12**, 219 (2000).
7. H. Modares and F. L. Lewis, Optimal tracking control of nonlinear partially-unknown constrained-input systems using integral reinforcement learning, *Automatica* **50**, 1780 (2014).
8. Y. Li, F. Wang, Z. Liu and Z. Chen, Leader-follower optimal consensus of discrete-time linear multi-agent systems based on q-learning, *Proceedings of 2021 Chinese Intelligent Systems Conference*, 492 (2022).
9. M. I. Abouheaf, F. L. Lewis, K. G. Vamvoudakis, S. Haesaert and R. Babuska, Multi-agent discrete-time graphical games and reinforcement learning solutions, *Automatica* **50**, 3038 (2014).

Distributed cooperative SLAM with adaptive Kalman filter and dynamic consensus

Chengwang Yang and Linying Xiang*

Northeastern University at Qinhuangdao
Qinhuangdao 066004, China
*xianglinying@neuq.edu.cn

In this paper, we investigate the problem of multi-agent Simultaneous Localization and Mapping (SLAM). We introduce an adaptive extended Kalman filter (AEKF), which enables the agent to estimate the noise information of the environment in real time, thus obtaining an accurate local map. At the same time, each agent interacts with its neighbor agents to calculate the global map by using a distributed information filter. The simulation results show that the map fusion algorithm with AEKF has better stability and precision than the traditional methods.

Keywords: Multi-agent system; distributed cooperative SLAM; adaptive extended Kalman filter; dynamic consensus.

1. Introduction

Recently, the issue of cooperative SLAM problem gradually becomes hot research topic in the field of agent cognitive.[1-3] Multi-agent cooperative SLAM problem refers to the process in which multiple agents start from different locations in the same unknown environment, perceive the environment with sensors carried by themselves respectively, and analyze, synthesize and integrate the data from different information sources through the interaction between agents into a global map.[4] Then the agent team can use the global map to make decisions, such as collaborative exploration or task assignment.[5]

The most common method to solve SLAM is the Kalman filter (KF), and its accuracy in estimating the trajectory and feature distribution in a particular environment has been proved.[6] The Information filter, which is the dual form of KF, is an ideal choice for distributed information fusion because of its additive measurement property.[7] However, these methods are only used effectively in accurate system models and known noise statistics. These requirements can be faced in the simulation case.[8] The adaptive Kalman filter (AKF) is an effective method to solve the problem of unknown noise covariance matrices in agent positioning.[9] Recently, many AKFs such as the innovation based AKF (IAKF),[10] the variational Bayesian-based AKF (VBAKF),[11] and the residual-based AKF[12] have been proposed. However, this approach requires off-line measurements, so the unknown noise covariance matrices cannot be estimated online.

Motivated by the above discussions, a new adaptive extended Kalman filter (AEKF) is introduced to solve the SLAM problem. In the AEKF, the predicted error covariance matrix and measurement noise covariance matrix are estimated adaptively. The AEKF does not require a window of data because the predicted error covariance matrix instead of process noise covariance matrix is estimated, which makes it suitable for the case of unknown and time-varying noise covariance matrices so that the agent can use the AEKF to get more exact local map. In addition, the local convergence of iteration is guaranteed with the proposed AEKF.

2. Problem Formation

Consider a team of N agents exploring an unknown environment. There are M different static landmarks in the environment. Assume that agent i observes $M_{i,k}$ landmarks at step k. Then, the discrete-time state-space model of the system is given as

$$r_{i,k} = \begin{bmatrix} r_{i,k}^x \\ r_{i,k}^y \\ \theta_{i,k} \end{bmatrix} = f(r_{i,k-1}) + \omega_{i,k-1}$$

$$= \begin{bmatrix} r_{i,k-1}^x + \frac{\Delta D_{i,k}}{\Delta \theta_{i,k}} \left[\cos(\theta_{i,k-1} + \Delta\theta_{i,k}) - \cos\theta_{i,k-1}\right] \\ r_{i,k-1}^y + \frac{\Delta D_{i,k}}{\Delta \theta_{i,k}} \left[\sin(\theta_{i,k-1} + \Delta\theta_{i,k}) - \sin\theta_{i,k-1}\right] \\ \theta_{i,k} + \Delta\theta_{i,k} \end{bmatrix} + \omega_{i,k-1}, \quad (1)$$

$$z_{i,k} = \begin{bmatrix} \rho_{i,k} \\ \varphi_{i,k} \end{bmatrix} = h(r_{i,k}, l_{i,k}) + v_{i,k} = \begin{bmatrix} \sqrt{\left(r_{i,k}^x - l_{i,k}^x\right)^2 + \left(r_{i,k}^y - l_{i,k}^y\right)^2} \\ \arctan\frac{r_{i,k}^y - l_{i,k}^y}{r_{i,k}^x - l_{i,k}^x} - \theta_{i,k} \end{bmatrix} + v_{i,k},$$

$$(2)$$

$$l_{i,k}^{new} = g(r_{i,k}, z_{i,k}) + v_{i,k} = \begin{bmatrix} r_{i,k}^x + \rho_{i,k} * \cos(\varphi_{i,k} + \theta_{i,k}) \\ r_{i,k}^y + \rho_{i,k} * \sin(\varphi_{i,k} + \theta_{i,k}) \end{bmatrix} + v_{i,k}, \quad (3)$$

where $r_{i,k} \in \mathbb{R}^3$ is the state of agent i at step k with $r_{i,k}^x$ the x-coordinate of the state, $r_{i,k}^y$ the y-coordinate of the state, and $\theta_{i,k}$ the attitude angle of agent i. $f(\cdot)$ is the nonlinear state function, $\Delta D_{i,k}$ is the length of the arc that agent i traveled from step $k-1$ to k, and $\Delta\theta_{i,k}$ is the change of attitude angle of agent i in this interval. $z_{i,k}$ is the measurement of agent i, which includes the distance $\rho_{i,k}$ and angle $\varphi_{i,k}$ between agent i and the landmark. $l_{i,k}$ is the coordinate of the landmark that agent i has observed and $h(\cdot)$ is the nonlinear measurement function. $l_{i,k}^{new}$ is the coordinate of the new landmark that agent i observed and $g(\cdot)$ is the nonlinear function. $\omega_{i,k-1}$ is a zero mean noise with covariance matrix $Q_{i,k-1}$ and $\nu_{i,k}$ is also a zero mean noise with covariance matrix $R_{i,k}$. The noises are modeled as uncorrelated Gaussian noise, i.e., $\omega_{i,k-1} \sim N(0, Q_{i,k-1})$, $\nu_{i,k} \sim N(0, R_{i,k})$, and their cross-covariance is zero, that is $Cov[\omega_{i,k-1}, \nu_{i,k}{}^T] = \mathbf{0}$.

3. Distributed Map Fusion Algorithm

In this paper, our distributed nonlinear filtering algorithm is composed of an adaptive extend Kalman filter and a distributed information filter.

3.1. Adaptive extend Kalman filter for single-agent

Since the measurement equation is nonlinear and the noise statistic is unknown, we introduce the AEKF[9] to obtain noise adaptively. The local map of agent i at step k are represented as

$$\hat{m}_{i,k} = \begin{bmatrix} \hat{r}_{i,k} \\ \hat{l}_{i,k} \end{bmatrix}, \quad \hat{P}_{i,k} = \begin{bmatrix} \hat{P}_{i,k}^{rr} & \hat{P}_{i,k}^{rl} \\ \hat{P}_{i,k}^{lr} & \hat{P}_{i,k}^{ll} \end{bmatrix}, \tag{4}$$

where $\hat{m}_{i,k} \in \mathbb{R}^{2M_{i,k}+3}$ is the local map estimation and $\hat{P}_{i,k}$ is the corresponding covariance. $\hat{r}_{i,k} \in \mathbb{R}^3$ denotes the estimation of the state vector and $\hat{l}_{i,k} \in \mathbb{R}^{2M_{i,k}}$ denotes the estimation of all the $M_{i,k}$ landmarks. $\hat{P}_{i,k}^{rr} \in \mathbb{R}^{3\times3}$ is the covariance of agent's position and $\hat{P}_{i,k}^{rl} \in \mathbb{R}^{3\times2M_{i,k}}$ is the agent to landmark covariance. $\hat{P}_{i,k}^{lr} \in \mathbb{R}^{2M_{i,k}\times3}$ is the landmark to agent covariance and $\hat{P}_{i,k}^{ll} \in \mathbb{R}^{2M_{i,k}\times2M_{i,k}}$ is the covariance of landmarks.

The time update process of the AEKF is given by

$$\tilde{r}_{i,k-1} = F_{i,k}\hat{r}_{i,k-1} + u_{i,k}, \tag{5}$$

$$\tilde{l}_{i,k-1} = \hat{l}_{i,k-1}, \tag{6}$$

$$\tilde{P}_{i,k-1}^{rr} = F_{i,k}\hat{P}_{i,k-1}^{rr}(F_{i,k})^T + Q_{i,k-1}, \tag{7}$$

$$\tilde{P}_{i,k-1}^{rl} = F_{i,k}\hat{P}_{i,k-1}^{rl}, \tag{8}$$

$$\tilde{P}_{i,k-1}^{lr} = (\tilde{P}_{i,k-1}^{rl})^T, \tag{9}$$

$$\tilde{P}_{i,k-1}^{ll} = \hat{P}_{i,k-1}^{ll}, \tag{10}$$

where $\hat{r}_{i,k-1}$ and $\tilde{r}_{i,k-1}$ denote the estimation and prediction of the state vector, respectively. $\hat{l}_{i,k-1}$ and $\tilde{l}_{i,k-1}$ denote the estimation and prediction of the landmarks, respectively. $\tilde{P}_{i,k-1}^{rr}$ is the covariance prediction of agent's position and $\tilde{P}_{i,k-1}^{rl}$ is the agent to landmark covariance prediction. $\tilde{P}_{i,k-1}^{lr}$ is the landmark to agent covariance prediction and $\tilde{P}_{i,k-1}^{ll}$ is the covariance prediction of landmarks. $\hat{P}_{i,k-1}^{ll}$ is the covariance estimation of landmarks that agent i observes. $F_{i,k}$ denotes the Jacobian matrix of $f(\cdot)$ at $\hat{r}_{i,k-1}$.

The measurement update process of the AEKF formulates is given by

$$K_{i,k}^{(t+1)} = \tilde{P}_{i,k-1}^{(t)}(H_{i,k}^{(t)})^T[H_{i,k}^{(t)}\tilde{P}_{i,k-1}^{(t)}(H_{i,k}^{(t)})^T + \hat{R}_{i,k}^{(t)}]^{-1}, \tag{11}$$

$$\hat{m}_{i,k}^{(t+1)} = \tilde{m}_{i,k-1} + K_{i,k}^{(t+1)}[z_{i,k} - h(^{(t)}\hat{r}_{i,k}, l_{i,k})], \tag{12}$$

$$\hat{P}_{i,k}^{(t+1)} = \tilde{P}_{i,k-1}^{(t)} - K_{i,k}^{(t+1)}H_{i,k}^{(t)}\tilde{P}_{i,k-1}^{(t)}, \tag{13}$$

where $K_{i,k}^{(t+1)}$ is the Kalman gain after $t+1$ times of noise adaptive process. $\tilde{P}_{i,k-1}^{(t)}$ is the covariance prediction after t times of noise adaptive process and $\hat{R}_{i,k}^{(t)}$ is the covariance estimation of the measurement noise. $H_{i,k}^{(t)}$ denotes the Jacobian matrix of $h(\cdot)$ at $\tilde{r}_{i,k-1}^{(t)}$ and $l_{i,k}$.

The noise update process of the AEKF is given by

$$\hat{R}_{i,k}^{(t+1)} = H_{i,k}^{(t+1)}\hat{P}_{i,k}^{(t+1)}(H_{i,k}^{(t+1)})^T + \left[z_{i,k} - h(\hat{r}_{i,k}^{(t+1)}, l_{i,k})\right]\left[z_{i,k} - h(\hat{r}_{i,k}^{(t+1)}, l_{i,k})\right]^T,$$

$$\tilde{P}_{i,k-1}^{(t+1)} = \hat{P}_{i,k}^{(t+1)} + \left(\hat{m}_{i,k}^{(t+1)} - \tilde{m}_{i,k-1}\right)\left(\hat{m}_{i,k}^{(t+1)} - \tilde{m}_{i,k-1}\right)^T.$$

3.2. Distributed map fusion algorithm

Inspired by,[13] the designed distributed map fusion algorithm includes two steps, i.e., measurement update and space update for each iteration. (Measurement update)
If $k \in \mathcal{T}_i$, $d_{i,k} = d_{i,k-1} + 1$,

$$\hat{I}_{i,k_+} = (1 - 1/d_{i,k})\hat{I}_{i,k} + (H_{i,k}^l \times L_{i,k})^T\hat{R}_{i,k}(H_{i,k}^l \times L_{i,k})/d_{i,k},$$
$$\hat{i}_{i,k_+} = (1 - 1/d_{i,k})\hat{i}_{i,k} + (H_{i,k}^l \times L_{i,k})^T\hat{R}_{i,k}z_{i,k}/d_{i,k}, \tag{14}$$

otherwise, $d_{i,k} = d_{i,k-1}$,

$$\hat{I}_{i,k_+} = \hat{I}_{i,k}, \quad \hat{i}_{i,k_+} = \hat{i}_{i,k}, \tag{15}$$

where $d_{i,k}$ is the degree of agent i representing the times that agents acquired new measurements in their local maps, up to step k.
(Space update)
If $d_{i,k} > 0$,

$$\hat{I}_{i,k+1} = \hat{I}_{i,k_+} + \sum_{j \in \mathcal{N}_{i,k}} d_{j,k} \mathcal{W}_{ij}(\hat{I}_{j,k_+} - \hat{I}_{i,k_+}),$$

$$\hat{i}_{i,k+1} = \hat{i}_{i,k_+} + \sum_{j \in \mathcal{N}_{i,k}} d_{j,k} \mathcal{W}_{ij}(\hat{i}_{j,k_+} - \hat{i}_{i,k_+}),$$

(16)

where the weight matrix $\mathcal{W}_{ij} \in \mathbb{R}^{N \times N}$ is

$$\mathcal{W}_{ij} = \begin{cases} 1/max\{d_{i,k}^{st}, d_{j,k}^{st}\}, & (i,j) \in \mathcal{E}_k, \\ 1 - \sum_{j \in \mathcal{N}_{i,k}} \mathcal{W}_{ij}, & i = j, \\ 0, & otherwise, \end{cases}$$

(17)

with $d_{i,k}^{st}$ being the space-time degree, which contains the number of map changes propagated by both agent i and its neighbors up to step k:

$$d_{i,k}^{st} = d_{i,k} + \sum_{j \in \mathcal{N}_{i,k}} d_{j,k}.$$

The global estimations of agent i are given as

$$\hat{P}_{i,k}^{ll} = \left(\hat{I}_{i,k}\right)^{-1}, \quad \hat{l}_{i,k} = \left(\hat{I}_{i,k}\right)^{-1}\hat{i}_{i,k},$$

(18)

$$\hat{I}_{i,k}^G = d_k \times \hat{I}_{i,k}, \quad \hat{i}_{i,k}^G = d_k \times \hat{i}_{i,k},$$

(19)

where $d_k = \sum_{i=1}^N d_{i,k}$.

The global estimation $\hat{r}_{i,k}^G$ and $\hat{P}_{i,k}^{rr|G}$ within the covariance matrix $(Y_{central,0} + \sum_{i=1}^N \sum_{t=1}^k Y_{i,t})^{-1}$ can be obtained as follows:

$$\hat{r}_{i,k}^G = \hat{r}_{i,k} + \hat{P}_{i,k}^{rl}(\hat{P}_{i,k}^{ll})^{-1}(L_{i,k}\hat{l}_{i,k}^G - \hat{l}_{i,k}),$$

(20)

$$\hat{P}_{i,k}^{rr|G} = \hat{P}_{i,k}^{rl}(\hat{P}_{i,k}^{ll})^{-1}H_{i,k}^l\hat{P}_{i,k}^{ll}(H_{i,k}^l)^T(\hat{P}_{i,k}^{rl}(\hat{P}_{i,k}^{ll})^{-1})^T + \hat{P}_{i,k}^{rr} - \hat{P}_{i,k}^{rl}(\hat{P}_{i,k}^{ll})^{-1}\hat{P}_{i,k}^{lr}.$$

4. Stability Analysis

Theorem 4.1. *Assume that before agent i runs the proposed distributed map fusion algorithm, each agent has zero (prior) information about the undiscovered landmark, and all the information about the landmark comes from the agent's observations, and the agent transmits and updates its local* *map information $i_{i,k}$ such that $d_{i,k-1} > 0$. Then the local estimations of the features' positions $\hat{l}_{i,k}$ and the estimation of covariance $\hat{P}_{i,k}^{ll}$ in (18) satisfy*

$$E[\hat{l}_{i,k}] = E[\hat{l}^G], \quad \hat{P}_{i,k}^{ll} = \hat{P}_k^{ll|G} \times d_k,$$

where $\hat{l}^G$ and $\hat{P}_k^{ll|G}$ are the centralized estimations.

Proof of Theorem 1. According to (18) and (19), we have that

$$E[\hat{l}_{i,k}] = \left(\hat{I}_{i,k}\right)^{-1} \hat{i}_{i,k} = \left(\hat{I}_{i,k}^G\right)^{-1} \times \hat{i}_{i,k}^G, \quad \hat{P}_{i,k}^{ll} = \left(\hat{I}_{i,k}\right)^{-1} = \left(\hat{I}_{i,k}^G \Big/ d_k\right)^{-1}.$$

Then, using the convergence condition of distributed map merging algorithms, we have that

$$E[\hat{l}_{i,k}] = \left[\sum_{i=1}^{N} \sum_{k \in \mathcal{T}_i} (H_{i,k}^l \times L_{i,k})^T \hat{R}_{i,k} (H_{i,k}^l \times L_{i,k})\right]^{-1}$$

$$\times \left[\sum_{i=1}^{N} \sum_{k \in \mathcal{T}_i} (H_{i,k}^l \times L_{i,k})^T \hat{R}_{i,k} \times z_{i,k}\right]$$

$$= E[\hat{l}^G],$$

$$\hat{P}_{i,k}^{ll} = \left\{\sum_{i=1}^{N} \sum_{k \in \mathcal{T}_i} [(H_{i,k}^l \times L_{i,k})^T \hat{R}_{i,k} (H_{i,k}^l \times L_{i,k})]^{-1} / d_k\right\}^{-1}$$

$$= \hat{P}_k^{ll|G} \times d_k.$$

$\square$

5. Simulation Results

In order to test the performance of the proposed algorithm, we have performed Monte-Carlo simulations with 3 agents in a scenario with 36 features. The simulation schematic diagram is shown in Fig. 1.

There are three triangles in Fig. 1, which represent three agents, respectively. The red dot denotes the actual value of the landmarks, the blue triangle the pose estimation of *agent* 1, the cyan triangle the pose estimation of *agent* 2, and the black triangle the pose estimation of *agent* 3. The solid red triangle under the three different colors represents the actual position of each agent. The ellipse inside each agent triangle represents the covariance matrix of its position and pose information. The red "+" represents the real location information of the environment feature points, the blue "+" near *agent* 1 represents the estimated value of landmarks information of *agent* 1. The cyan "+" near *agent* 2 and the black "+" near

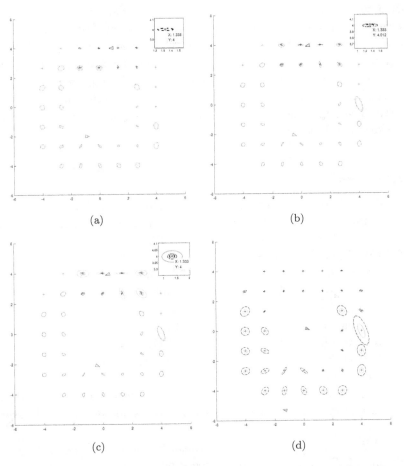

Fig. 1. The process of map fusion: (a) $k = 1$; (b) $k = 5$; (c) $k = 6$; (d) $k = 56$.

agent 3 represent the estimated value of landmarks information of *agent* 2
and *agent* 3, respectively. The green solid line, red dotted line and black
dotted line ellipse around the red "+" respectively belong to the covariance
matrix information of each agent's estimated value of landmarks information. It can be seen from Fig. 1 that all the agents have access to all 36
landmarks at $k = 56$.

6. Conclusion

In this paper, we have proposed a method for merging maps in a dynamic
way. We first use a new AEKF to solve the SLAM problem of a single

agent to obtain local maps when the process noise and measurement noise covariances in the multi-agent system are uncertain. Second, we use the distributed average tracking algorithm to fuse the local map and finally obtain the global map. Consensus is reached on the latest global map, using the map increments between the previous and the current time steps. In addition, the robustness and effectiveness of the method have been validated. The communication cost of our algorithm could be greatly improved by executing directed networks.

References

1. E. Nettleton, S. Thrun, H.F. Durrant-Whyte and S. Sukkarieh, Decentralised SLAM with low-bandwidth communication for teams of vehicles, *Field and Service Robotics* **24**, 179 (2006).
2. J.W. Fenwick, P.M. Newman and J.J. Leonard, Cooperative concurrent mapping and localization, in *Proceedings 2002 IEEE International Conference on Robotics and Automation*, 2002.
3. L. Marín, Á. Soriano, M. Vallés, Á. Valera and P. Albertos, Event based distributed Kalman filter for limited resource multirobot cooperative localization, *Asian Journal of Control* **21**, 1531 (2019).
4. A. Mourikis and S. Roumeliotis, Performance analysis of multirobot cooperative localization, *IEEE Transactions on Robotics* **22**, 666 (2006).
5. M. Bryson and S. Sukkarieh, Co-operative localisation and mapping for multiple UAVs in unknown environments, in *2007 IEEE Aerospace Conference*, 2007.
6. M.W.M.G. Dissanayake, P. Newman, S. Clark, H.F. Durrant-Whyte and M. Csorba, A solution to the simultaneous localization and map building (SLAM) problem, *IEEE Transactions on Robotics and Automation* **17**, 229 (2001).
7. P. Maybeck, *Stochastic Models, Estimation and Control* (Elsevier, 1979).
8. J.J. Leonard and H.F. Durrant-Whyte, *Directed Sonar Sensing for Mobile Robot Navigation* 1992.
9. Y.L. Huang, Y.G. Zhang, B. Xu, Z.M. Wu and J.A. Chambers, A new adaptive extended Kalman filter for cooperative localization, *IEEE Transactions on Aerospace and Electronic Systems* **54**, 353 (2018).
10. J.C. Fang and S. Yang, Study on innovation adaptive EKF for in-flight alignment of airborne POS, *IEEE Transactions on Instrumentation and Measurement* **60**, 1378 (2011).

11. S. Sarkka and A. Nummenmaa, Recursive noise adaptive Kalman filtering by variational Bayesian approximations, *IEEE Transactions on Automatic Control* **54**, 596 (2009).
12. M.J. Yu, INS/GPS integration system using adaptive filter for estimating measurement noise variance, *IEEE Transactions on Aerospace and Electronic Systems* **48**, 1786 (2012).
13. L. Xiao, S. Boyd and S. Lall, A space-time diffusion scheme for peer-to-peer least-square estimation, in *Proceedings of the Fifth International Conference on Information Processing in Sensor Networks*, 2006.

Learning competitive relationships with relative advantage enhanced with consumers' perspective: A heterogeneous network embedding method

Jinghui Zhang*, Qiang Wei and Guoqing Chen

School of Economics and Management, Tsinghua University
Beijing, 100084, China
zhangjh.18@sem.tsinghua.edu.cn

Competitive relationships analysis is of great importance in the fiercely competing ecommerce marketplace. Due to the large-quantity and high homogeneity of competitive products, it is challenging for merchants to customize marketing tactics to highlight its products' features with relative advantage to outperform others. This paper aims to design a machine learning method to analyze competitive relationships, including competitive entities identification and advantaged features detection. Specifically, this study incorporates an valuable data source reflecting consumers' perspective, i.e., online reviews, together with data source from merchants' perspective, i.e., the product descriptions, to capture the comprehensive competitive relationships on both product and feature levels. Furthermore, due to the multi-perspective of data sources, a heterogeneous network embedding method is developed. Data experiments and user experiments demonstrate the superiority of the proposed method.

Keywords: Competitive entity; competitive feature; relative advantage; heterogeneous network.

1. Introduction

A survey on e-commerce marketplace found that 84% of the merchants evaluated their market competition level as being very tough or tough.[†] Moreover, fiercer competition could be observed among products, e.g., given a search criteria or even in a segmented category, plenty of similar products might be listed to a consumer. Therefore, the merchants attempt to take advantage of the targeted marketing tactics, e.g., customizing their product descriptions, to help attract more consumers to stay ahead of the competition [1]. Nevertheless, there exist some major challenges.

---

*This work is supported by the National Key R&D Program of China (Grant No. 2020AAA0103801) and the National Natural Science Foundation of China (72172070).
[†]https://www.statista.com/statistics/1173855/evaluate-market-competition-ecommerce-companies-worldwide/

First, due to the large-quantity of similar products and limited marketing campaign cost, a merchant needs to accurately and agilely identify its top ranked competitive products/entities for effectively customizing the competitive tactics. Second, due to the high homogeneity in products as well as product descriptions, the competition focuses more on the granular feature level, e.g., one product might outperform a competitive product on some specific features, i.e., the competitive feature detection matters. Third, the locality and asymmetry of competition, i.e., also on feature level, makes it further challenging for a merchant to carefully detect and customize the competitive features with relative advantage, i.e., called advantaged features, with respect to different competitive entities. For instance, in the lipstick category with hundreds of homogeneous products, a middle-level lipstick might customize its targeted advertising, e.g., in description or snippet, by highlighting the "entry-lux" feature showing its relative advantage when displayed together with a low-price competitive product, but customizes a different campaign on promoting its "cost-effective" feature in competing a luxury one. Therefore, analyzing competitive relationships with relative advantage, including competitive entities identification and advantaged features detection, is of great importance to help merchants better understand the market competition and improve their marketing tactics.

Typically, the features in existing product descriptions are recognized and generated by merchants, i.e., called merchant-perspective features. The merchant-perspective features are crucial for competitive entities identification, since they reflect the primary functions and key characteristics of products, but they are little differentiated on homogenous products or even totally recognized by other merchants due to the exposure on marketplace. Therefore, they could hardly be used as advantaged features to distinguish a focal product to outperform its competitive entities.

In fact, consumers are the ultimate arbiters of competitive relationships in market [2], who assess similar products from their perspective, which may be quite different from merchants' perspective. Therefore, it is of great value to take advantage of information from consumers' perspective to facilitate competitive relationships analysis. Especially in the context that merchant-perspective features are quite similar, consumers may care more on some subjective feelings or subtle characteristics of products, which are not easily perceived by merchants. For the instance of a sub-category of lipsticks with almost the same merchant-perspective features, a lipstick is observed to outperform others because of a specific feature highlighted in its description, that is, "the warm berry-red shade matching well with coat", i.e., showing its relative advantage on the color-synesthesia, to better touch consumers in winter season. This type of tactic by highlighting the features reflecting consumers' perspective, i.e., called consumer-perspective features, seizes more and more attention. However, different from the merchant-perspective features that could be extracted from, e.g., existing product descriptions, new information source should be involved to extract the consumer-perspective features.

Therefore, incorporating the consumers' perspective together with merchants' perspective and conducting a granular analysis with relative advantage will benefit to capture the comprehensive competitive relationships (i.e., including competitive entities identification and advantaged features detection), which may further help merchants better customize and improve their targeted marketing tactics, in such a large-scaled competitive marketplace.

Recent studies on competitive relationships analysis have developed some intelligent methods on dealing with various information sources, e.g., utilizing predetermined linguistic patterns to detect the co-occurrence of entities in texts to identify potential competitors [3], detecting indirect associations based on similar features to identify competitive relationships [4, 5], etc. Nevertheless, existing methods have not well taken both merchants' perspective and consumers' perspective into a comprehensive consideration. In addition, so far we have found no literature on designing an intelligent solution on competitive relationships analysis from the relative advantage angle. To fill the research gap, this study aims to design a machine learning method to analyze competitive relationships, including competitive entities identification and advantaged features detection. Specifically, this study incorporates a data source reflecting consumers' perspective, i.e., online reviews, together with a data source from merchants' perspective, i.e., product descriptions, to capture the comprehensive competitive relationships. Furthermore, due to the multi-perspective of data sources, a heterogeneous network embedding solution is developed.

The rest of the paper is organized as follows. In Section 2, the technical details of the proposed method are introduced. Data and user experiments are discussed in Section 3. Final conclusions are presented in Section 4.

2. The Method

Considering the multi-perspective of product descriptions and online reviews, a heterogeneous network embedding model is constructed to depict the relationships of products, merchant-perspective features as well as consumer-perspective features. In addition, the products' co-occurrence in consumers' browsing data, e.g., "also-viewed" information, could be used as the ground-truth for facilitating the learning of products' competitive relationships.

Therefore, the representations of nodes in the model can be learnt through meta-path random walk and ranking learning. In doing so, the similarities between nodes are calculated to help identify competitive entities and detect advantaged features. The methodological framework is as shown in Fig. 1.

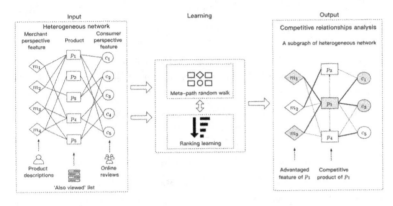

Fig. 1. The Framework of the Method.

Concretely, the heterogeneous network is defined as a graph $G = (V, E)$. V contains three types of nodes, including a set of products P, a set of merchant-perspective features M extracted from existing descriptions of P and a set of consumer-perspective features C extracted from online reviews of P. E contains two types of edges, i.e., E^{pm} with $p \in P$, $m \in M$ and E^{pc} with $p \in P$, $c \in C$, where e^{pm} in E^{pm} denotes that p has merchant-perspective feature m and e^{pc} in E^{pc} denotes that p has consumer-perspective feature c. In E^{pm}, the weight on edge e^{pm} is 1 if product p has feature m, otherwise 0. In E^{pc}, the weight of consumer-perspective feature of each product is calculated with TF-IDF.

Following the principle of Metapath2vec [8], two meta-paths are defined, i.e., "P-M-P" and "P-C-P", based on the tripartite graph, which means that products share the same features are more likely to be competing on these granular features. Thus, the heterogeneous random walks could be conducted on the predefined meta-paths to track the node sequences given the weight of the edges. Specifically, the Skip-Gram on the generated sequences is deployed to learn the representations of nodes. The objective is to maximize the conditional probability:

$$\arg\max_{\theta} P(v_{i-w}, \ldots, v_{i+w}|v_i; \theta) = \prod_{j=i-w, j \neq i}^{i+w} P(v_j|v_i; \theta), \quad (1)$$

where w is the length of the window. By incorporating negative sampling, the objectives based on the predefined meta-paths are then transformed to:

$$L_{pm} = \sum_{(i,j) \in E_{pm}} \left(\log \sigma \left(X_{v_j} \cdot X_{v_i} \right) + \sum_{t=1}^{N} log\sigma \left(-X_{v_t} \cdot X_{v_i} \right) \right), \quad (2)$$

$$L_{pc} = \sum_{(i,j) \in E_{pc}} \left(\log \sigma \left(X_{v_j} \cdot X_{v_i} \right) + \sum_{t=1}^{N} log\sigma \left(-X_{v_t} \cdot X_{v_i} \right) \right), \quad (3)$$

where $\sigma(x)$ is a sigmoid function, X_{v_i} is the embedding vector of v_i in the matrix X and v_t is sampled N times from $P(v)$, i.e., a pre-defined distribution.

Furthermore, for better analyzing competitive relationships, the co-occurrence of products in "also-viewed" is incorporated into learning as ground truth of competitive entities identification. However, due to the sparsity and noises in the data, a ranking learning treatment is designed to enhance the learning. Concretely, for a pair of product p_x and p_y, the competitive score can be defined as a dot production of their embedding vectors, i.e., $Comp_{xy} = X_{p_x} \cdot X_{p_y}$. With the "also-viewed" data, a basic fact can be found that, for a product p_x, if p_y is in p_x's "also-viewed" list while p_z is non-shown, then it could be expected that, $Comp_{xy} > Comp_{xz}$ may hold, which could be used as a ground truth label. Therefore, inspired by Bayesian Personalized Ranking [9], the probability considering the pairwise order $Comp_{xy} > Comp_{xz}$ given X can be defined as:

$$P \left(Comp_{xy} > Comp_{xz} \right) = \sigma \left(Comp_{xy} - Comp_{xz} \right). \quad (4)$$

Then, the ranking learning objective can be defined as follows:

$$O = \sum_{(p_x, p_y, p_z) \in D} ln\sigma \left(Comp_{xy} - Comp_{xz} \right), \quad (5)$$

where D is a set of triplets from P, and p_x is a focal product, p_y is the shown product, and p_z is the non-shown one. With the above ranking learning treatment, representations of products can be enhanced to better identify competitive entities and detect advantaged features. Then, Eq. (2), Eq. (3) and Eq. (5) can be unified together as one objective function as follows, to guarantee the overall performance of both representation learning and ranking learning.

$$L = O + \lambda_m \times L_{pm} + \lambda_c \times L_{pc} + \eta(||X_p||^2 + |||X_m|^2 + ||X_c||^2), \quad (6)$$

where λ_m and λ_c are parameters to balance the importance of each term, η is a regularization parameter and $|| \cdot ||^2$ is l_2 regularization to avoid overfitting. The final goal is to maximize the objective function L. The method is optimized by stochastic gradient ascent and the gradients are computed with back-propagation algorithm.

The representations obtained from the method are then used to identify competitive entities and detect advantaged features. Concretely, the products with higher similarity are likely to be competitive entities, since they share more similar features. Therefore, given a focal product, e.g., A, its top-ranked competitive entities with high similarities can be obtained. Furthermore, given the focal product A and an identified competitive product B, the advantaged features of A over B can be detected by comparing the similarities on feature level. Specifically, for a feature f, if its similarity to A is greater than its similarity to B, then feature f is deemed as an advantaged feature of A over B, mirroring a fact that merchants or consumers acknowledge the feature f to a larger degree in the descriptions or reviews of A than B. Moreover, the similarity difference, i.e., denoted as $sim(f, A) - sim(f, B)$, could be used as the degree measuring the relative advantage of A over B on f. Then, for focal product A and a competitive product B, the top ranked advantaged features with high similarity differences can be recognized and detected.

3. Experiments and Results

3.1. Data experiments on competitive entities identification

The experimental data, i.e., including the products in a specific cosmetics sub-category, the product descriptions and online reviews, as well as "also-viewed" list of products, were crawled from Jingdong.com (i.e., one of the largest e-commerce websites in China). The texts were preprocessed by segmenting, POS tagging and deleting stop words, and adjectives and nouns describing products were retained [10]. The derived dataset contains 60 products, 100 merchant-perspective features and 1,085 consumer-perspective features from 52,083 online reviews. The products in the sub-category are highly homogeneous and competitive. Moreover, the 100 merchant-perspective features are not compre-hensive enough to analyze competitive relationships compared with numerous consumer-perspective features which provide more fruitful dimensions and are quite different from merchant-perspective features. For each product, one product in the "also-viewed" list is retained to test set and the others are assigned to training set. For evaluation metrics, similar to [6], HR@k and nDCG@k are chosen. Six baseline methods are chosen for comparison, i.e., Cminer [5], Cominer [3], LR [4], LDA [11], TFGM [6] and Deep walk [7].

Figure 2 shows that the proposed method significantly outperforms the baseline methods. Concretely, LDA and Cminer perform the worst as they are unsupervised methods, i.e., hard to utilize the competitive ground truth information. Compared with LR, the superiority of the proposed method reflects on well capturing the relationships on granular feature level. Cominer does not perform satisfactorily because it only considers the co-occurrence in reviews. It is worthy to mention that, both Deep walk and TFGM do not perform as well as the proposed method since they could not well capture the heterogeneous network characteristic of the research problem. Furthermore, the ablation experiments, which is omitted due to the limited space, also justify the critical contribution of different components of the method, i.e., the "*P-M-P*" path, the "*P-C-P*" path, the ranking learning treatment, respectively.

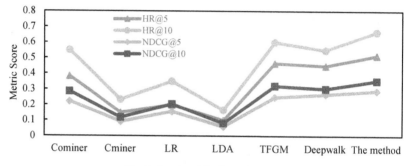

Fig. 2. Results of the Seven Methods.

3.2. User experiments on advantaged features detection

In order to validate the effectiveness of the proposed method on detecting advantaged features, user experiments were conducted, i.e., human evaluators were asked to annotate the advantaged features based on their subjective perceptions as consumers in a blinded-test manner. Four baseline methods, i.e., LDA, Frequency, LDA-difference and Frequency-difference are chosen, where they can extract the important features from different aspects and the latter two adopt the same difference treatment, i.e., as in the proposed method, to exquisitely locate the advantaged features.

Specifically, four comparative experiments were conducted between our method and each baseline method, respectively. In each experiment, five focal products were randomly chosen coupled with a top-ranked competitive product. For each competitive pair, top 5 ranked features detected by the method and the compared one were blindly mixed to form a 10 features list. In each experiment, 50 human evaluators were asked to annotate the top 5 features they perceived to show relative advantage of each focal product over the other. The evaluators were recruited from university female students with sufficient experience in shopping for cosmetics to ensure the credibility. Precision and Novelty are used to assess the performance of methods. Table 1 shows the significant superiority on detecting advantaged features of the proposed method over others.

Table 1. Results of the Four User Experiments.

Method	Precision@5	Novelty	Method	Precision@5	Novelty
Frequency	46.86%	25.51%	Frequency-diff	49.25%	19.05%
The method	**55.54%**	**48.17%**	The method	**54.47%**	**46.85%**
Method	Precision@5	Novelty	Method	Precision@5	Novelty
LDA	45.65%	0%	LDA-diff	49.42%	3.5%
The method	**54.35%**	**46.85%**	The method	**53.08%**	**46.15%**

4. Conclusion

Competitive relationships analysis, including competitive entities identification and advantaged features detection, from a relative advantage angle, is important for merchants to make targeted marketing tactics in such a fierce competing ecommerce marketplace. This paper proposes a heterogeneous network embedding learning method to, not only take consumers' perspective together with merchant's perspective into consideration, but also conduct a granular analysis with relative advantage. Data experiments and user experiments show that the proposed method outperforms other baseline methods.

References

1. Peteraf, Margaret A., and Mark E. Bergen. "Scanning dynamic competitive landscapes: a market-based and resource-based framework." *Strategic Management Journal* 24.10 (2003): 1027-1041.
2. Wilson, Dominic F. "Competitive marketing strategy in a volatile environment: theory, practice and research priorities." *Journal of Strategic Marketing* 7.1 (1999): 19-40.
3. Bao, Sheng, et al. "Competitor mining with the web." *IEEE Transactions on Knowledge and Data Engineering* 20.10 (2008): 1297-1310.
4. Pant, Gautam, and Olivia RL Sheng. "Web footprints of firms: Using online isomorphism for competitor identification." *Information Systems Research* 26.1 (2015): 188-209.
5. Valkanas, George, Theodoros Lappas, and Dimitrios Gunopulos. "Mining competitors from large unstructured datasets." *IEEE Transactions on Knowledge and Data Engineering* 29.9 (2017): 1971-1984.
6. Yang, Yang, et al. "Mining competitive relationships by learning across heterogeneous networks." *Proceedings of the 21st ACM international conference on Information and knowledge management.* 2012.
7. Perozzi, Bryan, Rami Al-Rfou, and Steven Skiena. "Deepwalk: Online learning of social representations." *Proceedings of the 20th ACM SIGKDD international conference on Knowledge discovery and data mining.* 2014.

8. Dong, Yuxiao, Nitesh V. Chawla, and Ananthram Swami. "metapath2vec: Scalable representation learning for heterogeneous networks." *Proceedings of the 23rd ACM SIGKDD international conference on knowledge discovery and data mining.* 2017.

9. Rendle, Steffen, et al. "BPR: Bayesian personalized ranking from implicit feedback." *arXiv preprint arXiv:1205.2618* (2012).

10. Hu, Minqing, and Bing Liu. "Mining and summarizing customer reviews." Proceedings of the tenth ACM SIGKDD international conference on Knowledge discovery and data mining. 2004.

11. Blei, David M., Andrew Y. Ng, and Michael I. Jordan. "Latent dirichlet allocation." *Journal of machine Learning research* 3 Jan (2003): 993-1022.

Formation problem of first-order multi-agent systems with bounded control input

Zhengquan Yang

College of Transport Science and Engineering, Civil Aviation University of China
Tianjin, 30000, China
zquanyang@163.com

Yang Li

Tianjin Yihualu Information Technology Co., Ltd.
Tianjin, 300131, China
liuhuafeiyu8@163.com

This paper aims to study consensus formation constraint set. A bonded consensus protocol for agents with continuous-time dynamics is put forward to achieve formation. The proposed protocol has a smooth bounded function, and composed of the formation part and the projection part. Besides, the correctness of protocol is proved by Lyapunov function. Finally, the effect of the algorithm is verified by a simulation.

Keywords: Formation; multi-agent systems; finite-time formation; asymptotic convergence.

1. Introduction

In recent years, the formation control is widely used to intelligent robot cooperative work, unmanned aerial vehicle formation and target search.[1,2]

Based on various concepts of graph theory and dynamic system, many different types of formation control methods are proposed,[3,4] and formation control problems are discussed from the perspective of randomness and certainty. Wen et al.[5] proposed an optimized leader-follower formation control for the multi-agent systems with unknown nonlinear dynamics. Wang et al.[6] considered the leader-follower formation control problem for general multi-agent systems with Lipschitz nonlinearity and unknown disturbances.

In reality, we may need to consider some constraints, such as space, angle, and finite-time constraints, etc.[7–9] Meysam et al.[8] introduced a solution to the distributed bearing only triangular formation control problem with angle-only inter-agent constraints. Ge et al.[9] proposed a control law based on artificial potential field method for formation tracking control of multi-agents in constrained space. Hong et al.[10] investigated global finite time stabilization for a class of nonlinear systems in normal form with parametric uncertainties. Yang et al.[11] studied the formation problem of second-order multi-agent with region constraint.

In real control systems, we need to control agents to a desired area. That is, to consider situations where the only concern of the final state is constraint rather than some specific geometry. Compared with those of the previous result, the features of this paper are as follows: First, in this paper, the first-order system is considered. Second, the new controller is bounded by employing a smooth bounded function (i.e., tanh function). The third, the bounded controller is used to solve the formation problem of multi-agent.

The organization of this paper is described as follows: Section 2 mainly introduces the research problems and graph theory. In Section 3, a bounded protocol with region constraint is presented to solve formation problem of multi-agent. In Section 4, numerical simulation result is given to verify the validity of the above results. Finally, conclusions are given in Section 5.

2. Preliminaries

Given $x \in \mathbb{R}^m$, where $\mathbb{R}^m$ is a m-dimensional vector space. T is used to represent the transpose of a vector or matrix. The 2-norm of the vector s is defined by $\|s\|$. Let $P_\Omega(x)$ denotes the projection of the vector x onto the closed convex set Ω. The projection distance of the vector x to the set Ω is described as:

$$dist(x, \Omega) = argmin_{\bar{x} \in \Omega} \|x - \bar{x}\|$$

The smooth bounded function $tanh$ is used in this paper. The $tanh(x)$ can be calculated by:

$$\tanh(x) = \frac{e^x - e^{-x}}{e^x + e^{-x}} = \begin{cases} [-1, 0), x < 0 \\ [0, 1], x \geq 0 \end{cases}$$

The function has the following properties: $tanh \in (0, 1]$ while $x > 0$, $tanh = 0$ while $x = 0$, otherwise, $tanh \in [-1, 0)$ while $x < 0$. Given an undirected graph $G(t) = (V, E(t), A(t))$ consists of a set V of vertices and a set $E(t)$ of edges. If $(i, j) \in E(t)$ and $(j, i) \in E(t)$ that means i and j are neighbors at the time t. The graph is connected, if there is a connection to any other adjacent vertices between i and j. $A(t) = [a_{ij}(t)] \in \mathbb{R}^{n \times n}$ is the weighted adjacency matrix of the graph $G(t)$, where $a_{ij} = 1$ if$(i, j) \in E(t)$, otherwise, $a_{ij} = 0$. The graph is undirected and connected, consequently, $a_{ij} = a_{ji}$.

In this paper, the $N(N > 2)$ agents are considered on multi-agent system with the dynamic, which can be expressed as follow:

$$\dot{x}_i(t) = u_i(t) \tag{1}$$

where $x_i(t) \in \mathbb{R}^m$ is the position vector of agent i and $u_i(t) \in \mathbb{R}^m$ means the vector of control inputs of each agent i. The controller u_i is designed to ensure the state of $x_i(t)$ lie in a corresponding non-empty and closed convex set $\Omega \in \mathbb{R}^m$. Meanwhile, It exists a $t_1 > t_0$ for all $t > t_1$, $x_i(t) \in \Omega$. A framework is defined as a pair $(\mathcal{G}, X)$ where $X = [x_1^T, x_2^T, \cdots x_N^T]^T \in \mathbb{R}^{mN}$. Ordering edges of $\mathcal{E}$ in some way, the rigidity function $r_G(X) : R^{2N} \to R^{|\mathcal{E}|}$ associated with the framework $(\mathcal{G}, X)$ is defined as:

$$r_G(X) = \frac{1}{2}[\cdots, \|x_i - x_j\|^2, \cdots]^T, (i, j) \in \mathcal{E} \tag{2}$$

Definition 2.1.[12] A framework $(\mathcal{G}, X)$ is rigid if there exists a neighborhood $\mathcal{U}$ of R^{2N} such that $r_G^{-1}(r_G(x)) \cap \mathcal{U} = r_\mathcal{K}^{-1}(r_\mathcal{K}(x)) \cap \mathcal{U}$ where $\mathcal{K}$ is the complete graph on N-vertices.

In this paper, we consider the region constraint on formation control of multi-agents. That is, all agents are given a region constraint $\Omega \in R^2$, which limits all multi-agents to enter the constraint area while reaching formation. To do that, give a point $X^* = [x_1^{*T}, x_2^{*T}, \cdots x_N^{*T}]^T, x_i^* \in \Omega$ such that $(\mathcal{G}, X)$ is infinitesimally rigid, the target formation is defined as

$$E_X := \{X : x_i - x_j = x_i^* - x_j^*, j \in N_i, i \in \mathcal{K}\} \tag{3}$$

That is, E_X is the set of all formations congruent to X^*.

Assumption 1. The constraint subset Ω of each agent is convex and nonempty. The intersection of constraint sets is non-empty and convex. The graph G is undirected and connected.

3. Formation Control

In this section, we will propose a bounded controller to make multi-agent realize asymptotic formation. Then, the control algorithm with convex set constraints is proposed:

$$u_i = -\sum_{j \in N_i} a_{ij} \tanh\left(x_i - x_j - r_{ij}^*\right) - \alpha \frac{(x_i - P_\Omega(x_i))}{\|x_i - P_\Omega(x_i)\|} \tag{4}$$

where N_i means the neighbors set of agent i, the neighbor $j \in N_i$, $\alpha > 0$ is a constant, smoothing function $tanh$ maps the error between agents i and j in the interval $(0,1)$, $r_{ij}^* = x_i^* - x_j^* \in \mathbb{R}^m$ indicates the desired formation vector from the ith agent to the jth agent. $P_\Omega(x_i(t))$ is the projection of vertex $x_i(t)$ on the set Ω, $\|x_i(t) - P_\Omega(x_i(t))\|$ represents the 2-norm, and the projection of Ω exists and is unique.

The proposed protocol is composed of the formaiton part and the projection part. Because these two parts are bounded functions, the controller is bounded.

Because $r_{ij}^* = x_i^* - x_j^*$, that is $x_i - x_j - r_{ij}^* = x_i - x_i^* - (x_j - x_j^*)$, so, $x_i - x_j - r_{ij}^* = \tilde{x}_i - \tilde{x}_j$ where $\tilde{x}_i = x_i(t) - x_i^*$ $\tilde{x}_j = x_j(t) - x_j^*$

Theorem 3.1. *Let Assumption 1 be satisfied. Under the algorithm (4), all agents of the system (1) achieve the asymptotical convergence of the formation shape, and $x_i(t) \in \Omega$ as $t \to \infty$.*

Proof. The proof is divided into two parts. First of all, we proved all agents move to their constraint region in a finite time. The second, we will prove that multi-agent can realize formation asymptotically. Considering the Lyapunov function $V_1(t)$ of system (1) as:

$$V_1(t) = \frac{1}{2} \| (x_i(t) - P_\Omega(x_i(t))) \|^2 \tag{5}$$

Deriving the derivative of time t for $V_1(t)$, together with Assumption 1, the result can be calculated as:

$$\dot{V}_1(t) = (x_i(t) - P_\Omega(x_i(t)))^T \left[-\sum_{j \in N_i} a_{ij} \tanh\left(x_i(t) - x_j(t) - r_{ij}^*\right) - \alpha \frac{(x_i(t) - P_\Omega(x_i(t)))}{\|x_i(t) - P_\Omega(x_i(t))\|} \right]$$

$$= -\sum_{j \in N_i} (x_i(t) - P_\Omega(x_i(t)))^T a_{ij} \tanh\left(x_i(t) - x_j(t) - r_{ij}^*\right) - \alpha \|x_i(t) - P_\Omega(x_i(t))\|$$

$$\leq (N - \alpha) \|x_i(t) - P_\Omega(X_i(t))\| \tag{6}$$

Combining the result of Eq. (6) with Eq. (5), the outcomes can be obtained as:

$$\dot{V}_1(t) \leq -(\alpha - N)\sqrt{2V_1(t)} \tag{7}$$

Moving the right root sign part of inequality to the left. It follows that:

$$\frac{\dot{V}_1(t)}{\sqrt{2V_1(t)}} \leq -(\alpha - N) \tag{8}$$

Integrating both sides of this inequality, we have

$$\int_{t_0}^{t} \frac{\dot{V}_1(t)}{\sqrt{2V_1(t)}} dt \leq \int_{t_0}^{t} -(\alpha - N) dt \tag{9}$$

$$\sqrt{2V_1(t)} - \sqrt{2V_1(t_0)} \leq -(\alpha - N)(t - t_0)$$

if $\alpha > N$, $V_1(t)$ converges to zero in finite time. Consequently, there is a constant $t_1 > t_0$ such that for all $t > t_1$, $\|x_i(t) - P_\Omega x_i(t)\| = 0$. as a result, under the control (4), $x_i(t) \in \Omega$.

So, the $x_i(t) \in \Omega$ while $t > t_1$ and the algorithm (4) can be expressed by:

$$u_i = -\sum_{j \in N_i} a_{ij} \tanh\left(x_i(t) - x_j(t) - r_{ij}^*\right) \tag{10}$$

From Eq. (10), because of $x_i - x_j - r_{ij}^* = \tilde{x}_i - \tilde{x}_j$, the $u_i(t)$ can be calculated by:

$$u_i = -\sum_{j \in N_i} a_{ij} \tanh\left(\tilde{x}_i - \tilde{x}_j\right) \tag{11}$$

Next, we will prove that multi-agent can realize formation. The new Lyapunov function $V_2(t)$ is considered as follow:

$$V_2(t) = \frac{1}{2} \sum_{i=1}^{N} \left(x_i(t) - x_i^*\right)^T \left(x_i(t) - x_i^*\right) \tag{12}$$

From the Eq. (11), the $V_2(t)$ can be described as:

$$V_2(t) = \frac{1}{2} \sum_{i=1}^{N} \tilde{x}_i^T(t) \tilde{x}_i(t) \tag{13}$$

Deriving the derivative of time t for $V_2(t)$, the outcomes can be calculated by:

$$\dot{V}_2(t) = \sum_{i=1}^{N} \tilde{x}_i^T \dot{\tilde{x}}_i$$

$$= \sum_{i=1}^{N} \tilde{x}_i^T \left[-\sum_{j \in N_i} a_{ij} \tanh(\tilde{x}_i - \tilde{x}_j) \right]$$

$$= -\sum_{i=1}^{N} \tilde{x}_i^T \sum_{j \in N_i} a_{ij} \tanh(\tilde{x}_i - \tilde{x}_j) \tag{14}$$

From the graph theory, similarly, the result can be expressed by:

$$\sum_{i=1}^{N} \tilde{x}_i^T(t) \sum_{j \in N_i} a_{ij} \tanh(\tilde{x}_i(t) - \tilde{x}_j(t))$$

$$= \frac{1}{2}\left[\sum_{i=1}^{N}\sum_{j=1}^{N} a_{ij}\tilde{x}_i^T(t)\tanh(\tilde{x}_i(t) - \tilde{x}_j(t)) + \sum_{i=1}^{N}\sum_{j=1}^{N} a_{ij}\tilde{x}_i^T(t)\tanh(\tilde{x}_i(t) - \tilde{x}_j(t))\right]$$

$$= \frac{1}{2}\left[\sum_{i=1}^{N}\sum_{j=1}^{N} a_{ij}\tilde{x}_i^T(t)\tanh(\tilde{x}_i(t) - \tilde{x}_j(t)) + \sum_{i=1}^{N}\sum_{j=1}^{N} a_{ji}\tilde{x}_j^T(t)\tanh(\tilde{x}_j(t) - \tilde{x}_i(t))\right]$$

$$= \frac{1}{2}\sum_{i=1}^{N}\sum_{j=1}^{N} a_{ij}(\tilde{x}_i(t) - \tilde{x}_j^T(t))\tanh(\tilde{x}_i(t) - \tilde{x}_j(t))$$

Thus, the Eq. (14) can be described as:

$$\dot{V}_2(t) = -\frac{1}{2}\sum_{i=1}^{N}\sum_{j=1}^{N} a_{ij}(\tilde{x}_i(t) - \tilde{x}_j(t))^{\mathrm{T}}\tanh(\tilde{x}_i(t) - \tilde{x}_j(t))$$

$$= -\frac{1}{2}\sum_{i=1}^{N}\sum_{j=1}^{N} a_{ij}(x_i(t) - x_j(t) - r_{ij}^*)^{\mathrm{T}}\tanh(x_i(t) - x_j(t) - r_{ij}^*)$$

$$\leq 0 \qquad\qquad (15)$$

Thus, from the above deduction, we can get $\|x_i(t) - x_j(t) - r_{ij}^*\| \to 0$ when $t \to \infty$, based on Lasalle's Invariance Principle. $\qquad\square$

4. Simulation

In this section, a simulation is given to verify the availability of our algorithm. This simulation consists of 92 agents moving on the 2D plane. The initial state of all agents are set randomly. Then, the Random network[13] is used to initialize the connection relationship for MAS. In this paper, we choose $N = 92, p = 0.5$.

The digital formation "2022" is chose as the target configuration for the group. The constraint region is a rectangle, which is described by $\Omega = \{(x, y) : 3 \leq x \leq 12, 2 \leq y \leq 6\}$. Figure 1 describes the final formation shape of multi-agent, and we can see the groups of 92 agents have moved into the constraint region. In Fig. 2, the trajectory of 92 agents can be observed, and the positions of all agents gradually approach the constraint area and finally enter the target area with the digital formation "2022", which achieves our expectation.

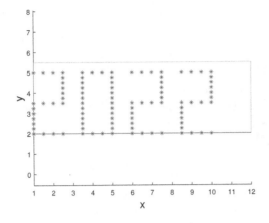

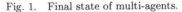

Fig. 1.   Final state of multi-agents.

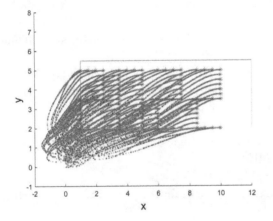

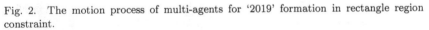

Fig. 2.   The motion process of multi-agents for '2019' formation in rectangle region constraint.

5. Conclusion

Assuming that the values of each agent are constrained to lie in a nonempty closed convex constraint set, a bonded protocol for agents with continuous-time dynamics is proposed. The proposed protocol is composed of the consensus part and the projection part respectively. Finally, the effect of the propose algorithm is verified by simulations.

References

1. A. Abdessameud and A. Tayebi, Formation control of VTOL unmanned aerial vehicles with communication delays, *Automatica*, **47**, 2383 (2011).
2. R. Cui, S. S. Ge, E. H. B How, and Y. C. Sang, Leader-follower formation control of underactuated autonomous underwater vehicles, *Ocean Engineering*, **37**, 1491 (2010).
3. K. Oh, M. Park, and H. Ahn, A survey of multi-agent formation control, *Automatica*, **53**, 424 (2011).
4. Z. Gao, and G. Guo Velocity free leader-follower formation control for autonomous underwater vehicles with line-of-sight range and angle constraints, *Information Sciences*, **48**, 359-378 (2011).
5. G. Wen, C. L. P. Chen, J. Feng, and N. Zhou, Optimized multi-agent formation control based on an identifier-actor-critic reinforcement learning algorithm, *IEEE Trans Fuzzy Syst*, **26**, 2719 (2018).
6. C. Y. Wang, Z. Y. Zuo, Q. H. Gong, and Z. T Ding, Formation control with disturbance rejection for a class of Lipschitz nonlinear systems, *Sci China Inf Sci*, **60**, 070202 (2017).
7. Z. Sun, S. Mou, M. Deghat, and B. D. O. Anderson, Finite Time Distance-based Rigid Formation Stabilization and Flocking, *Ifac Proceedings Volumes*, **47**, 9183 (2014).
8. B. Meysam, N.Adrian, and P. J. Bishop, Distributed control of triangular formations with angle-only constraints, *Systems Control Letters*, **59**, 147 (2010).
9. S. S. Ge, X. Liu, C. H. Goh, and L. G. Xu, Formation Tracking Control of Multiagents in Constrained Space, *IEEE Transactions on Control Systems Technology*, 24, 992 (2016).
10. Y. G. Hong, J. Wang, D. Cheng, Adaptive finite-time control of nonlinear systems with parametric uncertainty. *IEEE Trans. Autom. Control*, vol. 51, no. 5, pp. 858-862, 2006.
11. Z. Q. Yang, Q. Zhang, and Z. C. Zhang, Formation Control of Multi-Agent Systems with Region Constraint, *Complexity*, 2019, 1-6 (2019).
12. L. Asimow, and B. Roth, The rigidity of graphs. *Journal of Mathematical Analysis and Applications*, 68, 171 (1979).
13. P. Erdos, and A. Rényi, On random graphs I, *Publicationes Mathematicae*, 6, 290 (1959).

Entity alignment between knowledge graphs via contrastive learning

Xiaohui Chen, Jie Hu*, Shengdong Du and Fei Teng

School of Computing and Artificial Intelligence, Southwest Jiaotong University
Chengdu, Sichuan, 611756, China
*jiehu@swjtu.edu.cn
www.swjtu.edu.cn

Entity Alignment (EA) aims to identify entities representing the same entity in the real world between two knowledge graphs. Recently, entity embedding-based models become the mainstream models of EA. But these models have the following shortcomings: (1) the ratio of seed alignments seriously affects the performance of EA and the acquisition of them often requires a lot of labor costs (2) entity embeddings don't take into account the differences of different entities. To address these problems, an entity embedding-based model via contrastive learning is proposed for EA between KGs without utilizing pre-aligned seed entity pairs, which not only integrates entity attribute information in entity embeddings, but also enhances the discrimination between different entity embeddings. Experimental results on two real-world knowledge bases show that our proposed model has achieved a good improvement in the three common metrics for the entity alignment task, i.e., hits@1, hits@10, and MR.

Keywords: Knowledge graph; entity alignment; contrastive learning; embedding.

1. Introduction

Currently, knowledge graph (KG) technology has achieved results in several application areas. But in real applications, each KG is often incomplete due to the fact that they are constructed from different sources. As one of the most important tasks of KG fusion, the goal of entity alignment (EA) is to find entities between two knowledge graphs that point to the same real entity, which can enrich a KG from another complementary KG via EA. It is critical for downstream application tasks.

Some studies focus on improving the vector representation of TransE [1] for EA, but these methods require pre-aligned entity pairs called seed alignments [2-3]. In recent years, unsupervised entity alignment has gradually started to be studied, for example, Zhang et al. [4] proposed an embedding-based model using attribute (AttrE). However, the joint training process in AttrE [4] only

---

*Corresponding author.

draws the distance between the two embedding representations in the semantic space, which fails to capture the semantic spatial differences in representations of different entity embeddings.

In this paper, a new embedding model for entity alignment is proposed. It generates attribute embeddings and structure embeddings from attribute triples and relationship triples, respectively. But unlike AttrE [4], we introduce a contrastive learning framework while fusing the two types of information. The contrastive learning loss fuses attribute information by maximizing the cosine similarity of two embedding representations of the same entity, and minimizes the cosine similarity of relational embedding representations between different entities to increase the discrimination of different entities. Through contrastive learning, it not only integrates the relation semantics and attribute semantics of entities but also strengthens the discrimination of different entities.

2. Related Work

2.1. *Embedding-based entity alignment*

Early embedding-based entity alignment models are mainly based on TransE and its variants, such as IPTransE [2] and BootEA [3]. Unlike traditional TransE-based models, Zhang et al. [5] used a multi-view knowledge graph embedding (MultiKE) model. In addition to fusing attribute information to obtain semantic similarity for alignment with attributes, there are also scholars who used structural similarity between relations for entity alignment [6]. To obtain fine-grained matching of neighbors and attributes, Tang et al. [7] constructed interaction between neighbors and attributes based on BERT embedding to solve the knowledge graph alignment problem.

2.2. *Contrastive learning*

Contrastive learning is one of the most important methods of self-supervised learning [8]. Its purpose is to embed the augmented form of the same sample in the same space close to each other, and away from other samples. For example, in the text semantic matching task, two different representations of the same text are obtained as positive samples by the dropout method, and the similarity of the positive samples is maximized while the similarity of different texts is minimized to train the embedded representation of the enhanced text [9].

3. Proposed Model

Considering the difficulty of seed alignment acquisition and the differences of different entities, we proposed an EA model based on contrastive learning

(CL-EA) without seed alignments. First, we briefly explain the general architecture of our approach. Then, we describe the modules of our model in detail, which include embedding learning, contrastive learning, and entity alignment as Fig. 1 shown.

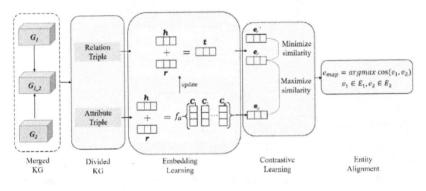

| Merged KG | Divided KG | Embedding Learning | Contrastive Learning | Entity Alignment |

Fig. 1. Overview of the proposed solution.

3.1. Embedding learning

Our model divides the triples in the merged knowledge graph into relation triples and attribute triples to learn the relation-based and attribute-based embedding representations of the same entity, respectively, and for the whole embedding representation, we will follow the formula in AttrE [4].

3.1.1. Entity Embedding based on attribute

We consider the predicate r as a mapping from the head entity h to the attribute a, i.e., $h + r \approx f_a(a)$, where $f_a(a)$ is a composite function based on attribute-value character combinations, a is the attribute value of a particular entity $a = \{c_1, c_2, c_3, ..., c_t\}$ and c is the character that makes up a. The composite function can encode an attribute value into a single vector of low dimension, where similar attribute values can be encoded into an approximate vector representation. In AttrE [4], the N-gram-based compositional function has been verified to be the best attribute encoding function, so we still use it for attribute encoding, which is represented as follows:

$$f_a(a) = \sum_{n=1}^{N} \left(\frac{\sum_{i=1}^{t} \sum_{j=i}^{n} c_j}{t - i - 1} \right), \tag{1}$$

where N is a hyper-parameter denoting the maximum number n of combination in the N-gram combination model, and t is the length of the attribute value.

Similar to TransE, the objective function L_{AE} that we need to minimize is as follows:

$$L_{AE} = \sum_{t_a \in T_a} \sum_{t_a' \in T_a'} \max\left(0, \left[\gamma + \alpha\left(f\left(t_a\right) - f\left(t_a'\right)\right)\right]\right), \tag{2}$$

$$\alpha = \frac{count(r)}{|T|}, \tag{3}$$

$$f\left(t_a\right) = \left\|\mathbf{h} + \mathbf{r} - f_a(a)\right\|, \tag{4}$$

where T_a is a set of true attribute triples obtained by observation, T_a' is a set of altered attribute triples. Here T_a' is got by randomly replacing the head entity h or the attribute value a of the attribute triples, and the altered triples obtained afterward are used as negative samples. $count(r)$ is the number of occurrences of relationship r, and $|T|$ is the total number of triples in the merge KG G_{1_2}. Weight α is more helpful to focus the model on aligned entity pairs, because usually between two KGs, aligned predicates occur more often than non-aligned ones. $f(t_a)$ is the scoring function of the attribute triples, which calculates the confidence score of the vector representation of the attribute values.

3.1.2. Entity embedding based on relation

To get entity embedding based on relation, it's necessary to use the hyper-parameter α to make the model focus more on aligned entity pairs, so that TransE can learn the structure embedding suitable for entity alignment. Meanwhile, the attribute embedding of the entity is used to "supervise" the relation embedding learning process. The objective function L_{RE} that needs to be minimized is as follows:

$$L_{RE} = \sum_{t_r \in T_r} \sum_{t_r' \in T_r'} \max\left(0, \gamma + \alpha\left(f\left(t_r\right) - f\left(t_r'\right)\right)\right) + \sum_{e \in G_1 \cup G_2} \left[1 - \cos\left(e_r, e_a\right)\right], \tag{5}$$

$$f\left(t_r\right) = \left\|\mathbf{h} + \mathbf{r} - \mathbf{t}\right\|, \tag{6}$$

where T_r is a set of true relation triples obtained by observation, T_r' is a set of altered relation triples and $cos(e_r, e_a)$ is the cosine similarity of vectors e_r and e_a.

Since we need to keep two different types of embedding representations of the same entity closer together, we assist in updating the structure embedding representations of the entity by minimizing the cosine similarity between them.

3.2. Contrastive learning

For contrastive samples construction, we first take the two types of embedding representations with rich semantic information obtained by iterative training of the embedding learning model as positive samples in the comparative learning, and the embedding representations of other entities in the same batch as negative samples. We devised a loss function L_{CL} based on contrastive learning as follows:

$$L_{CL} = \sum_{e \in E_1 \cup E_2} -\log \frac{\exp\left(\cos\left(e^r_i, e^a_i\right)/\tau\right)}{\exp\left(\cos\left(e^r_i, e^a_i\right)/\tau\right) + \sum_{e^r_j \in E'} \exp\left(\cos\left(e^r_i, e^r_j\right)/\tau\right)}, \quad (7)$$

where τ is a temperature hyper-parameter, $\mathbf{e}^r_i$ and $\mathbf{e}^a_i$ are the embeddings of the same entity based on relation and attribute, and $\mathbf{e}^r_i$ and $\mathbf{e}^r_j$ represent the embedding representation of different entities in the same batch during model training.

3.3. Entity alignment

Entity alignment is realized by computing the similarity between e_1 and e_2 with the following equation:

$$e_{map} = \operatorname*{argmax}_{e_2 \in E_2} \cos\left(e_1, e_2\right), \quad (8)$$

where $<e_1, e_{map}>$ is the pair of aligned entities we need.

4. Experiments

We adopt two widely used datasets [10] to evaluate our model: DY-NB and DW-NB. The statistical information of the datasets is listed in Table 1.

Table 1. Dataset statics.

Dataset	Subset	Entities	Aligned entities	Predicates	Relation triples	Attribute triples
DY-NB	DBpedia	58,858	15,000	211	87,676	173,520
	Yago	60,228		91	66,546	186,328
DW-NB	DBpedia	84,911	50,000	545	203,502	221,591
	Wikidata	86,116		703	198,797	223,232

Then, we compare CL-EA with IPTransE [2], BootEA [3], MultiKE [7] and AttrE [4]. IPTransE considers the information of multi-hop paths in KG, incorporates relational paths in knowledge embedding, and improves the performance of entity alignment through iterative updating and parameter sharing. BootEA proposes a parameter exchange strategy to expand the seed alignments, and adds the new aligned entity pairs generated in the iterative process to the training set to achieve the purpose of expanding the training set. MultiKE takes into account that KG has a variety of features, and embeds and fuses from four views of text, name, relationship and attribute. AttrE proposes an efficient attribute-based knowledge embedding model that embeds entities of two KGs into the same space through joint training of structure and relation.

For our model CL-EA, we set the hyper-parameter as follows: temperature coefficient τ = 0.05, margin γ = 1.0, the embeddings dimension d = 100 and batch size for training n = 100. The embedding learning module has been trained for 200 epochs, and then input the output embeddings into the contrastive learning module to train for 100 epochs.

4.1. Entity alignment results

As Table 2 shows, our proposed model CL-EA consistently outperforms previous baseline models. Meanwhile, the performance of models such as IPTransE, BootEA, and MultiKE that require seed alignments is severely affected by the proportion of seed alignments. AttrE is not affected by seed alignments and performs well because it is an unsupervised method, but our model outperforms AttrE on all three metrics.

Table 2. Entity alignment results.

Model	Seed:10%		Seed:20%		Seed:30%		Seed:40%		Seed:50%	
	Hits@ 1	Hits@ 10	Hits@ 1	Hits@ 10	Hits@ 1	Hits@ 10	Hits@ 1	Hits@ 10	Hits@ 1	Hits@ 10
DW-NB										
IPTransE	5.9	13.4	7.5	18.7	12.9	24.6	16.3	32.8	25.4	37.5
BootEA	8.1	16.1	12.5	20.1	17.9	28.3	21.4	35.1	25.4	27.5
MultiKE	80.2	87.5	82.5	88.9	84.0	90.0	84.8	91.2	85.2	95.0
AttrE	82.9	94.1	82.9	94.1	82.9	94.1	82.9	94.1	82.9	94.1
Proposed	**85.6**	**95.4**	**85.6**	**95.4**	**85.6**	**95.4**	**85.6**	**95.4**	**85.6**	**95.4**
DY-NB										
IPTransE	1.5	9.8	5.6	25.7	14.5	36.4	15.7	45.8	17.3	52.1
BootEA	2.1	14.1	8.4	38.1	15.7	48.3	17.2	57.1	19.2	58.1
MultiKE	81.8	88.0	82.1	89.2	84.9	90.8	87.2	92.0	89.2	93.5
AttrE	90.4	96.2	90.7	96.2	90.4	96.2	90.4	96.2	90.4	96.2
Proposed	**93.9**	**97.6**	**93.9**	**97.6**	**93.9**	**97.6**	**93.9**	**97.6**	**93.9**	**97.6**

4.2. Ablation study

In AttrE, the process of representation learning and the joint learning of structure embedding and attribute character embedding are trained alternately. But our model, unlike AttrE, first trains multiple iterations of representation learning on the knowledge triples of the KG to minimize $L_{AE} + L_{RE}$, and then enhances the embedding representation by contrastive learning to minimize L_{CL}. In order to verify whether the training order has an effect on the results, we performed relevant ablation experiments. The experimental results are shown in Table 3, where AttrE-noalter indicates that multiple iterations of representation learning are performed first and then joint learning is performed. This shows that our proposed contrastive learning-based entity alignment model is effective.

Table 3. Ablation experiment results.

Model	DW-NB			DY-NB		
	Hits@1	Hits@10	MR	Hits@1	Hits@10	MR
AttrE	82.9	94.1	196	90.4	96.2	28
AttrE-noalter	83.8	94.6	158	90.8	96.4	27
Proposed	**85.6**	**95.4**	**144**	**93.9**	**97.6**	**11**

4.3. Effect of temperature

The temperature τ in the contrastive loss can adjust the model's focus on difficult samples. A small value means that the model focuses more on the difference between the current sample and the most similar difficult sample, but in which there may be potentially positive samples. And a large value will cause the model to lose focus on difficult samples. Table 4 shows the experiment results in DY-NB with different temperatures.

Table 4. The experiment results with different temperatures.

τ	Hits@1	Hits@10	MR
0.02	92.5	97.2	18
0.05	93.9	97.6	11
0.07	93.5	97.6	14
0.10	92.2	97.0	13
0.12	92.3	97.2	12

5. Conclusion

Considering the sparseness of seed alignments, the difficulty of obtaining seeds, and the differences of different entities are ignored in current knowledge graphs fusion, we propose a knowledge graph entity alignment model based on contrastive learning. Compared with the previous unsupervised model, all three indicators have improved, especially MR has been improved significantly. In our model, the choice of relation-based embedding model and attribute-based embedding model have an important impact on the experimental results. Therefore, we will consider improving the triple embedding model to obtain more semantic embedding representation in our next stage work.

Acknowledgments

This work was supported by the Key Research and Development Program of Sichuan Province, China [Grant Number: 2022YFH0020, 2021YFG0136].

References

1. A. Bordes, N. Usunier, A. Garcia-Duran, J. Weston, Translating embeddings for modeling multi-relational data, in: Proceedings of the Advances in Neural Information Processing Systems, 2013, pp. 2787-2795.
2. H. Zhu, R. Xie, Z. Liu, M. Sun, Iterative entity alignment via joint knowledge embeddings, in: Proceedings of the International Joint Conference on Artificial Intelligence, 2017, pp. 4258-4264.
3. Z. Sun, W. Hu, Q. Zhang, Y. Qu, Bootstrapping entity alignment with knowledge graph embedding, in: Proceedings of the International Joint Conference on Artificial Intelligence, 2018, pp. 4396-4402.
4. BD. Trisedya, J. Qi, R. Zhang, Entity alignment between knowledge graphs using attribute embeddings, in: Proceedings of the AAAI Conference on Artificial Intelligence, 2019, pp. 297-304.
5. Q. Zhang, Z. Sun, W. Hu, M. Chen, L. Guo, Y. Qu, Multi-view knowledge graph embedding for entity alignment, in: Proceedings of the International Joint Conference on Artificial Intelligence, 2019.
6. Y. Peng, J. Zhang, C. Zhou, J. Xu, Embedding-based entity alignment using relation structural similarity, in: Proceedings of the 2020 IEEE International Conference on Knowledge Graph (ICKG), 2020, pp. 123-130.
7. X. Tang, J. Zhang, B. Chen, Y. Yang, H. Chen, C. Li, BERT-INT: a BERT-based interaction model for knowledge graph alignment, in: Proceedings of the 29th International Conference on International Joint Conferences on Artificial Intelligence, 2021, pp. 3174-3180.
8. A. Jaiswal, AR. Babu, MZ. Zadeh, D. Banerjee, F. Makedon, A survey on contrastive self-supervised learning, Technologies 9 (1) (2020) 2.
9. Y. Liu, P. Liu, SimCLS: A simple framework for contrastive learning of

abstractive summarization, in: Proceedings of the 59th Annual Meeting of the Association for Computational Linguistics, 2021, pp. 1065-1072.
10. R. Zhang, BD. Trisedy, M. Li, Y. Jiang, J. Qi, A comprehensive survey on knowledge graph entity alignment via representation learning, arXiv preprint arXiv:2103.15059 (2021).

Pixel-by-pixel classification of edges with machine learning techniques[a]

Pablo Flores-Vidal[*], Javier Castro[†] and Daniel Gómez[‡]

Estadística y Ciencia de los Datos, Facultad de Estudios Estadísticos
Universidad Complutense, Madrid, 28040, Spain
[*]pflores@ucm.es
[†]castroc@estad.ucm.es
[‡]dagomez@estad.ucm.es

The main purpose of this paper is to solve the edge detection (ED) problem through Machine Learning (ML) techniques. ED is one of the main IP techniques, and it has found applications in a wide range of tasks. For this purpose, it is proposed a pixel-by-pixel classification approach. Some of the predictors employed to build the classifiers include information about the pixel neighborhood and structures of connected pixels called edge segments. This approach allows working with the edge information provided by the Canny algorithm. In this paper are used the first 50 images of the Berkeley segmentation data set (BSDS500). The performance of our pixel-by-pixel classification approach was tested with logistic regression, neural networks, and support vector machines. The results showed evaluation measures significatively higher than standard Canny's, and this proved our pixel-by-pixel based classification as a promising approach able to improve edge detection performance.

Keywords: Edge detection; pixel-by-pixel classification; machine learning; Canny's.

1. Introduction

Edge detection (ED) is one of the main IP techniques, and it has found applications in a wide range of tasks, such as pathological diagnostics in medicine,[12] remote sensing,[3] military industry, surveillance,[20] and others.[9,27]

In the last decades, machine learning has been widely employed for IP problems.[6,15-17,22,24-26] Nevertheless, it is not easy to find learning approaches employed for low-level processing tasks. An example of research making use of ML on the ED problem can be seen in [10], where the aim was to classify edge segments –linked structures of edges–. In that research, the goal was limited in the sense that the edges could not be classified locally (pixel-by-pixel), an

[a]This research has been supported by the Spanish Ministry of Science [PGC2018-096509-B100].

approach that is specifically explored in this paper, and that was explored in Ref. 29.

As it is shown in this paper, there are several advantages for using ML for ED purposes, being one of them the use of more information that can be considered for the classification. The pixel-by-pixel classification allows classifying a pixel as "edge" or "non-edge" considering the pixel information and other local information of its neighborhood, and the segment to which that pixel belongs.

This paper is structured as follows: the first three subsections of the next section are devoted to some needed preliminaries. Section 3 is focused on our proposal: Classifying pixels with ML techniques using pixel-by-pixel approach. Firstly, the problem of building a new ground-truth version is explored, secondly, the process of collecting the predictors, and finally, the experiment's overall scheme is explained. The last sections are devoted to the results and conclusions.

2. Edge Detection with Machine Learning Techniques

2.1. Digital image

Let us denote a digital image by a matrix I,[14] and its pixel coordinates in the *spatial domain* by (i, j). For clarity's sake, the coordinates are integeres, where each point (i, j) represents a pixel with $i = 1, ..., n$ and $j = 1, ..., m$. Therefore, the size of an image, $n \times m$, is the number of its horizontal pixels multiplied by its number of verticals. The value of the spectral information depends on the digital image type that is considered. In this paper, the next image types are used:

- Binary map (I^{bin}): $I_{i,j} \in \{0,255\}$ (as well it is expressed as , $I_{i,j} \in \{0,1\}$).
- Gray-scale image (I^{gray}): $I_{i,j} \in \{0,1, ...,255\}$.
- Soft image (I^{soft}): $I_{i,j} \in [0,1]$. This is as well referred as a normalized gray-scale image.

2.2. Edge detection problem

In a digital image I, a pixel (i, j) is considered as an edge if in this pixel there is an important change of the intensity function $I_{i,j}$.[19,27] An Edge Detector is an algorithm that takes an image I as input and then converts it into a binary solution image[27] ($I_{i,j}^{sol}=1$ or "edge" and $I_{i,j}^{sol}=0$ or "non-edge"). In previous research,[29] Sobel operator was used, but in this research, is employed Canny's.

Canny's is a well-known example of an efficient ED algorithm[4] that can be considered complete in the sense that goes through all the ED steps: from the smoothing phase to the scaling The canny method pursues to define mathematically and optimize three criteria: that each extracted edge must be located the closest to the original one, that each 'real' edge produces one single edge, and finally, a high rate of true positives.

In this research, the focus on Canny's is placed on its last step, where is applied the hysteresis.[4] This performs the scaling step (i.e., the classification) by means of evaluating structures of connected pixels (aka segments) that are evaluated with two thresholds: α_{sup} and α_{inf}. Thus, Canny's scaling approach can be considered to produce a global evaluation of edges, contrarily to simpler ED operators as Sobel's, which employs local evaluation. Sobel was explored in Ref. 29, while in this research Canny's is employed. which is a more complex algorithm and brings the challenge of producing similar results to the ones obtained with hysteresis.

3.   A Pixel-by-Pixel based Classification with ML Techniques

Firstly, a data set of images with their respective ground-truth is needed. The common approach is that this ground-truth contains the "true" edges. In the case of the Berkeley Image segmentation data set[18] this ground-truth consists of human sketches. Then, with the information provided by this ground-truth the pixels labels are built.

For the learning process, one of the advantages of using supervised ML against non-supervised methods, is that they can deal with more variables to be included in the learning process, which ends up with the classification of pixels into "edge" or "non-edge" labels. Traditionally, this classification –extraction– of edges, is made by finding the suitable parameter's values involved, which could be done by means of non-supervised or supervised methods. In this research, over thirty predictor variables are used together to provide the needed information for taking the decision pixel-by-pixel. Nevertheless, one of the big issues of this research is that to make this classification, a proper ground-truth must be first built.

3.1.   Creating a new ground-truth version

Let $I_{i,j}^{Gt-human_k}$ be one of the K different human-made sketches, that are available for each image as a ground-truth. Then, as every image was drawn by K humans, i.e., K labels, they must be aggregated into one single label for ML purposes. In this paper, the next aggregation is proposed: the pixel label is considered as an edge if it has been drawn by at least h humans. This "aggregated" image is expected to avoid the subjective tendency of a single human, minimizing the possibility of wrong labels. However, this aggregation is not going to be the definitive image from which the labels are going to be built, because is not realistic to expect that a human is able to draw with absolute precision the location of an "edge". Here, it is important to remind that some Canny's ideas[4] generated the tradition of considering the edges the thinnest possible, i.e., 1-pixel thin, which can be considered a strong restriction. When evaluating the classified pixel with its human equivalent this strong constrain could be loosened in the matching process by allowing a $n \times n$ pixels window tolerance (for example, a 3×3 pixels window), as it is done in [8]. Because of this, the ground-truth image should be thickened to cover this $n \times n$ pixels window. An easy method to build this thickened image is through mathematical morphology.[23] More specifically, a dilation ($\oplus$) is applied over $I_{i,j}^{Gt-human_k}$ with a $square_n$ ($n \times n$ white pixels acting as a structural element). This process of building the definitive experiment's ground-truth is expressed by Eqs. (1) and (2). All this is shown in Fig. 1:

$$I_{i,j}^{dilatedhuman_k} = I_{i,j}^{Gt-human_k} \oplus square_n. \tag{1}$$

$$I_{i,j}^{h-dillabel} = \begin{cases} 1, & if \ \sum_{k=1}^{K} I_{i,j}^{dilatedhuman_k} \geq h. \\ 0, & otherwise. \end{cases} \tag{2}$$

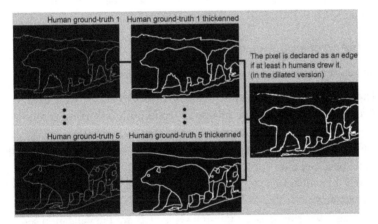

Fig. 1. First, the human ground-truth is dilated, and after, aggregated.

3.2. Collecting the predictors

For this research, the predictor variables are extracted from $I_{i,j}^{soft-Canny}$, which results after Canny's ED is applied over a grey image, but before the binarization –scaling– is performed. We distinguish between three predictor categories:

- **Pixel predictors.** These are the variables with information about the pixel. They include the intensity $I_{i,j}^{soft-Canny}$, the potential edge angle θ separated in $sin(\theta)$ and $cos(\theta)$, the pixel horizontal (i) and vertical (j), and the minimum distances from (i) and (j) to the top and left borders.

- **Neighbor predictors.** These are the predictors related to the pixel neighborhood. They include: the 3×3 neighbor's values of $I_{i,j}^{soft-Canny}$. Maximum, minimum, and average intensity of the 3 neighbor pixels of the pixel's row, maximum, minimum, and average intensity of the 3 neighbor pixels of the pixel's column, and maximum, minimum, and average intensity of the 3 neighbor pixels of both diagonals.
- **Segment predictors.** These variables are obtained from the segments that result from connecting the "edge candidates" of $I_{i,j}^{soft-Canny}$. In Refs. 10, 11 was presented the concept of edge segments. Collecting these variables is especially suitable in the case of Canny, as it uses global information. These segment predictors are "the length", "the intensity mean", "the maximum edginess", "the standard deviation", the "rule of thirds",[14] "the area of the rectangle containing the segment", and "the belonging itself of the pixel to a certain segment". Finally, five binary variables were included with information of the output of "classic" Canny (1= "edge", 0= "non-edge") and $thr_{sup}=\{0.2, 0.3, ..., 0.6\}$, and $thr_{inf} = 0.4\ thr_{sup}$.

3.3. The experiment's scheme

The experiment was conducted following these steps:

1. The 50 first images –sorted by number– of BSDS500[18,28] were used.
2. A modified version of the image's ground-truth was created following the method explained in 3.1, with $h = 2$ humans, and square$_3$.
3. The predictor variables explained in 3.2 were extracted taking as input the soft value obtained after applying the Canny algorithm. As a result of this step, a matrix with all cases –i.e., the pixels– as rows, and forty predictors as columns was created[b].
4. 30 images were used as the training set, and 20 for the validation set.
5. Logistic regression,[2] Neural networks (NN) and Support Vector Machines[1] (SVM) were employed over the training test. Dozens of models were tested. For logistic regression, all predictor variables, and Logic, Probit and Cloglog functions were employed. Moreover, different p-values were tested.[7] NN models were all built with one hidden layer varying the nodes from one to seven. Arctangent, exponential, and hyperbolic tangent activation functions were used. The independent variables of these NN models were the same as Logistic's. Finally, for the SVM models, linear, polynomial and gaussian

---

[b]The size of this matrix was 7720050 rows $\times$ 40 columns.

functions were tested, and 'box' boundaries ranged from 1 to 100. The SVM models used a random sample of 200.000 pixels[c] from the training set.

6. For the validation set of twenty images, the confusion matrix was computed. This was done 15 times as the classification is made using 15 different scoring thresholds (from 1% to 15% of the highest scorings). Three different F-measures were computed for each image: "F minimum" –representing the most different human–, "F mean" –representing the average human–, and "F maximum" –representing the closest human–. The matching between the outputs and the humans was made allowing a tolerance of 3×3 pixels window, following the procedure proposed in Ref. 8.

4. Results and Discussion

Both, Table 1 and Fig. 2 show that the proposed methodology, which is based on ED with ML techniques, outtakes classic Canny's performance by 14%. For the area under curve between percentages of edges ranging from 1% to 15 it reached an average of $F_{Max} = 0.562$ against $F_{Max} = 0.492$.

Table 1. Performance over BSDS500 of ML models and 'classic' Canny's.

Classifier/Algorithm	Human Max	Human Max (1% to 15%)	Human Mean	Human Mean (1% to 15%)	Human Min	Human Min (1% to 15%)
Logistic-Canny	.553	.542	.454	.450	.356	.357
Neural Networks-Canny	**.568**	**.562**	**.468**	**.467**	**.372**	**.372**
Support Vector Machine-Canny	.553	.544	.456	.451	.361	.359
'Classic' Canny	.557	.492	.458	.391	.354	.295

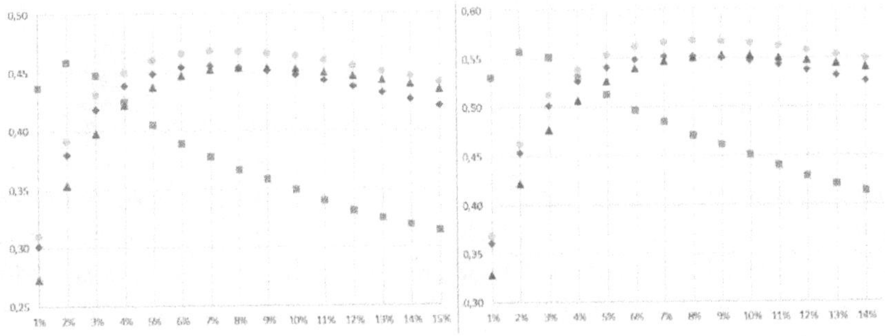

Fig. 2. Logistic, NN, SVM and "classic" Canny performances (Average and maximum F ranging from 1% to 15% of edges).

---

[c]The training size of SVM models was smaller due to the computational costs of this algorithm.

The best Logistic model found used 20 variables, the logit function, the stepwise method, and a p-value of 10^{-16}. The best NN model employed one hidden layer with 3 nodes, the same 20 variables as Logistic's, and used hyperbolic tangent as activation function. Finally, the best SVM model used Gaussian's, with a box size of 1.6, and 20 variables but some of them were different from the Logistic's, as in SVM case were not used the binary "classic" Canny variables neither the aggregations of neighbors. We can see in Fig. 3 three binarized images after learning the edges through the different methods. The best edge extraction was reached by the NN method. Notice that while the edges in "classic" Canny were thin, in the ML cases were thickened, which is consistent with the fact that all of them learned with a thickened version of the ground-truth.

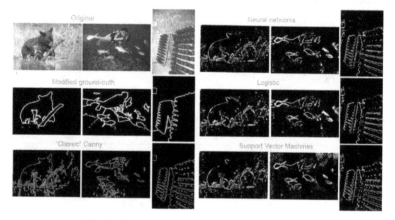

Fig. 3. Three examples among the outputs of the algorithms.

5. Conclusions

The proposed methodology shows that with ML techniques it is possible to improve Canny's. The edges extracted though ML were considered "better" edges in the sense that they contain less noisy artefacts than "classic" Canny. Moreover, in the case of our methods more pixels containing information about the texture were extracted. Furthermore, the same procedure has been proved to be easily adaptable to other ED algorithms, as it was already successfully applied as well over Sobel.[29] This improvement was partially possible due to an intelligent modification of the original ground-truth by means of allowing thicker edges. The utility of creating these thickened or dilated edges is justified by the fact that human vision is not able to match a certain edge to its exact pixel location.

A natural extension of this research could be related to considering more color or other channels with the extra difficulty of aggregating them in an intelligent manner. Finally, the idea of developing deep learning methods that make use of single pixels as input seems promising.

Acknowledgments

For conducting this research the code of Kermit Research Unit was quite helpful.[5]

References

1. VanderPlas, J. (2016). Python data science handbook: Essential tools for working with data. "O'Reilly Media, Inc.".
2. Breiman, L. (2017). Classification and regression trees. Routledge.
3. Campbell, J. B. and Wynne, R. H. (2011). Introduction to remote sensing. Guilford Press.
4. Canny, J. (1986). A computational approach to edge detection. IEEE Transactions on Pattern Analysis y Machine Intelligence, PAMI-8(6).
5. de Baets, B. and López-Molina, C. (2016). The kermit image toolkit (kitt), Ghent university, www.kermitimagetoolkit.net.
6. Dollar, P. and Zitnick, C. L. (2014). Fast edge detection using structured forests. IEEE transactions on pattern analysis and machine intelligence, 37(8):1558–1570.
7. Efroymson, M. (1960). Multiple regression analysis. Mathematical methods for digital computers, 191–203.
8. Estrada, F. J. and Jepson, A. D. (2009). Benchmarking image segmentation algorithms. International journal of computer vision, 85(2):167; 167–181; 181. doi:10.1007/s11263-009-0251-z pmid:.
9. Fathy, M. and Siyal, M. I. (1995). An image detection technique based on morphological edge detection y background differencing for real-time traffic analysis. Pattern Recognition Letters, 16(12):1321–1330.
10. Flores-Vidal, P. A., Gómez, D., Montero, J., and Villarino, G. (2017). Classifying segments in edge detection problems. In 2017 12th International Conference on Intelligent Systems y Knowledge Engineering (ISKE).
11. Flores-Vidal, P. A., Olaso, P., Gómez, D., and Guada, C. (2018). A new edge detection method based on global evaluation using fuzzy clustering. Soft Computing, pages 1–13.
12. Gao, G., Wan, X., Yao, et al. (2017). Reversible data hiding with contrast enhancement and tamper localization for medical images. Information Sciences, 385-386:250–265.

13. Goldstein, E. B. (2009). Sensación y percepción.
14. González, R. C. and Woods, R. E. (2008). Digital Image Processing, 3rd edition.
15. Ha, V. K., Ren, J., Xu, X., et al. (2018). Deep learning based single image super-resolution: A survey. In International Conference on Brain Inspired Cognitive Systems, 106–119. Springer.
16. He, Z.-W., Zhang, L., and Liu, F.-Y. (2020). Discostyle: Multi-level logistic ranking for personalized image style preference inference. International Journal of Automation and Computing, 17(5):637–651.
17. Kivinen, J., Williams, C., and Heess, N. (2014). Visual boundary prediction: A deep neural prediction network and quality dissection. Artificial Intelligence and Statistics, 512–521. PMLR.
18. Martin, D., Fowlkes, C., Tal, D., and Malik, J. (2001). A database of human segmented natural images y its application to evaluating segmentation algorithms y measuring ecological statistics. In Proceedings of the IEEE International Conference on Computer Vision, Vol. 2, 416–423.
19. Pal, S. K. and King, R. A. (1983). On edge detection of x-ray images using fuzzy sets. IEEE Transactions on Pattern Analysis y Machine Intelligence, PAMI-5(1):69–77.
20. Rosin, P. (1998). Thresholding for change detection. In Sixth International Conference on Computer Vision (IEEE Cat. No. 98, 274–279). IEEE.
21. Rosten, E. and Drummond, T. (2006). Machine learning for high-speed corner detection. In European conference on CV, 430–443. Springer.
22. Sen, P. C., Hajra, M., and Ghosh, M. (2020). Supervised classification algorithms in machine learning: A review. In Emerging technology in modelling and graphics, 99–111. Springer.
23. Soille, P. (2013). Morphological image analysis: principles and applications. Springer Science & Business Media.
24. Wu, Y.-H., Liu, Y., Zhang, L., and Cheng, M.-M. (2020). Edn: Salient object detection via extremely-downsampled network. arXiv preprint.
25. Zhao, C., Hao, Y., Sui, S., and Sui, S. (2018). A new method to detect the license plate in dynamic scene. In 2018 IEEE 7th Data Driven Control and Learning Systems Conference (DDCLS), pages 414–419. IEEE.
26. Zielke, T., Brauckmann, M., and Vonseelen, W. (1993). Intensity y edge-based symmetry detection with an application to car-following. CVGIP: Image Understanding, 58(2):177–190.
27. Ziou, D., Tabbone, S., et al. (1998). Edge detection techniques-an overview. Pattern Recognition and Image Analysis C/C of Raspoznavaniye Obrazov I Analiz Izobrazhenii, 8:537–559.

28. Berkeley Computer Vision page (09/23/2021). Berkeley Segmentation Data Set (BSDS500), https://www2.eecs.berkeley.edu/Research/Projects/CS/

29. Flores-Vidal, P. A., Castro, J., and Gómez, D. (2022). Post-processing of edge detection algorithms with machine learning techniques. Mathematical Problems in Engineering, 2022.

Formal modeling of mobile agent control system in uncertain environment

Xia Wang, Yang Xu and Keming Wang

School of Computing and Artificial Intelligence
Southwest Jiaotong University, Chengdu, China
{Kelly_wang@my, xuyang, kmwang}@swjtu.edu.cn

Jun Liu

School of Computing, Ulster University, Northern Ireland, UK
j.liu@ulster.ac.uk

Guanfeng Wu

National-Local Joint Engineering Laboratory of System Credibility
Automatic Verification, School of Mathematics, Southwest Jiaotong University
Chengdu, China
wl520gx@gmail.com

In a stochastic uncertainty environment, if the state transition of the mobile agent control system has only one preset plan, once this plan fails, the system will immediately enter the fault state. Therefore, multiple alternative plans can be provided in system design to improve system reliability, that is, alternatives can be implemented after the current plan fails. Considering the mobile agent control system in uncertain environment, this paper proposes a mobile agent control system with multiple alternative plans for system state transition. The nature of the system allows us to use one of the most recently developed open source model checkers for multi-agent system, MCMAS, to perform the model checking of safety verification task in designing the system. We formally model the proposed control system into Interpreted Systems Programming Language (ISPL) descriptions, which is actually the input of MCMAS. Finally MCMAS is used to validate the established ISPL model. The results show that the control system with multiple alternatives satisfies the required properties and can greatly improve the reliability of the system.

Keywords: Control system; uncertain environment; model checking; alternative plans.

1. Introduction

With the continuous development of computer technology, the function of intelligent control system has also been greatly improved. A mobile agent refers to an agent that can move as required to reach the target position in a certain environment. The intelligent control system is essential for ensuring the agent's safe operation in the environment. When the environment is determined, an intelligent algorithm is used to plan the movement of the agent,[2] which can complete the task quickly and with high accuracy. However, controlling the agent's movement in an uncertain environment is more difficult. Unknown anomalies, such as hardware failure, software failure, and obstacle interference, may arise as a result of the uncertain environment. Therefore, a successful industrial application of an agent mobility control system requires careful consideration of its safety and error tolerant in a stochastic uncertainty environment.

Formal method is a technology for modeling the system with strict mathematical semantics, which can well avoid the ambiguity in the system description.[3] Formal method has developed rapidly in recent decades, especially in the safety-critical field, and many specifications, such as EN50128, clearly put forward a strong recommendation to adopt formal methods in system design. In this paper, the formal modeling is used to model the mobile agent control system, and several alternative plans are added. It can effectively improve the safety and error tolerance of the control system. Finally, we use the model checker MCMAS to verify the established ISPL model of the control system with multiple alternative plans. The verification result demonstrates that the designed control system satisfies all of the required properties.

The rest of this paper is organized as follows. Section 2 depicts several work that related with this topic. Preliminaries are illustrated in Section 3. Section 4 introduces the framework. Section 5 presents and discusses a case. Section 6 concludes the work and outlines the future work.

2. Related Work

For the modeling of the control system, it is necessary to consider the risks and whether the emergency measures will interfere with the system operation and cause accidents under an uncertain environment. Many related studies have emerged in recent years. Wei et al. used the model checking to analyze whether some failures exist in the Flight Control System (FCS).[4] Lu et al. proposed the hierarchical Petri nets model for modeling and verification of emergency treatment processes.[5] Hou et al. built a formal model of emergency call systems with proper granularity.[7] Cheng gave an approach that provides the support for obtaining the constraint sets of all uncertain parameters in the abstract Linear Hybrid Automata (LHA) model when satisfying the safety requirements of the train control system.[6] However, few studies have focused on improving the system's error tolerance and reliability by adding alternative plans and modeling the control system with multiple alternative plans using formal method. This paper considers design and formal modeling of the control system with multiple alternative plans.

3. Preliminary

3.1. Interpreted System Programming Language (ISPL)

An Interpreted System (IS) is a formal description that has been proven to be an appropriate formalism for reasoning about knowledge and time in Multi-Agent System (MAS),[8] and that can be used to systematically model various types of MAS.[9]

Interpreted System Programming Language (ISPL) has multiple essential parts to represent the IS, i.e., the Environmental agent, the agents, the Initial state, Evaluation, and Formulaes.[1] In the agent (including the Environment agent), the Kripke model can be constructed utilising state variables, actions, protocols, and evolution. The possible world can be defined as the state variable. The marking function is represented by characteristics defined as actions in the labelling. The accessibility links between alternative worlds are denoted by the rules in evolution. The InitStates section defines the initial state of all agents. Finally, in the evaluation section, the atomic propositions and their valid states are declared independently. In the formula section, the properties are expressed as the logic formulas.

3.2. Computation Tree Logic (CTL)

Model checking is mainly used to check whether the formal model satisfies the requested properties in the specification. Computation Tree Logic (CTL)[10] is an important branching temporal logic that is sufficiently expressive for the formulation of system properties.

Definition 3.1. The definition of the CTL presents as follows,

$$\varphi ::= \rho \mid \neg\varphi \mid \varphi \wedge \varphi \mid EX\varphi \mid EG\varphi \mid EF\varphi \mid E(\psi U\varphi) \mid AX\varphi \mid AG\varphi \mid AF\varphi \mid A(\psi U\varphi)$$

where,

- $\rho \in PV$ is an atomic proposition. $\neg$ and $\wedge$ are the usual Boolean connective.
- E and A are the existential and universal quantifiers on paths.
- X, G and U are CTL path model connectives stands for 'next', 'globally' and 'until', respectively.

The CTL formula will be used to specify the required properties in the verification of the intelligent control system.

4. Formal Modeling of Control System in an Uncertain Environment

In an uncertain environment, circumstances anomalies, hardware problems, and human errors may cause the control system's original plan to fail, resulting in system failures. This paper proposes a Control System with Multiple Alternative Plans (CS_MAP) and modeling it by ISPL. It can be realized that when one plan fails, another plan can be activated immediately. Adding alternative plans can effectively improve system reliability.

Definition 4.1. The CS_MAP is defined as a tuple $CS\_MAP = (S, P_{i \to j}, Seq\_P)$.

where,

- S is the set of states, $S = \{S_0, ..., S_i, ..., S_j, ..., S_n\}$.
- $P_{i \to j} = \{P_{1 \to 2}, ..., P_{m-1 \to m}\}$ means that there are m plans that can be used to realize the system transition from state i to state j.
- Seq_P refers to the execution sequence of the plans in $P_{i \to j}$.

We may deduce from the Definition 4.1 that before modeling the CS_MAP system, designers first should determine which states exist in the system, which plans can accomplish the transition between the two states, and the execution sequence of the alternative plans.

The system is partitioned into several agents in ISPL-based modeling. A multi-agent system is formed when the system state is regarded as an agent and each plan represents an agent. List the system's required properties, and verify the CS_MAP system with the model checker MCMAS to see whether the system satisfies the requirements.

5. Case Study

Assuming that the agent moves in an uncertain environment, from state S_0 to S_1, Plan A is adopted first. Due to various factors (such as system failure, environmental obstruction), Plan A may fail. At this scenario, alternative plans B and C can be used to complete the process. As shown in Fig. 1.

Fig. 1.   The case of state transition.

When modeling a control system, it is necessary to clarify the timing between each state in the entire control process. According to the Definition 4.1, the state set of the system is $S = \{S_0, S_1\}$, $P_{0 \to 1} = \{Plan\ A, Plan\ B, Plan\ C\}$, and $Seq\_P : Plan\ A \to Plan\ B \to Plan\ C$. The system at S_0 adopts the Plan A first. If Plan A completes the state transition, the system enters the state S_1, and then enters the *Stop* state. Plan B is activated if Plan A fails. Plan C is activated if Plan B fails. If Plan C fails to execute, the system as a whole fails and enters the *Stop* state. The entire procedure is divided into the work of four agents: the Location agent records the agent's current location, the Plan A agent records the execution of Plan A, and the Plan B and C agents perform the same responsibilities as the Plan A agent. The Fig. 2 depicts the state transitions.

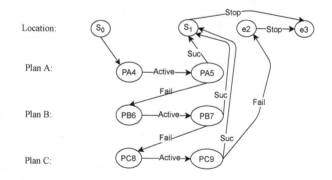

Fig. 2.   The state transition of the intelligent control system.

5.1. Formal modeling

We construct the formal model of the control system using the ISPL language, as illustrated in Fig. 3. Only the Plan A agent's description is presented here due to space limitations. Plan A includes two state, i.e., $PA4$

and $PA5$. The actions that can be executed by Plan A include *Active*, *Suc*, and *Fail*. '*Suc*' denotes success. The protocol indicates that when the system is in $PA4$ state, the system can choose the action *active*, that is, activate Plan A. When Plan A is activated, it enters state $PA5$. In $PA5$ state, the system can choose to act *Suc* or *Fail*. Evolution shows that when the system is in the $PA4$ state and adopts the action *Active* it will enter the $PA5$ state. In the $PA5$ state, if the Plan A successfully completes the state transition, the system enters the state S_1. If the Plan A fails and the system enters $PB6$.

```
Agent PlanA
Vars:
PA:{PA0, PA1, PA2, PA3, PA4, PA5,PA6, PA7, PA8, PA9, PA10};
end Vars
Actions = {Active_A,Success_A,Fail_A,PlanA_null};
Protocol:
PA=PA4 : {Active_A};
PA=PA5 : {Success_A,Fail_A};
Other: {PlanA_null};
end Protocol
Evolution:
PA=PA4 if PA=PA0 and Environment.Action=e_Location_S0 and Location.Action=Location_S0;
PA=PA5 if PA=PA4 and Environment.Action=e_Active_A and Action=PlanA_Active_A;
PA=PA1 if PA=PA5 and Environment.Action=e_Success_A and Action=PlanA_Success_A;
PA=PA6 if PA=PA5 and Environment.Action=e_Fail_A and Action=PlanA_Fail_A;
PA=PA7 if PA=PA6 and Environment.Action=e_Active_B and PlanB.Action=PlanB_Active_B;
PA=PA1 if PA=PA7 and Environment.Action=e_Success_B and PlanB.Action=PlanB_Success_B;
PA=PA8 if PA=PA7 and Environment.Action=e_Fail_B and PlanB.Action=PlanB_Fail_B;
PA=PA9 if PA=PA8 and Environment.Action=e_Active_C and PlanC.Action=PlanC_Active_C;
PA=PA1 if PA=PA9 and Environment.Action=e_Success_C and PlanC.Action=PlanC_Success_C;
PA=PA2 if PA=PA9 and Environment.Action=e_Fail_C and PlanC.Action=PlanC_Fail_C;
PA=PA3 if PA=PA2 and Environment.Action=e_Location_Fail and Location.Action=Location_Fail;
PA=PA3 if PA=PA1 and Environment.Action=e_Location_S1 and Location.Action=Location_S1;
PA=PA10 if PA=PA3 and Environment.Action=e_Location_Stop and Location.Action=Location_Stop;
PA=PA0 if PA=PA10 and Environment.Action=e_null;
end Evolution
end Agent
```

Fig. 3.   The ISPL model for Plan A agent.

5.2. *Verification*

Five CTL formulas are included in the model checking to depict the required properties, as follows.

Property 1 : Plan A is the preferred execution plan, hence all paths always exist at least one path will eventually activate Plan A.

CTL 1 : *AG EF Active_PlanA*.

Property 2 : All paths always satisfy the activation Plan A, and there is at least one path that satisfies the system eventually reaching the *stop* state.

234

CTL 2 : $AG(Active\_PlanA \rightarrow EF\ Location\_Stop)$;

Property 3 : In an uncertain environment, there is at least one path that will eventually activate Plan B.

CTL 3 : $EF Active\_PlanB$;

Property 4 : In an uncertain environment, there is at least one path that will eventually activate Plan C.

CTL 4 : $EF Active\_PlanC$;

Property 5 : After the execution of the plans, the system will always enter the S_1 state or the fault state, and will eventually enter the *stop* state.

CTL 5 : $AG(Location\_S1 \lor Location\_Fail \rightarrow AF\ Location\_Stop)$;

The verification result in MCMAS (shown in Fig. 4) demonstrates that the required properties are satisfied.

```
/home/swjtu/Desktop/mcmas-t-1.0.1-sc/mcmas-1.0.1-sc/mobile agent.ispl has been parsed successfully.
Global syntax checking...
Done
Encoding BDD parameters...
Building partial transition relation...
Building OBDD for initial states...
Building reachable state space...
Checking formulae...
Verifying properties...
  Formula number 1: (AG (EF Active_PlanA)), is TRUE in the model
  Formula number 2: (AG (Active_PlanA -> (EF Location_Stop))), is TRUE in the model
  Formula number 3: (EF Active_PlanB), is TRUE in the model
  Formula number 4: (EF Active_PlanC), is TRUE in the model
  Formula number 5: (AG ((Location_S1 || Location_Fail) -> (AF Location_Stop))), is TRUE in the model
done, 5 formulae successfully read and checked
execution time = 0.007
```

Fig. 4. The results of the verification in MCMAS.

6. Conclusion

This paper proposed an intelligent control system with multiple alternative plans in an uncertain environment. The designed control system is formally modeled using formal language ISPL, the system required properties are described based on CTL formulas, and the system model is verified by MCMAS. The result shows that the CS_MAP system satisfies the requirements.

Future research will consider specific alternative plans and the execution sequence of alternative plans, and propose corresponding selection strategies and criteria.

Acknowledgment

This work was supported by the National Natural Science Foundation of China (No. 62106206).

References

1. A. Lomouscio, H. Y. Qu, F. Raimondi. "MCMAS: A Model Checker for the Verification of Multi-Agent Systems," International Conference on Computer Aided Verification, 2009.
2. L. Xu. "Research Advances of Distributed Artificial Intelligence and Multi-agent Systems", BioTechnology, 2016, 14:113-114.
3. K. M. Wang, X. Wang, G. F. Wu, et al. "Consistency verification of safety-critical decision on routing operation of the train." in Proceedings of the 14th International FLINS Conference (FLINS 2020). 2020: 35-42.
4. Q. X. Wei, J. Jiao, and T. D. Zhao. "Flight Control System Failure Modeling and Verification based on SPIN." Engineering failure analysis, 2017, 82: 501-513.
5. F. M. Lu, Z. Qu, and B. Yang. "Hierarchy Modeling and Formal Verification of Emergency Treatment Processes." IEEE Transactions on Systems, Man, and Cybernetics: Systems 2013, 44(2): 220-234.
6. R. J. Cheng, J. Zhou, D. W. Chen, and Y. Song. "Model-based verification method for solving the parameter uncertainty in the train control system." Reliability Engineering and System Safety, 2016, 145: 169-182.
7. K. Y. Hou, Y. Li, Y. B. Yu, Y. Chen, and H. Zhou. "Discovering emergency call pitfalls for cellular networks with formal methods." Proceedings of the 19th Annual International Conference on Mobile Systems, Applications, and Services. 2021.
8. H. Y. Wang, Z. H. Duan, C. Tian. "APTL Model Checker for Verifying Multi-agent System", Journal of Software, 2019, 30(02):231-243.
9. M. Alam, S. R. Malik, Q. Javed, et al. "Formal Modeling and Verification of Security Controls for Multimedia Systems in the Cloud", Multimedia Tools and Applications, 2017, 76: 22845-22870.
10. C. Baier, J. P. Katoen. "Principles of model checking". MIT press, 2008.

Lightweight fusion channel attention convolutional neural network for helmet recognition

Chang Xu, Jinyu Tian and Zhiqiang Zeng*

*Department of Intelligent Manufacturing, WuYi University
JiangMen, 529030, China*
*zhiqiang.zeng@outlook.com

Recently, in the context of complex production and construction environments, the detection of unsafe behavior becomes more and more necessary to ensure the safety of construction projects. In this paper, a multi-level pyramidal feature fusion network based on an attention mechanism is proposed for the detection and identification of helmets worn by personnel. To improve the detection speed and accuracy, the network uses a residual block structure design and introduces the ECAttention channel attention mechanism to achieve cross-channel interaction. By doing so, it significantly reduces the complexity of the model while maintaining a high level of performance. To verify the effectiveness of the proposed detection network, this study compares some outstanding detection methods, drawing on existing public datasets and images obtained from the Internet. The results show the proposed network's detection efficiency is higher, demonstrating the ability to achieve real-time high-precision detection of helmets worn at production sites.

Keywords: Helmet detection; channel attention; multi-scale; feature fusion.

1. Introduction

During production, safety measures intended for the prevention of injury to operators are vital, as well the safety helmet, which is an important means to protect personnel. Typically, the environments in which they are necessary are intricate and hazardous, yet for various reasons, some operators ignore the importance of helmets. Therefore, there are still a large number of casualties caused by operators not wearing helmets as required.[1] Consequently, in such an environment, to better protect operators' safety, there is a need to detect and confirm when helmets are being worn. The traditional manual inspection is labor-intensive, error-prone, and cannot be monitored in real-time. Indeed, the incidences of workers not wearing helmets in accordance with safety regulations are many. To address this, the use of computer-generated vision to achieve real-time automatic detection of personnel and determining whether or not they are wearing helmets is an effective way to solve the above mentioned problem. This method can be divided into two types of methods: traditional machine learning and deep learning.

In traditional machine learning algorithms, helmet detection is performed by isolating color and shape features. For example, Talaulikar et al.[2] used threshold processing to segment the safety helmet from the background, followed by extracting the shape features of the safety helmet and acting Principal Component Analysis (PCA), before finally constructing an MLP classifier to achieve detection of the safety helmet as worn by onsite workers. Chiverton et al.[3] proposed a new shadow detection method by using the reflective characteristics of the safety helmet and subtracting the background to extract the helmet's feature image, using an SVM classifier to detect it. The above techniques primarily rely on human feature extraction, which, due to the single feature and poor generalization ability, cannot effectively detect safety helmets in complex construction environments. As a result, traditional detection methods have limited ability to solve the detection problem in the context of wearing safety helmets.

Currently, the majority of deep learning-based means of object detection can be divided into two categories: two-stage and one-stage object detection algorithms. The two-stage network encompasses region extraction and classification, which has higher accuracy overall. However, the presence of a large number of operations in the proposed extraction region leads to a slow detection speed.[4] Conversely, the one-stage network uses advanced features of the image to directly predict location and category, which improves the speed, but compared to the two-stage network, its small object detection is less effective and the localization accuracy is often insufficient.[4] In the actual helmet detection scenario, the two-stage network approach cannot achieve the necessary real time detection. In order to meet the accuracy and speed requirements of helmet wearing recognition for operational scenes, this paper first proposes a backbone network (ConCaNet) that can effectively extract image features. Based on this, the proposed technique incorporates YOLOv3[5] Neck (neck structure), YOLOv3 Head (detection head), and said ConCaNet to construct a one-stage helmet detection model. The experimental results showed that the final algorithm mAP_{50} detailed in this paper outperforms some outstanding detection network algorithms. In addition, it has improved detection accuracy for small, medium, and large objects. The proposed ConCaNet is applied to the helmet detection algorithm with the following main contributions:

(i) A multi-route parallel residual structure is designed for the network to learn features more efficiently. The introduction of a channel attention in the structure block allows the network to reduce the number of parameters while being able to maintain the correlation between channels.

(ii) ConCaNet has an extra scale compared to YOLOv3, and feature fusion is done in the FPN structure to increase the recognition accuracy of tiny objects, thereby mitigating the circumstances in which YOLOv3 misses detection for small targets as may be applicable here.

The structure of this paper is as follows: in Section 2, the proposed EFFCA (Effective Feature Fusion Channel Attention) module, ConCaNet network, and helmet detection model are described; detailed experimental results and analysis of ConCaNet on helmet detection tasks are detailed in Section 3; and finally, conclusions are stated in Section 4.

2. Helmet Detection Algorithm and Model

In this section, the multi-channel attention interaction enhancement module (EFFCA) as designed in this paper in 2.1 is proposed, which can exchange information between multiple channels, and the EFFCA module improves the network feature's extraction capability. The helmet detection backbone network, ConCaNet, is introduced in 2.2. Finally, details related to the application to the task of detecting helmets when worn or not worn are presented in 2.3.

2.1. *Effective Feature Fusion Channel Attention (EFFCA) module*

The EFFCA module contains the ECA[6] channel attention calculation operation, therefore, this section describes the module and the channel attention calculation process. In the ECA module, the input features first pass through the GAP (global average pooling) layer, followed by a convolutional layer with a convolutional kernel of size 1×1, a Sigmoid activation layer, before it is finally superimposed with the input features. The GAP can compress the feature maps on the channels into global features, thanks to which, EFFCA can learn the weight coefficients of each channel, as shown in Fig. 1 below. In the EFFCA module, the input features x will pass through the convolutional layers of convolutional kernels with sizes 1×1 and 3×3 in turn, followed by the ECA module to obtain $Output_1$. The input features

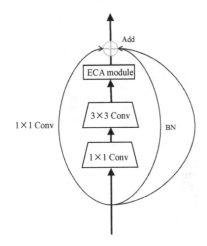

Fig. 1.   EFFCA block.

will also pass through the convolutional layers of convolutional kernel size 1×1 and BN (BatchNorm) operation, resulting in $Output_2$ and $Output_3$, respectively. Here the design of the 1×1 convolution can effectively integrate all channel information,[7] and the BN layer can effectively prevent the neural network gradient from disappearing.[8] Finally, with input features x, the EFFCA module output results in $x + Output_1 + Output_2 + Output_3$.

Inspired by He et al. in ResNet,[9] who used residual connections to train deep networks, a design for a four-way parallel structure in EFFCA is provided here. For a stacked block structure, it was assumed its learned features can be noted as $H_{(x)}$ when the input is x. In ConCaNet, the residual connected block represented in Fig. 2 is driven to learn features as $F_{(x)} = H_{(x)} - I_{(x)} - G_{(x)} - x$, where $I_{(x)}$ and $G_{(x)}$ represent the convolution and BN operations, respectively. Then, the original learned features may be expressed as $F_{(x)} + I_{(x)} + G_{(x)} + x$. This structure can make it easier for the network to learn features, and the structure in Fig. 1 allows the network to have better performance compared to those that learn the original features directly.

2.2. ConCaNet

The structure of the network model is shown in Fig. 2. The input image size is $224 \times 224 \times 3$, and the low-level features are first extracted by a two-layer convolution operation. The feature map then goes through an EFFCA

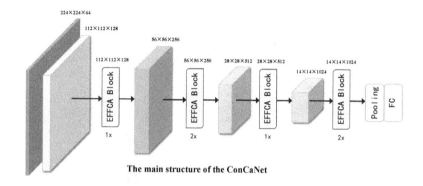

The main structure of the ConCaNet

Fig. 2.   ConCaNet structure diagram.

convolution block to calculate the channel attention, and the number of output channels in the convolution block is equal to the number of input channels. After each EFFCA block, a convolution layer is passed to boost the number of feature channels.

2.3. *Design of a network to detect helmets*

In object detection, the most basic network consists of a backbone network, a detection neck structure, and a detection head.[10] Briefly, the backbone network is used to extract image features, the neck structure is responsible for feature fusion, and the detection head eventually gives predicted values for the target location as well as the class to which it belongs. The structure of the helmet detection network is designed as shown in Fig. 3, where the input image size is $224 \times 224 \times 3$. The image is first fed into the feature

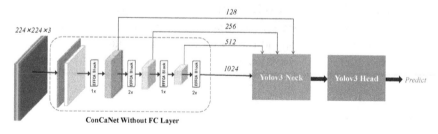

ConCaNet Without FC Layer

Fig. 3.   Detection network structure design – the helmet detection network can predict the object class and location while generating candidate regions in a one-stage object detection algorithm.

extraction network ConCaNet, where four scale feature maps are used in the network before being passed into the neck structure for fusion to improve the detection accuracy for small, medium, and large objects. The neck structure fuses the four scale features and sends them into the detection head structure to obtain the object location information and the predicted value of the class.

3. Experimental

3.1. *Introduction to the dataset*

The dataset used in this paper is obtained from the public safety helmet dataset of Baidu Paddle community and web crawler. The final COCO format dataset is built by using labelImg and other annotation tools. A total of 6000 photos make up the helmet dataset, which includes a training set, a validation set, and a test set. The training set accounts for 60%, the validation set for 20%, and the test set for 20%, all of which include data from tiny, middle, and large objects. Considering the application benefits and economic costs of the detection task, the detection objects are divided into two categories in this paper: those who wear helmets correctly are marked as Helmet category, and those who do not wear helmets are marked as Head. in addition, those who wear straw hats, bandanas, etc. as helmets in the dataset are marked as Head category, and those unused helmets are not marked in any way and are only treated as background.

3.2. *Experimental settings and results*

In the helmet detection task, the training image is randomly cropped to a section measuring 224×224 pixels, random horizontal flipping and random cropping stitching are used to increase the amount of training data, and label smoothing[11] is carried out to avoid overfitting. The AdamW optimizer[12] was applied for optimization, where the momentum was set to 0.9, weight decay to 0.05, and batch size to 128. After five preparatory iterations, the warm-up learning rate was set to 1×10^{-6} while the initial learning rate was set to 1×10^{-4}, but because the cosine learning rate strategy decreased, 311 iterations were trained on a single NVIDIA A100 GPU. The accuracy on the validation set was evaluated using images with a center crop of 224×224 pixels. For the helmet detection task, the algorithms performed to the standard as detailed in Table 1.

'Params', 'FPS', and 'FLOPs' represent the number of parameters, the frame rate, and the number of floating-point calculations per second, re-

Table 1. Comparison of metrics of different algorithms

Model	#Params(M)	#FPS(img/s)	#FLOPs(G)	#mAP_50	#mAPs	#mAPm	#mAPl
Cascade_Rcnn_r50	68.93	21.72	**234.47**	83.7	35.0	60.0	63.7
YOLOF_r50	42.09	24.28	98.19	87.3	39.5	64.6	**70.9**
YOLOv3_d53	61.53	22.92	193.87	**89.1**	41.6	62.9	54.4
ConCaNet	**37.65**	**29.66**	137.02	88.2	**42.3**	**64.7**	70.3

spectively. The proposed detection algorithm as detailed here is the best according to four metrics: Params; FPS; mAPs; and mAPm. In the mAPl metric, it is superior by 28.3% and 15.9% when compared to Cascade Rcnn r50 and YOLOv3 d53, respectively. ConCaNet is effective in detecting helmet objects of all three sizes. In terms of FPS, the proposed algorithm demonstrated the fastest detection speed, showing it can be applied in practical environments since it can meet the demand for detecting worn helmets in terms of accuracy.

4. Conclusion

The ConCaNet algorithm designed for the purpose of detecting helmets worn by operators, as proposed in this paper, can effectively learn data features while significantly reducing the number of necessary parameters, and improve the model detection performance using data enhancement, channel attention and multiple parallel residual mechanisms, and multi-scale feature fusion. This resulted in improved mAP50, which was 4.5% higher than in Cascade Rcnn. With a near match to the mAP50 of YOLOv3, the detection of small, medium, and large targets (relating to helmet size and proximity) was better with the ConCaNet as proposed in this paper. Future research will be conducted to investigate how the algorithm performs when subjected to adverse conditions including occlusion and bad weather and how this can be improved effectively.

References

1. S. Ajith, S. Chandrasekaran and V. A. Prabu, Safety and hazards management in construction sites - a review, *Journal of Technology* **35**, 175 (2020).
2. A. S. Talaulikar, S. Sanathanan and C. N. Modi, An enhanced approach for detecting helmet on motorcyclists using image processing and machine learning techniques (2019).
3. J. Chiverton, Helmet presence classification with motorcycle detection and tracking, *IET Intelligent Transport Systems* **6**, 259 (2012).

4. Y. Xiao, Z. Tian, J. Yu, Y. Zhang, S. Liu, S. Du and X. Lan, A review of object detection based on deep learning, *Multimedia Tools and Applications* **79**, 23729 (2020).

5. J. Redmon, S. Divvala, R. Girshick and A. Farhadi, You only look once: Unified, real-time object detection, in *Proceedings of the IEEE conference on computer vision and pattern recognition*, 2016.

6. Q. Wang, B. Wu, P. Zhu, P. Li and Q. Hu, Eca-net: Efficient channel attention for deep convolutional neural networks, in *2020 IEEE/CVF Conference on Computer Vision and Pattern Recognition (CVPR)*, 2020.

7. A. Howard, M. Sandler, G. Chu, L.-C. Chen, B. Chen, M. Tan, W. Wang, Y. Zhu, R. Pang, V. Vasudevan *et al.*, Searching for mobilenetv3, in *Proceedings of the IEEE/CVF International Conference on Computer Vision*, 2019.

8. W. Wang, X. Huang, J. Li, P. Zhang and X. Wang, Detecting covid-19 patients in x-ray images based on mai-nets, *International Journal of Computational Intelligence Systems* **14**, 1607 (2021).

9. K. He, X. Zhang, S. Ren and J. Sun, Deep residual learning for image recognition, in *Proceedings of the IEEE conference on computer vision and pattern recognition*, 2016.

10. K. Chen, J. Wang, J. Pang, Y. Cao, Y. Xiong, X. Li, S. Sun, W. Feng, Z. Liu, J. Xu *et al.*, Mmdetection: Open mmlab detection toolbox and benchmark, *arXiv preprint arXiv:1906.07155* (2019).

11. C. Szegedy, V. Vanhoucke, S. Ioffe, J. Shlens and Z. Wojna, Rethinking the inception architecture for computer vision, in *Proceedings of the IEEE conference on computer vision and pattern recognition*, 2016.

12. I. Loshchilov and F. Hutter, Decoupled weight decay regularization, *arXiv preprint arXiv:1711.05101* (2017).

Collaborative control model of automatic intersection based on vehicle networking environment

Jie Xian[1], Hailiang Zhao[2], Ling Yan[3] and Peiyao Liu[4]

School of Mathematics, Southwest Jiao tong University
Chengdu, 610031, China
[1]1482160005@qq.com, [2]hailiang@home.swjtu.edu.cn
[3]1021495347@qq.com, [4]liupeiyao@my.swjtu.edu.cn

In this paper, a control model is proposed to realize the coordinated control of traffic system composed of automatic intersection and intelligent vehicle. Firstly, conflict circle and vehicle motion model are proposed. Then the conflict model is constructed by using the circular contour of the vehicle. Avoid collisions only need to consider the constraint of two vehicles in the conflict circle. Finally, based on stability and traffic efficiency, a control model is proposed. The model takes the acceleration of the vehicle, the speed and time of entering the intersection as variables. The results show that compared with the traffic light control, the optimization strategy can effectively improve the traffic efficiency under the premise of meeting the safety and stability.

Keywords: Intelligent transportation; automatic intersection management; connected autonomous vehicle; vehicle collision avoidance; traffic efficiency.

1. Introduction

Intelligent vehicles are expected to improve traffic efficiency at non-signal intersections. At present, the research on automatic intersection management is mainly divided into cooperative resource reservation and trajectory planning.[1]

Cooperative resource reservation regards vehicle conflict as a competition for space-time resources, and achieves collision avoidance by constraining the arrival time of vehicles.[2-4] He Zhengbing et al. designed a freely steerable automatic intersection without signal,[5] the paper adopts the principle of FCFS, it causes excessive time delays. For such problems, Wu Wei et al based on spatial discrete method to assign vehicle occupancy time.[6] But arrival time constraints create nonlinear constraints that increase model complexity. It also ignores the important role of speed. Trajectory planning considers that the essence of vehicle collision is the intersection of two vehicle bodies, and a safe distance between vehicles is required for collision avoidance.[7-9] For example, Chai Linguo et al. proposed an intersection control algorithm based on the gap theory.[10] However, the vehicle distance constraint is too strong, makes the intersection resources underutilized. Except the above approach, there are other methods[11–12] for the traffic problems at intersection. But so far, many of these works do not carefully consider the intersection and vehicle as a system.

For the above problems, this paper considers the vehicle distance and the positional relationship between the vehicle and the conflict circle, so that avoid collisions only need to consider the constraint of two vehicles in the conflict circle, and some infeasible strategies in the methods provided by other articles can be feasible in this paper. The vehicle circle model is used to analyze the collision process, and the coordinated control system composed of intelligent intersections and intelligent vehicles is proposed. Finally, a simple method is given by using the principle of group solution and proximity. The validity of the model is demonstrated by an example of a two-way single-lane intersection.

2. Intersection Analysis

2.1. Model assumptions

For ease of description, only straight and left-turn vehicles are considered, which is relatively complex and typical, and the following assumptions are made.
- All intelligent vehicles are of the same type, and there is no non-intelligent interference on the road.
- All communications without delay.
- Vehicle lane change process has been completed, followed by lane direction.

2.2. Definition of conflict circle

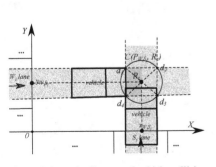

Fig. 1. Schematic diagram of vehicle collision and conflict circle.

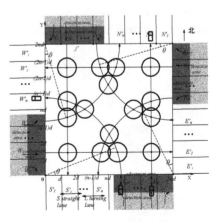

Fig. 2. Schematic diagram of a two-way intersection formed by n entrance lanes.

Obviously, the vehicle trajectory is a strip area. As shown in Fig. 1, there are four intersections between the two trajectory boundaries. Due to the different definitions of conflict domain in different literature,[8–10] for clarity, this paper gives the following definitions.

Definition 2.1. (*Conflict circle*) *Let the intersection point of the center lines of the two driving trajectories be P, and the distances from P to the four intersection points of the boundary are* d_1, d_2, d_3 *and* d_4 *respectively. Take P as the center and* $R_c = \max\{d_1, d_2, d_3, d_4\}$ *as the radius to make a circle* $C(P, R_c)$, *which is called the conflict circle of the two trajectories.*

Figure 1 shows an example of a collision circle, the size of which is related to both the vehicle and the collision type. Similar analysis can be done when the vehicle types are different. As shown in Fig. 2, for case of the two-way intersection, the number of conflict circles on each trajectory is 2(n-1).

3. Intersection Control Model

3.1. *Vehicle motion model*

For simplicity of control, set each entrance lane has a detection area and an adjustment area, the lengths are d_{det} and d_{adj} respectively, as shown in Fig. 1. Starts when the first vehicle arrives at the detection area, after a detection period T_{det}, all vehicles in the detection area will be considered. It is stipulated that the vehicle only adjusts the state with uniform acceleration in the adjustment area, and the rest of the road sections are driven at a uniform speed. The motion state of the vehicle is divided into three stages, for vehicle k on lane S_i, let its position at each stage be $(x_{1S_{ik}}, y_{1S_{ik}})$, $(x_{2S_{ik}}, y_{2S_{ik}})$, and $(x_{3S_{ik}}, y_{3S_{ik}})$ respectively. When S_i is a straight lane, the motion of vehicle k can be expressed as follows.

$$x_{mS_{ik}}(t) = \left(2n + \frac{1}{2} - i\right)d \quad (m = 1, 2, 3), \tag{1}$$

$$y_{1S_{ik}}(t) = \int_{t_0}^{t} v_{0S_{ik}} dt - (d_{adj} + d_{det}), \tag{2}$$

$$y_{2S_{ik}}(t) = \frac{v_{intS_{ik}}^2 - v_{0S_{ik}}^2}{2a_{S_{ik}}} - d_{adj}, \tag{3}$$

$$y_{3S_{ik}}(t) = y_{2S_{ik}} - \int_{t}^{t} v_{intS_{ik}} dt + d_{adj}, \tag{4}$$

where d is the lane width. $v_{0S_{ik}}$, $a_{S_{ik}}$ and $v_{intS_{ik}}$ represent the initial velocity, target acceleration and target velocity, respectively. t' represents the time for the vehicle to complete the state adjustment. When S_i is the turning lane, before entering the intersection, the vehicle motion formula on it is the same as in the straight lane. After entering the intersection, by the assumption, the vehicle is in uniform circular motion, the radius $R = \left(2n+\dfrac{1}{2}-i\right)d$, and the center is $(0,0)$. It

is known that $t_{intS_{ik}} = \dfrac{d_{det}}{v_{0S_{ik}}} + \dfrac{v_{intS_{ik}} - v_{0S_{ik}}}{a_{S_{ik}}} + \dfrac{2a_{S_{ik}}d_{adj} + v_{0S_{ik}}{}^2 - v_{intS_{ik}}{}^2}{2a_{S_{ik}}v_{intS_{ik}}}$, where $t_{intS_{ik}}$ is

the time to enter the intersection, so the vehicle position can be expressed as

$$x_{S_{ik}}(t) = R\,cos\left(\int_{t_{intS_{ik}}}^{t} \frac{v_{intS_{ik}}}{R}dt\right), \qquad (5)$$

$$y_{S_{ik}}(t) = R\,sin\left(\int_{t_{intS_{ik}}}^{t} \frac{v_{intS_{ik}}}{R}dt\right). \qquad (6)$$

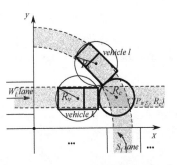

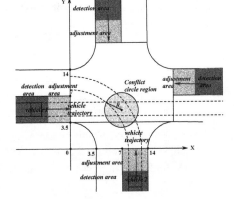

Fig. 3. Schematic diagram of the circular contour model of the vehicle.

Fig. 4. Schematic diagram of the intersection formed by a two-way single lane.

3.2. Determination of driving constraints

(1) Constraints for collision avoidance

As shown in Fig. 3, for convenience, the vehicle shape is equivalent to a circle, the center of the vehicle as the circular center, and the diagonal $2R_v$ as the diameter. Obviously, no collision means that the two circles have no intersection, that is, the distance between the centers of the two vehicles is greater than a certain distance. However, just as the case in Fig. 3, a vehicle has left the conflict circle and cannot collide again, but it still does not meet the requirements,[13] which leads to insufficient utilization of intersection resources. Therefore, this paper puts forward the following constraints.

$$\chi_\Omega(t)[(x_k(t) - x_l(t))^2 + (y_k(t) - y_l(t))^2] \geq \chi_\Omega(t)(2R_v)^2. \tag{7}$$

$\chi_\Omega(t) = \begin{cases} 1, & t \notin \Omega \\ 0, & t \in \Omega \end{cases}$, $\Omega = \Omega_k \cup \Omega_l$. Let $f(t)$ represents the Euclidean distance from the center of the vehicle to the center of the conflict circle at time t. $R_c + R_v$ is approximately the distance between the center of the vehicle and the center of the area when the vehicle reaches the boundary of the collision circle. Let $\Omega_q = \{t \mid R_c + R_v \leq f_q(t), f_q(t) < f_q(t + \Delta t)\}$ ($q = k, l$), the first inequality says that the time when the vehicle is outside the conflict circle, and the second one represents the time when the vehicle leaves the circle. The constraint will no longer work after the vehicle leaves the conflict circle.

(2) Velocity and acceleration constraints

Vehicle speed and acceleration cannot exceed road limits and vehicle dynamics constraints, that is, both must meet

$$v_{min} \leq v(t) \leq v_{max}, \tag{8}$$

$$a_{min} \leq a \leq a_{max}. \tag{9}$$

Where a_{min}, a_{max} and v_{min}, v_{max} are the minimum and maximum acceleration and speed that the vehicle can reach.

(3) Car-following constraints

When vehicles k-1 and k follow car-following behavior, let the distance between vehicles be d_{gap}, the minimum safe distance be d_{safe}. It is required that

$$d_{safe} \leq d_{gap} + \int_{t_0}^{t} \left[v_{0(k-1)} + \int_{t_0}^{t} a_{k-1} dt \right] dt - \int_{t_0}^{t} \left[v_{0k} + \int_{t_0}^{t} a_k dt \right] dt. \tag{10}$$

(4) Adjustment area constraint

To ensure the status adjustment can be completed in the adjustment area, it is required that

$$\frac{v_{int}^2 - v_0^2}{2a} \leq d_{adj}. \tag{11}$$

3.3. Determination of the objective function

Assuming that after T_{det}, the number of vehicles in the detection area on the D_i lane is D_{iA}. For the intersection shown in Fig. 2, the establishment process of the objective function is as follows.

(1) Construction of traffic efficiency index

Let S represent the distance of the collision circle from the entrance of the lane. In order to increase the traffic efficiency, it is necessary to increase the speed of vehicles and the utilization rate of the conflict circle as much as possible. So define the following two indicators.

$$E = \sum_{D=E,W,S,N} \sum_{i=1}^{n-1} \sum_{k=1}^{D_{iA}} (v_{max} - v_{intD_{ik}}), \qquad (12)$$

$$\sigma_T = \sum_{D=E,W,S,N} \sum_{i=1}^{n-1} \sum_{k=1}^{D_{iA}} \sum_{m=1}^{2(n-1)} \left| \frac{t_{intD_{ik}} + \dfrac{S_{D_i P_m}}{v_{intD_{ik}}} - t_{intD'_{ik}} - \dfrac{S_{D'_i P'_m}}{v_{intD'_{ik}}}}{2} \right|. \qquad (13)$$

(2) Construction of vehicle stability index

The acceleration index required for vehicle stability is defined as follows.

$$A = \sum_{D=E,W,S,N} \sum_{i=1}^{n-1} \sum_{k=1}^{D_{iA}} | a_{D_{ik}} |. \qquad (14)$$

In order to optimize the above three indicators, the objective function of the control model can be defined as follows.

$$min Z = p_1 F(E) + p_2 F(\sigma_T) + p_3 F(A), \qquad (15)$$

where p_i is the weight coefficient, and $F(x)$ is the elimination dimension function. The first item reflects vehicle transit time, the second item reflects the utilization of conflict circles, and the third item reflects vehicle stability.

3.4. The idea and concrete steps of obtaining satisfactory control strategy

The above problem is easy to find many feasible control strategies, and compare their revenue function values to obtain a more satisfactory strategy, which is a simple method. Speed can be classified into several grades, depending on the grades, two conflicting vehicles can be combined into several classes. Using the above method to obtain a satisfactory control strategy for each classification, two conflicting vehicles can be adjusted according to the principle of proximity.

Consider the traffic situation of two vehicles on the straight lane W and the turning lane S, as shown Fig. 4. The above situation can be extended to the situation where multiple vehicles pass through the intersection. Combined with reality, take the lane width as $3.5m$, the vehicle length as $4.7m$ and the width as $1.8m$. Combined with vehicle dynamics and road speed limit conditions, the acceleration and speed ranges are set as $[-3,3]m \cdot s^{-2}$ and $[4.5,16.67]m \cdot s^{-1}$, respectively. Divide the speed into three grades, namely $[4.5,8]$, $[8,12.5]$ and $[12.5,16.67]$, and set the length of the adjustment area as $100m$.

Let the initial velocities of vehicles 1 and 2 be $9m \cdot s^{-1}$, $12m \cdot s^{-1}$, and their distances to the conflict area are $5m$ and $48m$, respectively. The three feasible strategies are shown in Table 1. Let $p_1 = p_2 = p_3 = 3^{-1}$, and the value of the revenue function under each strategy is 4.781, 5.942 and 4.139, respectively.

Table 1. Examples of three feasible strategies under two working conditions.

Strategy	vehicle	acceleration / m•s^{-2}	speed / m•s^{-1}	time/s
1	1	2	10	11.136
	2	0	12	12.333
2	1	0	9	12.222
	2	-2	10	13.9
3	1	3	12	9.569
	2	2	15	1.816

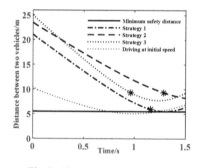

Fig. 5. Distance between vehicles.

The variation of the distance between vehicles is shown in Fig. 5. The black dots on each curve correspond to the critical point where a vehicle leaves the conflict circle. In Strategy 3, although the distance between the two vehicles will be reduced to a critical distance, one vehicle has already left the circle at that time, so there will be no collision. Therefore, the third strategy is not only feasible, but also the best among the three strategies according to the value of the revenue function. The control model proposed in this paper is compared with the traffic scene controlled by traditional traffic lights. When the number of vehicles in the detection area is known, the traffic time is taken as the evaluation index. The time interval of traffic lights is set to be $15s$, under the control of signal lights, it takes $18.531s$ for vehicles 1 and 2 to completely leave the intersection, while the optimization strategy 3 under the control model proposed in this paper only needs $12.047s$.

4. Conclusion

In order to reduce the complexity, this paper defines the conflict circle and the vehicle circle model, and establishes a constraint to avoid collisions based on the relative position function of the vehicle and the conflict circle, so that collision avoidance only needs to consider the constraints of the two vehicles in the conflict circle. The control model composed of automatic intersection and intelligent vehicle, considering vehicle stability and traffic efficiency can meet the needs of different scenarios. The experimental results show that the control model proposed in this paper can significantly improve the road traffic efficiency as well as the driving safety and stability compared with the signal light control.

References

1. L. Chen et al., Cooperative Intersection Management: A Survey[J], IEEE Transactions on Intelligent Transportation Systems, 2016, 17(2): 570-586.
2. Y. Xu et al., V2X Enabled Non-Signalized Intersections Management: A Function Approximation Approach, GLOBECOM 2020 - 2020 IEEE Global Communications Conference, 2020 IEEE. December 2020: 1-5.
3. C. Zhu, Research on cooperative driving of vehicles at automatic intersections under vehicle networking environment [D], 2018. (in Chinese)
4. Jiang Haorani et al., Automatic intersection vehicle timing optimization model based on virtual fleet [J/OL], Chinese Journal of Highway: 1-24 [2021-12-16]. (In Chinese)
5. Z. B. He et al., Erasing Lane Changes from Roads: A Design of Future Road Intersections[J], IEEE Transactions on Intelligent Vehicles, 2018, 3(2): 173-184.
6. W. Wu et al., Traffic control model for free steering lanes at intersections under autonomous driving environment [J], China Journal of Highways, 2019, 32 (12): 25-35. (In Chinese)
7. Kamal M. et al., A vehicle-intersection coordination scheme for smooth flows of traffic without using traffic lights[J], IEEE transactions on intelligent transportation systems, 2015, 16(3): 1136-1147.
8. Y. Wang et al., Road capacity and throughput for safe driving autonomous vehicles[J], IEEE Access, 2020, 8: 95779-95792.
9. M. Duan et al., Research on Multi - vehicle Cooperative Control of Unmanned Vehicle Crossroads [J], Automotive Technology, 2020 (4): 33-39. (In Chinese)

10. L. G. Chai et al., Intelligent vehicle intersection operation control method based on gap theory [J], Journal of system simulation, 2019, 31(9): 1875-1882. (In Chinese)

11. Y. Zheng, Research on vehicle cooperative control algorithm for non-signalized intersection under vehicle networking environment [D], Jilin University, 2020. (In Chinese)

12. Bas van der Bijl et al., A Practical Approach to Implementing Automated Intersection Management [J]. Traffic and Transportation Engineering: English version, 2019, 7(5): 212-217.

13. S. M. Chen et al., Research on the collision avoidance model and simulation of intelligent vehicles at the intersection of ramps [J]. Agricultural Equipment and Vehicle Engineering, 2016, 54(2): 44-50.

Treelet-edge-weighted graph neural network for premise selection in first-order logic

Xue Ma, Xiaomei Zhong*, Yongqi Lan, Xingxing He and Guoyan Zeng

National-Local Joint Engineering Lab of System Credibility Automatic Verification
School of Mathematics, Southwest Jiaotong University
Chengdu, China
x.he@home.swjtu.edu.cn

The performance of automated theorem provers for large-scale mathematical problems is greatly reduced compared with smaller-scale problems, premise selection is one of the effective solutions. Since current graph neural networks usually aggregate information of neighbor nodes to update the feature representation of the central node, the order information between child nodes and nodes' types in first-order logical formulas are ignored. To address the above problems, a new graph neural network model based on treelet and edge weights is proposed to encode first-order logical formulas in this paper. The experimental results show that the proposed model performs better in the premise selection task on the same dataset, which can improve the classification accuracy by about 2% compared with the best model of current graph neural network models.

Keywords: First-order logical formula; graph neural network; premise selection; treelet.

1. Introduction

With the development of automated theorem provers (ATPs), more and more mathematical theorems are converted into first-order logical formulas and proved by ATPs. At the same time, with the development of computer science and the expansion of practical applications of automated theorem proving, ATPs need to face more and more large-scale problems from large mathematical libraries, which have hundreds premises, but only a small number of premises are useful for the proof of the conclusion. This will result in slower performance of ATPs. One of effective ways to solve this problem is premise selection, that is, in the preprocessing stage of automated theorem proving, evaluating and selecting the useful premise from a

---

*Corresponding author.

large-scale premise set that is most likely to participate in the proof of the conjecture.

At present, there are some deep learning algorithms, such as convolutional neural networks,[1] long short-term memory neural networks,[2] and GNNs,[3] combined with ATPs to guide the premise selection task. Due to logical formulas can be naturally represented as directed acyclic graphs (DAGs) that preserve the syntax and semantic information of formulas, the combination of automated theorem proving and GNNs is one of the hottest research topics currently. The mainstream graph neural network frameworks often ignore the internal information of the first-order logical formulas, so that the first-order logical formulas cannot be well encoded. For example, there is an order between the corresponding child nodes in a logical graph, also, the importance of different node types in the premise selection task is generally different. Wang[4] proposes a method of order preservation for higher-order logical formulas. The method is extended to first-order logical formulas in this paper, and a graph neural network, i.e., treelet-edge-weighted graph neural network (TE-GNN), is designed for the premise selection task which can also encode the node types. The experimental results show that TE-GNN is able to perform better in the premise selection task.

The rest of this paper is organized as follows. Preliminaries are illustrated in Section 2. Section 3 introduces the framework. Section 4 introduces the dataset. Section 5 outlines experimental results. Section 6 concludes the work and future work. Acknowledgments are shown in Section 7.

2. Preliminary

2.1. Order-preserving embedding

Given a node v in graph $G = (V, E)$, let $\langle v, w \rangle \in E$ be an outgoing edge of v, and let $r_v(w) \in \{1, 2, \cdots\}$ be the rank of edge $\langle v, w \rangle$ among all outgoing edges of v. We define a treelet of graph G as a tuple of nodes $(u, v, w) \in V \times V \times V$ such that (1) both $\langle v, u \rangle$ and $\langle v, w \rangle$ are edges in the graph and (2) $\langle v, u \rangle$ is ranked before $\langle v, w \rangle$ among all outgoing edges of v. In other words, a treelet is a subgraph that consists of a head node v, a left child u and a right child w. We use τ_G to denote all treelets of graph G, that is, $\tau_G = \{(u, v, w) : (v, u) \in E, (v, w) \in E, r_v(u) < r_v(w)\}$.[4]

2.2. Edge type embedding

We use the names of logical connectives, quantifiers and equivalents as the types of nodes, and the types of predicates, functions, constants and variables are recorded as pred, func, const, and var. Each edge type contains the type of its corresponding parent node and child node. Figure 1 shows edge types of $\Phi : \forall x \forall y \left[(p(a, f(x)) \rightarrow q(b, y)) \vee q(f(x), g(a, y))\right]$.

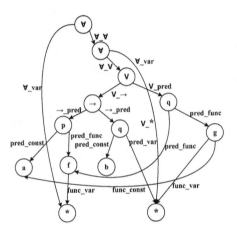

Fig. 1.   The edge types of formula Φ

3. Model

TE-GNN mainly includes four parts: initialization, message aggregation, message propagation, and graph aggregation. And then we use graph vector representations of premises and conjectures after graph aggregation as the input of binary classifier for classification prediction.

3.1. TE-GNN

In initialization, the model maps feature vectors x_v and x_e into initial state vectors $h_v{}^{(0)}$ and $h_e{}^{(0)}$ by embedding functions F_v and F_e.

$$h_v^{(0)} = F_v(x_v) \tag{1}$$

$$h_e^{(0)} = F_e(x_e) \tag{2}$$

where $h_v^{(0)} \in R^{d_{h_v}}$, $h_e^{(0)} \in R^{d_{h_e}}$, d_{h_v} and d_{h_e} are the dimensions of output state vectors. F_v and F_e are different lookup tables that store vectors of fixed dictionaries and sizes, they encode the input feature vectors to fix-size state vectors.

In message aggregation, TE-GNN aggregates the information of neighbor nodes from two parts. The first part gathers the node type information, and the second part gathers the order information and the parent-child information of the central nodes.

The node type information is added to the node state vector by calculating the weight. First, the weight between node u and node v is calculated as $a_{uv}^{(k)}$. In the k_{th} iteration, the information about node type of node v from node u is aggregated as $m_{vm}^{(k)}$:

$$h_{e_{uv}}^{(k)} = W_e^{(k)} \left(\left[h_u^{(k-1)}; h_{e_{uv}}^{(k-1)}; h_v^{(k-1)} \right] \right) \tag{3}$$

$$a_{uv}^{(k)} = \sigma \left(W_w^{(k)} \left(h_{e_{uv}}^{(k)} \right) \right) \tag{4}$$

$$m_{vm}^{(k)} = \sum_{u \in N(v)} a_{uv}^{(k)} F_m^{(k)} h_v^{(k-1)} \tag{5}$$

where $[;]$ represents the splicing between vectors, $W_e^{(k)} \in R^{d_{h_e} \times (2d_{h_v} + d_{h_e})}$ and $W_w^{(k)} \in R^{d_{h_e}}$ are different learnable parameter matrices. $\sigma(x) = 1/(1 + e^{-x})$ is the sigmoid activation function. $N(v)$ is the set of neighbor nodes of v, $F_m^{(k)}$ is designed as Multi-Layer Perceptron(MLP).

In the kth iteration, the information $m_{vp}^{(k)}$ and $m_{vc}^{(k)}$ from parent nodes and child nodes of node v is aggregated as $m_{v1}^{(k)}$:

$$m_{vp}^{(k)} = \frac{1}{d_D^-(v)} \sum_{(u,v) \in E} F_P^{(k)} \left(\left[h_u^{(k-1)}; h_v^{(k-1)} \right] \right) \tag{6}$$

$$m_{vc}^{(k)} = \frac{1}{d_D^+(v)} \sum_{(v,u) \in E} F_C^{(k)} \left(\left[h_v^{(k-1)}; h_u^{(k-1)} \right] \right) \tag{7}$$

$$m_{v1}^{(k)} = F_1^{(k)} \left(m_{vp}^{(k)} + m_{vc}^{(k)} \right) \tag{8}$$

where $d_D^-(v)$ and $d_D^+(v)$ represent the number of parent nodes and child nodes of v; $F_P^{(k)}$, $F_C^{(k)}$ and $F_1^{(k)}$ are designed as MLPs.

Given a DAG of a formula, any node in G maybe the top node, left child or right child of the treelet. Let $\tau_T(v)$, $\tau_L(v)$ and $\tau_R(v)$ be the set of treelets in G with node v as the top node, left child and right child:

$$\tau_T(v) = \{(u,v,w)|\langle v,u\rangle \in E, \langle v,w\rangle \in E, r_v(u) < r_v(w)\}$$

$$\tau_L(v) = \{(v,u,w)|\langle u,v\rangle \in E, \langle u,w\rangle \in E, r_u(v) < r_u(w)\}$$

$$\tau_R(v) = \{(u,w,v)|\langle w,u\rangle \in E, \langle w,v\rangle \in E, r_w(u) < r_w(v)\}$$

In the kth iteration, the information from $\tau_T(v)$, $\tau_L(v)$ and $\tau_R(v)$ are aggregated as $m_{vt}^{(k)}$, $m_{vl}^{(k)}$ and $m_{vr}^{(k)}$:

$$m_{vt}^{(k)} = \frac{1}{|\tau_T(v)|} \sum_{(u,v,w)\in\tau_T(v)} F_T^{(k)}\left(\left[h_u^{(k-1)}; h_v^{(k-1)}; h_w^{(k-1)}\right]\right) \quad (9)$$

$$m_{vl}^{(k)} = \frac{1}{|\tau_L(v)|} \sum_{(v,u,w)\in\tau_L(v)} F_L^{(k)}\left(\left[h_v^{(k-1)}; h_u^{(k-1)}; h_w^{(k-1)}\right]\right) \quad (10)$$

$$m_{vr}^{(k)} = \frac{1}{|\tau_R(v)|} \sum_{(u,w,v)\in\tau_R(v)} F_R^{(k)}\left(\left[h_u^{(k-1)}; h_w^{(k-1)}; h_v^{(k-1)}\right]\right) \quad (11)$$

where $|\tau_T(v)|$, $|\tau_L(v)|$, $|\tau_R(v)|$ represent the number of treelets that v is the top node, left child node and right child node; $F_T^{(k)}$, $F_L^{(k)}$, $F_R^{(k)}$ are designed as MLPs.

The information of central node from $\tau_T(v) \cup \tau_L(v) \cup \tau_R(v)$ can be summarized as $m_{v2}^{(k)}$, therefore, the information of the central node v from two parts can be summarized as $m_v^{(k)}$:

$$m_{v2}^{(k)} = F_2^{(k)}\left(m_{vt}^{(k)} + m_{vl}^{(k)} + m_{vr}^{(k)}\right) \quad (12)$$

$$m_v^{(k)} = m_m^{(k)} + m_{v1}^{(k)} + m_{v2}^{(k)} \quad (13)$$

where $F_2^{(k)}$ is designed as MLP. In the kth iteration, the state vector of node v is represented as:

$$h_v^{(k)} = m_v^{(k)} + h_v^{(k-1)} \quad (14)$$

After K iterations, the graph aggregation layer takes all the node state vectors on the graph as inputs and outputs a graph-level embedding h_g:

$$h_g = AvgPool\left\{h_v^{(K)} | v \in V\right\} \quad (15)$$

where $h_g \in R^{d_{hv}}$ and $AvgPool$ represents average pooling of the final state vectors of all nodes on the graph.

3.2. Binary classifier

In the premise selection model based on TE-GNN, the input of the binary classifier is a graph-vector pair (h_{prem}, h_{conj}), which respectively represents the premise and its corresponding conjecture.

$$z = F_{class}\left([h_{prem}; h_{conj}]\right) \tag{16}$$

where, $z \in R^2$ indicates whether the premise is useful for the proof of the corresponding conjecture. F_{class} is designed as MLP. Therefore, the probability whether the premise is useful in the proof of corresponding conjecture is

$$\hat{y} = softmax\left(z\right) \tag{17}$$

$$\hat{y}_i = \frac{e^{z_i}}{\sum_j e^{z_j}} \tag{18}$$

where, $softmax$ is a normalization function, $\hat{y}_i$ is the ith element of $\hat{y}$, z_i is the ith element of z.

4. Dataset

This paper adopts the same dataset as Liu,[5] which is created based on the MPTP2078 question bank. To construct negative samples equal to the number of positive samples, the negative samples have been sampled. The final dataset is shown in Table 1.

Table 1. Distribution of datasets.

	Train	Valid	Test
Positive	27663	3417	3432
Negative	27556	3485	3471
Total	55219	6902	6903

5. Experimental Results

The model is trained using Adam optimizer, and the model with the smallest loss on the valid set is selected as the optimal model and evaluated on the test set. Table 2 lists all the parameter settings in the experiment. Meanwhile, we use accuracy to evaluate the comparative experimental results, and additional indices[5] including recall, precision, and F1 are also added to evaluate the model.

Table 2. Setting of parameters.

Descriptions	Parameters
d_{h_v}	512
d_{h_e}	32
K	1
epochs	100
learning rate	0.001
learning decay	0.1
batch size	32
weight decay	0.0001

To evaluate the superiority of the proposed TE-GNN in premise selection task, this paper compares it with the current popular graph neural networks. The comparative experimental results are shown in Table 3, in which the optimal results are shown in bold. Experimental results show that TE-GNN has a stronger ability to represent first-order logical formulas than other popular graph neural network models.

Table 3. Comparison of experimental results on datasets.

Model	Accuracy	Precision	Recall	F1
GCN[6]	0.8625	0.8669	0.8547	0.8608
GAT[7]	0.8580	0.8629	0.8518	0.8573
GraphSAGE[8]	0.8615	0.8686	0.8501	0.8592
SGC[9]	0.8557	0.8579	0.8506	0.8543
Chebyshev[10]	0.8608	0.8660	0.8518	0.8588
TE-GNN	**0.8820**	**0.8821**	**0.8800**	**0.8811**

6. Conclusion

This paper proposed a TE-GNN model for premise selection task, which encodes the child node order information and node type information inside first-order logic formulas. Compared with the current popular graph neural network models, our proposed model clearly outperforms the premise selection task. Future research will consider more targeted models based on the characteristics of first-order logic formulas.

Acknowledgments

This research is supported by the National Natural Science Foundation of China (Grant Nos. 61603307 and 61673320), the Grant from MOE

(Ministry of Education in China) Project of Humanities and Social Sciences (Grant Nos. 19YJCZH048 and 20XJCZH016), and the Fundamental Research Funds for the Central Universities (Grant Nos. 2682020ZT107, JBK2102037 and JBK2003006).

References

1. N. Kalchbrenner, E. Grefenstette, and P. Blunsom. A convolutional neural network for modelling sentences. *arXiv preprint arXiv:*1404.2188, 2014.
2. G. Irving, C. Szegedy, A. A. Alemi, et al. Deepmath-deep sequence models for premise selection. *Advances in neural information processing systems*, 2016, 69.
3. A. Paliwal, S. Loos, M. Rabe, et al. Graph representations for higher-order logic and theorem proving. *Proceedings of the AAAI Conference on Artificial Intelligence.* 2020, 34(03): 2967-2974.
4. M. Wang, Y. Tang, J. Wang, et al. Premise selection for theorem proving by deep graph embedding. *Advances in neural information processing systems*, 2017: 2783-2793.
5. Q. H. Liu, Y. Xu, G. F. Wu, et al. Edge-Weight-Based Graph Neural Network for First-Order Premise Selection. *Journal of Southwest Jiaotong University*, 2022: 1-8. (in Chinese)
6. T. N. Kipf, and M. Welling. Semi-supervised classification with graph convolutional networks. *arXiv preprint arXiv:*1609.02907, 2016.
7. P. Veličković, G. Cucurull, A. Casanova, et al. Graph attention networks. *arXiv preprint arXiv:*1710.10903, 2017.
8. W. Hamilton, Z. Ying, and J. Leskovec. Inductive representation learning on large graphs. *Advances in neural information processing systems,*2017, 30.
9. F. Wu, A. Souza, T. Zhang, et al. Simplifying graph convolutional networks. *International conference on machine learning.* PMLR, 2019.
10. M. Defferrard, X. Bresson, and P. Vandergheynst. Convolutional neural networks on graphs with fast localized spectral filtering. *Advances in neural information processing systems*, 2016, 29.

The best of translation:
RNN-based machine translation and post-editing*

Xia He, Taiqian Chai, Xin Guan, Mengting Chen and Yuchen Kan

Faculty of Foreign Languages/Faculty of Computer Science and Software Engineering
Huaiyin Institute of Technology, Huai'an, 223001 Jiangsu Province, China
hxhg@hyit.edu.com
787533530@qq.com
1042743597@qq.com

Neural Machine Translation (NMT) is the most widely used machine translation method. At the same time, in order to ensure translation quality, the NMT output needs to be post-edited by human translators. In this paper, NMT recurrent neural language model (RNN) is used to train relevant datasets, and the training results are used for corpus machine translation test to obtain machine translated texts. Based on the differences between Chinese and English languages and relevant translation standards, we construct quantitative criteria to evaluate the "understandability" of the machine translation output, and conduct manual post-editing based on the evaluation results to minimize the loss of understandability, so as to optimize the machine translation output. The research in this paper has some implications on how to combine machine translation efficiency and manual translation optimization in the process of artificial intelligence natural language processing to improve the quality of translation.

Keywords: RNN machine translation; post-editing; translation quality; understandability.

1. Introduction

Machine translation translates natural language in written form or sound form into another natural language in written form or sound form by applying computer technology [6]. Since its development, neural machine translation has become the most widely used machine-translation method, and its excellent performance relies on a rich corpus and huge computer computing power [1]. RNN is one of such widely adopted network model for neural machine translation [3]. The model gives excellent performance in machine translation as it can be adapted to sentences of arbitrary length, and the inference time of the model is positively

*This paper is supported by the Excellent Foreign Language Project of Jiangsu Provincial Federation of Social Sciences: Practical Research on Interpretation Teaching Mode based on Flipped Classroom (Fund ID: 511715034) and partially supported by 2022 National College Students' Innovation and Entrepreneurship Training program and Exploration.

correlated with the sentence length [9]. Moreover, RNN conceives the words in a sentence as discrete signals, and as the signals are continuously input, the network performs recursive processing, continuously accumulating information and forming valuable contextual memory [8]. Therefore, the paper employs RNN network to train data and gives machine translation output. Although machine translation output can convey the basic information or meaning of the translation, the translation quality of machine translation often depends on whether the differences in vocabulary, grammatical structure, language family, and even culture between the translated incoming and outgoing languages could be carefully "understood" and taken care of in translation [2]. In order to optimize the results of machine translation, neural machine translation needs to be paired with human post-editing to obtain correct and logically organized text [5]. The combination of technical and human-linguistic cognitive aspects is used to achieve an optimized machine-translated translation [7].

The paper first introduces RNN model and the steps to realize NMT with the model. Then Four-scale Evaluation Table of Understandability in machine translation and post-editing for translation optimization are given. Based on the NMT output of the data trained by RNN model, Scheme of understandability problem of MT output and post-editing revision are displayed, followed by the result analysis. Last, the conclusion is given.

2. RNN-based NMT Realization

2.1. Preparation

This experiment uses the AI Change open source data set in the field of machine translation as the machine translation corpus. The AI Change data set is currently the largest English-Chinese bilingual data set in the spoken language field, providing more than 10 million English-Chinese sentences as a data set, and its double sentences have been manually compared, so the AI Change dataset has excellent quality assurance. There are eleven steps to normalize the dataset: English corpus case conversion is processed, standardize punctuation marks, remove special character processing in corpus, Chinese corpus is processed by word segmentation, set the strengths of each corpus to process, generate Chinese and English vocabulary, mark the end of the English corpus, mark the beginning and end of Chinese corpus, fill short sentences with symbols, create a sentence corresponding to each moment label of the decoder according to the Chinese sentence, convert the training sentence into a sequence of word IDs.

2.2. Network construction and create encoder and attention decoder

The machine translation in this experiment adopts the Encoder-AttentionDecoder architecture, where the Encoder adopts the LSTM model and the Decoder adopts the Attention+LSTM model. The essence of using the RNN structure is that the initial state of the Decoder RNN is equal to the last state of the Encoder RNN, and the input of the Decoder RNN at time t is the relationship vector spliced by " " $x\_t^{\wedge'}$ and Context "Vector" $c\_(t-1)$. In the process of creating the Encoder and inputting English sentences, a network of Chinese and English sentence encoding is constructed by finding the Embedding and then connecting an LSTM. In the Decoder part, the decoding process is continuously completed through LSTM with Attention. The function in the Decoder part only makes the LSTM calculate forward once every time it is called, and only outputs the current generated moment, rather than the entire output sequence generated. The overall output part is output in the training loop. The machine translation weight of this experiment is improved by using the attention mechanism to improve the Seq2Seq model: the output state relationship vector s_tof the Decoder at time t is spliced with the state relationship vectors h_1 to h_m of the Encoder at each time, and continuously passes through a tanh A fully connected layer and a linear summation layer performed by the function. That is h_i and S_t are spliced together, and then left-multiplied by a parameter matrix W to obtain a result vector. Apply the hyperbolic tangent function tanh to each element of all the obtained vectors, and adjust the value of each element of the vector to between -1~+1 to obtain a new vector. Finally, the inner product of the parameter vector V and the new vector is calculated as $\tilde{\alpha}\_ti$, where the matrices W and V are parameter matrices, which need to be learned from the training data. After calculating the results of $\tilde{\alpha}\_t1, \tilde{\alpha}\_t2,...,\tilde{\alpha}\_tm$ Softmax changes can be performed, and the results of changes are recorded as $\alpha\_t1, \alpha\_t2,...,\alpha\_tm$, and the formula is obtained: $[\alpha\_t1, \alpha\_t2,...,\alpha\_tm] = Softmax ([\tilde{\alpha}\_t1, \tilde{\alpha}\_t2,...,\tilde{\alpha}\_tm])$.

2.3. Training the model

Define functions to create Encoder and AttentionDecoder objects, create optimizers, and set learning rates and optimization parameters: learning efficiency (lr) = 0.001, batch size = 64, hidden layer size (hidden_dim) = 256, loss parameter (label-smoothing) = 0, 1, iterations = 10000. In each iteration, the training data is randomly scrambled, and within each batch size, attention decoding and force decoding are called multiple times to realize the overall output loop during decoding. Each time the next word is decoded, the real word in the training data is given as the input for the next word. After the training is completed, its loss rate is around 0.0001, and its training results can be used. And when the training of the dataset is completed, use the training data for translation through function calls.

3. Translation Quality Assessment and Post-editing

Arnold (1994) proposed the Four Level Scale of Understandability in assessing machine translation quality: Level 1: the sentence is well-meaning and easy to understand, and the structure obeys the grammar rules; Level 2: the meaning of the sentence is generally clear, retaining the original meaning, but there are some inaccurate or inappropriate translation; Level 3: there are grammatical errors or word selection wrongs, and can only be understood through careful thinking; Level 4: the translation is unable to read or to provide reliable original information, and it must be retranslated by human translation. We could see that the understandability of the translation could be branched with two sub-indicators: accuracy and fluency. The two dimensions also meet the basic criteria of translation, namely, fidelity and fluency. And also from which we could find space and clues for human translator posting-editing. To human reviewer, the inspection index is not only the surface language characteristics of the vocabulary dimension, but also the syntactic and chapter dimensions, including the complexity of sentence structure, the use of cohesive words and latent meaning analysis. This requires reviewers have enough capacity to apply the language logic while familiar with language differences. To give more substantial indicators for translation assessment and post-editing, we sub-divide accuracy and fluency level into four levels: entire, general, partial, and little. In this way, the machine translation evaluation criteria of this paper is formed: the evaluation scale based on "understandability". See Table 1.

Table 1. Four-scale evaluation table of understandability.

	accuracy	fluency	understandabiltiy
Level 1	entire	entire	Correct grammar, well-structured and well-defined sentence
Level 2	general	general	Generally clear meaning, with some inaccurate or inappropriate translation
Level 3	partial	partial	Grammar error, faulty wording, handicapped understanding
Level 4	little	little	Prevalent grammar and wording errors, not understandable

4. Result and Analysis

The machine translation output is post-edited in the problematic points, and the results are compared with those of machine translation. Result of MT output and post-editing revision based on "understandability" is presented in Table 2.

Table 2. Scheme of understandability problem of MT output and post-editing revision.

ID	ST_EN/ MT_CN	understandability /level	Loss of understadability (LOU)(%)	Post-editing HT_CN
1	If you are tired, go to bed. 你若累了，就去睡个觉。	Fluency/ General/1	0.02	如果你感到疲惫，就去休息吧。
2	It never rains but it pours. 不下雨则臭，一下一定是倾盆大雨。	Fluency /general/2	0.05	祸不单行
3	Having missed the train, I had to wait about an hour for the next one. 由于错过了火车，我不得不等下一班等一小时。	Fluency/ partial/3	0.1	因为错过了这一班火车，我只能等一个小时后的下一班火车。
4	Those chairs are in the way, and those two are exactly alike. 那些椅子挡住了去路,那两个是一模一样的。	Fluency/ partial/3	0.1	两张一模一样的椅子挡住了去路。
5	He doesn't have any children, and he does not have any friends. 他没有孩子，他一个朋友都没有。	Fluency/ partial/3	0.1	他没有孩子，甚至连一个朋友都没有。
6	I've been requested to help you. I've already told you the truth. 有人请我帮你，我已经告诉你真相了。	Accuracy/ fluency/ partial/3	0.15	好吧我告诉你，其实是有人请我帮你。
7	Great progress has been made. Don't ever underestimate Tom. 已经取得巨大进展。千万不可低估汤姆。	fluency/ partial/3	0.1	汤姆已经取得了很大进步，千万不要低估他。
8	He is a man of few words, but he always keeps his promise. 他这个人话不多，但总是遵守诺言。	Fluency/ entire/1	0.02	他平时沉默寡言，却是个一言九鼎的人。
9	A little walk will give you a good appetite for breakfast. 散散步将会给你很好的食欲吃早餐。	Fluency/ entire/1	0.08	散散步会让早餐吃得更香。
10	France is running a welfare state it can no longer afford. 法国是一個福利国家，但它却不再能够负担得起了。	Accuracy/ fluency/ partial/3	0.15	法国是一个福利制国家，但却不再能负担起沉重的社会福利了。

ID 1 is of level 1 with general fluency and 0.02 understandability loss and was post edited with the change of the tone in expression. According to the context, it is apparent that the dialogue takes place between people who are close to each other, and the keywords of exhaustion and rest are involved. Therefore, the tone of the dialogue should be more intimate, and the results of the machine translation emerge to be more rigid and cannot reflect the intimate relationship between the two parties of the dialogue.

ID 2 is of level 2 with general fluency and 0.05 understandability loss and was post edited with the usage of proverbs in expression. From the perspective of the difference in Western cultural background, this sentence should correspond to the Chinese "Bad luck will happen one after another." Therefore, the result of machine translation is adjusted to be more consistent with the expression habits of the translated language.

ID 3 is of level 3 with partial fluency and 0.1 understandability loss and was post edited by adding a conjunction. The first half of the sentence and the second half of the sentence are not closely connected, and the overall structure of the sentence is ignored, making the translation result too rigid. By adding a conjunction in post-editing, the cause-and-effect relationship can be explained.

ID 4 is of level 3 with partial fluency and 0.1 understandability loss and was post edited by changing the word order. The role of conjunctions in the machine-translated sentence is not properly considered, making the translation result too rigid. The sentence which has been adjusted reads more smoothly and conforms to the rules of grammatology.

ID 5 is of level 3 with partial fluency and 0.1 understandability loss and was post edited by adding a conjunction. In this sentence, the machine translation translated the meaning of each word correctly. Whereas, it did not properly consider the role of the connecting words in the sentence and did not closely link the first half of the sentence with the second half, making the translation result too rigid. The sentence which has been edited is more grammatically correct and reflects the transitive relationship between the first half of the sentence and the second half of the sentence.

ID 6 is of level 3 with partial accuracy and partial fluency and 0.15 understandability loss and was post-edited by changing the word order. From the perspective of discourse dimension, the content of the second sentence is the first sentence, that is, the truth of the matter is that someone has asked me to help you; from the lexical dimension, this is an oral language. In the expression, zhenxiang (真相) is too formal, and the selection qishi (其实) can achieve the effect of expression.

ID 7 is of level 3 with partial fluency and 0.1 understandability loss and was post edited by restructuring the sentence. In translating this sentence, it is best to adjust the language order. There is no "Tom" in the first sentence, but it is Tom that made the progress. In the first English sentence, passive voice is used where the doer of the action is omitted, and in the Chinese translation the doer, Tom, is give as the subject.

ID 8 is of level 1 with general fluency and 0.02 understandability loss and was post edited by doing lexical conversion into a Chinese idiom. Machine translation has achieved a clear meaning, easy to understand, in line with grammatical rules, but the expression "always keeps promise" does not conform to the idiomatic Chinese language expression habits. The adverb of degree "always" is usually followed by derogatory words or neutral words in Chinese expression, which is slightly inappropriate to describe good quality.

ID 9 is of level 1 with general fluency and 0.08 understandability loss and was post edited by doing lexical conversion. The machine translation has achieved overall clarity of sentence meaning and retained the original meaning, but it is slightly stiff in expression. "给你很好的食欲" is not in line with the Chinese expression. The dynamic grammar can be transformed into a static one, hidden verb "give" can be converted into a more daily expression.

ID 10 is of level 3 with partial accuracy and partial fluency and 0.15 understandability loss and was post edited by making amplification. The phrase "no longer afford" should be used to refer to social welfare payments in the preceding sentence. It cannot be reflected in the text making a certain barrier in reading and understanding. Machine translation output could show each word without error, and basically conforms to the grammatical rules. Thus the understandability loss is only within 0.02-0.15. However, there are still some shortcomings, such as partial word order errors, lacking conjunctive words to indicate cohesion and plain delivery, which may handicap the understandability to some extent, and those where the post-editing work could improve upon.

5. Conclusion

This paper builds a RNN-based NMT framework to give a NMT output of a given language data. It turns out that NMT out sacrifices some degree of understandability. Based on a four-scale evaluation scheme, human post-editing was added, thus saving the understandability loss and giving the best translation. The paper has its due significance in fields like natural language processing, AI, MT plus post-editing, translation teaching and learning.

References

1. Chenhui Chu, Rui Wang. *A Survey of Domain Adaptation for Machine Translation*. Journal of Information Processing, 2020, 28(0).
2. Koponen, M., Salmi, L. (2015). *On the correctness of machine translation: A machine translation post-editing task*. Journal of Specialised Translation, 23, 118-136.
3. Li Lobin, Gong Xiaonan, Gan Xiaolu, Cheng Kang, Hou Yongmao. *Prediction of maximum ground settlement triggered by shield tunnel based on recurrent neural network*. Journal of Civil Engineering, 2020, 53(S1): 13-19. DOI: 10.15951/j.tmgcxb. 2020.s1.003.
4. Myle Ott, Michael Auli, David Grangier, Marc'Aurelio Ranzato. *Analyzing Uncertainty in Neural Machine Translation*. CoRR,2018, abs/1803.00047.
5. O'Brien, S., Balling, L. W., et al. (2014). Post-editing of Machine Translation: Processes and Application. *Cambridge Scholars Publishing*, Newcastle upon Tyne.
6. Stahlberg Felix. *Neural Machine Translation: A Review*. Journal of Artificial Intelligence Research, 2020, 69.
7. TAUS. (2010b). *Post-editing in Practice. A TAUS Report. Technical report.* Retrieved July, 2019, from https://www.taus.net/think-tank/reports/postedit-reports/postediting-in-practice
8. Wang Lianzhu. *A review of research on machine learning applied to language intelligence*. Modern educational technology, 2018, 28(09): 66-72.
9. Xia Jiajia, Jiang Tao. *Research on financial risk early warning based on RNN recurrent neural network--Anhui Province as an example*. Journal of Hubei Academy of Arts and Sciences, 2021, 42(11): 26-32.

Deep learning-based facial expression recognition

Hadi Parayil Nisamudeen and Li Zhang*

Department of Computer Science, Royal Holloway, University of London
Surrey, TW20 0EX, UK
*li.zhang@rhul.ac.uk

This research utilizes several well-known Convolutional Neural Networks (CNNs) for facial expression recognition. By taking advantage of transfer learning, deep networks are able to perform a new classification task with a comparatively smaller training dataset. The experiment was efficiently executed by using these models to classify seven universally recognized emotions, i.e. neutral, happiness, sadness, angry, disgust, fear, and surprise. The models were also fine-tuned using a grid search strategy to identify optimal hyperparameter settings. Evaluated using the CK+ dataset, the transfer learning networks show reasonable performance.

Keywords: Facial expression recognition; deep learning; transfer learning.

1. Introduction

Facial expression recognition has been used widely in healthcare, e-learning and robotic applications. With the aid of the essences of artificial intelligence, deep learning methods such as Convolutional Neural Networks (CNNs) show great efficiency in tackling diverse image classification tasks [1, 2]. Specifically, such methods initially capture the image of the face regions and then generate "unique numeric representations" of the extracted faces. A theoretically simple, yet not so common attribute is to detect facial expressions, where the deep networks could analyze and conclude if the person is e.g. 'smiling' or 'frowning' based on the end-to-end facial features such as the teeth being visible and the squinting of their eyes to detect a 'laugh'. Although facial features do visibly show the expression of the person at that moment, emotions are much more than just physical expressions, as they have implications from the psychological perspective. Research has shown that however physical expressions do surprisingly play an impact on showing what emotion the person is feeling at that moment [3].

Although current implementations of facial emotion recognition do exist, the accuracy rates of the CNN-based methods vary by large margins, with different datasets, emotion categories, and different hyperparameter settings.

The aim of this research is to evaluate and compare different CNN models (both pre-existing and newly made), to evidently provide a conclusion to which deep learning methods can predict a variety of emotions more effectively. In this research, our proposed models under transfer learning and training from scratch strategies are able to differentiate seven key facial expressions, i.e. neutral, happiness, sadness, anger, disgust, fear and surprise. Several deep networks in combination with grid-search based hyperparameter search are used to conduct facial expression recognition using the CK+ dataset. The networks with identified learning configurations show great efficiency for the recognition of seven facial expressions.

2. Related Work

In machine learning, a multilayer perceptron neural network, in a nutshell, takes in the input data through the input layer, adjusts its weights and other hyper-parameters, produce an output prediction, and compare the generated output with the expected output using a loss function [4-6]. CNNs also known as ConvNets will adopt images as inputs directly by creating respective numeric representations, to perform image recognition tasks.

The advantage of a CNN is that the effort put up during the pre-processing stage of the data is much less compared to that of a feed forward network [7-10]. In addition, CNNs have the ability to easily extract spatial relationships with the help of built-in filters, which results in enhanced capabilities for image classification tasks.

CNNs vary in sizes, numbers of filters and kernel sizes. In particular, filters are used to detect specific features of an image, for example, the edges of a object, or even as detailed as the ears of a kitten. CNNs conduct feature learning using convolutional layers. There are also two types of pooling layer, i.e. Max Pooling and Average pooling, for dimension reduction. The Max pooling layer takes a patch of the Conv Layer and extracts the pixels with the maximum values. Such pixels provide the most important properties of that patch (hence called Max pooling), whereas Average Pooling takes on the average value of the pixels of that specific patch.

As mentioned before, the concept of a neural network is technically a mimicked version of the functioning of a human brain. In that perspective, humans gain information and create solutions quicker on new tasks, if they are not completely unfamiliar to the tasks and problems. That is, it is easier for humans to 'cross-utilize' knowledge if the tasks are more related to each other [11], and that's how transfer learning comes into play in a neural network.

Transfer learning easily overcomes the problem of isolated learning, thereby avoiding excess time consumption by taking advantage of existing knowledge (such as a model pretrained using ImageNet). This method makes training easier by making use of the information retrieved from training a specific problem, to train on a different, yet related problem. In this research, we employ transfer learning and pretrained CNNs for facial expression recognition.

Facial Recognition is also widely used in many domains, such as healthcare and product review. As an example, Face2Gene [12] is an application which recognizes genetic disorders from facial images based on the extracted 130 features using a CNN. It has been reported [13] that the application was successfully able to discover rare conditions such as Wiedemann–Steiner syndrome using facial image inputs. Such a technique has also been used to aid patients with autism spectrum disorder for facial expression interpretation [12]. This glass, called the 'Superpower Glass', tracks facial expressions and alerts the user with the detected expressions such as 'interested'.

According to psychosocial rehabilitation specialists, an 'emotion' is a state of complex feeling, which in turn results in physical and psychological changes [14]. Because of this, many existing works have also tried to detect emotions using EEG and ECG data, to gain information on the psychological states of the person while carrying out a certain task. However, such datatypes are not easily accessible, thus it hinders their wide applications.

According to the work of [15], this 'state of feeling' encompasses three major 'responses': subjective, psychological, and behavioral responses. Understanding of the physical attributes with respect to the behavioral response plays a major role for facial expression recognition [15]. Facial Action Coding System (FACS) is also widely studied from psychological perspective for interpreting and recognition of facial expressions [14]. In this research, we employ CNNs and transfer learning to interpret different emotion categories automatically using facial image inputs.

3. The Proposed Facial Expression Recognition System

In this research, we employ several CNN architectures, i.e. AlexNet, ResNet, MobileNet and NasNet, for facial expression recognition using the CK+ dataset. Specifically, AlexNet is one of the widely adopted CNN architectures. In contrast, ResNet employs shortcut connections on residual blocks to avoid overfitting and enhance performance. MobileNet is a light-weight CNN model with comparatively improved computational efficiency. NASNet (Neural Search Architecture Network) [16] is a highly efficient and strategic deep architecture generation model.

The above networks are evaluated using the CK+ dataset, which is imported using the CV2 library. This dataset is made available in a simple CSV file, with all the emotion labels numbered from 0 to 6. Opencv, PIL (Python Image Library), Pickle and TensorFlow packages are used to conduct face detection, import pretrained CNN models and perform other initial pre-processing procedures. We elaborate the pre-processing steps and transfer learning-based image classification in detail below.

3.1. *The data processing phase*

We aim to analyze the efficiency of several CNN architectures for facial expression recognition tasks. This section splits into different parts: The pre-processing prior to training the model, the training phase, and the detection phase.

The CK+ dataset is used in this research and it is imported using the CV2 library. The dataset is then split into NumPy arrays of X and Y values, and then reshaped into a 4-dimension array as per the model's concerns, using the np.reshape() method. The X and Y values are subsequently saved into a pickle. In addition, the pickles are saved using the pickle.dump() function, and can be later read using pickle.in(). Such pre-processing may help reduce the computational costs significantly during training.

3.2. *Model training phase*

As mentioned earlier, we adopt 4 CNNs in our experimental studies. However, only 3 of the 4 models, i.e. AlexNet, ResNet and MobileNet, are pre-trained and can be accessed using the TensorFlow Keras modules. NASNet is trained from scratch using the CK+ dataset. The input of all networks is a 227x227 image in RGB. Besides convolutional, dropout and normalisation layers, the final classi-fication layer is configured with 7 nodes, for the identification of 7 emotions. The SoftMax activation function is used to generate the classification result.

First of all, AlexNet, ResNet50, NASNet and MobileNet are available in Keras as pre-trained models, so they can be accessed using the keras.applications method. To make use of the pre-trained weights and biases, the convolutional blocks are extracted from these models, and new fully connected layers are added to the networks to learn from the new dataset.

After the creation of the models, the training data (the NumPy Arrays) are resized to their input dimensions using tensorflow.image.resize(). As the RAM of Colab only limits to a certain size of variables, the experiment only uses 6001 images of the randomly shuffled dataset. Finally, the model is compiled using

Sparse Categorical Entropy (a method used to detect non-binary categories) with ADAM as the optimizer and a maximum learning epoch of 20.

3.3. The prediction phase

The models are then trained on various number of iterations and batch sizes. To identify optimal network settings, we employ a grid-search strategy to monitor network performance. The haar-cascade method is also set up to tackle images which are not face–centered. This is done using CV2 CascadeClassifier() class, and utilizes the haarcascade_frontalface_alt2.xml file. To scan throughout the image to detect a face, a 'frame' is created. And is for-looped within the edges of the image. If a face is detected, a frame would be plotted around the face, else a 'Face Not Detected' message would prompt on the screen. The CascadeClassifier() class also has a detectMultiScale feature which allows the algorithm to detect faces of various sizes. The image is finally cropped into the detected face to be used for emotion prediction.

4. System Evaluation

To determine the best performant network, we test model efficiency using CK+. Each network was initially trained using 100 epochs, in order to identify the optimum epoch setting which has the minimum rate of validation loss. To implement this, Keras' EarlyStopping method is being used as a callback, which stops when the optimal minimum is found. These optimal settings are used for evaluating unseen test images. In addition, we also employ a vanilla network, which is a 5-layer CNN model. The vanilla model was trained on a weight decay of 0.9 and a learning rate of 0.0001. The network performances with respect to different learning hyperparameter settings in the training and test stages are provided in Tables 1 and 2.

Table 1. Training accuracy rates of different network settings for the CK+ dataset.

Model	Data Size	Image Size	Batch Size	Epochs	Learning Rate	Weight Decay	Accuracy	Loss	Val Accuracy	Val Loss
Vanilla Model	Full	48*48	NIL	49	1.00E-04	0.9	0.8018	0.5	**0.7549**	0.7
AlexNet	6001	227*227	NIL	4	1.00E-06	0.9	0.9244	0.39	0.53	1.3608
	6001	227*227	32	33	1.00E-05	0.8	0.9026	0.37	0.4933	1.36
	6001	227*227	32	60	1.00E-03	0.8	0.8223	0.41	0.4933	1.5
MobileNet	6001	96*96	32	26	1.00E-03	0.9	0.684	0.9048	0.5217	1.571
	6001	224*224	NIL	20	1.00E-05	0.7	0.81	0.9296	0.4875	1.56
ResNet50	Full	48*48	32	5	1.00E-06	0.9	0.8212	0.5023	**0.8835**	0.3813
	6001	224*224	32	20	1.00E-07	0.8	0.8009	0.4401	0.4617	1.77
	6001	224*224	32	26	1.00E-02	0.9	0.8019	0.453	0.4543	1.808
	6001	224*224	64	15	1.00E-03	0.9	0.797	0.558	0.5009	1.332
	6001	224*224	32	27	1.00E-04	0.9	0.8102	0.645	0.5109	1.31
	6001	224*224	64	27	1.00E-05	0.9	0.8007	0.9988	0.4522	1.7
NasNet	6001	224*224	NIL	100	1.00E-07	0.8	0.8023	0.4343	0.4297	1.62
	6001	224*224	32	550	1.00E-07	0.8	0.7997	0.4333	0.433	1.763

Table 2. Test accuracy rates for the CK+ dataset.

Model	Test Accuracy	Test Loss
Vanilla Model	75.66%	0.7329
AlexNet	46.10%	2.6136
ResNet50	39.31%	1.8835
ResNet50[28000]	69.36%	1.0587
MobileNetV2	17.12%	4.7947
NASNet	17.12%	7.8253

Table 2 indicates that the Vanilla network trained from scratch is the model with the best test accuracy rate of 75.66%, while ResNet50 is the best transfer learning model in comparison with AlexNet, NASNet and MobileNet.

5. Conclusions

This research employs vibrant CNN models for facial expression recognition. Networks trained from scratch illustrates competitive performance, while transfer learning networks show reasonable performance with less training data required. The complexities of these networks are different, which makes the sole purpose of this study sensible, so as to compare and find the best model. This method also supports the notion of how the increase in model complexity does not really make the model a better predictor. Deeper networks may require more training efforts to attain enhanced performance.

For future work, we will use a larger dataset for model training. Evolutionary algorithms will also be explored for parameter selection [17-29]. We also aim to detect fake smiles from real ones with the help of minute facial action changes and psychological studies such as a Duchenne Smile.

References

1. Mistry, K., Zhang, L., Neoh, S.C., Lim, C.P. and Fielding, B., 2016. A micro-GA embedded PSO feature selection approach to intelligent facial emotion recognition. *IEEE transactions on cybernetics*, *47*(6), pp. 1496-1509.

2. L. Zhang, K. Mistry, S.C. Neoh. and C.P. Lim. Intelligent facial emotion recognition using moth-firefly optimization, *Knowledge-Based Systems*. Volume 111, Nov. 2016, 248-267.

3. S.C. Neoh, L. Zhang, K. Mistry, M.A. Hossain, C.P. Lim, N. Aslam and P. Kinghorn. Intelligent Facial Emotion Recognition Using a Layered Encoding Cascade Optimization Model, *Applied Soft Computing*. 2015.

4. S. Slade, L. Zhang, Y. Yu and C.P. Lim, 2022. An evolving ensemble model of multi-stream convolutional neural networks for human action recognition in still images. *Neural Computing and Applications*, pp. 1-27.

5. Zhang, L., Lim, C.P., Yu, Y. and Jiang, M., 2022. Sound classification using evolving ensemble models and Particle Swarm Optimization. *Applied Soft Computing*, *116*, p. 108322.

6. Zhang, L., Lim, C.P. and Yu, Y., 2021. Intelligent human action recognition using an ensemble model of evolving deep networks with swarm-based optimization. *Knowledge-Based Systems*, *220*, p. 106918.

7. Tan, T.Y., Zhang, L. and Lim, C.P., 2020. Adaptive melanoma diagnosis using evolving clustering, ensemble and deep neural networks. *Knowledge-Based Systems*, *187*, p. 104807.

8. Tan, T.Y., Zhang, L., Lim, C.P., Fielding, B., Yu, Y. and Anderson, E., 2019. Evolving ensemble models for image segmentation using enhanced particle swarm optimization. *IEEE access*, *7*, pp. 34004-34019.

9. L. Zhang and C.P. Lim, 2020. Intelligent optic disc segmentation using improved particle swarm optimization and evolving ensemble models. *Applied Soft Computing*, *92*, p. 106328.

10. Xie, H., Zhang, L. and Lim, C.P., 2020. Evolving CNN-LSTM models for time series prediction using enhanced grey wolf optimizer. *IEEE Access*, *8*, pp. 161519-161541.

11. Goodfellow, I., Pouget-Abadie, J,. M. Mirza, B. Xu, D. Warde-Farley, S. Ozair, A. Courville, and Y. Bengio, ''Generative adversarial nets,'' in Proc. Adv. Neural Inf. Process. Syst., 2014, pp. 2672-2680.

12. K. Grifantini, 2020. *Detecting Faces, Saving Lives How facial recognition software is changing health care – EMBS*. [online] Embs.org. Available at: <https://www.embs.org/pulse/articles/detecting-faces-saving-lives/>

13. E. Dolgin, 2019. AI face-scanning app spots signs of rare genetic disorders, [Online] Nature. Available at: <https://www.nature.com/articles/d41586-019-00027-x#ref-CR1> [Accessed 28 April 2022].

14. P. Ekman and W.V. Friesen, 1978. Facial action coding system. *Environmental Psychology & Nonverbal Behavior*.

15. Hockenbury, D. and Hockenbury, S.E., 2007. *Discovering Psychology*. New York: Worth Publishers.

16. Zoph, B., Vasudevan, V., Shlens, J. and Le, Q.V., 2018. Learning transferable architectures for scalable image recognition. In *Proceedings of the IEEE conference on computer vision and pattern recognition* (pp. 8697-8710).

17. B. Fielding, T. Lawrence and L. Zhang. Evolving and Ensembling Deep CNN Architectures for Image Classification, In *Proceedings of International Joint Conference on Neural Networks (IJCNN)*. 2019.
18. B. Fielding and L. Zhang. Evolving Image Classification Architectures with Enhanced Particle Swarm Optimisation, *IEEE Access*, 6. pp. 68560-68575. 2018.
19. B. Fielding and L. Zhang. 2020. Evolving deep DenseBlock architecture ensembles for image classification. *Electronics*, 9(11), p. 1880.
20. Lawrence, T., Zhang, L., Rogage, K. and Lim, C.P., 2021. Evolving Deep Architecture Generation with Residual Connections for Image Classification Using Particle Swarm Optimization. *Sensors*, 21(23), p. 7936.
21. Lawrence, T., Zhang, L., Lim, C.P. and Phillips, E.J., 2021. Particle swarm optimization for automatically evolving convolutional neural networks for image classification. *IEEE Access*, 9, pp. 14369-14386.
22. P. Kinghorn, L. Zhang and L. Shao. A Hierarchical and Regional Deep Learning Architecture for Image Description Generation, *Pattern Recognition Letters*. 2019.
23. P. Kinghorn, L. Zhang and L. Shao. A region-based image caption generator with refined descriptions, *Neurocomputing*. 272 (2018) 416-424.
24. Yu, Y., Zhang, L., Wang, C., Gao, R., Zhao, W. and Jiang, J. (2019) Neural Personalized Ranking via Poisson Factor Model for Item Recommendation. *Complexity*, 2019. p. 3563674. ISSN 1076-2787.
25. D. Pandit, L. Zhang, S. Chattopadhyay, C.P. Lim, and C. Liu. 2018. *A Scattering and Repulsive Swarm Intelligence Algorithm for Solving Global Optimization Problems*. Knowledge-Based Systems.
26. L. Zhang, K. Mistry, C.P. Lim and S.C. Neoh. 2018. Feature selection using firefly optimization for classification and regression models. *Decision Support Systems*. 106 (2018) 64-85.
27. L. Zhang, W. Srisukkham, S.C. Neoh, C.P. Lim, and D. Pandit. 2018. Classifier ensemble reduction using a modified firefly algorithm: An empirical evaluation. *Expert Systems with Applications*, 93. pp. 395-422.
28. Y. Zhang, L. Zhang, S.C. Neoh, K. Mistry, and A. Hossain. 2015. Intelligent affect regression for bodily expressions using hybrid particle swarm optimization and adaptive ensembles. *Expert Systems with Applications*, 42 (22). pp. 8678-8697.
29. T. Lawrence and L. Zhang. IoTNet: An Efficient and Accurate Convolutional Neural Network for IoT Devices. *Sensors*, 19, 5541.

Ensemble transfer learning for plant leave disease identification

Ranjith Thaivalappil Karunan and Li Zhang*

Department of Computer Science, Royal Holloway, University of London
Surrey, TW20 0EX, UK
li.zhang@rhul.ac.uk

Plant diseases result in significant economic losses each year. The common plant diseases include early and late blight. As an example, early blight is caused by fungus while light blight is caused by a specific microorganism. If the plant diseases are detected in early stages with appropriate treatment, such economic loss could be prevented. Therefore, in this research, we propose an ensemble model combining three transfer learning networks, i.e. Resnet50, VGG-16, and MobileNetv2, for plant leaf disease identification. Evaluated using the Plant Village dataset, the proposed ensemble transfer learning model achieves impressive performance for the detection of healthy and unhealthy plant leaves with improved accuracy rates.

Keywords: Deep ensemble transfer learning; convolutional neural network; plant disease detection.

1. Introduction

In the modern era, deep learning is revolutionary in many fields for tackling image and language processing problems [1-6]. Deep learning shows significant capabilities in automated feature learning to aid classification and regression problems [7-10]. In this research, we use deep pre-trained networks and ensemble methods for undertaking plant leaf disease prediction.

Convolutional Neural Network (CNN) is a widely used for dealing with image classification and object detection problems. In this research, we employ pre-trained CNN such as Resnet50, VGG-16, and MobileNetv2, for the prediction of healthy and unhealthy conditions using leaf images as inputs. In particular, we focus on plant disease detection of potato, tomato, and pepper leaves. Firstly transfer learning is adopted to re-train the three networks using the new disease datasets. Ensemble learning is subsequently used to combine the three transfer learning networks to draw final conclusion on plant disease detection. The Plant Village dataset is used for model evaluation.

2. Related Work

Transfer learning and ensemble learning with hyper-parameter fine-tuning have been exploited by recent studies with respect to image segmentation and classification, and video classification problems [11-15]. There are various existing studies for plant disease detection e.g. Hassan et al. [1] and Ghazi et al. [2]. In particular, Hassan et al. [1] employed transfer learning for plant leaf disease detection. They also performed hyper-parameter optimization, in combination with different transfer learning methods.

3. The Proposed Methodology

We conduct plant disease detection using deep transfer ensemble learning. We introduce key steps and methods below.

3.1. *Data collection*

We employ the Plant Village dataset. The dataset was developed by Penn State University. This dataset contains 54,000 images of health and unhealthy leaf images. There are 14 types of plants with 36 different diseases. We focus on the detection of diseased and healthy conditions for three categories of plants, i.e. potato, pepper, and tomato plants in this work.

3.2. *Image pre-processing*

For pre-processing, we rescale the images and perform data augmentation operations. The data augmentation used includes random horizontal and vertical flip and random rotation. We resize the input image sizes to fulfil network input requirement.

3.3. *Transfer learning models*

Transfer learning is comparatively fast and efficient method as compared to developing a new network. In this research, we use three pre-trained networks, i.e. ResNet50, MobileNetv2, and VGG16 as the base classifiers. These networks are pre-trained using ImageNet and is widely used for image classification tasks. In particular, ResNet50 uses skip connection for solving vanishing gradient problems. The skip connection allows one to take an activation from one layer and fed it to any other layer.

The MobileNetv2 is a lightweight CNN that is very fast and smaller than many other transfer learning models. This model is very suitable for mobile devices because its small size. The details of these three networks are provided in Table 1.

Table 1. Network properties of ResNet50, MobileNetv2, and VGG16.

	No. of layers	Parameters in Million	In Mega-bytes
MobileNetV2	53	3.4	14
VGG16	16	138	528
ResNet50	50	25.6	98

3.4. The ensemble method

An ensemble model is used to combine the outputs of ResNet50, MobileNetv2, and VGG16 to reduce the generalization error. We employ a majority voting scheme as the ensemble strategy based on the outputs from all of the networks to improve accuracy rates [16].

4. Evaluation

The Plant Village dataset is used for model evaluation. A split of 80:10:10 is used to generate the training, validation and test sets. We employ 10 epochs and a batch size of 32 for model training. Table 2 shows the results of the transfer and ensemble learning models for plant disease detection after being trained using the plant disease cases with respect to potato, tomato and pepper plant leaves. Figure 1 shows the comparison of different networks.

Table 2. Plant disease detection results for transfer learning and ensemble networks.

	MobileNetv2	ResNet50	VGG16	Ensemble
Potato	0.8649	0.8660	0.8593	**0.9330**
Tomato	0.9423	**0.9752**	0.8240	0.9633
Pepper	0.7806	0.8662	0.6944	**0.8913**

As shown in Table 2 and Fig. 1, ResNet5 achieves the best performance among the three networks for the identification of healthy and diseased cases for all the three subsets. The ensemble transfer learning provides improved reliable with test accuracy rates of 93.3%, 96.33%, and 89.13% for the detection of disease cases for potato, tomato, and pepper plant leaves.

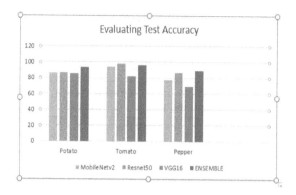

Fig. 1. Performance comparison between base and ensemble models.

4.1. Discussion

We employ well-known CNN architectures and transfers land ensemble learning to tackle plant leaf disease detection. The pre-trained CNNs are re-trained based on the pre-trained weights and extended to solving a new problem. Several final layers are trained using new training sets. The transfer learning models achieve good accuracy rates. Compared to designing a new CNN, transfer learning requires less effort and time with acceptable performance. The ensemble method combining the three transfer learning models further enhances the detection accuracy rates.

5. Conclusion

In this research, we employ an ensemble transfer learning network by integrating ResNet50, MobileNetv2, and VGG16 to reduce the generalization error for plant disease detection. Data augmentation techniques are used to improve the accuracy rates of the networks. By combining the three different base networks, the ensemble model is equipped with significant diversity and achieves better classification results. From our experiments, the best transfer learning base model is ResNet50 with the best test accuracy rate of 97%, while ensemble learning model provides the best accuracy rates between 89-97%. For future work, we will employ evolutionary algorithms for model architecture and hyper-parameter identification and fine-tuning [17-20]. Other deep networks and ensemble strategies will be employed to further test model efficiency [21-23].

References

1. Hassan, S.M., Maji, A.K., Jasiński, M., Leonowicz, Z. and Jasińska, E., 2021. Identification of plant-leaf diseases using CNN and transfer-learning approach. *Electronics*, *10*(12), p. 1388.
2. M.M. Ghazi, B. Yanikoglu and E. Aptoula. "Plant identification using deep neural networks via optimization of transfer learning parameters". *Neurocomputing*, 235, pp. 228-235. 2017.
3. Geetharamani, G. and Pandian, A., 2019. Identification of plant leaf diseases using a nine-layer deep convolutional neural network. *Computers & Electrical Engineering*, *76*, pp. 323-338.
4. C. Wall, F. Young, L. Zhang, E. Phillips, R. Jiang and Y. Yu, "Deep learning based melanoma diagnosis using dermoscopic images", *Developments of Artificial Intelligence Technologies in Computation and Robotics*, 2020.
5. S.C. Neoh, W. Srisukkham, L. Zhang, S. Todryk, B. Greystoke, C.P. Lim, A. Hossain and N. Aslam. "An Intelligent Decision Support System for Leukaemia Diagnosis using Microscopic Blood Images," *Scientific Reports*, 5 (14938). 2015.
6. W. Srisukkham, L. Zhang, S.C. Neoh, S. Todryk and C.P. Lim. "Intelligent Leukaemia Diagnosis with Bare-Bones PSO based Feature Optimization," *Applied Soft Computing*, 56. pp. 405-419. 2017.
7. L. Zhang, K. Mistry, S.C. Neoh. and C.P. Lim. "Intelligent facial emotion recognition using moth-firefly optimization," *Knowledge-Based Systems*. Volume 111, Nov. 2016, 248–267.
8. T. Tan, L. Zhang and C.P. Lim. "Adaptive melanoma diagnosis using evolving clustering, ensemble and deep neural networks," *Knowledge-Based Systems*. 2019.
9. T. Tan, L. Zhang, C.P. Lim. B. Fielding, Y. Yu, and E. Anderson. "Evolving Ensemble Models for Image Segmentation Using Enhanced Particle Swarm Optimization," *IEEE Access*. 2019.
10. L. Zhang, C.P. Lim and Y. Yu. "Intelligent human action recognition using an ensemble model of evolving deep networks with swarm-based optimization". *Knowledge-Based Systems*, 220, p. 106918. 2021.
11. P. Kinghorn, L. Zhang and L. Shao. "A Hierarchical and Regional Deep Learning Architecture for Image Description Generation," *Pattern Recognition Letters*. 2019.

12. L. Zhang and C.P. Lim. "Intelligent optic disc segmentation using improved particle swarm optimization and evolving ensemble models", *Applied Soft Computing*. 92, 106328. 2020.
13. P. Kinghorn, L. Zhang and L. Shao. "Deep learning based image description generation", In *IJCNN*, 919-926, 2017.
14. B. Fielding and L. Zhang. "Evolving Deep DenseBlock Architecture Ensembles for Image Classification". *Electronics*. Nov. 2020.
15. D. Farid, L. Zhang, C.M. Rahman, A.M. Hossain and R. Strachan. "Hybrid Decision Tree and Naïve Bayes Classifiers for Multi-class Classification Tasks," *Expert Systems with Applications*. Volume 41, Issue 4, Part 2, March 2014, 1937–1946. 2014.
16. S. Slade, L. Zhang, Y. Yu and C.P. Lim, 2022. An evolving ensemble model of multi-stream convolutional neural networks for human action recognition in still images. *Neural Computing and Applications*, pp. 1-27.
17. S. Slade and L. Zhang. "Topological Evolution of Spiking Neural Networks". In *Proceedings of IEEE WCCI*. 2018.
18. B. Fielding, T. Lawrence and L. Zhang. "Evolving and Ensembling Deep CNN Architectures for Image Classification". In *Proceedings of International Joint Conference on Neural Networks (IJCNN)*. 2019.
19. Zhang, L., Lim, C.P., Yu, Y. and Jiang, M., 2022. Sound classification using evolving ensemble models and Particle Swarm Optimization. *Applied Soft Computing*, *116*, p. 108322.
20. Y. Zhang, L. Zhang and M.A. Hossain. Adaptive 3D facial action intensity estimation and emotion recognition, *Expert Systems with Applications*, 42 (2015) 1446-1464.
21. Y. Yu, X. Chen, L. Zhang, R. Gao and H. Gao. "Neural Graph for Personalized Tag Recommendation". *IEEE Intelligent Systems*. 2020.
22. Lawrence, T., Zhang, L., Rogage, K. and Lim, C.P., 2021. Evolving Deep Architecture Generation with Residual Connections for Image Classification Using Particle Swarm Optimization. *Sensors*, *21*(23), p. 7936.
23. Lawrence, T. and Zhang, L., 2019. IoTNet: An efficient and accurate convolutional neural network for IoT devices. *Sensors*, *19*(24), p. 5541.

Part 3

Risk Analysis and Multi-criteria Evaluation

Assessing drivers' hazard prediction ability:
A multiple layer DEA application

Zegang Zhai

School of Transportation, Southeast University
Sipailou 2, Nanjing 210096, China
zhaizegang@seu.edu.cn

Qiong Bao

School of Transportation, Southeast University
Sipailou 2, Nanjing 210096, China
baoqiong@seu.edu.cn

Yongjun Shen

School of Transportation, Southeast University
Sipailou 2, Nanjing 210096, China
shenyongjun@seu.edu.cn

Hazard prediction ability refers to a driver's skill in anticipating and detecting potential road hazards. Drivers with good hazard prediction ability are able to effectively handle various traffic information of the road environment and evaluate predictive cues to help facilitate the early detection of hazards. Insight into the poor areas of hazard prediction ability for specific traffic scenarios provides drivers with valuable information about the kind of measures most urgently needed to improve their driving safety. In this study, a simulated driving experiment is conducted and the multiple layer DEA model is applied to assess drivers' hazard prediction ability. On the basis of the results, those under-performing drivers are distinguished. Moreover, by analyzing the weights allocated to each indicator from the model, the most problematic scenario and indicator are identified for each driver, which leads up to specific driver improvement recommendations (such as training programs).

Keywords: Driving safety; hazard prediction; simulated driving; multiple layer DEA.

1. Introduction

Hazard prediction is the skill of detecting, evaluating, and reacting to events on the road that have a high probability of producing a collision [1]. The skill of hazard prediction has been reported to be a specific driving ability that correlates with the risk of having a crash [2]. Hazard prediction assessment measures the ability to identify hazardous situations during the activity of driving. The assessment results can be used as a diagnostic and training tool to improve the skills of those drivers who lack the ability to detect hazards.

Driving simulator studies provide a safe and controllable environment to perform research on traffic safety, for example, evaluating vehicle designs, testing traffic control devices, evaluating new in-vehicle and cooperative infrastructure technologies, and analyzing drivers' behavior [3]. Over the past decades, many research efforts have focused on the application of driving simulators for safety issues [4, 5].

This study uses data from a fixed-based driving simulator to investigate the hazard prediction ability of various drivers in six typical traffic scenarios. For the analysis, the concept of composite indicators (CIs) or indexes, in which relevant information is combined in one figure, is employed. Specifically, the technique of multiple layer data envelopment analysis (MLDEA) is used for the index construction. This is the first time that this model is used for assessing drivers' hazard prediction ability. The results enable analysts to identify those underperforming drivers and to provide them with detailed suggestions for improving their driving performance with respect to hazard prediction.

The next section presents the appropriate indicators of hazard prediction ability and describes the data collection process. In Section 3, a description of the MLDEA methodology and its application is given. This paper closes with concluding remarks and topics for further research.

2. Experiment and Data

To analyze and evaluate the hazard prediction ability of a driver, we collected and sorted out six typical potential danger scenarios commonly met in urban roads, which include three road section scenes (passengers or pedestrians may cross the road from the front of the bus when the bus stops at the roadside; opposite vehicles may drive through the road when there is an accident in the opposite lane; vehicles parked on the roadside may suddenly start and change lanes) and three intersection scenes (pedestrians or non-motor vehicles may rush out of the visual blind area when there is a construction area at the entrance road; the large vehicles in front may block the left turning vehicles on the opposite entrance road when waiting for the traffic lights; the right turning vehicles on the right entrance road may be obscured when there is a construction area at the intersection). Then we built the road environment and traffic scene required for the simulation driving experiment based on 3D simulation modeling, so as to restore the driving environment from the real driver's perspective as much as possible.

Sixty novice drivers (of which 30 were men) between 20 and 25 years old (mean age = 22.3; SD = 1.75) participated in this study. The experiment was conducted on a medium fidelity driving simulator. It is a fixed-based driving simulator with a force-feedback steering wheel, brake pedal, and accelerator. The simulation included vehicle dynamics, visual and auditory feedback, and a performance measurement system. The visual environment was presented on a large screen, with rearview and side view mirror images.

In this study, five indicators are selected for each scenario, and thus a total of 30 indicators are utilized to characterize the driver's hazard prediction ability. From the perspective of detection process, we choose two indicators: (1) When does the driver notice the potentially dangerous area: the time difference between the time when the driver first looks at the potentially dangerous area and the time when the danger appears in front of the driver. (2) Gaze duration to the potentially dangerous area: the sum of the total gaze duration of the driver on the potentially dangerous area, which is used to characterize the driver's attention to the dangerous area. From the perspective of decision process, we choose three indicators: (3) When does the driver lift the accelerator pedal: the time difference between the moment when the driver lifts the accelerator pedal and the moment when the danger appears in front of the driver. (4) When does the driver put his/her foot above the brake pedal: the time difference between the time when the driver puts his/her foot above the brake pedal and the time when the danger appears in front of the driver. (5) When does the driver press the brake pedal: the time difference between the time when the driver presses the brake pedal and the time when the danger appears in front of the driver.

3. Multiple Layer DEA: Theory and Application

Indicators enhance understanding of situations and issues by transforming raw data into meaningful information [6, 7]. Recently, various indicators have been combined into so-called CIs or indexes [8, 9]. Simplistically, a CI synthesizes the information included in a selected set of indicators into one figure. In this study, a CI was created with respect to drivers' hazard prediction ability. Based on the index scores, drivers can be ranked in terms of relative performance tested by means of a simulator. Useful insight in underperformance area for each driver can be gained by analyzing the allocated indicator weights.

In recent years, there has been increasing interest in the methodology for creating a CI in which the assignment of weights to each indicator is an essential step [10]. One of the promising weighting methods is Data Envelopment Analysis (DEA), based on which the best possible indicator weights are determined for each decision-making unit (DMU) or driver in this case. In other words, the most optimal index score is obtained for each driver.

In the basic DEA-based CI model, by solving a linear programming problem as follows, the best possible indicator weights are determined. An index score between 0 and 1 was obtained for each unit, with a higher value indicating better relative performance.

$$CI_0 = \max \sum_{i=1}^{s} u_i y_{i0}$$

$$s.t. \sum_{i=1}^{s} u_i y_{ij} \leq 1, \quad j = 1, \dots, n \tag{1}$$

$$u_i \geq \varepsilon, \quad i = 1, \dots, m$$

In this constrained optimization problem, y_{ij} is the ith indicator of the jth driver, u_i is the weight given to indicator i, and ε is a small non-Archimedean number for restricting the model to assign a weight of 0 to unfavorable factors.

The model used in this study was the multiple layer DEA-based CI model (MLDEA-CI), which was able to take into account the layered hierarchy of indicators that often exists in reality [11-13]. Suppose that a set of n DMUs is to be evaluated in terms of s indicators (y) with a K layered hierarchy. The MLDEA-CI model can be formulated as follows:

$$CI_0 = \max \sum_{f_1=1}^{s} \hat{u}_{f_1} y_{f_1 0}$$

$$s.t. \sum_{f_1=1}^{s} \hat{u}_{f_1} y_{f_1 j} \leq 1, \quad j = 1, \dots, n$$

$$\frac{\sum_{f_1 \in A_{f_k}^{(k)}} \hat{u}_{f_1}}{\sum_{f_1 \in A_{f_{k+1}}^{(k+1)}} \hat{u}_{f_1}} = p_{f_k}^{(k)} \in \Theta, k = 1, \dots, K-1 \tag{2}$$

$$u_{f_K} \geq \varepsilon, \quad f_K = 1, \dots, s^{(K)}$$

where

$\hat{u}_{f_1}$ denotes set of most favorable optimal weights for DMU$_0$, obtained by solving model,

$s^{(k)}$ denotes number of categories in kth layer (k = 1, 2, . . ., K), $s^{(1)} = s$,

$A_{f_k}^{(k)}$ denotes set of indicators of fth category in kth layer,

$p_{f_k}^{(k)}$ denotes internal weights associated with indicators of fth category in kth layer, which sum to 1 within a particular category, and

Θ denotes restrictions imposed on corresponding internal weights.

In general, the MLDEA-CI model reflects the layered hierarchy of the indicators by specifying the weights in each category of each layer. Meanwhile, by restricting the flexibility of these weights, denoted Θ, consistency with prior knowledge and the ability to obtain acceptable, layer-specific weights are guaranteed, which cannot be realized in the one-layer model.

For this study, 60 drivers were evaluated based on the 30 driving indicators, structured in a three-layer hierarchy. The subscript 0 refers to the driver whose index score was to be obtained by solving the constrained optimization problem, which maximized the index value of the driver and satisfied the imposed restrictions. The first restriction guaranteed an intuitive interpretation of the composite indicator and implied that no driver in the data set could be assigned an index value larger than 1 under these weights. With respect to the second restriction, the layered hierarchy of the indicators was reflected by specifying the weights in each category of each layer and further restricting their flexibility. In this study, we restrict the weights or shares of indicators in the same category to be equal with 20% variability to still allow a high level of flexibility. In this way, realistic and acceptable weights were guaranteed. In addition, by the third restriction, all weights were constrained to be nonnegative.

4. Results

By applying the model, 30 hazard prediction ability performance indicators were combined into an index score for each driver by selecting the best possible indicator weights under the imposed restrictions. As a result, the index score for each driver was calculated in relation to scores for all the other drivers who took part in the experiment. Index values are between 0 and 1, with an index value equal to 1 identifying a best performer, whereas a score less than one implies underperforming drivers:

- Top five best-performing drivers: Drivers 57, 14, 43, 22, 52 and
- Last five underperforming drivers: Drivers 17, 21, 32, 16, 30

In addition to the overall index score of the drivers, more detailed insight can be gained from the assigned weights, which can be interpreted as indications of the importance shares of the corresponding indicators. The model not only pursues the optimal index score for each driver, but also guarantees acceptable weights through the imposed restrictions. Figure 1 shows the assigned weights and shares for the case of the driver 1. As can be seen, the performance with respect to the six scenarios in the overall index score obtain the share varying from 13.3% to 20.0%.

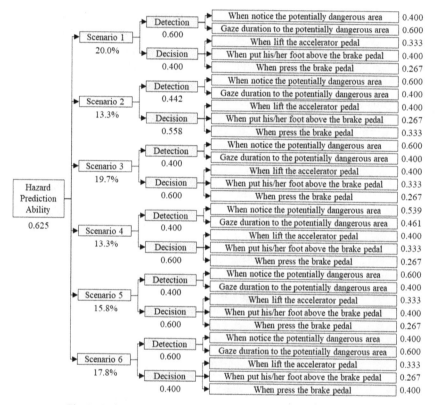

Fig. 1. Assigned weights and shares from the model for case of Driver 1.

More importantly, based on the principles of the MLDEA-CI model, an indicator will be assigned a high weight if the driver performed relatively well on that aspect. On the contrary, low weights provided valuable information about the aspects requiring more attention for improvement. Therefore, areas of underperformance can be detected for each driver and required improvement priorities can be formulated. Specifically, driver 1 did relatively well with respect to scenario 1 (with the highest share of 20.0%), whereas more attention should be paid to scenario 2 and scenario 4 (with the lowest share of 13.3%), especially for the gaze duration to the potentially dangerous area.

5. Concluding Remarks

To measure the multidimensional concept of the hazard prediction ability, which cannot be captured by a single scenario or indicator, this study investigated the construction of a composite indicator for driver evaluation. In doing so, a multiple-layer DEA-based composite indicator model was applied on a hierarchy of driving performance indicators. Based on this model, the most optimal index score between 0 and 1 for each of the 60 drivers was determined by combining 30 hierarchical indicators, with higher values indicating better relative performance. From the index scores, the underperforming drivers with an index score less than 1, were identified.

Apart from distinguishing the best-performing and underperforming drivers, their relative performance with respect to detection and decision process for each scenario was compared. In addition, based on the principles of the MLDEA-CI model, areas of underperformance were detected and required improvement priorities were formulated for each driver.

This study suggested that the MLDEA-CI model is appropriate for evaluating drivers' hazard prediction ability and for identifying the most problematic aspects during their driving. Drivers can be trained in different tasks in the simulator, according to each driver's weaknesses, thereby improving drivers' abilities and the level of road safety. Moreover, regarding the future usefulness of the results from this methodology, there are opportunities in terms of selecting candidates for driving jobs, identifying high-risk drivers, improving the rating process, rewarding low-risk drivers, etc.

Acknowledgments

This research was supported by the National Natural Science Foundation of China (Grant No. 52002063), the Natural Science Foundation of Jiangsu Province of China (Grant No. BK20190371), and the Humanities and Social Sciences Foundation of the Ministry of Education (Grant No. 21YJCZH129).

References

1. Crundall D, Chapman P, Trawley S, et al. Some hazards are more attractive than others: Drivers of varying experience respond differently to different types of hazard. *Accid Anal Prev*, 45: 600-609 (2012).
2. Darby P, Murray W, Raeside R. Applying online fleet driver assessment to help identify, target and reduce occupational road safety risk. *Saf Sci*, 47(3): 163-174 (2009).

3. Fisher, D., M. Rizzo, J.K. Caird, and J. Lee (eds.). *Handbook of Driving Simulation for Engineering, Medicine, and Psychology*, CRC Press, Boca Raton, Fla (2011).

4. Charlton, S.G. Driving While Conversing: Cell Phones That Distract and Passengers Who React. *Accid Anal Prev*, 41: 160-173 (2009).

5. Boyle, L. N., and J. D. Lee. Using Driving Simulators to Assess Driving Safety. *Accid Anal Prev*, 42: 785-787 (2010).

6. Litman, T.A. Well Measured: Developing Indicators for Comprehensive and Sustainable Transport Planning. Victoria Transport Policy Institute (2005).

7. Litman, T.A. Developing Indicators for Comprehensive and Sustainable Transport Planning. *Transportation Research Record*, 2017: 10-15 (2007).

8. Salzman, J. Methodological Choices Encountered in the Construction of Composite Indices of Economic and Social Well-being. Center for the Study of Living Standards (2003).

9. Al-Haji, G. Road Safety Development Index (RSDI): Theory, Philosophy and Practice. Department of Science and Technology. PhD dissertation. Campus Norrköping, Linköping University, Norrköping (2007).

10. Nardo, M., M. Saisana, A. Saltelli, S. Tarantola, A. Hoffman, and E. Giovannini. *Handbook on Constructing Composite Indicators: Methodology and User Guide*. Organisation for Co-operation and Development (2005).

11. Shen, Y., E. Hermans, D. Ruan, G. Wets, T. Brijs, and K. Vanhoof. A Generalized Multiple Layer Data Envelopment Analysis Model for Hierarchical Structure Assessment: A Case Study in Road Safety Performance Evaluation. *Expert System with Applications*, 38(12): 15262-15272 (2011).

12. Shen, Y., E. Hermans, T. Brijs, and G. Wets. Data Envelopment Analysis for Composite Indicators: A Multiple Layer Model. *Social Indicators Research*, 114(2): 739-756 (2013).

13. Shen Y, Hermans E, Bao Q, Brijs T, Wets G. Towards better road safety management: Lessons learned from inter-national benchmarking. *Accid Anal Prev*, 138: 105484 (2020).

Household micro-grid framework and gossip power optimization algorithm

Erliang Chai[1,*], Tailin Chen[1], Zhanru Fu[1] and Guibin Liao[2]

[1]*Shenzhen Power Supply Co., Ltd., Shenzhen, Guangdong 518048, China*
[2]*Shenzhen Microgrid Energy Management System Laboratory Co., Ltd.*
Shenzhen, Guangdong 518054, China
[*]499534027@qq.com

Baofeng Miao
Shenzhen Daidian Technology Development Co., Ltd.
Shenzhen, Guangdong 518081, China

Aiming at the problems of large data, high communication cost, vulnerable controller and poor expansibility which cause extra energy loss in the current centralized control of micro-grid, a novel topology of smart micro-grid for home applications is proposed. Moreover, a distributed optimization operation strategy based on Gossip algorithm is proposed to optimize the operation of micro-grid. In this strategy, the optimized operation of the micro-grid can be achieved only by exchanging information between adjacent controllers, while the central controller is not required. Therefore, the problems existing in centralized control can be effectively solved, and the control performance of the system is improved, which is beneficial to the micro-grid implementation of plug and play. Finally, the feasibility of the proposed micro-grid structure, model and operation method is verifed by the Matlab/Simulink simulation platform, simulation results are consistent with the consistent with the analysis. This paper aims to design a novel micro-grid for home applications to help achieve the goal of reducing carbon peaking at the micro level.

Keywords: Carbon Peaking and carbon neutrality goals; micro-grid; distributed control; gossip algorithm.

1. Introduction

As a large number of new energy sources are connected to the power grid, the power balance between supply and demand and power quality of the grid are impacted due to its intermittency and unpredictability [1]. The reason for the phenomenon of abandoning wind and light is the main network puts forward a series of standards for new energy grid connection in order to ensure its own stable operation, which is detrimental to the early achievement of Carbon Peaking and Carbon Neutrality goals. Therefore, it is important to achieve micro-grid operation control and energy management in micro-grid research as soon as possible [2, 3].

In order to solve the problem of micro-grid control, the central controller is usually used to send and receive instructions that the whole network can operate in a relatively optimal way in the traditional control methods [4]. However, the traditional control method needs to rely on the communication network for huge data processing in practice, which will not only greatly increase the cost of communication, but also reduce the stability of the whole system. And it is difficult to expand continually [5].

In recent years, distributed control method has been adopted in power system in order to solve the problem of centralized control, which is realized distributed cooperative control through data exchange between adjacent units or nodes. In [6], scholars adopted a distributed secondary control strategy to control voltage, frequency and reactive power in micro-grid. Based on the analysis of typical cogeneration systems, literature [7] presented a bus structure describing their composition and structure and established a 0-1 mixed integer linear programming model for daily dynamic economic adjustment of cogeneration micro-grid. Literature [8] proposed a distributed point-voltage control strategy based on Gossip algorithm, which effectively reduces voltage deviation without central controller. Taking air conditioner and water heater as representatives of household temperature control loads, two refined models of typical loads are proposed to analyze their energy storage characteristics, high control characteristics and fast response characteristics in literature [9]. However, the control of such thermal power effect equipment by start-stop action cannot actively play the role of" non-sensitive load of power quality" such as electric kettle, electric heater and ice storage air conditioner in regulating the balance of power send and demand.

In addition, in order to take advantage of the characteristics of power quality non-sensitive loads better, the team from the University of Hong Kong and Imperial College London proposed that the demand side follows the generation side [10] in 2012, and then first proposed the concept and equipment of electrical spring. Since then, electrical spring has been a series studied by scholars [11-13]. Therefore, based on the electrical spring technology, this paper proposed a new micro-grid structure for home applications and distributed micro-grid control strategy based on Gossip algorithm. Without central controller, the stable and efficient operation of micro-grid can be realized only through a small amount of communication between adjacent controllers. In other words, the new energy fluctuations are transferred to non-sensitive loads of power quality on the premise of fully utilizing new energy sources, and ensures the "sensitive loads" (such as lights, computers and washing machines, etc.) run normally. In addition, the decentralization characteristic of Gossip algorithm makes it more robust to packet loss, which can well meet the plug and play requirements of smart grid and solve the problems existing in traditional micro-grid.

The structure of this paper is as follows: In Section 2, smart micro-grid topology for home applications is conducted. Section 3 introduces vector control algorithm and cooperative control algorithm for micro-grid system. In Section 4, the effectiveness and reliability of the algorithm are verified by MATLAB simulation. Conclusion remarks are given in Section 5.

The equivalent circuit of the proposed converter is shown in Fig. 1, which includes one switch (S), one coupled inductor, three diodes $(D_1, D_2$ and $D_3)$, and four capacitors $(C_1, C_2, C_3$ and $C_4)$. The coupled inductor can be expressed by an ideal transformer series leakage inductance (LK) with a turn ratio of N.

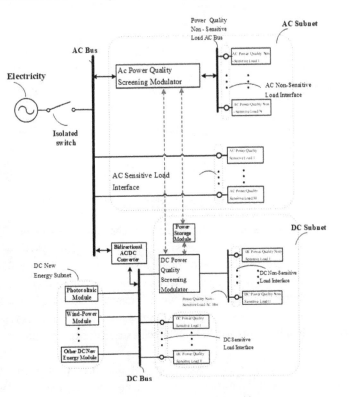

Fig. 1. Structure of smart household micro-grid system.

2. Structure of Smart Micro-grid for Home Applications

2.1. *Frame of system*

Figure 1 shows the framework of smart micro-grid for home applications. As shown in Fig. 2, micro-grid is consist of AC subnet, DC subnet and DC new energy subnet, among which the AC subnet and DC subnet are connected by bidirectional AC/DC converter. The AC bus is connected to the mains through the island switch. The AC sensitive power quality load module is connected to the AC bus directly, and the AC non-sensitive power quality load is connected to the AC bus through the AC power quality screening modulator. The DC new energy subnet and the DC sensitive power quality load are directly connected to the DC bus, and the DC non-sensitive power quality load and the power storage device are connected to the DC bus through the DC power quality screening modulator.

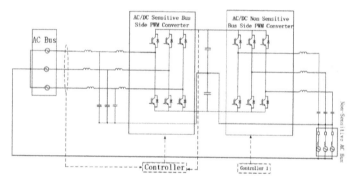

Fig. 2. Diagram of AC power quality selector and modulator.

In this paper, the loads are divided into two types: non-sensitive power quality and sensitive power quality. The non-sensitive power quality load whose bus voltage is controlled by the power quality screening modulator refers to the adjustable load that allows voltage fluctuation in a certain range, such as water heater, electric blanket, electric kettle, building icing equipment, etc. The sensitive power quality load whose power consumption is determined by users refers to the load that requires high voltage stability, such as rice cooker, computer, washing machine, TV, fan, etc.

The red dotted line in Fig. 1 indicates that the three controllers exchange information, thus coordinate the control of active power, reactive power and charge and discharge power of the energy storage device.

2.2. *AC power quality screening modulator*

The framework of smart micro-grid system for home applications is shown in Fig. 1. By adjusting the voltage of the non-sensitive load, the power quality screening modulator is able to balance the random vibration of the new energy generation to ensure the stable operation of the sensitive load. In this paper, the AC power quality screening modulator adopts AC-DC-AC PWM converter, and its frame is shown in Fig. 2.

2.3. *DC power quality screening modulator*

As Fig. 3 shown, DC power quality screening modulator is composed of bi-directional DC/DC converter and DC/DC converter. The bi-directional DC/DC converter controls the charge and discharge of electric energy in the electric energy storage device, and the DC/DC converter adjusts the voltage amplitude of the DC bus to weaken its influence on the non-sensitive load of power quality on the bus. AC-DC-AC PWM converter is composed of AC/DC PWM variable current converter on the sensitive bus side and DC/AC PWM variable current converter on the non-sensitive bus side. In order to improve the stability of the output power of the converter on the AC side, PWM converter is usually used to maintain the stability of the voltage amplitude of the DC bus on the AC/DC sensitive bus side and adjust the reactive power on the side. The main function of the PWM variable current converter on the DC/AC non-sensitive bus side is to adjust the voltage amplitude of the non-sensitive load AC bus.

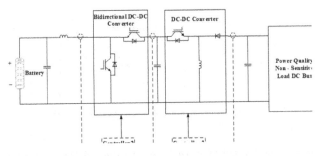

Fig. 3. Diagram of DC power quality selector and modulator.

3. Control Strategy

3.1. *Vector control*

In this paper, vector control technology is used to adjust active and reactive power independently. The basic control block diagram of AC power quality screening

298

modulator is shown in Fig. 4, where d and q represent the active and reactive component reference respectively. Firstly, active power and reactive power are calculated approximatively according to the electrical characteristics i_a, i_b, i_c, u_a, u_b and u_c of each phase. Secondly, the PI regulator is used to adjust the voltage amplitude and reactive power of the DC bus in the PWM converter of AC/DC sensitive bus side and the voltage amplitude of non-sensitive AC bus can be adjusted by controlling the active power in DC/AC non-sensitive bus side PWM converter. Non-sensitive AC load active power reference value P1* is generated by the Gossip algorithm. In Fig. 5, the basic control block diagram of AC power quality screening modulator is shown.

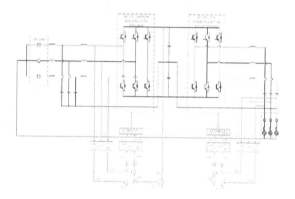

Fig. 4. Detailed control diagram of AC power quality selector and modulator.

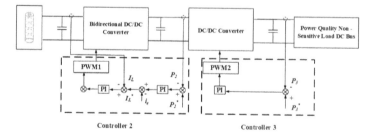

Fig. 5. Detailed control diagram of DC power quality selector and modulator.

3.2. Cooperative control

3.2.1. Gossip algorithm

In 1972, the question that "How many telephone connections would it take for n women in a group to have the information that everyone has" was brought up by

Hajnal et al. This discussion gave the first description of the Gossip problem, and since then the study of the Gossip problem officially entered the historical stage. The Gossip algorithm is a distributed algorithm carried out in a network of N nodes. In each round of the Gossip algorithm, each node communicates with the nearest node and exchanges information with these nodes. In addition, in a round of the Gossip algorithm, all nodes process the exchanged information locally to update their knowledge in preparation for the next round. Finally, after several iterations, all nodes have access to the entire system of their choice.

Suppose node i has information x_0 a, and the value of I ranges from 1, 2...n. All nodes in the system have a number of information, which can be any parameter at node i, such as voltage and power of the node. In each step of the iteration, each node exchanges information with its neighboring nodes and updates according to its own local information x_r^j ($j \in n_i$) to obtain x_{r+1}^j. The updating process is carried out according to Eq. (1).

$$x_{r+1}^i = w_{ii} \cdot x_r^i + \sum_{j \in n_i} w_{ij} \cdot x_r^j \tag{1}$$

In Eq. (1), w_{ii}, w_{ij} are weights and the matrix W which is called the weight matrix consist of elements i, j. The convergence of the algorithm depends on the value of each element of the weight matrix.

Elements of matrix W can be determined by Eq. (2):

$$W(ij) \begin{cases} 1 - \dfrac{2}{\lambda_1(L) + \lambda_{n-1}(L)} d_i, & i = j \\ \dfrac{2}{\lambda_1(L) + \lambda_{n-1}(L)}, & j \in n_i \\ 0 & j \notin n_i \end{cases} \tag{2}$$

In Eq. (2), L is the Laplacian matrix of the system communication topology graph G, λ_i represents the I eigenvalue of all eigenvalues sorted from large to small ($i = 1, 2, ..., n$). d_i is the degree of node i, which can be determined by Eq. (3).

$$L(ij) = \begin{cases} d_i & i = j \\ -1 & j \in n_i \\ 0 & j \notin n_i \end{cases} \tag{3}$$

In Eq. (3), if nodes i and j are not adjacent, $w_{ij} = 0$. In combination with the iterative update process shown in Eq. (1), it can be seen that the status update process of each node is independent of the status of non-neighboring nodes and only associated with the status of neighboring nodes. In addition, Gossip algorithm is a completely distributed algorithm due to the different correlations between them.

3.2.2. *Optimal operation model in micro-grid*

The purpose of optimal operation in micro-grid is to make the total power consumption of micro-grid be the lowest under the premise of fully utilizing new energy. The objective function is

$$F_i(P_i) = \alpha_i P_i^2 + \beta_i P_i + \gamma_i \quad i \in n \tag{4}$$

In Eq. (4), P_i represents the reference value of the active power of the i controller, α_i, β_i and γ_i are the power consumption coefficients of each converter respectively, then the optimization operation of the micro-grid is transformed into the problem of finding the minimum value and the objective function F_i:

$$min \sum_{i=1}^{n} F_i(P_i) \tag{5}$$

In order to realize the full utilization of new energy and the pure resistance and time-sharing constant power of the whole micro-grid, the micro-grid should also meet the following conditions:

$$\begin{cases} P_{maxv} - P_v = 0 \\ \sum_{i=1}^{n} Q_i = 0 \\ \sum_{i=1}^{n} P_i - P_{LD} = N_i \end{cases} \tag{6}$$

To construct the Lagrange function of Eqs. (5) and (6),

$$L(P_1, P_2, \ldots, P_n, \mu) = \sum_{i=1}^{n} Fi(Pi) + \sum_{i=1}^{n} Q_i$$
$$+ \mu \left(\sum_{i=1}^{n} P_i - P_{LD} - N_i \right) + (P_{maxv} - P_v) \tag{7}$$

The necessary condition for the existence of Lagrange extreme value can be established by (7)

$$\frac{\partial L}{\partial P_i} = \frac{\partial Fi}{\partial P_i} - \mu = 2\alpha_i P_i + \beta_i - \mu = 0 \tag{8}$$

When the partial derivatives of the power loss function of each converter are equal to the respective load regulating power, the sum of the objective function F_i has a minimum value, which can be obtained from Eq. (8),

$$\mu = \frac{\partial F_i}{\partial P_i} = 2\alpha_i P_i + \beta_i \qquad (9)$$

According to Eq. (9), the optimal active power reference value of the converter is

$$P_i = \frac{\mu - \beta_i}{\alpha_i} \qquad (10)$$

After several Gossip iterations, all μ_i values converge to the same value μ theoretical.

4. Simulation

In this paper, Matlab/Simulink is used to simulate the model and algorithm. The simulation results are shown in Figs. 6 and 7. Figure 6 shows the AC bus voltage of non-sensitive load with power quality. When t=50s, its voltage amplitude increases to 275V. At this time, all transducers jointly adjust the active power of non-sensitive load with power quality and the charge and discharge power of energy storage equipment to balance the fluctuation of new energy through the Gossip algorithm. As shown in Fig. 7, at t=50s, the use power of non-sensitive AC-DC load increases as the voltage increases, and the energy storage equipment changes from discharge state to charging state. As shown in Fig. 8, all of ff value converges to the same value. In other words, the micro-grid operates in the state of minimum power consumption. At the same time, the whole micro-grid presents pure resistance externally.

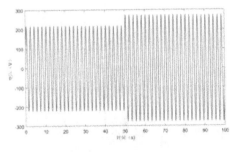

Fig. 6. Bus voltage of AC non-sensitive load.

302

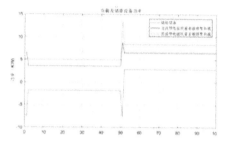

Fig. 7. Active power of non-sensitive loads.

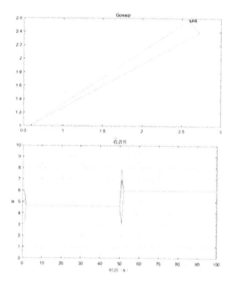

Fig. 8. Algorithm convergence.

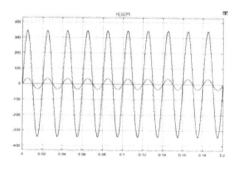

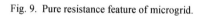

Fig. 9. Pure resistance feature of microgrid.

5. Conclusion

In this paper, an optimization model of smart micro-grid for home considering demand-side response is constructed by taking household non-sensitive load as demand-side resource. The demand-side resources and supply-side resources are treated equally to minimize the power consumption of the entire micro-grid, and ensure the external performance of pure resistance, stable operation of sensitive load, time-sharing constant power and complete grid connection of new energy. In addition, this paper realizes the optimization control of each converter, which solves the problem of large amount of data and high cost in the process of centralized control communication effectively. At the same time, the communication topology of the algorithm can be modified according to the needs of users, so that the system can adapt to different scenarios.

References

1. W. Yuan, C. Wang, X. Lei, Q. Li, Z. Shi, and Y. Yu, "Multi-area scheduling model and strategy for power systems with large-scale new energy and energy storage," in 2018 Chinese Automation Congress (CAC). IEEE, 2018, pp. 2419–2424.
2. K. Roy, K. K. Mandal, and A. C. Mandal, "Modeling and managing of micro grid connected system using improved artificial bee colony algorithm," International Journal of Electrical Power & Energy Systems, vol. 75, pp. 50–58, 2016.
3. Y. Han, H. Li, P. Shen, E. A. A. Coelho, and J. M. Guerrero, "Review of active and reactive power sharing strategies in hierarchical controlled microgrids," IEEE Transactions on Power Electronics, vol. 32, no. 3, pp. 2427–2451, 2016.
4. C. Chen, "Economic dispatch using simplified personal best oriented particle swarm optimizer," in 2008 Third International Conference on Electric Utility Deregulation and Restructuring and Power Technologies. IEEE, 2008, pp. 572–576.
5. P. Prakash and D. K. Khatod, "Optimal sizing and siting techniques for distributed generation in distribution systems: A review," Renewable and sustainable energy reviews, vol. 57, pp. 111–130, 2016.
6. C. Goldman, "Coordination of energy efficiency and demand response," 2010.
7. Q. Shafee, J. M. Guerrero, and J. C. Vasquez, "Distributed secondary control for islanded microgrids—a novel approach," IEEE Transactions on power electronics, vol. 29, no. 2, pp. 1018–1031, 2013.

8. D. He, D. Shi, and R. Sharma, "Consensus-based distributed cooperative control for microgrid voltage regulation and reactive power sharing," in IEEE PES Innovative Smart Grid Technologies, Europe. IEEE, 2014, pp. 1–6.

9. N. Hatziargyriou, A. Dimeas, A. Tsikalakis, J. P. Lopes, G. Karniotakis, and J. Oyarzabal, "Management of microgrids in market environment," in 2005 International Conference on Future Power Systems. IEEE, 2005, pp. 7–pp.

10. S. Y. Hui, C. K. Lee, and F. F. Wu, "Electric springs—a new smart grid technology," IEEE Transactions on Smart Grid, vol. 3, no. 3, pp. 1552–1561, 2012.

11. S.-C. Tan, C. K. Lee, and S. Hui, "General steady-state analysis and control principle of electric springs with active and reactive power compensations," IEEE Transactions on Power Electronics, vol. 28, no. 8, pp. 3958–3969, 2012.

12. S. Yan, S.-C. Tan, C.-K. Lee, B. Chaudhuri, and S. R. Hui, "Electric springs for reducing power imbalance in three-phase power systems," IEEE Transactions on Power Electronics, vol. 30, no. 7, pp. 3601–3609, 2014.

13. T. Yang, K.-T. Mok, S.-C. Tan, C. K. Lee, and S. Y. Hui, "Electric springs with coordinated battery management for reducing voltage and frequency fluctuations in microgrids," IEEE Transactions on Smart Grid, vol. 9, no. 3, pp. 1943–1952, 2016.

Expanddetector: A novel platform of android malware intelligent detection

Jianfei Tang* and Hui Zhao

Xinjiang Key Laboratory of Multilingual Information Technology
Xinjiang Key Laboratory of Signal Detection and Processing
School of Information Science and Engineering, Xinjiang University
Urumqi, 830046, China
*kid519388073@gmail.com

With the gradual popularity of Android apps, smartphones have become an important source of privacy. While malicious apps are becoming increasingly rampant, even some seemingly ordinary apps may leak your private data at any time, so identifying and detecting malware plays an important role in mobile security.

However, existing deep learning-based malware approaches suffer from poor scalability and high experimental costs. This is due to the diverse and complex detection steps, especially in the software analysis and feature extraction phases.To solve the above problems, we propose a highly scalable full-process automation platform-ExpandDetector-which simplifies the analysis process of the original program by a custom repackaged framework, generating good feature forms to facilitate later construction of datasets and analysis work.

Finally, we tested on the malware dataset CIC-AAGM2017, and ExpandDetector does not exceed 5% of the original in size after repackaging. With only static features extracted, ExpandDetector analyzes a larger (up to 60MB in size) and a smaller (In the case of extracting only static features, ExpandDetector takes about 15 seconds and 3 seconds to perform a complete analysis of a larger (up to 60MB in size) and a smaller (up to 30MB in size) individually. In cases where both static and dynamic features need to be extracted, ExpandDetector outperforms existing methods by 5% to 15% in terms of the completeness of the extracted features.

Keywords: Deep learning; android malware detection, software security engineering; hybrid analysis.

1. Introduction

With the popularity of mobile Internet, malware developed for Android system has become increasingly rampant. With the iterative update of Android system, the technology used by malware is also changing, and malware analysis has gradually become a strategic research topic. At the same time, the development of artificial intelligence also provides new ideas for research in the field of security.[1] Along with the development of deep learning in the fields of natural language processing, image and speech recognition, various malware detection methods based on deep learning are constantly being introduced.

The current detection process can be divided into the following main parts: 1) software analysis of the , 2) feature extraction, 3) feature fusion and encoding, and 4) selection of a suitable neural network.

In the analysis phase of s, the analysis methods for s are mainly divided into static and dynamic analysis. In static analysis, a large number of research methods choose to use third-party reverse engineering tools,[2-4] such as Jadx, Tool or dex2jar. However, the advantage of third-party tools is that they can perform a complete and systematic analysis of a single and provide patching, deshelling and detailed flow analysis as well as a nice graphical interface, but at the cost of long running time and high space overhead. For researchers who have not studied reverse engineering, the threshold for using these tools is high and the learning curve is expensive. Instead, in dynamic analysis, the main techniques are by using strace to capture the system calls of the and by reading the log messages in logcat.[5]

In this work, we propose ExpandDetector, a deep learning-based malware detection platform. ExpandDetector implements tools that aim to simplify and extend existing malware detection methods.

To simplify the malware detection process, we complete the feature collection derived from static analysis by repackaging the malware. At the same time, sensitive points that may trigger malicious behavior in dynamic analysis, such as Intent, API calls, etc., are marked instead of relying entirely on test cases. After completing static and dynamic analysis, various feature information of is categorized in a unified manner to provide a complete form of data structure, and the interaction between various processes is realized based on the framework itself using the tangent-oriented technology, which is systematized on the basis of putting each process module on, and provides a unified feature processing interface to facilitate researchers to extend and utilize the extracted feature information. Researchers can easily complete the whole process from feature extraction to neural network training through the ExpandDetector platform, without the need to understand the complex knowledge of decompiling, reverse engineering, IR middleware construction, and static analysis theory, reducing the learning threshold in this field.

Due to the rapid development of the deep learning field, it is impossible to encompass all feature forms and neural network templates, so to ensure the sustainability of the platform, ExpandDetector is designed to be scalable.

2. Related Work

In the Android malware detection method,[6-10] researchers first have to complete the parsing work, and usually the professional reverse engineering tools they would choose are usually Tool, dex2jar, jadx, etc. In Table 1, we compare the output types of these tools, and also compare each tool in terms of whether it supports concurrency, fine-grained analysis construction, and the requirement of prior knowledge. The output results cannot be effectively transformed into the required feature types, and a large number of intermediate files irrelevant to feature extraction are generated.

Table 1.   Partial malware and benign in the CIC-AAGM2017 dataset.

Tool name	Output Type	Usage	Can concurrently parse	Can fine-grained analysis be constructed	pre-knowledge	utilization rate
Tool	.xml and smail files	command line	No	No	RE, smail	72%
dex2jar	classes-dex2jar.jar	command line	No	No	RE, Java	18%
jadx	.java file	command line	No	No	RE, Java	4%
baksmali	smail file	command line	No	No	RE, smail	3%
Android Killer	Repackaged	GUI	No	No	RE, Java	2%
Smali Viewer	.jar	GUI	No	yes	RE, Java	1%

More critically, these tools do not provide the user with a complete analysis report of the , which means that it is difficult to write customized scripts to complete the work of feature extraction, resulting in the current feature extraction work in many detection methods is still focused on the analysis of the 's AndroidManifest.xml, which is obviously due to the fact that the output results of the third-party tools are not universal, causing This is obviously due to the fact that the output of third-party tools is not universal, which makes the subsequent feature extraction work difficult. At the same time, these third-party tools lack extensibility and do not have open interfaces to facilitate users to extend their analysis work.

After parsing, different researchers have different focus on feature selection in their methods, so we summarize some representative works. Niall et al.[6] proposed to utilize raw code sequences as a feature type to train neural network CNNs. Kim et al.[7] proposed training neural network MLPs using fusion coding of multiple features (transmission, opcode, API call,

Component, etc.). Vinayakumar et al.[8] proposed to train the neural network LSTM using static features permissions and dynamic features battery, binder, memory, respectively. Abada et al.[9] proposed to train neural network CNN using dynamic features system call.

In addition to the above feature types extracted by these detection methods, we also investigated other feature types related to malware detection, and finally we implemented 11 features of Android applications that are currently more commonly used in the feature extraction module of ExpandDetector, among which static features include permissions, hardware, Intent, and API Call, etc. Dynamic features include NetworkData, File Read/Write, BroadCast/Receivers, etc.

3. Overall Architecture

In this paper, we propose a new platform, ExpandDetector, which is the first platform that simplifies the traditional malware analysis process through repackaging and systematizes the whole process of parsing, feature extraction, feature fusion, and neural network modeling on this basis. ExpandDetector not only can can analyze malware in detail and extract multiple features through hybrid analysis, but also can concurrently process a large number of APKs in malware datasets and provide multiple malware feature forms, encoding methods and neural network templates, contributing a complete set of one-stop solutions for malware detection based on deep neural networks. Researchers can use ExpandDetector to quickly replicate others' experiments, or focus on a process innovation in malware detection methods and complement other process modules on ExpandDetector to quickly validate their own experimental methods. ExpandDetector consists of five modules: APK analysis module, dynamic execution module, feature extraction module, feature encoding module, and neural network module, respectively. Among them, APK Analysis module is a lightweight APK parsing module developed and built-in by us.

In Feature Extraction module, we have implemented 11 kinds of feature types of Android applications which are more commonly used now. In Feature Encoding module, 4 more commonly used encoding forms are implemented. Finally, 4 types of neural networks are implemented in the Netural Network module using standardized templates. The general framework of ExpandDetector in this paper is shown in Fig. 1, and the specific design of each module of the platform is described in detail below.

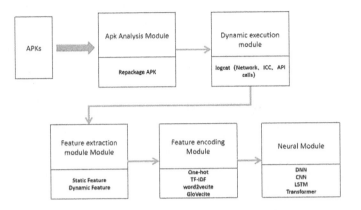

Fig. 1.   ExpandDetector architecture.

3.1. *Analysis module*

Android (Android Package Kit) file is essentially a compressed file, mainly divided into resc resource file and classes.dex file. In ExpandDetector, Analysis module will first repackage , in this process, ExpandDetector will collect static features and mark sensitive points of the program in this process. After repackaging the program will store a SF.txt file which holds the static features collected from the , meanwhile, the packaged enters the next analysis process.

Analysis is developed and implemented based on soot, a simplified Java bytecode optimization tool developed by McGill University's Sable Research Group. In Analysis, after decompressing the file, Analysis imports the resc resource file into the sub-module SourceAnalysis for parsing and collecting static features related to permissions, components, and Intent. Next, we convert each to be analyzed into Jimple code (intermediate representation of Soot), and then find and collect static features related to API calls, strings, third-party SDK information, etc. in Jimple. And insert the Jimple code probes into the runtime monitor in the Jimple code to track each method call. For example, we mark the component type of each detection class, the class of each detection callback, and the source or receiver property of each associated SDK API. The most important thing is to build the control flow graph CFG of the and write these collected to static features in the SF.txt file. The design of Analysis is shown in Fig. 2, and we will discuss the design and benefits of Analysis in detail in 3.5.1.

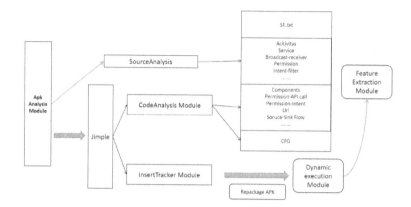

Fig. 2. The design of Analysis.

3.2. Dynamic execution module

After the application is repackaged by Analysis, we will run the application dynamically in the Android emulator AVD environment. We integrate the Monkey Runner test tool provided by Google, which will execute 1000 test cases for each application in the emulator environment, and finally collect the system calls through the strace tool that comes with Linux, and collect the feature information output in logcat through the sensitive points marked by the Tracker in the repackaging process.

3.3. Feature Extraction module

Various types of features in Android applications help to represent the behavior of the program more comprehensively is a currently accepted research strategy in the field of malware detection, while multiple features also help models to learn the intrinsic association between features. According to many current research approaches, we classify Android features into two main categories: static features and dynamic features. Static features mainly include permissions, intent, API calls, etc. Dynamic features mainly include network data, file reading and writing operations, etc. This part is realized by two sub-modules, StaticFeatureExtraction and Dynamic Feature Extraction in Feature Extraction module respectively, where StaticFeatureExtraction needs to rely on Analysis module, and Dynamic Feature Extraction depends on the output of Dynamic execution module.

To better integrate some hard-to-extract features, such as taint propagation path and dynamic data distribution behavior. We also integrate

FlowDroid and DroidBox[5] as third-party components, which are not started by default unless required by the user, as their startup can seriously affect the efficiency of ExpandDetector's operation. In addition, ExpandDetector is extensible. If ExpandDetector does not provide a suitable feature type, users can customize their own feature extraction scripts to extract the features they need inside ExpandDetector according to the extensible interface provided by ExpandDetector.

3.4. Feature Encoding module

After the previous program analysis and feature extraction, the extracted features need to be further encoded into feature vectors. There are many forms of feature encoding, and in ExpandDetector, we provide four common encoding forms: One-hot, Graph, text, and raw code. At the same time, in the feature encoding module, we still support users to implement their own encoding forms through ExpandDetector's extended interface.

3.5. Netural Network module

Currently, we provide models of traditional neural networks, such as DNN, CNN, RNN, etc. Since we all have different requirements for hyperparameters such as the number of layers and training time of the models, users can specify these hyperparameters according to their business needs, or they can directly use our default parameters. In addition, ExpandDetector modularizes the individual neural network models so that users can easily rely on these basic network models to form more complex neural networks.

4. Conclusions

For deep learning researchers without reverse engineering or security background, how can they focus more on innovation of a single process and get rid of complicated other experimental aspects, ExpandDetector gives the solution.

ExpandDetector effectively simplifies the static and dynamic analysis process through the process of APK repackaging, and using a multi-threaded mechanism can effectively use CPU resources to concurrently process large malware datasets and generate good feature forms.

Finally, in the next work, we consider extending the architecture of ExpandDetector to gradually get rid of the dependence on DroidBox and FlowDroid for part of the current feature extraction work and further reduce the time cost.

312

Acknowledgments

This work was supported by the National Natural Science Foundation of China (grant number 62166041).

References

1. R. R. Nabila Popal, Smartphone market share. *https://www.idc.com/promo/smartphone-market-share*, 29 July 2021.
2. K. W. Y. Au, Y. F. Zhou, Z. Huang and D. Lie, Pscout: analyzing the android permission specification. In *Proceedings of the 2012 ACM conference on Computer and communications security*, pages 217–228, 2012.
3. A. Martín, R. Lara-Cabrera and D. Camacho, Android malware detection through hybrid features fusion and ensemble classifiers: the andropytool framework and the omnidroid dataset. *Information Fusion*, 52:128–142, 2019.
4. O. Lhoták and L. Hendren, Scaling java points-to analysis using s park. In *International Conference on Compiler Construction*, pages 153–169. Springer, 2003.
5. P. Chaurasia, *Dynamic analysis of Android malware using DroidBox*. PhD thesis, Tennessee State University, 2015.
6. N. McLaughlin, J. Martinez del Rincon, B. Kang, S. Yerima, P. Miller, S. Sezer, Y. Safaei, E. Trickel, Z. Zhao, A. Doupé et al., Deep android malware detection. In *Proceedings of the seventh ACM on conference on data and application security and privacy*, pages 301–308, 2017.
7. T. Kim, B. Kang, M. Rho, S. Sezer and E. G. Im, A multimodal deep learning method for android malware detection using various features. *IEEE Transactions on Information Forensics and Security*, 14(3):773–788, 2018.
8. R. Vinayakumar, K. Soman, P. Poornachandran and S. Sachin Kumar, Detecting android malware using long short-term memory (lstm). *Journal of Intelligent & Fuzzy Systems*, 34(3):1277–1288, 2018.
9. A. Abderrahmane, G. Adnane, C. Yacine and G. Khireddine, Android malware detection based on system calls analysis and cnn classification. In *2019 IEEE Wireless Communications and Networking Conference Workshop (WCNCW)*, pages 1–6. IEEE, 2019.
10. Y.-S. Yen and H.-M. Sun, An android mutation malware detection based on deep learning using visualization of importance from codes. *Microelectronics Reliability*, 93:109–114, 2019.

Risk evaluation of differential security checks for metro

XueYing Liu

Intelligent Transportation System Research Center, Southeast University
Nanjing, Jiangsu, 210096, China
220205034@seu.edu.cn

Ning Zhang

Intelligent Transportation System Research Center, Southeast University
Nanjing, Jiangsu, 210096, China
331061643@qq.com

BoQing Chu

Beijing Metro
Beijing, 100044, China
15201581660@139.com

Guang Ji

Beijing Telesound Electronics Co. Ltd
Beijing, 100085, China
jiguang@telesound.com.cn

Metro security check risk evaluation plays an important role in identifying security check risks. The differential security check mode can improve passenger passage efficiency and metro service quality. In this paper, a multi-level comprehensive evaluation index system of differential security checks at stations is constructed, and the combination assignment method is selected as the method of determining index weights. Furthermore, a risk evaluation model of differential security checks in the metro based on the extension theory is established. The case study shows that the selected station of the Nanjing metro is in a relatively safe state.

Keywords: Metro; risk evaluation; differential security checks.

1. Introduction

The efficiency of the security check affects the passage and safety of the metro.[1] A full security check will increase the time for passengers to enter the station.[2] Differential security check is based on the risk level of passenger triage, and the implementation of different specifications of security check measures to maximize the effectiveness of the use of security resources. The drawbacks of fixed standards and unreasonable resource allocation of traditional security check forms have gradually become apparent. The existing security check model cannot meet the growing needs of metro station safety and security, so domestic and international have begun to gradually explore the differentiated security screening model.[3-5] The current research has certain achievements, but the metro differential security check evaluation model has just started. Firstly, there are fewer specialized studies on the risk influencing factors of metro security checks. Secondly, there is a lack of reasonable quantification of qualitative and quantitative indicators. In this paper, an extendable security risk evaluation model will be developed. This model will analyze four risk factors, and assess the risk level of metro stations. This will facilitate managers to take timely preventive and control measures according to the risk level, and improve the level of risk prevention and management.

2. Methodologies

2.1. Construction of evaluation system

LEC method is a semi-quantitative safety evaluation method. It is used to evaluate the magnitude of risk factors. Based on the results, the factors with the largest danger values are selected as risk assessment factors. The main factors affecting metro security checks include personnel factors, security equipment factors, environmental factors, and management factors.[6]

2.2. The establishment of an extendable security risk evaluation model

We use extension theory to establish a risk evaluation model for metro security inspection based on extension theory. The extension theory avoids the problem of imprecise quantification of indicators by other risk assessment methods, and can effectively deal with the problem of qualitative and quantitative conversion between qualitative and quantitative indicators. The subjective and objective combination assignment method is used to determine the index weights. Extension theory[7] combines object element theory and extendable set theory.

2.2.1. Determining security evaluation elements

Let there be m kinds of security objects and n impact indicators, then security evaluation can be described by n-dimensional object elements. The object element represents an ordered triad consisting of object N, feature C, and the quantity value V of the thing about the feature, and is written as $R = (N, C, V)$. The expression of R is Eq. (1).

$$R_{(m+1)(n+1)} = \begin{pmatrix} N & N_1 & N_2 & \cdots & N_m \\ C & V_1 & V_2 & \cdots & V_m \end{pmatrix} = \begin{pmatrix} N & N_1 & \cdots & N_m \\ C_1 & V_{11} & \cdots & V_{1m} \\ \vdots & \vdots & \ddots & \vdots \\ C_n & V_{n1} & \cdots & V_{nm} \end{pmatrix}. \tag{1}$$

2.2.2. *Determining classical domain elements and nodal domain elements*

According to the N_0 rating level standard, the security level of the metro differentiated security risk evaluation is divided into y levels and combined with the evaluation index system, the classical domain elements of risk evaluation are derived as Eq. (2). N_0 is the evaluation level standard. N_{0m} denotes the mth evaluation level in the evaluation scale. C_i is the ith evaluation indicator. $V_{0ij} = [a_{ij}, b_{ij}](i = 1,2, \ldots, n; j = 1,2, \ldots, m)$ is the range of values of level N_{0m} concerning indicator C_i. It is the classical domain of the range of data obtained for each classification to the corresponding evaluation indicator.

$$R_{0(m+1)(n+1)} = \begin{pmatrix} N_0 & N_{01} & N_{02} & \cdots & N_{0m} \\ C & V_{01} & V_{02} & \cdots & V_{0m} \end{pmatrix} = \begin{pmatrix} N & N_{01} & \cdots & N_{0m} \\ C_1 & (a_{11}, b_{11}) & \cdots & (a_{1m}, b_{1m}) \\ \vdots & \vdots & \ddots & \vdots \\ C_n & (a_{n1}, b_{n1}) & \cdots & (a_{nm}, b_{nm}) \end{pmatrix}. \tag{2}$$

The metro differential security check security risk evaluation section domain elements are shown in Eq. (3). N_p is the whole of the risk evaluation level. $V_{ip} = [a_{ip}, b_{ip}](i = 1,2, \ldots, n)$ is the range of values for indicator C_i.

$$R_p = (N_p, C, V_p) = \begin{pmatrix} N_p & C_1 & V_{1p} \\ & C_2 & V_{2p} \\ & \vdots & \vdots \\ & C_n & V_{np} \end{pmatrix} = \begin{pmatrix} N_p & C_1 & (a_{1p}, b_{1p}) \\ & C_2 & (a_{2p}, b_{2p}) \\ & \vdots & \vdots \\ & C_n & (a_{np}, b_{np}) \end{pmatrix}. \tag{3}$$

2.2.3. *Identifying the weight of each indicator*

The method we use to determine the weights is the combination of the weighting method. First, we use the analytic hierarchy process[8] to find the weight value of each indicator. Second, the entropy method[9] combined with the factor analysis method is used to find the weight value of each indicator. Finally, we use the additive integration method[10] to determine the final weight of each indicator.

2.2.4. Identifying the correlation function of each evaluation index

The correlation function of the ith indicator of the jth category of evaluation object regarding the category of the differentiated security level of urban rail transit is Eq. (4).

$$K_{jk}\left(V_{ij}\right) = \begin{cases} \dfrac{-\rho\left(v_{ij}, V_{0ik}\right)}{\left|V_{0ik}\right|}, v_{ij} \in V_{0ik} \\ \dfrac{\rho\left(v_{ij}, V_{0ik}\right)}{\rho\left(v_{ij}, V_{ip}\right) - \rho\left(v_{ij}, V_{0ik}\right)}, v_{ij} \notin V_{0ik} \end{cases} \tag{4}$$

$\rho(v_{ik}, V_{0ij})$ is the distance of the point v_{ik} from the finite interval $V_{0ij} = [a_{ij}, b_{ij}]$.

2.2.5. Calculating the integrated correlation

The integrated correlation of object N_k to be evaluated concerning rank j is expressed by Eq. (5).

$$K_j\left(N_k\right) = \sum_{i=1}^{n} \omega_i K\left(v_{ik}\right). \tag{5}$$

2.2.6. Grade rating

If $K_{j0}(N_k) = max\{K_j(N_k), j = 1, 2, \ldots, m\}$, N_k is rated as belonging to rank j.

$$\overline{K}\left(N_k\right) = \frac{K_j\left(N_k\right) - \min K_j\left(N_k\right)}{\max K_j\left(N_k\right) - \min K_j\left(N_k\right)}. \tag{6}$$

$$j^* = \frac{\sum_{i=1}^{t} \overline{jK_j}\left(N_k\right)}{\sum_{i=1}^{t} \overline{K_j}\left(N_k\right)}. \tag{7}$$

j^* is the risk level variable characteristic value, which is used to judge the degree of bias of the target toward the adjacent risk level.

3. Experiments

The case study uses a large metro station in Nanjing as the experimental object. The paper details the process of calculating the risk level of personnel factors, and the process of calculating the rest of the factors is the same. According to the situation of Nanjing metro security checks and expert scoring suggestions, the level of security risk for each indicator is determined, as shown in Table 1.

Table 1. Nanjing metro station security risk level table.

Indicators		A Security	B Relatively security	C Relatively danger	D Danger
			Security level value		
Personnel factors	Dedicated access door load degree	(0,0.8]	(0.8,1.2]	(1.2,2]	(2,3]
	Security check lane congestion	(0,1]	(1,1.67]	(1.67,2.33]	(2.33,5]
	Baggage exemption rate	(0,60]	(60,80]	(80,90]	(90,100]
	Baggage sampling rate	(7,10]	(4,7]	(1,4]	(0,1]
	Station level risk	(0,0.7]	(0.7,0.8]	(0.8,0.9]	(0.9,1]
	Length of service of security personnel	(5,10]	(3,5]	(1,3]	(0,1]
	Security personnel literacy	(6,8]	(4,6]	(2,4]	(1,2]
	Work intensity of security personnel	(6,8]	(4,6]	(2,4]	(1,2]
Security equipment factors	Inspection pass rate of equipment and facilities	(90,100]	(80,90]	(60,80]	(40,60]
	Equipment and facilities load intensity	(0,0.8]	(0.8,1.2]	(1.2,2]	(2,3]
	Equipment and facility failure rate	(0,15]	(15,25]	(25,40]	(40,80]
Environmental factors	Temperature and humidity index	(0,40]	(40,60]	(60,80]	(80,100]
	Noise pollution index	(0,60]	(60,75]	(75,90]	(90,110]
Management factors	Degree of perfection of management system	(80,100]	(60,80]	(40,60]	(0,40]
	Degree of implementation of management system	(80,100]	(60,80]	(40,60]	(0,40]
	Preparedness	(8,10]	(6,8]	(4,6]	(0,4]
	Resourcefulness	(8,10]	(6,8]	(4,6]	(0,4]
	Drill frequency and effectiveness	(8,10]	(6,8]	(4,6]	(0,4]

The classical and nodal domains determined using the object-element extension method are shown below.

$$R_{01} = \begin{bmatrix} N_{01} & C_1 & (5,10] \\ & C_2 & (6,8] \\ & C_3 & (6,8] \end{bmatrix}, \quad R_{02} = \begin{bmatrix} N_{02} & C_1 & (3,5] \\ & C_2 & (4,6] \\ & C_3 & (4,6] \end{bmatrix}, \quad R_{03} = \begin{bmatrix} N_{03} & C_1 & (1,3] \\ & C_2 & (2,4] \\ & C_3 & (2,4] \end{bmatrix}, \quad R_{04} = \begin{bmatrix} N_{04} & C_1 & (0,1] \\ & C_2 & (1,2] \\ & C_3 & (1,2] \end{bmatrix}, \quad R_p = \begin{bmatrix} P & C_1 & (0,10] \\ & C_2 & (1,8] \\ & C_3 & (1,8] \end{bmatrix}.$$

The weights derived from the combined assignment method are shown in Table 2. The weight of security personnel skills quality is $\omega_{161} = (0.37, 0.29, 0.34)$.

According to Eq. (4), the correlation degree between the evaluation object and each grade is calculated.

$$K_{161} = \begin{bmatrix} -0.300 & 0.250 & -0.125 & -0.417 \\ -0.222 & 0.400 & -0.300 & -0.533 \\ 0.400 & -0.600 & -0.800 & -0.866 \end{bmatrix}$$

The combined relevance of the evaluation objects is K_{16}.

$$K_{16} = \omega_{161} \times K_{161} = (-0.039, 0.005, -0.405, -0.603)$$

From the evaluation results, it can be seen that the risk level of the station's security personnel skill quality is level 2, which is a relatively safe state.

The evaluation results of the third level are used as the basis for the second level evaluation. Similarly, the risk evaluation results of personnel indicators, equipment and facilities indicators, environmental indicators, and management indicators can be obtained as $K_1 = (-0.503, -0.218, 0.072, -0.141)$, $K_2 = (0.144, 0.334, -0.286, -0.627)$, $K_3 = (-0.159, -0.254, 0.084, -0.239)$, $K_4 = (-0.019, 0.123, -0.332, -0.560)$.

Table 2. Security check security risk indicators weighting table.

Level 1	Weights	Level 2	Weights	Level 3	Weights
Personnel factors	0.476	Dedicated access door load degree	0.17		
		Security check lane congestion	0.18		
		Baggage exemption rate	0.22		
		Baggage sampling rate	0.21		
		Station level risk	0.13		
		Security personnel skills quality	0.09	Years of service	0.37
				Education level	0.29
				Work intensity	0.34
Security equipment factors	0.263	Inspection pass rate of equipment and facilities	0.26		
		Equipment and facilities load intensity	0.31		
		Equipment and facility failure rate	0.43		
Environmental factors	0.108	Temperature and humidity index	0.66		
		Noise pollution index	0.34		
Management factors	0.153	Safety management level	0.64	Degree of perfection of management system	0.43
				Degree of implementation of management system	0.57
		Station emergency response capability index	0.36	Preparedness	0.29
				Resourcefulness	0.32
				Drill frequency and effectiveness	0.39

The evaluation matrix of the first level is composed of the evaluation results of the second level, and the comprehensive results of the station security risk evaluation are obtained as follows.

$$K = \begin{bmatrix} -0.503 & -0.218 & 0.072 & -0.141 \\ 0.144 & 0.334 & -0.286 & -0.627 \\ -0.159 & -0.254 & 0.084 & -0.239 \\ -0.019 & 0.123 & -0.332 & -0.560 \end{bmatrix}, \ \omega = (0.476, 0.263, 0.108, 0.153),$$

$$K_p = \omega \times K = (-0.222, -0.025, -0.083, -0.344)$$

From the calculation results, it can be obtained that the comprehensive security risk level of the station using differential security checks is level 2, which means that it is a relatively safe state.

The safety level of each tier indicator is obtained separately by calculating the risk evaluation model for the station, as shown in Table 3.

Table 3. Extendable security risk evaluation grades.

Level 1	Grade	Level 2	Grade	Level 3	Grade
Personnel factors	3	Dedicated access door load degree	3		
		Security check lane congestion	3		
		Baggage exemption rate	2		
		Baggage sampling rate	3		
		Station level risk	3		
		Security personnel skills quality	2	Years of service	2
				Education level	2
				Work intensity	1
Security equipment factors	2	Inspection pass rate of equipment and facilities	1		
		Equipment and facilities load intensity	2		
		Equipment and facility failure rate	1		
Environmental factors	3	Temperature and humidity index	3		
		Noise pollution index	1		
Management factors	2	Safety management level	2	Degree of perfection in management system	2
				Degree of implementation of management system	1
		Station emergency response capability index	2	Preparedness	2
				Resourcefulness	1
				Drill frequency and effectiveness	2

From the calculation results of the first level of the station, the risk status of using a differential security check is graded 2 (relatively safe status). The personnel indicators and environmental indicators in the first level are graded 3 (relatively dangerous state), and the personnel indicators such as dedicated access door load degree, security check lane congestion, baggage sampling rate, and station level risk in the second level are graded 3 (relatively dangerous state). These four indicators all reflect that the large passenger flow greatly affects the effect of differential security checks in the Nanjing metro. We recommend that the sampling rate should be increased appropriately to reduce the safety risk and ensure the normal operation of the Nanjing metro while ensuring the efficiency of the passage.

4. Conclusion

We select the indicators from personnel, facilities, environmental, and management perspectives. Based on the extension theory, an extendable security risk evaluation model is established. Through experiments, we evaluate the differential security check risk levels of specific metro stations in Nanjing. The results show that the station is in a relatively safe state.

Acknowledgments

This research was supported by the National Key R&D Program of China (Grant No. 2020YFB1600701).

References

1. A. Popa, and J. Strer, Analysis of Passenger and Vehicle Flows with Microscopic Simulations as a Result of Security Checks at Ferry Terminals, *Transportation Research Procedia* **14**, (2016) pp. 1384-1393.
2. Y. L. Li, X. Gao, Z. W. Xu, and X. R. Zhou, Network-based Queuing Model for Simulating Passenger Throughput at an Airport Security Checkpoint, *Journal of Air Transport Management* **66**, (2018) pp. 13-24.
3. Majeske K, Lauer T. Optimizing Airline Passenger Prescreening Systems with Bayesian Decision Models, *Computers and Operations Research* **39**, (2012) pp. 1827-1836.
4. J. Cai, Z. J. Lin. Classified Security Check Ensures Safety at Israel Airport, *International Aviation* **3**, (2011) pp. 60-61.
5. Z. W. Zhao, Y. L. Tang, J. J. Ma. Study on Airport Security System Based on Passenger Classification, *China Transportation Review* **39**, (2017).

6. C. J. Soons, J. W. Bosch, G. Arends, and G. Van, P.H.A.J.M, Framework of a Quantitative Risk Analysis for the Fire Safety in Metro Systems, *Tunnelling and Underground Space Technology* **21**, no. 3 (2006) pp. 281.

7. C. Y. Yang, W. Cai, Study on Extension Engineering, Engineering Science, **2**, (2000) pp. 90-96.

8. S. Sipahi, and M. Timor, The Analytic Hierarchy Process and Analytic Network Process: An Overview of Applications, *Management Decision* **48**, no. 5 (2010) pp. 775-808.

9. O. Mohsen, and N. Fereshteh, An Extended VIKOR Method Based on Entropy Measure for the Failure Modes Risk Assessment – A Case Study of the Geothermal Power Plant (GPP), *Safety Science* **92** (2017) pp. 160-72.

10. H. Chen, J. Z. Zhao, Y. Liu, and T. Q. Jin, Equipment Support Ability Evaluation Based on Set Pair Theory and Subjective-objective Combined Weighting Method, *Zhuangbei Huanjing Gongcheng (Equipment Environmental Engineering)* **13**, no. 1 (2016) pp. 151-55.

Exploring consumers' discernment ability of autogenerated advertisements

Johannes Sahlin[1,2], Håkan Sundell[1], Gideon Mbiydzenyuy[1], Håkan Alm[1],
Jesper Holgersson[2,‡], Christoffer Suhonen[1] and Tommy Hjelm[1]

[1] *Department of Information Technology, University of Borås, Sweden*
[2] *School of Informatics, University of Skövde, Sweden*
{johannes.sahlin, hakan.sundell, gideon.mbiydzenyuy, hakan.alm}@hb.se
{s182303, s182959}@student.hb.se
‡jesper.holgersson@his.se

Autogenerated Advertisements (AGAs) can be a concern for consumers if they suspect that Artificial Intelligence (AI) was involved. Consumers may have an opposing stance against AI, leading companies to miss profit opportunities and reputation loss. Hence, companies need ways of managing consumers' concerns. As a part of designing such advices we explore consumers' discernment ability (DA) of AGAs. A quantitative survey was used to explore consumers' DA of AGAs. In order to do this, we administered questionnaires to 233 respondents. A statistical analysis including Z-tests, of these responses suggests that consumers can hardly pick out AGAs. This indicates that consumers may be guessing and thus do not possess any significant DA of our AGAs.

Keywords: Autogenerated ads; discernment ability; marketing.

1. Introduction

Autogenerated Ads (AGAs) may be a concern to consumers[4] when they discover that Artificial Intelligence (AI) is used in creating SMS and email ads (see Fig. 1). Consequently, consumers can develop stances against companies that use AI, and companies risk losing profit opportunities and reputation when AI is suspected through identifiable mistakes or oddities with the AGAs. Thus, companies are hesitant towards using AGAs in their marketing activities. In the literature, AI can give rise to several Consumers' Concerns (CC), for example; i) uniqueness neglection, in other words, AI not being able to account for one's uniqueness,[9] ii) AI lacking sympathy compared to human actors,[3] iii) data privacy issues[10] like data security,[8] misuse of information[8] and prediction of sensitive information, for example, sexual orientation,[7] and iv) algorithmic biases favoring companies or disfavoring certain consumer groups.[14] Due to such CC, consumers may balance privacy concerns against the benefits of the personalized recommendations in a privacy-personalization trade-off.[1] AGA pioneers relied on predefined templates to generate readable and attractive sentences to decrease the risk of becoming detected.[6] The approach of using template-based generation methods can vastly reduce human efforts but are rigid, lack diversity, and cannot adapt like modern, sophisticated methods.[6] However, the approach of employing modern, sophisticated methods shows 15% of nonsense generations.[6] Therefore, we suggest combining a template-based approach with sophisticated methods that may capture the best of both directions to meet the high production requirements, avoid reluctant consumers and secure profit opportunities and reputation. Business requirements demand an almost perfect attractiveness and full certainty of AGAs to stay undetected, in order to be accepted. However, combining template-based and sophisticated methods are insufficient to prevent the detection of AGAs. Marketing activities need well adjusted and reliable methods for managing CC and identification of anomalies and oddities from quantitative and qualitative views to improve the underlying generational models. For example, AI can generate anomalies and oddities that methods simply relying on quantitative evaluations may not capture, and thus undesirable ads may pass on to consumers. Thus, this article aims to describe consumers' DA of AGAs. To do so, the study has to first establish an environment for researching consumers' perceptions of AGAs. This is needed to identify CC of AGAs, from which advices can be developed on how to manage the identified CC of AGAs (see Fig. 2). We consider *consumer perception* as the consumers' awareness and understanding, which can be further broken down into sensations, discernment, apprehensions, consciousness, and notions of the phenomenon. A *notion* is defined by us as a belief about something. We consider *discernment ability* (DA) as the ability to reveal if an ad is an AGA, and can be viewed as an umbrella term for perceptiveness, insight, awareness and understanding. We argue that in order to understand the consumers' perceptions of AGAs, it is essential to determine how consumers distinguish AGAs. Moreover, studying consumers' notions about AGAs can also help establish knowledge about their beliefs. We consider *concerns* to be the activity of being involved with something, or worried about something - influenced by our perceptions, thoughts and subjective experiences. We consider *managing* to be the activity of succeeding in dealing or maintain control over something. The article describes consumers' DA of AGAs.

Fig. 1.   Example of an autogenerated SMS ad, with variables and values.

2. Method

To capture overall patterns of discernment we adopted a quantitative design when it comes to consumer discernment of AGAs (see Fig. 2). The quantitative survey was designed to study consumers' DA of AGAs. To understand consumers' DA an online questionnaire[11] was designed to survey consumers' DA of AGAs. The stop criteria for the data collection were based on time resources and were active for two weeks. Authentic ads were acquired from a Swedish e-commerce retailer. The selected ads upheld the sender's anonymity. The AGAs is a product of[12,13] proposed system for automatically breaking down ads into its components and generating a variety of synonymous messages (see Fig. 1) through the use of AI-assisted text generation algorithms. The generated AGAs were chosen randomly. The sampling used for the quantitative research was based on non-probability sampling methods to gain an exploratory sample. Using a combination of self-selection methods and convenience sampling resulted in 102 respondents who self-selected themselves by opting into the questionnaire. The questionnaire was posted on social media feeds (Facebook) on the authors' accounts. These pledges were redistributed three times each week from

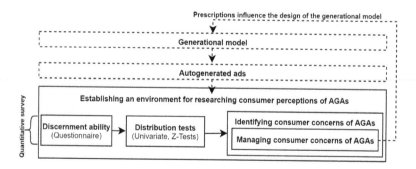

Fig. 2.   Illustration of our overall research process.

2021-04-21 to 2021-05-05. The pledge to participate was later shared further through friends and family. Further attempts were made to increase the amount by sending out a notification through a communication channel used by the University's pedagogical platform. This notification reached a lot of students and increased the sample by 135 respondents (in addition to the 102 above). Lastly, criterion sampling was applied inside the questionnaire to apply criteria as (1) frequent or accustomed to online shopping and (2) having received ads recently as SMS or email. If the participant opted no to these questions, they were not presented with the rest of the questionnaire. Four respondents were excluded, resulting in 233 total respondents (102+135-4 from above). The questionnaire was divided into three parts. The first part consisted of the criterion sampling questions. The second part consisted of demographics collection: in other words, age, sex, education, and occupation. The last part consisted of five AGA DA tests. For each test, respondents had a binary choice to discern whether they perceived the first or second option as AGAs or authentic, in other words intentionally disallowing a neutral option. The DA was analysed through univariate and bivariate analysis. To analyse the whole sample's DA, we used univariate analysis. When there were multiple groups, we used bivariate analysis. Here, the respondents were asked to discern which option was the AGA, and answers was coded into binary values where 1 represented proper discernment, and 0 represented faulty discernment. The percentage of correct discernment tests was calculated (total correct discernment divided by total tests). When the data set contained every respondent's percentage of correct DA level, we plotted the DA percentage values for each respondent into a histogram distribution chart. The same procedure was applied to different demographic groups. Z-tests[2] was conducted for inferential statistics regarding the DA of the demographic groups. Z-tests were also used to compare the mean values of two groups and test the acceptance of *the null hypothesis* (H_0). It is defined as that H_0 decides if there is a statistical significance in the mean values according to the groups used and is decided by the p-value relation to the z-value. Rejecting H_0 means the result is not statistically significant and can be achieved by chance, while accepting H_0 implies accepting the alternate hypothesis (H_a). Z-tests are suitable for comparing a numerical variable's averages under the assumption of a normal distribution. Each Z-test consisted of the following comparisons *Gender* (none responded with the option *other*, enabling binary grouping of males and females), *Academics or not, Hired or not* (students having a paid job were considered hired). The groups *gender, academics or not, hired or not* are defined and served to support H_0. The Z-tests are considered with a 95% confidence level.

3. Result and Analysis

The quantitative study yielded the following demographic data. Respondents were 234 in total. Age constituted; 18-29: 35,7% (81), 30-39: 41,9% (95), 40-49: 11,5% (26), 50-59: 8,8% (20), 60-69: 1,8% (4), 70+: 0,4% (1). Gender constituted; Male: 39,6% (90), Female: 60,4% (137), Other: 0% (0). Academics 58.5% (86) and non-academic 41.5% (147). The univariate analysis represents the whole sample, and the z-test results represent a more in-depth view of selected groups in the sample. In Table 1 each z-test is presented with details. Results of the online questionnaire yielded an DA level distribution based on the population, of: 0% (18), 25% (54), 50% (100), 75% (43), 100% (18), total: 233. The accuracy of the responses about DAs suggested that the mean, mode and median were approximately the same (0.5). Thus indicating the responses were indicative of a normal distribution (see Fig. 3). From the mean and standard deviation of the accuracy scores in Table 1, the responses from each group in the sample do not differ significantly.

Table 1.   Z-test summary. Sym for symmetrical, Asym for asymmetrical.

	Male or Female		Academic or not		Hired or not	
Size	92	141	86	147	117	116
Average	.505	.476	.509	.588	.504	.467
Std Dev	.228	.270	.237	.260	.249	.254
Skewness	-.043	.185	.039	.087	.175	.012
Skewness shape	Sym	Sym	Sym	Asym	Sym	Sym
Normality	9.257×10^{-7}	1.161×10^{-7}	5.94×10^{-6}	3.847×10^{-7}	4.217×10^{-7}	3.753×10^{-7}
Outliers	5	0	3	0	0	7
P-value	0.402686		0.0515185		0.267159	
Z-score	0.836835		-1.947136		1.109630	
H_0	Accepted		Accepted		Accepted	

Z-test - Male and Female. The aim of a Z-test here is to determine the extent to which responses differ as a result of gender. Thus, Z-test allows to test for H_0: There is no difference in respondents' DAs as a result of gender.

To test this, variables representing different samples were introduced; male (92) and female (141). Detail statistics of these variables are summarised in Fig. 3. From the accuracy scores calculated for these groups, the P-value was estimated to be .40, (p(x≤Z)=.79). A large P-value suggest that the chances that there is a difference in DA responses from the population due to gender are low, thus we accept H_0.

Z-test - Academic or not. The aim of a Z-test here is to determine the extent to which responses differ as a result of academic education level. Thus, Z-test allows to test for H_0: There is no difference in respondents' DAs as a result of academic education level. To test this, variables representing different samples were introduced; academic (86) and non-academic (147). Detail statistics of these variables are summarised in Fig. 3. From the accuracy scores calculated for these groups, the P-value was estimated to be .40, (p(x≤Z)=.79). A large P-value suggest that the chances that there is a difference in DA responses from the population due to academic education level are low, thus we accept H_0.

Z-test - Hired or not. The aim of a Z-test here is to decide the extent to which responses differ as a result of employment. Thus, Z-test allows to test for H_0: There is no difference in respondents' DAs as a result of employment. To test this, variables representing different samples were introduced; hired (86) and non-hired (147). Detail statistics of these variables are summarised in Fig. 3. From the accuracy scores calculated for these groups, the P-value was estimated to be .40, (p(x≤Z)=.79). A large P-value suggest that the chances that there is a difference in DA responses from the population due to employment are low, thus we accept H_0.

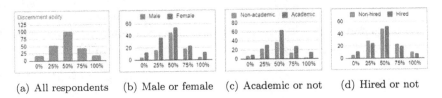

(a) All respondents (b) Male or female (c) Academic or not (d) Hired or not

Fig. 3. Discernment ability distribution tests.

4. Discussion and Conclusion

The study suggest that consumers cannot discern AGAs from authentic ads, indicating they may be guessing. The results contribute to the existing literature by exploring consumers' perceptions of AGAs. Moreover, adding to the discussion of how to design and implement value-creating AI-enabled marketing services, which is a topic of merit for scholars and practitioners. Through the univariate analysis consumer's DA of AGAs were measured, this study found that the respondents could not discern AGAs from authentic ads, at least in this situation. Also, this is shown by the average, median and mode values that indicate that the DA of the research population is close to 50% which perfectly correlate with a random probability outcome in a normal distribution under independent observations. The result of the z-tests indicated no significant difference between the samples' DA, and using the 95% confidence interval showed that all samples are within statistical boundaries. Also, the presented z-value for all the tests is in accepted boundaries to support H_0, implying no or minor differences between population characteristics. The average scores presented in the z-tests are similar to those presented in the univariate analysis, showing a 50% chance to discern the ad correctly. The law of large numbers (LLN) can be considered for quantitative measurements.[5] LLN states that an observed sample average from a large sample will be close to the actual population average and will get closer the larger the sample is. LLN also states that there is no guarantee that a small sample will reflect the actual population characteristics and that the true population will be balanced in the subsequent sample, and hence, a larger sample will always be preferable for more accuracy. Yet, as seen in the results, even though the sample is relatively small, there is a resemblance of a normal distribution in the DA of the sample population, which might indicate some degree of generalisability. Using a univariate analysis for deciding consumers' DA of AGAs was considered most feasible. Directions for future research include extending the topic of managing CC of AGAs by other views. In a future study, we suggest studying discernment motivations through content analysis with conceptual and co-occurrence analysis. Moreover, a qualitative perspective can be included for giving advice on how to manage consumers' concerns of AGAs.

References

1. Elizabeth Aguirre, Dominik Mahr, Dhruv Grewal, Ko De Ruyter, and Martin Wetzels. Unraveling the personalization paradox: The effect of information collection and trust-building strategies on online advertisement effectiveness. *Journal of retailing*, 91(1):34–49, 2015.
2. George Casella and Roger L Berger. *Statistical inference*. Cengage Learning, 2021.

3. Noah Castelo. *Blurring the Line Between Human and Machine: Marketing Artificial Intelligence.* PhD thesis, Columbia University, 2019.

4. Thomas Davenport, Abhijit Guha, Dhruv Grewal, and Timna Bressgott. How artificial intelligence will change the future of marketing. *Journal of the Academy of Marketing Science,* 48(1):24–42, 2020.

5. Frederik Michel Dekking, Cornelis Kraaikamp, Hendrik Paul Lopuhaä, and Ludolf Erwin Meester. *A Modern Introduction to Probability and Statistics: Understanding why and how,* volume 488. Springer, 2005.

6. J Weston Hughes, Keng-hao Chang, and Ruofei Zhang. Generating better search engine text advertisements with deep reinforcement learning. In *Proceedings of the 25th ACM SIGKDD International Conference on Knowledge Discovery & Data Mining,* pages 2269–2277, 2019.

7. Michal Kosinski, David Stillwell, and Thore Graepel. Private traits and attributes are predictable from digital records of human behavior. *Proceedings of the national academy of sciences,* 110(15):5802–5805, 2013.

8. Nir Kshetri. Big data's impact on privacy, security and consumer welfare. *Telecommunications Policy,* 38(11):1134–1145, 2014.

9. Chiara Longoni, Andrea Bonezzi, and Carey K Morewedge. Resistance to medical artificial intelligence. *Journal of Consumer Research,* 46(4): 629–650, 2019.

10. Kelly D Martin, Abhishek Borah, and Robert W Palmatier. Data privacy: Effects on customer and firm performance. *Journal of Marketing,* 81(1):36–58, 2017.

11. B.J. Oates. *Researching Information Systems and Computing.* ISBN 9781412902243.

12. Johannes Sahlin, Håkan Sundell, Håkan Alm, and Jesper Holgersson. Short message service campaign taxonomy for an intelligent marketing system. In *Developments of Artificial Intelligence Technologies in Computation and Robotics: Proceedings of the 14th International FLINS Conference,* pages 606–613. World Scientific, 2020.

13. Johannes Sahlin, Håkan Sundell, Håkan Alm, and Jesper Holgersson. Evaluating artificial short message service campaigns through rule based multi-instance multi-label classification. In *AAAI 2021 Spring Symposium on Combining Machine Learning and Knowledge Engineering,* volume 2846. Sun SITE Central Europe, 2021.

14. John Villasenor. Artificial intelligence and bias: Four key challenges. *Retrieved February,* 11:2019, 2019.

Bearing fault diagnosis based on STFT-SPWVD and improved convolutional neural network

Hongyi Liu, Guanfeng Wu and Peiyao Liu

National-Local Joint Engineering Laboratory of
System Credibility Automatic Verification
School of Mathematics, Southwest Jiaotong University, Chengdu, China
905759310@qq.com, wgf1024@swjtu.edu.cn, liupeiyao@my.swjtu.edu.cn

Qi Cao
School of Mathematics and Statistics
Chongqing Jiaotong University, Chongqing, China
320559979@qq.com

Aiming at the problem of poor fault diagnosis of rolling bearing, combined with the non-stationary characteristics of vibration signals, a bearing fault diagnosis method based on STFT-SPWVD and an improved convolutional neural network is proposed. Firstly, short-time Fourier transform and smoothed pseudo Wigner-Ville distribution are performed on the vibration signals of rolling bearings, and then through the analysis of the two methods, it is proposed to use the STFT-SPWVD method to obtain high time-frequency aggregation performance and no crossover. The time-frequency analysis results in distinct and distinct features. Finally, it is detected using an improved convolutional neural network. From the experimental results on the bearing dataset of Case Western Reserve University, it can be seen that the accuracy rate of the proposed method reaches 98.14%, which can better distinguish different faults.

Keywords: Time-frequency analysis; short-time Fourier transform; smoothed pseudo Wigner-Ville distribution; convolutional neural network.

1. Introduction

Rotating machinery is one of the most important parts of mechanical equipment and is widely used in various industries. Rolling bearing is the core part of mechanical equipment, and their operating status directly affects the working process of the entire rotating equipment. If a fault occurs, it will affect the entire production process and may cause casualties in severe cases [1]. Therefore, it is of great significance to achieve effective fault diagnosis for rolling bearings.

The data-driven fault diagnosis method is one of the commonly used methods. It uses the vibration data changes before and after the failure of the rolling bearing and adopts pattern recognition technology to improve the fault identification accuracy of the rolling bearing. Time-frequency analysis is one of the earliest methods for fault diagnosis of rotating machinery. It combines time-frequency analysis and diagnosis method with frequency-domain analysis, and it shows the instantaneous characteristics of vibration signals. For the non-stationary vibration signal of the rolling bearing, the local transformation method is used to represent the signal with the time-frequency of the joint function, which is the time-frequency analysis [2]. Time-frequency analysis is divided into linear time-frequency analysis and quadratic time-frequency analysis. Linear time-frequency analysis methods such as short-time Fourier transform(STFT) do not generate cross-terms when analyzing multi-component non-stationary signals. But the time-frequency aggregation performance of STFT is low. As a typical quadratic time-frequency analysis method, Wigner-Ville distribution(WVD) has the highest theoretical time-frequency resolution and many excellent math-ematical properties, but there is serious cross-term interference, which reduces the resolution of the signal's time-frequency distribution and blurs the original characteristics of the signal, which hinders its effective analysis and parameter extraction of the signal [3].

Through time-frequency analysis, the characteristics of different working states can be characterized, and on this basis, the classification of working conditions is realized by using a convolutional neural network. This paper combines STFT and SPWVD, and also the STFT-SPWVD joint method is proposed to perform time-frequency analysis on rolling bearings to obtain highly distinctive features. The improved convolutional neural network can be used to achieve high accuracy bearing fault diagnosis.

The rest of this paper is organized as follows. Section 2 depicts several works that are related to this topic. Section 3 introduces the related algorithms. Section 4 introduces the method proposed in this paper. Section 5 summarizes the experiments conducted in this paper and the results. Section 6 concludes the work.

2. Related Work

Zhong proposed an intelligent fault diagnosis model combining STFT and a convolutional neural network (CNN) [4]. Cai et al. proposed a hybrid approach combining WVD with CNN for power quality disturbance classification [5]. However, due to the bearing's complex and changeable working state, the vibration signal is significantly different from the theoretical or simulated signal, and the difference between different faults cannot be highlighted. Just using STFT or WVD is not enough.

Cheng et al. combined STFT and WVD by exploiting the property that STFT does not produce cross-terms [2]. In this way, the cross-terms generated in WVD are suppressed while maintaining high time-frequency resolution. Li et al. analyzed the vibration data of the centrifugal pump by using the STFT-WVD combined method, to realize the monitoring of the cavitation performance of the centrifugal pump [6]. Hao et al. used the normalized STFT-WVD method to extract the time-frequency characteristics of the surface natural pulsed electromagnetic field signal before the Lushan MS7.0 earthquake to study the time-frequency characteristics of the surface natural pulsed magnetic field before the big earthquake [7]. Liu et al. also used the normalized STFT-WVD method to analyze the time-frequency characteristics of very fast transient overvoltage (VFTO) [8].

3. Equations

3.1. *Short-time Fourier transform (STFT)*

STFT is one of the commonly used time-frequency analysis methods. The idea of STFT is to analyze the signal segment by segment. It uses a window function to slide the signal under study and then divides it into segments of equal length. The internal signal of the fragment is assumed to be stable. Then apply a Fourier transform to each segment to find the frequencies in that segment.

The STFT of a continuous-time signal $s(t)$ is defined as:

$$STFT_s(\tau, f) = \int\limits_{-\infty}^{+\infty} s(t)\omega^*(t-\tau)e^{-j2\pi f\tau}d\tau \tag{1}$$

where $\omega(t)$ is the window function, τ is the time position parameter of the window function, f is the frequency of the signal, and $\omega^*(t)$ is the conjugate of the complex function $\omega(t)$.

3.2. *Wigner-Ville distribution (WVD)*

As a commonly used time-frequency analysis method, the WVD is a quadratic transformation with many excellent properties. For a signal $x(t)$, its WVD is defined as:

$$W_x(t, f) = \int\limits_{-\infty}^{+\infty} x\left(t + \frac{\tau}{2}\right)x^*\left(t + \frac{\tau}{2}\right)e^{-j2\pi f\tau}d\tau \tag{2}$$

where τ is the time delay of the signal, f is the frequency of the signal, and $x^*(t)$ is the conjugate of $x(t)$.

3.3. Smoothed pseudo Wigner-Ville distribution (SPWVD)

SPWVD uses a windowing method for time and frequency based on the WVD to reduce the influence of cross terms. Therefore, SPWVD is defined as:

$$SPWVD_x(t,f) = \int\limits_{-\infty}^{+\infty}\int\limits_{-\infty}^{+\infty} x\left(t-u+\frac{\tau}{2}\right)x^*\left(t-u+\frac{\tau}{2}\right)e^{-j2\pi f\tau}h(\tau)g(u)d\tau du \qquad (3)$$

where τ is the time delay of the signal, f is the frequency of the signal, $x^*(t)$ is the conjugate of $x(t)$, $h(t), g(u)$ are the window functions.

3.4. STFT-WVD

To better perform time-frequency analysis and highlight the time-frequency characteristics, STFT-WVD combines STFT and WVD, which are defined as follows:

$$SW_x(t,f) = \min\{S_x(t,f),|W_x(t,f)|\} \qquad (4)$$

$$SW_x(t,f) = W_x(t,f)\bullet\{|S_x(t,f)|> c\} \qquad (5)$$

$$SW_x(t,f) = S_x^a(t,f)W_x^b(t,f) \qquad (6)$$

where $S_x(t,f)$ is the STFT expression and $W_x(t,f)$ is the WVD expression.

The first formula takes the smaller value of the value after STFT transformation and WVD, and this process is performed to eliminate the cross term of WVD transformation, which is called the minimum value method. The second formula sets a cross-term threshold to eliminate cross-terms, which is called binarization. The third formula sets the power exponent and eliminates the cross-term through the power exponent, which is called the power adjustment coefficient method.

4. STFT-SPWVD

It can be seen from the above work that different time-frequency analyses have their characteristics. As a linear time-frequency analysis method, STFT does not generate cross-terms when analyzing multi-component non-stationary signals. As a typical quadratic time-frequency analysis method, WVD has the theoretically highest time-frequency resolution and many excellent mathematical properties. However, due to the serious cross-term of WVD and the poor time-frequency aggregation of STFT, the time-frequency analysis results under different conditions are not significantly different. Although STFT and WVD are combined, to achieve high-accuracy fault diagnosis, it is necessary to highlight the characteristics of different types of faults, so that the difference is obvious.

In summary, using SPWVD with few cross-terms and relatively high time-frequency aggregation and STFT can obtain relatively stable time-frequency characteristics and other advantages. Combined with SPWVD, it is proposed to use the STFT-SPWVD joint method to perform time-frequency analysis on rolling bearings to obtain high-distinguishing features, and to use the improved CNN to achieve high-accuracy bearing fault diagnosis.

In this paper, the power adjustment coefficient method is used to construct the STFT-SPWVD method, and the expression is as follows:

$$SW_x(t, f) = S_x^a(t, f)SPW_x^b(t, f) \qquad (7)$$

where $S_x(t, f)$ is the STFT expression and $SPW_x(t, f)$ is the SPWVD expression.

A large part of the value is enhanced by the power exponent, but the exponent should not be taken too high. Considering that the value after STFT transformation is generally small, increase its weight appropriately, a and b take 1.5 and 1 respectively.

5. Experiment

5.1. Experimental data

This paper takes rolling bearings as the experimental object and uses the bearing dataset from Case Western Reserve University (CWRU) to test the improved method [9]. In this paper, the vibration of rolling bearings with a sampling frequency of 48kHz and horsepower of 3HP under seven working conditions, such as normal, inner race fault (0.007mm), inner race fault (0.014mm), inner race fault (0.021mm), outer race fault (0.007mm), outer race fault (0.014mm) and outer race fault (0.021mm) are selected signal data. The experimental environment is MATLAB R2021a, AMD R7 5800H processor, CPU main frequency 3.20 GHz, memory 16.0 GB, and Windows 10 operating system.

5.2. Data processing and analysis

First, the vibration signal data under each condition is cut into data with a length of 480256, and it is divided into 512 segments by the frame processing, and each segment can be used as a piece of data for the working condition. Observing the signal in the time domain, there are certain differences in the vibration signals between different working conditions, but it is not enough as the input of the classifier, and further analysis is required.

The following is a time-frequency analysis of the vibration signal under different working conditions. STFT, WVD, SPWVD, STFT-WVD, and STFT-

SPWVD are used to analyze the vibration signal respectively. The Hamming window with a length of 255 is used in STFT and SPWVD functions and the analysis results of different methods for a class of inner race fault (0.021mm) are selected as shown in Fig. 1.

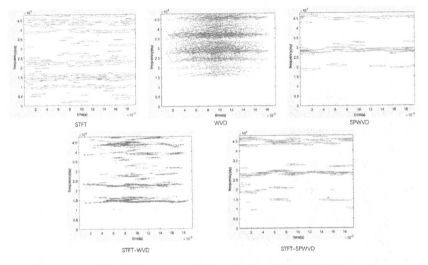

Fig. 1. Time-frequency analysis results from different methods.

It can be seen from Fig. 1 that the time-frequency analysis results of STFT have clear contours and no cross-terms, but the time-frequency aggregation is poor. The time-frequency analysis results of WVD have high time-frequency aggregation, but there are serious cross-terms. SPWVD suppresses the cross-term through the windowing function. Although the cross-term is reduced, the time-frequency aggregation is also reduced, which is not conducive to the classification of working conditions. STFT-WVD combines the two methods. Although the advantages of the two methods can be used to suppress the cross term of WVD through STFT and improve the time-frequency aggregation, there are still cross-terms, and the features are not prominent enough, which is not conducive to classification. It can be seen that STFT-SPWVD amplifies the time-frequency aggregation characteristics, with sharp contours and extremely low cross-terms, which significantly improves the time-frequency characteristics.

The vibration signals of normal, inner race fault (0.021mm) and outer race fault (0.007mm) are selected for time-frequency analysis using STFT-SPWVD. The results are shown in Fig. 2.

336

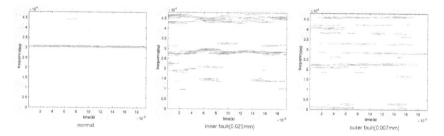

Fig. 2. Time-frequency analysis results of STFT-SPWVD under different working conditions.

It can be seen from Fig. 2 that the time-frequency analysis results of STFT-SPWVD under different working conditions have obvious differences and have a high degree of distinction.

5.3. Experimental test

CNN is one of the very mature and commonly used classification networks. In this paper, the time-frequency analysis results of seven working conditions obtained by STFT, WVD, STFT-WVD, and STFT-SPWVD are put into the improved CNN for training. and test. The network adopts 4 convolution layers, 4 pooling layers, 16 convolution kernels, and 2 fully connected layers. Through the training and testing of the network, the results are shown in Table 1.

Table 1. Comparison table of algorithm accuracy.

Algorithm	Accuracy
STFT	94.00%
WVD	92.85%
STFT-WVD	93.00%
STFT-SPWVD	98.14%

Table 1 shows that the accuracy of STFT-SPWVD reaches 98.14%. STFT-SPWVD has higher accuracy than the other three algorithms. It can be seen that the improved STFT-SPWVD method can effectively classify different working conditions, thereby realizing fault diagnosis.

6. Conclusion

Aiming at the problem of poor fault diagnosis of rolling bearing, combined with the non-stationary characteristics of vibration signal, a bearing fault diagnosis method based on STFT-SPWVD and an improved convolutional neural network is proposed. The combination of STFT and SPWVD amplifies the time-frequency aggregation characteristics, with clear outlines and extremely low cross-terms, which significantly improves the time-frequency characteristics and makes the difference between different working conditions amplify. Finally, the improved CNN is used for classification and diagnosis. Conducted on the bearing dataset of CWRU, the experiment has high accuracy and can realize fault diagnosis of rolling bearings.

Acknowledgment

This research is supported by the National Natural Science Foundation of China (Grant No. 62106206).

References

1. H. Q. Wang, Y. L. Ke, G. G. Luo, et al. "Compressed sensing of roller bearing fault based on multiple down-sampling strategy." *Measurement Science and Technology*, 2016, 27(2):025009.
2. X. Cheng, B. Xu, X. Xue, et al. "Suppression of cross-terms in Wigner-Ville Distribution based on short-term Fourier transform," 2015 12th *IEEE International Conference on Electronic Measurement & Instruments* (ICEMI), 2015, pp. 472-475, doi: 10.1109/ICEMI.2015.7494239.
3. H. J. Liu, X. H. Gao, R. J. Guo. "A Time-frequency Analysis Method for Linear Frequency Modulation Signal with Low Sidelobe and Nonaliasing Property." *Journal of Electronics & Information Technology*, 2019, 41(11): 2614-2622. doi: 10.11999/JEIT181190
4. D. Zhong, W. Guo and D. He, "An Intelligent Fault Diagnosis Method based on STFT and Convolutional Neural Network for Bearings Under Variable Working Conditions," 2019 *Prognostics and System Health Management Conference* (PHM-Qingdao), 2019, pp. 1-6, doi: 10.1109/ PHM-Qingdao46334.2019.8943026.
5. K. Cai, W. Cao, L. Aarniovuori, et al. "Classification of Power Quality Disturbances Using Wigner-Ville Distribution and Deep Convolutional Neural Networks," in *IEEE Access*, vol. 7, pp. 119099-119109, 2019, doi: 10.1109/ACCESS.2019.2937193.
6. Y. Li, G. Feng, X. Li, et al. "An experimental study on the cavitation vibration characteristics of a centrifugal pump at normal flow rate." *J Mech Sci Technol* 32, 4711–4720 (2018). https://doi.org/10.1007/s12206-018-0918-x.

7. G. C. Hao, Z. C. Cheng, J. Zhao, et al. "Time-frequency analysis of the Earth's natural pulse electromagnetic field signal before and after the Lushan MS 7.0 earthquake based on NSTFT-WVD transform." *Earth Science Frontiers*, 2016, 23(1): 275.

8. S. M. Liu, S. Li, C. Tan, et al. "Spectral analysis method of VFTO based on NSTFT-WVD transform." *Journal of North China Electric Power University*, 2018, 45(005): 52-61.

9. Case Western Reserve University bearing data center, 2022. Available from: `https://engineering.case.edu/bearingdatacenter/download-data-file`

Enable anomaly detection in electroplating*

Moussab Orabi*,**, Kim Phuc Tran*, Sébastien Thomassey* and Philipp Egger**

*Univ. Lille, ENSAIT, ULR 2461 - GEMTEX - Génie et Matériaux Textiles
F-59000 Lille, France
**Rosenberger Hochfrequenztechnik GmbH & Co. KG Hauptstraße 1
83413 Fridolfing, Germany

Customer requirements and specifications are becoming increasingly complex, resulting in more complicate production processes to meet these requirements. With this complexity come anomalies and deviations into processes. On the other hand, we are seeing a new generation of technology can handle complexity of process and discover unusual executions of large and complex processes by tracing their generated data and transforming it into insights and actions. Hence, using data in industry becomes inevitable, giving it a fundamental role in improving efficiency and effectiveness of any organization. However, it is not sufficient to store and analyze data, but also the ability to link it to operational processes and be able to pose right questions; moreover, a deep understanding of end-to-end processes, which may ultimately accelerate every aspect of detecting abnormal process executions and determining process parameters responsible for quality fluctuations. Anomaly detection in manufacturing has raised serious concerns. Any divergence in process may lead to a quality degradation in manufactured products, energy wastage and system unreliability. This paper proposes an approach for anomaly detection in electroplating processes by combining process steps ordering relationship and boosted decision tree classifiers, XGBoost system, that employs the dimensionality reduction using Kernel principal component analysis which turns out to be effective in handling nonlinear phenomena using the Gaussian kernel on a self-tuning procedure. This approach has ensured a good accuracy property while maintaining enough generalization characteristics to beat data size and complexity challenges in order to improve detection rate and accuracy. The approach was validated using a dataset representing electroplating executions in year 2021. The classified anomaly events produced by our approach can be used, for instance, as candidates for a generalized anomaly detection framework in electroplating.

Keywords: Anomaly detection; machine learning; XGBoost; KPCA; process discovery; manufacturing; electroplating.

*This work is supported by Rosenberger Hochfrequenztechnik GmbH & Co. KG.

1. Introduction

Anomaly has many meanings and definitions. However, in its broader aspects and loosely defined, as it was given by Kuhn:[1] "Any phenomenon that deviates from a common form, that displays inconsistency with what is expected, or that is generally considered 'odd' or 'peculiar' in some way". In terms of machine learning anomalies or outliers are instances in a dataset deviate from the majority of the data, this deviation could be caused by abnormal execution, noise in the data, deviation in the data caused by a system error, a data entry error, or even a fraud attempt. While business rules can be tolerant of unusual executions or even some noise, they are strict on fraud attempts and operational failures that lead to undesirable outcomes. By this definition, anomaly detection will be the task of successfully identifying those records within a given dataset. Removing outliers in the data set is the first application of anomaly detection in smart manufacturing, in addition, it is used in many different aspects of manufacturing operations such as anomaly detection in machine operations, detection of attacks in industrial systems, detection of mechanical anomalies before having an impact on product quality, Tran.[2] In manufacturing, more precisely in electroplating, anomaly detection is a key factor to improve process efficiency, considering the difficult of performing any quality check on processed products after each step of the process, as we have to wait until the end of the process to perform any check. In addition, anomaly detection gains considerable attention in batch production processes as multiple batches of the same product with the same process set-up parameters are produced. Therefore, the timing of detecting anomalies and intervention action is the key factor to reduce defective parts by stopping processing more batches. Even if a huge amount of data is generated at every process step, this data overload can make it difficult to uncover useful insights in order to make effective decisions. Moreover, the state of the preceding process steps of the one responsible for the anomaly, all drives us to search for detection approaches with retention capabilities. Among recent approaches to detect anomalies, there is the one using Hierarchical Transformers to detects anomalies by utilizing a hierarchical transformer structure to model log template sequences and parameter values, where noise in event logs is closely related to anomaly detection as in Ref. 3. It is worth noting that Long Short-Term Memory Networks (LSTM) achieves a higher level of detection accuracy and a lower percentage of false positive rate compared to the popular methods like Support Vector Machine (SVM) as it has been discussed by Tran,[4] where (LSTM) was proposed to meet the challenges of temporally dependent anomaly detection problems, due to their ability to maintain long term memories. Nevertheless, we barely find any research conducted on detecting anomalies in the electroplating field, although the Electroplating processes are well-defined. Furthermore, these methods need to consider the simultaneous event occurrence, which is normal in Electroplating. The rest of the paper is organized as follows. In Section 2, an illustration of the properties and characteristics of electroplating process, in Section 3 we go into the most common machine learning techniques for detecting anomalies. Then our proposal is presented in Section 4. Experimental results of detecting abnormal executions in electroplating processes are illustrated in the following Section 5. Finally, concluding remarks can be found in Section 6.

2. Problem Statement

As already mentioned in the introduction, electroplating processes are well defined, and they express the maximum potential of their performance if a series of parameters are respected. But due to the massive production conditions and the variety of processes, one execution of the same process can differ from another and cause a defective coating, which can be a spot on the surface, optic issue, adhesion, dimensional changes, coating thickness is low or high, pitting, micro-porosity, or generally tiny round concave holes found irregularly on the product surface a combination of them. It is worth noting that electroplating defects have some distinctive features, among which are:

(1) Sporadic failures: two executions with the same parameters, one producing defective products and the other not.
(2) Failures are rare but very expensive, which leads to an imbalanced data set.
(3) Quality check is only carried out on samples of the products.
(4) Quality check is only performed at the end of the process, as it cannot be done after each step.

Moreover, we need always to consider in batch processing, where multiple executions of the same process are running, that it is necessary to detect the failure as soon as possible in order to be able to adjust the process parameters early enough to avoid more defective batches. Considering an average QC response time of 1.5 hours and an average execution duration of 30 minutes, the deviation in parameters for a given batch may be propagated to the next two or three batches before receiving instructions from the QC team to stop processing and readjust those parameters. Thereby, it was necessary to use machine learning for detecting anomalies in processes at an early stage. The following section gives us a brief overview of the most popular machine learning anomaly detection techniques.

3. Literature Review

Several anomaly detection techniques in manufacturing processes have been proposed in the literature such as Recurrent Neural Networks (RNN) and their combinations have recently been widely applied to detect anomalies in manufacturing processes. Like Lindemann[5] used LSTM to detect anomalies and prediction in discrete manufacturing based on cooperative LSTM networks and the Bi-directional LSTM was applied to capture long-term dependence for machining tool wear prediction as in Ref. 6, Variational LSTM (VLSTM) was used to Enhanced Anomaly Detection for Industrial Big Data like in Ref. 7. Basically, the compression network is employed to mitigate the complexity of high-dimensional input data, while retaining adequate information to ensure detection accuracy.

4. Proposed Method for Anomaly Detection in Electroplating

4.1. Data description

At the factory where we are conducting these experiments, electroplating can be grouped according to the used technology and solutions into 4 types: Zinc mass plating, Rack plating, Technikum plating and Vibration plating. The number of executions is between 4277 for Technikum system and 83624 for the Zinc one in year 2021. Each process chain consists of a series of steps (between 27 and 42) that are executed sequentially, each execution has master data like process number, product, product quantity and time information like start and end time. Besides process data, we have step execution information which differs from step to step. All this data is a rich source and valuable information can provide deep insights into the process. The following diagram Fig. 1 shows the usage of process discovery and process mining in order to identify anomalies in processes use.

Figure 1 provides an overview of our approach to extract and prepare process data for anomaly detection, which is organized in five steps:

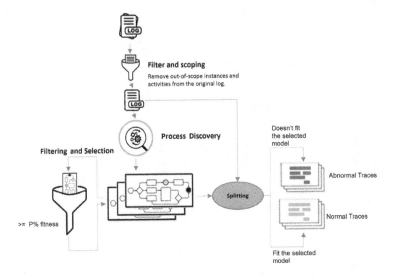

Fig. 1.   Process Discovery: Approach for discovering processes data form log files.

(1) Data extraction: to extract and clean process data from data sources.

(2) Scoping and filtering: Is a domain-dependent step by applying some filters where instances and activities that out-of-scope are removed from the original data set.

(3) Process discovery: this step is an essential one, where we discover each process instance and each instance's activity, these activities data will form the most important anomaly detection model features.

(4) Process selection: this step applies the fitness criteria in order to select the proper processes, where fitness refers to the ability to reproduce the log in normal execution

(5) Splitting: This is the final step where anomaly detection technique was applied to classify instances in anomalous and normal.

We collected data received from different types of sensors fixed on 156 galvanic bathes in the Zinc plating system. These sensors are collecting temperature, current values, solution conductivity, and other data. The format of the data is digital and is being collected every second. The collected data represents 83624 executions of 236 different processes. After collecting data, applying some cleansing and scoping on it, we filtered it on one particular process, the most executed one. Figure 2 shows the top 15 executed processes in 2021.

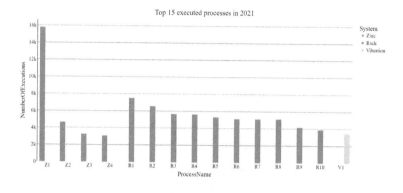

Fig. 2.   Process Executions: Top 15 executed processes in 2021.

4.2. Data prepossessing

When detecting anomalies, we know that manufacturer hardly wants to create an anomalous product. Hence, the anomalies are like a needle in a haystack making the data set significantly unbalanced, since failures ratio in Technikum, Vibration, Zinc and Rack were (0,001%, 0,015%, 0.21% and 0.027%) respectively. The problem of imbalanced label appears when anomalous classes are underrepresented. The naivest way to mitigate this problem is to generate new samples by random sampling with replacing the currently available samples. The Random Over Sampler provides such a possibility. As a result, the majority class does not take over the other classes during training process. Consequently, all classes are represented by the decision function. Not only the imbalanced data set problem we quickly face in anomaly detection, but the over-fitting problem too, especially when the data model has so many features. Over-fitting happens when the model learns signal as well as noise in the training data and would not perform well on new data on which the model was not trained. Traditional methods like cross-validation, stepwise regression to handle over-fitting, and perform feature selection work well with a small set of features but regularization techniques are great alternatives when dealing with a large set of features. In our data set, we applied Random Over Sampler to mitigate the imbalanced data challenge and L2 Regularization in order to reduce the possibility of Over-fitting, since it basically adds "squared magnitude" of coefficient as a penalty term to the loss function as the model complexity increases. As it is shown in the following loss function in Eq. (1).

$$J(\theta) = \frac{1}{2m} \left[\sum_{i=1}^{m} (h_\theta(x^{(i)}) - y^{(i)})^2 + \lambda \sum_{j=1}^{n} \theta_j^2 \right] \qquad (1)$$

4.3. Feature engineering

Before getting into the gist of this section, let's emphasize that Feature Engineering (FE) has been applied to numerous domains and proven an effectiveness in increasing the performance of machine learning algorithms. In our experiment, FE is part of various tasks aimed at increasing the efficiency of ML models and the effectiveness of anomaly detection in order to avoid production stops and yield losses. Nevertheless, when analyzing our data sets, we quickly faced two particular challenges:

High-dimensionality: Typically, the number of features p to be evaluated in FE can reach thousands and it can even be much larger than the number of instances n.

Collinearity: Some features may be strongly correlated with one another. Before digging furthermore, let's describe the data modeling approach that was used. After data extraction and cleansing, we had a data as followed: Each row represents one activity in a process execution, where process relevant data like process name and process article alongside the activity data from start time, duration, temperature, voltage, and current were located in one row. At the beginning, all possible features were collected, considering more than 210 different process variants, each has between 27 and 42 different steps, output a data set with more than 8000 features, therefore it was necessary to focus on only one process, the most executed one which reduced features to 1213. Afterward, the domain experts were asked to exclude non-relevant activities like loading and unloading which has no influence on the product manufacturing, this reduced the dataset to only 800 features. Finally, it comes to dimension reduction techniques the KPCA to apply dimension reduction. As we are dealing with an anomaly detection problem where outliers are the crucial part of the data, KPCA was a proper technique to use where it turns out to be effective in handling non-linear phenomena through the use of the Gaussian kernel on a self-tuning procedure by optimizing the reconstruction error using GridSearchCV. After tuning and applying KPCA the data dimensions were reduced to 310.

This is just the tip of the iceberg. There is so much more we can do with features Engineering in electroplating data.

5. Experimental Setup and Performance Analysis

In this section, we illustrate the performance of the proposed method of detecting anomalies in electroplating. In our experiment, the dataset was split into train, test, and evaluation as followed: The dataset represents 15356 executions of one process in 2021 and 2022. 310 features were extracted in order to train an XGBoost system that implements a gradient tree boosting algorithm, uses the previous data features ordered by activities relationships for producing a set of simple interpretable rules. These rules represent the rationale for generalizing its application over a massive number of unseen events in a distributed computing environment. XGBoost applies a good regularization technique to reduce over-fitting in the training phase as shown in8. The widely used measures to analyze the performance of a certain detection method like Accuracy, Recall, Precision and F-score were applied. Among these measures, DR (Recall or sensitivity) represents the true positive rate, Precision represents the probability of predicting a true positive from all positive predictions, Accuracy represents a general anomaly detection performance and F-score provides a configurable harmonic mean between Precision and Recall. The XGBoost was trained on two datasets, one without oversampling the anomalous samples and one with oversampling. The performance of the proposed model was evaluated based on 1345 normal and abnormal corresponding to 0.09% of the total dataset. The predict function for XGBoost outputs probabilities by default and not actual class labels. To calculate accuracy, we converted them to 0 and 1 labels, where a 0.5 probability corresponds to the threshold. Training using dataset without sampling leads to poor model performance, where precision, Recall, and F1-Score for class 1 where 0 even the accuracy was 0.99. On the contrary, XGBoost was able to correctly classify all the test data after training on the over-sampled dataset using Random Over-Sampler which depicts the importance of oversampling according to the F-score metric. It is clearly observed the performance improvement for the over-sampled data over the original one in anomaly detection which can be considered as an extreme case of the class imbalance problem.

6. Conclusion

In this paper, an illustration of the practical steps and techniques we used to extract, clean, and model the electroplating processes data as a preparation for anomaly detection was presented. Then we went through the data science process life cycle from feature selection to dimension reduction ending with applying machine learning methods on final transformed and normalized dataset with proper features which were formed by applying feature engineering techniques. Anomalies in an event log, in fact, normally are linked to specific root causes. However, while anomaly detection algorithms may be effective at identifying anomalies, they have a major drawback, as their output is hard to explain and identify aberrant variables. Thus, efforts are needed to develop the Explainable Artificial Intelligence-based event log Anomaly Detection in Online Process Mining.

References

1. T. S. Kuhn, *The Structure of Scientific Revolutions*, 3rd. (University of Chicago Press, 1996).
2. K. Tran, *Control Charts and Machine Learning for Anomaly Detection in Manufacturing* (Springer, 10 2021).
3. H. Shaohan, L. Yi, F. Carol, H. Rong, Z. Yining, Y. Hailong and L. Zhongzhi, Hitanomaly: Hierarchical transformers for anomaly detection in system log, *IEEE Transactions on Network and Service Management* **PP**, 1 (10, 2020).
4. K. Tran, H. Nguyen and S. Thomassey, Anomaly detection using long short term memory networks and its applications in supply chain management, *Science Direct* **11**, 2 (2019).
5. M. W. B. Lindemann, N. Jazdi, Anomaly detection and prediction in discrete manufacturing based on cooperative lstm networks, *IEEE International Conference on Automation Science and Engineering* **11**, p. 3 (2020).
6. Z. Rui, Y. Ruqiang, W. Jinjiang and M. Kezhi, *Learning to monitor machine health with convolutional bi-directional lstm networks*, *Sensors* **17**, p. 273 (01, 2017).
7. H. Y. X. Zhou and Q. Jin, Variational lstm enhanced anomaly detection for industrial big data, *IEEE* **11**, p. 4 (2021).
8. J. Henriques, F. Caldeira, T. Cruz and P. Simões, Combining k-means and xgboost models for anomaly detection using log datasets, *Electronics* **9** (2020).

Detection of oocyte nucleus motion based on mean drift algorithm

Zuqi Wang, Xiangfei Zhao, Xin Zhao and Yaowei Liu[†]

College of Artificial Intelligence, Nankai University, Tianjin, 300350, China
Institute of Intelligence Technology and Robotic Systems, Shenzhen Research Institute of
Nankai University, Shenzhen, 518083, China
[†]liuyaowei@mail.nankai.edu.cn
www.nankai.edu.cn

In this paper, a method for detecting the nucleus movement of oocytes during the enucleation process based on the mean drift algorithm is proposed, including the following steps: 1. Establish the target model ROI_{ini} and calculate the probability density histogram; 2. Establish the target candidate model ROI_{candi} and calculate the probability density histogram; 3. Use the Bhattacharyya coefficient to compare the similarity of the target model and the target candidate model; 4. Locate the moving target. This method is a universal nucleus motility detection method, which improves the limitations of the traditional mean drift target tracking algorithm, solves the problem of nucleus motion detection under the conditions of low microscopic image resolution, change in nucleus shape during enucleation, and large differences in the shape of different oocyte nuclei. This method can be used in the field of somatic cell nuclear transplantation, which can greatly improve the accuracy of oocyte enucleation, reduce cell damage, and further improve the development potential of recombinant cells.

Keywords: Mean drift algorithm; oocyte enucleation; motion detection.

1. Introduction

Somatic cell nuclear transfer is the transfer of somatic cell into enucleation oocytes, where the recombinant cells undergo and then program and develop into new embryos [1]. This method not only yields a large number of embryos with the same genetic trait, but also accelerates the reproduction of excellent species through genetic modification of somatic nuclei [2]. In the somatic cell nuclear transfer procedure, the enucleation operation has the most significant effect on the success rate of nuclear transplantation [3]. Enucleation is the

[†]This work is supported by the National Key R&D Program of China, grant number 2020YFB1313101; the National Natural Science Foundation of China (NSFC), grant number 62027812, U1813210, 62003174, 61903201, 62003173; the China Postdoctoral Science Foundation, grant number 2020M680865.

removal of the main genetic material from the oocyte, thus ensuring that the individual developed by the migrated nucleus has the highest genetic characteristics than the donor animal [4]. However, due to the invisible location of the nucleus during the blind aspiration enucleation process, it will lead to incomplete enucleation of oocytes or excessive cytoplasm removal. Incomplete enucleation of oocytes may cause their own parthenogenesis to activate, and removing too much cytoplasm will reduce the development rate of reconstituted embryos [5]. Therefore, it is necessary to visualize the nucleus and detect its motion during the enucleation process.

The visualization of oocyte nuclei can be achieved by cell fluorescence staining, and the method is quite mature. In terms of motion detection of targets, common techniques include optical flow method [6], background difference method [7] and mean drift method [8]. The implementation of the optical flow method is complex which is not suitable for accurate target tracking problems; The background difference method can only extract the outer outline of the target. Therefore, neither of the above two methods is suitable for detecting the movement of nucleus.

In recent years, many methods have been proposed for detecting nucleus motility after fluorescent staining. Yadi Li et al. screened out the nucleus by calculating the circular outline size [9], but this method largely depends on the difference of gray value between the nucleus and the surrounding environment, and failed in the case of irregular circular shape of the nucleus. Ke Li et al. proposed the Siamese-FC Neural Network tracking method [10], This method is suitable for fast-moving targets, but there is a possibility of tracking failure when the nucleus undergoes motion deformation during the enucleation process. Can Fahrettin Koyuncu et al. took a more precise approach by designing a merging algorithm to form a closed pattern to surround all fluorescent parts [11]. This detection method will define false boundaries for the uneven part of pixel intensity in the image, resulting in detection. Therefore, it is necessary to propose a fast, efficient and universal nuclear motility detection method.

The rest of the paper is organized as follows. Section 2 introduces the principle, steps and mathematical calculation formula of mean shift algorithm. Section 3 gives the results of the application of mean shift algorithm in the field of nuclear tracking. Section 4 is the summary of this paper.

2. Key Techniques

Figure 1 shows the specific process of the detecting the nucleus.

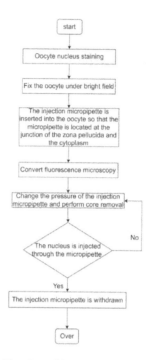

Fig. 1. Flowchart of the oocyte nucleus detection.

2.1.1. *Establish the target model*

In the start frame, set the initial target area ROI_{ini}, which is the nucleus portion of the image. Set y_0 represent the center of the motion target area, x_i represents the set of all pixels in the target area, and m represents the total number of eigenvalues, the probability density of the target model feature value u is estimated as in Eq. (1).

$$\hat{q}_u = C \sum_{i=1}^{n} k\left(\left\| \frac{y_0 - x_i}{h} \right\|^2 \right) \delta\left[b(x_i) - u \right]. \tag{1}$$

where $k(x)$ is the contour function of the kernel function, which is mainly used to assign weights to the relevant pixels; the role of $\left\| \frac{y_0 - x_i}{h} \right\|^2$ is to solve the problem caused by the change in the scale of the moving target, h is the width of the kernel function; $\delta\left[b(x_i) - u \right]$ is used to determine whether the value of pixel x_i in the target region belongs to the characteristic value of the u interval,

$b(x_i)$ represents the characteristic value of the pixel at sample point x_i. If so, the value is 1, and the opposite is 0; C is the normalization coefficient, $C = \dfrac{1}{\displaystyle\sum_{i=1}^{n} k\left(\left\|\dfrac{y_0 - x_i}{h}\right\|^2\right)}$, which makes $\displaystyle\sum_{u=1}^{m} q_u = 1$.

2.1.2. Establish a target candidate model

Enter an image of the next frame and set the target candidate area ROI_{candi}, the target candidate area is all areas that are likely to contain the tracked target.

Set the center coordinate of the target candidate region to y, which is also the center coordinate of the kernel function. All pixels in the center of the target candidate region are represented by the set x_i, so the probabilistic density estimate formula for the target candidate model as in Eq. (2).

$$\hat{p}_u = C_h \sum_{i=1}^{n} k\left(\left\|\frac{y_0 - y_i}{h}\right\|^2\right) \delta\left[b(x_i) - u\right], \tag{2}$$

where C_h is the normalization coefficient:

$$C_h = \frac{1}{\displaystyle\sum_{i=1}^{n_h} k\left(\left\|\dfrac{y - x_i}{h}\right\|^2\right)}. \tag{3}$$

2.1.3. Similarity determination

Set $\hat{q}_u$ and $\hat{p}_u$ to represent the target template and the candidate target template respectively, and define the formula for calculating the similarity between the models as in Eq. (4).

$$\rho = \rho\left(\hat{p}, \hat{q}\right) = \sum_{u=1}^{m} \sqrt{\hat{p}_u \, \hat{q}_u}. \tag{4}$$

Calculate the distance between the two model histograms as in Eq. (5).

$$d(y) = \sqrt{1 - \hat{\rho}(y)}. \tag{5}$$

The candidate model calculated from the different candidate regions in the current frame takes the candidate region with the largest value as the actual position of the target in the frame.

2.1.4. *Positioning of sports targets*

The candidate target model $\hat{p}(y_0)$ is calculated, and the Taylor series expansion is performed at $\hat{p}(y)$ and $\hat{p}(y_0)$, and the Bhattacharyya coefficient is approximated as in Eq. (6).

$$\rho\left(p(\hat{y}_0), \hat{q} \right) = \frac{1}{2} \sum_{u=1}^{m} \sqrt{\hat{p}_u(y_0)\hat{q}_u} + \frac{1}{2}C_h \sum_{i=1}^{n_k} w_i k \left(\left\| \frac{y - x_i}{h} \right\|^2 \right), \tag{6}$$

where w_i represents the pixel weight.

As in Eq. (7).

$$f_k = \frac{1}{2} C_h \sum_{i=1}^{n_k} w_i k \left(\left\| \frac{y - x_i}{h} \right\|^2 \right). \tag{7}$$

Then when the value of f_k is the largest, the weight w_i is the largest. After calculating the drift vector of f_k, the vector $M_{h,G(y)}$ of the process of iterating the candidate target region center position y_0 drift to the center position y of the actual motion target area can be obtained, and finally a new motion target center position y_1 can be obtained, as in Eq. (8).

$$y_1 = \frac{\sum_{i=1}^{n_h} x_i w_i g \left(\left\| \frac{\hat{y}_0 - x_i}{h} \right\|^2 \right)}{\sum_{i=1}^{n_h} w_i g \left(\left\| \frac{\hat{y}_0 - x_i}{h} \right\|^2 \right)}. \tag{8}$$

3. Results

The porcine oocyte was used in the experiments. In the starting frame, set the complete core image as the initial target area ROI_{ini}, and calculate the eigenvalue probability density histogram of the core part, as shown in Fig. 2.

Then entered the second frame image, set the target candidate model region as ROI_{candi}, as shown in Fig. 3. Calculate the eigenvalue probability density histogram of each ROI_{candi}, as shown in Fig. 4.

After that, Bhattacharyya coefficient is used as the similarity measure. The similarity between the target candidate region example and the real core in the first frame is 0.4328, 0.4492, 0.5058 and 0.9639.

According to the similarity calculated by Bhattacharyya coefficient, the candidate target corresponding to 0.9639 is the position of oocyte nucleus in frame 2, as shown in Fig. 5. The above steps are then performed in subsequent frames until the last frame of the video.

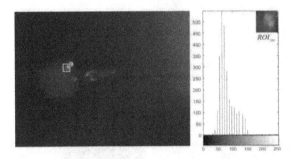

Fig. 2. Histogram of the probability density of the nucleus image and the nucleus portion of the initial frame.

Fig. 3. Schematic diagram of the candidate region of the second frame nucleus position.

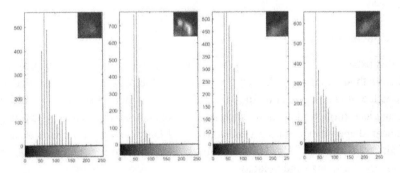

Fig. 4. Histogram of the probability density of the nucleus candidate region characteristic values in the second frame.

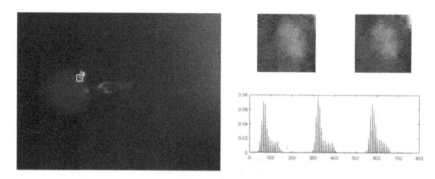

Fig. 5. The filtered out nucleus true position in frame 2 and the histogram of the nucleus image in frame 1 compared with the histogram of the nucleus image located in frame 2.

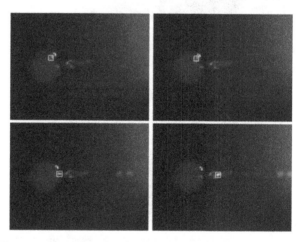

Fig. 6. The effect of tracking the position of the nucleus in real time during the operation of the algorithm.

4. Conclusion

In this paper, a nuclear motion tracking method based on mean drift is proposed. This method depends on the sampling points in the feature space and calculates the value of density function to realize target recognition. It solves the problems of nuclear motion detection, such as low resolution of microscopic image, nuclear shape change during enucleation, and large difference in nuclear shape of different oocytes. This method can be used for nuclear tracking problems with any shape, size and velocity.

References

1. P. Ross and C. Feltrin, Cloning animals by somatic cell nuclear trans plantation (2014).
2. Q. Meng, S.-E. Zhu, S.-M. Zeng and Z.-C. Zhang, Effects of reduction of cytoplasm quantity on the in vitro development of partheno genetic embryos from activated oocytes, *Scientia Agricultura Sinica*, 1109 (2003).
3. H. Liu, X. Zheng, R. Wang and J.-l. Zhang, The efffect of enucleation time and method on the enucleation efficiency using in vitro matured goat oocytes, *ACTA Agriculturae Boreali-sinica* **26**, 90 (2011).
4. C. P. Silva, K. Kommineni, R. Oldenbourg and D. L. Keefe, The first polar body does not predict accurately the location of the metaphaseii meiotic spindle in mammalian oocytes, *Fertility and sterility* **71**, 719(1999).
5. T. Dominko, A. Chan, C. Simerly, C. Luetjens, L. Hewitson, C. Martinovich and G. Schatten, Dynamic imaging of the metaphase II spindle and maternal chromosomesin bovine oocytes: implications for enucleation efficiency verification, avoidance of parthenogenesis, and successful embryogenesis, *Biology of reproduction* **62**, 150 (2000).
6. P. J. Burt and E. H. Adelson, The laplacian pyramid as a compact image code, *in Readings in computer vision*, (Elsevier, 1987) pp. 671–679.
7. Z. Zivkovic and F. Van Der Heijden, Efficient adaptive density estimation per image pixel for the task of background subtraction, *Pattern recognition letters* **27**, 773 (2006).
8. D. Comaniciu and P. Meer, Mean shift: A robust approach toward feature space analysis, *IEEE Transactions on pattern analysis and machine intelligence* **24**, 603 (2002).
9. G. Chen, A novel multi-cue based image fusion method combining multi-principle microscopy images towards Nuclear transfer technology, *The 7th IEEE International Conference on Nano/Molecular Medicine and Engineering*, (Thailand, 2013) pp. 11–15.
10. Z. Zhang, Y. Zhang, X. Cheng and K. Li, Siamese network for real-time tracking with action-selection, *Journal of Real-Time Image Processing* **17**, 1647 (2020).
11. C. F. Koyuncu, İ. Durmaz, R. Çetin-Atalay and Ç. Gündüz-Demir, A supervised learning model for live cell segmentation, *22nd Signal Processing and Communications Applications Conference (SIU)*, (Turkey, 2014) pp. 1971–1974.

Comprehensive minimum cost consensus for analyzing different agreed solutions

Diego García-Zamora* Álvaro Labella, Rosa M. Rodríguez and Luis Martínez

Department of Computer Sciences, University of Jaén
Jaén, Spain
* dgzamora@ujaen.es

Consensus Reaching Processes (CRPs) aim at guaranteeing that the decision-makers (DMs) involved in a Group Decision-Making (GDM) problem achieve an agreed solution for the decision situation. Among other proposals to obtain such agreed solutions, the Minimum Cost Consensus (MCC) models stand out because of their reformulation of the GDM problem in terms of mathematical optimization models. Originally, MCC models were limited to compute agreed solutions from a simple distance measure that cannot guarantee to achieve a certain consensus threshold. This drawback was lately fixed by the Comprehensive MCC (CMCC) models, which include consensus measures in the classic MCC approach. However, some real-world problems require analyzing the feasibility of the DMs to choose a certain alternative regarding the others, namely, the cost of achieving an agreed solution on a certain alternative. For this reason, this contribution introduces new CMCC models that drive DMs to an agreed solution on a given alternative and, in such a way, it provides a method to analyze the cost and appropriateness of guiding such group to a specific solution.

Keywords: Comprehensive minimum cost consensus; persuading model; group decision-making.

1. Introduction

The participation of multiple DMs in the resolution of a decision problem provides a heterogeneous view about such a problem, but also gives place to a significant phenomenon: the possibility of disagreements among the DMs. When discrepancies in GDM are neglected, it is possible that the reached solution does not satisfy some DMs, and they may even call into question the decision process.[1] The CRPs were proposed to avoid this situation. A CRP was initially proposed as a discussion process, usually coordinated by a moderator, which aims at smoothing such disagreements and obtaining a consensual solution to the decision problem that satisfies all members of the group. In order to model these consensus processes, the classic literature essentially considers two kinds of approaches[2] depending on if they use a feedback process, in which DMs are asked about if they want to accept the suggestions provided by the moderator, or without feedback, in which the participation of the DMs is omitted, and the changes are applied automatically without asking to achieve an optimal solution. Among the latter models, the well-known MCC models[3,4] stand out because of their simplicity and unique interpretation of the notion of consensus. Such MCC models are mathematical optimization problems that try to find a feasible agreed solution for a GDM problem according to a maximal allowed distance among the DMs' preferences and the collective opinion by preserving as much as possible the initial DMs' opinions. Over the years, these models have been studied in greater depth. Labella et al.[5] argued that the maximal distances between the DMs' preferences and collective opinion do not guarantee to reach a desired consensus threshold, and thus, it was necessary to include consensus measures in the optimization models, giving place to the CMCC models.[5]

Even though, classic GDM and its MCC models aim at providing collective solutions to decision problems, traditional literature usually neglects the study of the cost of guiding/persuading the group towards a predetermined solution, in spite of achieving a given alternative under agreement could be necessary in certain real-world problems.[6] Hence, it would be interesting to analyze how to include mechanisms to guide the CMCC model to obtain an agreement from DMs' opinions on choosing a certain alternative in the decision process.

For instance, we can think about a financial institution which desires to establish a certain policy P which needs the approval of the regional managers. For such a policy P, there are several alternatives $p_1, p_2, \ldots, p_n$ with different characteristics: some of them could be more beneficial to the DMs, namely, the regional managers, but others could be more profitable for the interests of the institution. In this context, the institution would be interested in analyzing how feasible it is to convince these managers about the election of a predetermined alternative p_k by analyzing the cost of guiding the involved DMs to choose such an alternative p_k.

Therefore, this contribution proposes CMCC models for GDM which aim at driving the involved DMs to agree their opinions for choosing a predetermined alternative in order to analyze the cost of agreement on different alternatives in a GDM problem. To do so, our proposal extends the CMCC model to include a *persuading constraint*, such that the Persuasive-CMCC (P-CMCC) output provides an agreed solution which minimizes the cost of modifying DMs' opinions and guarantees an agreed solution on a predefined alternative. Our proposal deals with Fuzzy Preference Relations (FPRs)[5] to model DMs' preferences, because they are the most widely used preference structures in the GDM and CRP specialized literature.

The remainder of this contribution is summarized below: Section 2 reviews some basic concepts related to the proposal. Section 3 introduces the P-CMCC models and their performance is shown in Section 4. Finally, Section 5 draws some conclusions and future works.

2. Preliminaries

A GDM problem is a situation in which a group of DMs has to reach a common solution for a certain decision problem.[2] Formally, such problems are modelled by a finite set of alternatives $A = \{A_1, A_2, \ldots, A_n\}$ of possible solutions for the considered problem and the DMs set $E = \{E_1, E_2, \ldots, E_m\}$ who rate the alternatives in A.

Butler and Rothstein[7] proposed several rules like the majority rule or the Borda Count to model these decision situations. However, when using such algorithms, some DMs involved in the decision problem could feel that their opinions were not sufficiently considered during the process because they fully disagree with the solution. To overcome such limitations, CRPs were developed, which support discussion processes and aim for DMs to modify their preferences to obtain a collective group opinion which satisfies all DMs up to a certain degree, the so-called consensus threshold μ.[2]

In the literature, several types of preference structures have been introduced to model the DMs' opinions. This contribution focuses on the well-known FPRs[5] because of their simplicity and easy construction. Formally, an FPR is a fuzzy set $P : A \times A \to [0,1]$ defined on the alternative set A whose membership function satisfies $P(A_i, A_j) + P(A_j, A_i) = 1$ for all $i, j \in \{1, 2, \ldots, n\}$, where $P(A_i, A_j)$ represents the degree of preference of the alternative A_i over A_j according to a certain DM.

In the literature about consensus models, MCC models[3,4] highlight as models without feedback mechanism because they allow to translate the discussion process into a mathematical programming problem in which the objective function is the cost of modifying the original preferences of the corresponding DMs. In addition, these models ensure that the absolute deviation between the modified opinions and the group collective opinion is lower than a certain parameter ε. Formally, if the original DMs' preferences are modeled by the numerical vector $(o_1, o_2, \ldots, o_m) \in \mathbb{R}^m$ and a vector

$(c_1, c_2, \ldots, c_m) \in \mathbb{R}^m_+$ is used to represent the cost of moving the opinion of each DM, the resulting consensus model would be given as:[3]

$$\min \sum_{k=1}^{m} c_k |x_k - o_k| \tag{MCC}$$
$$s.t. \ |x_k - \overline{x}| \leq \varepsilon, k = 1, 2, \ldots, m,$$

where $(x_1, \ldots, x_m)$ are the adjusted opinions of the DMs, $\overline{x}$ represents the collective opinion computed by using an arithmetic mean operator and ε is the maximum allowed absolute deviation between the modified opinions and the collective one.

Traditionally, the consensus computation has been established from two different kinds of consensus measures: those which compute the distance between DMs and group opinion and those based on the distances between DMs.[2] Nevertheless, classical MCC models use the distance between modified opinions and the collective one, i.e., $\max_{i=1,\ldots,m} |x_i - \overline{x}|$ to obtain agreed solutions which cannot guarantee to reach a predefined consensus threshold, but a maximal distance between the DMs' preferences and the collective opinion. For this reason, Labella et al.[5] generalized the former proposal by introducing CMCC models which include the above consensus measures:

$$\min \sum_{i=1}^{m} c_i |x_i - o_i|$$
$$s.t. \begin{cases} \overline{x} = F(x_1, \ldots, x_m) \\ |x_i - \overline{x}| \leq \varepsilon, i = 1, 2, \ldots, m \\ consensus(x_1, \ldots, x_n) \geq \mu, \end{cases} \tag{CMCC}$$

where $consensus(\cdot)$ represents the desired consensus measure and $\mu \in [0, 1[$ is the consensus threshold, which is fixed a priori.

3. CMCC Persuasion Model for Analyzing the Cost of Agreeing on Alternatives

This section is devoted to introducing P-CMCC models, which are able to guide DMs towards an agreement on selecting a certain alternative by modifying their preferences as little as possible. To do so, the CMCC models[5] are extended by including a linear constraint, which guarantees that the desired alternative will be chosen by the group. Since such models consider two types of consensus measures, depending on the distance between DMs and collective opinion and the distance between DMs, we propose two different nonlinear optimization P-CMCC models with nonlinear constraints.

Let $O_1, O_2, \ldots, O_m$ be the initial FPRs given by the DMs in $E = \{E_1, E_2, \ldots, E_m\}$, which contain their opinions about the alternatives $A = \{A_1, A_2, \ldots, A_n\}$. The cost of moving one unit the DM E_k's rating of the alternative A_i over A_j is modeled by using the values $c_{ij}^k \in [0, 1]$, which satisfies $\sum_{k=1}^{m} \sum_{i<j} c_{ij}^k = 1$. In order to guarantee that the chosen alternative is A_{i_0}, the corresponding consensus model is as follows:

- **Consensus model based on distance between DMs and collective opinion**

$$\min_{X_1, X_2, \ldots, X_m \in \mathcal{M}_{n \times n}([0,1])} \sum_{k=1}^{m} \sum_{i=1}^{n-1} \sum_{j=i+1}^{n} c_{ij}^k |x_{ij}^k - o_{ij}^k|$$

$$s.t. \begin{cases} \overline{x}_{ij} = \frac{1}{m} \sum_{k=1}^{m} x_{ij}^k & 1 \leq i < j \leq n, \\ |x_{ij}^k - \overline{x}_{ij}| \leq \varepsilon, & 1 \leq i < j \leq n, k = 1, 2, \ldots, m, \\ 1 - \frac{2}{mn(n-1)} \sum_{k=1}^{m} \sum_{i=1}^{n-1} \sum_{j=i+1}^{n} |x_{ij}^k - \overline{x}_{ij}| \geq \mu. & \\ x_{ij}^k + x_{ji}^k = 1 & 1 \leq i < j \leq n, k = 1, 2, \ldots, m. \\ \sum_{j=1}^{n} \overline{x}_{i_0, j} \geq \sum_{j=1}^{n} \overline{x}_{i, j} & i \neq i_0. \end{cases}$$

(P-CMCC:1)

- **Consensus model based on distance between DMs**

$$\min_{X_1, X_2, \ldots, X_m \in \mathcal{M}_{n \times n}([0,1])} \sum_{k=1}^{m} \sum_{i=1}^{n-1} \sum_{j=i+1}^{n} c_{ij}^k |x_{ij}^k - o_{ij}^k|$$

$$s.t. \begin{cases} \overline{x}_{ij} = \frac{1}{m} \sum_{k=1}^{m} x_{ij}^k & 1 \leq i < j \leq n. \\ |x_{ij}^k - \overline{x}_{ij}| \leq \varepsilon. & 1 \leq i < j \leq n, k = 1, 2, \ldots, m. \\ 1 - \frac{4}{m(m-1)n(n-1)} \sum_{k=1}^{m-1} \sum_{l=k+1}^{m} \sum_{i=1}^{n-1} \sum_{j=i+1}^{n} |x_{ij}^k - x_{ij}^l| \geq \mu. & \\ x_{ij}^k + x_{ji}^k = 1 & 1 \leq i < j \leq n, k = 1, 2, \ldots, m. \\ \sum_{j=1}^{n} \overline{x}_{i_0, j} \geq \sum_{j=1}^{n} \overline{x}_{i, j} & i \neq i_0. \end{cases}$$

(P-CMCC:2)

where $X_1, X_2, \ldots, X_m$ are the FPRs which contain DMs' modified preferences, i.e., $X_k = (x_{ij}^k) \in \mathcal{M}_{n \times n}([0, 1])$, where $x_{ij}^k + x_{ji}^k = 1 \ \forall i, j = 1, 2, \ldots, n, \ \forall k = 1, 2, \ldots, m, \overline{X}$ is the group collective opinion, the parameter $\varepsilon \in]0, 1]$ represents the maximum distance between DMs and collective opinion and $\mu \in [0, 1[$ is the consensus threshold. The GDM significance of the constraints in these models is as follows:

- The first one guarantees that the collective opinion is computed by the arithmetic mean.
- The second and the third constraints ensure that the desired consensus between the experts in the group is achieved.
- The purpose of the fourth one is to guarantee that the FPR structure is preserved during the optimization process.

• The last inequality guarantees that the overall preference of the alternative A_{io} over the others is greater than the same overall preference of any other alternative and, consequently, that the alternative A_{i_0} will be chosen by the group.

4. Case Study

Let us assume that is required to analyze the costs of guiding DMs to achieve an agreement on selecting a certain alternative regarding the costs obtained by the CMCC approach to analyze the feasibility of choosing such alternative.

Our example is based on a GDM problem that involves the financial company JaenBank, whose executive committee intends to implement a novel policy with the aim of reducing costs. Several possible measures $\{A_1, A_2, A_3, A_4\}$ are put to the financial directors of the different branches of the company $\{E_1, E_2, E_3, E_4\}$, who have to reach an agreement among themselves to implement the most convenient one according to their view. However, the top executives are interested in implementing the measure A_2, which could represent a better solution for the medium-long term. Since the financial directors are more interesting on the short-term feasibility of the policy, the top executives want to know a priori how much effort would be involved in convincing all directors to choose the A_2 policy according to their initial preferences. The financial directors have provided their opinions by means of FPRs as follows:

$$
E_1 = \begin{pmatrix} - & 0.5 & 0.4 & 0.8 \\ 0.5 & - & 0.4 & 0.8 \\ 0.6 & 0.6 & - & 0.85 \\ 0.2 & 0.2 & 0.15 & - \end{pmatrix} \quad
E_2 = \begin{pmatrix} - & 0.95 & 1.0 & 1.0 \\ 0.05 & - & 0.92 & 0.94 \\ 0.0 & 0.08 & - & 0.58 \\ 0.0 & 0.06 & 0.42 & - \end{pmatrix}
$$

$$
E_3 = \begin{pmatrix} - & 0.6 & 0.33 & 1.0 \\ 0.4 & - & 0.25 & 1.0 \\ 0.67 & 0.75 & - & 1.0 \\ 0.0 & 0.0 & 0.0 & - \end{pmatrix} \quad
E_4 = \begin{pmatrix} - & 0.57 & 0.72 & 0.58 \\ 0.43 & - & 0.67 & 0.51 \\ 0.28 & 0.33 & - & 0.34 \\ 0.42 & 0.49 & 0.66 & - \end{pmatrix}
$$

From these preferences, several consensus models are applied. Firstly, the previous GDM problem is solved by using the classical CMCC model, in which the consensus measure is based on the distance between the DMs' preferences and collective opinion. To do so, the consensus threshold is set as $\mu = 0.8$, the maximum allowed distance between DMs and collective opinion is $\varepsilon = 0.2$ and the cost of moving E_k's rating for the alternative A_i

over A_j is assumed to be $c_k = \frac{2}{mn(n-1)}$ for the sake of simplicity. Afterwards, by solving the same GDM problem with the P-CMCC:1 model, it is analyzed the cost of agreeing on each alternative to evaluate the feasibility of guiding the DMs to choose each one and provide valuable information to the executives.

Table 1. Comparative results between P-CMCC and CMCC.

Consensus model	Consensus parameters	Desired alternative	Cost	Ranking of alternatives
CMCC	$\mu = 0.8, \varepsilon = 0.2$	-	0.048	$A_1 \succ A_2 \succ A_3 \succ A_4$
P-CMCC:1	$\mu = 0.8, \varepsilon = 0.2$	A_1	0.048	$A_1 \succ A_2 \succ A_3 \succ A_4$
		A_2	0.072	$A_2 = A_1 \succ A_3 \succ A_4$
		A_3	0.081	$A_3 = A_1 \succ A_2 \succ A_4$
		A_4	0.173	$A_4 = A_1 = A_2 \succ A_3$

Remark 1. Note that the minimum cost solutions to the P-CMCC:1 model are ranked the same as the minimum cost solution to the CMCC model. From the decision-making point of view, this means that the easier way to drive the DMs to choose a predefined alternative is to convince them that such alternative is as good as the one that they initially prefer.

The results of the CMCC model (see Table 1) show that the best policy according to the financial directors' point of view (short-term and possibly selfish) is the first alternative, whose cost in a $0 - 1$ scale is equal to 0.048 and thus, the most feasible to agree their opinions. However, by analyzing the results of the persuading models, the cost of choosing the alternative A_2, the preferred one by the top executives (long-term view), is 0.072, which is a 50% extra relative cost regarding the DMs' most preferred alternative A_1. Therefore, the executive should decide if such an extra cost is worthy to adopt the desired policy. Regarding the rest of the alternatives, their selection implies not only a greater extra cost, but also more changes than the optimal solution. Particularly, the most unfeasible alternative is A_4 because its cost is the highest one and thus its selection requires the greatest change in the DMs' preferences.

5. Conclusions

This contribution has extended CMCC models to propose two automatic consensus models, namely P-CMCC:1 and P-CMCC:2, which allow analyzing the cost of driving the DMs involved in a decision process to reach a predetermined agreed solution. To do so, these models provide a measure of the cost of convincing DMs of choosing a certain alternative over the others. By comparing the cost obtained in either P-CMCC:1 or P-CMCC:2 with the solution obtained in CMCC, it is possible to determine if it would be worthy in practice to convince the DMs of adopting a concrete alternative instead of the one preferred by the group. In addition, the practical applications of these persuasion models have been shown in an illustrative example.

Future research may be addressed by using the concept of persuasive consensus models. It would be interesting to study such an approach in classical CRPs that use feedback mechanisms and take into account the DMs' attitude. Regarding formal issues, a linearized version of the model could be proposed to deal with GDM problems with many DMs.

Acknowledgments

This work is partially supported by the Spanish Ministry of Economy and Competitiveness through the Spanish National Project PGC2018-099402-B-I00, and the Postdoctoral fellow Ramón y Cajal (RYC-2017-21978), the FEDER-UJA project 1380637 and ERDF, by the Spanish Ministry of Science, Innovation and Universities through a Formación de Profesorado Universitario grant (FPU2019/01203) and by the Junta de Andalucía, Andalusian Plan for Research, Development, and Innovation (POSTDOC 21-00461).

References

1. S. Saint and J. R. Lawson, *Rules for Reaching Consensus. A Modern Approach to Decision Making* (Jossey-Bass, 1994).
2. I. Palomares, F. Estrella, L. Martínez and F. Herrera, Consensus under a fuzzy context: Taxonomy, analysis framework AFRYCA and experimental case of study, *Information Fusion* **20**, 252 (2014).
3. D. Ben-Arieh and T. Easton, Multi-criteria group consensus under linear cost opinion elasticity, *Decision Support Systems* **43**, 713 (2007).
4. G. Zhang, Y. Dong, Y. Xu and H. Li, Minimum-cost consensus models under aggregation operators, *IEEE Transactions on Systems, Man and Cybernetics-Part A: Systems and Humans* **41**, 1253 (2011).
5. A. Labella, H. Liu, R. Rodríguez and L. Martínez, A cost consensus metric for consensus reaching processes based on a comprehensive min-

imum cost model, *European Journal of Operational Research* **281**, 316 (2020).

6. B. Caillaud and J. Tirole, Consensus building: How to persuade a group, *American Economic Review* **97**, 1877 (2007).

7. C. Butler and A. Rothstein, *On Conflict and Consensus: A Handbook on Formal Consensus Decision Making* (Takoma Park, 2006).

Asymmetric distance-based comprehensive minimum cost consensus model

Wen He*, Rosa M. Rodríguez and Luis Martínez

Department of Computer Science, University of Jaén
Jaén, 23071, Spain
*whe@ujaen.es

Consensus reaching processes (CRPs) try to reach an agreement among decision makers involved in a Group Decision Making (GDM) problem to obtain an accepted solution for all of them. In CRPs without feedback, Minimum Cost Consensus (MCC) models stand out among the consensus models because of their simplicity to achieve the consensus automatically with the minimum cost, that is, to change as less as possible the initial decision makers' preferences. However, these MCC models cannot guarantee to achieve the consensus threshold, because they do not consider reaching a minimum consensus level amongst decision makers. To overcome this limitation, the Comprehensive MCC (CMCC) models have been recently proposed including a new constraint to achieve the consensus threshold. These models apply the same unit cost when the decision makers' preferences are increased or decreased, and in some GDM situations, it should not be the same. Therefore, we propose to use asymmetric costs in the CMCC models by applying an asymmetric distance that considers the direction of the change. These models are called, asymmetric distance-based CMCC models and are developed to deal with fuzzy preference relations.

Keywords: Comprehensive minimum cost consensus model; asymmetric distance; group decision making; fuzzy preference relations.

1. Introduction

In real world, due to the complexity of social and economic development, decisions are made by multiple decision makers giving rise to the Group Decision Making[1] (GDM) problems. Generally, GDM problems are modeled by preferences over a set of feasible alternatives provided by decision makers, aiming to achieve a common solution. However, this common solution could not satisfy all decision makers because some of them might feel that their opinions have been ignored. To overcome this drawback, it is necessary to require a Consensus Reaching Process (CRP)[2] to achieve agreed solutions before making a decision. A CRP is a dynamic iterative process supervised by a moderator, where decision makers modify their initial preferences in different rounds to increase the degree of agreement and reach a consensual solution acceptable to all. CRPs can be classified into two types: with feedback, in which decision makers change their opinions according to the suggestions provided by the moderator to increase the consensus degree in the next round; and without feedback, in which decision makers' opinions are modified automatically to increase the consensus degree. Within the latter ones, the outstanding and widely used model is the Minimum Cost Consensus (MCC)[3] model, which was introduced by Ben-Arieh and Easton to control the minimum cost of reaching consensus. Since then, it has become a hot research topic in CRPs.[3-6] Afterwards, Zhang et al.[6] studied how the use of different aggregation operators to obtain the collective opinion influences in the degree of agreement within the group. However, the unit cost used in all these models is the same, which does not always apply in all situations. Considering that the unit cost might be asymmetric cost, Cheng et al.[4] extended the MCC model to add a directional constraint by means of applying asymmetric costs according to the decision maker's preferences are increased or decreased. Subsequently, Labella et al.[5] pointed out that these MCC models ignore a minimum level of agreement between decision makers and proposed the Comprehensive MCC (CMCC) models including an additional minimum consensus level constraint to guarantee to achieve the consensus threshold. Therefore, considering such a situation in which the direction of the change can have different costs, we propose new Asymmetric Distance-based CMCC (AD-CMCC) models to deal with Fuzzy Preference Relations (FPRs), which utilizes asymmetric distances to identify the directions that will be applied in the asymmetric costs of adjusting decision makers' preferences.

The remainder of this paper is organized as follows. Section 2 reviews some concepts that help to come up with new models. Section 3 introduces the AD-CMCC models, which use asymmetric distances to model the objective and constraint functions. Section 4 briefly shows an illustrative example to prove the feasibility and performance of the proposed model. Finally, some conclusions and future works are pointed out in Section 5.

2. Preliminaries

This section briefly reviews some concepts such as asymmetric distance, CRP for GDM dealing with FPRs, and CMCC model. All of them are the basis for proposing new AD-CMCC models.

2.1. Asymmetric distance

Compared with the general distance, the asymmetric distance[7] does not satisfy the symmetry property because it implies direction.

Definition 2.1.[7] Let X be a non-empty set and $\mathbf{R}$ be the set of all real numbers. The function $d : X \times X \to \mathbf{R}$ is an asymmetric distance if d satisfies

- **Non-negativity:** $\forall x, y \in X$, $d(x,y) \geq 0$ and $d(x,x) = 0$;
- **Weak symmetry:** $\forall x, y \in X$, $d(x,y) = d(y,x) = 0$ implies $x = y$;
- **Triangle inequality:** $d(x,z) \leq d(x,y) + d(y,z)$ for all $x, y, z \in X$.

If the symmetry property, i.e., $\forall x, y \in X$, $d(x,y) = d(y,x)$, is added to the above definition, then it becomes to the general distance. The widely used asymmetric distance[7] in the existing literature is given as follows:

$$d(x,y) = \max\{y - x, 0\} = (y - x)^+ . \tag{1}$$

2.2. A GDM dealing with FPRs

The classical solution process of a GDM problem is a selection process,[1] which aims to select an appropriate alternative/s among a set of feasible alternatives. However, there may be cases where decision makers do not accept the solution because some of them may feel that their opinions have not been taken into account. To overcome this limitation, a CRP[2,5] needs to be added before the selection process to achieve an agreed solution within the group.

Usually, a GDM problem is constructed by the following elements:[8] (i) a problem to be solved; (ii) a set of feasible alternatives, i.e., $\mathcal{A} = \{\mathcal{A}_1, \mathcal{A}_2, \ldots, \mathcal{A}_n\}$ $(n \geq 2)$; and (iii) a group of multiple decision makers, i.e., $E = \{e_1, e_2, \ldots, e_m\}$ $(m \geq 2)$, to expressing their individual opinions over the alternatives set $\mathcal{A}$. The information is often represented by a reciprocal FPR[9] matrix $P = (p_{ij})_{n \times n}$ verifying $p_{ij}, p_{ji} \in [0,1]$ and $p_{ij} + p_{ji} = 1$, in which p_{ij} $(\forall i, j = 1, 2, \ldots, n)$ is interpreted as the preference degree of alternative $\mathcal{A}_i$ over $\mathcal{A}_j$: (i) $p_{ij} > 0.5$ indicates that $\mathcal{A}_i$ is preferred to $\mathcal{A}_j$; (ii) $p_{ij} = 1$ indicates that $\mathcal{A}_i$ is absolutely preferred to $\mathcal{A}_j$; and (iii) $p_{ij} = 0.5$ indicates indifference between $\mathcal{A}_i$ and $\mathcal{A}_j$.

2.3. CMCC model

Consensus models can be classified into two categories: (i) with feedback, when decision makers are asked to change their preferences following the guidance provided by the moderator and (ii) without feedback, when the preferences are changed automatically. Among the consensus models with non-feedback, the MCC models stand out as linear programming models that find an optimal solution to achieve the consensus with the minimum cost. However, Labella et al.[5] pointed out that this is not enough to guarantee to achieve the consensus threshold, and thus, they proposed CMCC models which include an additional constraint to achieve a minimum consensus level amongst decision makers. The CMCC model dealing with FPRs is defined as follows:

$$(\mathbf{M-1}) \quad \min \quad \sum_{i=1}^{n-1} \sum_{j=i+1}^{n} \sum_{k=1}^{m} c_k |p_{ij}'^k - p_{ij}^k|$$

$$\text{s.t.} \quad \begin{cases} p_{ij}^c = \sum_{k=1}^{m} \omega_k p_{ij}'^k; & \\ & k = 1, 2, \ldots, m, \\ |p_{ij}^c - p_{ij}'^k| \le \varepsilon, & i = 1, 2, \ldots, n-1, \\ & j = i+1, \ldots, n; \\ \mathbf{C}\left(P_1', P_2', \ldots, P_m'\right) \ge \alpha, & \end{cases}$$

where $P_k = \left(p_{ij}^k\right)_{n \times n}$, $P_k' = \left(p_{ij}'^k\right)_{n \times n}$ and $P_c = \left(p_{ij}^c\right)_{n \times n}$ represent the initial opinions, the adjusted consensus opinions, and the collective opinions, respectively. And ω_k is the kth decision maker's weight satisfying $\omega_k \in [0, 1]$ and $\sum_{k=1}^{m} \omega_k = 1$. $\mathbf{C}(\cdot)$ represents the consensus level achieved, the parameter α is a predefined consensus threshold, ε is the maximum acceptable distance between decision makers' opinion and the collective opinion.

It should be pointed out that $\mathbf{C}(\cdot)$ can be calculated by the distance between decision makers' opinions or the distance between each decision maker's opinion and the collective opinion (see[5] for more details).

3. Novel AD-CMCC Model Dealing with FPRs

Distance plays a key role in the CMCC model, where the involved distances are computed by symmetric distances as $|p_{ij}'^k - p_{ij}^k|$ and $|p_{ij}^c - p_{ij}'^k|$, respectively. However, Cheng et al.[4] pointed out that the cost of increasing or decreasing the preferences should be different in some GDM problems, which implies using asymmetric costs. Therefore, we propose new AD-CMCC models that extends the CMCC models to consider the asymmetric costs and asymmetric distance.

For sake of clarity and simplicity, let c_i^U and c_i^D represent unit costs in the increasing and decreasing directions identified by asymmetric distances $d(x, y) = (y - x)^+$, then the AD-CMCC model dealing with FPRs is defined as follows:

$$(\mathbf{M-2}) \quad \min \sum_{k=1}^{m} \sum_{i=1}^{n-1} \sum_{j=i+1}^{n} \left[c_k^U \left(p_{ij}'^k - p_{ij}^k \right)^+ + c_k^D \left(p_{ij}^k - p_{ij}'^k \right)^+ \right]$$

$$\text{s.t.} \begin{cases} p_{ij}'^k - \left(p_{ij}'^k - p_{ij}^k \right)^+ + \left(p_{ij}^k - p_{ij}'^k \right)^+ = p_{ij}^k, & \begin{aligned} k &= 1, 2, \ldots, m, \\ i &= 1, 2, \ldots, n, \\ j &= 1, 2, \ldots, n; \end{aligned} \\ p_{ij}^c = \sum_{k=1}^{m} \omega_k p_{ij}'^k; & \\ 0 \le \left(p_{ij}^c - p_{ij}'^k \right)^+, \left(p_{ij}'^k - p_{ij}^c \right)^+ \le \varepsilon, & \begin{aligned} k &= 1, 2, \ldots, m, \\ i &= 1, 2, \ldots, n, \\ j &= 1, 2, \ldots, n; \end{aligned} \\ \mathbf{C}\left(P_1', P_2', \ldots, P_m' \right) \ge \alpha, & \end{cases}$$

where $\mathbf{C}(\cdot)$ represents the achieved consensus level based on the asymmetric distance, the parameters α and ε are the same as $\mathbf{Model-1}$.

Therefore, due to the different extensions of the consensus measures $\mathbf{C}(\cdot)$ introduced by Labella,[5] the following AD-CMCC models dealing with FPRs can be proposed:

(i) $\mathbf{C}(\cdot)$ is computed based on the asymmetric distance[10] between each decision maker's opinion and the collective opinion:

$$(\mathbf{M-2_1}) \quad \min \sum_{k=1}^{m} \sum_{i=1}^{n-1} \sum_{j=i+1}^{n} \left[c_k^U \left(p_{ij}'^k - p_{ij}^k \right)^+ + c_k^D \left(p_{ij}^k - p_{ij}'^k \right)^+ \right]$$

$$\text{s.t.} \begin{cases} p_{ij}'^k - \left(p_{ij}'^k - p_{ij}^k \right)^+ + \left(p_{ij}^k - p_{ij}'^k \right)^+ = p_{ij}^k, & \begin{aligned} k &= 1, 2, \ldots, m, \\ i &= 1, 2, \ldots, n, \\ j &= 1, 2, \ldots, n; \end{aligned} \\ p_{ij}^c = \sum_{k=1}^{m} \omega_k p_{ij}'^k; & \\ 0 \le \left(p_{ij}^c - p_{ij}'^k \right)^+, \left(p_{ij}'^k - p_{ij}^c \right)^+ \le \varepsilon, & \begin{aligned} k &= 1, 2, \ldots, m, \\ i &= 1, 2, \ldots, n, \\ j &= 1, 2, \ldots, n; \end{aligned} \\ 1 - \frac{2}{n(n-1)} \sqrt[\lambda]{\sum_{k=1}^{m} \sum_{i=1}^{n} \sum_{j=1}^{n} \omega_k \left(\left(p_{ij}^c - p_{ij}'^k \right)^+ \right)^\lambda} \ge \alpha, & \lambda \ge 1. \end{cases}$$

Noticing that in the last constraint $\mathbf{C}(\cdot)$ can also use $\left(p_{ij}^{\prime k} - p_{ij}^{c}\right)^{+}$ instead of $\left(p_{ij}^{c} - p_{ij}^{\prime k}\right)^{+}$ without changing the result.

(ii) $\mathbf{C}(\cdot)$ is computed based on the asymmetric distance[10] between decision makers' opinions:

$$(\mathbf{M}-\mathbf{2_2}) \quad \min \quad \sum_{k=1}^{m} \sum_{i=1}^{n-1} \sum_{j=i+1}^{n} \left[c_k^U \left(p_{ij}^{\prime k} - p_{ij}^{k}\right)^{+} + c_k^D \left(p_{ij}^{k} - p_{ij}^{\prime k}\right)^{+} \right]$$

s.t.
$$
\begin{cases}
p_{ij}^{\prime k} - \left(p_{ij}^{\prime k} - p_{ij}^{k}\right)^{+} + \left(p_{ij}^{k} - p_{ij}^{\prime k}\right)^{+} = p_{ij}^{k}, & \begin{aligned} k &= 1, 2, \ldots, m, \\ i &= 1, 2, \ldots, n, \\ j &= 1, 2, \ldots, n; \end{aligned} \\[2ex]
p_{ij}^{c} = \sum_{k=1}^{m} \omega_k p_{ij}^{\prime k}; & \\[2ex]
0 \le \left(p_{ij}^{c} - p_{ij}^{\prime k}\right)^{+}, \left(p_{ij}^{\prime k} - p_{ij}^{c}\right)^{+} \le \varepsilon, & \begin{aligned} k &= 1, 2, \ldots, m, \\ i &= 1, 2, \ldots, n, \\ j &= 1, 2, \ldots, n; \end{aligned} \\[2ex]
1 - \dfrac{2}{n(n-1)} \sqrt[\lambda]{\sum_{i=1}^{n} \sum_{j=1}^{n} \sum_{k=1}^{m} \sum_{l=1}^{m} \frac{\omega_l + \omega_k}{m-1} \left(\left(p_{ij}^{\prime l} - p_{ij}^{\prime k}\right)^{+} \right)^{\lambda}} \ge \alpha, & \lambda \ge 1.
\end{cases}
$$

Similarly, in the last constraint $\mathbf{C}(\cdot)$ can also use $\left(p_{ij}^{\prime l} - p_{ij}^{\prime k}\right)^{+}$ to replace $\left(p_{ij}^{\prime k} - p_{ij}^{\prime l}\right)^{+}$ for computation.

4. Illustrative Example

Due to the limited space, we will only apply the model $\mathbf{M}-\mathbf{2_1}$ with $\lambda = 1$ to show the applicability and effectiveness of the proposed AD-CMCC models dealing with FPRs. In this problem, there are three decision makers e_1, e_2, e_3 associated with the same weights $(\omega_1, \omega_2, \omega_3)^T = \left(\frac{1}{3}, \frac{1}{3}, \frac{1}{3}\right)^T$, and with respectively unit costs $\left(c_1^U, c_2^U, c_3^U\right)^T = (2, 4, 3)^T$ and $\left(c_1^D, c_2^D, c_3^D\right)^T = (5, 4, 2)^T$. The initial assessments over the four alternatives $\mathcal{A} = \{\mathcal{A}_1, \mathcal{A}_2, \mathcal{A}_3, \mathcal{A}_4\}$ using reciprocal FPRs, $P_k = \left(p_{ij}^k\right)_{4\times 4}$ $(k = 1, 2, 3)$, are shown as follows:

$$
P_1 = \begin{pmatrix} 0.5 & 0.6 & 0.3 & 0.3 \\ 0.4 & 0.5 & 0.2 & 0.9 \\ 0.7 & 0.8 & 0.5 & 1 \\ 0.7 & 0.1 & 0 & 0.5 \end{pmatrix}; \quad
P_2 = \begin{pmatrix} 0.5 & 0.7 & 0.5 & 0.9 \\ 0.3 & 0.5 & 0.5 & 0.6 \\ 0.5 & 0.5 & 0.5 & 0.1 \\ 0.1 & 0.4 & 0.9 & 0.5 \end{pmatrix}; \quad
P_3 = \begin{pmatrix} 0.5 & 0.7 & 0.4 & 0.5 \\ 0.3 & 0.5 & 0.9 & 0.1 \\ 0.6 & 0.1 & 0.5 & 0.7 \\ 0.5 & 0.9 & 0.3 & 0.5 \end{pmatrix}.
$$

Table 1. The minimum cost according to different values of ε and α of $\mathbf{M} - \mathbf{2_1}$.

cost	$\alpha = 0.65$	$\alpha = 0.7$	$\alpha = 0.75$	$\alpha = 0.8$	$\alpha = 0.85$	$\alpha = 0.9$	$\alpha = 0.95$
$\varepsilon = 0.05$	9.299	9.299	9.299	9.299	9.549	9.950	10.450
$\varepsilon = 0.1$	7.725	8.000	8.350	8.800	9.250	9.799	10.425
$\varepsilon = 0.15$	7.199	7.649	8.100	8.550	9.150	9.750	10.425
$\varepsilon = 0.2$	6.949	7.400	7.900	8.500	9.100	9.750	10.425
$\varepsilon = 0.25$	6.699	7.250	7.850	8.450	9.075	9.750	10.425
$\varepsilon = 0.3$	6.599	7.190	7.800	8.400	9.075	9.750	10.425

The results are shown in Table 1. Obviously, $\mathbf{C}\,(\cdot)$ is highly dependent on the value of ε, therefore, we can conclude that:

(i) Obviously, for a fixed α, the minimum cost decreases as the value of ε increases; For a given ε, the minimum cost increases as the value of α increases.

(ii) There are some special cases. For instance, for $\varepsilon = 0.05$, if $\alpha \leq 0.8$, the minimum cost is a constant 9.299; Similarly, $\alpha = 0.95$, the minimum cost is a constant 10.425 when $\varepsilon \geq 0.1$.

5. Conclusions and Future Work

Consensual solutions are becoming increasingly important in GDM problems, driving to include CRPs in the solving process. There are CRPs with feedback and without feedback. In the latter case, it stands out the MCC models, which aims to achieve consensus with minimal cost. Recently, a CMCC model has been proposed to guarantee the consensus between decision makers. However, the cost of increasing or decreasing the decision makers' preferences are usually equal and sometimes they might be different. Thus, in this contribution, AD-CMCC models that deal with FPRs using an asymmetric distance have been presented, where the asymmetric distance provides the direction to apply the asymmetric costs when decision makers' preferences are increased or decreased.

In future research, we will study the application of the proposed model to linguistic information.

Acknowledgments

This work is partially supported by the Spanish Ministry of Economy and Competitiveness through the Spanish National Project PGC2018-099402-B-I00, and the Postdoctoral fellow Ramón y Cajal (RYC-2017-21978), the FEDER-UJA project 1380637 and ERDF.

References

1. M. Roubens, Fuzzy sets and decision analysis, *Fuzzy sets and systems* **90**, 199 (1997).
2. C. L. Butler and A. Rothstein, *On conflict and consensus: A handbook on formal consensus decisionmaking* (Citeseer, 2007).
3. D. Ben-Arieh and T. Easton, Multi-criteria group consensus under linear cost opinion elasticity, *Decision support systems* **43**, 713 (2007).
4. D. Cheng, Z. Zhou, F. Cheng, Y. Zhou and Y. Xie, Modeling the minimum cost consensus problem in an asymmetric costs context, *European Journal of Operational Research* **270**, 1122 (2018).
5. Á. Labella, H. Liu, R. M. Rodríguez and L. Martinez, A cost consensus metric for consensus reaching processes based on a comprehensive minimum cost model, *European Journal of Operational Research* **281**, 316 (2020).
6. G. Zhang, Y. Dong, Y. Xu and H. Li, Minimum-cost consensus models under aggregation operators, *IEEE Transactions on Systems, Man, and Cybernetics-Part A: Systems and Humans* **41**, 1253 (2011).
7. F. Plastria, Asymmetric distances, semidirected networks and majority in fermat–weber problems, *Annals of Operations Research* **167**, 121 (2009).
8. J. Kacprzyk, Group decision making with a fuzzy linguistic majority, *Fuzzy sets and systems* **18**, 105 (1986).
9. K. Nakamura, Preference relations on a set of fuzzy utilities as a basis for decision making, *Fuzzy sets and systems* **20**, 147 (1986).
10. X. Blasco, G. Reynoso-Meza, E. A. Sánchez Pérez and J. V. Sánchez Pérez, Asymmetric distances to improve n-dimensional pareto fronts graphical analysis, *Information Sciences* **340-341**, 228 (2016).

Correlation analysis of traffic accidents based on multiple model fusion

Jian Wang* and Jin Guo

*School of Information Science and Technology, Southwest Jiaotong University
Chengdu, 611756, China*
* wj_xnjd@my.swjtu.edu.cn
www.swjtu.edu.cn

Shanshan Dong, Bin Bian and Hongjun Wang†

*School of Computing and Artificial Intelligence, Southwest Jiaotong University
Chengdu, 611756, China*
† wanghongjun@swjtu.edu.cn
www.swjtu.edu.cn

For a long time, China's transportation safety production situation has been generally stable. However, the situation is still grim, with frequent accidents, and the number of deaths and accidents in road traffic accidents is still high. Therefore, it will be of great use to analyze and study the causes of traffic accidents. The main work of this paper is to explore the correlation between accident factors and traffic accident severity. According to the relevant knowledge of machine learning, the influence and correlation of human, vehicle, road and environmental factors on the severity of traffic accidents are analyzed by using three correlation coefficients and the maximum information coefficient of statistics. The aim is to improve the current road safety situation and thus reduce the occurrence of traffic accidents. The results show that the severity of traffic accidents has the greatest correlation with the types of casualties and whether there is police intervention, and has a great correlation with pedestrians, the number of vehicles causing traffic accidents and the level of roads.

Keywords: Traffic accident; correlation analysis; maximal information coefficient.

1. Introduction

The analysis of the causes of traffic accidents is of great practical importance to reduce casualties and property losses, and to help road safety workers to grasp the characteristics of traffic accidents and thus to improve the current road safety situation. At present, most scholars only attribute traffic accident causation to a single factor for their research,[1,2] ignoring the fact that the traffic system is a complex dynamic system. Although these indicators are simple and intuitive, they cannot deal with the data in essence or from the perspective of connection, and cannot find the main contradiction of traffic accidents.[3]

The correlation coefficient is a statistical indicator reflecting the closeness of the relationship between variables, and this paper is to explore the closeness between accident factors and accident severity, so it is feasible to apply the correlation analysis method to the analysis and research of traffic accidents.

To sum up, this paper uses statistical correlation coefficients such as Pearson, the three major coefficients, to quantitatively describe the correlation between traffic accident factors and traffic accident severity, and to integrate the results obtained from multiple models in a scientific and reasonable way.

The contributions of this paper are as follows: first, through experiments, it is proved that it is feasible to apply the three correlation coefficients and the maximum information coefficient of statistics to the analysis and research of traffic accident data. Second, to improve road safety to provide a scientific basis to help road safety workers to grasp the characteristics of traffic accidents and improve the current road safety situation.

2. Related Work

According to literature research, corresponding studies on traffic accident data have been conducted at home and abroad, and a more systematic analysis of traffic accident classification, accident characteristics, influencing factors and other research contents have been conducted from different perspectives. Among the many factors affecting transportation accidents, association rule theory and rough set theory analysis are widely used.[4] Many scholars have also chosen the correlation degree analysis among gray factors in gray theory to conduct their research. Gray theory is an applied mathematical discipline that studies phenomena in which information is partly clear and partly unclear and carries uncertainty. In the objective world, a large number of gray systems exist.

As early as 1998, Chai et al.[5] used gray prediction and correlation analysis in gray theory to calculate predictions for three years of traffic accident data in a city so as to determine the primary and secondary relationships among factors. So far, many other scholars have proposed derivative algorithms for grayscale correlation, including.[6] In-depth analysis of traffic accident causation using a fusion of T-S fuzzy fault trees and Bayesian networks has also been used, followed by the identification of major causative factors using Bayesian networks and two-way inference of the importance and posterior probability of the underlying events.

Most of the traffic accident severity research methods use gray theory, and as the dimensionality of accident data increases, machine learning models can improve the efficiency of data analysis and visual interpretation of the results. For this reason, this paper applies the three major correlation coefficients of statistics and the maximum information coefficient in the analysis and study of traffic accident data.

3. Model

In this section, we focus on the models used. In this paper, we mainly use the statistical three main correlation coefficients, and since the three main correlation coefficients are applicable to linear data or simple monotonic nonlinear data, in order to make our experimental results more credible, we also use the maximum information coefficient, which is applicable to both linear and nonlinear data and has good robustness. In the experimental part, we apply these models to traffic accident data sets, where $D = \{X, Y\}, X = \{x_1, x_2, ..., x_n\}, Y = \{y\}$, X represents the accident factors that affect traffic accidents, and Y represents the severity of traffic accidents.

3.1. Pearson simple correlation coefficient

In this paper, we use Pearson correlation coefficient to measure the linear correlation between traffic accident influencing factor X and traffic accident severity Y, which can be calculated by: $r_p = \frac{\sum_{i=1}^{n}(x_i - \bar{x})(y_i - \bar{y})}{\sqrt{\sum_{i=1}^{n}(x_i - \bar{x})^2 \sum_{i=1}^{n}(y_i - \bar{y})^2}}$, where $\bar{x}$ and $\bar{y}$ represent the average value of samples respectively. The value range of correlation coefficient r_p is [-1,1], that is, $|r_p| \leq 1$. The larger $|r_p|$, the higher the correlation between the two variables x_i and y_i.[7]

3.2. Spearman rank correlation coefficient

Based on the rank order magnitude of the traffic accident influencing factor X and the severity of the traffic accident Y, which can be specifically expressed as: $r_s = \frac{\sum_{i=1}^{n}(r_i - \bar{r})(s_i - \bar{s})}{\sqrt{\sum_{i=1}^{n}(r_i - \bar{r})^2 \sum_{i=1}^{n}(s_i - \bar{s})^2}}$, where r_i and s_i represent the rank of x_i and y_i respectively.

3.3. Kendall rank correlation coefficient

Kendall correlation coefficient was proposed by Kendall[8] in 1938 as a new method to calculate the rank correlation coefficient. In addition, Kendall correlation coefficient has three subdivisions that need attention. In this paper, harmony coefficient is selected to represent the correlation between accident factors and traffic accident severity according to the dataset used in this paper. The calculation formula is: $r_k = 1 - \frac{4\sum_i}{n(n-1)}$, where n is the sample size, $\sum_i$ is the total number of transpositions.

3.4. Maximum Information Coefficient

Maximum Information Coefficient (MIC) is a modern correlation analysis method. Reshef et al.[9] firstly proposed the MIC based on mutual information theory on Science in 2011, also known as Maximum Mutual Information Coefficient, which can be calculated by: $r_m = \max_{|X|*|Y|<B} \left(\frac{\max_d \left(\sum_{x \in X, y \in Y} P(x,y) \log T \right)}{\log \min (|X|,|Y|)} \right)$, of which $T = \frac{P(x,y)}{\sum_{x \in X} P(x,y) \sum_{y \in Y} P(x,y)}$, $P(x,y) = \frac{C_{x,y}}{C}$, $B = f(data\_size) = n^{0.6}$.

In the calculation method of MIC measurement, the grid of $m * n$ will be used to divide the data space. $P(x,y)$ is the frequency estimation of the data points falling in the (x,y) grid, where $C_{x,y}$ is the total number of data points falling in the (x,y) grid and C is the total number of data points and d is different grid.

3.5. Fusing

In machine learning, different results are obtained by applying different algorithms on the same dataset, and some method of fusing multiple results is needed to balance the single model to make incorrect predictions.[10] The fusion approach used in this paper can be represented by the equation. $r_f = \frac{|r_p|+|r_s|+|r_k|+r_m}{4}$. Since the values of r_p, r_s and r_k are all in (-1,1), it is necessary to take the absolute values, and finally take the average to obtain r_f.

4. Experiments

In this section, the dataset is first introduced, followed by and comparative analysis of the results of the four algorithms, and finally the experimental results are fused and briefly analyzed by a custom fusion method.

4.1. Datasets

The dataset comes from the UK official sector collecting traffic data from 2000 to 2016, recording more than 1.6 million accidents, making it one of the most comprehensive traffic data available. 370 datasets were generated from the traffic data, and 12 datasets were selected for experiments, whose details are given by Table 1.

Table 1. Description of experimental datasets.

No.	Dataset	Objects	Features
D1/6	Accidents0514_130/135	10000	30
D7/12	Casualties0514_10/15	10000	14

4.2. Results

In this section, correlation analysis is performed on 12 datasets using four different algorithms and the results are tallied. The top 12 attributes with the highest correlation are selected from each algorithm on each dataset, as shown in Table 2, Table 3. A_n denotes the attribute name, and the value in parentheses is the relevance value of that attribute. Finally, the results obtained by the four algorithms on each dataset were fused, and the results are shown in the lower part of Table 3.

5. Conclusion

In this paper, correlation analysis is applied to the study of traffic accident data, incorporating the results of multiple algorithms as the final result, from which accident factors with high correlation with accident severity are derived. The occurrence of traffic accidents is related to the level of the road, the control of the intersection and the presence or absence of police intervention to guide that section of the road. The most important correlation is with the type of casualty, pedestrian status, pedestrian location and type and number of vehicles involved in the accident.

Table 2. Result table.

Results of Pearson

DataSet	D1	D2	D3	D4	D5	D6	D7	D8	D9	D10	D11	D12
1	A8(0.1443)	A8(0.1223)	A8(0.1122)	A8(0.1095)	A8(0.1199)	A8(0.1235)	B1(0.1011)	B10(0.1379)	B10(0.1379)	B7(0.1102)	B1(0.0948)	B7(0.0898)
2	A17(0.0752)	A17(0.0865)	A17(0.0940)	A17(0.0540)	A17(0.0740)	A17(0.0703)	B7(0.0768)	B1(0.1104)	B1(0.0940)	B10(0.0940)	B7(0.0936)	B10(0.0669)
3	A18(0.0748)	A18(0.0838)	A18(0.0409)	A18(0.0536)	A18(0.0738)	A18(0.0509)	B8(0.0565)	B7(0.0836)	B7(0.0816)	B1(0.0680)	B8(0.0768)	B1(0.0480)
4	A9(0.0666)	A9(0.0837)	A9(0.0323)	A9(0.0517)	A9(0.0665)	A9(0.0459)	B10(0.0515)	B8(0.0403)	B8(0.0369)	B9(0.0439)	B10(0.0476)	B9(0.0463)
5	A19(0.0546)	A19(0.0700)	A19(0.0226)	A19(0.0502)	A19(0.0476)	A19(0.0433)	B9(0.0515)	B9(0.0395)	B9(0.0313)	B8(0.0197)	B9(0.0415)	B8(0.0266)
6	A7(0.0325)	A7(0.0592)	A7(0.0179)	A7(0.0429)	A7(0.0358)	A7(0.0247)	B12(0.0268)	B12(0.0240)	B12(0.0287)	B11(0.0179)	B12(0.0119)	B11(0.0257)
7	A20(0.0293)	A20(0.0405)	A20(0.0154)	A20(0.0362)	A20(0.0333)	A20(0.0246)	B11(-0.0216)	B11(-0.0072)	B11(0.0283)	B12(0.0044)	B11(-0.0061)	B12(0.0026)
8	A21(0.0263)	A21(0.0396)	A21(0.0152)	A21(0.0277)	A21(0.0317)	A21(0.0216)	B6(-0.0265)	B6(-0.0139)	B5(-0.0250)	B5(-0.0257)	B5(-0.0197)	B5(-0.0197)
9	A22(0.0154)	A22(0.0230)	A22(0.0124)	A22(0.0197)	A22(0.0290)	A22(0.0213)	B5(-0.0304)	B5(-0.0444)	B6(-0.0336)	B6(-0.0295)	B6(-0.0292)	B6(-0.0215)
10	A2(0.0115)	A2(0.0218)	A2(0.0123)	A2(0.0177)	A2(0.0146)	A2(0.0180)	B2(-0.1039)	B3(-0.1047)	B3(-0.1073)	B2(-0.0431)	B2(-0.0624)	B2(-0.0392)
11	A1(0.0114)	A1(0.0099)	A1(0.0109)	A1(0.0138)	A1(0.0135)	A1(0.0176)	B3(-0.1273)	B2(-0.1184)	B2(-0.1146)	B3(-0.0562)	B3(-0.0834)	B3(-0.0694)
12	A23(0.0104)	A23(0.0055)	A23(0.0031)	A23(0.0031)	A23(0.0034)	A23(0.0103)	B4(-0.1479)	B4(-0.1316)	B4(-0.1400)	B4(-0.0820)	B4(-0.1013)	B4(-0.0781)

Results of Spearman

DataSet	D1	D2	D3	D4	D5	D6	D7	D8	D9	D10	D11	D12
1	A8(0.1446)	A9(0.1244)	A8(0.1216)	A8(0.1097)	A8(0.1191)	A8(0.1238)	B1(0.2107)	B1(0.1907)	B1(0.1893)	B1(0.1465)	B1(0.1929)	B1(0.1074)
2	A9(0.1008)	A8(0.1110)	A9(0.1179)	A9(0.0740)	A9(0.0839)	A9(0.0947)	B7(0.0787)	B7(0.1482)	B7(0.1470)	B7(0.1090)	B7(0.0958)	B7(0.0907)
3	A17(0.0658)	A7(0.0463)	A17(0.0937)	A17(0.0521)	A17(0.0668)	A17(0.0580)	B8(0.0598)	B8(0.0846)	B8(0.0821)	B8(0.1055)	B8(0.0554)	B8(0.0759)
4	A18(0.0656)	A17(0.0313)	A18(0.0936)	A18(0.0465)	A18(0.0647)	A19(0.0518)	B9(0.0560)	B9(0.0500)	B9(0.0458)	B9(0.0537)	B9(0.0544)	B9(0.0524)
5	A19(0.0619)	A19(0.0242)	A19(0.0783)	A19(0.0431)	A19(0.0518)	A18(0.0440)	B10(0.0479)	B10(0.0457)	B10(0.0457)	B10(0.0189)	B12(0.0216)	B10(0.0323)
6	A7(0.0578)	A22(0.0235)	A7(0.0581)	A7(0.0424)	A7(0.0509)	A7(0.0357)	B12(0.0304)	B12(0.0399)	B12(0.0315)	B6(0.0176)	B10(0.0175)	B12(0.0274)
7	A20(0.0390)	A18(0.0209)	A20(0.0459)	A20(0.0412)	A20(0.0473)	A20(0.0343)	B5(0.0000)	B5(0.0273)	B5(0.0273)	B12(0.0175)	B5(-0.0067)	B5(0.0268)
8	A21(0.0147)	A20(0.0104)	A21(0.0456)	A21(0.0410)	A21(0.0445)	A21(0.0283)	B6(-0.0036)	B6(-0.0070)	B11(-0.0153)	B5(0.0112)	B11(-0.0099)	B6(-0.0044)
9	A1(0.0130)	A21(0.0102)	A1(0.0307)	A1(0.0161)	A1(0.0373)	A1(0.0238)	B11(-0.0239)	B11(-0.0081)	B6(-0.0161)	B11(-0.0188)	B6(-0.0161)	B11(-0.0063)
10	A23(0.0130)	A27(0.0057)	A22(0.0235)	A2(0.0148)	A2(0.0365)	A2(0.0149)	B2(-0.0813)	B2(-0.1045)	B2(-0.0916)	B2(-0.0244)	B2(-0.0429)	B2(-0.0237)
11	A22(0.0126)	A1(0.0049)	A27(0.0057)	A22(0.0069)	A22(0.0307)	A22(0.0138)	B3(-0.1591)	B3(-0.1567)	B3(-0.1576)	B3(-0.0874)	B3(-0.1142)	B3(-0.0844)
12	A27(0.0087)	A23(0.0046)	A23(0.0046)	A27(0.0041)	A27(0.0041)	A27(0.0136)	B4(-0.1601)	B4(-0.1572)	B4(-0.1579)	B4(-0.0879)	B4(-0.1145)	B4(-0.0863)

Results of Kendall

DataSet	D1	D2	D3	D4	D5	D6	D7	D8	D9	D10	D11	D12
1	A8(0.1436)	A9(0.1127)	A8(0.1209)	A8(0.1091)	A8(0.1183)	A8(0.1232)	B1(0.1960)	B1(0.1766)	B1(0.1764)	B1(0.1372)	B1(0.1784)	B1(0.0996)
2	A9(0.0967)	A8(0.1105)	A9(0.1127)	A9(0.0707)	A9(0.0800)	A9(0.0904)	B7(0.0783)	B7(0.1456)	B7(0.1444)	B7(0.1061)	B7(0.0952)	B7(0.0902)
3	A17(0.0632)	A7(0.0445)	A17(0.0761)	A17(0.0474)	A17(0.0647)	A17(0.0539)	B8(0.0591)	B8(0.0842)	B8(0.0818)	B8(0.1048)	B8(0.0736)	B8(0.0742)
4	A18(0.0610)	A17(0.0299)	A18(0.0760)	A18(0.0446)	A18(0.0597)	A18(0.0426)	B9(0.0544)	B9(0.0485)	B9(0.0445)	B9(0.0520)	B9(0.0527)	B9(0.0507)
5	A19(0.0566)	A19(0.0221)	A19(0.0731)	A19(0.0398)	A19(0.0469)	A19(0.0325)	B10(0.0470)	B10(0.0470)	B10(0.0339)	B10(0.0187)	B10(0.0403)	B10(0.0301)
6	A7(0.0528)	A18(0.0210)	A7(0.0559)	A7(0.0393)	A7(0.0463)	A7(0.0290)	B12(0.0291)	B12(0.0396)	B12(0.0306)	B12(0.0168)	B12(0.0207)	B12(0.0266)
7	A20(0.0377)	A22(0.0197)	A20(0.0426)	A20(0.0393)	A20(0.0416)	A20(0.0290)	B5(0.0000)	B5(-0.0057)	B5(0.0271)	B5(0.0104)	B5(-0.0058)	B5(0.0263)
8	A21(0.0135)	A20(0.0135)	A21(0.0412)	A21(0.0389)	A22(0.0356)	A21(0.0258)	B6(-0.0031)	B6(-0.0065)	B6(0.0146)	B6(-0.0131)	B6(-0.0060)	B6(-0.0038)
9	A22(0.0124)	A21(0.0101)	A22(0.0295)	A22(0.0155)	A21(0.0258)	A22(0.0233)	B11(-0.0230)	B11(-0.0070)	B11(0.0133)	B11(-0.0162)	B11(-0.0093)	B11(-0.0052)
10	A1(0.0105)	A27(0.0057)	A1(0.0230)	A1(0.0122)	A2(0.0134)	A1(0.0149)	B2(-0.0777)	B2(-0.0995)	B2(-0.0877)	B2(-0.0236)	B2(-0.0413)	B2(-0.0228)
11	A2(0.0104)	A1(0.0042)	A2(0.0210)	A2(0.0063)	A27(0.0121)	A2(0.0134)	B3(-0.1543)	B3(-0.1516)	B3(-0.1533)	B3(-0.0854)	B3(-0.1113)	B3(-0.0824)
12	A27(0.0086)	A2(0.0020)	A27(0.0057)	A27(0.0041)	A1(0.0031)	A27(0.0111)	B4(-0.1558)	B4(-0.1519)	B4(-0.1538)	B4(-0.0861)	B4(-0.1118)	B4(-0.0841)

Table 3. Result table.

DataSet.	D1	D2	D3	D4	D5	D6	D7	D8	D9	D10	D11	D12
						Results of MIC						
1	A1(0.0684)	A4(0.0620)	A2(0.0687)	A2(0.0637)	A2(0.0654)	A3(0.0628)	B1(0.0450)	B1(0.0401)	B1(0.0351)	B1(0.0326)	B1(0.0418)	B1(0.0198)
2	A2(0.0681)	A2(0.0617)	A3(0.0679)	A3(0.0621)	A3(0.0617)	A1(0.0622)	B5(0.0162)	B5(0.0169)	B5(0.0166)	B5(0.0098)	B5(0.0098)	B5(0.0089)
3	A3(0.0671)	A3(0.0610)	A1(0.0672)	A1(0.0607)	A1(0.0612)	A2(0.0621)	B7(0.0162)	B7(0.0168)	B7(0.0159)	B7(0.0096)	B7(0.0093)	B7(0.0062)
4	A4(0.0657)	A1(0.0602)	A4(0.0602)	A4(0.0600)	A4(0.0578)	A4(0.0608)	B2(0.0155)	B2(0.0166)	B2(0.0151)	B2(0.0094)	B2(0.0087)	B2(0.0057)
5	A5(0.0593)	A5(0.0503)	A5(0.0560)	A5(0.0511)	A5(0.0543)	A5(0.0513)	B4(0.0141)	B4(0.0156)	B4(0.0150)	B4(0.0067)	B4(0.0086)	B4(0.0055)
6	A6(0.0436)	A6(0.0307)	A6(0.0351)	A6(0.0431)	A6(0.0400)	A7(0.0346)	B3(0.0061)	B3(0.0148)	B3(0.0145)	B3(0.0056)	B3(0.0075)	B3(0.0050)
7	A7(0.0434)	A7(0.0285)	A7(0.0343)	A7(0.0419)	A7(0.0375)	A6(0.0333)	B6(0.0040)	B6(0.0054)	B6(0.0051)	B6(0.0025)	B6(0.0034)	B6(0.0025)
8	A8(0.0196)	A9(0.0143)	A10(0.0166)	A10(0.0103)	A10(0.0135)	A8(0.0137)	B10(0.0046)	B10(0.0085)	B10(0.0073)	B10(0.0054)	B10(0.0048)	B10(0.0047)
9	A9(0.0115)	A8(0.0107)	A8(0.0137)	A8(0.0100)	A8(0.0124)	A10(0.0090)	B11(0.0024)	B11(0.0039)	B11(0.0020)	B11(0.0024)	B11(0.0023)	B11(0.0022)
10	A10(0.0114)	A12(0.0051)	A12(0.0131)	A12(0.0089)	A12(0.0081)	A9(0.0088)	B9(0.0022)	B9(0.0023)	B9(0.0020)	B9(0.0016)	B9(0.0020)	B9(0.0022)
11	A11(0.0112)	A10(0.0051)	A9(0.0129)	A9(0.0084)	A9(0.0078)	A12(0.0054)	B12(0.0011)	B12(0.0023)	B12(0.0009)	B12(0.0013)	B12(0.0012)	B12(0.0018)
12	A12(0.0108)	A13(0.0047)	A14(0.0118)	A14(0.0072)	A14(0.0071)	A11(0.0047)	B8(0.0010)	B8(0.0010)	B8(0.0009)	B8(0.0008)	B8(0.0010)	B8(0.0008)
						Results of fusion of four models						
1	A8(0.1130)	A9(0.0881)	A8(0.0946)	A8(0.0846)	A8(0.0927)	A8(0.0960)	B1(0.1382)	B1(0.1295)	B1(0.1237)	B1(0.0961)	B1(0.1270)	B7(0.0692)
2	A9(0.0689)	A8(0.0861)	A9(0.0825)	A9(0.0505)	A9(0.0595)	A9(0.0660)	B4(0.1198)	B4(0.1143)	B4(0.1166)	B7(0.0825)	B4(0.0841)	B1(0.0687)
3	A17(0.0510)	A7(0.0343)	A2(0.0806)	A7(0.0401)	A17(0.0514)	A7(0.0481)	B3(0.1142)	B10(0.1121)	B10(0.1115)	B10(0.0811)	B3(0.0794)	B4(0.0626)
4	A18(0.0504)	A17(0.0255)	A1(0.0801)	A19(0.0378)	A18(0.0495)	A4(0.0375)	B2(0.0698)	B3(0.1075)	B3(0.1102)	B4(0.0657)	B7(0.0730)	B3(0.0612)
5	A7(0.0466)	A2(0.0204)	A7(0.0565)	A18(0.0342)	A1(0.0466)	A3(0.0373)	B7(0.0596)	B2(0.0845)	B2(0.0753)	B3(0.0586)	B10(0.0577)	B10(0.0554)
6	A19(0.0433)	A1(0.0199)	A17(0.0460)	A25(0.0335)	A7(0.0337)	A17(0.0217)	B8(0.0449)	B7(0.0644)	B7(0.0626)	B9(0.0380)	B9(0.0393)	B9(0.0379)
7	A20(0.0265)	A18(0.0182)	A18(0.0369)	A17(0.0335)	A19(0.0336)	A1(0.0201)	B9(0.0411)	B9(0.0351)	B9(0.0325)	B2(0.0242)	B2(0.0390)	B2(0.0228)
8	A1(0.0258)	A19(0.0172)	A19(0.0316)	A20(0.0271)	A23(0.0259)	A2(0.0199)	B10(0.0371)	B8(0.0305)	B12(0.0248)	B5(0.0166)	B12(0.0311)	B11(0.0228)
9	A2(0.0258)	A4(0.0155)	A20(0.0208)	A6(0.0216)	A20(0.0255)	A5(0.0190)	B12(0.0218)	B12(0.0294)	B11(0.0236)	B6(0.0165)	B12(0.0139)	B8(0.0200)
10	A3(0.0168)	A3(0.0152)	A6(0.0203)	A2(0.0159)	A4(0.0251)	A18(0.0167)	B11(0.0174)	B5(0.0180)	B8(0.0210)	B8(0.0145)	B5(0.0131)	B12(0.0145)
11	A4(0.0164)	A5(0.0126)	A23(0.0171)	A3(0.0155)	A25(0.0234)	A10(0.0150)	B5(0.0111)	B6(0.0143)	B5(0.0183)	B11(0.0104)	B6(0.0104)	B5(0.0105)
12	A5(0.0148)	A22(0.0082)	A3(0.0170)	A1(0.0152)	A14(0.0222)	A6(0.0137)	B6(0.0098)	B11(0.0053)	B6(0.0125)	B12(0.0100)	B11(0.0066)	B6(0.0076)

Table 4. Final results.

No.	AttributeID	Value	Attribute
1	A8	0.0949	Did_Police_Officer_Attend_Scene_of_Accident
2	A9	0.0689	Number_of_Vehicles
3	A7	0.0432	2nd_Road_Number
4	A17	0.0382	Number_of_Vehicles
5	A1	0.0346	Location_Northing_OSGR
6	A18	0.0343	2nd_Road_Class
7	B1	0.4554	Casualty_Type
8	B4	0.3754	Pedestrian_Location
9	B3	0.3541	Pedestrian_Movement
10	B10	0.3033	Vehicle_Reference
11	B7	0.2743	Sex_of_Casualty
12	B2	0.2104	Casualty_Class

References

1. H. Sitao, X. Qiaojun and Z. Yanru, Characteristics and causes of traffic accidents on freeway upgrade sections, *Journal of Transport Information and Safety* (2013).

2. Q. Yuanyuan, Correlation analysis between failure of automobile mechanical parts and traffic accidents, *Internal Combustion Enging & Parts*.

3. L. Zhong and Y. Rende, On causes of traffic accidents based on the theory of principal components analysis, *Journal of Shandong Jiaotong University* **14** (2006).

4. T. Rui, Y. Zhaosheng and Z. Maolei, Method of road traffic accidents causes analysis based on data mining, in *2010 International Conference on Computational Intelligence and Software Engineering*, 2010.

5. C. Tao, L. Yucun and Y. Guo, Grey predict ion and relativity analysi of the traffic accidents, *Journal of North China Institute of Techhnology*, 1 (1998).

6. L. Zhenning, C. Cong, C. Yusheng, Z. Guohui, W. Qiong, L. Cathy and Q. Z. Sean, Examining driver injury severity in intersection-related crashes using cluster analysis and hierarchical bayesian models, *Accident Analysis & Prevention* **120**, 139 (2018).

7. J. Lin and L. Yan, Discrimination of several correlation and their implementation in r software, *Statistics & Information Forum* **34** (2019).

8. M. Kendall, A new measure of rank correlation, *Biometrika* **30**, 81 (1938).

9. D. N. Reshef, Y. A. Reshef, H. K. Finucane, S. R. Grossman, G. Mcvean, P. J. Turnbaugh, E. S. Lander, M. Mitzenmacher and P. C. Sabeti, Detecting novel associations in large data sets, *Science* **334**.

10. Y. Wenlu, Z. Yinghui, W. Hongjun, D. Ping and L. Tianrui, Hybrid genetic model for clustering ensemble, *Knowledge-Based Systems* **231** (2021).

Recognition of train hydraulic brake oil level and reservoir water level based on FCOS and HSV algorithm

Jianyang Zhao

School of Computer and Software Engineering, Huaiyin Institute of Technology
Huaian, 223001, China
jianyang@hyit.edu.cn
www.hyit.edu

Qiuyang Chen and Kaixin Pan

School of Computer and Software Engineering, Huaiyin Institute of Technology
Huaian, 223001, China
974078446@qq.com

Biao Li, Jingsong Shan, Chengfu Sun and Weihong Ding

School of Computer and Software Engineering, Huaiyin Institute of Technology
Huaian, 223001, China
321520656@qq.com

With the continuous development of economy and the improvement of scientific and technological level, computer image processing technology has developed greatly in recent years, and is widely used in various industries. Image processing technology plays a supervisory role in environmental pollution and ecological damage to a great extent, making efficient use of resources and promoting the implementation of sustainable development policies. Our project is about how to realize the automatic recognition of train hydraulic brake oil level reading. In this regard, we propose a model algorithm based on FCOS and HSV algorithm. In addition, based on this model algorithm, we applied it to the reservoir water level recognition, meanwhile, realized the reservoir water level recognition algorithm. Automatic recognition technology replaces people's inefficient and high-risk work, which plays a great role in promoting sustainable development.

Keywords: FCOS algorithm; HSV algorithm; automatic recognition technology; train hydraulic brake oil level; reservoir water level.

1. Introduction

In recent years, with the improvement of economic conditions and the increase of the number and speed of trains, urban rail trains have become an indispensable means of transportation in people's lives. However, the new type of urban rail train has a short time interval, which makes the train slow down and brake frequently. Due to the limitation of space size and the pursuit of lightweight, miniaturization and low energy consumption of key train systems, air braking systems are generally not installed on urban rail trains. Hydraulic braking system is widely used in trains because of its small size, light weight and good safety performance under the same braking effect. In the actual working environment, the problem of insufficient oil in the chassis on the train often leads to the stagnation of rail transit. In order to avoid similar incidents and to enable the train to work continuously, an intelligent device which can track and detect the oil level of the train hydraulic brake in real time is needed.

To solve the above-mentioned problem, we propose a recognition algorithm based on FCOS and HSV color models. At the same time, we extended the algorithm to recognize the water level of the reservoir, and achieved remarkable results. Therefore, this algorithm provides a method for automatically identifying the position of liquid level, resolves the problem of large error and low efficiency in manual reading, and plays a certain role in promoting the sustainable development.

2. Implementation of Recognition Algorithm

2.1. Data sets construction

In this project, the data sets used are captured and collected by the cooperative railway company, which contains images of the train hydraulic brake level in three directions: front, right and left. Fifty pictures were collected for each direction of oil level image. The oil level image data in the three directions are gathered and divided into data sets and test sets according to a 3:1 scale. The following figure shows some examples of the oil level image data collection.

Fig. 1. Some examples of the oil level image data collection.

2.2. Annotation of data sets

Prior to training of the network model, the training picture dataset first needs to be annotated, which allows manual marking of the location and class of the target to be detected. The aim is, in the course of training, to give convolutional neural networks the true value of the target for learning. Software is generally used for the annotation of data sets, at present there are some commonly used software such as labelme, labelImg, VOTT, etc.

We adopt labelme software to label the desired sample sets for the project, and the annotated image sample examples are shown in the below figure.

Fig. 2. Example of labelme Software Marking Single Picture.

2.3. Model algorithm

Firstly, for the network model, we use FCOS network model and PYTORCH for model training. Resnet18 is used for the basic network, SCP-PANET is used for the neck structure and ADAMW is used as the optimizer. FCOS target detection algorithm detects the target of image. FCOS target detection algorithm can avoid the complex operation about rectangular box and save the memory occupancy during training. In addition, FCOS can directly return the target boundary frame of each pixel during training. The object of the pixel regression is a four-dimensional vector, as shown in Formula (1):

$$\eta^* = (l^*, t^*, r^*, b^*) \tag{1}$$

l^*, t^*, r^*, b^* represents the distance from the pixel to the edges of the boundary box. The FCOS network model can make use of the pixel points for regression, which increases the number of positive samples that can be used for training, thus improving the final detection accuracy of the model.

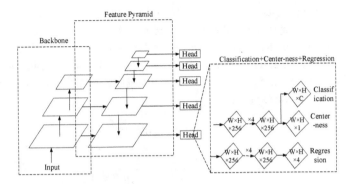

Fig. 3. FCOS network model architecture diagram.

In the training of the model, the loss function plays a vital role. It can provide the learning direction for the whole network and make the model converge gradually. Different loss functions will have different effects on the final convergence effect of the model. The loss function of FCOS includes three parts:

$$L(p_{x,y}, t_{x,y}, centerness_{x,y}) = \frac{1}{N_{pos}} \sum_{x,y} L_{cls}(p_{x,y}, c_{x,y}^*) + \frac{\lambda_1}{N_{pos}} \sum_{x,y} 1c_{x,y}^* > 0 L_{reg}(t_{x,y}, t_{x,y}^*)$$

$$+ \frac{\lambda_2}{N_{pos}} \sum_{x,y} 1c_{x,y}^* > 0 L_{center-ness}(centerness_{x,y}, centerness_{x,y}^*) \quad (2)$$

In the formula (2), $1c_{x,y}^*$ takes 1 when it is a positive sample and 0 when it is a negative sample, So L_{reg} and $L_{center-ness}$ are calculated only for positive samples. λ is the weight coefficient, which is taken as 1 in the paper. The image of loss function in the model training is shown in Fig. 4 below.

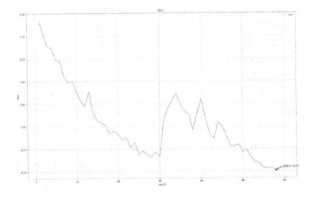

Fig. 4. The image of loss function in the model training.

In the second place, we used HSV color-space model to process oil level image. RGB color space is the most common choice in pictures, but the high correlation between R, G, B components makes it not the most effective method in image processing. Therefore, if R, G, B ∈ [0, 1], and the transformed h is normalized, then H, S, V ∈ [0, 1], RGB->HSV transformation formula is rewritten as formula (3),(4),(5):

$$V = \max(R, G, B) \tag{3}$$

$$S = \begin{cases} \dfrac{V - \min(R, G, B)}{V}, & if\ V \neq 0 \\ 0, otherwise \end{cases} \tag{4}$$

$$H = \begin{cases} 60(G - B)/(V - \min(R, G, B)), & if\ V = R \\ 120 + 60(B - R)/(V - \min(R, G, B)), & if\ V = G \\ 240 + 60(R - B)/((V - \min(R, G, B)), & if\ V = B \\ 0, & if\ R = G = B \end{cases} \tag{5}$$

According to the HSV color space model, the range of colors would be obtained intuitively, which is very helpful for us to process the oil level image.

3. Recognition of Train Hydraulic Brake Oil Level Image

3.1. *Image processing*

In the first place, we need to denoise the oil level image. We use the mean-shift filter algorithm to filter the noise in the image. After filtering and binarization, we get several pre-processed oil level images.

Secondly, according to the minimum circumscribed rectangle method of OpenCV, we determine the width, height, coordinates and rotation angle of the scale in each oil level image processed by FOCS model.

Then, after recognizing the scale of each corrected oil level image, the scale image is processed. On the one hand, the scale image is segmented by local adaptive threshold. Figure 5 shows the image after threshold segmentation. This method can make the local image areas with different brightness, detail texture and contrast in the oil level image have the corresponding local binarization threshold. On the other hand, the oil level image is analyzed by HSV color space model. Figure 6 shows the image processed by HSV color model.

Fig. 5. The result image of threshold segmentation.   Fig. 6. The oil level image processed by HSV color model.

3.2. Calculation and analysis of oil level

The calculation of oil level is divided into the following steps:

The first step is to obtain oil level coordinates and oil level range of each oil level gauge in the corresponding oil level image.

The second step is to calculate the reading of the oil level image according to the preset algorithm. The formula of the preset algorithm is as follows:

$$dushu = \frac{oil\_index}{index} \times kedu\_vector \tag{6}$$

In the formula (6), DUSHU is the reading of oil level image, OIL_INDEX is the height of the oil level surface, INDEX is the height of oil level range and KEDU_VECTOR is the actual range of the oil level scale.

Fig. 7. Scene images of oil level to be recognized.   Fig. 8. Calculation result of the test train hydraulic brake oil level.

Input the oil level coordinates and oil level range of each oil level gauge in the corresponding oil level image, as well as the actual range of the oil level gauge into the preset algorithm to obtain the reading of each oil level image. Figure 7 shows the oil level scene image to recognized by the algorithm. The calculation results of oil level image in the experiment are shown in Fig. 8. Figure 8 shows the recognition results of the oil level container of the train hydraulic brake with a depth of 17.1mm.

4. Application of Algorithm Extension to Reservoir Water Level Recognition

According to the algorithm model of train hydraulic brake oil level, we extended it to the identification of reservoir water level, and achieved good results. We use the FCOS model to locate the position of the water gauge in the reservoir, and then obtain each character of the water gauge and segment it. We use the feature that each character is white and there must be a line of black background between the next character to segment. Finally, the height of the water level is calculated. Figure 9 shows the water gauge intercepted after FCOS model, and Fig. 10 shows the calculation results of reservoir water level.

Fig. 9. The water gauge intercepted after FCOS model.

Fig. 10. The calculation results of reservoir water level.

5. Conclusion

The recognition of train hydraulic brake oil level and reservoir water level based on FCOS and HSV algorithm has the following advantages and disadvantages:

The advantage of this algorithm is that the oil level image is analyzed by HSV color model, and the pictures with poor illumination can also be processed normally. There is no need to adjust any parameters in the whole process, which can not be achieved by traditional methods.

The disadvantage of this algorithm is that when we locate the position of oil gauge and water gauge through FCOS model, the calculation of parameters is complex.

References

1. Wang N, Gao Y, Chen H, et al. NAS-FCOS: Fast neural architecture search for object detection[C]//Proceedings of the IEEE/CVF Conference on Computer Vision and Pattern Recognition. 2020: 11943-11951.
2. Zhang F, Zeng Y. D-FCOS: traffic signs detection and recognition based on semantic segmentation[C]//2020 IEEE International Conference on Power, Intelligent Computing and Systems (ICPICS). IEEE, 2020: 287-292.
3. Zhi Tian, Chunhua Shen, Hao Chen, et al. FCOS: Fully Convolutional One-Stage Object Detection[C].
4. Xiaogang Zheng, Ridong Chen, Xingnian Liu. Numerical simulation of water level surge based on sediment mass algorithm[C].//The 2nd International Conference on the Material Point Method for Modelling Soil-Water - Structure Interaction.
5. Lin F, Chang W Y, Lee L C, et al. Applications of image recognition for real-time water level and surface velocity[C]//2013 IEEE International Symposium on Multimedia. IEEE, 2013: 259-262.
6. Li Bing. Study on the Sustainable Developments of Shandong Agricultural Products Exports[C].//2008 Conference on Regional Economy and Sustainable Development.
7. Wang P L, Wang S H, Wang X. Recognition of Main Transformer Oil Conservator Oil Level Representation Number Based on FCM Segmentation[C].//2021 IEEE 5th Information Technology, Networking, Electronic and Automation Control Conference (ITNEC). IEEE, 2021, 5: 479-483.
8. Zhao X, Jiang F, Wang G, et al. Study on Displacement Recognition and Capacity Table Calibration of Oil Tank[J]. Science Technology and Engineering, 2012.
9. Tian Z, Shen C, Chen H, et al. FCOS: Fully Convolutional One-Stage Object Detection[C].// 2019 IEEE/CVF International Conference on Computer Vision (ICCV). IEEE, 2020.
10. N. Alegre, P. Jeffrey, B. McIntosh, et al. Strategic options for sustainable water management at new developments: the application of a simulation model to explore potential water savings[C].//Wastewater Reclamation and Reuse IV. 2003: 9-15.

BERT-RS: A neural personalized recommender system with BERT

Kezhi Lu*, Qian Zhang, Guangquan Zhang and Jie Lu

Australian Artificial Intelligence Institute
Faulty of Engineering and Information Technology
University of Technology Sydney
Sydney, NSW, 2007, Australia
*lukezhi@bjtu.edu.cn
{qian.zhang-1, guangquan.zhang, jie.lu}@uts.edu.au

Accurate user preferences and item representations are essential factors for personalized recommender systems. Explicit feedback behaviors, such as ratings and free-text comments, are rich in personalized preference knowledge and emotional evaluation information. It is a direct and effective way to obtain individualized preference and item latent representations from these sources. In this paper, we propose a novel neural model named BERT-RS for personalized recommender systems, which extracts knowledge from textual reviews and user-item interactions. First, we preliminary extract the semantic representation for users and items from the textual comments based on BERT. Next, these semantic embeddings are used for user and item latent representations through three different deep architectures. Finally, we carry out personalized recommendation tasks through the score prediction based on these representations. Compared with other algorithms, BERT-RS demonstrates outstanding experimental performance on the Amazon dataset.

Keywords: Collaborative filtering; recommender systems; BERT; personalized recommendation.

1. Introduction

In the information age, the recommender system (RS) is crucial to solving the problem of information overload in Internet services. Providing personalized recommendations is the central goal for the RS. Meanwhile, the core in the personalized RS is accurately identifying the user's preferences and linking them with items or online services.[1] To this day, the collaborative filtering (CF) method has been used to obtain and predict users' similar preferences through the past interaction information between users and items (e.g., click and rating), which has been successfully and widely used in RS.[2]

CF-based algorithms recommend relevant products according to users' similar preferences.[3-5] The CF-based model generally has two key points: (1) construct the similarity representation between users and items according to the past interaction records; (2) construct the model to train and recommend relevant items. For example, the neural collaborative filtering (NCF) method uses nonlinear neural networks with different structures based on matrix factorization (MF) to construct the representation of users and items.[3,6] However, the NCF model can not deeply analyze the potential preference information and emotional factors according to textual comments. As a result, in this paper, we propose a novel model utilizing reviews knowledge and user-item interactions to construct user/item representations for personalized recommendations.

Review texts contain rich knowledge of personal preferences and sentiments, which can facilitate the accurate representation of users and items. In NLP, various BERT-based models show their state-of-the-art performance in multiple tasks such as Named Entity Recognition (NER) and Question Answering (QA).[7] Inspired by this, we fuse the BERT with neural architectures to extract semantic embeddings from reviews content and construct the personalized user/item representations based on them for RS.

In general, BERT-RS has three different parts. Firstly, we extract and fine-tune the preliminary semantic embeddings from reviews based on the BERT. Secondly, we fuse semantic information to construct user and item personalized representations through three different neural architectures, i.e., BERT, GMF, and MLP. Lastly, we carry out personalized recommendation tasks through the score prediction based on these representations. The main contributions of this paper are summarized as follows:

- We propose BERT-RS, a novel method for personalized recommendations utilizing textual reviews based on BERT, GMF, and MLP, which shows that auxiliary knowledge of user reviews helps improve performance.
- Our proposed method not only captures the characteristic and emotional knowledge of users and items at the semantic level but also extracts the interactive knowledge between them.
- The outstanding experimental performance in the Amazon dataset compared with NCF proves the reliability of our method.

2. Related Work

This section will briefly introduce related research work about CF-based and BERT model for recommender systems.

CF-based methods obtain and predict users' similar preferences through utilizing the past interactive information between users and items (e.g., click and rating), which is successfully and widely used in recommendation systems. For example, the Tapestry system (Goldberg et al., 1992) is one of the first industrial systems to utilize CF-based methods for the recommendation task.[2] Later, various CF-based algorithms emerged and were applied to the industrial RS. In particular, the matrix factorization (MF) method is further improved by mapping user-item representations into a shared latent space.[8,9] With the development of neural networks, NCF forms user-item representations by integrating CF with multi-layer perceptrons (MLP), which shows state-of-the-art performance on different datasets for RS.[3] In the meantime, in various NLP tasks, the pre-trained language representations model effectively improves their performance.[10] For example, Devlin et al. (2018) propose a novel Bidirectional Encoder Representations from Transformers (BERT) as a new language representation model,[7] which demonstrates its state-of-the-art performance for various downstream NLP tasks, such as QA and NER. Recently, Qiu et al. (2021)[11] pre-trains user and item representations based on BERT for cross-domain recommendations. Inspired by these works, in this paper, we fuse the BERT model to extract the latent semantic embeddings in reviews for user/item representations and propose a new model for downstream recommendations.

3. Methods: BERT-RS

BERT-RS includes five main components: Figure 1A mainly introduces the preprocessing steps of comment content; Fig. 1B-1D illustrates three different nonlinear neural networks to construct personalized user/item representations. Figure 1E shows the final prediction layer of BERT-RS for the recommendation.

3.1. Preprocessing steps as input layer

Given a comment text r, we mark its head with a token, [CLS], and its tail with [SEP]. As shown in Fig. 1A, each word in the sentence is represented by position embeddings, segment embeddings, and token embeddings. These three embeddings of each word in the sentence are added and put into the layer normalization (LN) as the final embeddings. Finally, each review forms an embedded representation of $R_{l \times d}^{ui}$. l represents the length of the review content, d represents the dimensions for each word embedding, and u, i represent the user and item respectively.

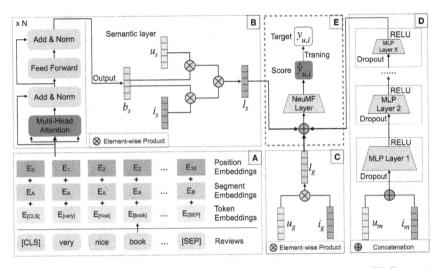

Fig. 1.   Overview and framework of BERT-RS. (A) Preprocessing steps. (B) Semantic layer. (C) GMF layer. (D) MLP layer. (E) Prediction layer.

3.2. Semantic layer for user/item representations

As illustrated in Fig. 1B, this paper mainly utilizes the BERT model to extract the semantic information in the review. BERT model is mainly composed of n Transformer layers. $\boldsymbol{S}_k$ denotes the input embeddings in the k-th Transformer layer. It should be noted that $\boldsymbol{R}_{l \times d}^{ui}$ is the 0-th input embedding. As shown in Fig. 1B, each Transformer layer has three key components, which are the Multi-Head Self-Attention layer, Add & Norm layer, and Feed-Forward layer.

3.2.1. Multi-head self-attention layer

In normal attention network, three different matrices are set as $\boldsymbol{Q}_{L_q \times d}$, $\boldsymbol{K}_{L_k \times d}$, and $\boldsymbol{V}_{L_v \times d}$ respectively ($L_k = L_v$). The formula is defined as:

$$Attention(\boldsymbol{Q}, \boldsymbol{K}, \boldsymbol{V}) = Softmax(\boldsymbol{Q}\boldsymbol{K}^T / \sqrt{d})\boldsymbol{V} \qquad (1)$$

Compared with the normal Attention layer, the Multi-head Self-Attention layer integrates multiple sub-layers to extract the Attention information, which is defined as:

$$Multi - Head - Attention(\boldsymbol{S}_k) = [head_1; ...; head_h]\boldsymbol{W}^* \qquad (2)$$

$$head_j = Attention(\boldsymbol{S}_k \boldsymbol{W}_j^Q, \boldsymbol{S}_k \boldsymbol{W}_j^K, \boldsymbol{S}_k \boldsymbol{W}_j^V) \qquad (3)$$

h represents the total number of Multi-heads. W_j^Q, W_j^K, and W_j^V represent $d \times d/h$ dimensional parameters. W^* represents the $d \times d$ dimensional parameters.

3.2.2. Feed-forward layer

We define this sub-layer as following:

$$FF(I) = GELU(IW^{FF1} + b^{FF1})W^{FF2} + b^{FF2} \tag{4}$$

where I represents the $L_i \times d$ dimensional input. W^{FF1}, b^{FF1}), W^{FF2}, and b^{FF2} are parameters with $d \times d$, $4d \times d$, $4d$, and d dimension respectively. GELU represents the GELU activation function. The Add & Norm layer adds embeddings and performs LN, which is the same as the previous research work.[12] We define layer normalization as LN. The final output of the Transformer layer is defined as:

$$S^{k+1} = LN(I^k + FF(I^k)) \tag{5}$$

$$I^k = LN(S^k + Multi - Head - Attention(S^k)) \tag{6}$$

where S^{k+1} represents the final contextual semantic representation for reviews. Then this representation was inputted into a pooler layer, which consists of a linear layer and a Tanh activation function. As shown in Fig. 1B, we define the output as b_s. After that, we construct our semantic personalized user/item embedding (u_s, i_s) through element-wise product operation. Finally, we obtain the user and item semantic interaction embedding, l_s. The detailed formula is defined as:

$$b_s = Tanh(S^{k+1}W^{p1} + b^{p1}) \tag{7}$$

$$l_s = (u_s \odot b_s) \odot (i_s \odot b_s) \tag{8}$$

where $\odot$ represents the element-wise product.

3.3. Neural user/item representations based on GMF

As illustrated in Fig. 1C and inspired by NCF,[3] we define the user latent embedding of GMF layer as u_g and item latent embedding as i_g. The detailed function is defined as:

$$l_g = u_g \odot i_g \tag{9}$$

3.4. Neural user/item representations based on MLP

As can be shown in Fig. 1D and inspired by NCF,[3] we define the user latent embedding of MLP layer as u_m and item latent embedding as i_m. This layer mainly consists of different MLP layers, which is defined as:

$$z_1 = \phi_1(u_m, i_m) = [u_m, i_m]^T, \tag{10}$$

$$\phi_L(z_{L-1}) = \alpha_L(W_L^T z_{L-1} + b_L), \tag{11}$$

where W_L^T, b_L and α_L represent the weight matrix, bias vector, and activation function respectively. We use the RELU function as the activation function for the MLP layer and define the output of MLP layer representation as l_m.

3.5. Prediction layer

As illustrated in Fig. 1E, concerning the prediction layer, we concatenate the outputs of these three layers as the final embedding and utilize a linear layer to predict the target score, $\hat{y}_{ui}$, for the recommendation. Then, we use the sigmoid activation function as a probabilistic function to map $\hat{y}_{ui}$ in the range of $[0, 1]$. The final loss function, L, is defined as:

$$L = \frac{1}{n} \sum_{(u,i) \in Y} y_{ui} \times ln\hat{y}_{ui} + (1 - y_{ui}) \times ln(1 - \hat{y}_{ui}) \tag{12}$$

where Y denotes the interaction set of user, u, and item, i. n represents the total number of interactions.

4. Experiments

4.1. Datasets and evaluation metrics

We take experiments based on the real-world and public Amazon dataset.[13] This dataset includes reviews and rating data that is suited for our task. Specifically, we randomly sample 10000 users with at least 20 comments per-user in the book category and pick each item with no less than ten reviews. In the training stage, we convert the interaction records between a user and an item to a value of 1. At the same time, we negative sample with the same number of user comments and set their interactive value to 0. Finally, we shuffle 70% of the interactive information as the training set and 30% as the test set. Table 1 shows the statistics of the final dataset.

Table 1. Statistics of the dataset.

Datasets	Category	User	Item	Reviews	Sparsity
Amazon	Books	3764	17647	83599	99.87%

We adopt two widely used top-K ranking metrics, i.e., Hit Ratio@K (HR) and Normalized Discounted Cumulative Gain@K (NDCG) as our final evaluation metrics.[1] In detail, we choose HR@K and NDCG@K with $K \in [1, 3, 5, 10]$ to show the evaluation results compared with baselines.

4.2. Results

In the semantic layer of our experiment, we use the pre-trained BERT-base-uncased model as our initial model. Then we fine-tune this model through our reviews the same as the original BERT step with MLM and NSP tasks.[7] The configuration parameters are the same as the BERT-base-uncased model using 12 Transformer layers and 768 hidden sizes. In the MLP layer, we use 3 MLP layers and 32 dimensions as predictive factors that are the same as the GMF layer. About the optimizer, we utilize Adam with a learning rate of 1×10^{-4}. Table 2 shows the final results following:

Table 2. Performance comparison on Amazon dataset.

Method	HR@10	NDCG@10	HR@5	NDCG@5	HR@3	NDCG@3	HR@1	NDCG@1
BERT-RS	**0.534**	**0.393**	**0.446**	**0.365**	**0.390**	**0.342**	**0.276**	**0.276**
NCF	0.460	0.315	0.355	0.281	0.298	0.258	0.202	0.202
MLP	0.440	0.286	0.336	0.252	0.269	0.225	0.164	0.164
GMF	0.438	0.289	0.333	0.255	0.274	0.231	0.171	0.171

Compared with the other methods, HR@K and NDCG@K evaluation results of BERT-RS were significantly improved by nearly 30%. In particular, in the HR@1 and NDCG@1 results, our method improved by 36.63%.

5. Conclusion

In this paper, we propose a novel neural personalized user/item representations method, named BERT-RS, making use of reviews content based on BERT, GMF, and MLP, which demonstrates that the auxiliary information of user reviews helps to improve recommendation. In the final experimental results, our method has significantly improved in both HR and NDCG compared with baselines, which proves the effectiveness of our method.

References

1. J. Lu, Q. Zhang and G. Zhang, *Recommender Systems: Advanced Developments* (World Scientific, 2020).
2. D. Goldberg, D. Nichols, B. M. Oki and D. Terry, Using collaborative filtering to weave an information tapestry, *Communications of the ACM* **35**, 61 (1992).
3. X. He, L. Liao, H. Zhang, L. Nie, X. Hu and T.-S. Chua, Neural collaborative filtering, in *Proceedings of the 26th International Conference on World Wide Web*, 2017.
4. Q. Zhang, W. Liao, G. Zhang, B. Yuan and J. Lu, A deep dual adversarial network for cross-domain recommendation, *IEEE Transactions on Knowledge and Data Engineering* (2021).
5. T. Wang and Y. Fu, Item-based collaborative filtering with bert, in *Proceedings of The 3rd Workshop on e-Commerce and NLP*, 2020.
6. J. Lu, J. Xuan, G. Zhang and X. Luo, Structural property-aware multi-layer network embedding for latent factor analysis, *Pattern Recognition* **76**, 228 (2018).
7. J. Devlin, M.-W. Chang, K. Lee and K. Toutanova, Bert: Pre-training of deep bidirectional transformers for language understanding, *ArXiv Preprint ArXiv:1810.04805* (2018).
8. A. Paterek, Improving regularized singular value decomposition for collaborative filtering, in *Proceedings of KDD Cup and Workshop*, 2007.
9. Y. Koren, Factorization meets the neighborhood: a multifaceted collaborative filtering model, in *Proceedings of 14th ACM SIGKDD International Conference on Knowledge Discovery and Data Mining*, 2008.
10. A. Vaswani, N. Shazeer, N. Parmar, J. Uszkoreit, L. Jones, A. N. Gomez, Ł. Kaiser and I. Polosukhin, Attention is all you need, *Advances in Neural Information Processing Systems* **30** (2017).
11. Z. Qiu, X. Wu, J. Gao and W. Fan, U-bert: Pre-training user representations for improved recommendation, in *Proc. of the AAAI Conference on Artificial Intelligence. Menlo Park, CA, AAAI*, 2021.
12. J. L. Ba, J. R. Kiros and G. E. Hinton, Layer normalization, *ArXiv Preprint ArXiv:1607.06450* (2016).
13. J. Ni, J. Li and J. McAuley, Justifying recommendations using distantly-labeled reviews and fine-grained aspects, in *Proceedings of the 2019 Conference on Empirical Methods in Natural Language Processing and the 9th International Joint Conference on Natural Language Processing (EMNLP-IJCNLP)*, 2019.

398

Research on the coordination of logistics service supply chain with the participation of Non-car Operating Carrier*

Xiaoping Qiu

School of Transportation and Logistics, Southwest Jiaotong University
Chengdu, China
qxp@home.swjtu.edu.cn

Yanjiao Wu

National United Engineering Laboratory of Integrated and Intelligent Transportation
Chengdu, China
1502608005@qq.com

Shasha Liu

School of Transportation and Logistics, Southwest Jiaotong University
Chengdu, China
410432275@qq.com

To promote the cooperation between the Non-car operating carrier and road transportation enterprises, a modified revenue sharing contract is used in this paper to coordinate the logistics service supply chain involving non-car operating carrier under transport demand and cost disruption. And numerical examples are used to verify the theoretical results and analyze the impact of disruption management. We can obtain that the modified revenue sharing contract can achieve arbitrary allocation of supply chain profits.

Keywords: Non-car operating carrier; logistics service supply chain; disruption management; supply chain coordination; revenue sharing contract.

1. Introductions

Non-car operating carriers (NCOC) have the characteristics of strong resource integration ability and wide brand effect as logistics coordinator. They use Internet platform and organizational model innovation to effectively promote the intensive integration of resources in the freight market [1]. The NCOC undertakes the customer's transportation business according to the market demand. After

*This work is supported by the National Natural Science Foundation of China (Grant No. 61673320), National Key R&D Program of China (Grant No. 2019YFB2101802), International S&T cooperation program (Grant No. 2020-GH02-00064-HZ) of Chengdu.

that, he signs a certain amount of transportation contracts with different Road Transportation Enterprises (RTEs) in a more favorable negotiated freight rate [2]. RTEs provide different types of transport products in the market. And each transport product may be provided by more than one enterprise. Thus, the logistics service supply chain (LSSC) composed of NCOC and RTEs is formed.

Currently, the relevant research on NCOC mainly focuses on partner selection, supply chain coordination and platform pricing [3-5]. Besides, research on the problem of simultaneous disruption of demand and cost is common. For example, Pi et al. [6] studied pricing and service strategies for dual-channel supply chains under demand disruptions. Choi [7], Wang et al. [8], Cao et al. [9] studied the effect of cost or demand on the decision-making of the participants in LSSC. In addition, Tang et al. [10] studied the optimal strategies for dual-channel supply chain. However, the above research does not consider the transport cost and demand disruption faced in the LSSC involving NCOC. Therefore, based on the research of Cao et al. [9], this paper focuses on the coordination mechanism of the secondary LSSC composed of NCOC and n RTEs under transport demand and cost disruption, which provides ideas for realizing good cooperation and maximizing benefits between RTEs and NCOC.

The remainder of this paper is organized as follows. Section 2 presents the problem and assumptions. The models under disruption of transport cost and demand are presented in Section 3. The numerical examples are used to verify the theoretical results in Section 4 and the conclusions are drawn in Section 5.

2. Problem Description and Assumptions

All parties are independent, and they all aim at maximizing their own profits in the specific decision-making process. Now the assumptions are shown as follows.

(1) The price demand relationship between NCOC and RTE is determined and known.

(2) The decision-making process between NCOC and RTEs can be regarded as a Stackelberg game, in which RTEs are followers because they do not know the current market demand information. The NCOC is leader since he has an Internet information platform, which can timely get the changes in market demand. The NCOC provides a revenue-sharing contract $\{(w_i, \phi_i)\}$ to RTEs, in which the contract i is a sub-contract, including the negotiated freight price w_i and the revenue share ratio ϕ_i. Then, RTEs freely choose their preferred sub-contracts. Finally, the NCOC decides the negotiated traffic volume.

(3) In the traffic volume and price function, the effect of substitute elastic parameter on price is negative, that is the transport i and j have substitutability. It affects the profit of the NCOC.

3. Model Analysis

3.1. Decisions under disruption of transport cost and demand

Assume that the NCOC doesn't pay the cost when there is no disruption, then the market price of the transport product i signed with the cargo owner satisfies Eq. (1).

$$p_i = a_i - q_i - \sum_{j \neq i} d_{ji} q_j, 0 < d < 1, i, j = 1, 2, \ldots, n \tag{1}$$

Where a_i represents the market size of transport product i provided by the RTE i with the transport cost c_i, that is the possible maximum demand. q_i is the negotiated traffic volume. d_{ji} represents the substitution elasticity of actual demand among different transport products under the price p_i, and is also a sensitivity index used to measure the influence of the quantity of transport product j on the price of transport product i.

Assuming that the market size of demand changes from a_i to $a_i + \Delta a_i$, and the transport cost of RTEs changes from c_i to $c_i + \Delta c_i$ under the disruption of transport cost and demand. Then the transport price under disruption can be obtained as shown in Eq. (2).

$$\overline{p_i} = a_i + \Delta a_i - q_i - \sum_{j \neq i} d_{ji} q_j \tag{2}$$

Assume $a_i + \Delta a_i > q_i + \sum_{j \neq i} d_{ji} q_j$ to ensure $\overline{p_i} > 0$, where q_i represents the market demand of transport product i under disruption, q_i^0 represents the vector of the optimal negotiated traffic volume when there is no disruption. $\Delta q_i = q_i - q_i^0$ represents the negotiated traffic volume deviation of the NCOC caused by the disruption. It is assumed that the NCOC bears all the cost of volume deviation. Then the revenue $R_i(q)$ and profit Π_{fi} of the NCOC can be obtained, which are shown in Eq. (3) and Eq. (4).

$$R_i(q) = q_i (a_i + \Delta a_i - q_i - \sum_{j \neq i} d_{ji} q_j) \tag{3}$$

$$\Pi_{fi} = (1 - \phi) R_i(q) - \omega_i q_i - [c_{ui} (q_i - q_i^0)^+ + c_{si} (q_i^0 - q_i)^+] \tag{4}$$

Where $(x)^+ = \max(0, x)$, $c_{ui} > 0$ and $c_{si} > 0$ respectively represent the marginal incremental cost of increased and decreased traffic volume that deviates from the original transport plan.

And the profit Π_{ri} of RTE i can be calculated as shown in Eq. (5).

$$\Pi_{ri} = \phi R_i(q) - (\omega_i - c_i - \Delta c_i)q_i \tag{5}$$

The profit Π_i of the supply chain at node i is shown in Eq. (6).

$$\Pi_i = R_i(q) - (c_i + \Delta c_i)q_i - [c_{ui}(q_i - q_i^0)^+ + c_{si}(q_i^0 - q_i)^+] \tag{6}$$

Then the total profits of the supply chain can be obtained as Eq. (7).

$$\Pi_T = \sum_{i=1}^{n}\left[\left(a_i + \Delta a_i - q_i - \sum_{j\neq i} d_{ji}q_j - c_i - \Delta c_i\right)q_i\right]$$
$$- \left[\sum_{i=1}^{n} c_{ui}\cdot\left(q_i - q_i^0\right)^+ + \sum_{i=1}^{n} c_{si}\cdot\left(q_i^0 - q_i\right)^+\right] \tag{7}$$

Let $q^* = \left(q_1^*, q_2^*, \cdots, q_n^*\right)$ represents the vector of the optimal negotiated traffic volume under disruption. It is easily known that q^* satisfies Eq. (8) or Eq. (9).

$$2q_i^* + \sum_{j\neq i}^{n}\left(d_{ji} + d_{ij}\right)q_j^* = a_i - c_i + \Delta a_i - \Delta c_i + c_{ui} \tag{8}$$

$$2q_i^* + \sum_{j\neq i}^{n}\left(d_{ji} + d_{ij}\right)q_j^* = a_i - c_i + \Delta a_i - \Delta c_i - c_{si} \tag{9}$$

These equations form equation set $Dq^* = \overline{A}$, where

$$D = \begin{pmatrix} 2 & d_{12}+d_{21} & d_{13}+d_{31} & \cdots & d_{1n}+d_{n1} \\ d_{12}+d_{21} & 2 & d_{23}+d_{32} & \cdots & d_{2n}+d_{n2} \\ d_{13}+d_{31} & d_{23}+d_{32} & 3 & \cdots & d_{3n}+d_{n3} \\ \vdots & \vdots & \vdots & \cdots & \vdots \\ d_{1n}+d_{n1} & d_{2n}+d_{n2} & d_{3n}+d_{n3} & \cdots & 2 \end{pmatrix}, \quad q^* = \begin{pmatrix} q_{1*}^* \\ q_{2*} \\ q_{3*} \\ \vdots \\ q_n^* \end{pmatrix}, \quad \overline{A} = \begin{pmatrix} \overline{A_1} \\ \overline{A_2} \\ \overline{A_3} \\ \vdots \\ \overline{A_n} \end{pmatrix},$$

$\overline{A_i} \in \{A_i^1, A_i^2\}$, $A_i^1 = a_i - c_i + \Delta a_i - \Delta c_i + c_{ui}$, $A_i^2 = a_i - c_i + \Delta a_i - \Delta c_i - c_{si}$. The equation set can be transformed as Eq. (10). Then we can get the optimal solution q^* by programming in Matlab by solving the inverse of D.

$$\begin{cases} 2q_1 + \left(d_{12} + d_{21}\right)q_2 + \cdots + \left(d_{1n} + d_{n1}\right)q_n = \left(1 - t_1\right)A_1^1 + t_1 A_1^2 \\ \vdots \\ \left(d_{1n} + d_{n1}\right)q_1 + \left(d_{2n} + d_{n2}\right)q_2 + \cdots + 2q_n = \left(1 - t_n\right)A_n^1 + t_n A_n^2 \\ t_i\left(t_i - 1\right) = 0 \\ \left(t_i - 1/2\right)\left(q^i - q_i^o\right) \leq 0 \end{cases} \tag{10}$$

Proposition 1. When the demand-price relationship for different types of transport products in the market satisfied $\overline{p_i} = a_i + \Delta a_i - q_i - \sum_{j\neq i} d_{ji}q_j$, the total profit of the supply chain is the largest at the optimal negotiated traffic volume q^* which is the solution of Eq. (10).

Proposition 1 gives the optimal negotiated traffic volume under centralized decision-making when there are transport demand and cost disruption. When they make decentralized decisions, all the members will adjust their decisions under the transport demand and cost disruption. Therefore, the original coordination mechanism must be modified to maximize the profit of the supply chain.

3.2. Supply Chain Coordination

This section coordinates the supply chain with a similar revenue-sharing contract. Set $S\left(q_i^*\right) = c_{ui} \cdot \left(q_i^* - q_i^0\right)^+ + c_{si} \cdot \left(q_i^0 - q_i^*\right)^+$, ϕ_i represents the revenue share ratio of a RTE, then the transport price is calculated by Eq. (11).

$$w_i\left(q^*\right) = \left(1 - \phi_i\right)\left(c_i + \Delta c_i\right) + \phi_i\left(\sum_{j \neq i}^{n} R_j^i\left(q^*\right) - \frac{S\left(q_i^*\right)}{q_i^*}\right) \tag{11}$$

Where $0 < \phi_i < \dfrac{\Pi_i}{\Pi_i + q_i^* \sum\limits_{j \neq i}^{n} R_j^i\left(q^*\right)}$, $R_j^i\left(q^*\right) = \partial R_j / \partial q_i$. The NCOC can use

revenue-sharing contracts to induce RTEs to sign agreements on traffic volume $q^* = \left(q_1^*, q_2^*, \ldots, q_n^*\right)$ to maximize the total profit of the supply chain when transport costs and demand are disrupted at the same time. Proposition 2 embodies this.

Proposition 2. In the case of decentralized decision-making in which transport costs and demand are disrupted at the same time, the RTE selects its most preferred contract from the modified contract $\left\{\left(w_i, \phi_i\right)\right\}$, then the supply chain can be coordinated, and the profits of the supply chain can be allocated arbitrarily, and the modified revenue sharing contract is disruption-resistant.

Proof. Based on the contract terms given above, the profit $\overline{\Pi_{ri}}$ of RTE i can be expressed as Eq. (12).

$$\begin{aligned} \Pi_{ri}\left(q^*\right) &= \phi_i R_i + \left(w_i - c_i - \Delta c_i\right)q_i^* \\ &= \phi_i R_i - \phi_i\left(c_i + \Delta c_i\right)q_i^* + \phi_i\left(q_i^* \sum_{j \neq i}^{n} R_j^i\left(q^*\right) - S\left(q_i^*\right)\right) \\ &= \phi_i\left[\Pi_i + q_i^* \sum_{j \neq i}^{n} R_j^i\left(q^*\right)\right] \end{aligned} \tag{12}$$

According to the overall profit maximization condition of the supply chain, the following equation is established.

$$\sum_{j\neq i}^{n} R_j^{i}\left(q^*\right) = c_i + \Delta c_i + c_{si} - R_i^{i} \tag{13}$$

$$\Pi_i + q_i^* \sum_{j\neq i}^{n} R_j^{i}\left(q^*\right) = \Pi_i + \left(c_i + \Delta c_i - c_{si} - R_i^{i}\right)q_i^* = R_i - c_{si}q_i^o - R_j^{i}q_i^* \tag{14}$$

The profit of the RTE is positive since $R_i^{i} < 0$, as shown in Eq. (15).

$$\Pi_{ri} = \phi_i \left[\Pi_i + q_i^* \sum_{j\neq i}^{n} R_j^{i}\left(q^*\right)\right] = \phi_i \left(R_i - c_{si}q_i^o - R_i^{i}q_i^*\right) > 0 \tag{15}$$

The profit Π_f of the NCOC is

$$\begin{aligned}
\Pi_f\left(q^*\right) &= \sum_{i=1}^{n} \Pi_{fi}\left(q^*\right) = \sum_{i=1}^{n}\left((1-\phi_i)R_i - w_i q_i^*\right) \\
&\quad - \left[\sum_{i=1}^{n} c_{ui}\cdot\left(q_i^* - q_i^0\right)^{+} + \sum_{i=1}^{n} c_{si}\cdot\left(q_i^0 - q_i^*\right)^{+}\right] \\
&= \sum_{i=1}^{n}\left[(1-\phi_i)\left(\Pi_i + q_i^* \sum_{j\neq i}^{n} R_j^{i}\left(q^*\right)\right) - q_i^* \sum_{j\neq i}^{n} R_j^{i}\left(q^*\right)\right] \tag{16}
\end{aligned}$$

Then the results of $\dfrac{\partial \Pi_{ri}}{\partial \phi_i} > 0$ and $\dfrac{\partial \Pi_f}{\partial \phi_i} < 0$ can be obtained, that is the arbitrary allocation of the optimal profit of the supply chain can be realized by adjusting the revenue sharing ratio of the RTE.

4. Case Analysis

This section uses some numerical examples to verify the theoretical results obtained earlier, and then analyzes the impact of disruption management under changes in demand and costs. The parameters are set as follows: $a_1 = a_2 = 30$, $c_1 = 8, c_2 = 9$, $\Delta a_1 = \Delta a_2 = \{-3,3\}$, $c_{ui} = c_{si} = 1$, $\Delta c_1 = \Delta c_2 = \{-2,2\}$, $d_{12} = 0.3$, $d_{21} = 0.5$. Assume that under symmetric information, both RTEs and NCOC agree to share the supply chain benefits in a ratio of 8:2, i.e. $\phi_1 = \phi_2 = 0.8$.

In the case of disruption, according to Proposition 1, given the above values, there are 8 cases in total, of which the negotiated traffic volume is different from the initial traffic volume plan in 6 cases. According to Proposition 2, the impact of disruption on the parameters in the revenue sharing contract and the total profit of the supply chain is shown in Table 1.

Table 1. Parameters in the revenue sharing contract under the impact of disruption.

Case	Δa_1	Δa_2	Δc_1	Δc_2	q_1^*	q_2^*	p_1^*	p_2^*	w_1^*	w_2^*	Supply chain total profit	
											Initial plan	New plan
1	-3	-3	-2	-2	8.10	7.26	15.27	17.31	-0.54	-1.84	149.94	149.94
2	-3	-3	2	2	5.95	5.12	18.49	20.10	0.48	-0.52	88.51	92.80
3	-3	3	-2	-2	5.45	11.31	15.87	20.05	-1.90	-1.08	193.51	194.94
4	-3	3	2	2	4.05	9.88	21.91	13.46	-1.17	0.37	132.09	133.51
5	3	-3	-2	-2	12.14	4.64	18.54	18.71	-0.18	-3.91	198.51	199.94
6	3	-3	2	2	10.71	3.21	20.68	20.57	1.03	-3.10	137.08	138.51
7	3	3	-2	-2	10.24	9.41	18.06	20.52	-1.23	-2.88	242.08	246.37
8	3	3	2	2	8.10	7.26	21.27	23.31	0.26	-1.04	180.66	180.66

In Case 1, there are 3 feasible solutions which are $q^* = [8.57; 6.07]$, $q^* = [6.90; 7.73]$ and $q^* = [7.38; 6.55]$. After comparing the total supply chain profit with the initial solution, it is found that the total supply chain profit under the initial solution is greater than these 3 solutions, so the negotiated traffic volume in this case selects the initial solution. The solver in other cases is similar to Case 1, with a minimum of 1 feasible solution and a maximum of 3 feasible solutions, but the optimal solution is selected after comparison with the initial solution.

It can be seen from Table 1 that in the first and eighth cases, when the transport demand and cost change in the same direction within a certain range, the initial transport plan is not affected, because the demand and the transport cost disruption limit each other, and cancel each other out. Therefore, the optimal profit of the supply chain remains stable, and only the market price needs to be adjusted, which reveals that the initial volume plan has a certain robustness. In case 2, the market demand is decreasing, the transport cost is increasing, and the negotiated volume of both transport products by the NCOC is decreasing. In case 7, the market demand is increasing, the transport cost is decreasing, and the negotiated traffic volume of the NCOC for both transport products is increasing. In cases 3 and 6, the demand and cost change in different directions, and the negotiated traffic volume of the two transport products also changes in the opposite direction.

5. Conclusion

This paper uses revenue-sharing contract to coordinate a secondary LSSC composed of RTEs and a NCOC under the disruption of transport demand and cost. The following conclusions can be drawn. When the demand and cost change in the same direction within a certain range, the initial transport plan does not need to be adjusted, which shows that the initial transport plan has a certain robustness. Conversely, when the disruption degree is large, the traffic volume needs to be adjusted to realize the supply chain coordination. Besides, the change of market demand synchronously affects the change of negotiated traffic volume. And the modified revenue sharing contract can realize the arbitrary allocation of supply chain profits by adjusting the revenue sharing ratio of the RTE.

References

1. Qiu ZQ, Zhang Y, Yuan HX, et al. Non-Car Operating Carrier Model Based on "Internet plus"[C]. 6th International Conference on Transportation Engineering (ICTE2019), 2019, 11-16.
2. Hu Z, Ma R. Dynamic Pricing Method of Non-Truck Operating Common Carrier under Cost-Core Multivariate Conditions[C]. 2020 IEEE International Conference on Information Technology, Big Data and Artificial Intelligence (ICIBA), 2020, 1: 1477-1482.
3. Kang Fengwei, Li Xuemei, Li Jinyu, et al. Game Research into Subjects of Rail-road intermodal Transport under Different Decision Models[J]. Journal of the China Railway Society, 2020, 42(11):22-28.
4. Liu Shuai, Jiang Li. A research on partner selection of Non-Truck Operating Carrier based on PCA-BP Neural Network[J]. Railway Transport and Economy, 2018, 40(10):45-50.
5. Nie Fuhai, Li Diansheng. Study of Pricing Strategies for Non-car Operating Carriers Platform under Asymmetric Information[J]. Industrial Engineering and Management, 2020, 25(5):121-128.
6. Pi ZY, Fang WG, Zhang BF. Service and Pricing Strategies with Competition and Cooperation in a Dual-channel Supply Chain with Demand Disruption[J]. Computers & Industrial Engineering, 2019, 138(1):106-130.
7. Choi TM. Facing Market Disruptions: Values of Elastic Logistics in Service Supply Chains[J]. International Journal of Production Research, 2021, 59(1):286-300.
8. Wang Jiahao, Chen Zigen, Xin Congying, et al. Coordination Strategy of Port Logistics Service Supply Chain Considering Demand Disruption[J]. Journal of Dalian Maritime University, 2021, 47(4):47-55.
9. Cao E, Wan C, Lai M. Coordination of a Supply Chain with One Manufacturer and Multiple Competing Retailers Under Simultaneous Demand and Cost Disruptions[J]. International Journal of Production Economics, 2013, 141(1):425-433.

10. C.H. Tang, H.L. Yang, E.B. Cao, et al. Channel Competition and Coordination of a Dual-channel Supply Chain with Demand and Cost Disruptions[J]. Applied Economics, 2018, 50(46):4999-5016.

Evaluation of a financial technology project decision in the Central Bank of Oman by the multistage one-shot decision-making approach[*]

Mohammed Al-Shanfari

Graduate School of International Social Sciences, YOKOHAMA National University
Yokohama, 240-8501, Japan
al-ahmed-yh@ynu.jp

The research paper aims to determine the effectiveness of the MOSDMA (the multistage one-shot decision-making approach) in an application of a financial information technology project from the central bank of Oman. The study cases from this organization are the first to utilize the MOSDMA. Qualitative and quantitative data sources were gathered to reconstruct the problem and apply the MOSDMA. The results show the high effectiveness of the proposed approach in supporting the decision makers in re-evaluating such problems in actual practice. Moreover, such a scenario-based approach could bring confidence in, satisfaction with, and ownership of the decision, irrespective of the future outcomes.

Keywords: Decision support system; one-shot decision theory; multistage decision making; IT project; decision tree.

1. Introduction

For years, numerous approaches and theories have been suggested to deal with decision making under uncertainty (e.g., [1-10]). Most theories follow the Bernoullian framework of the weighted average and are based on the generalized theory of probability. Various experiments on psychological behavior have revealed that individuals systematically violate the axioms for the expected utility and the subjective expected utility (e.g., [11, 12]) and do not perform a weighting and summing process. Likewise, substantial empirical evidence has uncovered that salient (attention-grabbing) information has a vital role in human decision making (e.g., [13, 14]). Guo illustrated in [15, 16] that a decision alternative could be assessed based on some associated event (called the focus of a decision), which is most salient to the decision maker due to its resultant payoff and probability.

---

[*]Work received no external funding.

Thus, Guo proposed a new theory called the one-shot decision theory (OSDT) [15]. The OSDT has been applied to newsvendor problems for innovative products [17-19], duopoly markets of innovative products [20, 21], production planning problems [22], private real estate investment [23], and auction problems [24]. The one-shot theory is generalized to the focus theory of choice (FTC) in [25, 26]. OSDT can appeal to intuition, is easy to apply, and is explicable. Since it is incredibly close to the human way of thinking, a decision made with OSDT is a product of human-centric decision making incorporating the decision maker rather than just the decision analyst. In a recent development of the OSDT, Guo and Li [27] propose a multistage one-shot decision-making approach (MOSDMA) to handle the multistage decision-making problem under uncertainty. Li and Guo [28] proposed a decision model for individual multi-period consumption–investment problems using MOSDMA.

This paper proposes to apply the MOSDMA to a financial information technology project from the Central Bank of Oman. The objective is to determine the effectiveness of MOSDMA applications in re-evaluating a former decision in real practice. The study cases from this organization are the first to utilize the MOSDMA. This work supports the gap between the theory and practice aspects of decision-making models. Thus, offering insights on real-world applications for further improvements in IT project decision making and other fields such as quality management, decision governance, and any activity related to decision evaluation. Similarly, it can contribute as a method for evaluating historical decisions (such as lesson learned activities, auditing, consulting, and governance) and usage in upcoming uncertain situations. With respect to the theoretical contribution, this paper extends MOSDMA for a multiple criteria evaluation problem involving quantitative and qualitative data.

This paper is arranged as follows. In Section 2, the case study is introduced. Then, Section 3 presents the modeling and the solutions employed. Finally, the discussion and conclusion are given in Section 4.

2. The Case Study: A Financial Information Technology Project in the Central Bank

The case in review is a technology project between financial institutions in Oman and the Central Bank of Oman (CBO). Typically, the non-routine decision problems are raised to an independent committee for a group consensus.

In 2007, the CBO identified a need to implement a new Banking Oversight and Research IT System (BORS) to automate existing manual practices related to one of the bank core responsibilities. The management believed that developing an IT system would be the obvious decision when it was commenced as part of the national electronic government strategy. Eventually, the bank went through the vendors' selection process to develop and implement IT automation for the first attempt. It was found that the BORS project had not been yielding the desired objectives since its initiation in 2007. The project was under review after the termination of the second vendor in 2012. It was decided intuitively in 2012 to continue the full IT automation for the third attempt with limited employment of such decision-making approaches. Some of the reasons the previous two vendors were terminated include inadequate requirements analysis and inadequate process re-engineering. The alternative (abandon the project) was not realized as a valid course of action. In contrast, other alternatives, like improving the processes separately in a business process re-engineering (BPR), were not considered. Next, the paper will re-evaluate this decision problem by the MOSDMA.

3. Modeling and Solutions

3.1. Modeling the decision problem by the decision tree

A decision-making simulation is employed with a focus group of three personnel who aid in supplying, designing, and harvesting qualitative and quantitative data sources. First, the group agrees on the decision tree scenarios of the two alternatives. Then they supply their subjective probabilities and the weight of each considered objective through collaborative group workshops.

The (IT automation) alternative has 16 possible paths (numbered from P1 to P16), while the (Abandon) alternative has one certain value (P17), as expressed in a decision tree in Fig. 1. The event branches in the decision tree, high (H), medium (M), and low (L), are assigned to two uncertainties, namely, system reliability and employee adoption.

To find the probability of each scenario, the average of the three personnel responses is taken using a customized probability scale card with 11 scales corresponding to a level and a probability. The lowest scale rating is 1, which signifies the lowest level, "impossible," and denotes a probability of 0 to the event. Similarly, a scale rating of 11 signifies the highest level, "Certain," and denotes a probability of 1.

Four objectives are considered: payoff as cost and benefit (CB), security and efficiency (SE), social impact (SI), and employee satisfaction (ES) using a weighted sum method scorecard as outlined in Table 1. The main wight assigned for CB, SI, SE, and ES objectives are 0.2, 0.4, 0.1 and 0.3, respectively.

The payoff objective is achieved for all the outcomes based on a simple premise: Payoff = potential benefits − applicable costs. After finalizing the payoff details, the team decides on each path's objective values and normalizes them based on the weighted sum scorecard described in Table 1. The values are normalized by multiplying them to the corresponding main weight of the objective. For example, in Path 1, the CB, SI, SE, and ES values of −3,874,488, VL, H, and VL are normalized to the scores 3, 1, 2, and 1 and then to the scores

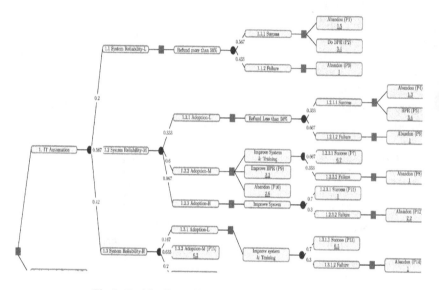

Fig. 1. Decision Tree with final probabilities and outcome.

Table 1. Weighted sum method scorecard.

Objectives	Aim	1[a]	2	3	4	5	6	7[b]
Cost/Benefits (CB) in USD[d] (weight=0.2)	Max.	−6,000,000 or less	−3,000,000 to −5,999,999	−2,999,999 to 999,999	1,000,000 to 3,999,999	4,000,000 to 7,999,999	8,000,000 to 11,999,999	12,000,000 or More
Security & Efficiency (SE) (weight=0.4)	Max.	VL[c]	L		M		H	VH
Social impact (SI) (weight=0.1)	Min.	VH	H		M		L	VL
Employee satisfaction (ES) (weight=0.3)	Max.	VL	L		M		H	VH

Note: [a]The scale 1 indicates the least favorite outcome. [b]The scale 7 indicates the most favorite outcome.
[c]VL = Very High, L = Low, M = Medium, H = High, VH = Very High
[d]UDS = United States Dollars

multiplied by the weights of the objectives 0.6, 0.4, 0.2, and 0.3, which yield a final outcome of 1.5. Subsequently, the final outcomes and the final probabilities are positioned in the decision tree presented in Fig. 1 to solve the decision problem using the MOSDMA.

3.2. Solving the problem by the multistage one-shot decision-making approach (MOSDMA)

Twelve types of focus points can be chosen in the MOSDMA to match the types of decision makers. In this paper, the Active Focus Point (AFP) is chosen according to the decision maker's style and appetite in this case. First, a decision $a \in A$ on a decision node A is considered at stage 1 (the final decision stage). The satisfaction function $u(x, a)$ and the relative likelihood function $\pi(x)$ are then obtained by normalizing the outcomes and probabilities as follows:

$$u(x, a) = r(x, a) / \max_{x \in X} r(x, a), \tag{1}$$

where $x \in X$ stands for a state.

$$\pi(x) = p(x) / \max_{x \in X} p(x) \tag{2}$$

The active focus point (AFP) of $a \in A$ is given as

$$x(a) = \operatorname*{argmax}_{x \in X} \min \{\pi(x), u(x, a)\} \tag{3}$$

Which means that, for $a \in A$, $x(a)$ is a state that can yield a relatively high outcome with a relatively high probability. It reflects the optimistic mental set of a decision maker. After finding out all active focus points of $a \in A$, the optimal decision on the decision node A denoted as $a(A)$ is selected by

$$a(A) = \operatorname*{argmax}_{a \in A} u(x(a), a), \tag{4}$$

which means that the decision maker chooses one decision that can lead to the best outcome amongst the favorite scenarios. Instead of determining the expected utility of each decision and comparing them with each other on a decision node, rolling back in stochastic dynamic programming, in the MOSDMA, the active focus point of each decision in the final stages is found and compared by their outcomes corresponding to the active focus point and rolled back to the initial decision stage. The AFP finds a state (scenario) with a higher likelihood level and a higher satisfaction level. Note that $r(x, a)$, $u(x, a)$, $p(x)$ and $\pi(x)$ for this application are listed in Fig. 2, and the detailed calculation procedure, including rolling back, is introduced in the following section.

412

Stage 4

r(x,a) / p(x) / u(x,a) / π(x)	Path	1.2.1.1	1.2.1.2	1.2.2.1	1.2.2.2	1.2.3.1	1.2.3.2
r(x,a)	Outcome	3.4	1	6.2	1	1	2.2
p(x)	Probability	0.333	0.667	0.667	0.333	0.7	0.3
u(x,a)	Satisfaction	1	0.294	1	0.161	0.455	1
π(x)	Likelihood	0.5	1	1	0.5	1	0.429
	AFP	0.5	0.294	1	0.161	0.455	0.429

Stage 3

	Path	1.1.1	1.1.2	1.2.1	1.2.2	1.2.3
r(x,a)	Outcome	3.4	1	3.4	6.2	1
p(x)	Probability	0.567	0.433	0.111	0.4	0.047
u(x,a)	Satisfaction	1	0.294	0.548	1	0.161
π(x)	Likelihood	1	0.765	0.278	1	0.117
	AFP	1	0.294	0.278	1	0.117

Stage 2

	Path	1.1	1.2	1.3
r(x,a)	Outcome	3.4	6.2	6.2
p(x)	Probability	0.113	0.227	0.148
u(x,a)	Satisfaction	0.548	1	0.652
π(x)	Likelihood	0.5	1	0.652
	AFP	0.5	1	0.652

Stage 1

	Path	1	2
r(x,a)	Outcome	6.2	3.6

Fig. 2. MOSDMA results using the active focus point (AFP).

In Fig. 2, the results are examined using (1), (2), (3), and (4) following the decision tree shown in Fig. 1. There are four stages where the event ID, such as 1.2.3, corresponds to the same one in Fig. 1. Stage 4, 3, and 2 are reduced to the main chance nodes, and Stage 1 is the main initial decision node. By using (1) and (2) to normalize the values, (3) is applied to obtain AFP between siblings' branches from Stage 4 to Stage 2, as highlighted in gray color in Fig. 2. (4) is then used at the initial stage (Stage 1) for the final decision after migrating the outcome values only. For example, to obtain the active focus point (AFP) between Sibling Branches 1.2.3.1 and 1.2.3.2, first, the minimum value of $\{\pi(x), u(x, a)\}$ is found at each branch. The minimum is 0.455 for Branch 1.2.3.1 and 0.429 for Branch 1.2.3.2. From these two minimums, the maximum value is 0.455, which means the AFP between these two siblings is Branch 1.2.3.1. Next, Branch 1.2.3.1 values are migrated to the parent branch (1.2.3). The outcome r(x,a) migrates with the same value of 1; however, probability p(x) is multiplied by this parent branch's probability presented in Fig. 1 ($0.7 \times 0.067 = 0.047$). The rolling back process in Stage 4 is repeated in Stage 3. Consequently, the minimum values of $\{\pi(x), (x,a)\}$ for Branches 1.2.1, 1.2.2, and 1.2.3 are 0.278, 1, and 0.117, respectively. This means that Branch 1.2.2 is the AFP among its sibling branches. Similarly, other AFP results at Stage 3 are found, and their values are migrated to their parent's branches in Stage 2, as done earlier. The outcome and probability values for the parent branch (Branch 1.2) after migration from the child (Branch 1.2.2) are 6.2 and 0.227 (0.567×0.4), respectively. Repeating the same process in Stage 3, the AFPs in Stage 2 is branch 1.2. After migrating the outcomes of Branch 1.2 to the final stage, the decision maker compares outcomes scores of 6.2 and 3.6 using (4). In the case of an optimistic mentality, the highest outcome amongst the favorite scenarios is the alternative with a score of 6.2, which is the alternative to continue with the (IT automation). This explanation satisfies the participants.

4. Discussion and Conclusion

The optimistic mentality of the decision makers is considered to apply the active focus point (AFP) following the MOSDMA. The AFP generates a relatively high outcome with a relatively high probability. This new approach systematically reviews the alternatives while capturing the decision maker's satisfaction levels in relevant scenarios. Recently, the project reached an undesired outcome, and the management had to abandon the project. The participants who favored (continue IT automation with a new vendor) in 2012 felt some satisfaction and confidence when this alternative was also chosen over the alternative (abandon) in this exercise.

Since this is an old case, limited choices of participants were available. Some limitations of this study could include the participant's biases and level of commitment to re-evaluating their old decision. Moreover, new updates, preceding knowledge, and teamwork in an open group composition may have affected the participant's responses compared to private inputs or inputs given under the pressure of current and future decision problems. This paper did not add new possible alternatives to the re-evaluation.

In conclusion, this study successfully applied the MOSDMA by evaluating a past decision problem. The study demonstrated that the approach could help evaluate previous decisions and its potentials to make an informed one with proper justifications aligned to stakeholders' satisfaction levels. This organization is the first to contribute to applying the proposed MOSDMA in actual practice.

Research on MOSDMA is still early and requires more theoretical and applied studies. Though the project reached an undesired outcome, this re-evaluation regains the participants' confidence in, satisfaction with, and ownership of the decision made in 2012. It also enlightened the group on the strength of proper evaluations with such approaches. Future studies may consider more complex problems, add more alternatives, and improve on the limitations of this paper.

References

1. D. Dubois, H. Prade, and R. Sabbadin, European Journal of Operational Research **128**, 459 (2001).
2. I. Gilboa, Journal of Mathematical Economics **16**, 65 (1987).
3. P. Guo and Y. Wang, Information Sciences **190**, 17 (2012).
4. D. Kahneman and A. Tversky, Econometrica **47**, 263 (1979).
5. P. Guo and H. Tanaka, European Journal of Operational Research **203**, 444 (2010).
6. P. Guo, H. Tanaka, and H.-J. Zimmermann, Fuzzy Sets and Systems **111**, 71 (2000).
7. H. Derakhshanfar, J. J. Ochoa, K. Kirytopoulos, W. Mayer, and C. Langston, Engineering, Construction and Architectural Management **28**, 1952 (2020).
8. H. Gaspars-Wieloch, Cent Eur J Oper Res **22**, 779 (2014).
9. M. Espinilla, J. Montero, and J. T. Rodríguez, International Journal of Computational Intelligence Systems **7**, 1 (2014).
10. A. Piegat and W. Sałabun, Appl. Comp. Intell. Soft Comput. **2014**, 14:14 (2014).
11. M. Allais, Econometrica: Journal of the Econometric Society 503 (1953).
12. D. Ellsberg, The Quarterly Journal of Economics 643 (1961).
13. N. Lacetera, D. G. Pope, and J. R. Sydnor, American Economic Review **102**, 2206 (2012).
14. M. R. Busse, N. Lacetera, D. G. Pope, J. Silva-Risso, and J. R. Sydnor, American Economic Review **103**, 575 (2013).
15. P. Guo, IEEE Transactions on Systems, Man, and Cybernetics - Part A: Systems and Humans **41**, 917 (2011).
16. P. Guo, in *Human-Centric Decision-Making Models for Social Sciences*, edited by P. Guo and W. Pedrycz (Springer, Berlin, Heidelberg, 2014), pp. 33–55.
17. P. Guo and X. Ma, European Journal of Operational Research **239**, 523 (2014).

18. X. Zhu and P. Guo, Optim Lett **14**, 1393 (2020).
19. X. Zhu and P. Guo, Math Meth Oper Res **86**, 255 (2017).
20. P. Guo, IJIDS **2**, 213 (2010).
21. P. Guo, R. Yan, and J. Wang, International Journal of Computational Intelligence Systems **3**, 786 (2010).
22. X. Zhu and P. Guo, 4OR-Q J Oper Res **18**, 151 (2020).
23. P. Guo, International Real Estate Review **13**, 238 (2010).
24. C. Wang and P. Guo, European Journal of Operational Research **261**, 994 (2017).
25. P. Guo, European Journal of Operational Research **276**, 1034 (2019).
26. P. Guo, European Journal of Operational Research (2022).
27. P. Guo and Y. Li, European Journal of Operational Research **236**, 612 (2014).
28. Y. Li and P. Guo, Fuzzy Sets and Systems **274**, 47 (2015).

Scoped literature review of artificial intelligence marketing adoptions for ad optimization with reinforcement learning

Johannes Sahlin*,†, Håkan Sundell*, Gideon Mbiydzenyuy* and Jesper Holgersson†,‡

*Department of Information Technology, University of Borås, Sweden
†School of Informatics, University of Skövde, Sweden
{johannes.sahlin, hakan.sundell, gideon.mbiydzenyuy}@hb.se
‡jesper.holgersson@his.se

Artificial Intelligence (AI) and Machine Learning (ML) are shaping marketing activities through digital innovations. Competition is a familiar concept for any digital retailer, and the digital transformation provides hopes for gaining a competitive edge over competitors. Those who do not adopt digital innovations risk getting outcompeted by those who do. This study aims to identify AI marketing (AIM) adoptions used for ad optimization with Reinforcement Learning (RL). A scoped literature review is used to find ad optimization adoptions research trends with RL in AIM. Scoping this is important both to research and practice as it provides spots for novel adaptations and directions of research of digital ad optimization with RL. The results of the review provide several different adoptions of ad optimization with RL in AIM. In short, the major category is Ad Relevance Optimization that takes several different forms depending on the purpose of the adoption. The underlying found themes of adoptions are Ad Attractiveness, Edge Ad, Sequential Ad and Ad Criteria Optimization. In conclusion, AIM adoptions with RL is scarce, and recommendations for future research are suggested based on the findings of the review.

Keywords: Advertisement; artificial intelligence; reinforcement learning.

1. Introduction

Precision marketing emphasizes *relevance* as an important aspect of the marketing method to retain, cross-sell and upsell existing customers. Therefore, marketers solicit personal preferences directly from recipients to achieve precision marketing. Marketers also collect and analyze behavioural and transactional data to improve relevance. Marketing's holy grail is to target consumers with faultlessly customized offers at the best occasion with the right channel. In this pursuit, marketing should consider each consumer a unique person with different needs and desires; what drives one consumer to visit a business (or purchase a product) very likely varies with another consumer. Marketing strategies that do not consider the uniqueness of the consumer are deemed to be ineffective. Mass marketing has, over time, transformed into being digital through many different channels with many different strategies, and is now transforming into artificial intelligence marketing (AIM). Artificial intelligence (AI) is considered as the main driver of innovation in marketing today, and is expected to transform marketing even further in the future. The transformation of marketing requires marketers to adapt their services and business models according to changes in society, and consequentially in consumer behaviour and expectations. Through online marketing and harsh competitive realities, a paradigm shift has occurred in marketing, which stipulates increasing importance to understand each consumer's needs and demands while accurately and quickly responding to market dynamics. At the core of this shift lies data analytics and AI. AI has proven to be a powerful tool and has transformed many industries due to its capabilities to solve problems using conventional mathematical models. AI provide a potential solution for identifying and anticipating consumer needs in real-time. Adopting AI applications into marketing may provide more special (and precise) offers that consumers want and use.

This study suggests scoping the literature of AIM adoptions applied with reinforcement learning (RL). Scoping the literature of AIM and RL may reveal gaps of application areas where AIM is applied. Those gaps can then be used to set future research projects and agendas. Those efforts, in turn, may lead to improved situations and novel procedures for performing AIM. Research into AIM innovations is crucial as it can directly provide value to marketers, consumers and organizations. For marketers, it may translate to improved working methods, e.g., more powerful tools or better support. For consumers, it could be less annoyance and increased precision and relevancy of ads. For businesses, it could lead to improved efficiency in many forms, e.g., increased sales or less churn. This study aims to perform a scoped systematic review for identifying RL procedures for AIM while studying AIM adoptions and application areas. Surveying the adoptions of RL in ads is crucial as it can map the existing adoptions and highlight research opportunities. The following section will provide a short introduction to AIM and essential related concepts to RL. Then the systematic review procedures will be presented, and the results of the method will be presented. Finally, the conclusions and a discussion of the found results will be provided.

2. Methodology

This study used a scoping systematic review with purposive, criterion and snowball sampling approaches for satisfying the aim. A systematic review structures a flow of information through different phases: identification, screening, eligibility and inclusion. Below, the following aspects tied to the method are highlighted; criterion sampling & snowball sampling, eligibility criteria, information sources, inclusion and exclusion criteria, data collection process, synthesis of results, and additional analysis of the synthesized results. Scoping reviews do not assess study quality. Scoping reviews attempt to provide an initial indication of the potential size and nature of the available literature on a particular topic. Researchers may conduct such a review to examine the extent, range and nature of research activities, determine the value of undertaking a full systematic review, or identify research gaps in the extant literature. Scoping reviews can use a structured approach, which ensures consistency. This review was based on the following recommendations of: (1) start by identifying the research question, (2) identify relevant studies from different sources, (3 and 4) encompass study selection and data charting, and, finally, (5) analyse the data. *Criterion sampling* involves selecting cases that meet some predetermined criterion of importance. In the sense of literature review, *snowball sampling* is a way of finding literature by using a key document on your subject as a starting point. Then one inspects the bibliography in the key document to find other relevant titles to the subject. Then through the newly selected titles, one inspects these new titles' bibliographies to find yet more relevant titles. Notably to mention is that the snowball sampling, for this review, used the same *eligibility criteria* across all literature. This study aims at surveying adoptions of RL in advertising. The articles where investigated of concepts related ML adoptions of RL in advertising, or variations close to this initial search point. The *information sources* used for the identification of literature were (1) Scopus, (2) Web of Science, and IEEE Xplore. These information sources were searched during the all available years. *Publication type* was set to journal or conference, and *access* was set to open access. The keywords used for searching the information sources used the following rationale: "reinforcement learning" and "advertisement". Only English language articles were selected. The *data collection* took place between the dates 2021-11-13 - 2021-11-14. In Table 1, the found articles are presented, grouped by information source or technique used to capture additional sources. Unfortunately, one article from Scopus at the time of data collection was rendered corrupt and therefore excluded. Additionally, in Table 1 the articles filtered after the screening and eligibility are presented. The literature were then processed for information regarding adoptions of RL in advertising settings. The gathered literature from the initial database search were then screened for relevance through investigations of titles and abstracts to begin. The criteria for relevance, consisted of determining if the literature were in the study domain, i.e., applying RL and the domain of advertisement. After this, the literature were assessed for eligibility by investigating the full-text of the article. Full-texts that did not use RL algorithms were excluded. The data collected were then analyzed for adoptions used and themed. Themes were qualitatively conceptualised as patterns of shared meaning across the data, being underpinned or united by a central concept which were important to the understanding of the theme. These themed adoptions were then presented through a concept-author matrix, See Table 2, for visualizing the allocation of the adoption throughout the selected literature.

3. Results and Analysis

The literature review resulted in twelve articles after the identification, screening and eligibility procedures. In Table 1, the results from each database are broken down into the search phases of identification, screening and eligibility. The results show the inclusion and exclusion of articles through the phases. In Table 2, the concept by author relation is presented.

Basically, all RL approaches for ad optimization is for increasing relevance by apply relevance optimization. Zhao et al.[14] applied RL for providing recommendations in a e-commerce setting. Click-through rate (CTR), measures how well your ad is performing in the sense of relevance. CTR prediction aims to recall the ad that users are interested in and to lead users to click. Vargas et al.[10] applied RL to determine which content is more demanded (e.g., receive more clicks). Zhang et al.[12] focused on the ranking

Table 1. Search results by each database through search phases.

Database	Identification	Screening	Eligibility
Scopus	34	7	7
WoS	9	0	0
IEEE	5	0	0
Snowball	6	6	6

Table 2. Concept-author matrix.

Concept	Article
Ad Relevance Optimization	Zhao et al.[14], Vargas et al.[10], Zhang et al.[12], Liang[6]
Edge Ad Optimization	Lou et al.[7]
Ad Attractiveness Optimization	Wang et al.[11]
Sequential Ad Optimization	Hao et al.[5]
Ad Criteria Optimization	Du et al.[4], Afshar et al.[1], Cai et al.[3], Zhao et al.[13], Cai et al.[2]

ads in large-scale search engines with RL. Liang[6] used RL for extracting effective features from massive advertising data and predicting advertising precision accurately and efficiently.

Ad Attractiveness Optimization. Wang et al.[11] investigated how a model-based RL framework could generate ad texts for increased CTR. Wang et al.[11] goes beyond measuring CTR but connects it to generational aspects compared to other CTR works (e.g., Zhao et al.,[13] Vargas et al.[10] and Zhang et al.[12]). The underlying argument by Wang et al.[11] is that attractive and relevant ads can significantly increase the probability that consumers respond to their value propositions.

Edge Ad Optimization. A digital roadside billboard is a helpful tool for advertising. They can easily make a more profound impression on potential customers like drivers and passengers. Billboards can bring graphic advertising content dynamically. Existing ad strategies mainly focus on what ad content should be delivered and select locations for the static billboards. To maximize the profit for the advertiser, Lou et al.[7] decide to use dynamic billboards where an agent decides what to display. Changing ads dynamically according to the situation, is the problem called the *dynamic ad problem*.[7] Here, an agent will repeatedly observe the current state s_t of the environment and take action a from all available actions in this state. Then, the state of the environment will transfer to s_{t+1}, and the agent will get a reward r_t from the environment for its action. Each billboard observes its environment, such as the locations of the potential consumers and the preferences of the potential consumers. Since every billboard has its agent, it can be viewed as multi-agent RL as there are many billboards.

Sequential Ad Optimization. Ads are vital for advertisers to reach their consumers. Usually, the objective is to maximize the advertiser's cumulative revenue over time under a budget constraint. An ad usually needs to be exposed to the consumer multiple times, until the consumer finally puts an order. Yet, existing ad systems mainly focus on single ad exposures, ignoring the benefits of multiple exposures contributing to the final conversion, thus usually falling into suboptimal solutions. Hao et al.[5] formulate the sequential advertising strategy optimization as a dynamic knapsack problem targeted with RL.

Ad Criteria Optimization. Ad criteria optimization aims to intelligently set criteria to maximize other criteria, e.g., expenses under a budget or setting discount while maximizing profit. Du et al.[4] found that a RL approach functions well to optimize bidding strategies in the computational advertising industry, which maximizes one criterion while keeping another criterion below a given threshold. Afshar et al.[1] applied RL for buying online ad placements in real time auctions and maximize profit. Zhao et al.[13] and Cai et al.[2] focus on the real-time bidding problem, they propose model-based RL models from the perspective of advertisers to learn the bidding strategy in real-time bidding (RTB) display advertising, for the aim of boosting the performance of advertisers. Cai et al.[3] target the issue of allocating impressions to sellers in e-commerce websites for increased profit, where impressions are the total number of exposures to your ad.

4. Discussion and Conclusion

This study scoped RL adoptions in advertising. The study has provided several adoption areas where RL has been used in AIM for improved ads. However, the scoping indicates that RL's adoption in ad optimization is weak, and there are plenty of gaps to incorporate RL in AIM further. Besides scoping the adoptions, this study serves to find future research agendas. Based on the review, we suggest targeting gaps previous research has not covered. Wang et al.[11] showed how pretrained language models and RL can be used to increase the attractiveness of ads when working with CTR. Wang et al.[11] argue that template-based approaches are too rigid, but their study with complete statistical learning showed that 15% of the output of the generative text models are nonsense. This justifies our hybrid design,[8,9] that suggests combining rule-based generation with statistical learning for generating ads, as businesses cannot accept such a notable falloff. We further suggest combining the rule-based approach with statistical learning by using an RL agent to control the rule-based model and, at the same time, consider consumer traits. The agent may observe the environment of consumer groups as the agent builds ads. By combining the rule-based model with an agent, there is a chance to join many of the adoption areas, e.g., attractiveness optimization,[11] criteria optimization,[4] and edge optimization[7] at once. Edge ad optimization, similar to Lou et al.,[7] could be performed with edge machine learning. Conceptually, actors could push their intentions to consumer devices and let the devices build ads with local device data, for increased precision with small intrusion into integrity. Another direction to study regarding ad optimization is how to design ad optimization that allow machines and humans to collaborate.

References

1. Reza Refaei Afshar, Jason Rhuggenaath, Yingqian Zhang, and Uzay Kaymak. A reward shaping approach for reserve price optimization using deep reinforcement learning. In *The International Joint Conference on Neural Networks (IJCNN2021)*, 2021.

2. Han Cai, Kan Ren, Weinan Zhang, Kleanthis Malialis, Jun Wang, Yong Yu, and Defeng Guo. Real-time bidding by reinforcement learning in display advertising. In *Proceedings of the Tenth ACM International Conference on Web Search and Data Mining*, pages 661–670, 2017.

3. Qingpeng Cai, Aris Filos-Ratsikas, Pingzhong Tang, and Yiwei Zhang. Reinforcement mechanism design for e-commerce. In *Proceedings of the 2018 World Wide Web Conference*, pages 1339–1348, 2018.

4. Manxing Du, Redouane Sassioui, Georgios Varisteas, Mats Brorsson, Omar Cherkaoui, et al. Improving real-time bidding using a constrained markov decision process. In *International Conference on Advanced Data Mining and Applications*, pages 711–726. Springer, 2017.

5. Xiaotian Hao, Zhaoqing Peng, Yi Ma, Guan Wang, Junqi Jin, Jianye Hao, Shan Chen, Rongquan Bai, Mingzhou Xie, Miao Xu, et al. Dynamic knapsack optimization towards efficient multi-channel sequential advertising. In *International Conference on Machine Learning*, pages 4060–4070. PMLR, 2020.

6. Haiqing Liang. A precision advertising strategy based on deep reinforcement learning. *Ingénierie des Systèmes d'Information*, 25(3), 2020.

7. Kaihao Lou, Yongjian Yang, En Wang, Zheli Liu, Thar Baker, and Ali Kashif Bashir. Reinforcement learning based advertising strategy using crowdsensing vehicular data. *IEEE Transactions on Intelligent Transportation Systems*, 2020.

8. Johannes Sahlin, Håkan Sundell, Håkan Alm, and Jesper Holgersson. Short message service campaign taxonomy for an intelligent marketing

system. In *Developments of Artificial Intelligence Technologies in Computation and Robotics: Proceedings of the 14th International FLINS Conference (FLINS 2020)*, pages 606–613. World Scientific, 2020.

9. Johannes Sahlin, Håkan Sundell, Håkan Alm, and Jesper Holgersson. Evaluating artificial short message service campaigns through rule based multi-instance multi-label classification. In *AAAI 2021 Spring Symposium on Combining Machine Learning and Knowledge Engineering*, volume 2846. Sun SITE Central Europe, 2021.

10. Ana M Vargas et al. Linear bayes policy for learning in contextual-bandits. *Expert systems with applications*, 40(18):7400–7406, 2013.

11. Xiting Wang, Xinwei Gu, Jie Cao, Zihua Zhao, Yulan Yan, Bhuvan Middha, and Xing Xie. Reinforcing pretrained models for generating attractive text advertisements. In *Proceedings of the 27th ACM SIGKDD Conference on Knowledge Discovery & Data Mining*, pages 3697–3707, 2021.

12. Yusi Zhang, Zhi Yang, Liang Wang, and Li He. Autor3: Automated real-time ranking with reinforcement learning in e-commerce sponsored search advertising. In *Proceedings of the 28th ACM International Conference on Information and Knowledge Management*, pages 2499–2507, 2019.

13. Jun Zhao, Guang Qiu, Ziyu Guan, Wei Zhao, and Xiaofei He. Deep reinforcement learning for sponsored search real-time bidding. In *Proceedings of the 24th ACM SIGKDD international conference on knowledge discovery & data mining*, pages 1021–1030, 2018.

14. Xiangyu Zhao, Liang Zhang, Zhuoye Ding, Long Xia, Jiliang Tang, and Dawei Yin. Recommendations with negative feedback via pairwise deep reinforcement learning. In *Proceedings of the 24th ACM SIGKDD International Conference on Knowledge Discovery & Data Mining*, pages 1040–1048, 2018.

Examining QFD based omnichannel capacity of service industries with interval type-2 hesitant DEMATEL-TOPSIS

Luis Martínez* and Rosa M. Rodríguez†

Department of Computer Science, University of Jaén
Jaén 23071, Spain
*martin@ujaen.es
†rmrodrig@ujaen.es
www.ujaen.es

Hasan Dinçer‡ and Serhat Yüksel§

The School of Business, İstanbul Medipol University
İstanbul, 34810, Turkey
‡hdincer@medipol.edu.tr
§serhatyuksel@medipol.edu.tr
www.medipol.edu.tr

Tuba Bozaykut Bük

Mikado Sustainable Development Consultancy
İstanbul, 34394, Turkey
tuba.bozaykut@mikadoconsulting.com
www.mikadoconsulting.com

The aim of this study is to examine the omnichannel capacity of the banking industries in E7 economies. For this purpose, quality function deployment approach is taken into the consideration. The analysis of this study consists of five different stages. Customer requirement dimensions are weighted in the first stage with the help of interval type-2 hesitant fuzzy DEMATEL method. On the other side, type-2 hesitant fuzzy TOPSIS approach is used in other stages to measure omnichannel capacity of the customer requirements, evaluate new service development process, assess the innovative channels and rank E7 countries with respect to the omnichannel performance. The main novelty of this study is to evaluate the omnichannel capacity of the service industry with a novel fuzzy decision-making model. In this process, the main reason of using type-2 hesitant fuzzy information is to model the hesitancy of the experts so that uncertainties in this process can be handled more effectively.

Keywords: Omnichannel; banking; quality function feployment; type-2 hesitant fuzzy DEMATEL; type-2 hesitant fuzzy TOPSIS.

1. Introduction

Omnichannel banking are labelled as the "new generation banking" that has a higher capacity for answering customer needs (Jayamaha, 2016). Thereby, current banking management by taking customer requirements into the center must design omnichannel strategies both taking into consideration technological and social dimensions. Previous studies related to omnichannel capacities indicate consistency as a critical dimension in terms of service continuity (Parise et al., 2016), price consistency, processing speed (Jayamaha, 2016) and customer satisfaction (Maiya, 2017). It means that, this dimension is related to the continuous and uninterrupted services regardless of which channel is used. Another important channel feature is the customization to design products and services that can answer customer expectations through developing collaboration with technology firms. Therefore, technological cooperation, optimization (Schmidt et al., 2017), technological partnerships are all significant for creating a personalized omnichannel experience.

Omnichannel capacity of the banking industries in E7 economies are evaluated in this study. For this purpose, a novel fuzzy decision-making model is generated. In this model, five different stages of QFD approach are taken into consideration. Interval type-2 hesitant fuzzy DEMATEL method is used to examine customer requirement dimensions. On the other hand, in the following stages, type-2 hesitant fuzzy TOPSIS approach is taken into consideration. The main novelty of this study is to measure the omnichannel capacity of the service industry by considering a novel fuzzy decision-making model. Hence, by considering the analysis results, appropriate strategies can be presented for the performance improvements of the service companies.

The proposed model has also some superiorities by comparing with the previous ones. In this context, a hybrid model is created by using both DEMATEL and TOPSIS techniques. In other words, calculations in all processes in the model are made using a model. This situation contributes to increasing the objectivity of the findings. In this process, the main reason of using type-2 hesitant fuzzy information is to model the hesitancy of the experts so that uncertainties in this process can be handled more effectively. Additionally, DEMATEL approach has also benefits over other similar techniques. For instance, impact relation map among the criteria can be created. This situation provides a significant advantage in comparison for the models where DEMATEL was not considered. Moreover, TOPSIS methodology considers the distances to both positive and negative optimal solutions. Hence, more appropriate results can be achieved in this model.

2. Methodology

This part includes the information about IT2 hesitant fuzzy DEMATEL and TOPSIS.

2.1. IT2 Hesitant Fuzzy DEMATEL

Decision making trial and evaluation laboratory is known as DEMATEL method that can identify the significance levels of the variables. DEMATEL approach has been extended to deal with interval type-2 fuzzy sets (Abdullah and Zulkifli, 2015) that follows five steps in its analysis process:

1. The evaluations of the decision makers are obtained under the hesitancy in the first step. Moreover, these evaluations are converted into the interval type-2 fuzzy sets.

2. The initial direct-relation fuzzy matrix is constructed by considering the evaluations collectively. This step also includes the generation of the initial direct-relation fuzzy matrix $(\widetilde{Z})$. Equations (1) and (2) are taken into the consideration for this purpose.

$$\tilde{Z} = \begin{bmatrix} 0 & \tilde{z}_{12} & \cdots & & \cdots & \tilde{z}_{1n} \\ \tilde{z}_{21} & 0 & \cdots & & \cdots & \tilde{z}_{2n} \\ \vdots & \vdots & \ddots & & \cdots & \cdots \\ \vdots & \vdots & \vdots & & \ddots & \vdots \\ \tilde{z}_{n1} & \tilde{z}_{n2} & \cdots & & \cdots & 0 \end{bmatrix} \tag{1}$$

$$\tilde{Z} = \frac{\tilde{Z}^1 + \tilde{Z}^2 + \tilde{Z}^3 + \cdots \tilde{Z}^n}{n} \tag{2}$$

3. The pairwise matrix is normalized. In this process, the Eqs. (3)-(5) are used.

$$\tilde{X} = \begin{bmatrix} \tilde{x}_{11} & \tilde{x}_{12} & \cdots & & \cdots & \tilde{x}_{1n} \\ \tilde{x}_{21} & \tilde{x}_{22} & \cdots & & \cdots & \tilde{x}_{2n} \\ \vdots & \vdots & \ddots & & \cdots & \cdots \\ \vdots & \vdots & \vdots & & \ddots & \vdots \\ \tilde{x}_{n1} & \tilde{x}_{n2} & \cdots & & \cdots & \tilde{x}_{nn} \end{bmatrix} \tag{3}$$

$$\tilde{x}_{ij} = \frac{\tilde{z}_{ij}}{r} = \left(\left(\frac{Z_{a_{ij}}}{r}, \frac{Z_{b_{ij}}}{r}, \frac{Z_{c_{ij}}}{r}, \frac{Z_{d_{ij}}}{r}; H_1(z_{ij}^U), H_2(z_{ij}^U) \right), \left(\frac{Z_{e_{ij}}}{r}, \frac{Z_{f_{ij}}}{r}, \frac{Z_{g_{ij}}}{r}, \frac{Z_{h_{ij}}}{r}; H_1(z_{ij}^L), H_2(z_{ij}^L) \right) \right) \tag{4}$$

$$r = max \left(max_{1 \leq i \leq n} \sum_{j=1}^{n} Z_{d_{ij}}, max_{1 \leq i \leq n} \sum_{j=1}^{n} Z_{d_{ij}} \right) \tag{5}$$

4. The total influence fuzzy matrix is created with the help of the Eqs. (6)-(10).

$$X_{\acute{a}} = \begin{bmatrix} 0 & a'_{12} & \cdots & \cdots & a'_{1n} \\ a'_{21} & 0 & \cdots & \cdots & a'_{2n} \\ \vdots & \vdots & \ddots & \cdots & \cdots \\ \vdots & \vdots & \vdots & \ddots & \vdots \\ a'_{n1} & a'_{n2} & \cdots & \cdots & 0 \end{bmatrix}, \ldots, X_{\hbar} = \begin{bmatrix} 0 & h'_{12} & \cdots & \cdots & h'_{1n} \\ h'_{21} & 0 & \cdots & \cdots & h'_{2n} \\ \vdots & \vdots & \ddots & \cdots & \cdots \\ \vdots & \vdots & \vdots & \ddots & \vdots \\ h'_{n1} & h'_{n2} & \cdots & \cdots & 0 \end{bmatrix} \quad (6)$$

$$\tilde{T} = \lim_{k \to \infty} \tilde{X} + \tilde{X}^2 + \cdots + \tilde{X}^k \quad (7)$$

$$\tilde{T} = \begin{bmatrix} \tilde{t}_{11} & \tilde{t}_{12} & \cdots & \cdots & \tilde{t}_{1n} \\ \tilde{t}_{21} & \tilde{t}_{22} & \cdots & \cdots & \tilde{t}_{2n} \\ \vdots & \vdots & \ddots & \cdots & \cdots \\ \vdots & \vdots & \vdots & \ddots & \vdots \\ \tilde{t}_{n1} & \tilde{t}_{n2} & \cdots & \cdots & \tilde{t}_{nn} \end{bmatrix} \quad (8)$$

$$\tilde{t}_{ij} = \left(a''_{ij}, b''_{ij}, c''_{ij}, d''_{ij}; H_1(\tilde{t}_{ij}{}^U), H_2(\tilde{t}_{ij}{}^U) \right), \left(e''_{ij}, f''_{ij}, g''_{ij}, h''_{ij}; H_1(\tilde{t}_{ij}{}^L), H_2(\tilde{t}_{ij}{}^L) \right) \quad (9)$$

$$[a''_{ij}] = X_{\acute{a}} \times (I - X_{\acute{a}})^{-1}, \ldots, [h''_{ij}] = X_{\hbar} \times (I - X_{\hbar})^{-1} \quad (10)$$

5. In the last step, the defuzzified total influence matrix is generated by considering the Eqs. (11)-(14).

$$Def_T = \frac{\frac{(u_U - l_U) + (\beta_U \times m_{1U} - l_U) + (\alpha_U \times m_{2U} - l_U)}{4} + l_U + \left[\frac{(u_L - l_L) + (\beta_L \times m_{1L} - l_L) + (\alpha_L \times m_{2L} - l_L)}{4} + l_L \right]}{2} \quad (11)$$

$$Def_T = T = [t_{ij}]_{n \times n}, \ i, j = 1, 2, \ldots, n \quad (12)$$

$$\tilde{D}_i{}^{def} = r = \left[\sum_{j=1}^{n} t_{ij} \right]_{n \times 1} = (r_i)_{n \times 1} = (r_1, \ldots, r_i, \ldots, r_n) \quad (13)$$

$$\tilde{R}_i{}^{def} = y = \left[\sum_{i=1}^{n} t_{ij} \right]'_{1 \times n} = (y_j)'_{1 \times n} = (y_1, \ldots, y_i, \ldots, y_n) \quad (14)$$

$\tilde{D}_i{}^{def}$ represents the sum of all vector rows and the sum of all vector columns is identified by $\tilde{R}_i{}^{def}$. Within this framework, high $\left(\tilde{D}_i + \tilde{R}_i \right)^{def}$ value means being closer to the central point.

2.2. IT2 Hesitant Fuzzy TOPSIS

"Technique for Order Preference by Similarity to Ideal Solution" is explained as TOPSIS. The main purpose of this methodology is to rank the alternatives based on their importance levels. In other words, this technique is taken into consideration to find the best alternative among many different factors. The main superiority of TOPSIS by comparing with similar approaches in the literature is that the distances to both negative and positive ideal solutions are used. This situation has a positive impact on reaching more precise results. In this study, this model is considered with hesitant interval type-2 fuzzy sets. The collective hesitant evaluations of decision makers are provided for the fuzzy decision matrix in the calculation process. Moreover, the positive and negative ideal solutions are determined. Thus, the best alternative is defined by looking at the distance from this ideal solution (Cevik Onar et al., 2014).

1. The fuzzy positive-ideal solution (A^+) and fuzzy negative ideal solution (A^-) are identified as in the Eq. (15).

$$A^+ = max(v_1, v_2, v_3, \dots v_n); A^- = min(v_1, v_2, v_3, \dots v_n) \qquad (15)$$

2. The values of D^+ and D^- are calculated by considering the Eqs. (16) and (17).

$$D_i^+ = \sqrt{\sum_{i=1}^{m}(v_i - A_i^+)^2} \qquad (16)$$

$$D_i^- = \sqrt{\sum_{i=1}^{m}(v_i - A_i^-)^2} \qquad (17)$$

3. The closeness coefficient (C_i) is defined with the help of the Eq. (18).

$$CC_i = \frac{D_i^-}{D_i^+ + D_i^-} \qquad (18)$$

3. An Application on the Banking Industries of E7 Economies

Stage 1: Weighting the criteria of customer requirements in the banking sector using IT2HF DEMATEL

The first stage is related to the weighting the criteria of customer requirements in the banking sector. For this purpose, IT2HF DEMATEL methodology is taken into consideration. Within this framework, three decision makers are appointed to provide their evaluations on the criteria and alternatives by using a linguistic term set. The expert team consists of the top managers in the banking industry who have at least 22-year experience. These evaluations are converted into interval type-2 fuzzy numbers. Table 1 gives information about the weights of the criteria related to the customer requirements.

Table 1. Defuzzified total relation matrix and the weights for the customer requirements.

	C1	C2	C3	C4	r	y	r+y	r-y	Weights
Functionality (C1)	0.72	0.87	0.85	0.83	3.26	3.32	6.58	-0.06	0.266
Customer Interaction (C2)	0.73	0.55	0.70	0.65	2.63	3.16	5.78	-0.53	0.234
Operational Facilities (C3)	0.90	0.81	0.62	0.73	3.05	3.06	6.11	-0.01	0.246
Cost and Earnings (C4)	0.98	0.93	0.89	0.65	3.45	2.85	6.30	0.60	0.254

Influence degrees of each criterion demonstrates that Cost and earnings (C4) is the most influencing factor while customer interaction (C2) is the most influenced component among the criteria. However, functionality (C1) is the most weighted criteria with 26.6 percentage as customer interaction (C2) has the weakest importance with 23.4%.

Stage 2: Measuring the Omnichannel capacity on the customer requirements in banking sector based on the house of quality with IT2HF TOPSIS

Following stage computes the omnichannel capacity according to the customer requirements in the E7 banking sector. For this reason, the first step of QFD called as house of quality is used for measuring the potential impacts of omnichannel capacity on each criterion of customer requirements. Final ranking and weighting results of omnichannel capacity have been calculated and the results are seen in Table 2.

Table 2. Weighting results of the omnichannel capacity.

Alternatives	D+	D-	Ci	Ranking	Weighting
Consistency (A1)	0.244	0.945	0.795	1	0.419
Customization (A2)	0.234	0.881	0.790	2	0.417
Operational Infrastructure (A3)	1.006	0.224	0.182	3	0.096
Information and Communication Capacity (A4)	0.948	0.140	0.129	4	0.068

According to the results, consistency (A1) is the best performing factor and the most weighted in the set of criteria. In addition to this aspect, customization (A2) has the second highest importance. However, Information and Communication capacity (A4) is the weakest factor in the ranking and weighting results.

Stage 3: Measuring the new service development process on the omnichannel capacity of banking sector with IT2HF TOPSIS

Stage 3 defines the second step of QFD for the integrated analysis. A set of alternatives used in the first step of QFD is considered as a set of criteria in the fuzzy decision matrix. Thus, the integrated QFD could be applied to analyze the omnichannel capacity of banking industry. The summarized results of the method are seen in Table 3.

Table 3. Weighting results of the new service development process.

Alternatives	D+	D-	Ci	Ranking	Weighting
Design (A1)	0.253	0.715	0.739	1	0.333
Analysis (A2)	0.344	0.571	0.624	2	0.282
Development (A3)	0.783	0.285	0.267	4	0.120
Commercialization (A4)	0.520	0.741	0.587	3	0.265

Stage 4: Measuring the innovative channels on the new service development process of banking sector with IT2HF TOPSIS

Stage 4 examines the next step of integrated QFD. The results of step 3 of QFD are illustrated in Table 4.

Table 4. Weighting results of the innovative channels.

Alternatives	D+	D-	Ci	Ranking	Weighting
Competitors (A1)	0.142	1.155	0.890	1	0.303
Suppliers (A2)	0.469	0.730	0.608	2	0.207
Customers (A3)	1.128	0.175	0.134	6	0.046
Employees (A4)	0.750	0.457	0.379	4	0.129
Top Managers (A5)	0.589	0.734	0.555	3	0.189
Owners (A6)	1.008	0.598	0.373	5	0.127

The results clarify that competitor (A1) is the best alternative for the innovative channels of banking sector while customers (A3) is the weakest factor.

Stage 5: Measuring the E7 banking industry on the innovative channels with IT2HF TOPSIS

The final step of QFD is to rank the banking industries of E7 economies according to the innovative channels by considering the integrated QFD. Table 5 examines the ranking results of each E7 economies.

Table 5. Ranking results of the omnichannel capacity for the E7 banking industry.

Alternatives	D+	D-	Ci	Ranking
Brazil (A1)	0.490	0.229	0.318	5
China (A2)	0.389	0.364	0.484	3
India (A3)	0.123	0.658	0.843	1
Indonesia (A4)	0.570	0.182	0.242	6
Russia (A5)	0.678	0.157	0.188	7
Mexico (A6)	0.403	0.396	0.496	2
Turkey (A7)	0.388	0.360	0.481	4

Overall results provided from the integrated QFD demonstrate that omnichannel capacity of Indian banking industry (A3) is the best among the E7 economies. However, Russia (A5) has the weakest performance by considering the omni-channel capacity of banking sector accordingly.

4. Conclusion

Based on the analysis results, it is strongly recommended that the issues, such as speed of the transaction, queue time, ease of use should be mainly considered by the banks to satisfy customer requirements. Similarly, banks should also give importance to the consistency factors, such as the continuity of the services and price consistency of different services to increase their omnichannel capacity. For this purpose, cost management analysis should be carried out by the banks effectively. With the help of this issue, the banks can determine their prices in a successful manner. Therefore, omnichannel marketing strategies can be more successful. In addition to them, a comprehensive evaluation should be conducted for the banks to understand the strategies of the competitors. Hence, more appropriate strategies can be created, and this situation provides a competitive advantage for the banks.

In this study, some important points are underlined to increase omnichannel capacity of the banks. Therefore, it can be said that this study mainly provides opportunities for the countries that have low performance in omnichannel capacity. Additionally, a novel fuzzy decision-making model is constructed in this study. However, the main limitation is focusing on only emerging economies. The performance of the banking industry also plays a critical role for the success of other country groups. Therefore, in the future studies, analyzing this situation for developed economies also make contribution to the literature. Furthermore, the proposed model can also be improved in new studies. Within this framework, new fuzzy sets can be taken into consideration.

Acknowledgments

This study is constructed in the scope of The GEBİP award program (Outstanding Young Scientists Awards) by TURKISH ACADEMY OF SCIENCES.

References

1. L. Abdullah, and N. Zulkifli. Integration of fuzzy AHP and interval type-2 fuzzy DEMATEL: An application to human resource management. *Expert Systems with Applications*, **42** 9, 4397-4409, (2015).
2. S. Cevik Onar, B. Oztaysi, and C. Kahraman. Strategic decision selection using hesitant fuzzy TOPSIS and interval type-2 fuzzy AHP: a case study. *International Journal of Computational intelligence systems*, 7 5, 1002-1021, (2014).
3. R. Jayamaha. Thriving in a Digital World: Non-Banks have Challenged Retail Business of Banks. *World Bank Group*, 22-50, (2016).
4. R. Maiya. How to be a truly digital bank. *Journal of Digital Banking*, 1 4, 338-348, (2017).
5. S. Parise, P. J. Guinan, and R. Kafka. Solving the crisis of immediacy: How digital technology can transform the customer experience. *Business Horizons*, **59** 4, 411-420, (2016).
6. J. Schmidt, P. Drews, and I. Schirmer. Digitalization of the Banking Industry: A Multiple Stakeholder Analysis on Strategic Alignment. *Twenty-third Americas Conference on Information Systems, Boston*, 1-10, (2017).

Intelligent assessment approach to garment fit degree for garment e-mass customization using probabilistic neural network

Zhujun Wang* and Yingmei Xing

School of Textile and Garment, Anhui Polytechnic University
Wuhu, Anhui, China
ahpuwzj@ahpu.edu.cn
www.ahpu.edu.cn

Xuyuan Tao, Xianyi Zeng† and Pascal Bruniaux

GEMTEX Laboratory, Ecole Nationale Superieure des Arts et Industries Textiles
Roubaix, France
†xianyi.zeng@ensait.fr

This paper presented a new approach to garment fit assessment using probabilistic neural network, aiming to promote the implementation of garment e-mass customization in the new era of Industry 4.0. The proposed method was supported by several PNN models. The inputs of each PNN model were the garment ease allowance at the feature position as well as the parameters of fabric mechanical properties collected in a 3D virtual design environment. At the same time, the output of the PNN model was the real garment fitting data. The experimental results revealed that the present approach's performance was feasible and could predict the fast and precise gar. Furthermore, a new interactive fashion design and manufacturing system for customized garments can be developed by using the proposed models.

Keywords: Garment e-mass customization; Industry 4.0; garment fit degree assessment; probabilistic neural network.

1. Introduction

Nowadays, the fashion industry has been experiencing Industry 4.0, aiming to provide fashion products and services for consumers more accurate, fast, sustainable, and smart [1]. In this context, there has been a tendency for fashion brand companies to meet the fierce market compe by implementing e-mass customization (e-MC). Meanwhile, thanks to the advance in emerging digital technologies (i.e., virtual reality, augmented reality, extended reality, etc.) [2-4], commercially available garment computer-aided design (CAD) software systems, such as Lectra 3D prototype, Clo 3D, and Vidya, have been applied intensively as a powerful tool to support garment e-MC recently. The outstanding advantages of

434

these software/solutions mainly exist in the following aspects: (1) enhancing human-computer interactions between consumers, designers, and products; (2) prominently decreasing the costs for the companies by employing virtual garment samples instead of the physical garment samples in the design process; (3) promoting the implementation of clean, green, and sustainable manufacturing for enterprises by reducing the material wastes. Due to these, big fashion companies like Decathlon, Nike, and Adidas have broadly utilized the 3D garment CAD for offering highly customized garments [5-8].

Furthermore, as the 3D garment CAD can effectively overcome the limitations of traditional 2D garment design methods by 3D digitalized model [9], they have also attracted extensive attention in academia. For example, Kuzimichev et al. developed a method to reconstruct the historical garment based on virtual technology [10]. Mulat et al. put forward a bra pattern design process for customizing female seamless soft armour based on innovative 3D reverse engineering approaches [11-13]. These studies provided good cases of the application of virtual reality-based 3D garment CAD. However, a convincing fashion product demonstration based on virtual try-on that powerfully supports consumers' purchasing decision-making is still a challenging issue for the success of garment e-MC [14]. Therefore, we put forth a machine learning-based assessment approach to garment fit, aiming to enhance the reliability and precision of virtual reality-based garment design by acting on the interactions between the design parameters in a 3D virtual design environment and the real garment fitting data.

2. General Research Scheme

2.1. Brief introduction of probabilistic neural network

The probabilistic neural network (PNN) is denoted as a Bayesian decision rules-based artificial neural network (ANN) [15,16]. PNN is usually composed of four layers of neurons which are the input layer, pattern layer, summation layer, and output layer, see Fig. 1. Compared with other types of ANN, the number of parameters for creating the PNN model is relatively fewer. Furthermore, the learning process of PNN can be greatly shortened without bringing negative influences on the prediction performance contributing to its inherently parallel structure. Hence, PNN has been employed as a powerful computational tool for dealing with pattern recognition and classification problems in the clothing industry [17].

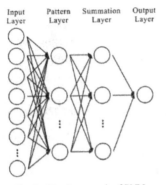

Fig. 1. The framework of PNN.

2.2. General research scheme

The proposed machine learning-based assessment approach to garment fit was supported by several PNN-based predictive models of garment fit degrees. For various garment styles, the concrete PNN models corresponding to the feature positions were determined based on the domain knowledge of fashion designers. For each predictive model of garment fit degree at a specific feature position, the output was the real garment fit degree, while the inputs were the garment design parameters collected from a 3D garment CAD, involving the garment ease allowances and the parameters of fabric mechanical properties.

In the process of garment fit degree assessment, we firstly estimated the garment fit degree at each feature position using the PNN model. Afterwards, we can obtain the overall garment fit degree by aggregating the predictive fit degrees of all the feature positions according to Eq. (1).

$$wf = \sum_{i=1}^{k} w^i lf^i, i \in \{1, \dots k\} \tag{1}$$

Where, wf refers to the overall garment fit degree; lf^i is the predictive fit degree of the i-th feature position; w^i represents the weight value of the i-th feature position.

3. Data Acquisition

3.1. Subjects recruitment

In this study, a sensory experiment based on real try-on was performed to collect the real garment fitting data. Considering the target markets of the companies involved in our research programs, we invited 14 male subjects with various figure types in China to participate in this experiment. The figure types of the subjects corresponded to 14 kinds of representative figure types demonstrated in the China National Standard (GB/T 1335.1-2008), which were 160/80A, 160/84A, 160/88A, 165/84A, 165/88A, 165/92A, 170/84A, 170/88A, 170/92A, 175/84A, 175/88A, 175/92A, 180/88A, and 185/92A, respectively.

3.2. Anthropometric data acquisition and 3D mannequin construction

Considering the accuracy and efficiency, the anthropometric data of the subjects were procured using Vitus Bodyscan. And then, the scanned 3D mannequins were imported into the 3D garment CAD named CLO 3D for further research.

3.3. Experimental garment style and fabrics

The general principles of the proposed approach can be suitable for all kinds of garment styles. Due to the length limitation, we elaborated on it using a real case of coat (see Fig. 2) from the companies involved in our research programs in this paper. The key dimensions of the coats were present in Table 1. The mechanical properties parameters of the fabrics for making the coats were demonstrated in Table 2.

Fig. 2. The coat involved in this study.

Table 1. Key dimensions of the coats.

Size	Garment length	Bust girth	Shoulder width	Sleeve length	Waist girth	Hip girth
38	81	108	40	55	104.4	106.4
40	83.5	112	41	56.5	108.4	110.4
42	86	116	42	58	112.4	114.4
44	88.5	120	43	59.5	116.4	118.4
46	91	124	44	61	120.4	122.4

Table 2. The parameters of fabric mechanical properties.

Sample number	Composition	Thickness (cm)	Stretch	Shear	Bending	Bulking stiffness
1	100% Cotton	0.06	56	14	22	29
2	100% Polyester	0.07	13	8	9	0
3	97% Polyester, 3% Spandex	0.04	27	9	38	78
4	65% Cotton, 35% Polyester	0.07	42	7	32	20
5	100% Polyester	0.08	30	8	8	79

3.4. Garment fitting data

A physical try-on experiment was conducted to collect the real garment fitting data. In a laboratory with constant temperature ($20 \pm 2\,°C$) and relative humidity ($65 \pm 5\%$), each subject performed his try-on with the experimental garments and perceived the fit degrees in static and dynamic scenarios, just like what he usually does in off-line ment fitstores. Meanwhile, they recorded the garment fitting data represented by {1,2,3,4,5}, corresponding to the linguistic values {"too tight/short(1)", "tight/short(2)", "perfect(3)", "loose/long(4)", "too loose/long(5)"}. Finally, these data were used to formed the output training dataset to construct the proposed model.

4. Construction of the PNN Model for Assessing Garment Fit Degree

4.1. General framework of the assessment model for garment fit degree

For a specific feature position k, the general framework of the PNN-based assessment model for garment fit degree was illustrated in Fig. 3. The input layer was composed of 6 input neurons, including the garment ease data and the fabric property parameters shown in Table 2. The output of the model was the predicted garment fit degree.

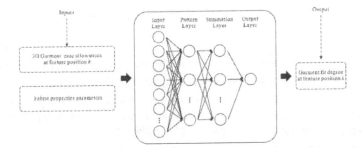

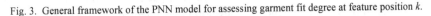

Fig. 3. General framework of the PNN model for assessing garment fit degree at feature position k.

438

4.2. Learning dataset

In this study, according to the style characteristics of the coat, seven feature positions were determined to assess the garment fit degree, involving the bust girth, collar girth, waist girth, hip girth, garment length, and sleeve length. For each feature position, 350 records of data were collected. To evaluate the proposed model close to reality, avoid the problem of over-fitting and guarantee the prediction accuracy of the proposed model, we utilized the K-fold ($K = 10$) cross-validation approach in establishing the garment fit degree assessment model. Concretely, the collected dataset was randomly divided into $K (= 10)$ smaller sets initially. And then, $K - 1 (= 9)$ small sets composed of 315 records, were utilized as the training dataset, in turn, to train the model, with the remaining part of the original dataset as the validation dataset. Finally, the PNN-model was determined after $10 - fold$ cross-validation.

4.3. Performance evaluation

Since the garment patterns are the business secrets of the companies, there are no real-time garment fitting data or datasets corresponding to the garment patterns in the public database which we can directly utilize for the baseline in our experiments. Therefore, the prediction accuracy of our proposed PNN models was compared with those of the models based on the BP ANN using the experimental data collected in Section 3. Table 3 shows the comparison results. From Table 3, it can be easily observed that the performance of the PNN models is better than those of BP ANN models at any feature positions.

Table 3. Performance comparison for coat fit degree assessment.

Model	Bust girth	Collar girth	Shoulder width	Waist girth	Hip girth	Garment length	Sleeve length
PNN	98%	96%	98%	98%	90%	85%	78%
BP ANN	96%	88%	96%	96%	88%	65%	86%

5. Conclusions

In this study, we put forth a new assessment approach to garment fit degree based on principle component analysis integrated probabilistic neural networks, aiming to enhance the implementation of garment e-mass customization. The proposed approach was expounded by using a real case of coat fit degree assessment. From the experimental results, we can find the PNN-based model shows better performance than the classical BP ANN-based model. The proposed model can be further improved and extended to develop a new interactive fashion design and manufacturing system for customized garments in future research.

Acknowledgments

This work is supported by the Social Science Planning Project in Anhui (grant No. AHSKQ2019D085), the Open Project Program of Anhui Province College Key Laboratory of Textile Fabrics, Anhui Engineering and Technology Research Center of Textile (grant No. 2021AETKL04), the Key Teaching and Research project of Colleges and Universities in Anhui (grant No. 2020jyxm0153), and the Scientific Research Project of Anhui Polytechnic University (grant No. Xjky2022064).

References

1. Charnley, F.; Knecht, F.; Muenkel, H.; Pletosu, D.; Rickard, V.; Sambonet, C.; Schneider, M.; Zhang, C. Can Digital Technologies Increase Consumer Acceptance of Circular Business Models? The Case of Second Hand Fashion. *Sustainability* **2022**, *14*, doi:10.3390/su14084589.
2. Erra, U.; Scanniello, G.; Colonnese, V. Exploring the effectiveness of an augmented reality dressing room. *Multimedia Tools and Applications* **2018**, *77*, 25077-25107, doi:10.1007/s11042-018-5758-2.
3. Lau, K.W.; Lee, P.Y. Shopping in virtual reality: a study on consumers' shopping experience in a stereoscopic virtual reality. *Virtual Reality* **2019**, *23*, 255-268, doi:10.1007/s10055-018-0362-3.
4. Wedel, M.; Bigné, E.; Zhang, J. Virtual and augmented reality: Advancing research in consumer marketing. *International Journal of Research in Marketing* **2020**, *37*, 443-465, doi:https://doi.org/10.1016/j.ijresmar.2020.04.004.
5. Liu, N.; Chow, P.-S.; Zhao, H. Challenges and critical successful factors for apparel mass customization operations: recent development and case study. *Annals of Operations Research* **2020**, *291*, 531-563, doi:10.1007/s10479-019-03149-7.
6. Turner, F.; Merle, A.; Gotteland, D. Enhancing consumer value of the co-design experience in mass customization. *Journal of Business Research* **2020**, *117*, 473-483, doi:https://doi.org/10.1016/j.jbusres.2020.05.052.
7. Yan, Y.; Gupta, S.; Schoefer, K.; Licsandru, T. A Review of E-mass Customization as a Branding Strategy. *Corporate Reputation Review* **2020**, *23*, 215-223, doi:10.1057/s41299-019-00087-9.
8. Wang, Z.; Wang, J.; Zeng, X.; Sharma, S.; Xing, Y.; Xu, S.; Liu, L. Prediction of garment fit level in 3D virtual environment based on artificial neural networks. *Textile Research Journal* **2021**, *91*, 1713-1731, doi:10.1177/0040517520987520.

9. Mosleh, S.; Abtew, M.A.; Bruniaux, P.; Tartare, G.; Xu, Y.; Chen, Y. 3D Digital Adaptive Thorax Modelling of Peoples with Spinal Disabilities: Applications for Performance Clothing Design. *Applied Sciences* **2021**, *11*, 4545.

10. Kuzmichev, V.; Moskvin, A.; Moskvina, M. Virtual Reconstruction of Historical Men's Suit. *Autex Research Journal* **2018**, *18*, doi:10.1515/aut-2018-0001.

11. Abtew, M.A.; Bruniaux, P.; Boussu, F.; Loghin, C.; Cristian, I.; Chen, Y. Development of comfortable and well-fitted bra pattern for customized female soft body armor through 3D design process of adaptive bust on virtual mannequin. *Computers in Industry* **2018**, *100*, 7-20, doi:https://doi.org/10.1016/j.compind.2018.04.004.

12. Abtew, M.A.; Bruniaux, P.; Boussu, F.; Loghin, C.; Cristian, I.; Chen, Y.; Wang, L. Female seamless soft body armor pattern design system with innovative reverse engineering approaches. *The International Journal of Advanced Manufacturing Technology* **2018**, *98*, 2271-2285, doi:10.1007/s00170-018-2386-y.

13. Abtew, M.A.; Bruniaux, P.; Boussu, F.; Loghin, C.; Cristian, I.; Chen, Y.; Wang, L. A systematic pattern generation system for manufacturing customized seamless multi-layer female soft body armour through dome-formation (moulding) techniques using 3D warp interlock fabrics. *Journal of Manufacturing Systems* **2018**, *49*, 61-74, doi:https://doi.org/10.1016/j.jmsy.2018.09.001.

14. Plotkina, D.; Saurel, H. Me or just like me? The role of virtual try-on and physical appearance in apparel M-retailing. *Journal of Retailing and Consumer Services* **2019**, *51*, 362-377, doi:https://doi.org/10.1016/j.jretconser.2019.07.002.

15. Specht. Probabilistic neural networks for classification, mapping, or associative memory. In Proceedings of IEEE 1988 International Conference on Neural Networks, 24-27 July 1988; pp. 525-532 vol.521.

16. Specht, D.F. Probabilistic neural networks. *Neural Networks* **1990**, *3*, 109-118, doi:https://doi.org/10.1016/0893-6080(90)90049-Q.

17. Mohebali, B.; Tahmassebi, A.; Meyer-Baese, A.; Gandomi, A.H. Chapter 14 - Probabilistic neural networks: a brief overview of theory, implementation, and application. In *Handbook of Probabilistic Models*, Samui, P., Tien Bui, D., Chakraborty, S., Deo, R.C., Eds. Butterworth-Heinemann: 2020; https://doi.org/10.1016/B978-0-12-816514-0.00014-Xpp. 347-367.

Part 4

Intelligent Wearable Systems and Advanced Computations for Sustainable Development

Application of deep dictionary learning in automatic classification of woven fabric texture

Bo Xing[a,b,*] and Qingqing Shao[a]

[a] College of Textiles, Donghua University, Shanghai, 201620, China
[b] Univ. Lille, ENSAIT, GEMTEX-Génie et Matériaux Textiles, Lille, 59000, France
*bo.xing@ensait.fr

Jun Wang

Key Laboratory of Textile Science and Technology, Ministry of Education
College of Textiles, Donghua University, Shanghai, 201620, China
junwang@dhu.edu.cn

Xianyi Zeng

Univ. Lille, ENSAIT, GEMTEX-Génie et Matériaux Textiles, Lille, 59000, France
xianyi.zeng@ensait.fr

This paper introduces fabric texture dataset which contains 300 labelled images to facilitate research in developing presentation algorithm for this challenging scenario. The next contribution of this research is a novel multilevel deep dictionary learning-based fabric texture classification algorithm that can discern different kinds of texture. An efficient layer by layer training approach is formulated to learn the deep dictionaries followed by different classifiers as types of texture for fabric. By changing the number of layers in proposed algorithm, performances in different classifiers are compared. It is possible to integrate the proposed algorithm with real-time systems because it is supervised and has high classification accuracy with 93.6%.

Keywords: Fabric texture; deep dictionary learning; image classification.

1. Introduction

Fabric analysis includes various items, including wear resistance, water resistance, air permeability, and fabric textural analysis. Among those, fabric textural analysis is the most important item, which provides information on fabric weave patterns, such as type, structure, and properties, prior to further analysis and research. Presently, woven fabric textures recognition is dependent on manual operations using human eyes aided with equipment. Traditionally, this manual inspection is performed by an expert who requires expertise and experience. However, it is accompanied with several drawbacks such as extensive labor, inefficiency, and time-consuming, but also leads to subjective human factors, such as mental and physical stress, dizziness, and tiredness, etc., which ultimately affects the recognition results. Therefore, it is indispensable to develop an automated inspection system for the recognition of woven fabric textures to produce high-quality products that meet the needs of customers.

In recent years, fabric textures recognition has gained much attention and made great achievements. Usually, methods for weave textures recognition can be divided into two broad categories, i.e., texture-based statistical method and model-based method. The texture-based statistical method uses preprocessed images. Seçkin et al.[1] proposed a method based on intertwined frame vector, using intertwined frames and center pixel to acquire information about fabric structure from different directions, and later, used Binarization to divide images into subimages for obtaining gray-scale features. The method was robust for extracting interlacing points in the weaving structure, but the work was limited to only simple woven fabrics. The recognition method based on model uses a recognition or classification algorithm to identify and match the fabrics patterns. Fan et al.[2] presented a method for yarn segmentation, texture orientation, and texture classification using K-means clustering method, gradient accumulation of gray levels, and Gabor filters. This method was not suitable for images that had an unclear texture as it neglected the importance of lighting effect while capturing the images.

There are several limitations to the recognition methods of woven fabric textures. The existing studies relied heavily on handcrafted features engineering. The rotational variations in fabric directly influenced the texture features extraction during image acquisition.

Inspired by these previous works and to address the shortcomings, we propose a model based on data augmentation and deep dictionary learning for the classification of woven fabric texture. The proposed method includes deep dictionary learning and classifier. In particular, a number of dictionary layers are analyzed to obtain better classification performance. Also, it is aimed to determine the classifier that provides the best classification performance in different layers. The proposed model performed end-to-end fabric texture classification using the woven fabric images that we had developed.

2. Experiments Details

The woven fabric images were collected to form a data set. We obtained 300 images of pieces of fabric. Out of these 300 images, we resized the images as 56×56 pixel, while the images were applied through various techniques of data augmentation to generate a total of 18,000 samples. We kept 15,000 images for our training samples and 3,000 images for testing dataset. A few sample images in each class are shown in Fig. 1. These images were subdivided into three classes, namely plain, satin, and twill weave fabrics.

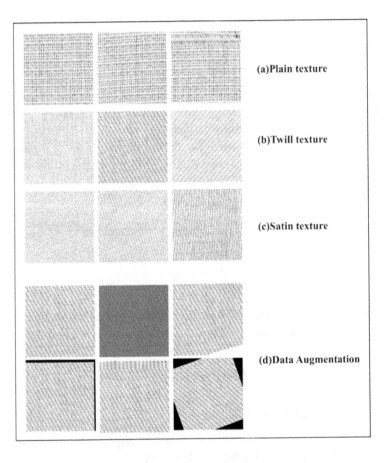

Fig. 1.   Few samples from dataset.

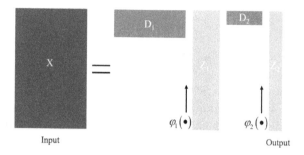

Fig. 2.   Basic deep dictionary learning model.

3. Method

3.1. Deep dictionary learning

A single level of dictionary learning[3] plays an important role in latent representation of data and dictionary atoms which is provided by multilevel dictionaries in the deep dictionary learning structure. In classic dictionary learning, X, D_1 and Z are data, dictionary and sparse representation respectively. In the synthesis, dictionary is firstly learned. Then, sparse representation is obtained according to the dictionary.

$$X = D_1 Z \tag{1}$$

Multilayers basic deep dictionary learning is shown in Fig. 2. Mathematical representation is given in Eq. (2):

$$X = D_1 D_2 Z \tag{2}$$

Features of the dictionaries are differentiated in accordance with number of levels. Nonlinear activation (φ) with the dictionary learning problem can be formulated as follows.

$$X = D_1 \varphi \left(D_2 \varphi \left(\ldots \varphi \left(D_N Z \right) \right) \right) \tag{3}$$

3.2. Proposed method

In this study, we proposed a method to classify the textures of woven fabric by using a deep dictionary learning algorithm.

Following the suggested model and training algorithm proposed by Tariyal et al.[4] we reimplemented the algorithm in the PyTorch framework. We took the gradient of the norm with respect to γ, require that it equals zero, and solve for the optimal γ. Therefore, solving the optimal γ yields

$$z_2 = \left(D_1 D_1^T\right)^{-1} D_1 z_1 \tag{4}$$

Similarly, we can solve for the optimal D_1 using Least Squares and we obtain:

$$D_1 = \left(z_2 z_2^T\right)^{-1} z_2 z_1^T \tag{5}$$

In a similar manner, we can extend the above formulations to a batch of observed signals.

3.3. Activation functions and classifiers

Experiments were performed using the Identity activation, the Tanh activation, the ELU activation, and the ElliotSig activation. The choice of the activation function must be an injective function since its inverse function is required.

Activation function	Expressions
Identity	$\varphi(x) = x$
Tanh	$\varphi(x) = \tanh(^x/_\alpha)$
ELU	$\varphi(x) = \begin{cases} x & x \geq 0 \\ \alpha\left(e^x - 1\right)x < 0 \end{cases}$
ElliotSig	$\varphi(x) = {^x}/_{(\alpha - |x|)}$

The MLP,[5] KNN,[6] and Linear SVM[7] we proposed are basic classifiers. We concatenated the representations across all the dictionary layers and feed this vector as the input to the classifiers. By feeding this vector, we incorporate both low-level information (earlier representations) and high-level information (later representations) into the classifiers.

4. Results and Discussion

Some sample reconstructions are shown in Fig. 3, and the classification performance is listed in Table 1. As we can see from the reconstruction, the deeper the Deep Dictionary Model is, the more artifacts from other image categories tend to show. One of the reasons causing these artifacts is because of the imperfect reconstruction between layers. Therefore, it is reasonable to expect more distorted image reconstructions with deeper Deep Dictionary models.

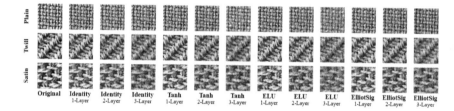

Fig. 3. A visualization of the reconstructions for Deep Dictionary models with varing depth and activation functions.

Table 1. Comparison of the reconstruction and classification performance for varying Deep Dictionary activation functions and classifiers.

Activa.Func-Layers	Recons.Loss	MLP-accurary (%)	KNN-accurary (%)	LSVM-accurary (%)
Identify-1	1.122	66.7	27.8	58.3
Identify-2	5.763	69.4	35.1	55.6
Identify-3	30.786	63.9	55.6	58.3
Tanh-1	2.367	69.1	70.1	81.2
Tanh-2	5.964	70.3	77.8	66.7
Tanh-3	10.452	75.0	61.1	72.2
ELU-1	2.557	66.7	66.7	81.5
ELU-2	8.621	77.8	69.4	80.6
ELU-3	18.249	75.0	70.8	84.4
ElliotSig-1	1.512	78.5	82.4	86.5
ElliotSig-2	6.841	83.2	85.9	82.1
ElliotSig-3	12.118	**93.6**	81.2	80.6

The results obtained from the proposed algorithm are described comparatively in this section. The lowest classification performance has an accuracy rate of 27.8%, when taking into account Table 1. The highest classification accuracy was achieved by classifying the deep dictionary learning structure with three layers with ElliotSig and MLP. The classification performance of this structure is 93.6%, which is highest in Table 1. Deep dictionary learning structure with single layer reached maximum 81.2% classification accuracy via layer by layer. This performance was achieved through Tanh activation function with Linear SVM classifier. The classification accuracy of deep dictionary learning with two layers structures was 85.9%. This performance was obtained with ElliotSig and KNN. When Table 1 is examined, it is observed that the average classification results according to the layer number are close to each other. The average performance of the layers is 69.63%, 71.16% and 72.64%, respectively.

5. Conclusions

In this study, comparative analysis of classification of woven fabric texture images was performed. With the proposed method, categories of texture can be determined. Thanks to the proposed method, it has a high performance and classification capability without any pre-processing and post-processing. A detection performance of 93.6% was achieved. The deep dictionary learning method, including when fabric textures are close, can sort textures with high accuracy. Types of activation functions, number of layers of deep dictionary learning structure, and selected classifiers affect performance directly.

Acknowledgments

This study was funded by the China Scholarship Council Fund.

References

1. Ahmet Çağdaş Seçkin and Mine Seçkin. Detection of fabric defects with intertwined frame vector feature extraction. *Alexandria Engineering Journal*, 61(4):2887–2898, 2022.
2. Zhen Fan, Senlin Zhang, Jun Mei, and Meiqin Liu. Recognition of woven fabric based on image processing and gabor filters. In *2017 IEEE 7th Annual International Conference on CYBER Technology in Automation, Control, and Intelligent Systems (CYBER)*, pages 996–1000. IEEE, 2017.
3. Ivana Tošić and Pascal Frossard. Dictionary learning. *IEEE Signal Processing Magazine*, 28(2):27–38, 2011.
4. Snigdha Tariyal, Angshul Majumdar, Richa Singh, and Mayank Vatsa. Deep dictionary learning. *IEEE Access*, 4:10096–10109, 2016.
5. Matt W Gardner and SR Dorling. Artificial neural networks (the multilayer perceptron)—a review of applications in the atmospheric sciences. *Atmospheric environment*, 32(14-15):2627–2636, 1998.
6. James M Keller, Michael R Gray, and James A Givens. A fuzzy k-nearest neighbor algorithm. *IEEE transactions on systems, man, and cybernetics*, (4):580–585, 1985.
7. William S Noble. What is a support vector machine? *Nature biotechnology*, 24(12):1565–1567, 2006.

Human action recognition based on transformer

Kehan Wu* and Jian Wu

School of Computing and Artificial Intelligence, Southwest Jiaotong University
Chengdu, 611756, China
*KehanWu@my.swjtu.edu.cn
www.swjtu.edu.cn

Yueying Li, Ran Hao and Hongjun Wang†

School of Computing and Artificial Intelligence, Southwest Jiaotong University
Chengdu, 611756, China
† wanghongjun@swjtu.edu.cn
www.swjtu.edu.cn

Human action recognition (HAR) has received extensive attention in artificial intelligence today. In view of the huge advantages of transformers in capturing global context information and extracting effective features compared with traditional deep neural networks, in this paper, we propose to utilize transformer to solve HAR problems and to our knowledge, this is the first time to solve HAR problems by transformer in sensor datasets. Experiments on 12 real sensor datasets with three evaluation metrics demonstrate the superiority of using transformer against four classic or state-of-the-art models.

Keywords: Action recognition; transformer; deep learning.

1. Introduction

Action recognition has become a current focus in artificial intelligence. When interpreting complicated behaviours, it appears that recognising a person's behaviour is critical. As a result, human action recognition has attracted a lot of attention, especially in real-world environments.

In this study, we propose a HAR model based on transformer. Transformers do not handle data sequentially. Any place in the input sequence is given context by the attention mechanism. Training times are reduced. And the accuracy of classification has been improved.

The contributions of this paper are as follows. Firstly, we creatively applied the transformer model for HAR on real sensor datasets for the first time. Secondly, Experiments conducted on 12 real sensor datasets show that transformer model has better accuracy in action recognition than other classic models.

The remainder of this paper is laid out as follows. In Section 2, we review the related works for HAR. In Section 3, we describe the designed model in detail. In Section 4, we provide a detailed illustration of the experiment setup. Results are illustrated and analyzed respectively in Section 5. The study is concluded in Section 6.

2. Related Work

Recent deep learning action recognition methods are DBN, RNN, CNN.

The related works of DBN on HAR are as follows. A real-time human action recognition approach based on a modified DBN model was presented by Zhang et al.[1] The DBN model was used by Zhang et al.[2] as human action classifiers, with the potential to be used in the creation of EMG-based user interfaces. Nickfarjam and Ebrahimpour-komleh[3] proposed a supervised strategy for HAR based on the power of simple features and advantages of multi-input topology of DBN.

This part introduces the related work about RNN. For skeleton-based action recognition, Du et al.[4] presented an end-to-end hierarchical RNN. Traditional CNN-RNNs regard all frames equally essential, making them error-prone when dealing with noisy frames. Wang et al.[5] presented a temporal spiking recurrent neural network to overcome this challenge. We often need to process high-dimensional input data such as video, text. However, if we use RNN models for training, there are problems of high memory usage and high computational cost. To solve this issue, Pan et al.[6] presented the TR-LSTM, a revolutionary compact LSTM model.

The last part is about CNN. Simonyan and Zisserman[7] introduced a two-stream deep Convolutional Networks architecture for HAR in Videos. To make better use of the spatio-temporal information in the dual flow model, Feichtenhofer et al.[8] proposed an updated two-stream model in which there is a novel convolutional fusion layer and a novel temporal fusion layer that incorporates 3D Conv + 3D Pooling.

Ji et al.[9] created a unique 3D CNN model for HAR. Varol et al.[10] created a long-term temporal convolutions architecture by superimposing 3D CNN over lengthier video clips to describe motion at full temporal scale. Training 3D convolutional kernels is complicated and requires vast volumes of training footage. To address this problem, Sun et al.[11] proposed a factorized spatiotemporal convolutional network.

3. Transformer Model for Action Recognition

In view of the huge advantages of transformers in capturing global context information and extracting effective features, we apply *transformer* to HAR. In this section, we focus on the detail of the proposed model. The framework is shown in Fig. 1.

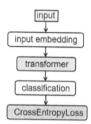

Fig. 1. The framework of action recognition model.

The sequence data with batch_size=128,seq_len=30 is taken as input and passed through a input embedding layer to modify the dimensionality of the input. The formula of the input embedding layer is $Y = xA^T + b$, where A is the weight matrix, and b is bias.

Then passing through a Rectified Linear Unit, the output of is adjusted. The function is $f(x) = max(0, x)$.

Then through *transformer* part for deep learning. The *transformer* part consists of 3 identical layers. Each *transformer* layer is made up of two sub-layers: a multi-head self-attention mechanism and a fully connected feed-forward network, each of which adds a residual connection and normalization. The detailed framework of the *transformer* model is shown in the Fig. 2.

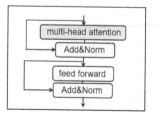

Fig. 2. The framework of transformer.

After that through a classification layer, outputting n-dimensional vector. The vector and label together, through the CrossEntropyLoss function, the loss is calculated. The formula is $L = -[y \lg \hat{y} + (1-y) \lg(1 - \hat{y})]$, where $\hat{y}$ is the predicted value, and y is the label value.

4. Experiments

The predictive model was evaluated by 12 datasets. In this section, the experimental settings were presented first, then the results were illustrated by three evaluation metrics.

4.1. Datasets

We have continuous ambient sensor data for 12 rooms, which have a feature of spatio-temporal continuity. Each room has two data sets, one sequential and one non-sequential. The non-sequential dataset is statistically derived from thirty rows of data in the sequential dataset.

4.2. Experimental settings

To prove the superiority of the *transformer* model for HAR, five-fold cross-validation experiments were set up. In this paper, 5 models were applied to perform classification on 12 datasets, respectively were Decision Tree (DT), Support Vector Machine (SVM), Gated Recurrent Unit (GRU), Conditional Random Fields (CRF) and *Transformer*.

4.3. Evaluation metric

In order to the performance and feasibility of the model, three evaluation metrics were used.

4.3.1. Accuracy

For a binary confusion matrix, the results can be classified into four categories: true positive (TP), false negative (FN), false positive (FP), true negative (TN). The formula is: $Accuracy = \frac{TP+TN}{TP+FN+FP+TN}$.

4.3.2. F1 score

The F1 score can be viewed as a harmonic mean of precision and recall. precision and recall have equal impact on F1 score. $precision = (TP +$

$TN)/(TP + FP)$, $recall = TP/(TP + FN)$. The F1 score is calculated as follows: $F1 = \frac{2*precision*recall}{precision+recall}$.

4.3.3. Jaccard_score

Jaccard similarity coefficient comparing similarities and differences between predicted values and labels. The formula of jaccard_score is $J(A,B) = \frac{|A \bigcap B|}{|A \bigcup B|}$, where A, B are two sets.

5. Results

The performance of five different models on 12 datasets is analyzed using five-fold cross-validation and compared. The results of 12 datasets were shown in table below, in which the number in brackets shows the ranking of the model on the corresponding dataset by comparing the evaluation metrics. The penultimate column of the table shows the average of the evaluation metrics of each model on the 12 datasets. The last column of the table shows the average rank.

Table 1. Accuracy score of the five models on the 12 datasets.

Model	csh101	csh102	csh105	csh107	csh108	csh110	csh114	csh116	csh118	csh119	csh120	csh121	avg.accu	avg.rank
SVM	0.8899(4)	0.8553(5)	0.9095(4)	0.9120(3)	0.8483(3)	0.9331(4)	0.9155(3)	0.9106(4)	0.9384(3)	0.9398(3)	0.8639(5)	0.9162(3)	0.9027	3.6666
transformer	0.9278(1)	0.9088(1)	0.9384(1)	0.9303(1)	0.8672(1)	0.9479(1)	0.9357(1)	0.9481(1)	0.9469(1)	0.9472(2)	0.9097(1)	0.9345(1)	0.9293	1.0833
GRU	0.9013(3)	0.8759(2)	0.9322(2)	0.9182(2)	0.8428(4)	0.9382(3)	0.9282(2)	0.9345(3)	0.9464(2)	0.9483(1)	0.8697(4)	0.9269(2)	0.9143	2.5000
DT	0.8805(5)	0.8724(4)	0.9014(5)	0.8983(4)	0.8051(5)	0.9417(2)	0.9091(4)	0.9366(2)	0.9275(5)	0.9220(4)	0.8737(2)	0.8919(4)	0.8967	3.8333
CRF	0.9168(2)	0.8733(3)	0.9270(3)	0.8836(5)	0.8547(2)	0.9173(5)	0.9071(5)	0.8963(5)	0.9283(4)	0.9058(5)	0.8699(3)	0.8790(5)	0.8966	3.9166

Table 2. F1 scores of the five models on the 12 datasets.

Model	csh101	csh102	csh105	csh107	csh108	csh110	csh114	csh116	csh118	csh119	csh120	csh121	average
SVM	0.8282(3)	0.7992(5)	0.8820(4)	0.8430(3)	0.7774(2)	0.9320(2)	0.8715(2)	0.7864(3)	0.8875(2)	0.8537(3)	0.8571(2)		0.8523
transformer	0.8804(1)	0.8595(1)	0.9209(1)	0.8848(1)	0.7818(1)	0.9353(1)	0.8963(1)	0.8110(1)	0.9191(1)	0.8885(1)	0.8804(1)	0.8584(1)	0.8764
GRU	0.8257(4)	0.8015(3)	0.8963(3)	0.8534(2)	0.7220(4)	0.9170(5)	0.8595(4)	0.7414(4)	0.9076(3)	0.8833(3)	0.8143(4)	0.8560(3)	0.8398
DT	0.8072(5)	0.8000(4)	0.8561(5)	0.8114(5)	0.6871(5)	0.9175(4)	0.8326(5)	0.7347(5)	0.8798(5)	0.8424(5)	0.8091(5)	0.8206(5)	0.8165
CRF	0.8753(2)	0.8355(2)	0.9073(2)	0.8148(4)	0.7637(3)	0.9192(3)	0.8659(3)	0.8043(2)	0.8929(4)	0.8442(4)	0.8713(2)	0.8257(4)	0.8517

Table 3. Jaccard scores of the five models on the 12 datasets.

Model	csh101	csh102	csh105	csh107	csh108	csh110	csh114	csh116	csh118	csh119	csh120	csh121	average
SVM	0.7203(3)	0.6768(5)	0.7926(4)	0.7528(3)	0.6462(2)	0.8773(2)	0.7805(2)	0.6736(3)	0.8416(2)	0.8171(2)	0.7534(3)	0.7867(2)	0.7599
transformer	0.7992(1)	0.7653(1)	0.8569(1)	0.8088(1)	0.6614(1)	0.8844(1)	0.8209(1)	0.7132(1)	0.8566(1)	0.8211(1)	0.7941(1)	0.7958(1)	0.7981
GRU	0.7194(4)	0.6847(4)	0.8177(3)	0.7621(2)	0.5896(4)	0.8532(5)	0.7673(4)	0.6341(4)	0.8400(3)	0.8119(3)	0.7003(4)	0.7837(3)	0.7470
DT	0.7013(5)	0.6875(3)	0.7572(5)	0.7159(4)	0.5477(5)	0.8558(4)	0.7297(5)	0.6330(5)	0.7963(5)	0.7561(5)	0.6981(5)	0.7326(5)	0.7176
CRF	0.7968(2)	0.7296(2)	0.8379(2)	0.7056(5)	0.6370(3)	0.8569(3)	0.7736(3)	0.6954(2)	0.8179(4)	0.7640(4)	0.7817(2)	0.7329(4)	0.7608

Analyzing these tables, it can be concluded that the *transformer* model has shown better performance on each dataset than other 4 comparison models in terms of action recognition.

5.1. Convergence proof

We visualize the loss on the 12 datasets. The charts are shown in Fig. 3. By analyzing the images, we can see that the model converges within 100 iterations. This shows that our model converges fast and the convergence time is short, which means the proposed model is feasible.

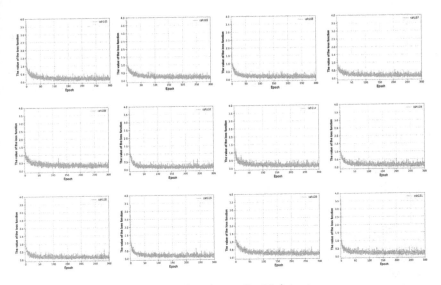

Fig. 3. Loss function on the 12 datasets.

6. Conclusion

In this paper, due to the spatio-temporal continuity of sensor data and the ability of the transformers model to capture contextual relationships, we propose the transformers model for action recognition and conduct comparative experiments with several other classical model. The experimental results show that the transformers model has excellent performance in action recognition, which provides a reliable reference for action recognition work in the future.

References

1. H. Zhang, F. Zhou, W. Zhang, X. Yuan and Z. Chen, Real-time action recognition based on a modified deep belief network model, in *2014 IEEE International Conference on Information and Automation (ICIA)*, 2014.
2. J. Zhang, C. Ling and S. Li, Emg signals based human action recognition via deep belief networks, *IFAC-PapersOnLine* **52**, 271 (2019).
3. A. Nickfarjam and H. Ebrahimpour-Komleh, Shape-based human action recognition using multi-input topology of deep belief networks, in *2017 9th International Conference on Information and Knowledge Technology (IKT)*, 2017.

4. Y. Du, W. Wang and L. Wang, Hierarchical recurrent neural network for skeleton based action recognition, in *Proceedings of the IEEE conference on computer vision and pattern recognition*, 2015.

5. W. Wang, S. Hao, Y. Wei, S. Xiao, J. Feng and N. Sebe, Temporal spiking recurrent neural network for action recognition, *IEEE Access* **7**, 117165 (2019).

6. Y. Pan, J. Xu, M. Wang, J. Ye, F. Wang, K. Bai and Z. Xu, Compressing recurrent neural networks with tensor ring for action recognition, in *Proceedings of the AAAI Conference on Artificial Intelligence*, (01)2019.

7. K. Simonyan and A. Zisserman, Two-stream convolutional networks for action recognition in videos, *Advances in neural information processing systems* **27** (2014).

8. C. Feichtenhofer, A. Pinz and A. Zisserman, Convolutional two-stream network fusion for video action recognition, in *Proceedings of the IEEE conference on computer vision and pattern recognition*, 2016.

9. S. Ji, W. Xu, M. Yang and K. Yu, 3d convolutional neural networks for human action recognition, *IEEE transactions on pattern analysis and machine intelligence* **35**, 221 (2012).

10. G. Varol, I. Laptev and C. Schmid, Long-term temporal convolutions for action recognition, *IEEE transactions on pattern analysis and machine intelligence* **40**, 1510 (2017).

11. L. Sun, K. Jia, D.-Y. Yeung and B. E. Shi, Human action recognition using factorized spatio-temporal convolutional networks, in *Proceedings of the IEEE international conference on computer vision*, 2015.

Online classification and diagnosis of COVID-19 symptoms by using an intelligent wearable system

Nkengue Marc Junior*, Xianyi Zeng†, Ludovic Koehl‡ and Xuyuan Tao§

Univ. Lille, ENSAIT, Laboratoire Génie et Matériaux Textile (GEMTEX)
F-59000, Lille, France
*marc-junior.nkengue@ensait.fr
†xianyi.zeng@ensait.fr
‡ludovic.koehl@ensait.fr
§xuyuan.tao@ensait.fr

We introduce in this paper ResvidNet, a new architecture of one-dimensional convolution neural network (CNN) to COVID-19 detection. The proposed architecture consists of an enhance version of ResNet18. The results are compared with common one-dimensional Convolutional Neural Network, a Deep Neural Network, and ResNet18, and show a better performance of ResVidNet in term of accuracy and robustness, compared to the Neural Networks mentioned above.

Keywords: Machine learning; data augmentation; deep learning; multiclass classification; COVID-19; signal processing.

1. Introduction

Three years after its emergence, the severe acute respiratory syndrome coronavirus 2 (Sars-CoV-2) or COVID-19 infected more than 470 million people, caused more than 6 million deaths [1]. The virus mostly affects the respiratory and the heart system. Despite the progress made so far to significantly reduce the propagation, thanks to the vaccine and follow-up of barrier gestures, we are far from getting rid of the virus. This is mainly due to the high infection rate, the proliferation of its variants that can potentially escape vaccination coverage, and the inability to detect the virus in real-time and thus, control its proliferation. This context fastened the emergence of remote monitoring and diagnosis tools in the IoMT (Internet of Medical Things) field [2, 3] and Artificial Intelligence [4-6]. These contributions have reduced healthcare facilities pressure (such as medical doctors, healthcare staff, etc.), but there still much to do. Indeed, since the diagnosis were either too simplistic by the wearables systems, or the data used by AI frameworks can't be acquired in real-time for the monitoring and the diagnosis, almost none of them are reliable for real-time monitoring and diagnosis. Our contribution will be the design of a wearable system coupling and an AI framework to efficiently monitor and diagnose COVID-19 in real-time. This paper will focus on the classification framework developed for the overall system, which helps us to detect COVID-19 patients, named ResVidNet, in a real-time scenario. The rest of the paper is organized as follows: Section 2 overviews related works. Section 3 offers a description of our proposed framework and methodology. In Section 4, we present the results obtained with a real-world dataset and Section 5 concludes our paper.

2. Related Works

Since the emergence of the virus, many researchers in artificial intelligence and IoMT had provided tools for the monitoring and the detection of the virus. Some of them develop artificial intelligence framework based and data, such as chest X-rays images [4] or Computed Tomography (CT) images [5], to detect the virus presence in the respiratory tract (in general): nose, throat and lungs. In [6], the researchers presented COV-ECGNET, to detect COVID-19 influence in ECG, by using ECG images as input. Although they are robust and accurate, the difficulty of acquisition of data such as X-rays, CT, radiographs images or ECG images, prevent these frameworks to be use in a real-time scenario. In IoMT, wearables systems which measured physiological parameters like temperature, heart rate, pulse and blood oxygen saturation (SPO_2) were designed [2, 3]. The real advantage of those solutions is their near real-time data acquisition. However, their accuracy should be discussed since the diagnosis method consists of simply checking if the physiological parameter does not cross a certain value, instead of using raw signals for the diagnosis and the monitoring.

3. Proposed Framework

The proposed system in this manuscript will combine an intelligent textile for quick and real-time data acquisition, and a framework which get raw data as input for the monitoring and diagnosis operation. In this paper, we present ResvidNet, a convolutional neural network to detect COVID-19, by using raw ECG signals from wearables sensors in real-time, since ECG images are difficult to get in a real time scenario.

3.1. Data description and pre-processing

3.1.1. Data description

The original dataset used in this study is an ECG image dataset of cardiac and COVID-19 patients [7]. It consists of 1937 distinct patient records, with five distinct classes: Normal, COVID-19, myocardial infarction (MI), abnormal heartbeat (HB) and history of myocardial infarction (PMI). The data were collected using the ECG device **EDAN SERIES-3**. The device collected 12 leads ECG trace images, sampling at 500 Hz. We used the 4-lead ECG, since it is one of the most prominent parameters used for COVID-19 detection by describe heart activity. Each 4-lead sample has a 2.5 second duration, since the total duration length is 10 seconds on the 12 lead ECG image.

3.1.2. *Pre-processing*

The pre-processing was done by following three steps:
- **Image segmentation:** An image segmentation near the 4-lead signal area has been performed. Since background pixels can influence the deep learning model, they are removed by a Gaussian filter. A Black and White image, with the signal in the foreground is obtained by applying a threshold
- **Image to signal conversion:** The program detects the foreground pixel which represents the signal and normalize them into an array. The signal has been sampling to 125 Hz, since the sample rate of the wearable sensor used. The smooth clean data have been generated by a low-pass Butterworth filter. The signal length will be 10 seconds.
- **Balance and data augmentation:** The data augmentation has been done by applying different operations, like jittering, scaling, permutation, magnitude and time warping, resampling [8]. We were able to generate up to 23000 signals per class, and 115000 signals overall.

3.2. *The proposed framework*

The framework developed, ResvidNet, is inspired by the time series version of ResNet18 [9], with few enhancements. The framework architecture illustrated by Fig. 1, can be split into three parts:
- **The *Input part*:** The input part consists of two layers: *one-dimensional Convolution Layer* (*Conv1D*), and one *Gaussian Noise Layer* (*GaussianN*). Conv1D involved a 256x15 filter that slid across the signals to extract features from the raw waveform. GaussianN was used to improve the model robustness against noise. Indeed, most real signals are imbued with noise. Since add a noise removal part can make our framework much heavier, adding a Gaussian Noise not only, make the framework more robust, but can also increase the accuracy and prevent overfitting [10]. The standard deviation used is 0.01, since a greater value can heavily reduce accuracy, and lower value will not make a significant difference.

- **The *Block part*:** The block part is an assembly of 6 residual blocks. Each residual block start with a batch Normalization layer, follow by 4 sub-residual blocks. Each sub-residual block consists on a Convolutional Layer, a Rectified linear activation (ReLU) units, a L2 regularization unit and a Dropout layer. ReLU units were applied to speed up the training, by further normalising the values. The Dropout layer, and the L2 regularization were used to reduce overfitting on the training data. The 6th sub-residual block is following by another Convolutional Layer. The result is sum up with the output of the *Input part* of the framework. The sum pass through another ReLU and Dropout layer. The Last layer of the residual block is a MaxPooling layer (MaxPool1D). The MaxPool1D was used to down sample the signal by taking every 5 values in a vector and reducing it to 2 values, forcing the Model to keep only the most relevant features and help decreasing the memory usage.

- **The *Fully Connected part*:** After the flattening of the block part's output, the fully connected layer transformed the data in to a 5x1 vector of numerical values corresponding to the outputs for each class The SoftMax function was used to represent these values as a probability by normalising them between 0 and 1.

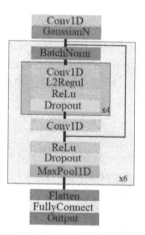

Fig. 1. ResVidNet architecture.

The training set was randomly split into 80% training, 10% test and 10% validation. The adaptive momentum estimation (Adam) optimizer, with a cyclic learning rate between 0.00001 and 0.001, was used to optimize the network parameters. Only the model with the best weights was saved after the training.

4. Results

4.1. *Multi-class classification and classification explanation*

The framework performance can be measured by using the loss curve (Fig. 2), the accuracy curve (Fig. 3), and the classification report (Table 1).

Table 1. Classification report

Class	Precision	Recall	F1-Score	Support
Normal	0.892276	0.880874	0.886538	2426
HB	0.932099	0.911993	0.921936	2318
MI	0.932619	0.938061	0.935332	2228
PMI	0.953762	0.937603	0.945614	2420
COVID-19	0.879567	0.925047	0.901734	2108
Macro	0.9180646	0.9187156	0.9182308	

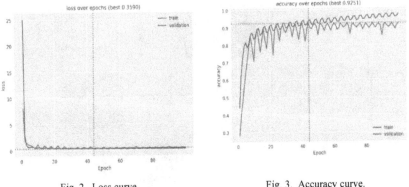

Fig. 2. Loss curve.   Fig. 3. Accuracy curve.

Fig. 2 shows a convergence of the validation loss curve to the training loss curve, and thus, asserting the robustness of ResVidNet. The framework accuracy is 91.8% (Table 1), showing the fact that ResVidNet is accurate. These results further assert the hypothesis about the effects of the enhancements we had provided.

The accuracy and the robustness of ResVidNet been asserted, the next step is the classification explanation. An approach call Gradient Weighted Class Activation Mapping (Grad-CAM), is proposed in [11]. Grad-CAM visualize the gradients of the final layer of the Network in a heatmap. The heatmap can be used for analysing factors that influence the classification result, and thus, help visualize where the network is looking. By using Fig. 4, we could establish a

462

correlation between the signal class and the features responsible of the classification. Indeed, If we consider L = [0,1,2,3,4], a list which contains the classes index (with 0 as *Normal* class index, 1 as *HB* class index, 2 as *PMI* class index, 3 as *MI* class index and 4 as *COVID-19* class index); then for i in L, the signal values in a timelapse of $[0.5i, 0.5(i + 1)]$ seconds are the most important features of the signal, and the ones which triggered the classification.

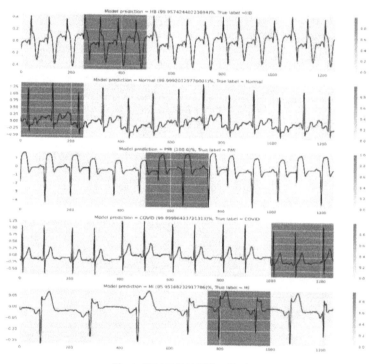

Fig. 4. GRAD-CAM Visualization.

4.2. Test with a wearable sensor

The framework was tested using this time, a real wearable sensor data design in [12]. It was wore by 3 healthy persons, and the results were 3 Normal ECG detected. It further asserted the accuracy and the robustness of ResVidNet, and the fact that it can be used in real-time.

4.3. Comparison with other Neural Networks

In order to assert the enhancements effects of ResVidNet, a comparison was made between ResvidNet, Convolutional Neural Network (CNN) [13], and ResNet [9].

The metrics used for the comparison the overall accuracy and the overall loss (Table 2) and the accuracy curve (Fig. 5) of each model.

Table 2. Accuracy and Loss comparison

Neural Network	Accuracy	Loss
CNN	77.2 %	0.6138
ResNet	87.1 %	0.8671
ResVidNet	91.8 %	0.37

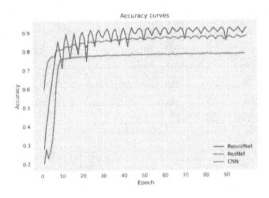

Fig. 5. Accuracy curves comparison.

As except, ResVidNet is more accurate and robust than ResNet and CNN as shows by Table 2 and Fig. 5.

5. Conclusion and Perspectives

In this paper, we've presented ResvidNet, a framework which predict COVID-19 by using raw ECG signal. The framework offers a very good performance with a 91.8 % accuracy overall, and 87.95 % for COVID-19 alone. Despite its very good performance and its reliability in a real-time scenario, our framework is far from perfect. The GRAD-CAM visualization doesn't explain entirely the relation between the features of the signal. Also, ResVidNet cannot predict if the patient is asymptomatic or not. Using only one parameter to predict COVID-19 is not enough to achieve a real diagnosis, since respiratory condition is also an important factor for COVID-19 detection. The accuracy can also be improved by using a wearable sensor with a greater sampling rate. Our future work will focus on both heart and respiratory information's, to improve ResVidNet diagnosis ability, and thus, create a real time accurate framework for COVID-19 monitoring and diagnosis, reliable and explainable.

References

1. Organization, W.H. *WHO Coronavirus (COVID-19) Dashboard.* 2022 2022 [cited 2020 2020]; Available from: https://covid19.who.int/.

2. Ding, X., et al., *Wearable sensing and telehealth technology with potential applications in the coronavirus pandemic.* IEEE reviews in biomedical engineering, 2020. **14**: p. 48-70.

3. Mirjalali, S., et al., *Wearable Sensors for Remote Health Monitoring: Potential Applications for Early Diagnosis of Covid-19.* Advanced Materials Technologies, 2022. **7**(1): p. 2100545.

4. Al-Waisy, A.S., et al., *COVID-CheXNet: hybrid deep learning framework for identifying COVID-19 virus in chest X-rays images.* Soft computing, 2020: p. 1-16.

5. Feng, Z., et al., *Early prediction of disease progression in COVID-19 pneumonia patients with chest CT and clinical characteristics.* Nature communications, 2020. **11**(1): p. 1-9.

6. Rahman, T., et al., *COV-ECGNET: COVID-19 detection using ECG trace images with deep convolutional neural network.* Health Information Science and Systems, 2022. **10**(1): p. 1.

7. Khan, A.H., M. Hussain, and M.K. Malik, *ECG Images dataset of Cardiac and COVID-19 Patients.* Data Brief, 2021. **34**: p. 106762.

8. Um, T.T., et al., *Data augmentation of wearable sensor data for parkinson's disease monitoring using convolutional neural networks,* in *Proceedings of the 19th ACM International Conference on Multimodal Interaction.* 2017, Association for Computing Machinery: Glasgow, UK. p. 216–220.

9. Jing, E., et al., *ECG Heartbeat Classification Based on an Improved ResNet-18 Model.* Computational and Mathematical Methods in Medicine, 2021. **2021**: p. 6649970.

10. Neelakantan, A., et al., *Adding gradient noise improves learning for very deep networks.* arXiv preprint arXiv:1511.06807, 2015.

11. Selvaraju, R.R., et al. *Grad-cam: Visual explanations from deep networks via gradient-based localization.* in *Proceedings of the IEEE international conference on computer vision.* 2017.

12. Tao, X., et al., *Bluetooth Low Energy-Based Washable Wearable Activity Motion and Electrocardiogram Textronic Monitoring and Communicating System.* Advanced Materials Technologies, 2018. **3**(10): p. 1700309.

13. Li, D., et al. *Classification of ECG signals based on 1D convolution neural network.* in *2017 IEEE 19th International Conference on e-Health Networking, Applications and Services (Healthcom).* 2017.

Latest research trends of wearable sensor based data modeling for fall risk prediction in community-dwelling elderly

Manting Chen[1], Hailiang Wang[2], Lisha Yu[3], Eric H. K. Yeung[4],
Jiajia Luo[1] and Yang Zhao[1,*]

[1]*School of Public Health (Shenzhen), Sun Yat-sen University, Shenzhen, China*
[2]*School of Design, The Hong Kong Polytechnic University, Hong Kong, China*
[3]*Shenzhen Enstech Technology Co. Ltd., Shenzhen, China*
[4]*Department of Physiotherapy, The University of Hong Kong-Shenzhen Hospital
Shenzhen, China*
zhaoy393@mail.sysu.edu.cn

Fall has been recognized as the major cause of accidental death for people aged 65 and above. Timely prediction of fall risk can help identify the elderly prone to falls and trigger prevention interventions. Recent advancement in wearable sensor technology and big data analysis offers the opportunities of accurate, affordable, and easy-to-use approaches to fall risk prediction. In this paper, we focused on assessing the current state of body-worn sensor technology with machine learning methods for fall risk prediction. Fifteen out of 523 research articles were finally identified and included in this review. A systematic comparison was conducted from several aspects, including sensor types, functional tests, modeling methods, prediction effectiveness, etc. Additionally, we discussed the future trends of fall risk prediction via sensor technology, and highlighted several challenging issues encountered in the area.

Keywords: Fall risk assessment; sensor technology; community-dwelling elderly; machine learning methods.

1. Introduction

With the accelerated growth of elderly population, the burden of healthcare dramatically increases worldwide. The existing literature indicates that the world's proportion of elderly increase from 10% to 16%, and about one of every six individuals in the world will be 65 years old or above by 2050 [1]. Among the critical health problems faced by elderly population, fall has been cited as the major cause of accidental death for them. It is reported that approximately 33.3% of community-dwelling elderly experience at least one fall per year [2]. The fall risk increases as the individual ages, since aging degrades lower limb function and results in falls among elderly. Risk prediction and preventive strategies for

---

*Corresponding author.

falls have been an important research area. The overall objective is to identify elderly individuals with high fall risk, and facilitate the decision-making of appropriate interventions to ultimately reduce the occurrence of falls [3]. While continuously screening the fall risk could help avoid unnecessary health deterioration, there are several reasons for the lack of fall risk assessment in current practice ranging from over-reliance on unreliable subjective measures, lack of cost-effective assessment technology, to inadequate professional health-care resources [4]. Therefore, accurate, affordable, easy-to-use fall risk prediction approaches that can be undertaken regularly are in urgent need [5].

Wearable sensors may comprehensively depict the patterns of different motions (e.g. Spatio-temporal characteristics of balance or gait), which provides sophisticated information about internal fall risk factors, e.g., dysfunctional patterns of gait or required motor tasks that are of interest to conceptualize fall prevention strategies [5, 6]. To date, sensor technology integrated with machine learning (ML) methods is widely applied in health monitoring and management. More recently, some research works have investigated the potential use of instrumented fall-risk assessment and prediction tools based on the features extracted from body-worn inertial measurement units (IMU) during standard functional tasks [7-9]. For these studies, machine learning methods were adopted to automatically identify fallers (F) and non-fallers (NF) based on the extracted features. Specifically, the subjects were labeled as F/NF by using at least one of the following methods: assessment results from the standard functional test (e.g. Berg Balance Scale and Tinetti), self-reported fall occurrence within a follow-up period, or related hospitalization history.

In this study, we aim to assess the current state of body-worn sensor technology with machine learning methods for fall risk prediction, with a focus on community-dwelling elderly. A systematic comparison was conducted from several aspects, including sensor types, sensor placement, functional tests, modeling methods, participants, etc. We also investigated the performance of various fall risk prediction approaches, including accuracy, sensitivity, and speci-ficity for different combinations of machine learning methods, sensors, and place-ments. Finally, we discussed the future trends of fall risk prediction via sensor technology, and highlighted several challenging issues encountered in the area.

2. Methods

2.1. Search strategy

The potentially relevant articles on the study of fall risk assessment in community-dwelling elderly population through wearable sensors were identified via a literature search. Keywords search was performed in PubMed, Scopus and Web of Science databases.

The following search string groups were employed: ('accelerometer' OR 'wearable sensors' OR 'gyroscope' OR 'magnetometers') AND ('fall' OR 'fall risk assessment') AND ('gait analysis' OR 'signal processing' OR 'feature extraction') AND ('aged OR geriatric OR gerontology OR senior OR elder OR old OR older adult') AND ('general' OR 'community-dwelling'). These search strings were validated by reviewing the retrieval of representative research works.

2.2. Selection and exclusion criteria

Articles were included in this review if they met all of the following criteria: 1) All studies on healthy aged people or intended to be applied on an aged population; 2) Articles that used wearable sensors combined with functional tests for the investigation of falls; 3) Articles that presented the keywords defined by the search string on the abstract or title; 4) Full original papers published in peer-reviewed journals between November 2017 and November 2021 in English.

Articles were excluded from the review if they meet one or more of the following criteria: 1) Articles that do not include healthy aged population as subjects; 2) Articles that used sensors combined with activity daily life (ADL); 3) The subjects aged less than 65 years old [10]; 4) Articles that are review studies; 5) No machine learning method was adopted in the approach for fall risk prediction.

3. Result

3.1. Study selection

The search strategy retrieved 523 papers. After the exclusion of duplicated articles found in different sources, 304 remained in the review. From those, 148 were removed after screening the abstract against the eligibility criteria, which left 156 papers to be checked in full text. 141were excluded after full-text checking due also to inclusion/exclusion criteria. Finally, 15 papers were shortlisted for this review. The flowchart, including the steps considered for the selection of articles in this review, is shown in Fig. 1.

3.2. Types of sensors

Inertial sensors were used in the 15 investigations. It is worth noting that most of the articles used the combination of two or more sensors to capture motion signals.

IMU consisting of multiple sensors (accelerometer, gyroscope, and magneto-meter) was the choice in 7 out of the 15 articles. For these 7 articles, all of them used accelerometers, and gyroscopes to acquire data. By reviewing all the types of sensors, it was found that accelerometer was the choice in 6 out of the 15 articles.

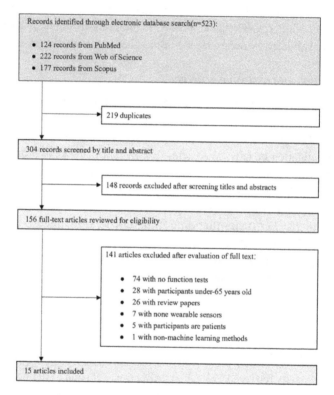

Fig. 1. Flowchart used in the selection of articles for systematic review.

3.3. Placement of sensors

A wearable sensor can be placed at multiple spots on a human body to measure the movement of different key points, depending on the application requirements. The detailed information of the sensors adopted in the reviewed articles is summarized in Fig. 2. 100 Hz was observed as the most frequently used sampling frequency. It was noticed that the spine region (lower back and sternum) was employed in 8 articles for quantifying center of mass movement and trunk movement. 8 articles utilized sensors placed bilaterally on lower limbs (foot/shank/ upper leg) for recording spatial/temporal gait parameters combined with 4 articles in the pelvis (with a total of 15 studies). The rest articles reported the spots that were less commonly used, such as the neck and chest. It should be noted that several articles used a combination of sensors placed in different spots of the body. From Fig. 2, it was observed that placing an IMU in the spine region was the most commonly used in the reviewed studies.

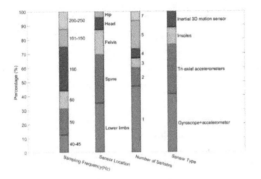

Fig. 2. Summary of sensor information of the reviewed articles.

3.4. Machine learning methods

A diverse collection of machine learning methods were employed to predict fall risk, including logistic regression [7, 11, 12], Support Vector Machine (SVM) [13-15], Random forest predictive model [16], neural networks [13], Elastic Net [17], ridge regression [17], lasso regression [9, 18], Convolutional Neural Network (CNN) [19] and Hierarchical classification model [20]. In general, statistical features characterizing gait pattern of the elderly were extracted from the pre-processed sensor data. The extracted features together with a quantitative assessment measure of fall risks will then be trained via the machine learning methods for fall risk prediction.

3.5. Performance analysis

In terms of the prediction effectiveness of the fall risk prediction approach, different evaluation metrics were used in the reviewed articles. However, it might not be fair to compare all these studies using a single evaluation metric, e.g. sensitivity. The primary reason is the inconsistency among the datasets, acquisition processes, participants, experiment environments, sensor types, sensor locations, and machine learning methods considered in different studies. To provide a complete picture of the difference comparison, we summarized the key information in Table 1.

470

Table 1. Performance Analysis of ML methods using Different Sensors and Locations.

ML Algo	Sensor	Sensor Placement	Accuracy	Specificity	Sensitivity	References
Logistic regression	Accelerometer + Gyroscope	chest, lower back, and each foot	NA	82.1%	48.1%	[7]
		mid-point of the left and right anterior shank (shin)	72.7%	54.50%	90.91%	[11]
		spine(sternum)	NA	69%	56%	[12]
SVM	Accelerometer + Gyroscope	spine(low back), upper legs, and lower legs	89.40%	84.90%	92.70%	[14]
		shanks	90.50%	92.90%	85.70%	[15]
	Tri-axial accelerometers, pressure-sensing insoles	Insole, left and right shanks, pelvis, and head (LS, Insole)	94.40%	100.00%	85.70%	[13]
Lasso regression	Tri-axial accelerometer	spine(lower back)	NA	79%	74%	[18]
		spine(lower back)	NA	NA	NA	[9]
Neural network	Pressure-sensing insoles and tri-axial accelerometer	head, pelvis, and left and right shanks	57%	65%	43%	[8]
Random forest	Tri-axial accelerometer	spine(sternum)	81.6± 0.7%	80.3 ± 0.2%	86.7 ± 0.5%	[16]
Ridge regression	Inertial 3D motion sensor	posterior pelvis and bilaterally to the foot segment	NA	NA	NA	[17]
CNN	Accelerometer + Gyroscope	spine(lower back)	76%	NA	NA	[19]
Hierarchical classification	Accelerometer + Gyroscope	hip	96%	NA	NA	[20]

4. Discussion

It was observed that SVM or Logistic regression using data from accelerometer and gyroscope on the low back and shanks [14, 15] [7, 11, 12] were the commonly used method for fall risk prediction. Overall, SVM performed better than the compared machine learning methods. For example, SVM achieved the accuracy of 90.50%, specificity of 92.90% and sensitivity of 85.70% by using the data from accelerometer and gyroscope on shanks in [15]. In the study conducted by Howcroft et al. [14], SVM achieved the accuracy of 94.40%, specificity of 100.00% and sensitivity of 85.70% by using the data collected from tri-axial accelerometers and pressure-sensing insoles on left shank and feet. In another related work, SVM outperformed the competitors via using the data from an accelerometer and gyroscope on the low back, upper legs, and lower legs [14, 15]. Specifically, this work incorporated 38 significant features as predictor variables from 196 community-dwelling elderly. Among those features, the representative outcome measures were Fall Efficacy Scale (FES) Score, Information Processing Speed, Step Length, Gait Velocity, Stand-Sit Jerk, Knee Extension Range, Sit-Stand-Sit Jerk, Turning Angular Velocity MAX, Visual-Equilibrium Score Mediolateral and Knee Flexion Range.

5. Conclusions

Aging is highly correlated with the decline in physical, cognitive, and sensory functionalities. These functionalities impairments increase the chances of fall, leading to fatal negative consequences. To date, a wide range of sensor technology with data analytical tools have been examined for fall risk prediction. In this paper, we present an overview of the latest fall risk assessment approach via machine learning methods by using wearable sensor data in community-dwelling elderly. We conducted a systematic comparison by looking into different aspects of the related works, including sensor types, modeling methods, prediction effectiveness, etc. Our analysis showed that the accelerometer and gyroscope from IMUs are the most frequently utilized sensors. The most desired locations of sensors for function tests are lower limbs and spine. Over half of the reviewed papers only take a single sensor for data acquisition. It was observed that SVMs using the accelerometer and gyroscope performed better than the compared machine learning methods. Focusing on SVM, we compared sensitivity between different studies in order to identify significant features related to high fall risk.

In practice, the obtained sensor-based data usually contains numerous noises and unwanted vibration interface. The signal data of elderly can be even more complex to find relevant harmonic ratios due to their unstable gait. It is challenging to extract features revealing the gait pattern of elderly. Additionally, there is still a gap between new technology and user acceptance among elderly.

References

1. Population Ageing: An Inescapable Future. https://www.globalissues.org/news/2022/01/05/29746.
2. Usmani, S.; et al., Latest Research Trends in Fall Detection and Prevention Using Machine Learning: A Systematic Review. *Sensors (Basel)* **2021**, *21*, (15).

3. Porta, S.; et al., Relevance of sex, age and gait kinematics when predicting fall-risk and mortality in older adults. *J. Biomech.* **2020**, *105*, 109723.

4. Sun, R.; Sosnoff, J.J., Novel sensing technology in fall risk assessment in older adults: a systematic review. *BMC Geriatrics* **2018**, *18*, (1), 14.

5. Bezold, J.; et al., Sensor-based fall risk assessment in older adults with or without cognitive impairment: a systematic review. *Eur Rev Aging Phys a* **2021**, *18*, (1), 15.

6. Montesinos, L.; et al., Wearable Inertial Sensors for Fall Risk Assessment and Prediction in Older Adults: A Systematic Review and Meta-Analysis. *IEEE Trans. Neural Syst. Rehabil. Eng.* **2018**, *26*, (3), 573-582.

7. Sample, R.B.; et al., Identification of key outcome measures when using the instrumented timed up and go and/or posturography for fall screening. *Gait Posture* **2017**, *57*, 168-171.

8. Howcroft, J.; Kofman, J.; Lemaire, E.D., Prospective Fall-Risk Prediction Models for Older Adults Based on Wearable Sensors. *IEEE Trans Neural Syst Rehabil. Eng.* **2017**, *25*, (10), 1812-1820.

9. Shahzad, A.; et al., Quantitative Assessment of Balance Impairment for Fall-Risk Estimation Using Wearable Triaxial Accelerometer. *IEEE Sens. J.* **2017**.

10. CDC Older Adult Fall Prevention. https://www.cdc.gov/falls/.

11. Greene, B.R.; Redmond, S.J.; Caulfield, B., Fall Risk Assessment Through Automatic Combination of Clinical Fall Risk Factors and Body-Worn Sensor Data. *IEEE J. Biomed. Health. Inf.* **2017**.

12. Atrsaei, A.; et al., Instrumented 5-Time Sit-To-Stand Test: Parameters Predicting Serious Falls beyond the Duration of the Test. *Gerontology* **2021**.

13. Howcroft, J.; Lemaire, E.D.; Kofman, J., Prospective elderly fall prediction by older-adult fall-risk modeling with feature selection. *Biomed. Signal Process. Control* **2018**, *43*, 320-328.

14. Qiu, H.; et al., Application of Wearable Inertial Sensors and A New Test Battery for Distinguishing Retrospective Fallers from Non-fallers among Community-dwelling Older People. *Sci Rep* **2018**, *8*, (1), 16349.

15. Diao, Y.; et al., A Novel Environment-Adaptive Timed Up and Go Test System for Fall Risk Assessment With Wearable Inertial Sensors. *IEEE Sens. J.* **2021**, *21*, (16), 18287-18297.

16. Lockhart, T.E.; et al., Prediction of fall risk among community-dwelling older adults using a wearable system. *Sci Rep-Uk* **2021**, *11*, (1).

17. Choi, J.; et al., Wearable Sensor-Based Prediction Model of Timed up and Go Test in Older Adults. *Sensors (Basel)* **2021**, *21*, (20).

18. Yu, L.; et al., Assessing elderly's functional balance and mobility via analyzing data from waist-mounted tri-axial wearable accelerometers in

timed up and go tests. *BMC Med. Inf. Decis. Making* **2021**, *21*, (1).

19. Buisseret, F.; et al., Timed Up and Go and Six-Minute Walking Tests with Wearable Inertial Sensor: One Step Further for the Prediction of the Risk of Fall in Elderly Nursing Home People. *Sensors-Basel* **2020**, *20*, (11).

20. Hellmers, S.; et al., Towards an Automated Unsupervised Mobility Assessment for Older People Based on Inertial TUG Measurements. *Sensors-Basel* **2018**, *18*, (10).

474

Designing wearables for assistive correction of children's sitting posture

Zhebin Xue[1,*], Qing Li[1] and Munir Ashraf[2]

[1]Collage of Textile and Clothing Engineering, Soochow University
Suzhou, China
[2]Functional Textile Research Group, School of Engineering and Technology
National Textile University, Faisalabad, Pakistan
*zhebin.xue@hotmail.com

Poor sitting posture in a long term can severely threaten children's physical and mental health. Clothes as an intimate but non-invasive existence on human body, is supposed to be a perfect carrier of wearable components by establishing personalized and meanwhile comfortable interaction between functional modules and the wearer. The current paper attempts to develop a knitwear based wearable system which is able to detect the wearer's back bending and chest-desk distance, and then send instructive alert so as to help the kid to cultivate good sitting habits. According to users' feedback to the prototype, the proposed wearable system is generally satisfactory, but further exploration is also needed to improve function and design.

Keywords: Smart wearables; sitting posture correction; knitwear; fabric sensor; distance detection.

1. Introduction

Poor sitting posture may have a life-long impact on a child. However, currently, children's poor sitting posture has become a worldwide problem. For example, according to a recent research on reading and writing posture of 365 first-year students from 5 elementary schools in Beijing, up to 80% of the tested students had posture problems [1], which deserves the attention from the whole society. Due to an increasing concern about children's posture problems and their potential harm, it is believed that posture correction related research is urgently needed and highly demanding [2].

The majority of the current posture correction wearables are small detachable accessories which are convenient to use but cannot get too close to the body thus they sometimes cannot get the real human data and their sensitivity is difficult to be guaranteed [3, 4]. Actually garment is known as "the second skin of human body" [5]. As an intimate but non-invasive existence on human body, clothes is

---

*Corresponding author.

supposed to be a perfect carrier of wearable components which carries out a direct conversation with the human body thus can establish personalized and meanwhile comfortable interaction between functional modules and the wearer. Using garment as the carrier of the smart posture correction system can provide the wearer with a stable and accurate sitting posture detection and alert. Thus a long-term use of it can help the kid to develop a right sitting posture, which compared with conventional external force-led correction methods, is an active way of correction and is believed to be more agreeable to use for especially kids.

The current research proposes to design a knitwear based wearable system for the instructive correction of kids' sitting posture during study. Standardized investigations will be carried out to explore the critical physical problems connected with poor sitting posture, according to which specific design to sensor, clothes and HCI (human-computer interaction) method will be conducted. A prototype of the proposed design will be obtained, on which a feedback investigation will be carried out on target subjects to see the acceptance of the research idea. Finally, through subjects' feedback, the current prototype is reflected and new ideas will be developed to improve the function and design.

To date, there are few study focusing on the smart clothing approach to sitting posture correction for kids. It is hoped that the current attempt can be considered an instructive step forward towards a more profound exploration of smart wearables for children's physical and mental need.

The rest of the paper is organized in the following. Section 2 illustrates the conceptualization and method of the design. Section 3 shows the feedback of the prototype based on which a reflection is carried out to further improve the current design. Section 4 presents a summary of the research and discusses the prospective development of the research.

2. Development of an Instructive Wearable for Sitting Posture Correction

Figure 1 shows the general framework of the development of an instructive wearable system for children's sitting posture correction.

After interviewing a number of first-year pupils and their teachers in a primary school, a few parents as well as some pediatricians in Wuxi, China, it was found that both parents and teachers were very concerned about the children's sitting posture. At school, teachers generally said that when students in the class were writing, they need to constantly remind children whose head was down, but the students would easily return to poor postures after a few minutes or sometimes just ignore the reminders. Some parents said that they often observed that their children unconsciously bowed their heads while doing their homework, and were

476

very worried that this would affect their children's vision. Generally speaking, the first-year children have weak self-control and cannot notice whether they are hunched or bowed, as showed in Fig. 2. Therefore, when the design idea was presented to some parents and teachers, most of them showed positive attitude towards it.

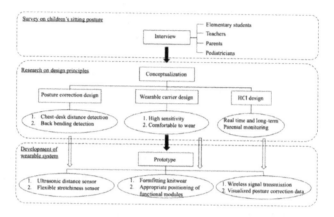

Fig. 1. General research framework.

Fig. 2. Poor sitting posture.

2.1. Sitting posture problem

Based on the information collected from the survey, the sitting posture problem has been analyzed as follows.

2.1.1. Short chest-desk distance

The most common poor sitting posture is that the child's chest getting too close to the desk while reading and writing. This posture oppresses the chest and could do harm to child's chest and cardiopulmonary development in a long term, which is a big threat to health and can easily develop other poor postures such as bowing, bending etc.

2.1.2. Hunchback

Hunchback is also a common abnormal sitting posture for children. During class or while doing homework, the child's relaxed body muscles tend to cause hunchback, which makes the eyes too close to the desk, and in turns the neck is excessively bent, finally leading to myopia, cervical spondylosis and other diseases. In particular, children's spine curvature is not fixed, and the hunchback in the long run, may cause abnormal curvature of the spine, leading to damage to the spinal cord and nerve roots, and even the risk of paralysis [6]. The thoracic and rib deformation caused by the hunchback is harmful to respiratory and digestive system functions, and affects body shape, which may cause psychological problems such as child inferiority [7].

Other posture problems vary from person to person. To solve common problems, only the above two main posture problems are selected for research.

2.2. Design principles

Figure 1 shows the development of the design principles of the posture correction wearable system. Based on the posture problems discussed in the above, the instructive wearable system consists of three parts, the wearable carrier (i.e., the clothes), and the two major functional modules, respectively the posture warning module and the parental monitoring module.

2.2.1. Wearable carrier

As mentioned in Fig. 1, there are two major concerns about the choice of the wearable carrier. The one is the sufficient sensitivity of the sensors when they are positioned on the carrier. The other is the basic and important issue about clothes, which is the comfort of it. In the current study, as shown in Fig. 2, a form-fitting knitwear for kids is selected as the carrier of the wearable components of the design, which is supposed to provide sufficient support to the sensors and meanwhile be comfortable to wear.

2.2.2. Posture warning module

• Chest-desk distance reminder

Based on the size of the standard desk and chair and the average body shape of the seven-year-old child, this study has determined the approximate contact area between the chest and the desk when the child is sitting. As shown in Fig. 3, an ultrasonic distance sensor is positioned at the corresponding area of the clothes' front chest, and is connected to the micro controller (at the back) and LED light (at the wrist). Thus constitutes a detecting-feedback system. When the child's chest is too close to the desk (less than the set value), the light at the wrist would start flashing to remind the child of the poor posture he (or she) is in. The closer the distance, the higher the flashing frequency of the LED, and when the child returns to the correct sitting posture, the light goes out.

- Hunchback reminder

The hunchback is reflected by the stretching of the fabric at the corresponding part of the back of the garment. Therefore, based on the above discussion, this study weaves conductive yarns at the corresponding positions on the back of the knitwear (the part where the back bends), and uses the elasticity of the knitted fabric itself to make the fabric a stretch sensor, so as to monitor with sufficient sensitivity the bending degree of the wearer's back. The sensor is connected to the micro controller and a vibration motor (positioned on the back of the neck) to constitute a monitoring-feedback system. Intermittent vibration is indicated when the degree of stretching exceeds the set value. The larger the stretching value, the higher the vibration frequency. When the posture is corrected, the vibration stops. When the back is bent, in order to prevent the garment from moving upward which will largely affect the sensitivity of the stretch sensor, the bottom of the knitwear is relatively fixed by some findings with the lower garment (e.g. the pants or skirts, etc.). Figure 3 shows the detailed design of the wearable system.

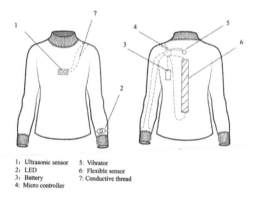

1: Ultrasonic sensor   5: Vibrator
2: LED   6: Flexible sensor
3: Battery   7: Conductive thread
4: Micro controller

Fig. 3. Prototype of sitting posture correction wearable.

2.2.3. *Parental monitoring*

The number of correction times will be recorded by the micro controller, and the data will be transmitted in real time to the human-computer interaction interface on mobile terminals through wireless transmission to realize data visualization. The collated data will be summarized every 24 hours. So the parents can not only monitor the children's posture, but also have a daily, monthly even annually view about the development of the posture correction.

3. Feedback and Reflection

In order to investigate the feasibility of the research and understand the experience and acceptance of the target users, an experience feedback survey was conducted on the proposed prototype. In the survey, five first-year students and their parents were invited to participate in a one-month trial of the prototype. The Children are required to wear the designated wearable prototype throughout the day, meanwhile, their parents should install relevant APP on their mobile phones to receive the data. A feedback interview will be carried out on them after a month.

3.1. *Overall acceptance*

In order to investigate the participants' acceptance after the experience of the wearable, their feedback were analyzed according to a three dimensional appraisal system. the three evaluation criteria that are believed to strongly connected with the overall acceptance of the prototype are wearing comfort, functionality, and long-term fidelity, respectively.

3.1.1. *Wearing comfort*

Since any smart clothes, in the first place are clothes, wearing comfort as a appraisal criterion comes first and shall be the most important. This criterion involves both physical and aesthetic evaluation of the prototype. The knitted prototype is soft and elastic, thus quite comfortable to wear. And the garment style is designed for easy wear. Most children said that the clothe looked good and was quite comfortable, while one child felt uncomfortable at the chest since the distance sensor is rigid and he didn't wear underwear.

3.1.2. *Functionality*

According to the parents, the prototype can make an accurate reminder on their child's poor sitting posture. Besides, the relevant data can be sent to the mobile phone, which is convenient to monitor. But some problems were found too. For example, sometimes the sensor seems to be over sensitive, but sometimes it is dull to posture change.

3.1.3. Long-term fidelity

After a month trial, most of the parents found that the clothes could help their children improve sitting habits. According to the visualized data, it can also be found that the number of children's posture reminders were significantly reduced, which indicated a satisfactory effect. At the end of the interview, most parents shows fidelity to a long-term use of this wearable.

To sum up, the proposed wearable system is generally accpetable in assisting children correcting their sitting posture. All the tested parents show fidelity on the prototype. Although they posed some minor negative comments, all of them are faithful to see the beta version of the design.

3.2. Reflection

3.2.1. Reflection on posture warning modules

According to the subjects' feedback on the rigidity of the distance sensor, the current prototype is not designed for direct contact with the body. Underwear is need before putting on this clothes. But as an improvement, the beta version of the prototype will have a double layer design to keep the rigid sensor on the shell, while the inner layer of the clothes being comfortable skin touch. The shape, area and position of the stretch sensor on the back could be modified to provide sufficient sensitivity and avoid noise at the same time in the beta version.

3.2.2. Optimization of HCI

All the parents at test were quite satisfied with the HCI interface on the mobile. But some of them also gives us some inspiration to further improve the interaction experience. For example, the posture correction data can be more visualized by involving real time posture animation. In order to better motivate the children and improve interaction with their parents, the beta version can involve a reward and punishment mechanism according to which a correction mission will be set within a time span, succeeding or failing the mission will lead to reward or punishment.

4. Conclusion

Compared with conventional elastic force based correction method, the proposed smart wearable provides an active and superior solution to children's posture correction in that it can accurately detect sitting posture and produce instructive alert which is more mentally acceptable to children of early age and at the same time the wearing comfort can be ensured. A prototype was made and went through feedback survey on the target users. A generally satisfactory result is obtained that most subjects welcome this new design, while some minor negative comments and suggestions concerning both the posture correction modules and HCI interface are collected and reflected, and will be taken into account in the development of the beta version of the wearable system.

The current design is just one of many ideas for the development of smart posture correction garments. With the development of smart wearable technology, smart posture-correction clothing will be able to face more people, more scenarios, and assist people to adjust their body in a smart and comfortable way.

References

1. X. Zheng, Sensor principle and model design based on sitting posture correction, *China Science and Technology Information* 14, 90 (2016).
2. H. L. Bi, Z. J. Zhang, and Y. J. Chen. SmartGe: identifying pen-holding gesture with smartwatch. *IEEE Access* 8, 28820 (2020).
3. X. Q. Zhang, Analysis of prevention of spinal bending anomalies in children and adolescents, *China Health Industry* 9, 155 (2012).
4. H. F. Zhang, L. Q. Cao, F. Gong et al. Interpretation of intelligent garment manufacturing system and intelligent garment system and reflections on the standard formulation, *Silk* 12, 47 (2021).
5. Chen, C., Ning, P., Zeng, Y., and Bao, X. (2021, January). Research on the Correlation between Body Mass Index and Physical Health Index of Medical College Students. In *IEEE. 2021 International Conference on Information Technology and Contemporary Sports (TCS)* (Guangzhou, China, 2021).
6. Q. Tang, B. B. Zhang, and X. Y. Zhang, Design of wearable intelligent clothing for infants, *Journal of Textile Research* 08, 156 (2021).
7. H. Shi, J. Fu, X. Liu et al. Influence of the interaction between parental myopia and poor eye habits when reading and writing and poor reading posture on prevalence of myopia in school students in Urumqi, China. *BMC ophthalmology* 21.1 (2021).

482

Nano-scPLA: An efficient nucleating agent and reinforcement for sustainable green polymer poly(lactic acid)[*]

Minjie Tong, Bomou Ma[†] and Xueli Wang

Innovation Center for Textile Science & Technology, College of Textiles
Donghua University, Shanghai, 201620, China
†mabomou@dhu.edu.cn
www.dhu.edu.cn

Polylactic acid (PLA) is one of the most promising green polymer and has a wide range of application in textile, food packaging, and plastics industries due to its sustainable, environment-friendly and biodegradable character. However, it is often restricted by its low crystallinity and crystallization rate, which affects the heat resistance and mechanical properties. The purpose of this research is to investigate the effect of nano-stereocomplex PLA (nano-scPLA) on the crystallization of Poly(lactic acid). The results show that nano-scPLA prepared from low molecular weight of poly($_L$-lactic acid) (PLLA) and poly($_D$-lactic acid) (PDLA) possesses a crystallinity of 53.9%, and most of them (98.8%) is stereocomplex crystal structure. This nano-scPLA has a prominent promotion of PLLA crystallization, and the crystallinity of the resulting composite films is increased to 48.5% from amorphous. Furthermore, their tensile strength is also increased from 17.5MPa to 60MPa. Based on the results, nano-scPLA is proved to be an efficient nucleating agent and reinforcement for PLA matrix. The prepared films are expected to be applied as a sustainable packaging materials.

Keywords: Nanoparticles; composite PLA films; nucleating agent; reinforcement.

1. Introduction

Biodegradable polymers are gaining attention from the viewpoint of environment protection and sustainable development. Poly(lactic acid)(PLA), a kind of linear aliphatic thermoplastic polyester which made from starch through fermentation and polycondensation, attracts much attention due to its degradable, biocompatible and renewable, and is regarded as a promising alternative for petroleum-based polymers [1]. However, the widespread application of PLA is still restricted by its low crystallinity and crystallization rate,

---

[*]Work partially supported by grant 2232020A4-06 of the Open Project Funds from Shanghai Key Laboratory of Lightweight Composite, 2232020D-10 of the Fundamental Research Funds for the Central Universities and BK20180624 of the Natural Science Foundation of Jiangsu Province.

which plays a decisive role on the mechanical and physical properties of the final products [2]. Up to now, many approaches have been applied to improve the crystallinity and crystallization rate of PLA materials, i.e. adding nucleating agent, blending with plasticizer and improving the optical purity of PLA [3, 4]. Among those methods, adding nucleating agent is seemed as easy and efficient. Qian used cellulose nanowhisker as additive and the crystallinity of resulting films fabricated by solution casting method researches 30.7% [5]. Aliotta investigated the effect of Boron Nitride and nanofillers (Talc, Calcium Carbonate) on crystallization property of PLA, the results show that crystallinity of molded PLA composite is increased to 22.3% when loading 20(wt.)% $CaCO_3$ [6]. Shazleen melt-blended PLA and cellulose nanofiber (CNF), found that both the crystallinity and crystallization rate of PLA increased, and the crystallinity of PLA composite is increased to 44.2% when adding 3(wt.)% CNF [7]. Although those nano additives increased the crystallinity of PLA composite, the incompatible interface leads to the decrease of tensile strength and elongation at break. Therefore, it is very important and significant to promote the crystallinity and mechanical property of PLA simultaneously. Liu studied the effect of polyamidamine grafted graphene oxide (PgGO) on the crystallization property of PLA [8]. Compared with pure PLA, the crystallization rate of PLA/PgGO is prominently improved and the spherulitic size is remarkably reduced, but there is no data about mechanical property of the composite. Gazzotti demonstrated the reinforcement of CNC-g-PLA (cellulose nanocrystal grafted PLA) for PLA matrix, while the cold crystallization temperature of CNC-g-PLA/PLA composite increased, which indicates a poor crystallization property [9]. Wang prepared carbon nanotubes/PLA nanocomposites by twin-screw extrusion, found that both the value of tensile strength and elongation at break increased, but the crystallinity of PLA is low, only 8.69% when the mechanical property is best [10]. Recently, sc-PLA (stereocomplex PLA), consisting of equivalent PLLA and PDLA, attracts more attentions due to its high melting point and heat distortion temperature. Many researchers have conducted numerous works on the preparation of sc-PLA microparticles, films and fibers [11, 12, 13]. Ji confirmed that the SC crystallites can effectively promote the nucleation of PLA [14]. However, sc-PLA film was used as nucleating agent to directly blend with PLA, which makes the SC crystallites cannot be uniformly dispersed in PLA matrix.

In this research, nano-scPLA was prepared by precipitation after blending PLLA and PDLA in chloroform and was added to PLLA matrix as nucleating agent. Its effect on crystallinity and mechanical property of the composites was fully investigated.

2. Experimental

2.1. Materials

PLLA was Ingeo 6202D produced from Nature Works, its M_v is 5.3×10^4 g/mol measured with Ubbelohde. PDLA was synthesized in the lab according to the previous method [14], the M_v is controlled around 1.0×10^4 g/mol by polymerization conditions. D-lactide (D-LA) with an optical purity of 99% was purchased from Jinan Daigang Biomaterials Co., Ltd. Stannous octoate, chloroform and ethyl alcohol was purchased from Sinopharm Chemical Reagent Co., Ltd.

2.2. Preparation of nano-scPLA

PLLA (1g) and PDLA (1g) were separately dissolved in 100ml of chloroform. The solutions were mixed and stirred at room temperature. Then the mixed solution was dropwise added to a ethanol bath with stirring, as shown in Fig. 1a. The precipitation was washed with ethanol and DI water successively, and freeze dried to afford nano-scPLA powder, its SEM images is shown in Fig. 1b and c.

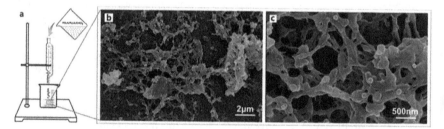

Fig. 1. Diagram of the nano-scPLA formation (a) and the SEM images (b,c).

2.3. Nano-scPLA/PLLA composite films

A certain amount of nano-scPLA powder was added to 10(wt.)% PLLA/ chloroform solution, and controlling the weight ratio of nano-scPLA at 0.5%, 1%, 2%, 5% respectively. Then the homogeneous solutions was poured into a culture dish and evaporated at fume hood overnight, and the resulting film was dried at 50°C for 24h to remove the residual solvent and obtain the composites.

2.4. Characterization

Solution viscosities were measured in chloroform with an Ubbelohde viscometer at 25°C and the value of M_v were calculated by the Eq. (1) [15].

$$[\eta] = 5.45 \times 10^{-4} M_v^{0.73} \tag{1}$$

Scanning electron microscopy (SEM) images were obtained *from Jeol* Jsm-5600lv. Differential scanning calorimeter (DSC) analyses were conducted on TA Q20 at a heating rate of 10°C/min from 30°C to 250°C. The wide X-ray diffraction (XRD) analyses were performed on Rigaku D/Max-2550. Mechanical property was measured with WDW3020 materials testing system with a crosshead speed of 5mm/min. The composite films were cut into strips of 80mm×10mm, and five strips were measured for each sample.

3. Results and Discussion

Stereocomplex PLA is the association of pair of optically active PLLA and PDLA, has a melting temperature between 210 and 230°C, which is about 50°C higher than that of pure enantiomeric form. The aim of this research is to investigate the promotion of nano-scPLA for PLLA crystallization and mechanical property of the resulting composite films. Many literatures have reported the preparation of nano- and micro-scPLA particles by different approach [16, 17]. Here, the nano-scPLA was prepared by simple blending and precipitation method. SEM images of the prepared nano-scPLA is show in Fig. 1b and c. It can be seen that the size of nano-scPLA is around 300nm with an irregular shape, which is different from the scPLA particles prepared by spray drying and thermal induced phase separation. That is ascribed to the strong agitation during the precipitation process.

Figure 2 presents the DSC and XRD results of the prepared nano-scPLA. As shown in Fig. 2a, it indicates that the melting temperature of nano-scPLA is 208°C, which is higher than that of pure PLLA and PDLA. However, this value is low compared with other scPLA materials [13]. It is ascribed to the low molecular weight of PDLA. If the PDLA with high molecular weight was used to blend with PLLA, the precipitation present flocculent and no particle obtained. Besides, there is no melting peak of PLA homogeneous crystal, this confirms that all the crystal in nano-scPLA is SC crystallites. In order to further prove the conclusion, the XRD analysis was conducted, as shown in Fig. 2b. The strong diffraction peak appears at 12.6, 21.3 and 24.5° are assigned to the SC crystalline, whereas the weak peaks appear at 17.1° corresponding to the PLA homo-crystal [18]. This demonstrates that most of the crystal is SC crystalline in the prepared nano-scPLA. According to the analysis of crystallinity, the crystalline degree of nano-scPLA is 53.9%, and the fraction of SC crystalline reaches 98.8%. When the nano-scPLA was added to PLLA/chloroform solution, the homo-crystal dissolves in chloroform and the SC-crystal as nucleating agent promotes the crystallization of PLLA macromolecules. The WAXD results of different nano-scPLA/PLLA composite films is shown in Fig. 3a. The characteristic diffraction peaks at 14.8°, 16.7°, 19.1° and 22.3°, which is assigned to (010), (110), (203) and (210) reflections of homo-crystal. While the characteristic diffraction peaks at 12.1° and 21.0°, which can be assigned to (110) and (300)/(030) reflections of SC crystals [19]. This confirms that the composite films consist of two crystal structures. Besides, the peak intensity of all the samples is increased with the increase of nano-scPLA content. Specifically, the pure PLLA film is almost amorphous, while the crystallinity of composite film with 5% nano-scPLA reaches 48.5%. This proves that nano-scPLA has an efficient promotion of PLA crystallization.

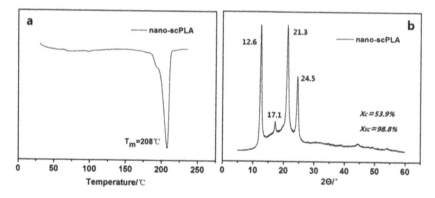

Fig. 2. DSC and XRD profiles of the prepared nano-scPLA.

Materials mechanical property is closely associated with the crystallinity. Here, the stress and strain of all films is performed, and the results is shown in Fig. 3b. It shows that tensile strength and break elongation of pure PLLA films is 17.5MPa and 26%, respectively. Compared with the previous publication, the tensile strength is low, and the break elongation is high [20]. This may be ascribed to the residual chloroform in PLLA matrix. The tensile strength gradually increases and reaches 60MPa when the content of nano-scPLA is 5%. While the break elongation presents a decreasing tendency. This is because the addition of nano-scPLA promotes the PLA crystallization, which contributes to the high tensile strength and low break elongation of the composite films.

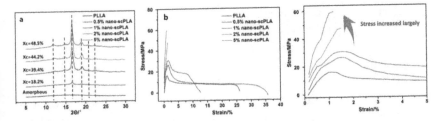

Fig. 3. XRD results (a) and mechanical properties (b) of the resulting composite films.

4. Conclusions

In order to promote the crystallization of PLLA matrix, the nano-scPLA prepared by precipitation method was introduced into PLLA matrix by solution blending. DSC and XRD results reveal that crystallinity and stereocomplex degree of nano-scPLA is 53.9% and 98.8%, respectively. The crystallinity of nano-scPLA/PLLA composite films is increased to 48.5% when loading 5% nano-scPLA. The tensile strength is increased from 17.5MPa to 60MPa. Specifically, nano-scPLA is an efficient nucleating agent and reinforcement for PLLA matrix.

Acknowledgments

This work was financially supported by the Open Project Funds from Shanghai Key Laboratory of Lightweight Composite (Grant No. 2232020A4-06), the Fundamental Research Funds for the Central Universities (Grant No. 2232020D-10) and the Natural Science Foundation of Jiangsu Province (Grant No. BK20180624).

Declaration of competing interest

The authors declare no competing financial interest.

References

1. T. Hottle, M. Bilec, A. Landis, Sustainability assessments of bio-based polymers, Polymer Degradation and Stability. 98 (2013) 1898-1907.

2. R. Ming, G. Yang, Y. Li, R. Wang, H. Zhang, H. Shao, Flax fiber-reinforced polylactide stereocomplex composites with enhanced heat resistance and mechanical properties, Polym. Composite. 38 (2017) 472-478.

3. P. Chen, K. Yu, Y. Wang, W. Wang, H. Zhou, H. Li, J. Mi, X. Wang, The

effect of composite nucleating agent on the crystallization behavior of branched poly (lactic acid), J. Polym. Environ. 26 (2018) 3718-3730.

4. H. Simmons, P. Tiwary, J. Colwell, M. Kontopoulou, Improvements in the crystallinity and mechanical properties of PLA by nucleation and annealing, Polymer Degradation and Stability. 166 (2019) 248-257.

5. S. Qian, H. Zhang, W. Yao, K. Sheng, Effects of bamboo cellulose nanowhisker content on the morphology, crystallization, mechanical, and thermal properties of PLA matrix biocomposites, Compos. Part B-Eng. 133 (2018) 203-209.

6. L. Aliotta, P. Cinelli, M.C. Righetti, M.B. Coltelli, A. Lazzeri, Effect of different nucleating agent on crystallinity and properties of polylactic acid, AIP Conference Proceedings 1981 (2018) 20036.

7. S. Shazleen, T. Yasim-Anuar, N. Ibrahim, M. Hassan, H. Ariffin, Functionality of Cellulose Nanofiber as Bio-Based Nucleating Agent and Nano-Reinforcement Material to Enhance Crystallization and Mechanical Properties of Polylactic Acid Nanocomposite, Polymers. 13 (2021).

8. X. Liu, Y. Sheng, D. Wu, R. Zhang, H. Cui, Synthesis of PAMAM-GO as new nanofiller to enhance the crystallization properties of polylactic acid, Mater. Lett. 235 (2019) 27-30.

9. S. Gazzotti, H. Farina, G. Lesma, R. Rampazzo, L. Piergiovanni, M.A. Ortenzi, A. Silvani, Polylactide/cellulose nanocrystals: The in situ polymerization approach to improved nanocomposites, Eur. Polym. J. 94 (2017) 173-184.

10. L. Wang, J. Qiu, E. Sakai, X. Wei, The relationship between microstructure and mechanical properties of carbon nanotubes/polylactic acid nanocomposites prepared by twin-screw extrusion, Composites Part a-Applied Science and Manufacturing. 89 (2016) 18-25.

11. A. Michalski, T. Makowski, T. Biedroń, M. Brzeziński, T. Biela, Controlling polylactide stereocomplex (sc-PLA) self-assembly: From microspheres to nanoparticles, Polymer 90 (2016) 242-248.

12. A. Gupta, V. Katiyar, Cellulose Functionalized High Molecular Weight Stereocomplex Polylactic Acid Biocomposite Films with Improved Gas Barrier, Thermomechanical Properties, Acs Sustainable Chemistry & Engineering. 5 (2017) 6835-6844.

13. G. Pan, H. Xu, B. Mu, B. Ma, J. Yang, Y. Yang, Complete stereocomplexation of enantiomeric polylactides for scalable continuous production, Chem. Eng. J. 328 (2017) 759-767.

14. N. Ji, G. Hu, J. Li, J. Ren, Influence of poly(lactide) stereocomplexes as nucleating agents on the crystallization behavior of poly(lactide)s, RSC

Adv. 9 (2019) 6221-6227.

15. A. Schindler, D. Harper, Polylactide. II. Viscosity–molecular weight relationships and unperturbed chain dimensions, Polymer Science: Polymer Chemistry. 17 (1979) 2593-2599.

16. V. Arias, K. Odelius, A.C. Albertsson, Nano-stereocomplexation of polylactide (PLA) spheres by spray droplet atomization, Macromol. Rapid. Comm. 35 (2014) 1949-1953.

17. Z. Chen, Y. Chang, Z. Jiang, Facile fabrication of polylactic acid stereo-complex microspheres, Mater. Lett. 211 (2018) 146-148.

18. M. Nofar, D. Sacligil, P.J. Carreau, M.R. Kamal, M.C. Heuzey, Poly (lactic acid) blends: Processing, properties and applications, Int. J. Biol. Macromol. 125 (2019) 307-360.

19. L. Cheng, C. Hu, J. Li, S. Huang, S. Jiang, Stereocomplex-affected crystallization behaviour of PDLA in PDLA/PLDLA blends, CrystEngComm 21 (2019) 329-338.

20. H. Wu, S. Nagarajan, J. Shu, T. Zhang, L. Zhou, Y. Duan, J. Zhang, Green and facile surface modification of cellulose nanocrystal as the route to produce poly(lactic acid) nanocomposites with improved properties, Carbohyd. Polym. 197 (2018) 204-214.

A coupled-inductor-network-based high-step-up converter for renewable energy

Zhanru Fu[1], Ye Fan[1], Erliang Chai[1], Tailin Chen[1], Guibin Liao[2], Baofeng Miao[3] and Mei Xiong[3]

[1]*Shenzhen Power Supply Co., Ltd., Guangdong, 518028, China*
[2]*Shenzhen Microgrid Energy Management System Laboratory Co., Ltd., Guangdong, 518000, China*
[3]*Shenzhen Daidian Technology Development Co., Ltd., Guangdong, 518000, China*

A novel DC-DC converter with high voltage gain for sustainable energy is proposed, which provides a new substituted topology for low and medium power applications fields where high-voltage conversion is required. The proposed Sepic-based converter combines a coupled-inductor voltage multiplier circuit, which can achieve higher voltage gain and lower voltage stress of power devices when the duty ratio and input voltage are same as the traditional Sepic converter. Moreover, the input current ripple in the proposed converter is decreased, which results in low voltage and high performance semiconductors devices, and then leads to the high efficiency and stability. In this paper, the proposed DC-DC converter is analysed and deduced in detail. Then, simulations and experimental results are presented to verify the feasibility of the proposed DC-DC converter.

Keywords: DC-DC converter; high gain; coupled inductor.

1. Introduction

High boost converters play an indispensable role in modern renewable energy integrated grids. However, limited by the characteristics of simple circuit structures and simple control schemes, traditional boost converters cannot achieve the high voltage required in the modern renewable energy field.[1] In order to achieve a high voltage gain, Dragan Maksimovic and Slobodan Cuk have proposed the concept of a wide-gain converter.[2] Existing wide-gain converters mainly include isolated wide-gain converters and non-isolated wide-gain converters.[3] Among them, non-isolated converters have attracted many attentions. The method of adopting the switched capacitor structure[4] can improve the voltage gain, and has a simple structure and high efficiency. Using a coupled inductor technique,[5,6] its voltage gain can be extended by adjusting its duty cycle or increasing the turns ratio of the coupled inductance, but its inherent leakage inductance will in another way increase the loss of the converter. Aiming at the advantages and disadvantages of coupled inductors, based on the traditional Sepic boost converter topology, this paper improves the existing methods and proposes an improved high-gain DC-DC converter for sustainable energy.[7] The coupled inductor is coupled into Sepic converter for further improving the voltage gain. Meanwhile, the leakage inductance of the coupled inductor is used to form a resonant circuit, so that the switch is turned on under zero current, which then improves the efficiency of the converter.

2. Proposed Converter Topology

The equivalent circuit diagram of the proposed converter is shown in Fig. 1, which includes a switch S, a coupled inductor, three diodes D_1, D_2 and D_3, and four capacitors C_1, C_2, C_3 and C_4. The coupled inductor can be represented by an ideal transformer series leakage inductance L_k with a turns ratio of n, where $n = n_1/n_2 = n_1/n_3$, n_1 represents the number of turns of the primary winding, and n_2 and n_3 are the number of turns of the secondary winding respectively.

In order to facilitate the modal analysis, the converter operates at a high switching frequency, and it is assumed as,

1) all components in the converter are ideal except for the leakage inductance of the coupled inductor;

2) values of all capacitors are large enough. The voltages across all capacitors are assumed constant within one switching cycle, which is sufficient to keep their voltages constant and the converter to operate stable. On this basis, the main waveform of CCM (continuous conduction mode) working in one switching cycle is shown in Fig. 2.

Mode 1 $[t_0, t_1]$: As shown in Fig. 3(a), switch S turned on. Diode D_3 reverse biased while D_1 and D_2 conduct at time t_0. The input power V_{in} begins to transfer energy to the coupled-inductor-network. C_1 and L_k form a resonant loop. Meanwhile, the energy is delivered to C_2 and C_3 through the coupled-inductor-network, D_1 and D_2. Capacitor C_4 supplies the load. This mode lasts until switch S turned OFF. State equations during this mode are as follows.

$$\begin{cases} V_{N_2} = V_{in}, \\ V_{L_k} = V_{C_1} - V_{N_1}, \\ i_S = i_{N_2} + i_{L_k}, \\ V_{C_2} = V_{C_3} = V_{N_3} = n_{13} V_{N_1}, \end{cases} \tag{1}$$

where $n_{12} = n_1/n_2$ and $n_{13} = n_1/n_3$ are turns ratios of the three-winding coupled inductor.

Mode 2 $[t_1, t_2]$: As shown in Fig. 3(b), switch S is off. Diodes D_1, D_2 and D_3 conduct at time t_1. When the switch S turned off, the current flowing in the coupled inductor winding N_3 cannot be abruptly changed, and diodes D_1 and D_2 shunt

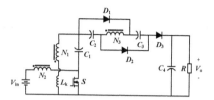

Fig. 1.   Schematic of the proposed converter.

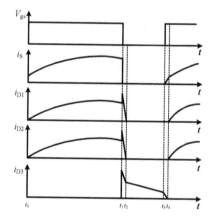

Fig. 2.   The main working waveforms of the converter.

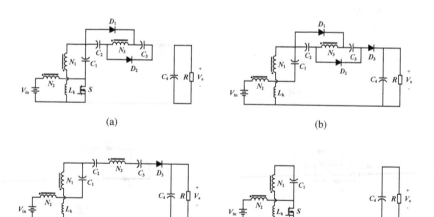

(a)   (b)

(c)   (d)

Fig. 3.   Equivalent circuit for each switching mode.

part of the current in the coupled inductor. The input power V_{in} and the coupled-inductor-network supply the load together, and charge C_1. State equations in this mode are a follows,

$$\begin{cases} V_{N_2} = V_o + V_{C_1} - V_{in} - V_{C_2}, \\ V_{L_k} = V_o - V_{N_1} - V_{C_2}. \end{cases} \qquad (2)$$

Mode 3 [t_2, t_3]: At t_2, switch S is still off, the operating mode of the converter changes to Mode 3. In this mode, all diodes are reversed-biased except diode D_3, as shown in Fig. 3(c). The energy stored in coupled-inductor-network and capacitors C_2 and C_3 along with the energy produced by the input source is delivered to capacitor C_4 and supply the load. State equations in this mode are shown as follows:

$$\begin{cases} V_{N_2} = V_o + V_{C_1} - V_{in} - V_{C_2} - V_{C_2} - V_{N_3}, \\ V_{L_k} = V_o - V_{N_1} - V_{C_2} - V_{C_2} - V_{N_3}. \end{cases} \qquad (3)$$

Mode 4 [t_3, t_4]: As shown in Fig. 3(d), switch S is turned on under zero current, and the current flowing through the leakage inductance of the coupled inductor decreases linearly at time t_3. At t_4, the current in the coupled inductor drops to zero, and the current through diode D_3 also drops to zero. Then the coupled inductor starts to be charged by the input power supply V_{in}, and its state expression is the same as the working Mode 1.

3. Performance Analysis

3.1. Voltage conversion ratio

In order to simplify the derivation process of the voltage gain when the converter is working in a stable status, the leakage inductance of the coupled inductor and the loss of the semiconductor device are ignored in the analysis process. With small ripple approximation, and applying the voltage-second balance principle on the coupled-inductor-network. The following equations can be obtained as

$$\begin{cases} V_{in}D = (V_o + V_{C_1} - V_{in} - V_{C_2} - V_{C_3} - V_{N_3})(1 - D), \\ (V_{C_1} - V_{N_1})D = (V_o - V_{N_1} - V_{C_2} - V_{C_3} - V_{N_3})(1 - D). \end{cases} \qquad (4)$$

In terms of (4), the capacitor voltages V_{C_1}, V_{C_2}, V_{C_3} and the output voltage V_o can be derived as

$$
\begin{cases}
V_{C_1} = \dfrac{1-D}{D+2n_{13}-Dn_{13}}V_o, \\[2ex]
V_{C_2} = \dfrac{n_{13}(1-D)}{D+2n_{13}-Dn_{13}}V_o, \\[2ex]
V_{C_3} = \dfrac{n_{13}(1-D)}{D+2n_{13}-Dn_{13}}V_o, \\[2ex]
V_o = \dfrac{D+2n_{13}-Dn_{13}}{n_{12}(1-D)}V_{in}.
\end{cases}
\tag{5}
$$

From (5), it can be found that the duty cycle D and the turns ratio of the coupled inductor are the main variables of the voltage gain of the converter, and with the increase of the turns ratio of the coupled inductor, the voltage gain of the proposed converter increases significantly as shown in Fig. 4.

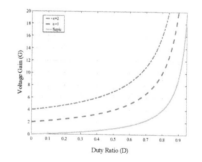

Fig. 4.　The relationship between the voltage gain and duty ratio.

3.2. Voltage stresses of components

During Mode 1, diodes D_1, D_2 and switch S are OFF, and the maximum voltages of D_1, D_2 and S can be obtained as

$$
V_{D_1} = V_{D_2} = \frac{n}{D+2n-Dn}V_o,
\tag{6}
$$

$$
V_S = \frac{1}{D+2n-Dn}V_o,
\tag{7}
$$

During Mode 2, diode D_3 is OFF, and the maximum voltage of D_3 can be obtained as

$$
V_{D_3} = V_o,
\tag{8}
$$

Table 1.   Components' Voltage Stresses.

Component	C_1	C_2/C_3	S	D_1/D_2	D_3
Voltage Stress	$\frac{1-D}{D+2n-Dn}V_o$	$\frac{n(1-D)}{D+2n-Dn}V_o$	$\frac{1}{D+2n-Dn}V_o$	$\frac{n}{D+2n-Dn}V_o$	V_o

Based on the derivations above, the voltage stresses of components are summarized in Table 1.

4. Simulation Verifications

To verify the feasibility and validity of the proposed converter, PSIM software is applied for the simulation.

The preassigned parameters are as listed as: input voltage $V_{in} = 20V$, permitted fluctuation range $x_C = 1\%$, $x_L = 10\%$, duty ratio $D = 0.6$, period $T_s = 100\mu s$ and resistive load $R = 100\Omega$. The high harmonic frequency of the capacitance and leakage inductance of coupled inductor are approximately equal to the switching frequency of the converter. The converter parameters are chosen as follow: $C_1 = C_2 = C_3 = 220\mu F$. Figure 5 presents the simulation results for $D = 0.6$. From the top to the bottom, the subfigures show driving voltage V_g, input voltage V_{in}, voltages across switches V_S, voltages across diodes V_D and output voltage V_o, respectively. In order to compare the voltage stress of each component, the output voltages of both converters are set as 100V. It is obvious that the input voltage of the Sepic converter is 66.67V, which is larger than that of the proposed converter, that is, the proposed topology has a higher voltage gain. Moreover, by comparing the voltage stress of the two converter power components, it can be found that the

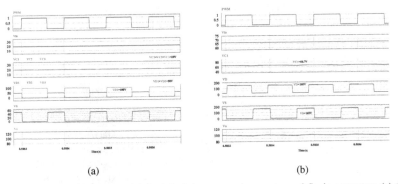

(a)   (b)

Fig. 5.   Simulation waveforms with D=0.6 of the proposed converter and Sepic converter: (a) the proposed converter, (b) Sepic Converter.

voltage stresses of the switch tube, diode and capacitor of the proposed converter is significantly reduced.

5. Experimental Verification

To verify the proposed converter, a hardware prototype is built as shown in Fig. 6. The experimental parameters and important specifications of power components of the proposed converter are listed in Table 2.

Figure 7 shows the open-loop experimental results of the proposed converter. The driving signal, input voltage V_{in} and output voltage V_o are shown. In this experiment, the actual output voltage is 96V, whereas the theoretical value is 100V. This discrepancy is expected and acceptable. Thus, the experimental result demonstrates the functionality and feasibility of the proposed converter.

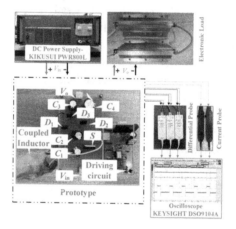

Fig. 6.   Prototypes and experimental setup.

Table 2.   Experimental Parameters.

Parameters	Value
Input voltage V_{in}	20 [V]
Output voltage V_o	100 [V]
Output power P_o	100 [W]
Switching frequency f_s	50 [kHz]
MOSFET	IXTQ88N30P / 40 [mΩ]
Diodes D_1, D_2, D_3	MBRF20200CT / 1 [V] / 0.05 [mΩ]
Capacitors C_1, C_2, C_3	110 [μF] / 100 [V] / 500 [mΩ]
Capacitors C_4	220 [μF] / 250 [V] / 500 [mΩ]

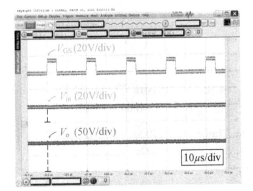

Fig. 7. Experimental waveform.

6. Conclusion

A newly design coupled-inductor-based Sepic converter is proposed, which can well utilize the leak inductance of coupled inductor to realize a high voltage. A detailed analyses and deduction are presented and with persuasive simulations and experiments, which well verify the feasibility of the proposed converter.

References

1. M. Forouzesh, Y. P. Siwakoti, S. A. Gorji, F. Blaabjerg and B. Lehman, Step-up dc–dc converters: A comprehensive review of voltage-boosting techniques, topologies, and applications, *IEEE Transactions on Power Electronics* **32**, 9143 (2017).
2. D. Maksimovic and S. Cuk, Switching converters with wide dc conversion range, *IEEE Transactions on Power Electronics* **6**, 151 (1991).
3. G. Zhang, Z. Li, B. Zhang and W. A. Halang, Power electronics converters: Past, present and future, *Renewable and Sustainable Energy Reviews* **81**, 2028 (2018).
4. T. Tanzawa, Innovation of switched-capacitor voltage multiplier: Part 1: A brief history, *IEEE Solid-State Circuits Magazine* **8**, 51 (2016).
5. S.-W. Lee and H.-L. Do, Quadratic boost dc–dc converter with high voltage gain and reduced voltage stresses, *IEEE Transactions on Power Electronics* **34**, 2397 (2019).
6. J. Liu, J. Wu, J. Qiu and J. Zeng, Switched z-source/quasi-z-source dc-dc converters with reduced passive components for photovoltaic systems, *IEEE Access* **7**, 40893 (2019).
7. J. Falin, Designing dc/dc converters based on sepic topology, *Analog Applications*, 19 (2008).

A high-frequency input CCM PFC converter for bypass switch cabinet

Erliang Chai[1], Tailin Chen[1], Zhanru Fu[1], Baofeng Miao[2], Mei Xiong[2]
and Guibin Liao[3]

[1]*Shenzhen Power Supply Co., Ltd., Guangdong, 518028, China*
[2]*Shenzhen Daidian Technology Development Co., LTD., Guangdong, 518000, China*
[3]*Shenzhen Microgrid Energy Management System Laboratory Co., Ltd. Guangdong, 518000, China*

Note that bypass truck is used to repair power device online, however, it is difficult to drive a bypass truck into a complex narrow environment. Thus, a mobile bypass switch cabinet is required in such special conditions. Therein, a high-frequency converter with high power factor correction (PFC) is required to reduce the device size for mobility. Thus, a high-frequency input continuous conduction mode (CCM) power factor correction (PFC) converter based on LC resonance principle for AC-DC converter is proposed. In the case of high-frequency input, the converter achieves PFC of CCM through LC resonant network, and minimizes the switching frequency, thus reducing the switching loss. In this paper, the structure, working modes, circuit analysis and control method of the proposed converter are studied in detail. Finally, based on the actual conditions, the function and superiority of the topology are verified by simulation. The results verify that the converter can be applied to AC-DC converter in a bypass switch cabinet to achieve low switching loss and high power factor at high frequency input.

Keywords: Bypass switch cabinet; high-frequency input; CCM; power factor correction; LC resonance.

1. Introduction

In order to protect the user's electricity, the bypass non-stop operation method of non-stop maintenance is often used. The principle of bypass non-stop operation is presented which is to build a new path for electrical energy across both ends of the equipment to be serviced to ensure normal power supply on the user side after isolation of the serviced equipment.[1] The working principle of the bypass operation of the serviced transformer using mobile boxcar operation method is shown in Fig. 1. Bypass operation can avoid the impact of planned maintenance outages on the continuity of power supply to users and improve power quality.

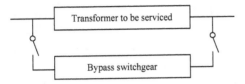

Fig. 1. Schematic diagram of bypass operation.

However, since many urban low-voltage distribution rooms are in the negative underground level, and the environment in which the low-voltage distribution room located has many obstacles and little space, the need to bypass the low-voltage switch cabinet will be difficult to enter the load transfer truck, difficult to transfer the construction of the linked lines, the construction impact is large. Besides, the safety problem is serious. Therefore, it is necessary to study a mobile bypass switch cabinet that can be moved.

$$A_e \cdot A_c \propto S/f \cdot J \cdot B_m \tag{1}$$

Power electronic converters, as a medium for electrical energy conversion, have been widely used in various important fields in recent years.[2] Due to the demand for light weight and integration of electrical equipment in production life, scholars are demanding more and more power density of power electronic converters, and the development of power electronic converters tends to miniaturization, high frequency and high efficiency.[3] Therefore, it is of great significance to apply power electronic converters in bypass switch cabinet to realize the miniaturization of switch cabinet and make it mobile and movable. The schematic block diagram of the bypass cabinet replaced with a converter is shown in Fig. 2. The conventional bypass cabinet runs the on-board transformer in parallel with the transformer to be serviced, and then withdraws the latter from operation to achieve non-stop maintenance. As shown in Fig. 2, the bypass cabinet replaced with a converter can be divided into three parts, AC-AC, AD-DC, and DC-AC, respectively.

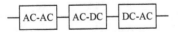

Fig. 2. Schematic diagram of bypass cabinet replaced by converter.

According to (1),[4] the volume of the transformer and the frequency are inversely related, i.e., the higher the frequency the smaller the transformer volume. Therefore, the first stage AC-AC raises the frequency from 50Hz to 50kHz-500kHz, which is commonly used in switching power supplies, and performs power factor correction and voltage boosting in the second stage AC-DC to ensure power quality while improving the flexibility of bypass switch cabinet applications. For the second stage AC-DC rectifier converter, the most traditional topology is the full-bridge rectifier converter,[5] but the power factor is extremely low.[6] Its output voltage usually has periodic fluctuations that cannot be eliminated, making it difficult to be used in applications with high requirements for voltage stabilization. It is difficult to be used in loads requiring high voltage stability such as precision instruments.[7] Cascading a conventional full-bridge rectifier converter with a boost link such as a Boost converter yields a Boost PFC converter,[8] which can realize both boost and PFC functions.[9] However, the switching frequency of this converter is usually several hundred times the input voltage frequency. The frequency of wireless power transmission is usually tens of kHz to tens of kHz,[10,11] then the switching frequency is at least several tens of MHz, which will generate huge switching losses and greatly reduce the efficiency of the system.[12]

2. Topology and its Operational Analysis

The high-frequency input CCM PFC converter based on the LC resonance principle proposed in this paper consists of a resonant network in the front stage and a DC-DC converter in the back stage. Among them, as shown in Fig. 3, the rear stage can use a variety of DC-DC converters, such as Buck

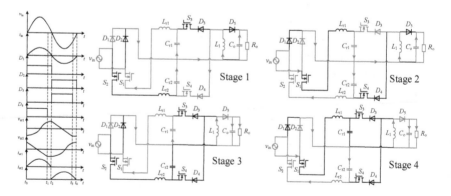

Fig. 3. Operating waveform and stages of high-frequency input CCM PFC converter based on LC resonance.

converter, Buck-Boost converter, Zeta converter, etc., which improves the flexibility of rectifier converter output voltage regulation. The pre-stage of this topology consists of two rectifier diodes, two switches, two resonant inductors and two resonant capacitors. The rear stage is composed of a DC-DC converter to realize flexible voltage output.

Stage 1 $[t_0, t_1]$: As shown in Fig. 3, at this time, the input voltage v_{in} is positive, S_1 and S_4 turn on, S_2 and S_3 turn off. v_{in} changes from negative to positive at the moment of t_0. As S_1 and D_1 are on, a power supply-inductor-capacitor series circuit is formed here. L_{r1} resonates with the C_{r1} to produce LC resonance, whose resonant frequency is equal to the frequency fin of the input voltage, and the input current i_{in} waveform tracks v_{in}, is in phase with v_{in}, and shows the form of a sinusoidal waveform. C_{r1} charges the L_1 through S_4 and D_4, and the energy is transferred from the front stage to the back stage. D_5 is cutoff, and C_o provides energy for the load R_o. When the voltage v_{Cr2} of C_{r2} decreases to the controller given value v_{Cr2min}, S_4 turns off and the stage 1 ends. Stage 2 $[t_1, t_2]$: After C_{r2} is discharged, S_4 turns off and D_4 cuts off. Stage 3 $[t_2, t_3]$ and Stage 4 $[t_3, t_4]$ are similar with Stage 3 $[t_2, t_3]$ and Stage 4 $[t_3, t_4]$ respectively.

As shown in (2), the *Laplace* equations for any series resonant circuit and for the inductor voltage and capacitor voltage, are presented respectively, where V_{in} is the input voltage, V_{Lr} is the voltage across the resonant inductor, V_{Cr} is the voltage across the resonant capacitor, I_{Lr} is the resonant inductor current, and $V_{Cr.min}$ is the initial voltage of the resonant capacitor or the minimum value given by the controller.

$$
\begin{cases}
V_{in}(s) = V_{Lr}(s) + V_{Cr}(s) \\
V_{Lr}(s) = sL_r I_{Lr}(s) - L_r I_{Lr}(0) \\
V_{Cr}(s) = \frac{I_{Lr}(s)}{sC_r} + \frac{V_{Cr.min}}{s} \\
V_{in}(t) = \hat{V}_{in} \sin(\omega t + \alpha) \\
\omega = \omega_S = 1/\sqrt{L_r C_r} \\
I_{Lr}(0) = 0
\end{cases}
\tag{2}
$$

(2) is calculated and substituted into the characteristic impedance $Z_{LC} = \sqrt{L_r/C_r}$ of LC series resonant network, (3) can be obtained, where $-\pi \leq \alpha \leq \pi$. Combining (2) and (3) and substituting $C_r = 1/(\omega Z_{LC})$, (4) can be obtained. The Laplace inverse transformation of (4) yields (5).

$$
\hat{V}_{in} \left[\frac{s \sin(\alpha) + \omega \cos(\alpha)}{s^2 + \omega^2} \right] = \frac{s^2 + \omega^2}{s} L_r I_{Lr}(s) + \frac{V_{Cr.min}}{s}
\tag{3}
$$

$$\begin{cases} I_{\mathrm{Lr}}(s) = -\frac{\omega}{Z_{\mathrm{LC}}(s^2+\omega^2)} V_{\mathrm{Cr.min}} + \frac{s^2\omega\sin(\alpha)+s\omega^2\cos(\alpha)}{Z_{\mathrm{LC}}(s^2+\omega^2)^2} \hat{V}_{\mathrm{in}} \\ V_{\mathrm{Cr}}(s) = \frac{sV_{\mathrm{Cr.min}}}{s^2+\omega^2} + [\frac{s\omega^2\sin(\alpha)+\omega^3\cos(\alpha)}{(s^2+\omega^2)^2}]\hat{V}_{\mathrm{in}} \end{cases} \tag{4}$$

$$\begin{cases} i_{\mathrm{Lr}}(t) = i_{\mathrm{in}}(t) = \frac{\hat{V}_{\mathrm{in}}\omega t}{2Z_{\mathrm{LC}}} \sin(\omega t - \alpha) + (\frac{\hat{V}_{\mathrm{in}}\sin(\alpha)-2V_{\mathrm{Cr.min}}}{2Z_{\mathrm{LC}}})\sin(\omega t) \\ v_{\mathrm{Cr}}(t) = \frac{\hat{V}_{\mathrm{in}}}{2}\cos(\alpha)\sin(\omega t) - \frac{\hat{V}_{\mathrm{in}}}{2}\omega t\cos(\omega t + \alpha) + V_{\mathrm{Cr.min}}\cos(\omega t) \end{cases} \tag{5}$$

To find the voltage conversion ratio of this converter, the energy formula for C_{r} and the energy consumed by the load are listed in (6), where ΔE_{Cr} represents the energy stored in C_{r}, E_{o} is the energy consumed by the load, and ω is the angular frequency. And the efficiency is assumed to be 1. So the voltage conversion is $\frac{V_{\mathrm{o}}}{\hat{V}_{\mathrm{in}}} = \sqrt{\frac{R_{\mathrm{o}}(V_{\mathrm{Cr.max}}^2 - V_{\mathrm{Cr.min}}^2)}{2\pi Z_{\mathrm{LC}}\hat{V}_{\mathrm{in}}^2}}$.

$$\begin{cases} \Delta E_{\mathrm{Cr}} = \frac{C_{\mathrm{r}}}{2}(V_{\mathrm{Cr.max}}^2 - V_{\mathrm{Cr.min}}^2) \\ E_{\mathrm{o}} = \frac{V_{\mathrm{o}}^2}{R_{\mathrm{o}}} \times \frac{\pi}{\omega} \\ \frac{V_{\mathrm{o}}^2}{R_{\mathrm{o}}} \times \frac{\pi}{\omega} = \frac{C_{\mathrm{r}}}{2}(V_{\mathrm{Cr.max}}^2 - V_{\mathrm{Cr.min}}^2) \\ \omega = \omega_{\mathrm{S}} = 1/\sqrt{L_{\mathrm{r}}C_{\mathrm{r}}} \end{cases} \tag{6}$$

3. Control Design

In this section, the corresponding control method is designed for this converter. In this converter, S_1 and S_2 alternately conduct with a duty cycle of 0.5. S_3 and S_4 alternately conduct, and S_4 with conduct only when S_1 conducts, and switch tube S_3 with conduct only when S_2 conducts, and the duty cycle of S_3 and S_4 depends on the reference value of V_{o}. The specific conduction modes of the switches are shown in Table 1. Therefore, the control of this converter is shown in Fig. 4. Among them, since there is a certain delay in the hardware for signal processing, it is necessary to design a corresponding delay link in the actual control to achieve the effect of fine-tuning the switching signal.

Table 1. Conduction mode of the switches.

Stage	Switch S_1	Switch S_2	Switch S_3	Switch S_4
1	ON	OFF	OFF	ON
2	ON	OFF	OFF	OFF
3	OFF	ON	ON	OFF
4	OFF	ON	OFF	OFF

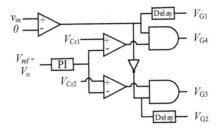

Fig. 4. Control method of high-frequency input CCM PFC converter based on LC resonance.

4. Simulation Verification

The accuracy of the resonant inductor and resonant capacitor is very important in this converter, but it is impossible to avoid the influence from the parasitic parameters in real experiments. Therefore, this paper simulates and verifies the power factor correction function of this converter considering the parasitic parameters in order to prove the theoretical correctness of this converter. Table 2 shows the parameter data used in the simulation session. Based on the simulation of this converter in PSIM platform, the waveforms of v_{in}, i_{in} and V_o are obtained as shown in Fig. 5 and Fig. 6. It can be seen that i_{in} is sinusoidal and in phase with v_{in}, and the PF exceeds

Table 2. Main parameters in the simulation.

Parameter	Value	Parameter	Value
v_{in}	50V 500kHz	R_o	100Ω
L_r	21.5577uH	C_r	4.7nF
L_1	220uH	C_o	2200uF

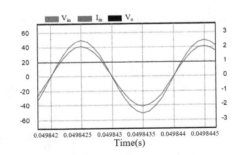

Fig. 5. Simulation result of the PFC function.

504

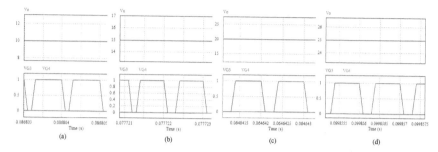

(a) (b) (c) (d)

Fig. 6.   Simulation Waveforms for different output voltages and duty cycles of S_3 and S_4. (a) $V_o = 10V$; (b) $V_o = 15V$; (c) $V_o = 20V$; (d) $V_o = 25V$.

0.998, which achieves PFC in CCM. The input voltage amplitude is 50V and V_o can be 10V, 15V, 20V, 25V. It can be seen that the output voltage can be flexibly adjusted by changing the duty cycle of the S_3 and S_4 and designing different parameters of L_r and C_r for different applications.

5. Conclusion

This paper proposes a CCM PFC converter based on the LC resonance principle for high frequency input applications. The converter achieves power factor correction in CCM, reduces the switching frequency as much as possible, makes the switching frequency equal to the LC resonant frequency and the input voltage frequency, reduces the switching losses, and reduces the influence of potential parasitic parameters on the circuit at high frequencies. Finally, the design of the control method is verified by simulation considering the parasitic parameters, and the applicability and superiority of the converter are proved.

References

1. G. Zhang, Z. Li, B. Zhang and W. A. Halang, Power electronics converters: Past, present and future, *Renewable and Sustainable Energy Reviews* **81** (2018).
2. X. Liu, X. Li, Q. Zhou and J. Xu, Flicker-free single-switch quadratic boost led driver compatible with electronic transformers, *IEEE Transactions on Industrial Electronics* **66**, 3458 (2019).
3. F. Chao, L. Qiang and F. C. Lee, Digital implementation of adaptive synchronous rectifier (sr) driving scheme for high-frequency llc converters with microcontroller, *IEEE Transactions on Power Electronics* **PP**, 1 (2017).

4. S. Perin, Transformer design review — important step in the technical risk management of the transformer procurement and design/manufacturing process, in *2014 Australasian Universities Power Engineering Conference (AUPEC)*, 2014.

5. W. Qi, S. Li, H. Yuan, S. C. Tan and R. Hui, High-power-density single-phase three-level flying-capacitor buck pfc rectifier, *IEEE Transactions on Power Electronics*, 10833 (2019).

6. J. Liu, J. Zhang, T. Q. Zheng and J. Yang, A modified gain model and the corresponding design method for an llc resonant converter, *IEEE Transactions on Power Electronics* **PP**, 1 (2017).

7. T. F. Wu, C. H. Chang, L. C. Lin, G. R. Yu and Y. R. Chang, Dc-bus voltage control with a three-phase bidirectional inverter for dc distribution systems, *IEEE Transactions on Power Electronics* **28**, 1890 (2013).

8. K. I. Hwu, Y. T. Yau and Y. C. Chang, Full-digital ac-dc converter with pfc based on counting, *IEEE Transactions on Industrial Informatics* **11**, 122 (2017).

9. W. Qi, S. Li, H. Yuan, S. C. Tan and R. Hui, High-power-density single-phase three-level flying-capacitor buck pfc rectifier, *IEEE Transactions on Power Electronics*, 10833 (2019).

10. W. Zhong, H. Li, S. Y. R. Hui and M. D. Xu, Current overshoot suppression of wireless power transfer systems with on–off keying modulation, *IEEE Transactions on Power Electronics* **36**, 2676 (2021).

11. H. Liang, H. Wang, K. L. Chi and R. Hui, Analysis and performance enhancement of wireless power transfer systems with intended metallic objects, *IEEE Transactions on Power Electronics* **PP**, 1 (2020).

12. X. Yu, J. Su, S. Guo, S. Zhong and J. Lai, Properties and synthesis of lossless snubbers and passive soft-switching pwm converters, *IEEE Transactions on Power Electronics* **PP**, 1 (2019).

Intelligent computational techniques for implementation of sustainable circular economy: Review and perspectives

Xianyi Zeng

GEMTEX Laboratory, ENSAIT Textile Institute, University of Lille
Lille, 59000, France
xianyi.zeng@ensait.fr
www.gemtex.fr

Zhebin Xue

College of Textile and Clothing, Soochow University
Suzhou, China
zhebin.xue@suda.edu.cn

This paper gives a comprehensive review on scientific and economic interests of intelligent computational techniques applied to construction of sustainable circular economy as well as the current methodologies and tools used and their cooperation with other digital tools such as IoT and cloud platform in the context of Industry 4.0. More emphasis has been placed on the areas of environmental impacts evaluation, remanufacturing and resource sustainability management and optimization, which are playing a key role in circular economy beyond classical manufacturing themes. Based on this review, a short analysis has been provided on the perspectives of this research theme in the future.

Keywords: Circular economy; sustainable development; Industry 4.0; intelligent computational techniques; cloud platform; IoT.

1. Introduction

The circular economy is a model of production and consumption, which involves sharing, leasing, reusing, repairing, refurbishing and recycling existing materials and products as long as possible [1]. Considered as a technology-focused concept that can generate economic gains while alleviating pressure on the environment, circular economy has attracted numerous organizations in public, private and civic sectors and, increasingly, academia alike [2]. However, current approaches on circular economy are strongly practitioner-led and lack a whole system thinking related to sustainability, i.e. how to avoid simply shifting emissions from one part of the system to another.

The most efficient solution for sustainable circular economy is to integrate Industry 4.0 by optimally eliminating toxic materials and reusing and eliminating wastage through the lifecycle of products and systems [3]. In various manufacturing areas, Industry 4.0 provides data ubiquity and interconnectivity, promoting rich information for decision-making, foreseeing failure, adapting to changes, reducing product development time, increasing product customization, and optimizing human-machine interactions. The main tools of Industry 4.0 include: additive manufacturing, artificial intelligence, artificial vision, big data and advanced analysis, cybersecurity, Internet of Things, robotics, and Virtual and Augmented Reality [4]. Of these Industry 4.0 tools, the AI techniques are playing a key role in all optimization issues during the product manufacturing and consumption processes and constitute the computational foundation of the other tools. Especially, they have shown special advantages for promoting sustainable circular economy by increasing production efficiency, reducing material and resource consumption and enhancing level material recyclability. In this context, the AI techniques (e.g. machine learning, deep learning) have been massively applied to different stages of the product lifecycle for facilitating the traceability of the environmental footprint of products, allowing manufacturers to control and monitor their products throughout their entire lifecycle, optimizing circular supply chain performance, increasing automatization, supporting planning, scheduling and optimization of remanufacturing processes with accurate AI-based predictive models, enabling earlier detection of defective products, reducing material, energy and water consumption and emissions to environment [5]. In practice, the key issue of successively applying the AI techniques to sustainable circular economy in various manufacturing areas is to establish an appropriate cooperation with IoT, cloud platforms, robotics and Virtual and Augmented Reality, in order to successively acquire reliable measured data and realize optimized interactions between real manufacturing scenarios and the corresponding digital environments, and conduct optimized actions in the digital environments.

In the following sections, we will review the current research work on intelligent computational techniques applied to environmental impacts evaluation, remanufacturing as well as resource sustainability management and optimization. Beyond conventional intelligent manufacturing subjects (e.g. planning and scheduling, automatization), these three application areas represent the most important issues in construction of sustainable circular supply chains for manufacturing sectors.

2. AI Techniques Applied to the Environmental Footprint Traceability

Life cycle Assessment (LCA) is a multi-criteria analysis that evaluates numerous environmental and social impacts caused by human activities [6]. In a sustainable circular economy, the LCA approaches usually focus on traceability of environmental impacts caused by products during their different stages of manufacturing, transaction, transport and consumption, in order to define labelling of product environmental footprints. In practice, the development of a decision-making system based on the LCA at all levels is important for realizing sustainable planning (e.g. raw material and supplier selection, production unit implementation) in an industrial company and its related supply chain. It can provide efficient support to industrial decision-makers by suitably combining all environmental impact indicators (e.g. eutrophication potential, global warming potential, human toxicity potential, energy and water consumption) [7] with overall economic costs and social impact indicators (e.g. noise level, impact of low employee's income) [8]. In the process of LCA, the Life Cycle Inventory (LCI) (i.e. the identification and quantification of the input (material and process technical parameters) and output flows (environmental impact indicators) from the production process under analysis throughout the product life) is the most delicate and challenging stage dealing with complex computations and human operation [9]. However, most of the exiting LCA tools are based on historic product data and cannot take into account online changes of product status in order to realize rapid corrective actions. Moreover, it is usually difficult to collect relevant data for LCA computations. In this context, intelligent techniques have been used for characterizing complex relations between the input and output flows of the LCI with missing data and uncertainty, and combining various environmental impact indicators and related economic and social indicators to provide decision making support in different industrial scenarios. Some typical studies are shown below.

Artificial Neural Networks (ANNs), decision trees and decision forest have been used to compare and predict the greenhouse emissions in order to find the best materials in automotive parts [10]. The Monte Carlo tree search (MCTS) method and deep reinforcement learning (MCTS-DNN) have been used to show the environmental consequences of predictive maintenance of products (wind turbines) [11]. ANNs have also been used for remote online monitoring and predicting the emissions of pollutants (greenhouse gases) from diesel generators at telecommunication base stations in cooperation with the IoT technologies [12]. The LCA computation has been realized in cooperation with process simulation and genetic algorithms (GAs). The process simulation has been used for estimating the emissions and quantifying their uncertainty (real data are missing) while the GAs generate alternatives of optimal process parameters that reduce environmental impacts (multi-criteria decision support) [13]. ANNs and fuzzy clustering have been used to evaluate environmental influence of cutting process parameters and develop a decision support tool for selecting the optimal environmental solution from various alternative schemes [14].

Currently, more and more researchers have been interested in developing real-time and automatic LCA systems by combining IoT technologies, manufacturing models and dynamic exploitation of product data collected by ERP [15]. In this context, the new LCA computations should be more product-oriented, capable of covering all key product features in the LCI input and taking into account changes of the relations between the LCI input and output. Moreover, multiple data sources (measured from the IoT technologies, extraction from product databases, and experts' environmental audits) should be considered in the final integrated indicators in order to obtain more accurate online environmental impacts for all stages of the product lifecycle. Based on the concept of real-time and automatic LCA, a Product Lifecycle Management System using the intelligent techniques (knowledge representation, data mining, robotic solution, pattern recognition, etc.) has been developed to predict the time to failure for railcar wheel bearing and enhance the performance of a product during the product lifecycle [16].

3. AI Techniques Applied to Remanufacturing

In a circular economy, after each cycle, used products need to be returned to a remanufacturer for identification, inspection, sorting and reprocessing [17]. The identification aims to determine the product type (properties, functions and components). The inspection, determines the quality of the used product and is carried out on certain predefined criteria. The sorting pursues to choose the economically and ecologically best reprocessing strategy for an examined used product. The decisions or selections in these remanufacturing processes for product design, network design and supply chain coordination can be supported by using digitalization and learning machine [18]. With relevant AI tools, a reverse supply chain starting with the return and collection of used products can be optimally established. Concretely, pattern recognition and machine learning can be used to improve selection results of used products by reducing manual errors, and predict product defects and quality levels automatically in inspection. Intelligent decision support systems can be used to define relevant multiple and changing sorting criteria and select the best strategy of remanufacturing under complex and uncertain conditions.

Compared with manufacturing, uncertainty in the quality state of used products (inspection) is a major complexity driver in remanufacturing. The condition of a returning product is highly variable and cannot be predicted.

Another challenging factor is the product variety especially when differing product types, their variants, and generations are jointly inspected and sorted. The application of the AI techniques will enable the technical inspection system more flexible and adaptive to various scenarios through a learning phase. In practice, the reinforcement-learning approach, for view-planning has been implemented for autonomous quality control in inspection of starter motors [19]. Also, unknown quality defects of used products can be identified by using case-based learning with a well-defined similarity degree (e.g. one-shot learning) in order to check whether the identified quality defects are already known [20].

In remanufacturing, the AI techniques have also been used for design optimization of repair and restoration with used products in order to retain their original function and performance [21]. The AI optimization algorithms (Particle Swarm Optimization, ANNs, fuzzy models and GAs, etc.) have been used to fund the optimal setting of process parameters, and observe and diagnose failures and erratic, subsequently fixing those failures and behaviors by optimally adjusting the parameters. Moreover, expert systems have been established for formulating repair and restoration strategies.

4. AI Techniques Applied to Resources Sustainability

Circular economy requires the creation of manufactured products through economically-sound processes that minimize negative environmental impacts while conserving energy and natural resources. To advance sustainable energy, the industry has supplied a wide variety of choices, including wind energy, fossil fuels, solar energy, and bioenergy. The AI techniques have been applied to: 1) sustainable buildings and smart grids for the purpose of reducing energy consumption (optimized planning of buildings by reducing CO_2 emissions); 2) AI-based evaluation of renewable energy technologies based on their cost of energy production, carbon footprint, affordability of renewable resources, and energy conversion efficiency; 3) AI-based energy optimization in order to minimize greenhouse gas emissions and cut energy usage by simultaneously reducing costs and side effects of energy consumption (e.g. optimized multi-layer perception and hybridized support vector regression for predicting load demand and energy usage, optimization of energy inputs and greenhouse gas emissions with multi-objective GAs) [22].

AI-based sustainable water management is also an important issue for circular economy. It deals with optimization of water treatment and supply, water pricing and tariff management, water quality evaluation with AI-based decision support systems (e.g. neuro-fuzzy inference system, visual recognition systems), in order to reduce water consumption and dynamically optimize water processing quality and efficiency [23]. A study conducted on ecological water governance implementation using AI found that including algorithms (decision tree-based SVM classification methods, particle swarm optimization) into the system yields higher-quality information and better prediction models for accurate evaluation of water quality [24]. AI can also be used for tracking water use and demand as well as forecasting water quality, estimating water infrastructure maintenance, monitoring dam conditions, water-related diseases and disasters and water reuse [25].

5. Conclusion and Perspectives

In the current research and industrial practices on circular economy, the importance of intelligent computational techniques has been validated through numerous real cases. Especially, thanks to their flexibility and quick adaptability, AI-based decision support systems have effectively shown their advantages for optimizing choices at different strategic and operational levels in a reverse supply chain starting from used products, and processing uncertainties caused by undetermined product origins and status. However, most of research work in this area has been realized to solve individual problems in specific stages of product transformation, and it lacks a generalized design thinking enabling to systematically support the whole circular supply chain for all stages of the product life cycle. Moreover, the current computational techniques are mostly classical ones, in which the specificities of circular economy have not been fully taken into account.

The AI techniques should be more extensively cooperated with the other digital tools, especially IoT, cloud platform management and product/material/ process digital simulations for product functionalities. The AI techniques should be systematically integrated into a traceability system, enabling to realize online monitoring of performance evolution for the whole product life cycle, and dynamically correct actions in different transformation processes according to the performances of measured data and simulations derived from product prediction.

References

1. *Circular economy: definition, importance and benefits* (Report of European Parliament, 02-12-2015), https://www.europarl.europa.eu/news/en/headlines/ economy/20151201STO05603/circular-economy-definition-importance-and-benefits

2. A.P.M. Velenturf and P. Purnell, Principles for a sustainable circular economy, *Sustainable Production and Consumption* **27** (2021).

3. A. Belhadi et al., A self-assessment tool for evaluating the integration of circular economy and industry 4.0 principles in closed-loop supply chains, *Int. J. Production Economics* **245** (2022).

4. I. Laskurain-Iturbe, G. Arana-Landín, B. Landeta-Manzano and N. Uriarte-Gallastegi, Exploring the influence of industry 4.0 technologies on the circular economy, *Journal of Cleaner Production* **321** (2021).

5. A. Rejeb, Z. Suhaiza, K. Rejeb, S. Seuring and H. Treiblmaier, The Internet of Things and the circular economy: a systematic literature review and research agenda, *Journal of Cleaner Production* **350** (2022).

6. X. Zeng and B. Rabenasolo, Developing a sustainable textile/clothing supply chain by selecting relevant materials and suppliers, *Research Journal of Textile and Apparel*, **17**, 2 (2013).

7. J.B Guinée, Life Cycle *Assessment: an Operational Guide to the ISO Standards: Parts 1 and 2*, Ministry of Housing, Spatial Planning and Environment and Centre of Environmental Science, Den Haag and Leiden, the Netherlands (2001).

8. E.S. Andrews et al., *Guidelines for Social Life Cycle Assessment of Products,* UNEP-SETAC Life-Cycle Initiative (2009).

9. F. Schlegl, J. Gantner, R. Traunspurger, S. Albrecht, P. Leistner, LCA of buildings in Germany: proposal for a future benchmark based on existing databases, **Energy Build.** **194** (2019).

10. M. Akhshik et al., Prediction of greenhouse gas emissions reductions via machine learning algorithms: Toward an artificial intelligence-based life cycle assessment for automotive lightweighting, Sustainable Materials and Technologies **31** (2022).

11. A. Carlson, T. Sakao, Environmental assessment of consequences from predictive maintenance with artificial intelligence techniques: importance of the system boundary, *Procedia CIRP* **90** (2020).

12. G. Bonire, A. Gbenga-Ilori, Towards artificial intelligence-based reduction of greenhouse gas emissions in the telecommunications industry, *Scientific African* **12** (2021).

13. J.J. Lopez-Andrés et al., Environmental impact assessment of chicken meat production via an integrated methodology based on LCA, simulation and genetic algorithms, *Journal of Cleaner Production* **174** (2018).

14. Y. Wang and S. Xiu, An intelligence evaluation method of the environmental impact for the cutting process, *Journal of Cleaner Production* **227** (2019).

15. A.M. Ferrari, L. Volpi, D. Settembre-Blundo and F.E. García-Muina, Dynamic life cycle assessment (LCA) integrating life cycle inventory (LCI) and Enterprise resource planning (ERP) in an industry 4.0 environment, *Journal of Cleaner Production* **286** (2021).

16. I. Daniyan, R. Muvunzi, K. Mpofu, Artificial intelligence system for enhancing product's performance during its life cycle in a railcar industry, *Procedia CIRP* **98** (2021).

17. M. Schlüter et al., AI-enhanced identification, inspection and sorting for reverse logistics in remanufacturing, *Procedia* **98** (2021).

18. M.I. Rizova, T.C. Wong and W. Ijomah, A systematic review of decision-making in remanufacturing, Computers & Industrial Engineering **147** (2020).

19. J.P. Kaiser, S. Lang, M. Wurster and G. Lanza, A concept for autonomous quality control for core inspection in remanufacturing, *Procedia CIRP* **105** (2022).

20. A.M. Deshpande, A.A. Minai and M. Kumar, One-shot recognition of manufacturing defects in steel surfaces, *Procedia Manufacturing* **48** (2020).

21. N.A. Aziz, N.A.A. Adnan, D.A. Wahab and A.H. Azman, Component design optimization based on artificial intelligence in support of additive manufacturing repair and restoration: current status and future outlook for remanufacturing, *Journal of Cleaner Production* **296** (2021).

22. T. Saheb, M. Dehghani and T. Saheb, Artificial intelligence for sustainable energy: a contextual topic modeling and content analysis, *Sustainable Computing: Informatics and Systems* **35** (2022).

23. M.H. Al-Adhaileh and F.W. Alsaade, Modelling and prediction of water quality by using artificial intelligence, *Sustainability* **13** (2021).

24. Y. Wei, Application of artificial intelligence in the process of ecological water environment governance and its impact on economic growth, *Mathematical Problems in Engineering* **2021** (2021).

25. G. Chhipi-Shrestha, K. Hewage, R. Sadiq, Fit-for-purpose wastewater treatment: conceptualization to development of decision support tool (I), *Science of the Total Environment* **607-608** (2017).

Interactive game-based device for sustainability education among teenagers

Qinglei Bu, Lechen Wu, Eng Gee Lim, Jie Sun* and Quang Zhang

School of Advanced Technology, Xi'an Jiaotong-Liverpool University
Suzhou, China
Jie.Sun@xjtlu.edu.cn

Education for sustainable development (ESD) is critical to teenagers, who are regarded as future citizens. However, it is not easy to achieve because sustainability is normally merged into other subjects and does not attract as much attention as that of the traditional subjects. Moreover, the importance and education contents of ESD vary among schools and teachers, which leads to fluctuation in awareness levels. This study aims to design an Interactive Game-based Device to attract and establish a relatively unified modular platform for ESD education among teenagers from different regions. To prompt participation through an immersive experience, the role-acting performance, intelligent voice synthesis, and audio-visual feedback are applied in this device design. The preliminary studies show that the awareness of sustainability is increased through entertainment and interaction.

Keywords: Audio-visual interaction; education for sustainable development; intelligent product design.

1. Introduction

Assigned to schools and universities since 1990s, Education for Sustainable Development (ESD) has been conducted for more than two decades.[1] Originated to promote sustainability awareness, ESD expands its content with more professional and interdisciplinary knowledge.[2] The key motivation for sustainability is to change the attitudes and behaviors of learners during daily life. However, it is not easy to implement this idea because sustainability cannot be achieved merely by announcing political regulations or applying new technology to the industry.[3] It needs the knowledge of interdisciplinary theory and methods, supporting students with an overall perspective. Moreover, to guarantee a greener planet with environmental-friendly development in the future needs the curtailment of people's desires and effective implementation of ESD education education. How to find a more efficient way in ESD becomes the challenge problem.

Researchers have explored different teaching and learning methods in ESD. Kunzli et al.[4] first focused on the teenagers' ability to negotiate and make decisions in sustainable activities through vision and participation orientation, while the method is traditional with feasible assessment. Stables[5] brought new technology into class, the lecture notes-based class with questioning-developing procedures increased the vividness of the knowledge, and students know how to use the energy efficiently. Based on Julien et al.,[6] the role-plays and exercises were introduced into primary school. It further enhanced the critical thinking ability from the perspective of sustainable systems. A similar method was also utilized,[7] role-playing and place-based activities were designed to train students with long-term, foresighted thinking. Generally, the interactive learning-based method is an efficient and joyful method when designing ESD cases.[1] With the rapid progress of communication technology, smartphones get involved in daily human life from many aspects. Schneider and Schaal[8] considered an instructional location-based smartphone game in ESD, which attracted students' attention and promoted the decision-making competencies in situations related to sustainability. However, these games or interactive platforms are not specially designed to meet teenagers' needs and interests. Despite previous researchers putting a significant effort into educating teenagers when designing these location-based games, they could not attract them with continuing learning and strengthening sustainability awareness in the future.

In order to attract users' interest, some interactive devices for elder people[9,10] and children[11] have been proposed. With the development of new technologies, intelligent voice synthesis-based Internet of Things (IoT), have been developing quickly in recent years. Based on users' speaking, the device can react with activating functions or giving feedback. It is more convenient and friendly to users with lower learning cost. Many applications based on this technology in smart homes and schools show board advantages. Specifically, applications based on IoT in interactive education show great performance because they can attract teenagers' interests and enhance the immersive experience.[12-14]

Although these devices can attract different users' attention, they are not designed for teenagers' ESD purpose. Thus, proposing a new and functional interactive tool with IoT and intelligent technology for ESD education is worthwhile. Compared with previous works, the intelligent voice synthesis has been embedded with an audio-visual feedback system to stimulate teenagers' interests and create an immersive environment, where the storyline-based sustainability scenarios were designed. Based on this design idea, we proposed the interactive game-based device that combines speech interaction and role-acting performance to enhance ESD among teenagers.

2. Interactive Game-based Device

The Interactive Game-based Device includes an embedded screen display, which is located on the top of the box. It can be operated using two modes: 1) Intelligent voice synthesis-based learning mode, 2) Storyline-based game mode. The former is for teenagers to ask some sustainability questions through the voice synthesis function. The latter is designed to play the interactive game using buttons and joystick in specific scenarios.

2.1. Hardware design

The main structure of the devices is a 3D printed box as Fig. 1(a). The hardware components, including a screen display, one radio frequency identification (RFID) reader, two speakers, two buttons, one joy stick and printed circuit board (PCB), are installed in the box. Raspberry Pi was selected as the main microcontroller to communicate with different components. The green and red button stands for the choice "Yes" and "No", which are introduced to lead the game in different directions. Multiple characters, like turtle or birds, are provided to choose different storylines and increase the attractiveness of role-playing. An example of the green turtle as the character token embedded with RFID chips is shown in Fig. 1(b). With the help of RFID reader on the left side of the device, the dif-

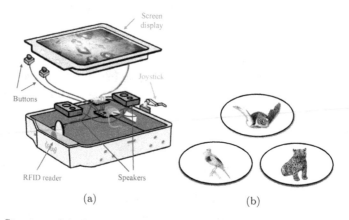

(a)   (b)

Fig. 1.   Structure of the Interactive Game-based Device: (a) Main device, (b) Token for characters.

ferent tokens for characters can be identified exclusively and create diverse storylines displayed on the screen.

2.2. Software design

The development platform in this study in the Raspberry Pi is the Android Thing, which is an Internet operating system developed by Google. Two leading technologies, automatic speech recognition (ASR) and text-to-speech synthesis (TTS), are applied to realize intelligent voice synthesis. The former is trying to recognize teenagers' voice and converts a raw acoustic signal into phonetically meaningful text. The latter is defined as the artificial production of human voices, which can convert the text into speech.

In terms of ASR, teenagers will be firstly instructed to say some sentences. Such sentences will be preprocessed to remove noises such as chatter, coughs and sneezes, and some unnecessary interference will be deleted. The processed audio signals will go for features extraction and balance the time-frequency ranges by converting analogue to digital signals. These extracted features will be compared with a standard library template, and search for the most likely phonemes using accuracy examination. This procedure is repeated until the words are connected in a complete text sentence and recorded as text. The complete framework is shown in Fig. 2.

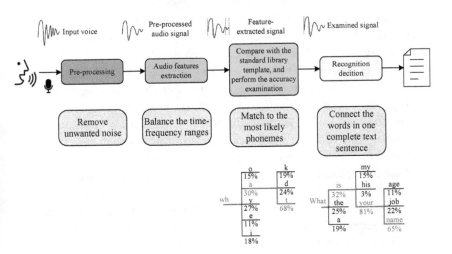

Fig. 2.   Framework of automatic speech recognition.

As for TTS, plenty of speech interaction is needed, especially in learning mode. The relevant text will be converted into artificial production of human voices. The researcher in this study adjusted the voice library parameters and found the speed and intonation that suits teenagers. Finally, the output of artificial human voices can respond to teenagers' questions naturally and smoothly.

2.3. Mode design

This device has two modes: the intelligent voice synthesis-based learning mode and game mode. In the first mode, the device can interact with children with intelligent voice synthesis for speech interaction. The token is not needed in this mode. Teenagers can directly communicate with the device by asking some sustainability related questions. The device can search for the answer in the cloud server and give feedback with the audio statement. Additionally, some graphic pictures, including educational videos relevant to this topic, can also be displayed to enhance the interaction.

In game mode, this Interactive Game-based Device will introduce the user guide via the speaker, mainly containing stand-alone and online functions. It is labelled as blue and red routines in Fig. 3, respectively. At the beginning, one of the character tokens was chosen and put the token near the RFID reader area to activate the game mode. After that, the network connection can be chosen manually to active online or stand-alone function. If the stand-alone function is chosen, the scenes and storylines are recalled in the secure digital (SD) memory card, and the game will start with a background introduction through voice guidance. The scene of the background will display on the screen simultaneously to enhance the immersive experience. The green and red buttons are provided to make a choice between agreement or disagreement after each short segment video, and each choice can create different storylines. In some particular scenarios, the children can rotate joystick during the game with a more interactive experience. One example will be explained in the following case.

The networked Raspberry Pi can access our cloud database to update the resources when the online function is chosen. The storyline can be updated and enhanced through real-time processing and the playback function. Meanwhile, the intelligent voice synthesis is also activated through the cloud server. Keywords that stand for "Yes" or "No" can be identified with the same function as green and red buttons.

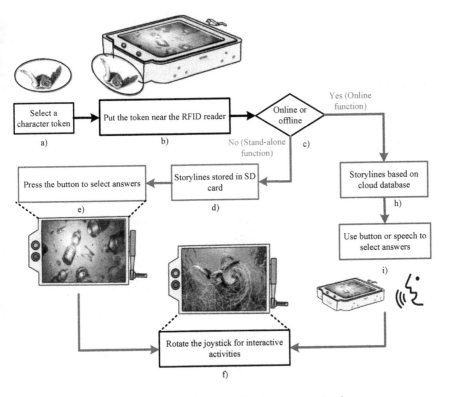

Fig. 3. Flowchart of the storyline-based game mode.

There are mainly two possible endings for both online and stand-alone functions, the happy one and the bad one, which is determined by teenagers' answers. The game play record for each selection can be stored in the cloud server with an online feedback report, which is helpful for users and educators to evaluate the sustainability consciousness and plan for future educations.

A case story based on the green turtle is introduced as an example. The designed storyline will start to ask questions like " how to deal with domestic waste, especially plastic products". If teenagers choose the littering or ignore waste classification, a scene with plenty of plastic waste in the ocean will be displayed as shown in Fig. 3e). Wrong answers to more questions will be shown in a video (Fig. 3f)) in which the green turtle is trapped by plastic mesh. In this situation, the joystick can be rotated to help the turtle escape from the mesh. This procedure tries to simulate how difficult the turtle can survive. If teenagers cannot rotate the joystick in time, the turtle will be trapped. As a bad ending, relevant green turtle death data due to the ocean waste will be displayed on the screen. Different storylines and characters have similar gamification but varied backgrounds, which will not be described in detail.

3. Conclusion

In this study, an Interactive Game-based Device is designed to improve sustainability education among teenagers. IoT-based Raspberry Pi can perform real-time processing. Combined with audio-visual support, it provides teenagers with a more immersive experience. The different choices will also be recorded in the cloud database, and the feedback report will be generated to help educators for reference. This design is dedicated to ESD among teenagers and has the potential to establish a relatively unified modular platform. We plan to collect more user data and improve the device to enhance education for sustainable development.

References

1. R. J. Brazier, How education can be used to improve sustainability knowledge and thinking among teenagers, *Australian Journal of Environmental Education* **30**, 280 (2014).
2. W. Riess, M. Martin, C. Mischo, H.-G. Kotthoff and E.-M. Waltner, How can education for sustainable development (esd) be effectively implemented in teaching and learning? an analysis of educational science recommendations of methods and procedures to promote esd goals, *Sustainability* **14**, p. 3708 (2022).
3. S. Janakiraman, S. L. Watson and W. R. Watson, Using game-based learning to facilitate attitude change for environmental sustainability, *Journal of Education for Sustainable Development* **12**, 176 (2018).
4. C. Künzli David, F. Bertschy, G. de Haan and M. Plesse, Learning to shape the future through education for sustainable development. an educational guide towards changes in primary school (2008).
5. K. Stables, Educating for environmental sustainability and educating for creativity: actively compatible or missed opportunities?, *International Journal of Technology and Design Education* **19**, 199 (2009).
6. M.-P. Julien, R. Chalmeau, C. V. Mainar and J.-Y. Léna, An innovative framework for encouraging future thinking in esd: A case study in a french school, *Futures* **101**, 26 (2018).

7. E. Frisk and K. Larson, Educating for sustainability: Competencies & practices for transformative action, *Journal of Sustainability Education* **2** (2011).

8. J. Schneider and S. Schaal, Location-based smartphone games in the context of environmental education and education for sustainable development: fostering connectedness to nature with geogames, *Environmental Education Research* **24**, 1597 (2018).

9. S. Jie, Y. Haoyong, T. L. Chaw, C. C. Chiang and S. Vijayavenkataraman, An interactive upper limb rehab device for elderly stroke patients, *Procedia CIRP* **60**, 488 (2017), Complex Systems Engineering and Development Proceedings of the 27th CIRP Design Conference Cranfield University, UK 10th – 12th May 2017.

10. X. Yang, Y. Zou, J. Sun and Y. C. Liang, Interactive upper limb training device for arm-reaching and finger pointing exercise, in *Adjunct of the 2019 International Conference on Multimodal Interaction*, ICMI '19 (Association for Computing Machinery, New York, NY, USA, 2019).

11. Y. Bian, X. Wang, D. Han and J. Sun, Designed interactive toys for children with cerebral palsy, in *Proceedings of the Fourteenth International Conference on Tangible, Embedded, and Embodied Interaction*, TEI '20 (Association for Computing Machinery, New York, NY, USA, 2020).

12. M. J. Liberatore and W. P. Wagner, Virtual, mixed, and augmented reality: a systematic review for immersive systems research, *Virtual Reality* **25**, 773 (2021).

13. A. Theodorou, B. Bandt-Law and J. J. Bryson, The sustainability game: Ai technology as an intervention for public understanding of cooperative investment, in *2019 IEEE Conference on Games (CoG)*, 2019.

14. L. Wu, E. G. Lim, Q. Zhang, A. Avliyoqulov, J. Sun, L. Kong and Z. Chen, Interactive story box for children with cerebral palsy, in *Companion of the 2022 ACM SIGCHI Symposium on Engineering Interactive Computing Systems*, EICS '22 Companion (Association for Computing Machinery, New York, NY, USA, 2022).

Sustainability driven apparel supplier selection

Zhongyi Zhu, Zhebin Xue* and Xianyi Zeng

College of Textile and Clothing Engineering, Soochow University
Suzhou, Jiangsu province, 215000, China
zhebin.xue@suda.edu.cn

The sustainability problem of the textile and apparel industry has always been a hot social issue. Among many sustainable strategies, the sustainable benefits brought by supply chain management are increasingly evident, among which supplier selection is the most critical part of each link of supply chain management. Integrating sustainability into the process of supplier selection increases the difficulty for apparel enterprises to choose suitable suppliers. This paper analyzes and integrates the criteria of a sustainable apparel supplier (SAS) selection system from the triple bottom line (TBL) perspective and proposes a sustainable selection method based on the triple bottom line principle. First, we systematically collect sustainable supplier selection criteria and establish a hierarchy of criteria suitable for the apparel industry. Then, the Fuzzy Analytic Hierarchy Process (FAHP) is used to determine the weight of sustainable supplier selection in the apparel industry. Finally, the potential suppliers were ranked by the Technique for Order Preference by Similarity to an Ideal Solution (TOPSIS), and a practical case verifies the feasibility of the model. This paper will provide apparel enterprises with a new idea of supplier selection based on the sustainable concept.

Keywords: Apparel sustainable; supplier selection; TBL; FAHP; TOPSIS.

1. Introduction

Globally, consumers attach great importance to the pollution problem of the apparel industry. Sustainable development has become the future primary trend in the apparel industry, and many apparel enterprises have begun to transform into sustainable development [1, 2]. The apparel industry is a supply-driven commodity chain; supply chain management is essential for sustainable development. Apparel enterprises have realized the importance of having excellent suppliers in a highly competitive environment, affecting product launch time, quality, cost, corporate image, sustainability, etc. In short, the quality of suppliers is crucial to customer satisfaction, corporate performance, and enterprise competitiveness.

The fashion industry is time-sensitive, and the life cycle of products is concise [3]. Therefore, delivery time, response-ability, and problem-solving are critical in procurement decision-making. Many well-known apparel enterprises, such as Zara and H&M, have researched the supply chain on a global scale. Suppliers are vital to the apparel industry's survival because they affect consumer satisfaction [4]. Therefore, choosing suppliers has become one of the critical issues to be solved by apparel enterprises. The existing research on supplier selection mainly focuses on two kinds of problems, namely, the construction of criterion systems and the determination of selection methods, and the apparel industry is no exception. The construction of the criteria system is mainly based on the TBL. It classifies the criteria from the three dimensions of economy, environment, and society selects the criteria that meet the enterprise, and determines the corresponding weight of the criteria [5, 6]. For the supplier selection method, with the development time, the supplier selection method for sustainable apparel gradually shifts from a single method to an integrated method, and more fuzzy factors in the supplier selection process are considered [7]. In terms of determining the criteria weight, AHP has always been a popular choice [8]. As people attach importance to fuzziness in research, FAHP has become a better alternative [8, 9]. It has been proven that the FAHP is the most suitable method for evaluating and making multicriteria decisions when it involves many interdependent criteria. Regarding ranking, TOPSIS, VIseKriterijumska Optimizacija I Kompromisno Resenje (VIKOR), and their variants are more widely used methods [10, 11]. Therefore, this paper adopts the FAHP-TOPSIS integrated method to construct the supplier selection decision model.

The specific structure of this paper is as follows. First, through the extensive collection of sustainable supplier selection and SAS selection criteria, experts and scholars were called to classify and screen the content in the criteria dimensions, forming a three-dimensional hierarchy of SAS selection criteria. Then, aiming at the fuzziness of the index, the FAHP method is used to determine the index weight of the three dimensions. Finally, the weighted TOPSIS method is used to rank potential suppliers. This paper will verify the practicability of the above methods through practical cases.

2. Materials and Methods

This paper constructs a complete SAS selection model in three stages. Stage I is used to build a comprehensive system of SAS selection criteria. Based on the supply chain operation reference (SCOR) model, this part develops a criteria system for SAS selection through qualitative analysis. Stage 2 is the process of deciding the weight of each criterion. The FAHP method determines the weight of 10 second-level and 22 third-level criteria of the three-level dimension. In stage 3, the sustainability ranking of the selected suppliers is obtained by introducing weights to the standardized matrix according to the TOPSIS method. To verify the operability and practicability of the above methods, a case study of a garment manufacturer was carried out, and the final ranking results were consistent with the ideal results of the expert group, which proved the feasibility of the model.

2.1. Establish a criteria system for selecting SAS's

This study's criteria system for evaluation and use was established based on the SCOR model and Delphi method. The SCOR model, also known as the Supply Chain Operation Reference model, was approved in 1996 and endorsed by the Supply Chain Council (SCC) [12]. The expert panel comprises 13 professionals from 12 different apparel companies related to supplier selection, including purchasing managers, merchandise planning supervisors, business unit managers, purchasing managers, and fabric purchasers. (Expert Panel X).

In establishing the criteria system, the sustainable supplier selection criteria are extensively collected through exhaustive enumerations. According to the characteristics of the apparel industry, such as solid timeliness, short product life cycle, and expert groups' opinions, the criteria are classified and screened. After that, in the form of a questionnaire survey, the expert panel evaluated and scored the screened criteria to obtain a further refined criteria system.

2.2. Determine the criteria weight

This paper uses the FAHP to determine the weight of the established criteria system. The procedure of the triangular fuzzy number-based analytic hierarchy process (TFN-FAHP) is as follows:
(1) Fuzzify each criterion based on the FAHP method
(2) Establish a fuzzy pairwise comparison matrix
(3) Test the consistency of the fuzzy comparison matrix
(4) Calculate the initial weight of each criterion
(5) Defuzzify and calculate the final weight
(6) Normalize to obtain the final weight set

$$W' = [d(1), d(2), ..., d(k)]^T. \tag{1}$$

2.3. Ranking selected suppliers

TOPSIS (Technique for Order Preference by Similarity to an Ideal Solution) is used to sort suppliers. TOPSIS ranks the limited evaluation objects according to their proximity to the ideal target. The TOPSIS process is as follows.

(1) Establish the original evaluation matrix
(2) Standardize the data of the evaluation matrix
(3) Establish a standardized matrix
(4) Establish a weighted standardized evaluation matrix
(5) Calculate the score of the weighted standardized evaluation matrix
(6) Determine the best (T⁺) and worst (T⁻) solutions
(7) Determine the distance between each scheme and the best and worst solutions
(8) Calculate the score of each scheme

$$S_i = \frac{D_i^-}{D_i^+ + D_i^-}.$$ (2)

2.4. Case study

To verify the feasibility of the above calculation steps and the criteria system's practicability, this paper uses an apparel enterprise as an example to conduct a case study. First, this paper investigated nine experts (expert group Y) related to supplier selection from 7 apparel enterprises to determine the weight of each criterion in the criteria system for supplier selection of sustainable apparel. According to the questionnaire results, the FAHP was used to determine the weight of 22 sub-criteria. The weight of the criteria system determined by this method can be suitable for most apparel manufacturers. After that, five experts related to supplier selection (expert group Z) of the case enterprise scored the six apparel suppliers (suppliers A, B, C, D, E, F) of the enterprise according to the established index system to obtain the unweighted standardized TOPSIS matrix. The weighted index determined by the FAHP was combined with the standardized matrix to obtain the weighted standardized matrix, and finally, the sustainability ranking of the six suppliers was obtained. To verify whether the obtained supplier ranking meets the requirements of the enterprise, expert group Z was invited to score their ideal suppliers with sustainable potential. The results were normalized and compared with the rankings obtained through this study to verify the feasibility of this study.

3. Results and Discussion

3.1. *Establishment of a criteria system for SAS selection*

In this stage, the SCOR model is first used to extensively collect supplier selection criteria related to sustainability, and 40 comprehensive sustainable supplier selection criteria suitable for the apparel industry are obtained after screening and exclusion combined with the characteristics of the apparel industry. Then, according to the interview results of the expert group, the criteria of the three dimensions of the TBL are classified as economic (cost, reliability, flexibility, development capacity), environmental (environmental capacity, environmental management system, green image), and social (social performance, internal management, external image). Finally, according to the results of the expert questionnaire, the threshold is set to make the top 40% of the third-level criteria contained in each second-level criterion the final member of the index system to determine 22 third-level criteria, as shown in Fig. 1 (on the right are descriptions of the criteria). A relatively comprehensive hierarchy of the criteria system for SAS selection is determined through the above methods.

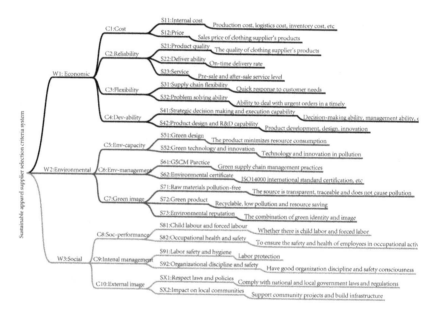

Fig. 1. Hierarchical criteria system.

3.2. FAHP calculated weight results

In this stage, the study compared and evaluated the importance of each criterion in the supplier selection process through expert group Y and determined the weight of 22 sub-criteria by FAHP according to the questionnaire results. The weights determined according to Eq. (1) are as follows. The weights of W1, W2, and W3 are 0.3513, 0.3276, and 0.3211, respectively. The weights of C1-C10 are 0.0894, 0.1015, 0.0771, 0.0833, 0.1111, 0.1102, 0.1064, 0.11062, 0.1136, and 0.1013, respectively. The weights of S11-SX2 are 0.0464, 0.0430, 0.0366, 0.0323,

0.0326, 0.0376, 0.0395, 0.0445, 0.0388, 0.0540, 0.0571, 0.0566, 0.0536, 0.0393, 0.0356, 0.0316, 0.0569, 0.0493, 0.0599, 0.0537, 0.0549, and 0.0463, respectively.

3.3. TOPSIS calculates the ranking of suppliers to be selected

The original evaluation matrix was obtained by scoring 22 three-level criteria of 6 suppliers by expert group Z. The weights of all criteria obtained through FAHP are combined with the standardized matrix to obtain the weighted standardized matrix. Equation (2) is used to obtain the score of each supplier that is not normalized. After normalization, the results and ranking are shown in Table 1.

Table 1. Normalized results and supplier ranking.

	D_i^-	D_i^+	Not normalized	Normalized	Rank
A	0.0170	0.0214	0.4428	0.1451	6
B	0.0180	0.0181	0.4976	0.1630	4
C	0.0159	0.0185	0.4622	0.1514	5
D	0.0213	0.0170	0.5569	0.1825	1
E	0.0195	0.0160	0.5494	0.1800	2
F	0.0179	0.0151	0.5432	0.1780	3

3.4. Expert panel verification

To verify the validity of the ranking results obtained from the above process, expert group Z was invited again to give intuitive ratings to selected suppliers. This process requires five expert panel members (a, b, c, d, e) to give subjective scores on the performance of 6 suppliers according to their own experience, take average values, and compare them with this research model after normalization. The results are shown in Table 2. Variance analysis of the results showed that P value=0.7516>0.05, indicating no significant difference between the expert results and the results of this research model, which was consistent. In terms of ranking, compared with the research model, the results of the expert group showed that the first and second rankings differed from the fifth and sixth rankings, but there was no significant difference in numerical value.

Table 2. Intuitive scoring results of experts.

	A	B	C	D	E	F
a	0.1537	0.1608	0.1537	0.1773	0.1844	0.1702
b	0.1545	0.1705	0.1614	0.1750	0.1727	0.1659
c	0.1674	0.1697	0.1560	0.1651	0.1720	0.1697
d	0.1514	0.1670	0.1492	0.1804	0.1782	0.1737
e	0.1585	0.1702	0.1515	0.1795	0.1725	0.1678
Average	0.1571 (5)	0.1677 (4)	0.1543 (6)	0.1755 (2)	0.1759 (1)	0.1695 (3)
This study	0.1451 (6)	0.163 (4)	0.1514 (5)	0.1825 (1)	0.18 (2)	0.178 (3)

Note: The numbers in "()" are the rankings.

3.5. Discussion

The sustainable problem of the apparel industry urgently needs to be solved. An excellent sustainable supplier can help enterprises establish a good business image and attract many consumer groups. This study focuses on constructing a reasonable and practical supplier selection method.

In this study, a case study was conducted on a supplier of an apparel company to verify the feasibility of the calculation steps and the model's practicality. The case systematically evaluates six fabric suppliers of the apparel company and comprehensively ranks the suppliers through 22 criteria in three dimensions. According to the FAHP-TOPSIS model above, supplier D is the best supplier with a performance of 0.1825, followed by supplier E with a performance of 0.1800, which is almost the same as supplier D and can be regarded as the best substitute supplier. Third, supplier F, whose performance is 0.1780, has a large gap between the top two. The comparison results with the final expert panel verification show that the supplier selection process established in this study can help enterprises make sustainable supplier selections.

This study successfully established a hybrid multiobjective decision-making model using the FAHP and TOPSIS methods, which can help the apparel industry select suppliers with sustainable properties. The process involved three expert groups (X Y Z); group X is used to formulate the criteria system, and group Y is dedicated to determining the criteria weight. Group Z comes from the apparel company and has completed two tasks. The first task is to score six suppliers according to the criteria system. The second task is to score six suppliers intuitively. The above example analysis results show that the model is feasible.

4. Conclusion

For apparel manufacturers, supplier selection is an essential link. Because of the complex fabric and accessories and the changeable market environment, manufacturers will have to frequently face the problem of choosing or changing suppliers. Moreover, in the current grim context of COVID-19 spreading around the world, suitable suppliers are even more critical for manufacturers to help reduce costs and build an excellent sustainable image. However, there are too many subjective factors and not enough comprehensive factors in the supplier selection process of the apparel industry, and the bias of decision-makers often makes enterprises fall into difficulty. This study aims to establish a robust, effective, and easy-to-operate sustainable supplier selection model. The FAHP and TOPSIS methods are used to help apparel manufacturers choose suppliers with a sustainable nature under a fuzzy decision environment. In this study, a comprehensive system of sustainable supplier selection criteria was established, and the FAHP method was used to evaluate the performance of the selected criteria and determine the weight. Next, the potential suppliers are ranked by the TOPSIS method. The process was validated with a real case study from an apparel manufacturer. This study provides an effective method for apparel manufacturers to help them make supplier selection decisions.

References

1. Peng Shao and Yuanyuan Zhang, *Green Consumption Policy system and its enlightenment to green clothing consumption.* Journal of Textile Science, 2022. **43**(01): p. 208-215.
2. Liang Jianfang and Cheng Wanying, *Research status and dilemma analysis of sustainable clothing consumption behavior.* Silk, 2020. **57**(06): p. 18-25.
3. Chan, F.T. and H.K. Chan, *An AHP model for selection of suppliers in the fast changing fashion market.* The International Journal of Advanced Manufacturing Technology, 2010. **51**(9): p. 1195-1207.
4. Ben-Daya, M., E. Hassini, and Z. Bahroun, *Internet of things and supply chain management: a literature review.* International Journal of Production Research, 2019. **57**(15-16): p. 4719-4742.
5. Zhang, J., et al., *Research on sustainable supplier selection based on the rough DEMATEL and FVIKOR methods.* Sustainability, 2020. **13**(1): p. 88.
6. Hou, Y., et al., *Assessing the Best Supplier Selection Criteria in Supply Chain Management During the COVID-19 Pandemic.* Frontiers in Psychology, 2021. **12**.
7. Amindoust, A. and A. Saghafinia, *Textile supplier selection in sustainable supply chain using a modular fuzzy inference system model.* The Journal of The Textile Institute, 2017. **108**(7): p. 1250-1258.
8. Guarnieri, P. and F. Trojan, *Decision making on supplier selection based on social, ethical, and environmental criteria: A study in the textile industry.* Resources, Conservation and Recycling, 2019. **141**: p. 347-361.
9. Wang, C.-N., T.-D.T. Pham, and N.-L. Nhieu, *Multi-layer fuzzy sustainable decision approach for outsourcing manufacturer selection in apparel and textile supply chain.* Axioms, 2021. **10**(4): p. 262.
10. Jia, P., et al., *Supplier selection problems in fashion business operations with sustainability considerations.* Sustainability, 2015. **7**(2): p. 1603-1619.
11. Karami, S., R. Ghasemy Yaghin, and F. Mousazadegan, *Supplier selection and evaluation in the garment supply chain: an integrated DEA–PCA–VIKOR approach.* The Journal of the Textile Institute, 2021. **112**(4): p. 578-595.

12. Ganji Jamehshooran, B., M. Shaharoun, and H. Norehan Haron, *Assessing supply chain performance through applying the SCOR model.* International Journal of Supply Chain Management, 2015. **4**(1).

Research on the system of smart wearable design factors for aging in place in the sustainable perspective

Yudian Zhang

School of Art and Design, Zhejiang Sci-Tech University, China
zoey0712@126.com

Ruoan Ren

School of Design, Jiangnan University, China
6200706020@stu.jiangnan.edu.cn

Zhengyang Lu[*,†]

Key Laboratory of Advanced Process Control for Light Industry
Jiangnan University, China
†7191905018@stu.jiangnan.edu.cn

Smart wearable is expected to give the elderly more peace of mind and experience in a comfortable home environment. This not only satisfies their desire to live relatively independently, but also avoids the waste of resources caused by the lack of timely detection and feedback of aging and health problems, and contributes to the sustainable development of society. In order to meet the current demand for high development of smart wearable products for the elderly at home, and to lay out the limited design resources on the key design factors so as to enhance the consumer experience, a design element system is constructed from a sustainable perspective. The textual measures of academic literature and product evaluations are used to analyze the relevant theoretical foundations and the current state of the market category products. Based on this, the user's needs at the instinctive, behavioral and reflective levels are captured through expert panel interviews, and the initial requirement importance is calculated. The QFD quality house model is used to translate the needs into design factors and score them based on the relationship degree of the needs, and finally construct the design factor system of smart wearable for the elderly at home in a sustainable perspective.

Keywords: Sustainable; smart wearable; aging in place; design factors; system; user needs.

---

[*]Work partially supported by the Postgraduate Research & Practice Innovation Program of Jiangsu Province (grant number KYCX20_1891).
[†]Corresponding author.

1. Introduction

Design for Sustainability originates from the concept of sustainable development and is a theoretical reflection on the relationship between environmental, social and economic elements in the design community.[1] Sustainable design calls for designers to discover more real social problems and to take social responsibility by proposing solutions based on the root causes of the phenomenon. Many countries around the world are currently facing the problem of aging population. Reducing the waste of public resources and improving the environment for aging in place from a sustainable perspective has become an urgent research topic.

International research on smart wearable design for the elderly has been not uncommon, but most studies have mainly examined scenarios from therapy,[2] rehabilitation,[3] and protection.[4-6] Few studies focus on smart wearable design in home care scenarios. RK Nath indicated that the advent of the Internet of Things has made possible the design of connected and integrated smart health monitoring systems. These smart health monitoring systems can be implemented in smart home environments to provide long-term care for the elderly.[7] Li Junde said that widespread use of smart wearables can reduce the social burden due to the increasing demand for healthcare and assistance for the elderly.[8] There is little literature that examines the system of smart wearable design factors for aging in place from a sustainable perspective.[9] However, the current high development demand of smart wearable for aging in place poses a challenge for its design methodology and resource allocation.[10] Based on this, this study adopts a variety of research and analysis methods to improve the construction of the current design element system of smart wearable for the elderly at home from the perspective of sustainability, so as to provide a scientific basis for the sustainable development of society in the future.

2. Method

2.1. Knowledge graph literature analysis

With the emergence of formatted and digital journals, data interpretation of literature has become more intuitive, visual and clear. Based on the idea of semantic network, knowledge mapping connects different nodes among knowledge ontologies according to their original relationships, forming a standardized form of sharing and representing knowledge clearly in a machine-readable way. Knowledge mapping allows a more comprehensive grasp of the knowledge system that has been established in a field.[11] In this study, VOS viewer software is used for data visualization and analysis of knowledge graphs.

This software constructs and presents bibliometric maps by the difference in size, distance, and density between different nodes.

2.2. Category product evaluation analysis

Consumer evaluations of products are a high-quality source of reference data for product development program development.[12] Traditional evaluation data collection methods tend to lead to incomplete data sources and insufficient sample sizes, which in turn lead to one-sided product development. The development of big data and intelligent data analysis technology has helped researchers to collect and process product evaluation text data in a more efficient way. In this study, the ROST-CM6 text content mining software platform developed by Professor Shen Yang's team at Wuhan University was used to analyze the word frequency and sentiment of product evaluations in the home monitoring smart wearable category.

2.3. Focus group interview

Experts from related fields were invited to form panels to participate in open-ended interviews about product requirements.[13] The results of the knowledge mapping and category product evaluation analysis were presented to the panel of experts as base material before the start of the interviews to enhance the comprehensiveness of the interview information. The two authors of this paper were present during the interviews as interview guides and recorders and joined the discussion at the end of each session. After the basic organization of the audio data from the interviews, the data were coded for metrological analysis through the rooting theory research method. To ensure the validity of the need factors, the need keywords that were mentioned 2 or more times were retained for recording, and vice versa were removed. The weight of need word frequency to total word frequency was recorded as the need importance score.

2.4. QFD quality house model

The QFD (Quality Function Deployment) method is a quantitative analysis method that translates requirements into design elements to guide design and production. The basic principle of the QFD method is to optimize the user experience by using a quality house matrix to identify the design elements that contribute most to meeting customer needs through data analysis and processing. The "left wall" and the ceiling of the QFD matrix model are user requirements and design elements respectively. The relevance of each set of user requirements and design elements was scored by a scoring panel. The relevance was rated by

534

a panel of 3 experienced practitioners in the field of home care smart wearable. The relevance ratings were divided into four categories: strong relevance, moderate relevance, weak relevance, and no relevance, with scores of 5, 3, 1, and 0, respectively. The three grades of strong, moderate, and weak are indicated by corresponding scores in the table, and the table of items judged to be irrelevant is not filled with scores. The design point importance Hj is calculated by Eq. (1), and Rij is the relationship between the i-th requirement and the j-th design requirement.

$$H_j = \sum_{i=1}^{n} W_i R_{ij} (j = 1,2,3, \ldots, m) \tag{1}$$

3. Results

3.1. Analysis of academic literature

The Web of Science core database was used as the source of data acquisition. The keywords "home", "elderly", and "wearable" were used to search all the documents collected before July 5, 2022, and a total of 193 results were obtained by manual sorting and filtering. After quantitative analysis by the VOS viewer software platform, relevant literature data are presented in the form of a visual graphical network according to timeline attributes. As shown in Fig. 1, the node colors from light to dark represent the data information on the timeline from early to recent. The co-occurrence mapping results of keyword clustering concisely and intuitively show that the main research directions in the field are: algorithm, assessment, fall, need, healthcare, usability, society, parameter, etc.

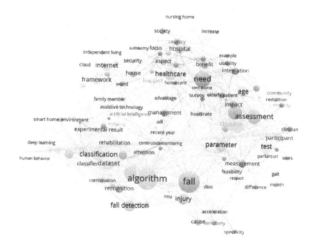

Fig. 1. Knowledge graph of timeline attributes.

The frontier research directions in the field are: framework, classification, dataset, iot, low cost, artificial intelligent, etc.

3.2. Category product evaluation analysis

In Taobao, Jingdong and other 4 comprehensive e-commerce platforms, we searched and filtered products with the combination of "home", "elderly" and "smart wearable" as keywords. A total of 233 valid product evaluation texts were obtained. The text data in ".txt" format was input into ROST-CM6 software. The text content was processed by the software's word separation and key word frequency analysis functions, and 54 high-frequency feature words and their frequency were obtained. Among them, product function-related feature words (such as heart rate, positioning, alarm, reminder, blood oxygen, sleep, etc.) accounted for 33.33% of the total; product use-related feature words (such as convenient, charging, put on and take off, setting, voice, etc.) accounted for 24.07% of the total; product appearance-related feature words (such as compact, exquisite, technology, fashion, etc.) accounted for 16.67% of the total; product technology-related feature words related to product technology (such as big data, cloud computing, sensors, etc.) accounted for 9.26% of the total. It can be seen that the function and use of smart wearable products for the elderly at home are the two points that consumers are most concerned about.

The sentiment of the category product evaluation text content was analyzed by ROST-CM6 software. The results showed that positive emotions accounted for 47.56% of the total emotion texts, intermediate emotions for 21.95% and negative emotions for 30.49%. It is evident that the majority of the customer base can satisfy their value needs through the purchase and use of products in this category in the market. However, there is still a relatively high proportion of customers who are conservative or negative about their feelings after using such products. Further analysis revealed that the negative emotions were mainly focused on the use of the product, with "inconvenience", "heavy", "difficult" and other negative emotion keywords appearing many times.

3.3. Design factors system construction

The expert panel interview was used to capture the needs and calculate the importance of the needs. The expert panel consisted of one age-appropriate product manager, two smart wearable designers and two PhD candidates in product design. The duration of this open-ended interview was 80 minutes. Guided by the previous focus group interview method, the final 3 primary needs,

Table 1. System of need factors.

Primary requirements	Frequency /times	Primary requirements	Frequency /times	Rank	Needs Importance
A1 Instinctive layer - percept experience	58	B1 Health Aids	18	3	0.13
		B2 Comfort	8	8	0.06
		B3 Risk Warning	26	1	0.19
		B4 Social evaluation	6	9	0.04
A2 Behavioral layer - situational use	51	B5 Usage Cost	14	4	0.10
		B6 Safety	11	6	0.08
		B7 Easy to use	21	2	0.15
		B8 Low extra burden	5	11	0.04
A3 Reflection layer - lifestyle	281	B9 Home Life	12	5	0.09
		B10 Community Life	9	7	0.07
		B11 Re-learning	5	10	0.04
		B12 Reemploy	2	12	0.01

Table 2. Deductive derivation of design factors.

Primary requirements	Secondary requirements	Design factors
A1 Instinctive layer	B1 Health Aids	C1 Proactive disease self-testing
		C2 Passive life monitoring
	B2 Comfort	C3 Flexible skin-friendly material
	B3 Risk Warning	C4 Hazardous Environment Alert
		C5 Lost and Found Alert
		C6 Fraud Alert
		C7 Behavioral guidance under risk
	B4 Social evaluation	C8 Appearance high value sense
	B5 Usage Cost	C9 Low cost
		C10 Durability
A2 Behavioral layer	B6 Safety	C11 Information Privacy Protection
		C12 Medical device qualification
	B7 Easy to use	C13 Simple operation logic
		C14 Low educational barriers
		C15 Easy after-sales maintenance
	B8 Low extra burden	C16 Everyday appearance
		C17 High battery duration
		C18 Lightweight
A3 Reflection layer	B9 Home Life	C19 Smart Home Connected
	B10 Community Life	C20 Community Information Release
	B11 Re-learning	C21 Hobby Forum
		C22 Online skills learning
	B12 Re-employment	C23 Public service volunteer job matching
		C24 Skills Job Matching

12 secondary needs and their corresponding word frequencies and need importance are shown in Table 1.

User needs are transformed into design factors through deductive derivation, as shown in the Table 2. In the process of deductive derivation, the relationship between needs and design factors may not be one-to-one, but will be merged and fractured according to the specific situation.

The results calculated by the previous QFD quality house model construction are shown in Fig. 2. The first 8 items of the scoring result are the core design elements to be focused on in the design, which are C2, C7, C1, C5, C19, C6, C13, C14. Items ranked 9-16 are partially referred to as sub-core design factors in the design process according to the actual situation.

The research framework of the design element system is obtained by connecting the modules in a flow sequence, as shown in Fig. 3.

User demand	Importance of demand	C₁	C₂	C₃	C₄	C₅	C₆	C₇	C₈	C₉	C₁₀	C₁₁	C₁₂	C₁₃	C₁₄	C₁₅	C₁₆	C₁₇	C₁₈	C₁₉	C₂₀	C₂₁	C₂₂	C₂₃	C₂₄
B₁	0.13	5	5		1	1						1													
B₂	0.06		5						1	1	1							1	3	1					
B₃	0.19	3	3		5	5	5	5			1		1	1						1	1				1
B₄	0.04		3						5	3	3	1	3	1		1	3	1	1	1	3		1		1
B₅	0.10		3	3	3	3	3	3	5	5	3	3	3	3	3		3	3	3						
B₆	0.08		1	1	1	1	1	1			5	5				1									
B₇	0.15	1				1	1	3					5	5	5	1	1	1	3	1	1	1			1
B₈	0.04	1	1	1	1	1	1	1					1	1	1	5	5	5	1						
B₉	0.09	5	5								1	1	1		1	1			1	5	3	3	3	1	1
B₁₀	0.07					1														5	3	3	3	1	1
B₁₁	0.04											3								3	5	5	1	1	
B₁₂	0.01										1	1								3	3	1	5	5	
Importance ranking of design elements		1.71	1.86	0.76	1.50	1.65	1.59	1.82	0.64	0.76	0.68	1.23	1.04	1.54	1.54	1.38	0.45	0.78	0.95	1.61	1.11	0.90	0.88	0.39	0.58
		3	1	18	9	4	6	2	21	18	20	11	13	7	7	10	23	17	14	5	12	15	16	24	22

Fig. 2. Design factors system.

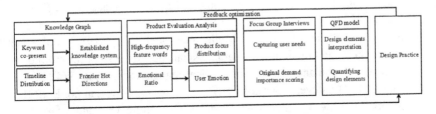

Fig. 3. Research framework for the construction of design element system.

4. Conclusion

In the background of aging, smart wearable is expected to become an important tool to enhance the quality of life of the elderly. Smart wearable plays an important role in health monitoring and entertainment life of the elderly in home aging life, reducing the burden of family and society and alleviating the current challenges of aging under the society. This study constructs a home aging smart wearable design factors system through knowledge mapping, product evaluation analysis, focus group interview, and quality house model analysis. It provides a theoretical and methodological reference for the design of smart wearable for aging in place, so that the elderly can effectively enjoy the benefits brought by the progress of wearable technology and promote sustainable social development.

Acknowledgments

This work is supported by the Postgraduate Research & Practice Innovation Program of Jiangsu Province (grant number KYCX20_1891).

References

1. Zhu, C., Sheng, W., and Liu, M. (2015). Wearable sensor-based behavioral anomaly detection in smart assisted living systems. IEEE Transactions on Automation Science & Engineering, 12(4), 1225-1234.
2. Zhang, Y., Sun, W., and Chen, J. (2022). Application of Embedded Smart Wearable Device Monitoring in Joint Cartilage Injury and Rehabilitation Training. Journal of Healthcare Engineering, 2022.
3. Yassine, A. (2021). Health monitoring systems for the elderly during COVID-19 pandemic: measurement requirements and challenges. IEEE Instrumentation & Measurement Magazine, 24(2), 6-12.
4. Mukherjee, S., Suleman, S., Pilloton, R., Narang, J., and Rani, K. (2022). State of the Art in Smart Portable, Wearable, Ingestible and Implantable Devices for Health Status Monitoring and Disease Management. Sensors, 22(11), 4228.
5. Rezayi, S., Safaei, A. A., and Mohammadzadeh, N. (2019). Requirement specification and modeling a wearable smart blanket system for monitoring patients in ambulance. Journal of Medical Signals and Sensors, 9(4), 234.
6. Chan, M., D Estève, Fourniols, J. Y., Escriba, C., and Campo, E. (2012). Smart wearable systems: current status and future challenges. Artificial Intelligence in Medicine, 56(3), 137-156.
7. Nath, R. K., and Thapliyal, H. (2021). Wearable Health Monitoring System for Older Adults in a Smart Home Environment.
8. Chen, W. (2021). The influence of consumers' purchase intention on smart wearable device: a study of consumers in east china. International Journal of Science and Business, 5.

9. Pascali, C. D., Francioso, L., Giampetruzzi, L., Rescio, G., Signore, M. A., and Leone, A., et al. (2021). Modeling, fabrication and integration of wearable smart sensors in a monitoring platform for diabetic patients. Sensors, 21(5), 1847.

10. Qaroush, A., Yassin, S., Al-Nubani, A., and Alqam, A. (2021). Smart, comfortable wearable system for recognizing arabic sign language in real-time using imus and features-based fusion. Expert Systems with Applications, 184, 115448.

11. Pentland, A. (2000). Looking at people: sensing for ubiquitous and wearable computing. Pattern Analysis & Machine Intelligence IEEE Transactions on, 22(1), 107-119.

12. Chan, M., Campo, E., D Estève, and Fourniols, J. Y. (2009). Smart homes — current features and future perspectives. Maturitas, 64(2), 90-97.

13. Lee, Y. D., and Chung, W. Y. (2009). Wireless sensor network based wearable smart shirt for ubiquitous health and activity monitoring. Sensors & Actuators B Chemical, 140(2), 390-395.

Part 5

Feature Classification and Data Processing

Fully reusing clause method based standard contradiction separation rule

Peiyao Liu[1,*], Yang Xu[1], Shuwei Chen[1] and Feng Cao[2]

[1]*School of Mathematics, Southwest Jiaotong University, Chengdu, 611756, China*
[2]*School of Information Engineering, Jiangxi University of Science and Technology
Ganzhou, 341000, China*
*liupeiyao@my.swjtu.edu.cn

Standard contradiction separation rule in first-order logic breaks through binary and static properties which are two remarkable features of canonical resolution. Standard contradiction separation rule offers multiple advantages, such as multi-clause, dynamic abilities and guidance, etc. In order to further take advantage of these abilities, we propose a fully reusing clause method based standard contradiction separation rule and design a deduction algorithm based on the fully reusing clause method in this paper. This algorithm is applied to the leading first-order prover, Vampire, to form V_FRC, the feasibility and superiority of this algorithm are illustrated though an experiment.

Keywords: Prover; first-order logic; deduction algorithm; standard contradiction separation.

1. Introduction

The essential feature of variants[1,2,3] of binary resolution is that only two clauses involved in each deduction step, and only one literal complementary pair from parent clauses is eliminated.[4] This feature also implies that binary resolution must be a static inference method, while also generating a mass of redundant clauses which may lead the search space explosion during the deduction process.[5] Although the appearance of redundancy elimination techniques[6,7] and related heuristic strategies[8,9] reduces the search space to a certain extent, this leads to additional deduction overhead. In 2018, standard contradiction separation (in short S-CS) rule for first-order logic was proposed,[10] which has multiple advantages of multi-clause, dynamic and guidance, etc.[11] The basic idea is that S-CS rule takes multiple clauses (two or more) as parent clauses, and selects multiple literals (one or more) from each parent to construct a contradiction, then infers the clause formed from the disjunction of the non-selected literals of the parent clause.[12] Meanwhile, binary resolution is a special case of S-CS rule.

In order to fully bring abilities of S-CS rule into full play, this paper proposes a fully reusing clause method based S-CS rule that takes better advantage of the guidance and synergy abilities of S-CS rule. On the other hand, we design a deduction algorithm based on the fully reusing clause method, FRC algorithm. An related experiment also is provided to illustrate the feasibility and superiority of FRC algorithm. We design a contrast experiment between Vampire and V_FRC, where V_FRC is a prover that is formed by applying FRC algorithm into the leading first-order prover Vampire.[13] The experiment uses CASC-J10[14] problems (FOF division) to evaluate the performance of V_FRC, and the experimental result shows that FRC algorithm is an effective deduction algorithm and fully reusing clause method can take better advantage of the guidance and synergy abilities of S-CS rule.

2. Preliminaries of Standard Contradiction Separation Rule in First-order Logic

This section first introduces the related concepts of first-order logic, and then introduces standard contradiction separation (S-CS) rule. We assume that the reader is already familiar with related concepts of first-order logic. This section only repeats some basic concepts, and Ref. 10 provides a more detailed introduction.

We restrict our discussion to conjunctive normal form (CNF) of first-order logic, a subset of first-order predicate that eliminates quantifiers and allows only conjunctions of clauses (which are disjunctions of elementary literals) as formulae. A literal is either an atom or a negated form, where an atom is an n-ary predicate (denoted P) with n terms. A term (denoted by t is either a variable (denoted x), a constant (denoted a), or an n-ary function (denoted f) with n terms. By the way, we use T to denote the set of all terms and use V to denote the set of all variables. A term is called ground term if it contains no variables. A clause (denoted by C) is a disjunction of a finite set of literals (denoted l or its negation $\sim l$). The empty clause is denoted by $\emptyset$. Especially if clause C has only one literal, the clause is called a unit clause. A formula (denoted by S) is a conjunction of a finite clauses. A substitution (denoted by σ) is a mapping from V to T with the property that $\{x|\sigma(x) \neq x\}$ is finite.

Definition 2.1. (Contradiction)[10] Let $S = \{C_1, C_2, \dots, C_m\}$ be a clause set. If $\forall (l_1, l_2, \dots, l_m) \in \prod_{i=1}^{m} C_i$, there exists at least one complementary pair among $\{l_1, l_2, \dots, l_m\}$, then $S = \bigwedge_{i=1}^{m} C_i$ is called a standard contradiction (in short, SC).

Definition 2.2.[10] Suppose a clause set $S = \{C_1, C_2, \ldots, C_m\}$ in first-order logic. The following inference rule that produces a new clause from S is called a standard contradiction separation rule, in short, an S-CS rule:

For each C_i ($i = 1, 2, \ldots, m$), firstly apply a substitution σ_i to C_i (σ_i could be an empty substitution but not necessary the most general unifier), denoted as $C_i^{\sigma_i}$; then separate $C_i^{\sigma_i}$ into two sub-clauses $C_i^{\sigma_i-}$ and $C_i^{\sigma_i+}$ such that

(1) $C_i^{\sigma_i} = C_i^{\sigma_i-} \vee C_i^{\sigma_i+}$, where $C_i^{\sigma_i-}$ and $C_i^{\sigma_i+}$ have no common literals;

(2) $C_i^{\sigma_i+}$ can be an empty clause itself, but $C_i^{\sigma_i-}$ cannot be an empty clause;

(3) $\bigwedge_{i=1}^{m} C_i^{\sigma_i-}$ is a standard contradiction, that is $\forall (x_1, \ldots, x_m) \in \prod_{i=1}^{m} C_i^{\sigma_i-}$, there exists at least one complementary pair among $\{x_1, \ldots, x_m\}$.

The resulting clause $\bigvee_{i=1}^{m} C_i^{\sigma_i+}$, denoted as $\mathbb{C}_m^{s\sigma}(C_1, \ldots, C_m)$, is called a standard contradiction separation clause (S-CSC) of $C_1, \ldots, C_m$, and $\bigwedge_{i=1}^{m} C_i^{\sigma_i-}$ is called a separated standard contradiction (S-SC).

The final deduction result (usually empty clause $\emptyset$) is derived from a series of deduction steps. Definition 2.3 describes deduction sequence based S-CS rule.

Definition 2.3.[10] Suppose a clause set $S = \{C_1, C_2, \ldots, C_m\}$ in first-order logic. $\Phi_1, \Phi_2, \ldots, \Phi_t$ is called a standard contradiction separation based dynamic deduction sequence (S-CS deduction) from S to a clause Φ_t, denoted as D^s, if

(1) $\Phi_i \in S$, $i = 1, 2, \ldots, t$; or

(2) there exist $r_1, r_2, \ldots, r_{k_i} < i$, $\Phi_i = \mathbb{C}_{k_i}^s(\Phi_{r_2}, \Phi_{r_2}, \ldots, \Phi_{r_{k_i}})$.

The soundness and completeness of S-CS rule are guaranteed by the following two theorems.

Theorem 2.1. (Soundness)[10] Suppose a clause set $S = \{C_1, C_2, \ldots, C_m\}$ in first-order logic. $\Phi_1, \Phi_2, \ldots, \Phi_t$ is an S-CS based dynamic deduction from S to a clause Φ_t. If Φ_t is an empty clause, then S is unsatisfiable.

Theorem 2.2. (Completeness)[10] Suppose a clause set $S = \{C_1, C_2, \ldots, C_m\}$ in first-order logic. If S is unsatisfiable, then exists an S-CS based dynamic deduction from S to an empty clause.

3. Fully Reusing Clause Method

S-CS rule separates a clause set $S = \{C_1, C_2, \ldots, C_m\}$ into two parts in the process of contradiction separation: contradiction and contradiction separation clause. For each clause $C_i \in S$ ($i = 1, \ldots, m$), C_i is separates into C_i^- and C_i^+ by S-CS rule. When $\bigwedge_{i=1}^{m} C_i^-$ is unsatisfiable, a corresponding contradiction is formed, and $\bigvee_{i=1}^{m} C_i^+$ is the contradiction separation clause.

The clause involved in the S-CS deduction is called *involved clause*. In an involved clause, these literals that are separated into the contradiction are called *selected literals*. Actually, the crucial point of contradiction construction is how to separate these involved clauses into the two parts, i.e., which literals in one involved clause should be selected into standard contradiction and other non-selected literals join S-CSC, after the corresponding substitutions. There is one literal from each involved clause in the contradiction is called *decision literal* that plays an important role on constructing the contradiction. After each separation of one clause, a literal from this clause need to be selected as the decision literal. We use symbol D_l to denote a set of decision literals in the contradiction. During the S-CS deduction, literal set D_l determines which literals in subsequent clauses are added to the contradiction, and the add condition is that the literal that can form a complementary pair with any literal in D_l will be added to contradiction.

For a first-order logic unsatisfiable problem, the final goal of S-CS deduction is to generate empty clause $\emptyset$, so the less the number of literals in the S-CSC, the more conducive to generate empty clause $\emptyset$. Therefore, it is helpful for constructing the contradiction that more literals from a subsequent clause are added to the contradiction. From the above analysis, we deduce a conclusion that the more different literals in D_l, the more conducive to generate empty clause $\emptyset$. In order to make D_l have more different literals, a clause should be reused multiple times in a contradiction construction. Because a clause may have more than one literal that qualifies as the decision literal. On the other hand, one literal may also form the complementary pair with multiple literals in D_l. It is noted that the same clause or literal with different substitutions will be regarded as different clause or literal. This is the main motivation for fully reusing clause method based S-CS rule.

The detail of fully reusing clause method based S-CS rule is described as follows. We first introduce a concept of *repetition value* that measure the number of reuse of a clause or a literal.

Definition 3.1. (Repetition value) Suppose a contradiction CT, and CT has a set of decision literal D_l which consisting of n different literals. There is a clause $C = l_1 \vee l_2 \vee \cdots \vee l_m$ which has m literals. If there exists k_i literals in D_l that can form complementary pair with literal l_i $(i = 1,2,\ldots,m)$, then the *repetition value* $Rv(l_i)$ of l_i is k_i. And the repetition value $Rv(C)$ of C is $\sum_{i=1}^{m} k_i$.

Next, we introduce the definition of *separation clause rule*.

Definition 3.2. (Separation clause rule) Suppose a contradiction CT with corresponding S-CSC, and CT has a set of decision literal D_l. A clause $C = l_1 \vee$

$l_2 \vee \cdots \vee l_m$ as a subsequent clause for S-CS deduction be separated into two parts after a substitution σ, this process of the separation be divided into two steps.

Step 1. The literal l_i $(i = 1,2,\ldots,m)$ that can form a complementary pair with the l_* in D_l be added to contradiction CT after a substitution $\sigma = \bigcup_{i=1}^{m} \sigma_i$, which also is called *pairing condition*.

Step 2. If there is no literal that do not satisfy pairing condition, then break. Otherwise go to Step 3.

Step 3. Select one literal from the other literals that do not satisfy pairing condition as the decision literal, update D_l and add this literal into contradiction CT. The last remaining literals that be called *remaining literals* of C add to the S-CSC.

The process of reusing a clause may generate many redundant clauses or make the number of literals in the S-CSC grow too fast. Therefore, there are some conditions to avoid these situations in actual implementation.

Definition 3.3. There two thresholds N_R and Nf which are the number of non-selected literals in the clause and the number of functions in the clause after separation respectively. After a clause C is separated, if the number of non-selected literals in clause C exceeds N_R or the number of functions in clause C exceeds Nf, then this separation of clause C is called *invalid separation*.

In general, N_R and Nf in Definition 3.3 can be set by some heuristic strategy. The fully reusing clause method based S-CS rule is used to construct one contradiction.

Given a clause set $S = \{C_1, C_2, \ldots, C_m\}$ in first-order logic, then the steps of fully reusing clause method based S-CS rule are described as follows. D_l denotes the set of decision literal, G_2 denotes the set of all binary clause in S and G_3 denotes the set of all non-unit and non-binary clauses in S, whose initialization are empty.

Step 1. All unit clauses in S are put into D_l, all binary clause in S are put into G_2, and all non-unit and non-binary clauses in S are put into G_3.

Step 2. Traverse each clause C_2 of G_2. Count the repetition value $Rv(C_2)$ of C_2, apply separation clause rule to reuse C_2 $Rv(C_2)$ times. Each separation of C_2 generates a newly clause C_R. If C_R is $\emptyset$, then it is add to S; otherwise UNSAT.

Step 3. End traverse of G_2. Traverse each clause C_3 of G_3. Count the repetition value $Rv(C_3)$ of C_3, apply separation clause rule to reuse C_3 $Rv(C_3)$ times. Each separation of C_3 generates a newly clause C_R. If C_R is $\emptyset$, then it is added to S; otherwise UNSAT.

Step 4. Go to Step 2.

Step 5. End traverse of G_3. Exit!

4. Experiment

We design a deduction algorithm based fully reusing clause method, FRC algorithm. In order to evaluate the feasibility and superiority of FRC algorithm, we apply FRC algorithm into Vampire to form V_FRC. By testing CASC-J10 problems (FOF division) to compare the performance between Vampire and V_FRC. The experimental environment is on a PC with 3.6GHz Inter(R) Core (TM) i7-7700 processor and 16 GB memory, OS Ubuntu 20.04 64-bit. The test time for a single problem is 300 seconds (CPU time) which is the standard test time for TPTP library). In the experiments, the version of Vampire is 4.5.1.

About the experimental result, V_FRC has solved 462 problems with 12 more than Vampire 4.5.1, which has solved 450 problems. The list of 12 problems that are solved by V_FRC but not by Vampire 4.5.1 shows in Table 1.

Table 1. The list of 12 problems solved by V_CRA but not by Vampire 4.5.1.

No	Problem	Time(s)	No	Problem	Time(s)
1	BOO109+1	293.74	7	NUM736+4	129.01
2	LCL650+1.010	192.63	8	NUM781+4	129.12
3	NUM671+4	115.79	9	NUM782+4	115.93
4	NUM695+4	152.24	10	NUN056+1	162.31
5	NUM697+4	163.96	11	SEU357+2	110.51
6	NUM801+4	163.86	12	SEU410+1	143.20

The experimental result shows that FRC is able to improve the reasoning capability and efficiency of Vampire and it is an effective deduction algorithm. Fully reusing clause method based S-CS rule can take better advantage of the guidance and synergy abilities of S-CS rule.

5. Conclusion

In order to take better advantage of the abilities of S-CS rule, especially guidance and synergy. We propose a fully reusing clause method based S-CS rule. This method is able to contribute more decision literals for contradiction, and has better ability for constructing the contradiction that more literals from a subsequent clause are added to the contradiction. The deduction algorithm (FRC) base fully reusing clause method is applied into Vampire to form V_FRC. The contrast experiment between Vampire and V_FRC shows that the performance of V_FRC is better than that of Vampire. It also shows that the fully reusing clause method is feasible and superior.

Acknowledgments

This work has been partially supported by the National Natural Science Foundation of China (Grant No. 61976130) and the General Research Project of Jiangxi Education Department (Grant No. GJJ200818).

References

1. L. Bachmair, H. Ganzinger, D. McAllester, C. Lynch, Chapter 2 - resolution theorem proving, *Handbook of Automated Reasoning*, pp. 19–99, 2001.
2. H. de Nivelle, J. Meng, Geometric resolution: a proof procedure based on finite model search, IJCAR 2006: Automated Reasoning, pp. 303–317.
3. J. Slaney, B. W. Paleo, Conflict Resolution: A first-order resolution calculus with decision literals and conflict-driven clause learning, *Journal of Automated Reasoning*, 60 (2): 133–156, 2018.
4. J.A. Robinson, A machine-oriented logic based on the resolution principle, *Journal of the ACM*, 12 (1): 23–41, 1965.
5. S. Schulz, Learning search control knowledge for equational deduction, Ph.D. Thesis, Technische Universität München, 2000.
6. B. Löchner, A redundancy criterion based on ground reducibility by ordered rewriting, IJCAR 2004, pp. 45–59.
7. B. Kiesl, M. Suda, A unifying principle for clause elimination in first-order logic, Automated Deduction - CADE 26, pp. 274–290, 2017.
8. J. Jakubův, K. Chvalovský, M. Olšák, B. Piotrowski, M. Suda, J. Urban, ENIGMA anonymous: symbol-independent inference guiding machine (system description), arXiv:2002.05406 [cs], 2020.
9. M. Rawson, G. Reger, Old or heavy? Decaying gracefully with age/weight shapes, Automated Deduction – CADE 27, pp. 462–476, 2019.
10. Y. Xu, J. Liu, S. Chen, X Zhong, X. He, Contradiction separation based dynamic multi-clause synergized automated deduction, *Information Sciences*, 462: 93–113, 2018.
11. Y. Xu, S. Chen, J. Liu, X Zhong, X. He, Distinctive features of the contradiction separation based dynamic automated deduction, the FLINS 2018 International Conference, pp. 725–732, 2018.
12. F. Cao, Y. Xu, J. Liu, S. Chen, J, Yi, A multi-clause dynamic deduction algorithm based on standard contradiction separation rule, *Information Sciences*, 566: 281–299, 2021.

13. L. Kovács, A. Voronkov, First-order theorem proving and vampire, the CAV 2013 International Conference, pp. 1–35, 2013.
14. G. Sutcliffe, The CADE ATP System Competition, http:/tptp.org/CASC/ J10/. Accessed 8 March 2022.

A lifelong spectral clustering based on Bayesian inference

Zongshan Huang, Yan Yang* and Yiling Zhang

School of Computing and Artificial Intelligence, Southwest Jiaotong University
Chengdu, 611756, China
*yyang@swjtu.edu.cn
www.swjtu.edu.cn

Clustering analysis is a significant technique of data mining. With the rise of lifelong learning, lifelong clustering has become a research topic. Lifelong clustering builds libraries shared among multiple tasks, and these tasks achieve effective information transmission by interacting with the shared knowledge libraries. However, selecting optimal hyper-parameters in the knowledge transfer process often employs the actual clustering division in the dataset as a reference, which is unavailable during the clustering process. Moreover, the hyper-parameters for each task are typically set to constant values because of computational difficulty. Therefore, this paper explores a clustering method based on Bayesian inference, where the parameter setting is priori information, and the clustering divisions obtained by the parameters are posteriori information. In our method, hyper-parameters corresponding to the maximum a posteriori (MAP) probability are selected in each task. Then, we apply this method to Lifelong Spectral Clustering to select hyper-parameters and propose a new algorithm, called Maximum a Posteriori Lifelong Spectral Clustering (MAPLSC). Finally, experiments on several real-world datasets show the effectiveness of our method and the average clustering performance of Lifelong Spectral Clustering is improved.

Keywords: Lifelong learning; Bayesian method; maximum a posteriori estimation; spectral clustering.

1. Introduction

Clustering analysis is an important unsupervised analysis method in data mining technology, in which the samples are classified according to the feature similarity rather than samples' categories and labels. Cluster analysis can be used for data mining in sustainable development research, such as distinguishing the sustainable development level of different regions, classifying demonstration regions according to different evaluation dimensions, etc. In clustering, lifelong clustering can handle continuous tasks. Lifelong Machine Learning[1] was proposed by Thrun and Mitchell, which is a continuous learning process. That is, after completing N tasks, the knowledge base stores and maintains the knowledge learned from the past N tasks.[2] In the existing lifelong clustering studies, some researchers use the actual clustering division of clustering samples as a reference to find the best hyper-parameters, which is unavailable in unsupervised learning. Moreover, these tasks usually utilize unified hyper-parameters because of computational difficulty and the limitation of unknown cluster labels; as a result, clustering can not achieve the best results.

To solve these problems, in this paper, we make two contributions:

(1) We propose a lifelong clustering method based on Bayesian inference, using Bayesian probability as the basis for hyper-parameter selection. When every new task arrives, the clustering algorithm runs with all pairs of parameters in grid search manner. Then the posteriori probability for each pair of parameters is calculated for selecting the clustering result corresponding to the maximum a posteriori probability.

(2) We apply the method to the Lifelong Spectral Clustering Model[3] and propose a Maximum a Posteriori Lifelong Spectral Clustering algorithm. Our algorithm can adaptively select hyper-parameters in an online and unsupervised manner.

2. Related Work

2.1. Spectral clustering

Spectral clustering is a clustering method based on graph theory. Graph G can be represented by $G(V, E)$, where V is the set of vertices in G, including n vertexes $(v_1, v_2, \ldots, v_n)$, E is the set of edges in G. In an undirected graph, the weight of the edge connecting vertices i and j is represented by $w_{i,j}$; KNN method is usually utilized to calculate the adjacency matrix W, as Eq. (1). Then the Laplacian matrix L of the graph is calculated by $L = D - W$, where D is W's degree matrix. After unitization, the eigenvalues of normalized L can be transformed into the cluster indicator matrix F. The K-means clustering takes F's rows as input samples, and its result is also the result of spectral clustering.

$$ w_{i,j} = \begin{cases} \exp(-\frac{\|v_i - v_j\|_2^2}{2\sigma^2}), & v_i \in KNN(v_j) \text{ or } v_j \in KNN(v_i) \\ 0, & \text{else} \end{cases} \tag{1} $$

Jianbo Shi et al.[5] utilized the Normalize Cut (NCut) method to cut the graph. Under this condition, the spectral clustering's objective function can be expressed as:

$$\max_{F} tr(F^\top KF), \text{s.t.} F^\top F = I_k \tag{2}$$

where K is calculated according to: $K = D^{-\frac{1}{2}}WD^{-\frac{1}{2}}$.

2.2. Lifelong spectral clustering

G. Sun et al.[3] proposed a Lifelong Spectral Clustering (L^2SC) algorithm. Firstly, F is decomposed by $F = EB$, where B represents the common characteristics of multiple tasks. Secondly, considering the relationship between tasks, L is obtained by graph joint clustering. Then F is replaced by the orthogonal basis library B and the feature embedding library L, which are shared among clustering tasks to transmit information. Equation (3) presents the new objective function for m-th task.

$$\max_{B,L,(E^t)_{t=1}^m} \frac{1}{m} \sum_{t=1}^{m} tr((B^\top (E^t)^\top K^t E^t B) + \lambda_t tr(L^\top \hat{X}^t E^t B))$$

$$+\mu \|L\|_{2,1} \text{ s.t. } B^\top B = I_k \text{ and } L^\top L = I_k \text{ and } E^{t^\top} E^t = I_k \tag{3}$$

in which $\hat{X}^t$ is calculated according to $\hat{X} = (D_1)^{-\frac{1}{2}} X (D_2)^{-\frac{1}{2}}$, where $D_1 = diag(X\mathbf{1})$, $D_2 = diag(X^\top \mathbf{1})$.

When a new task comes, the matrix E, B, and L are alternately computed and updated until the objective function converges. The way to alternately update the matrix is as follows:

When X is a rank p matrix, its projection on Stiefel manifold is: $\pi(X) = \arg\max_{Q^\top Q=I} \|X - Q\|_F^2 = U I_{n,k} V^\top$, where X's singular value decomposition is $U\Sigma V^\top$.

(1) Fixing L and B, E^m is updated by Eq. (4), where η is the step size.

$$E = \pi(E + \eta \nabla f(E)) \tag{4}$$

(2) Fixing L and $\{E^t\}_{t=1}^m$, B is updated by:

$$B = \arg\max_{B^\top B=I} tr(B^\top (M_m/m + L^\top C_m/m)B) \tag{5}$$

where $M_m = \sum_{t=1}^{m} (E^t)^\top K^t E^t$, $C_m = \sum_{t=1}^{m} \lambda_t \hat{X}^t E^t$ in task m.

(3) Fixing B and $\{E^t\}_{t=1}^m$, L is updated with the objective function about L:

$$\min_{L^\top L=I_k} \|L - (C_m B + \mu \Theta^{-1} L)\|_F^2 \tag{6}$$

where Θ is a diagonal matrix with all $\Theta_{i,i} = \frac{1}{2\|l_i\|_2}$, in which l_i represents the i-th row of L.

Finally, the clustering indicator matrix F is calculated by $F = EB$ using matrices E^m and B. K-means takes F as input to obtain clustering results.

3. Maximum a Posteriori Lifelong Spectral Clustering Algorithm

In the L^{2}SC algorithm, two libraries replace the representation of the original F, whose weights are represented by hyper-parameters λ and μ. The choice of clustering parameters usually relies on actual clustering division, which is unavailable in unsupervised learning. Meanwhile, the best hyper-parameters in each task may be different.

Therefore, we propose a Maximum a Posteriori Lifelong Spectral Clustering (MAPLSC) algorithm to select hyper-parameters in an online and unsupervised manner adaptively. It uses the maximum a posteriori probability of Bayesian inference as the basis for selecting optimal parameters.

Specifically, as for a hyper-parameter λ, the priori probability refers to the probability obtained based on experience and analysis, represented by $P_\lambda(Y|X)$. The posteriori probability is the probability after the clustering result is known, represented by $P(\lambda|Y)$. The λ with the maximum a posteriori probability is calculated with:

$$
\begin{aligned}
\lambda_{MAP} &= \arg\max_\lambda P(\lambda|Y) \\
&= \arg\max_\lambda \frac{P(Y|\lambda)P(\lambda)}{P(Y)} \\
&= \arg\max_\lambda P(Y|\lambda)P(\lambda) \\
&= \arg\max_\lambda \prod_{i=1}^{k}(P(Y_i|\lambda) \cdot P(\lambda))
\end{aligned}
\tag{7}
$$

where k is cluster number, $P(Y)$ is independent of λ so that it can be removed.

When there are two hyper-parameters: λ and μ, the priori probability is $P_{\lambda,\mu}(Y|X)$, and the posteriori probability is $P(\lambda, \mu|Y)$. $P(\lambda, \mu)$ takes the same value for each pair of λ and μ, so the desired hyper-parameters are:

$$(\lambda_{MAP}, \mu_{MAP}) = \arg\max_{\lambda,\mu} P(\lambda, \mu|Y)$$

$$= \arg\max_{\lambda,\mu} \sum_{i=1}^{k} \log P(Y_i|\lambda, \mu) \qquad (8)$$

In MAPLSC, the hyper-parameter pairs with different values are the prior information with equal probability, and the clustering divisions obtained by hyper-parameters are the posteriori information. Models are built for each value of λ and μ. Then L^{2}SC algorithm is run for every model. Finally, taking Eq. (8) as the selection standard, each task selects the values of λ and μ corresponding to the maximum a posteriori probability. The clustering result with selected λ and μ is the ultimate result for this task.

Algorithm 3.1 Maximum A Posteriori Probability Lifelong Spectral Clustering

Input: Clustering Tasks:$X^1, \ldots, X^T$
    Parameter Range: $\mu\_list(\forall\mu > 0)$, $\lambda\_list(\forall\lambda > 0)$
Initialize: Libraries:$B = \mathbf{1}_{k\times k}$, $L = \mathbf{0}_{d\times k}$
    $len1 = len(\lambda\_list)$, $len2 = len(\mu\_list)$
1: **while** new clustering task X^t comes **do**
2:    The maximum a posteriori probability $map^t = 0$.
3:    **for all** $\lambda \in \lambda\_list$ **do**
4:      **for all** $\mu \in \mu\_list$ **do**
5:        Initialize variables for this model to use later;
6:        **while** the objective function does not converge **do**
7:          Update E^t with (4);
8:          Update B with (5);
9:          Update L with (6);
10:        Calculate F with $F = E^t B$;
11:        Use F in K-means cluster, get $Ypred_{\lambda,\mu}$;
12:        Calculate posteriori probability $ptp_{\lambda,\mu}$ with (8);
13:        **if** $ptp_{\lambda,\mu} > map^t$ **then**
14:          $map^t = ptp_{\lambda,\mu}$
15:          $Ypred_{map}^t = Ypred_{\lambda,\mu}$
16:    $Ypred^t = Ypred_{map}^t$
Output: $Ypred^1, \ldots, Ypred^T$

4. Experiments

4.1. Datasets, evaluation indexes, and compared methods

We execute our experiments on commonly used datasets in clustering analysis: WebKB4,[a] Reuters[b] and 20NewsGroups.[c] The WebKB4 dataset is web page data from four universities. Reuters dataset is the text dataset of Reuters, which contains short news and their corresponding topics. 20NewsGroups dataset is the dataset of news articles containing 20 topics.

In the experiments, three commonly used clustering indexes are utilized to evaluate the performance: purity, normalized mutual information (NMI), and rand index (RI). We also record the running time of the algorithms.

MAPLSC algorithm is based on L^2SC, so the clustering performance is compared with the L^2SC algorithm. In addition, our algorithm is compared with three single-task spectral clustering models and five multi-task clustering models: Spectral Clustering (stSC),[6] Spectral clustering-union (uSC)[6] and One-step spectral Clustering (OnestepSC);[7] Multi-task Bregman Clustering (MBC),[8] Smart Multi-task Bregman Clustering (SMBC),[9] Smart Multi-task Kernel Clustering (SMKC),[9] Multi-Task Spectral Clustering (MTSC)[4] and Multi-Task Clustering with Model Relation Learning (MTCMRL).[10]

4.2. Experiment results

For each task, parameter values are chosen from the list [0.001, 0.01, 0.1, 1, 10, 100]. All results are the indexes' average and standard deviation values after ten operations. The clustering performance on the WebKB4 dataset is shown in Table 1. Performance on the Reuters dataset is shown in Table 2. Performance on the 20NewsGroups dataset is shown in Table 3.

There are differences in experimental data and operating environment, so this paper uses the results running in the local environment under the same condition to compare performance with L^2SC more reasonably. Table 1 and Table 2 show that the performance of the proposed algorithm on the WebKB4 dataset and Reuters dataset is sometimes better than that of L^2SC, and the average indexes value of MAPLSC exceeds that of L^2SC, which is because L^2SC runs under different pa-

---

[a]http://www.cs.cmu.edu/afs/cs.cmu.edu/project/theo20/www/data/
[b]http://www.cad.zju.edu.cn/home/dengcai/Data/TextData.html
[c]http://qwone.com/jason/20Newsgroups/

rameter settings where some are unsuitable. The first and third tasks of 20NewsGroups have three categories, while the second and fourth tasks have four categories, leading to negative transfer. Table 3 shows that on the 20NewsGroups dataset, our algorithm performs better in most tasks, which means that our parameter selection method can better cope with the negative transfer. The algorithms' running time is shown in Table 4. The speed of the MAPLSC algorithm is slower than that of the L²SC algorithm because it needs to calculate the posteriori

Table 1. Comparison of Evaluation Index on WebKB4 dataset (mean ± standard deviation)

Metrics		stSC	uSC	OnestepSC	MBC	SMBC	SMKC	MTSC	MTCMRL	L²SC	MAPLSC
Task1	Purity(%)	62.66±0.00	59.78±0.31	66.89±0.63	63.95±4.07	64.62±4.05	60.59±3.70	65.92±0.68	74.40±1.16	79.75±0.27	**80.00±0.00**
	NMI(%)	13.95±0.00	13.15±1.68	14.56±3.44	26.44±3.73	25.53±2.74	14.14±6.38	25.73±0.08	38.71±1.47	47.80±0.43	**47.88±0.03**
	RI(%)	59.89±0.00	58.83±0.04	64.76±1.06	61.64±3.58	62.58±2.65	59.45±1.62	62.85±0.76	**73.47±0.64**	72.57±0.17	72.65±0.05
Task2	Purity(%)	62.00±0.00	67.00±0.28	68.40±0.02	68.12±1.81	68.06±0.92	60.73±2.56	69.00±0.84	72.08±2.19	**80.30±0.20**	80.28±0.19
	NMI(%)	16.72±0.00	20.28±1.81	20.56±2.39	27.22±3.92	27.02±3.61	13.58±3.52	26.57±1.63	33.42±3.25	**42.41±0.43**	41.67±0.24
	RI(%)	57.12±0.00	60.38±2.06	64.81±1.52	68.04±2.46	68.32±3.29	58.31±1.19	66.57±0.85	**69.94±1.72**	69.46±0.40	69.18±0.28
Task3	Purity(%)	69.21±0.27	59.80±0.27	69.80±0.55	64.86±5.36	68.04±2.28	66.01±4.13	68.23±0.55	**76.47±3.15**	74.70±0.44	74.51±0.00
	NMI(%)	29.24±0.30	15.60±2.42	22.55±2.36	26.50±3.97	28.32±3.86	22.09±5.95	29.33±0.99	40.97±5.26	**46.33±1.17**	45.59±0.00
	RI(%)	66.37±0.19	61.84±0.60	66.16±0.22	65.86±4.09	67.34±3.23	65.02±2.41	65.56±0.87	76.34±4.85	**78.50±0.68**	78.05±0.00
Task4	Purity(%)	69.61±0.00	70.42±0.23	71.31±0.92	72.18±4.17	71.21±4.08	69.82±2.58	69.93±0.46	**78.23±2.68**	76.15±1.87	78.17±0.83
	NMI(%)	33.78±0.00	33.15±0.49	36.84±0.59	39.97±5.24	39.53±2.74	30.31±4.17	45.64±0.66	**49.23±2.17**	46.46±2.40	48.53±1.13
	RI(%)	66.93±0.00	67.50±0.54	68.69±0.94	70.27±3.59	70.29±2.65	67.62±1.85	60.72±1.15	79.01±1.54	77.31±2.40	**79.19±0.27**
All Tasks	Avg.Purity(%)	65.87±0.07	64.25±0.27	69.10±0.53	67.28±3.85	67.98±2.83	64.29±3.24	68.27±0.64	75.19±2.25	77.73±2.86	**78.34±2.69**
	Avg.NMI(%)	23.42±0.07	20.55±1.60	23.63±2.19	30.03±4.22	30.10±4.05	20.03±4.50	31.82±1.07	40.58±3.04	45.75±2.74	**46.05±3.13**
	Avg.RI(%)	62.63±0.05	62.14±0.81	66.11±0.94	66.45±3.43	70.29±2.65	62.60±1.76	63.93±0.91	74.69±2.19	74.46±4.40	**74.83±4.66**

Table 2. Comparison of Evaluation Index on Reuters dataset (mean ± standard deviation)

Metrics		stSC	uSC	OnestepSC	MBC	SMBC	SMKC	MTSC	MTCMRL	L²SC	MAPLSC
Task1	Purity(%)	95.63±0.00	85.44±0.00	94.66±0.00	73.30±9.27	89.90±1.40	95.75±0.72	**97.57±0.00**	**97.57±0.00**	93.22±4.59	92.48±4.86
	NMI(%)	82.72±0.00	60.54±0.20	75.89±1.52	61.39±2.32	77.92±3.31	84.17±2.05	**89.49±0.00**	**89.49±0.00**	81.42±9.11	79.71±9.94
	RI(%)	94.64±0.00	82.22±0.00	91.44±1.06	73.83±7.26	88.35±1.77	94.35±0.88	**96.83±0.00**	**96.83±0.00**	91.63±5.70	91.00±5.74
Task2	Purity(%)	84.62±0.00	70.00±0.00	86.92±0.00	70.19±0.73	92.88±0.38	90.96±1.15	96.15±0.54	97.31±0.54	**96.70±0.00**	**96.70±0.00**
	NMI(%)	62.91±0.00	53.17±0.00	64.45±0.00	53.43±7.81	79.53±2.74	75.76±2.65	84.80±1.62	88.93±2.46	**99.18±0.00**	**99.18±0.00**
	RI(%)	80.83±0.00	55.95±0.00	82.52±0.00	71.77±1.08	90.44±0.44	88.12±1.35	95.07±0.55	96.41±0.77	**99.18±0.00**	**99.18±0.00**
Task3	Purity(%)	75.26±0.00	82.63±0.00	76.05±1.86	72.36±9.78	75.24±2.98	76.50±2.07	90.79±0.37	79.45±0.00	83.70±8.60	**88.05±8.22**
	NMI(%)	54.00±0.00	59.85±0.00	61.74±1.44	46.35±6.70	54.11±5.41	52.72±2.79	73.37±0.66	**79.45±0.00**	58.30±13.88	65.08±13.34
	RI(%)	70.14±0.00	78.01±0.00	74.64±1.54	74.34±3.64	70.01±4.33	72.73±2.89	88.33±0.49	**93.13±0.00**	78.37±11.39	84.31±10.53
All Tasks	Avg.Purity(%)	85.17±0.00	79.36±0.00	85.88±0.62	71.95±6.59	86.01±1.59	87.74±1.32	94.96±0.46	96.36±0.18	92.05±8.90	**96.50±3.08**
	Avg.NMI(%)	66.54±0.00	79.36±0.18	67.35±0.99	53.72±5.61	70.52±3.33	70.88±2.50	83.63±1.14	85.96±0.82	78.81±20.67	**86.41±11.90**
	Avg.RI(%)	81.87±0.00	78.73±0.90	82.87±0.87	73.31±7.33	82.93±2.18	85.07±1.71	93.54±0.52	95.45±0.26	89.73±11.74	**95.48±4.25**

Table 3. Comparison of Evaluation Index on 20NewsGroups dataset (mean ± standard deviation)

Metrics		stSC	uSC	OnestepSC	MBC	SMBC	SMKC	MTSC	MTCMRL	L²SC	MAPLSC
Task1	Purity(%)	63.89±0.15	44.52±0.49	66.53±1.98	47.69±2.13	50.45±5.41	73.89±1.36	77.27±0.78	81.59±1.45	96.40±0.07	**96.46±0.00**
	NMI(%)	30.77±0.33	4.35±0.33	38.74±1.10	19.29±2.76	24.80±3.18	37.75±2.68	45.35±0.83	49.38±1.55	85.81±0.26	**86.12±0.00**
	RI(%)	61.27±0.30	56.32±0.24	65.54±1.48	48.93±7.45	54.19±0.72	72.09±1.17	74.31±0.69	78.45±1.47	95.31±0.09	**95.38±0.00**
Task2	Purity(%)	53.54±0.48	40.89±0.00	55.97±0.13	48.56±2.96	50.46±1.31	66.81±1.44	63.55±0.78	65.06±0.77	**74.21±2.95**	73.60±0.00
	NMI(%)	34.68±0.20	9.92±0.00	32.86±0.08	21.27±3.45	23.23±7.97	40.76±2.88	42.52±0.33	44.21±0.39	68.11±2.46	**69.10±0.00**
	RI(%)	60.08±0.66	65.51±0.00	62.54±0.17	64.31±2.16	63.82±4.60	76.26±1.01	70.23±0.21	72.19±0.18	81.82±1.87	**81.93±0.00**
Task3	Purity(%)	59.07±0.00	54.74±0.00	59.87±1.68	49.85±3.05	52.34±1.49	60.40±2.15	68.86±1.26	77.86±0.69	97.43±0.10	**97.46±0.00**
	NMI(%)	34.58±0.09	17.63±0.00	39.25±1.93	20.53±5.41	23.37±4.01	30.24±1.12	38.81±1.56	46.05±1.31	88.27±0.50	**88.36±0.00**
	RI(%)	61.08±0.01	58.10±0.00	61.47±1.51	48.35±2.76	52.67±0.89	65.23±0.98	64.06±1.30	75.14±0.58	96.65±0.14	**96.68±0.00**
Task4	Purity(%)	51.51±0.14	52.35±0.45	54.37±0.29	46.33±2.86	75.18±4.77	68.69±0.35	67.35±0.35	74.85±0.89	86.51±0.97	**86.80±0.00**
	NMI(%)	32.53±0.32	26.13±0.87	34.12±0.73	21.37±3.48	44.09±4.78	41.15±0.95	44.03±0.31	54.02±0.65	86.51±0.97	**86.59±0.00**
	RI(%)	52.54±0.19	64.70±0.25	54.70±0.29	46.61±2.70	78.99±2.71	74.68±0.41	70.35±0.41	74.56±0.79	96.46±0.30	**96.59±0.00**
All Tasks	Avg.Purity(%)	56.99±0.19	48.12±0.23	59.18±1.02	48.11±2.75	57.01±4.35	67.45±1.33	69.25±0.64	74.91±0.93	**91.12±11.29**	91.02±11.62
	Avg.NMI(%)	33.03±0.24	14.51±0.30	36.24±0.96	20.62±3.78	28.12±4.98	37.48±1.93	42.68±0.76	48.39±0.98	82.18±9.45	**82.59±9.04**
	Avg.RI(%)	58.73±0.20	61.16±0.12	61.46±0.89	52.05±3.77	62.42±2.23	72.07±0.89	69.74±0.41	76.15±0.85	92.56±7.19	**92.65±7.17**

Table 4. Comparison of Running Time (mean ± standard deviation)

	stSC	uSC	OnestepSC	MBC	SMBC	SMKC	MTSC	MTCMRL	L²SC	MAPLSC
WebKB(/seconds)	1.22±0.01	1.21±0.03	600.91±26.60	6.97±1.08	5.77±0.14	34.79±0.47	69.72±1.26	14.51±1.30	2.69±0.02	3.00±0.27
Reuters(/seconds)	0.87±0.20	1.31±0.22	1410.47±47.47	3.91±0.19	5.47±0.14	16.86±0.84	71.79±1.20	8.26±0.28	1.32±0.01	2.19±0.20
20NewsGroups(/seconds)	2.92±0.07	5.27±0.02	3500.16±77.70	19.19±1.04	26.54±1.30	316.22±3.53	44.01±3.53	384.52±19.55	9.95±0.29	12.66±0.57

probabilities and select the maximum one, but its running time is shorter than some single-task algorithms and all other multi-task algorithms.

5. Conclusion

Cluster analysis can help research related to sustainable development, in which lifelong clustering can handle continuous tasks. This paper proposes a Maximum a Posteriori Lifelong Spectral Clustering algorithm. Our algorithm relies on the maximum a posteriori probability method in the Bayesian Inference, which is more suitable for the unsupervised scene. So it can adaptively choose better hyper-parameters in each task during the clustering process. Experiments show that the performance of the proposed method is superior to that of the grid search method, and the hyper-parameters selected by the algorithm perform well in lifelong clustering. In the future, we will explore the selection of the number of cluster centers and task replay to optimize the algorithm further to improve lifelong clustering performance.

Acknowledgments

This work is supported by the National Natural Science Foundation of China (No. 61976247).

References

1. S. Thrun and T. M. Mitchell. Lifelong robot learning. Robotics and Autonomous Systems 15, 25–46 (1995).
2. B. Liu. Lifelong machine learning: a paradigm for continuous learning. Front. Comput. Sci. 11, 359–361 (2017).
3. G. Sun, Y. Cong, Q. Wang, J. Li, and Y. Fu. Lifelong Spectral Clustering. AAAI 34, 5867–5874 (2020).
4. Y. Yang, Z. Ma, Y. Yang, F. Nie, and H. T. Shen. Multitask Spectral Clustering by Exploring Intertask Correlation. IEEE Transactions on Cybernetics 45, 1083–1094 (2015).
5. J. Shi and J. Malik. Normalized cuts and image segmentation. IEEE Trans. Pattern Anal. Machine Intell. 22, 888–905 (2000).

6. A. Y. Ng, M. I. Jordan, and Y. Weiss. On spectral clustering: analysis and an algorithm. Proceedings of the 14th International Conference on Neural Information Processing Systems: Natural and Synthetic 849–856 (MIT Press, 2001).

7. X. Zhu, W. He, Y. Li, Y. Yang, S. Zhang, R. Hu, and Y. Zhu. One-Step Spectral Clustering via Dynamically Learning Affinity Matrix and Subspace. Proceedings of the AAAI Conference on Artificial Intelligence 31, (2017).

8. J. Zhang and C. Zhang. Multitask Bregman clustering. Neurocomputing 74, 1720–1734 (2011).

9. X. Zhang, X. Zhang, and H. Liu. Smart Multitask Bregman Clustering and Multitask Kernel Clustering. ACM Trans. Knowl. Discov. Data 10, 8:1-8:29 (2015).

10. X. Zhang, X. Zhang, H. Liu, and J. Luo. Multi-Task Clustering with Model Relation Learning. Proceedings of the Twenty-Seventh International Joint Conference on Artificial Intelligence 3132–3140 (2018).

Unsupervised clustering ensemble for traffic level prediction

Jian Wang* and Jin Guo

School of Information Science and Technology, Southwest Jiaotong University
Chengdu, 611756, China
*wj_xnjd@my.swjtu.edu.cn
www.swjtu.edu.cn

Yueying Li, Ran Hao and Hongjun Wang†

School of Computing and Artificial Intelligence, Southwest Jiaotong University
Chengdu, 611756, China
†wanghongjun@swjtu.edu.cn
www.swjtu.edu.cn

Traffic accidents are still an important cause of death. Predicting the severity of possible traffic accidents is helpful to speed up the decision-making of accident treatment plans and reduce casualties. Therefore, it is expected to establish a sufficient and reliable severity prediction model in traffic accidents. Up to now, there are a lot of research about traffic accident prediction. But traditional methods are susceptible to noise and not efficient enough. To conquer this challenge, we utilized a multi-diversified clustering ensemble approach to predict traffic accidents. Finally, 12 real datasets and 7 algorithms are used to carry out extensive comparison experiments, whose results show that clustering results generated by MDEC_HC have better robustness and accuracy.

Keywords: Clustering ensemble; traffic accident prediction; machine learning.

1. Introduction

People should be concerned about road traffic accidents, not only because it has become the eighth leading cause of death, but also because of the uncertainty of their occurrence.[1] Predicting the severity of possible traffic accidents is helpful to speed up the decision-making of accident treatment plans and reduce casualties.[2,3]

In previous works, clustering has been used for traffic accident prediction, but its effect is not ideal. Clustering ensemble improves the quality and robustness of clustering results. Therefore, we utilize a multi-diversified clustering ensemble approach called MDEC.[4] MDEC focused on the potential diversity of similar-different metrics, tackled the problem of how to produce and aggregate mass diversity indicators.

The contributions of this paper can be summarized as follows. Firstly, we creatively applied clustering ensemble to traffic accident prediction. Secondly, experiments conducted on some real-world datasets verify that MDEC is indeed effective and stable for predicting the severity of possible traffic accidents.

The remainder of this paper is organized as follows. The related work is reviewed in Section 2. The proposed model is presented in Section 3. The experimental results are shown in Section 4. Finally, conclusions are reported in Section 5.

2. Related Work

2.1. *Traffic accident prediction*

In the 1980s, primarily statistical was first used to predict road accidents to model the incidence of road accidents.[5] Each statistical model had advantages and strong limitations in its application.

Machine learning technology is widely used in traffic accidents and has excellent performance.[6-9] Deep learning methods are used to predict basic traffic parameters, including speed, volume, and so on. As a kind of deep learning technology, the Artificial Neural Network (ANN) model saves labor costs in the process of model training and prediction, but requires large and heterogeneous data sources for robust models. On the other hand, in predicting the severity of traffic accidents, the interpretability of the current ANN is poor,[7] which can not provide traffic experts with enough learnable information.

Except machine learning, meta-learning offers an effective solution to learn how to learn, and develop quickly, which is used for traffic accident prediction model might be a new choice.[10,11]

2.2. *Clustering ensemble*

Clustering is an unsupervised method of discovering natural groupings between samples and patterns. So the clustering method can save time and labor costs.[12] Since a single clustering method uses a specific optimization method, it needs to be evaluated before being used.

In real-world, multi-source, noisy data is hard to avoid. In recent years, clustering ensemble has attracted more and more attention because of the possibility of obtaining robust results even in the environment of multi-data sources and noise interference.[13] Ye et al.[14] found that traditional cluster ensemble just used the labels produced by base learning algorithms and applied nonnegative matrix factorization to clustering ensemble-based on these dark knowledge. Some researchers pay attention to the limitation of influence from low-quality base clusterings. For example, Huang et al.[15] focused on ensemble-driven cluster uncertainty estimation and local weighting. Limitations of scale application because of efficiency bottleneck also receive attention.[16] Huang et al.[17] dealt with the extensibility and nonlinear separability of the integration generation stage and consensus function stage in the integrated clustering.

3. Model

MDEC is proposed to tackle high dimensional data better, by exploiting the metrics and subspaces diversity, whose framework is shown in Fig. 1. Let sample M times, which leading to M datasets and M random subspaces.

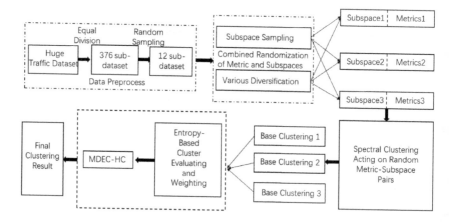

Fig. 1.   The framework of MDEC.

MDEC_HC is the MDEC framework joint with hierarchical clustering. The Integration Driven Cluster Index (ECI) is an indicator of the reliability of every cluster in an integration and computed as

$$ECI(C_i) = exp\left(-\frac{\sum_{m=1}^{M}(-\sum_{j=1}^{K_m} p(C_i, C_j^m) \log_2 p(C_i, C_j^m))}{M}\right), \quad (1)$$

where $p(C_i, C_j^m) = \frac{|C_i \bigcup C_j^m|}{|C_i|}$ is the ratio of samples in C_i appearing in C_j^m, and $p(C_i, C_j^m) \in [0, 1]$. C_i is the ith cluster, C_j^m is the jth cluster in the mth base clustering in the ensemble, and K_m denotes the total number of clusters in the m-base clustering.

The locally weighted cross-correlations matrix B is computed as below

$$B = \left\{ \frac{1}{M} \sum_{m=1}^{M} w_i^m \cdot \delta_{ij}^m \right\}_{N \times N}, \tag{2}$$

$$w_i^m = ECI(WhichCls^m(x_i)), \tag{3}$$

$$\delta_{ij}^m = \begin{cases} 1 \; if \; WhichCls^m(x_i) = WhichCls^m(x_j) \\ 0 \qquad\qquad otherwise \end{cases}, \tag{4}$$

where $WhichCls^m(x_i)$ indicates the x_i belongs to which cluster in the mth base clustering. δ_{ij}^m demonstrates whether x_i and x_j appear in the same cluster of the underlying the mth base clustering. w_i^m weights each cluster in accordance with the ECI value.

4. Experiments

In this section, we use 12 real traffic accident datasets derived from a huge traffic accident dataset and compare our algorithm with 6 state-of-the-art algorithms to evaluate the prediction model. Firstly, the experimental Settings are briefly introduced, and then two evaluation indexes are adopted to illustrate the results.

4.1. Datasets

The origin of the 12 datasets is a huge traffic accident dataset, which includes 1.6 million accident information. To get the result rapidly, we divide the big dataset into 375 and choose 12, which is presented in Table 1.

4.2. Experimental settings

To prove the superiority of the MDEC_HC model in traffic accident prediction, ten-fold cross-validation experiments are established. For each dataset, seven algorithms are used for the experiment. The comparison algorithms in this paper include: MDEC_HC,[4] NMFCE,[14] MDEC_SC,[4] MDEC_BG,[4] USENC,[17] LWEA,[15] LWGP.[15]

Table 1.   Summary of generated datasets.

No.	Dataset	Objects	Features
D1	Casualties_212	10000	14
D2	Casualties_210	10000	14
D3	Casualties_206	10000	14
D4	Casualties_201	10000	14
D5	Casualties_199	10000	14
D6	Casualties_180	10000	14
D7	Casualties_175	10000	14
D8	Casualties_170	10000	14
D9	Casualties_169	10000	14
D10	Casualties_153	10000	14
D11	Casualties_151	10000	14
D12	Casualties_140	10000	14

4.3. Evaluation metric

To evaluate the application of MDEC better, this paper uses two evaluation indexes, namely accuracy and entropy.

4.3.1. Accuracy

Accuracy is the ratio between the number of specimens accurately predicted and the number of specimens predicted, which can be computed as $accuracy = \frac{TP+TN}{total}$. TP is the number of special samples, whose prediction and actual are positive. TN is the number of special samples, whose prediction and actual are negative. So that the smaller the value, the better the predicted results.

4.3.2. Entropy

Entropy is a measure of the magnitude of the uncertainty contained in the information, which is defined as $entropy = -\sum_{i=1}^{N} p_i \log_2 p_i$. So that the bigger the value, the better the predicted results.

4.4. Results

In this section, the accuracy and entropy of 7 algorithms are analyzed on 12 datasets to evaluate the application effect of MDEC in traffic accident prediction.

4.4.1. Accuracy

The results are shown in Table 2, which has a comparison of accuracy and stabilize between 7 traffic accident prediction algorithms on 12 datasets. And we use numbers in parentheses indicates to form a ranking list. According to the analysis results, MDEC_HC always ranks top two, and the probability of being number one is 83.3%. It is obvious that MDEC_HC is more accurate most time. And even though in D11 and D12, the gap between MDEC_HC and the top one is small.

Table 2. Comparison of accuracy between 7 traffic accident prediction algorithms on 12 datasets.

Dataset	MDEC_HC	NMFCE	MDEC_SC	MDEC_BG	USENC	LWEA	LWGP
D1	**0.706(1)**	0.411(7)	0.469(3)	0.692(2)	0.437(5)	0.443(4)	0.437(5)
D2	**0.719(1)**	0.673(2)	0.477(4)	0.575(3)	0.454(7)	0.456(5)	0.456(5)
D3	**0.677(1)**	0.418(5)	0.388(7)	0.431(3)	0.408(7)	0.421(4)	0.409(6)
D4	**0.689(1)**	0.451(6)	0.431(7)	0.662(2)	0.462(4)	0.468(3)	0.462(4)
D5	**0.628(1)**	0.413(7)	0.434(6)	0.499(2)	0.445(4)	0.445(5)	0.454(3)
D6	**0.535(1)**	0.446(6)	0.390(7)	0.519(2)	0.479(3)	0.473(4)	0.473(4)
D7	**0.716(1)**	0.507(4)	0.588(2)	0.523(3)	0.440(6)	0.442(5)	0.440(6)
D8	**0.738(1)**	0.402(7)	0.511(2)	0.475(3)	0.428(4)	0.428(4)	0.428(4)
D9	**0.679(1)**	0.516(2)	0.434(5)	0.429(6)	0.504(3)	0.428(7)	0.435(4)
D10	0.541(2)	0.440(6)	**0.564(1)**	0.370(7)	0.442(4)	0.442(4)	0.443(3)
D11	0.536(2)	0.399(7)	**0.570(1)**	0.503(3)	0.499(4)	0.446(6)	0.450(5)
D12	**0.691(1)**	0.471(3)	0.344(7)	0.527(2)	0.458(5)	0.460(4)	0.458(5)
AvgRank	1.17	5.17	4.33	3.17	4.67	4.58	4.5

4.4.2. Entropy

The results based on entropy are shown in Table 3. It is obvious that MDEC_HC and MDEC_SC are ranked ahead of all other algorithms. MDEC is always in the top three. MDEC's average rank is 1.67, which is behind MDEC_SC. But at the same time, it is more consistent.

On the 12 datasets, the algorithm shows comparable accuracy and entropy with the other algorithms. Still, there are also some relatively low, such as D6. This is because the original dataset has a long period of traffic accidents and considers different related factors. We use the aggregation method to gain stable results. Above all, it is obvious that MDEC_HC is better at predicting traffic accidents.

Table 3. Comparison of entropy between 7 traffic accident prediction algorithms on 12 datasets.

Dataset	MDEC_HC	NMFCE	MDEC_SC	MDEC_BG	USENC	LWEA	LWGP
D1	**0.379(1)**	0.399(7)	0.384(3)	0.383(2)	0.397(4)	0.397(4)	0.397(4)
D2	**0.285(1)**	0.345(4)	0.309(2)	0.341(3)	0.350(6)	0.346(5)	0.350(6)
D3	0.337(2)	0.355(5)	**0.326(1)**	0.352(3)	0.355(5)	0.354(4)	0.355(5)
D4	0.381(2)	0.402(4)	**0.380(1)**	0.383(3)	0.402(4)	0.402(4)	0.402(4)
D5	0.378(2)	0.398(3)	**0.367(1)**	0.398(3)	0.401(5)	0.401(5)	0.401(5)
D6	0.336(2)	0.357(7)	**0.332(1)**	0.352(3)	0.356(6)	0.355(4)	0.355(4)
D7	0.364(3)	0.378(4)	**0.361(1)**	0.362(2)	0.378(4)	0.378(4)	0.378(4)
D8	0.356(2)	0.380(5)	**0.354(1)**	0.374(3)	0.380(5)	0.379(4)	0.380(5)
D9	0.327(2)	0.356(4)	**0.320(1)**	0.345(3)	0.356(4)	0.358(7)	0.357(6)
D10	**0.238(1)**	0.347(4)	0.306(2)	0.337(3)	0.347(4)	0.347(4)	0.347(4)
D11	**0.355(1)**	0.362(4)	0.360(3)	0.356(2)	0.365(5)	0.368(6)	0.368(6)
D12	**0.273(1)**	0.381(7)	0.311(2)	0.376(3)	0.380(4)	0.380(4)	0.380(4)
Avg Rank	1.67	4.83	1.58	2.75	4.67	4.58	4.75

5. Conclusion

Effective prediction of traffic accidents and classification of their severity are conducive to improving safety guarantees. In this paper, using the clustering ensemble model to predict traffic accidents is novel. Extensive experiments are carried out on 12 real traffic accident datasets using 7 algorithms, whose results show that MDEC_HC is more stable, and its results are more accurate. Compared with previous work, a more sufficient and reliable severity prediction model in traffic accidents is established and would be beneficial to guide the follow-up treatment of traffic accidents.

References

1. W. H. Organization *et al.*, Global status report on road safety 2018: summary (2018).
2. J. Lee, T. Yoon, S. Kwon and J. Lee, Model evaluation for forecasting traffic accident severity in rainy seasons using machine learning algorithms: Seoul city study, *Applied Sciences* **10** (2020).
3. S. Ebrahim and Q. Hossain, An artificial neural network model for road accident prediction: A case study of khulna metropolitan city, *International Conference on Civil Engineering for Sustainable Development(ICCESD)* **5193**, 1 (2018).
4. D. Huang, C.-D. Wang, J.-H. Lai and C.-K. Kwoh, Toward multidiversified ensemble clustering of high-dimensional data: From subspaces to

metrics and beyond, *IEEE Transactions on Cybernetics* (2021).

5. K. El-Basyouny and T. Sayed, Collision prediction models using multivariate poisson-lognormal regression, *Accident Analysis & Prevention* **41**, 820 (2009).

6. H. Wenhao, H. Haikun, L. Man, H. Weisong, S. Guojie and X. Kunqing, Deep architecture for traffic flow prediction, in *International Conference on Advanced Data Mining and Applications*, 2013.

7. M. I. Sameen and B. Pradhan, Severity prediction of traffic accidents with recurrent neural networks, *Applied Sciences* **7** (2017).

8. J. Baek and and K. Sohn, Deep-learning architectures to forecast bus ridership at the stop and stop-to-stop levels for dense and crowded bus networks, *Applied Artificial Intelligence* **30**, 861 (2016).

9. D. Impedovo, V. Dentamaro, G. Pirlo and L. Sarcinella, Trafficwave: Generative deep learning architecture for vehicular traffic flow prediction, *Applied Sciences* **9** (2019).

10. J. Zhang, J. Song, Y. Yao and L. Gao, Curriculum-based meta-learning, in *Proceedings of the 29th ACM International Conference on Multimedia*, 2021.

11. J. Zhang, J. Song, L. Gao, Y. Liu and H. T. Shen, Progressive meta-learning with curriculum, *IEEE Transactions on Circuits and Systems for Video Technology* (2022).

12. D. Rajjat, F. Thorben and D. Elena, An adaptive clustering approach for accident prediction, in *2021 IEEE International Intelligent Transportation Systems Conference (ITSC)*, 2021.

13. W. Yang, Y. Zhang, H. Wang, P. Deng and T. Li, Hybrid genetic model for clustering ensemble, *Knowledge-Based Systems* **231** (2021).

14. Y. Wenting, W. Hongjun, Y. Shan, L. Tianrui and Y. Yan, Nonnegative matrix factorization for clustering ensemble based on dark knowledge, *Knowledge-Based Systems* **163**, 624 (2019).

15. H. Dong, W. Chang-Dong and L. Jian-Huang, Locally weighted ensemble clustering, *IEEE Transactions on Cybernetics* **48**, 1460 (2018).

16. L. Hongfu, W. Junjie, L. Tongliang, T. Dacheng and F. Yun, Spectral ensemble clustering via weighted k-means: Theoretical and practical evidence, *IEEE Transactions on Knowledge and Data Engineering* **29**, 1129 (2017).

17. H. Dong, W. Chang-Dong, W. Jian-Sheng, L. Jian-Huang and K. Chee-Keong, Ultra-scalable spectral clustering and ensemble clustering, *IEEE Transactions on Knowledge and Data Engineering* **32**, 1212 (2019).

568

Graph learning for incomplete multi-view spectral clustering

Win Sandar Htay*, Yan Yang† and Yiling Zhang‡
School of Computing and Artificial Intelligence, Southwest Jiaotong University
Chengdu, China
*sandar@my.swjtu.edu.cn
†yyang@swjtu.edu.cn
‡yee@my.swjtu.edu.cn

Multi-view clustering has been attracting the attention of researchers in recent years and is one of the popular machine learning and unsupervised learning techniques. In conventional multi-view clustering, it is challenging to handle multi-view clustering containing missing views, called incomplete multi-view clustering. To address this problem, we propose a novel Graph Learning for Incomplete Multi-view Spectral Clustering (namely GIMSC) algorithm to perform incomplete multi-view clustering tasks. GIMSC can simultaneously integrate individual graph learning, fusion graph learning and spectral clustering into a unified framework, which is able to learn the consensus representation shared by all views via incomplete graphs construction. GIMSC learns the adaptive local structure for all views pre-constructed by k-nearest neighbor. Then, we construct the fusion graph with auto-weighted learning to explore the consensus similarity matrix for incomplete graphs with different sizes, which will reduce the negative influence of outliers. We introduce an index matrix to achieve the transformation among incomplete and complete graphs with respect to each view. An iterative optimization algorithm is proposed to solve the optimization procedure. In experiments, we extensively conduct our method on four incomplete multi-view datasets, showing the proposed method outperforms the existing state-of-the-art methods.

Keywords: Incomplete multi-view clustering; graph learning; graph fusion; spectral clustering.

1. Introduction

With the progress of the Internet and communication technology (ICT), a huge amount of data has emerged from various sources or multiple views [1]. For example, a web site is characterized by links, texts, images, etc. [2], it also can be represented as different views. Clustering with such kinds of data is generally adverted to as multi-view clustering (MVC). Existing MVC approaches normally focus on all views of data that are required to complete. However, the requirement is frequently challenging to satisfy because some views of samples are missing in real-world applications, called incomplete multi-view clustering (IVC) [1]. The graph construction in IVC is essential to achieve clustering. However, it is not possible to construct a complete graph to fully connect all the data points due to the lack of some views. Trivedi et al. [13] proposed to complete an incomplete graph of the view where the instance associated with the Laplacian matrix of the complete view is missing. Even though, the biggest limitation of this method is that it is required to complete at least one view [1, 4]. Yang et al. [5], Gao et al. [2], a filling method is used to complete the missing instances of the corresponding view by taking the average of features values. However, if the multi-view data has a large number of missing information in each view, this approach may decrease the clustering performance in practice. The methods [1, 7, 12] introduced the missing information recovery-based technique. Although various methods have been proposed to handle IVC problems e.g., [1, 2, 6], they still have many problems to be addressed. For example, most existing methods (a) cannot work if the data is more than two views e.g., [6], (b) require many parameters to obtain the optimal results e.g., [7, 8, 12], (c) cannot handle the integration of different sizes of incomplete graphs e.g., [3] and (d) require at least one view to be complete e.g., [1, 4]. Our wok can solve all these problems.

The contributions in this paper include: (1) we propose a novel unified framework called Graph Learning algorithm for Incomplete Multiview Spectral Clustering, which can handle complete and incomplete multi-view cases simultaneously, (2) the proposed method integrates the consensus graph construction and spectral clustering into a unified framework for all kinds of incomplete multi-view data. To achieve explicit clustering performance, GIMSC learns the consensus similarity graph matrix of different incomplete views and integrates multiple graphs of all views to generate a unified graph, (3) we assign different weights for different incomplete graphs to avoid the influence of noise and outliers. Additionally, in our proposed method, there is no limitation to the number of views and any number of views to be complete.

The rest of the paper is organized as follows. Section 2 briefly describes some related works to our proposed method. Section 3 presents the proposed method, algorithm and Section 4 offers some analysis of the optimization steps in details. Next in Section 5, for several multi-view datasets, experimental results and analysis of the proposed method are conducted. Finally, in Section 6, we discuss the conclusion of the whole paper.

2. Related Works

2.1. *Preliminary concept of multi-view spectral clustering*

Spectral clustering is able to partition both graphical and non-graphical data.

In spectral clustering, data points should be linked to each other without convex borders, as opposed to traditional clustering approaches, which cluster data points are based on their compactness [1, 3]. The problem of multi-view spectral clustering can be expressed, $F \in R^{n \times c}$ as follow:

$$\min_{F, F^T F = I} \sum_{v=1}^{m} Tr(F^T L_Z F) \tag{1}$$

where $Z\,(Z \geq 0)$ denotes the symmetric similarity graph matrix from the data and has non-negative instances.

Many multi-view spectral clustering algorithms have been presented, e.g., Xu et al. [1] proposed a more general framework to address the incomplete multi-view clustering problem. To construct the graph of individual view, low-rank representation is adopted which gives better clustering performance in revealing the intrinsic subspace structure of data. Then, the final clustering results are obtained by performing K-means on the common representation [1, 2, 3, 7].

3. The Proposed Method

3.1. Graph learning for incomplete multi-view spectral clustering

In this section, we present the proposed incomplete multi-view clustering method, GIMSC. GIMSC is a novel framework that can simultaneously integrate fusion graph construction and spectral clustering for incomplete multi-view cases, which give explicit clustering results. Different from the existing IVC method, an efficient and effective graph representation learning strategy is introduced based on the local manifold learning to obtain the optimal common representation.

3.2. Learning an initial graph construction

We first introduce how to construct an effective nearest neighbor graph matrix $Z^v \in R^{n_v \times n_v}$ which only contains the un-missing instances in the vth view, where any elements Z_{ij}^v defines the similarity between data points Y_i and Y_j in the vth view and n_v is the number of un-missing elements in the vth view. Then the graph Z^v of each view is obtained by the following formulation [5, 10]:

$$Z_{ij} = \left(-\frac{A_{ij}}{2\beta} + e_1\right)_+, \qquad s.t.\, Z_{ij}^v \geq 0\,, 1^T Z_i^v = 1 \tag{2}$$

3.3. Multiple graph fusion

After generating the graphs for all views, the general concept is to fuse the different sizes of multiple incomplete graphs into a unified graph via $U^v =$

$G^{vT}Z^vG^v$. $G^v \in R^{n_v \times n}$ is an index matrix used to determine the relationship between complete and incomplete graphs. G^v can be obtained by removing the rows of original data points whose all elements are zero in diagonal matrix D. Index matrix G^v is defined as follows:

$$G_{ij}^v = \begin{cases} 1, & \text{if } Y_j^v \text{ is the unmissing data instance } X_i^v \\ 0, & \text{otherwise} \end{cases} \tag{3}$$

An automatically weighted graph fusion is presented by assigning the different weights to different views. The graph fusion problem can be formulated as follows:

$$\min_{U^*} \sum_{v=1}^m w_v \| U^* - G^{vT}Z^vG^v \|_F^2, \quad s.t. \ u_{ij}^* \geq 0, \ 1^T u_i^* = 1, w_v \geq 0, \ 1^T w = 1 \tag{4}$$

where the weight w_v represents the importance of v-th view. According to Theorem 1, the weight of each view is automatically determined as w_v [3, 5].

$$w_v = \frac{1}{2\|U^* - G^{vT}Z^vG^v\|_F} \tag{5}$$

3.4. Learning data clustering

This subsection intends to solve the final clustering problem. Matrix U of the Laplacian matrix L_U is defined as $L_U = D_U - (U^T + U)/2$, where D_U is the diagonal matrix which denotes $D_{ii} = \frac{U_{ij}+U_{ji}}{2}$. However, it is difficult to satisfy the requirement, the following Theorem 2 can handle this problem [3, 9, 10].

Theorem 2. *The number of connected components k in the graph correlated with unified matrix U^* is equal to the multiplicity of the eigenvalue 0 of the Laplacian matrix L_{U^*}.*

According to Ky Fan's Theorem [11], the cost function can be calculated as:

$$\sum_{v=1}^m \sigma_v = \min_{F, F^T F=I} Tr(F^T L_{U^*} F) \tag{6}$$

where $\sigma_v \geq 0$ is smallest eigenvalues of the symmetric positive semi-definite matrix L_{U^*}. F is the embedding matrix. The final objective function can be formulated as follow by combining Eq. (6) and Eq. (4):

$$\min_{U^*, F} \sum_{v=1}^m w_v \| U^* - G^{vT}Z^vG^v \|_F^2 + \lambda Tr(F^T G^{(v)T} L_Z G^v F)$$

$$\text{s.t } Z_{ii}^v = 0, Z_{ij}^v \geq 0, 1^T Z_i^v = 1, U_{ij}^* \geq 0, \ 1^T U_i^* = 1, F^T F = I \tag{7}$$

4. Optimization for GIMSC

4.1. *Optimization procedure for problem (7)*

Suppose that $Z^1, \ldots, Z^m$ has been constructed by solving above subsection. The unified matrix U^* is obtained by using Eq. (7). An alternating iterative optimization algorithm is presented to solve it as shown below:

Update U^*, when w and F are fixed for U^*, Suppose $c^v = G^{vT} Z^v G^v$, $Tr(F^T L_U \cdot F) = \frac{1}{2} \Sigma_{i,j} \| f_i - f_j \|_2^2 u_{ij}^*$, and define $s_i \in R^{n \times 1}$ $s_{ij} = \| f_i - f_j \|_2^2$. The following problem is to be solved:

$$\min_{U^*} \sum_{v=1}^{m} w_v \| U_{ij}^* - c_{ij}^v \|_F^2 + \frac{\lambda}{2} s_i^T u_{ij}^* \tag{8}$$

Then the problem (8) can be formulated as follows:

$$\min_{U^*} \left\| U_i^* - \frac{\sum_{v=1}^{m} w_v c_i^v - \frac{\lambda}{4} s_i}{\sum_{v=1}^{m} w_v} \right\|_2^2, \quad s.t. \ U_{ij}^* \geq 0, 1^T U_i^* = 1 \tag{9}$$

Update F, when fixing the other variables, w_v and U^*, the cluster indicator matrix F of each view can be obtained by minimizing the following formula:

$$\min_{F} Tr(F^T L_U \cdot F), \quad s.t. F^T F = I \tag{10}$$

The optimal solution of F is calculated by the k eigenvectors of L_{U^*} corresponding to the k smallest eigenvalues. In summary, the details of solving proposed GIMSC method are summarized in Algorithm 1.

Algorithm 1 Optimization of GIMSC

Input: Incomplete Multiview data, $Y = \left[X_1^{(v)}, X_2^{(v)}, \ldots, X_{n_v}^{(v)} \right]$,

  Parameters $\lambda, \beta,$

Initializing Z^v with k-NN in the step of graph construction,

Initialize Z^v by constructing the SIG matrices using Eq. (2),

Initialize U^* by averaging of all Z^v.

$w_v = \frac{1}{m}$, where $m = total \ number \ of \ views,$

for v = 1 to m,

  do: Normalize X^v

end for

while not converged **do:**

for m = 1 to m, do

update w_v by Eq. (5)

update U^* by solving Eq. (9)

update F by solving Eq. (10)

end for

Until stop criterion is met.

Output: F by applying k-means algorithm on U^*

---

5. Experiments

5.1. *Experimental setting*

In this section, we conduct extensive experiments to verify the effectiveness of the proposed method on four real-world datasets, Mfeat [7], WebKB [9], ORL [1], Caltech7 [7] which are listed in Table 1. In our studies, 10%, 20%, 30% and

Table 1. Information of the benchmark datasets.

Dataset	Samples	Features	Views	Categories
Caltech7	1474	512/928	2	7
MFeat	2000	76/240/216/64/47/6	6	10
WebKB	203	1703/203/23	3	4
ORL	400	256/256/256/256	4	40

Table 2. Comparison of clustering performance in term of ACC and Purity.

Dataset	Method/IR	Accuracy				Purity			
		10%	20%	30%	40%	10%	20%	30%	40%
Caltech7	BSV	27.07	22.68	33.79	30.46	71.03	62.21	68.79	58.14
	MIC	39.69	34.53	32.36	35.75	79.51	77.54	70.62	77.75
	IMG	50.83	46.74	45.78	45.62	78.20	78.83	79.50	79.52
	DAIMC	41.66	38.67	44.78	37.86	82.02	80.05	82.90	79.17
	IMSCAG	63.22	54.25	52.85	52.62	84.79	85.82	85.07	85.24
	AWGSC	76.27	71.47	71.61	68.71	64.90	65.13	65.73	64.97
	Ours	**78.27**	**75.66**	**72.63**	**69.15**	**95.05**	**93.49**	**92.27**	**92.02**
Mfeat	BSV	34.90	27.30	19.25	20.35	38.50	31.15	23.80	20.40
	MIC	58.25	54.25	51.75	41.95	58.50	54.25	51.75	43.20
	IMG	64.14	53.95	51.34	46.35	64.14	54.48	51.38	47.15
	DAIMC	82.20	82.15	68.75	47.20	82.20	82.15	68.75	52.90
	IMSCAG	85.32	83.31	83.07	76.03	**87.00**	83.31	83.07	84.03
	AWGSC	81.65	80.40	**78.30**	79.30	75.69	81.61	71.60	72.87
	Ours	**85.60**	**83.47**	77.60	**82.75**	85.25	**83.60**	**83.15**	**84.75**
ORL	BSV	25.50	24.00	21.50	22.50	29.00	25.50	23.25	24.00
	MIC	56.50	49.00	41.50	34.00	61.50	53.25	45.25	37.50
	IMG	47.68	43.10	40.00	39.15	53.18	48.40	46.50	45.18
	DAIMC	54.50	55.50	45.50	38.50	60.50	60.00	52.00	43.75
	IMSCAG	73.55	72.20	61.80	66.45	78.00	73.60	65.05	69.30
	AWGSC	64.62	64.28	63.10	60.45	49.59	50.33	46.64	44.43
	Ours	**79.45**	**72.32**	**68.70**	**75.35**	**79.15**	**74.95**	**68.15**	**69.50**
WebKB	BSV	37.07	36.21	37.93	33.62	50.86	42.24	50.86	45.69
	MIC	50.86	39.66	43.97	37.07	53.45	41.38	50.00	43.97
	IMG	41.03	38.45	42.33	38.79	43.10	39.48	44.05	40.43
	DAIMC	68.10	59.48	61.21	49.14	75.86	68.97	70.69	62.07
	IMSCAG	74.66	78.10	75.00	69.68	85.86	88.45	85.34	73.79
	AWGSC	72.50	61.37	58.27	63.69	32.53	33.69	32.13	28.60
	Ours	**91.91**	**85.31**	**82.75**	**80.09**	**95.93**	**90.52**	**89.66**	**73.86**

40% of data instances are randomly removed from all views to generate instances with incomplete views. The proposed algorithm can handle the following incomplete cases: (1) arbitrarily missing views including no samples to have at least one view (2) paired samples i.e., some samples have features of all views and still available samples have feature of one view. Same as [7], extensive experiments are conducted by comparing with the following baseline algorithms: BSV [6], MIC [5], IMG [6], DAIMC [5], IMSCAG [1], AWGSC [7]. We use three evaluation criteria [3] to measure the clustering performance, namely clustering accuracy (ACC), normalized mutual information (NMI), and purity. The best clustering results are in bold numbers. The experimental results are reported in Table 2 with incomplete ratios.

5.2. Experimental analysis

As shown in Table 2, the proposed GIMSC method is superior to all baseline algorithms in all cases with all kinds of incomplete tasks. According to the results of ACC, Purity and NMI, our methods shows smoothly that the best clustering performance in all missing rates except from ACC of 30% over Mfeat dataset. The results in Fig. 1 shows that our proposed algorithm converges within 10 iterations. IR in represents incomplete ratios. Figure 2 NMI results of our method achieve the best in all incomplete ratios.

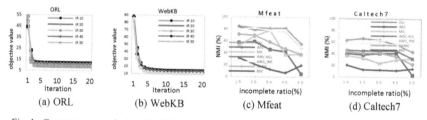

(a) ORL   (b) WebKB   (c) Mfeat   (d) Caltech7

Fig. 1. Convergence analysis with different incomplete ratios over two datasets

Fig. 2. NMI results of different incomplete ratios on two datasets

6. Conclusion

Incomplete multi-view spectral clustering method is proposed for solving the difficult clustering problem on incomplete multi-view data. Different from many existing methods, we propose a way to combine all basic incomplete graphs to obtain a complete consensus graph which can give the final clustering results. The proposed method simultaneously integrates graph construction, fusion graph construction and spectral clustering for incomplete multi-view clustering. Compared with the traditional methods, the proposed method is more versatile since it can handle all kinds of complete and incomplete tasks. Experimental results generally reveal that the proposed system outperforms different state-of-the-arts methods, showing that it is ability to dealing with the incomplete multi-view clustering works. Our data indicate that finding efficient and effective clustering techniques may help to solve the problems associated with memory, energy consumption, and the time needed to operate technology. We also find that to introduce continual learning into our proposed method to handle the sequential clustering tasks.

Acknowledgments

This work is supported by the National Natural Science Foundation of China (No. 61976247).

References

1. Wen, J., Xu, Y., and Liu, H. (2018). Incomplete multi-view spectral clustering with adaptive graph learning. *IEEE transactions on cybernetics, 50*(4), 1418-1429.
2. Gao, H., Peng, Y., and Jian, S. (2016, November). Incomplete multi-view clustering. In *International Conference on Intelligent Information Processing* (pp. 245-255).
3. Kang, Z., Shi, G., Huang, S., Chen, W., Pu, X., Zhou, J. T., and Xu, Z. (2020). Multi-graph fusion for multi-view spectral clustering. *Knowledge-Based Systems, 189*, 105102.
4. Wang, Y., Chang, D., Fu, Z., and Zhao, Y. (2021). Incomplete Multi-view Clustering via Cross-view Relation Transfer. *arXiv preprint arXiv:2112.00739*.
5. Zhou, W., Wang, H., and Yang, Y. (2019, April). Consensus graph learning for incomplete multi-view clustering. In *Pacific-Asia Conference on Knowledge Discovery and Data Mining* (pp. 529-540).
6. Zhao, H., Liu, H., and Fu, Y. (2016, July). Incomplete multi-modal visual data grouping. In *IJCAI* (pp. 2392-2398).
7. Zhang, P., Wang, S., Hu, J., Cheng, Z., Guo, X., Zhu, E., and Cai, Z. (2020). Adaptive Weighted Graph Fusion Incomplete Multi-View Subspace Clustering. *Sensors, 20*(20), 5755.
8. Pan, E., and Kang, Z. (2021). Multi-view Contrastive Graph Clustering. *Advances in Neural Information Processing Systems, 34*.

9. Wang, H., Yang, Y., and Liu, B. (2019). GMC: Graph-based multi-view clustering. *IEEE Transactions on Knowledge and Data Engineering, 32*(6), 1116-1129.

10. Nie, F., Wang, X., Jordan, M., and Huang, H. (2016). The constrained Laplacian rank algorithm for graph-based clustering. In *Proceedings of the AAAI conference on artificial intelligence* (Vol. 30, No. 1).

11. Fan, K. (1949). On a theorem of Weyl concerning eigenvalues of linear transformations I. *Proceedings of the National Academy of Sciences of the United States of America, 35*(11), 652.

12. Liu, J., Teng, S., Fei, L., Zhang, W., Fang, X., Zhang, Z., and Wu, N. (2021). A novel consensus learning approach to incomplete multi-view clustering. *Pattern Recognition, 115*, 107890.

13. Rai, P., Trivedi, A., Daumé, H., and DuVall, S. L. (2010). Multiview clustering with incomplete views. In *Proceedings of the NIPS Workshop on Machine Learning for Social Computing*.

Class-imbalance data preprocessing based on Generative Adversarial Networks

Linghao Zhang[*], Bo Pang[†], Chao Tang[‡] and Jie Zhang[§]

State Grid Sichuan Electric Power Research Institute
Power Internet of Things Key Laboratory of Sichuan Province
Chengdu, Sichuan 610000, China
[*] 16100178@qq.com
[†] pang-bo@outlook.com
[‡] 121648256@qq.com
[§] 506048990@qq.com

Yuxin Zhong[‖] and Hongjun Wang[¶]

School of Computing and Artificial Intelligence, Southwest Jiaotong University
Chengdu, China 610000, China
[‖] 2835210096@my.swjtu.edu.cn
[¶] wanghongjun@swjtu.edu.cn

In real-world, there are vast class-imbalanced datasets, while most existing algorithms are designed for balanced classes. Furthermore, traditional data augmentation methods mostly need to utilize Markov chain and infer hidden variables during the training process. To break this situation, this paper designed a method of using Generative Adversarial Networks (GAN) to produce more data samples for classification task. GAN utilizes back propagation instead of Markov chain, in which the parameter update of generator is not directly from the data samples, but from discriminator. Finally, experiments on 10 datasets are conducted with 3 classification models and the results demonstrate the high performance of using algorithms to classify preprocessed data.

Keywords: Class-imbalance; data augmentation; Generative Adversarial Networks.

1. Introduction

Class-imbalance is a challenge for classification in machine learning field, which has attracted extensive attention in application fields such as disease detection,[1] fraud detection[2] and fault diagnosis.[3] When samples in each class are unbalanced, problem of class-imbalance will happen.

Most classification methods are built under the assumption of balanced classes. But balanced dataset in real-world is little, and the classification results of minority class are more important. In real business scenarios, such as earthquake prediction, the proportion of samples is unbalanced. If the model tends to predict that the earthquake does not occur, the model may misjudge. Thus, solving class imbalance is important.

Data augmentation (DA) is a technique that can add samples for minority classes and improve the variety of training samples. It has developed very rapidly in neural networks research. However, conventional methods need to utilize Markov chain[4] and need to infer hidden variables during the training process.[5] Therefore, Generative Adversarial Networks (GAN)[6] is proposed to achieve data augmentation. GAN utilizes back propagation instead of Markov chain, in which the parameter update of generator is not directly from the data samples, but from discriminator. In addition, there is no need to infer hidden variables during training process for GAN.

This paper aims to give the GAN community a higher level of awareness of this growing area of work. GAN is not only a generative model but also a kind of unsupervised learning, which makes two neural networks namely generator and discriminator compete with each other. With the increasing interest and work on this topic, this is an appropriate time to write such a paper: (i) research GAN's data augmentation, and (ii) guide interest in this field with high efficiency.

The major contributions are as follows. Firstly, GAN model is introduced into data augmentation to improve the number and diversity of the minority class, and parameter is optimized. Secondly, experiments have been carried out on a variety of real-world datasets, which demonstrate that data generated by GAN have superior quality.

The framework of this paper is shown here. Firstly, related work is shown in Section 2. Then, Section 3 describes the proposed model. Next, the experimental settings, results and analysis are shown in Section 4. Finally, Section 5 is conclusion.

2. Related Work

Data augmentation produces more data samples based on datasets with limited data, which can increase the diversity of training samples and the robotness of the model. Neural networks often have many parameters, and the number of many neural networks is more than one million. To make neural networks work correctly, a large amount of data samples are needed, however, in many practical projects, it is difficult to find sufficient data to complete the training task, which will cause class-imbalance problem. Increasing the number of data samples can reduce the dependence of the model on some attributes, so that the trained model can have better fitting results for unknown data sets. The main methods of data augmentation utilize neural networks to generate new data samples, which can be broadly classified in terms of the neural networks they utilize: CNN,[7] RNN,[8] GAN.[9-13] Besides, meta-learning[14,15] can be used for data augmentation.[16]

GAN is a generative model, and its main inspiration comes from a concept of game theory, which is zero sum game. It competes continuously through generation network and discrimination network, and finally the distribution of data will be learned. Compared with other generative models like Boltzman, GAN only uses back propagation without complex Markov chain. It can produce clearer and more real samples.

Up to now, many methods based on GAN for data augmentation are proposed. Frid et al.[9] proposed a training scheme that further enlarges the data size and its diversity by applying GAN for synthetic data augmentation, but it can only perform well on classifying liver lesion. Huang et al.[10] proposed a GAN-based data augmentation network (AugGAN). This network is used for image-to-image translation, but it has many layers and in each one there are three hyper-parameters, which are hard to adjust and will take large amount of time. Waheed et al.[11] proposed an Auxiliary Classifier Generative Adversarial Network (ACGAN) based model to generate X-ray images, but because of the time constraints and difficulty in gathering enough data, only a small dataset is used. Tran et al.[12] proposed a data augmentation optimized for GAN, and it aligns with the original GAN, which can lead to learn the distribution of the augmented data correctly. Ma et al.[13] proposed a multi-modal conditional generative adversarial network, which can generate the multi-modal data with different modalities. However, the data collection may suffer from label noise.

3. Model

The generative model is described, which specifies the data augmentation process, and the framework is shown in Fig. 1. Firstly, GAN generate new data and judge whether they are true. Secondly, the dataset is classified (a training set and a validation set). Then, the new sets can be used for training. Finally, the validation set is used to validate.

GAN includes one generator Gt and one discriminator Dt. Generator receives a random noise vector nd, and the goal of generator is to generate a

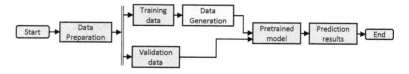

Fig. 1. The framework of class-imbalance data classification.

fake sample X_{fake}. Discriminator judges whether a sample is a real sample or a fake sample. The objective function of GAN is

$$V(Gt, Dt) = E_{x \sim P_r}[logDt(x)] + E_{x \sim P_f}[log(1 - Dt(x))], \quad (1)$$

where P_r and P_f are the probability distribution of real samples and fake samples, respectively. $logD(x \sim P_r)$ is the output result of real samples.

Gradient descent method is used to make the binary cross entropy between loss function of real data and 1 smaller, and make that between loss function of fake data and 0 smaller. Thus, the loss function of Dt is

$$\nabla \theta_{dt} \frac{1}{b} \sum_{i=1}^{b} [logDt(rs^{(i)}) + log(1 - Dt(Gt(nd^{(i)})))], \quad (2)$$

where b is branch size, nd are noisy scalars, rs are real samples, θ_{dt} is the parameter for discriminator.

When training the generator, after generating m noisy scalars, gradient descent method is used to make the binary cross entropy between loss function of fake data and 1 smaller. Thus, the loss function of Gt is

$$\nabla \theta_{gt} \frac{1}{b} \sum_{i=1}^{b} [log(1 - Dt(Gt(nd^{(i)})))], \quad (3)$$

where θ_{gt} is the parameter for generator.

4. Experiments

The model was evaluated by 10 datasets. The experimental settings were presented first, then the results were illustrated by two evaluation metrics.

4.1. Datasets

Experiments were performed on 10 datasets. For each dataset, there are original data and preprocessed data that are produced by the GAN model, whose detail information was presented by Table 1. The original data distribution is shown in Table 2, and each percentage represents the ratio of samples of each class to the total samples in each dataset.

Table 1. Dataset with original data and preprocessed data.

No.	Original Objects	Generated Objects	Features	Class
D1	20867	31804	10	12
D2	45211	46797	16	2
D3	13611	16628	16	7
D4	695	801	29	4
D5	65532	74153	11	4
D6	6118	7899	52	6
D7	10129	27238	16	4
D8	779	938	13	3
D9	6321	6658	12	2
D10	1000	1150	20	2

Table 2. Original data distribution.

No.	Distribution(%)										
D1	41.1	0.1	0.9	3.4	10.5	18.8	4.3	5.0	8.0	0.4	5	2.5
D2	88.3	11.7									
D3	9.7	3.8	12.0	26.1	14.2	15.9	19.3				
D4	48.4	11.8	16.5	23.3							
D5	57.4	22.9	19.6	0.1							
D6	17.8	8.0	12.2	10.1	10.2	41.7					
D7	81.2	4.5	7.4	6.9							
D8	59.1	8.2	32.7								
D9	89.3	10.7									
D10	30.0	70.0									

4.2. Experimental settings

To verify the superiority of the preprocessed data during classification task, ten-fold cross-validation experiments were set up. 3 models were applied to perform classification task on 10 datasets, respectively were support vector classifier (SVM), k-nearest neighbors (KNN) and DecisionTree (DT).

Two evaluation indices were used to verify the difference between the classification effect of original data and preprocessed data.

Accuracy[17] is the same ratio of the real tags to the predicted labels:

$$accuracy = \frac{\sum_{i=1} \&(t_i, map(c_i))}{n}, \tag{4}$$

where c_i and t_i are the obtained labels and true labels, respectively. Each r_i to the equivalent label from the original dataset is represented as $map(c_i)$.

F1-score measures the accuracy of binary classification model:

$$F1\text{-}score = 2 \times \frac{precision \times recall}{precision + recall}, \tag{5}$$

where *precision* and *recall* are the same ration of the positive data predicted correctly to the predicted and the actual positive data, respectively.

582

4.3. Results

The results and analysis are shown. Firstly, the average accuracy and F1-score of 3 algorithms on 10 datasets for original data and generated samples is compared. Then, a Friedman test of accuracy is performed.

In the experiment, 3 algorithms were applied to 10 datasets for classification, and the results of accuracy and F1-score are shown in Table 3 and Table 4, where the numbers in brackets are the rankings. It can be seen that the results over preprocessed data are better on each dataset.

Table 3. Accuracy comparison of preprocessed data and original data among three algorithms.

Dataset	Preprocessed Data			Original Data		
	SVC	KNN	DT	SVC	KNN	DT
D1	0.9987 (2)	0.9731(4)	0.9990(1)	0.5515(6)	0.7991(5)	0.9914(3)
D2	0.9969(1)	0.9737 (2)	0.8520(6)	0.8832(4)	0.8925 (3)	0.8737(5)
D3	0.9716(2)	0.8686(5)	0.9292(3)	0.9780(1)	0.5246(6)	0.9251(4)
D4	1.0000(1.5)	0.8523(3)	1.0000(1.5)	0.6571(4)	0.4783(6)	0.6000(5)
D5	0.9936(5)	0.9986 (2)	0.9999(1)	0.9850(6)	0.9951(4)	0.9983(3)
D6	0.9633(1)	0.7127(3)	0.9190(2)	0.4739(5)	0.2386(6)	0.5441(4)
D7	1.0000(3.5)	1.0000(3.5)	1.0000(3.5)	1.0000(3.5)	1.0000(3.5)	1.0000(3.5)
D8	0.9574(1)	0.8617(2)	0.8404(3)	0.8205(4)	0.6026(6)	0.7436(5)
D9	0.9805(4)	0.9474(5)	1.0000(1.5)	0.9858(3)	0.8592(6)	1.0000(1.5)
D10	0.8100(4)	0.7000(6)	0.7600(5)	0.9652(1)	0.9217(2)	0.8783(3)
Ave. Rank	2.5	3.55	2.75	3.75	4.75	3.7

Table 4. F1-score comparison of preprocessed data and original data among three algorithms.

Dataset	Preprocessed Data			Original Data		
	SVC	KNN	DT	SVC	KNN	DT
D1	0.9990(1.5)	0.9830(3)	0.9990(1.5)	0.3373(6)	0.7963(5)	0.9915(4)
D2	0.9944(1)	0.9552(2)	0.7783(3)	0.4972(6)	0.6636(5)	0.6810(4)
D3	0.9756(1.5)	0.8809(5)	0.9445(3)	0.9756(1.5)	0.5167(6)	0.9189(4)
D4	1.0000(1.5)	0.8622(3)	1.0000(1.5)	0.5254(4)	0.2612(6)	0.4369(5)
D5	0.9883(3)	0.9990(2)	0.9999(1)	0.7354(6)	0.7462(5)	0.9705(4)
D6	0.9690(1)	0.7481(3)	0.9287(2)	0.2874(5)	0.1396(6)	0.4265(4)
D7	1.0000(3.5)	1.0000(3.5)	1.0000(3.5)	1.0000(3.5)	1.0000(3.5)	1.0000(3.5)
D8	0.9682(1)	0.8838(2)	0.8719(3)	0.5638(5)	0.4625(6)	0.7395(4)
D9	0.9639(4)	0.9102(5)	1.0000(1.5)	0.9645(3)	0.4621(6)	1.0000(1.5)
D10	0.9640(1)	0.9202(2)	0.8771(3)	0.7333(4)	0.5951(6)	0.7143(5)
Ave. Rank	1.9	3.05	2.3	4.4	5.45	3.9

Friedman test determines whether there are large differences in many population distributions. For Table 4, $F_F = 9.47$. The p value is 3.20×10^{-6}, thus the null hypothesis is rejected at a high level of significance.

5. Conclusion

In this paper, the method of using machine learning model to classify class-imbalance data is first designed and practiced, in which GAN is utilized for data augmentation. Furthermore, two evaluation indicators are used to measure the results of the data classification. Extensive experiments are conducted on 10 real class-imbalance datasets with 3 classification models. The results demonstrate that the classification model conducted on data expanded by GAN model has high accuracy and F1-score, and provides a reliable reference for future class-imbalance data classification work.

Acknowledgment

This research work was supported by Science and Technology Project of State Grid Sichuan Electric Power Company (52199722000Y).

References

1. D. Devarriya, C. Gulati, V. Mansharamani, A. Sakalle and A. Bhardwaj, Unbalanced breast cancer data classification using novel fitness functions in genetic programming, *Expert Systems with Applications* **140**, p. 112866 (2020).
2. Z. Li, M. Huang, G. Liu and C. Jiang, A hybrid method with dynamic weighted entropy for handling the problem of class imbalance with overlap in credit card fraud detection, *Expert Systems with Applications* **175**, p. 114750 (2021).
3. Q. Shi and H.Z hang, Fault diagnosis of an autonomous vehicle with an improved svm algorithm subject to unbalanced datasets, *IEEE Transactions on Industrial Electronics* **68**, 6248 (2021).
4. H. Park, S. Lee, S. Kim, J. Park, J. Jeong, K.-M. Kim, J.-W. Ha and H. J. Kim, Metropolis-hastings data augmentation for graph neural networks, *Advances in Neural Information Processing Systems* **34**, 19010 (2021).
5. Y. Zhang and Q. Liu, On iot intrusion detection based on data augmentation for enhancing learning on unbalanced samples, *Future Generation Computer Systems* **133**, 213 (2022).

6. L. Goodfellow, J. Pouget-Abadie, M. Mirza, B. Xu, D. Warde-Farley, S. Ozair, A. Courville and Y. Bengio, Generative adversarial nets, *Advances in neural information processing systems* **27** (2014).

7. R. Poojary, R. Raina and A. K. Mondal, Effect of data-augmentation on fine-tuned cnn model performance, *IAES International Journal of Artificial Intelligence* **10**, p. 84 (2021).

8. M. Zohrer and F. Pernkopf, Virtual adversarial training and data augmentation for acoustic event detection with gated recurrent neural networks., in *Interspeech*, 2017.

9. M. Frid-Adar, E. Klang, M. Amitai, J. Goldberger and H. Greenspan, Synthetic data augmentation using gan for improved liver lesion classification, in *2018 IEEE 15th international symposium on biomedical imaging (ISBI 2018)*, 2018.

10. S. W. Huang, C. T. Lin, S. P. Chen, Y. Y. Wu, P. H. Hsu and S.-H. Lai, Auggan: Cross domain adaptation with gan-based data augmentation, in *Proceedings of the European Conference on Computer Vision (ECCV)*, 2018.

11. A. Waheed, M. Goyal, D. Gupta, A. Khanna, F. Al-Turjman and P. R. Pinheiro, Covidgan: data augmentation using auxiliary classifier gan for improved covid-19 detection, *Ieee Access* **8**, 91916 (2020).

12. N.-T. Tran, V.-H. Tran, N.-B. Nguyen, T.-K. Nguyen and N.-M. Cheung, On data augmentation for gan training, *IEEE Transactions on Image Processing* **30**, 1882 (2021).

13. F. Ma, Y. Li, S. Ni, S.-L. Huang and L. Zhang, Data augmentation for audio-visual emotion recognition with an efficient multimodal conditional gan, *Applied Sciences* **12**, p. 527 (2022).

14. J. Zhang, J. Song, L. Gao, Y. Liu and H. T. Shen, Progressive meta-learning with curriculum, *IEEE Transactions on Circuits and Systems for Video Technology* (2022).

15. J. Zhang, J. Song, Y. Yao and L. Gao, Curriculum-based meta-learning, in *Proceedings of the 29th ACM International Conference on Multimedia*, 2021.

16. E. D. Cubuk, B. Zoph, D. Mane, V. Vasudevan and Q. V. Le, Autoaugment: Learning augmentation strategies from data, in *Proceedings of the IEEE/CVF Conference on Computer Vision and Pattern Recognition*, 2019.

17. W. Yang, Y. Zhang, H. Wang, P. Deng and T. Li, Hybrid genetic model for clustering ensemble, *Knowledge-Based Systems* **231**, p. 107457 (2021).

A missing value filling model based on feature fusion enhanced autoencoder

Xinyao Liu, Shengdong Du*, Fei Teng and Tianrui Li

School of Computing and Artificial Intelligence, Southwest Jiaotong University
Chengdu, Sichuan 611756, China
* sddu@swjtu.edu.cn

With the advent of the big data era, the data quality problem is becoming more and more prominent, and data missing filling is one of the key techniques to improve data quality, which has attracted much attention from researchers. One of the typical research works is to use neural network models, such as autoencoders, but these methods are difficult to explore both data association features and data common features. To solve the above problems, a missing value filling model based on a feature fusion enhanced autoencoder is proposed. It designs a novel neural network hidden layer with the mutual enhancement of de-tracking neurons and radial basis function neurons. The de-tracking neurons can reduce the problem of invalid constant mappings and effectively explore the data association features; the automatic clustering capability of radial basis function neurons can better learn the data common features. And an automatic iterative optimization of the missing value dynamic clustering filling strategy is designed to achieve multidimensional feature fusion learning and dynamic collaborative filling. The effectiveness of the proposed model is verified by experimental comparison with traditional missing value filling methods on multiple datasets with different missing rates.

Keywords: Missing value filling; autoencoder; feature fusion.

1. Introduction

Data quality is one of the key challenges in data analysis research and application, and if not handled well, it will be "Garbage In Garbage Out".[1] Therefore, we need to properly handle the missing data values during data preprocessing. The missing value filling method can find a reasonable replacement or supplement for the missing data, thus maintaining the feature distribution of the original dataset and improving the data quality. Missing value filling has received wide attention because of its important application value, and many researchers have proposed different missing value filling methods from various perspectives.[2,3] To fill the missing data values effectively, the key issue is how to dig deeply into the internal features of the missing data and find reasonable values for filling the missing values through sufficient internal feature analysis. In general, missing value filling requires finding two key types of features in the missing data set: One is data common features, i.e., filling in with the most similar data. The other is is data association feature, i.e., filling by association between attributes.

Due to the simplicity of the autoencoder filling model structure, researchers have made various improvements based on the AutoEncoder (AE).[4-7] However, the above methods are difficult to explore the association features and common features among data sample attributes at the same time. Especially when using classical AE to fill the missing values, it is easy to learn invalid constant mappings and thus affect the filling effect.

To address the above problems, a Feature Fusion Enhanced Autoencoder Model for Missing Value Filling (FFEAM) is proposed in this paper. Firstly, a new neural network hidden layer is designed to learn data features from different dimensions by de-tracking neurons and radial basis function neurons. The de-tracking neurons can reduce the invalid constant mapping problem of the autoencoder and effectively explore the association features among data attributes; the automatic clustering ability of radial basis function neurons can better learn the common features among missing samples. The output of the two types of neurons are constrained by referring to each other so that the model can learn features from two dimensions of data association features and data common features. Secondly, an automatic iterative optimization of missing values dynamic clustering (MVDC) filling strategy is developed. In this strategy, each training will be based on the current data for automatic clustering, and the selected centroids and widths will be provided to the radial basis function neurons, while the missing values will be treated as variables along with the parameters of the model to be trained dynamically with the optimization function, allowing the accuracy and filling precision of the model to be continuously improved.

The rest of this paper is organized as follows: Section 2 introduces related work. Section 3 introduces the architecture of FFEAM. Section 4 verifies the effectiveness of the proposed model through comparative experiments. Finally, conclusions are presented in Section 5.

2. Related Work

Current mainstream methods for filling missing values in data are divided into two categories: statistical models and machine learning models. In the first category, the most classical method is the mean filling method, which uses the average or plural of the data to fill in the missing values.[8] In the research of missing value filling models based on machine learning, K-Nearest Neighbors (KNN) is one of the classical methods, and its main idea is to select the top K categories with the least variance by sorting the variance between the categorical samples and the training samples from smallest to largest.[9] Yi et al. proposed a missing value filling method based on spatio-temporal multi-view learning, which automatically fills missing records of geosensing data by learning from multiple views from both local and global perspectives of spatio-temporal.[10]

Currently, deep learning-based missing value filling methods are becoming a hot research topic. Four variants of AE models are proposed by Ravi et al.[5] In order to reasonably weaken the tracking of the input by the autoencoder, Lai et al. developed the de-tracking autoencoder.[4] Lai et al. continued their improvement by proposing the Association Enhanced Autoassociative Neural Network (CE-AANN),[7] which can well uncover the association features among data attributes.

The above methods such as Mean[8]and KNN[9] mostly analyze and process the missing data from the data common feature dimension. The deep neural network is from filling in the missing values of the dimension of association features between data attributes. Based on the above summary of related research work, the currently proposed missing value filling models are difficult to perform fusion learning from the above two dimensions simultaneously.

3. The Architecture of FFEAM

The architecture of FFEAM is shown in Fig. 1. The FFEAM designs a novel hidden layer, in which two types of neurons are developed and constructed, e.g., m_1 de-tracking neurons and m_2 radial basis function neurons.

The whole FFEAM calculation process is described below. It first prefills using random forest. Then the weights and thresholds of the FFEAM are initialized. Meanwhile, based on the MVDC dynamic filling strategy, the missing values are set as variables, and the k-means clustering algorithm is used to find h centroids μ_h in the current data set after pre-filling, and the width σ_g is calculated by Eq. (1).

$$\sigma_g = \frac{c_{max}}{\sqrt{2h}}(g = 1, 2, ..., h).$$ (1)

Where c_{max} denotes the maximum distance between h centers and h represents the number of centers.

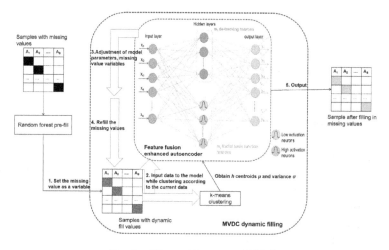

Fig. 1. The architecture of FFEAM.

Next, the data association features are discovered using the de-tracking neurons in the novel hidden layer. The output of the de-tracking neuron is shown in Eq. (2).

$$net_{ikj} = \text{relu} \left(\sum_{l=1, l \neq j}^{s} w_{lk}^{(1)} \cdot x_{il} + b_k^{(1)} \right), \, j = 1, 2, ..., s, k = 1, 2..., m_1. \quad (2)$$

Where net_{ikj} represents the output of the kth de-tracking neuron after eliminating the corresponding input x_{ij}, s represents the number of attributes, m_1 is the number of de-tracking neurons.

The output of the radial basis function hidden layer neuron is shown in Eq. (3).

$$net_{igj} = \exp \left[-\frac{\|x_{ij} - \mu_g\|}{2\sigma_g^2} \right], \, j = 1, 2, ..., s, g = 1, 2, ..., m_2. \quad (3)$$

Where m_2 is the number of radial basis function neurons. μ_g is the centroid of the g radial basis function hidden layer neurons, which is found according to the k-means algorithm. σ_g is the width of the g radial basis function hidden layer neurons, and is found according to Eq. (1). When the input sample is close to the center, the activation of the neuron is approximately 1, which belongs to the neuron with high activation.

After the new hidden layer, two outputs will be obtained in the output layer of the neural network: one going to the output of the de-tracking neuron y_{ij}, and the other is the reference output r_{ij} corresponding to the radial basis function neuron in the hidden layer.

The model loss function is as follows.

$$L = \frac{1}{2} \sum_{i=1}^{n} \sum_{j=1}^{s} [(y_{ij} - x_{ij})^2 + (y_{ij} - r_{ij})^2]. \tag{4}$$

Through the above computational process, the model minimizes the error between the output y_{ij} and the input x_{ij} while being as close as possible to the reference output of the radial basis function neuron. Through the mutual constraint of the two types of outputs, the model is able to effectively learn the association features and common features in the sample data while weakening the de-tracking of the outputs to the corresponding inputs.

4. Experimental Setup and Analysis of Results

4.1. *Experimental setup*

The Root Mean Square Error (RMSE) as in Eq. (5) and the Mean Absolute Error (MAE) as in Eq. (6) are used as evaluation indicators of filling performance.

$$RMSE = \sqrt{\frac{1}{n} \sum_{i=1}^{n} (x_i - y_i)^2}, \tag{5}$$

$$MAE = \frac{1}{n} \sum_{i=1}^{n} |x_i - y_i|. \tag{6}$$

Where n is the total number of samples, y_i denotes the filled value, and x_i denotes the true value corresponding to that filled value.

To test the performance of FFEAM, experiments are conducted based on three UCI datasets, and missing rates are set to 20%, 30%, 40%, and 50%, respectively. Two more complex real datasets (missing rate set to 20%), as detailed in Table 1. And the effectiveness of the model is verified by comparing the filling performance with the mean filling method, Autoencoder,[3] and CE-AANN.[7]

Table 1. Description of the dataset.

Data set name	Sample size	Number of attributes
Wine	178	14
Cloud	1024	10
Seeds	210	7
Traffic data of Baoan District	1102	10
AI4I 2020 Predictive Maintenance Dataset Data Set	10000	14

4.2. Analysis of experimental result

Experiments are first conducted based on three UCI datasets, and Table 2 shows the results. From Table 2, it can be seen that FFEAM outperforms the other comparison models in terms of missing value filling. Compared with the classical mean-value filling method and the benchmark AE filling model, FFEAM achieves the lowest RMSE and MAE with higher filling accuracy under different missing rate conditions.

Table 2. Comparison of filling errors of different models.

Data set name	Model name	RMSE				MAE			
		20%	30%	40%	50%	20%	30%	40%	50%
Wines	MEANS	32.616	42.534	52.027	48.024	3.405	5.035	6.931	7.420
	AE	32.669	42.502	51.894	47.605	3.432	5.056	7.007	7.469
	CE-AANN	25.764	35.115	44.731	44.193	2.605	4.084	5.669	6.547
	FFEAM	**22.780**	**24.553**	**29.518**	**35.272**	**2.383**	**3.226**	**4.044**	**5.456**
Cloud	MEANS	60.972	69.023	86.299	87.653	13.607	19.073	25.100	29.261
	AE	59.680	53.559	72.482	72.233	6.804	7.858	15.558	15.345
	CE-AANN	17.148	29.276	**28.669**	37.128	3.473	5.255	6.504	10.627
	FFEAM	**15.516**	**28.777**	28.944	**32.532**	**2.942**	**5.388**	**5.920**	**8.655**
Seeds	MEANS	0.600	0.697	0.782	0.822	0.155	0.220	0.292	0.332
	AE	0.606	0.719	0.794	0.821	0.158	0.234	0.299	0.339
	CE-AANN	0.363	0.564	0.444	0.589	0.073	0.141	0.147	0.199
	FFEAM	**0.261**	**0.336**	**0.379**	**0.482**	**0.066**	**0.109**	**0.127**	**0.179**

Next, two more complex real dataset comparison experiments are conducted. The experimental results are shown in Table 3. From Table 3, it can be seen that the performance of FFEAM in filling the missing values on the real datasets is also better than the benchmark comparison models, with the lowest RMSE and MAE.

Table 3. Comparison of filling errors of different models in real data sets.

Data set name	Model Name	RMSE	MAE
Traffic data of Baoan District	MEANS	1687.9270	286.815
	AE	1694.582	278.533
	CE-AANN	1067.15	158.45
	FFEAM	**593.246**	**85.458**
AI4I 2020 Predictive Maintenance Dataset Data Set	MEANS	24.716	3.183
	AE	24.714	3.195
	CE-AANN	21.633	3.153
	FFEAM	**15.426**	**2.601**

The main reason for the good performance of FFEAM is that it constrains the overdependence of the network output on the input by introducing de-tracking neurons, avoiding the invalid constant mapping of directly learning to output reproducing the input. And at the same time, through radial basis function neurons, clustering computation is performed on the sample data, and the interaction design between de-tracking neurons and radial basis function neurons allows the model to perform fusion learning of data association features and data common features.

5. Conclusions

This paper presented a new missing value filling model FFEAM to address the key problems faced by the classical autoencoder model in the application of missing value filling. The model constructed a new hidden layer of neural network by introducing two types of neurons. Through the mutual constraints of the two types of outputs, the model was motivated to combine the characteristics of the two types of neurons and exploit the association features between sample attributes and the common features of samples on the basis of removing self-tracking, so as to achieve multi-dimensional data feature fusion learning and improve the missing filling performance of the model. In addition, the MVDC filling strategy was designed, which automatically clusters each training according to the current data, while setting the missing values as variables to optimize iterative training with the model parameters to improve the model filling effect. The experimental results showed that FFEAM has better filling performance compared to the benchmark models. The current research mostly focuses on numerical missing value filling methods, and how to effectively learn the implicit information inside non-numerical attributes is a key issue to be addressed in future research.

Acknowledgments

This work was supported by the National Key R&D Program of China (2020AAA0105101).

References

1. Rose L, Fischer K. Garbage in, garbage out: Having useful data is everything[J]. Measurement: Interdisciplinary Research Perspective, 2011, 9(4): 222-226.
2. Vatanen T, Osmala M, Raiko T, et al. Self-organization and missing values in SOM and GTM. Neurocomputing, 2015, 147(5): 60-70.

3. Abdella M, Marwala T. The use of genetic algorithms and neural networks to approximate missing data in database. Proceedings of the IEEE 3rd International Conference on Computational Cybernetics, 2005: 207-212.

4. Lai X, Wu X, Zhang L, et al. Imputations of missing values using a tracking-removed autoencoder trained with incomplete data[J]. Neurocomputing, 2019, 366(13): 54-65.

5. Ravi V, Krishna M. A new online data imputation method based on general regression auto associative neural network. Neurocomputing, 2014, 138: 106-113.

6. Gautam C, Ravi V. Counter Propagation Autoassociative Neural Network based Data Imputationz. Information Sciences, 2015, 325: 288-299.

7. Lai X,Wu X, Zhang L, et al. Imputation Using a Correlation-Enhanced Auto-Associative Neural Network with Dynamic Processing of Missing Values. Proceedings of the International Symposium on Neural Networks. Springer, Cham, 2019: 223-231.

8. Meeyai S. Logistic Regression with Missing Data: A Comparison of Handling Methods, and Effects of Percent Missing Values. Journal of Traffic and Logistics Engineering, 2016, 4(2): 128-134.

9. Chen Yuming, Li Wei. Grain vectors and K-nearest neighbor grain classifiers. Computer Research and Development, 2019, 56(12): 2600-2611.

10. Yi X, Zheng Y, Zhang J, et al. ST-MVL: filling missing values in geosensory time series data. Proceedings of the Proceedings of the Twenty-Fifth International Joint Conference on Artificial Intelligence. 2016: 2704-2710.

Influence of potential multi-condition data on soft sensor modeling

Jiwei Qian, Yishui Zhang, Zhenglei He[*], Yi Man[†], Jigeng Li and Mengna Hong

State Key Laboratory of Pulp and Paper Engineering
South China University of Technology
Guangzhou, 510640, China
202020128109@mail.scut.edu.cn
[*]hezhenglei@scut.edu.cn
[†]manyi@scut.edu.cn

In the context of Industry 4.0, a large amount of industrial data is collected, which provides a good basis for soft sensing modeling. However, industrial data may have potentially multiple working conditions that make the data vary locally. Therefore, the prediction performance of the global model largely depends on the division of training data and test data. To illustrate this, Gaussian mixture model (GMM) is used for data partitioning, and then training data and test data are obtained proportionally in different partitions. Finally, support vector regression (SVR) and multilayer perceptron (MLP) are built under different training and test data to observe the changes of R^2, RMSE and MAPE. The results show that model's performance is largely affected by partitioning, and in order to obtain stable and usable models, data partitioning needs to be reasonably considered.

Keywords: Multiple working conditions; data-driven; data partitioning; soft sensor.

1. Introduction

Advances in sensor technology have made it easy to capture large amounts of industrial data. Soft sensor modeling has been extensively studied in process industries, such as chemical industry,[1,2] paper/pulp industry,[3,4] and steel industry.[5,6] It usually takes easy-to-measure variables as input and hard-to-measure variables as output. Soft sensor models can be roughly divided into two types: mechanistic soft sensor models and data-driven soft sensor models.[7] As the relevant variables of a key measurement through soft sensor could be highly numerous in process industry, it is difficult to find the connections by mechanistic models. Instead, data-driven models using intelligent techniques such as machine learning approaches, are more promising in this field as it can quickly handle the high-dimensional data and achieve the optimal results.[8]

Currently, there are two data-driven offline soft sensing modeling strategies. The first strategy is to build soft sensor models directly on the whole data set.

The second strategy is to partition the data set in a supervised (or unsupervised) manner and then build the corresponding sub-models on different sub-data sets. The obvious difference between these two strategies is the presence or absence of data partitioning. These two strategies are also known as global modeling and local modeling, respectively. Local modeling takes into account the possible local characteristics of the data and usually achieves better prediction results. However, it requires clear signals that make the researcher aware of the need for multiple local models rather than one global model. If a global model is built by the researcher for some objective reason or without attention. Then are the evaluation metrics' results of the global model obtained by the conventional modeling process reliable? How much does the presence of local characteristics of the data affect the performance of the global model? Is it necessary to consider the local characteristics of the modeled data to ensure robustness? The above issues will be discussed and analyzed according to the actual modeling results below.

2. Industrial Case Study: Papermaking Process

2.1. *Data collection*

The data used in this study are process data and quality data from an industrial paper mill. The process data can be measured directly by online sensors. However, each sensor has a different sampling frequency and time point, so further processing is required. The quality data is obtained by offline laboratory testing with severe time lag and low frequency compared to process data. It needs to exactly match the corresponding process data.

2.2. *Data processing*

During the papermaking process, online sensors are located at different locations throughout the paper machine. The sampling frequency and time points of the different sensors vary greatly. Therefore, data from different sensors needs to be processed. We use a processing method that converts fine-grained data into coarse-grained data. This is achieved by defining a time interval (*e.g.*, 30 or 60 seconds) and then calculating the average of all data collected by the sensors during that time interval. The processed data are shown in the middle of Fig. 1. The ordinate represents the order in which the different sensors were installed on the paper machine, the abscissa represents the time series, and the boxes represent the time corresponding to the recorded data. The actual data matches are shown as black line connections, depending on the specific time when the

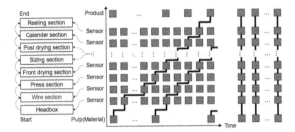

Fig. 1. Process data and quality data in papermaking industry.

raw paper passed through the different sensors. Finally, the sorted data set is shown on the right side of Fig. 1.

2.3. *Data division and modeling*

Figure 2 shows the modeling process of this paper. First, the data set is divided into multiple sub-data sets by Gaussian mixture model (GMM). And then, each sub-data set is divided proportionally into sub-training data and sub-test data. Finally, the sub-training data and sub-test data are merged separately. When the number of clusters is 1, the modeling process is no different from the regular modeling process. It can be considered that the original data set is divided into multiple sub-data sets according to certain rules when the number of cluster increases. The division of data ensures the diversity of training data and test data. On the one hand, the model is guaranteed to take into account all possible data distributions. On the other hand, the comprehensiveness of the test data is ensured.

Intelligent algorithms are effective methods for hyperparameter tuning, such as genetic algorithm,[9] particle swarm optimization,[10] artificial fish swarm,[11] *etc.* In this paper, genetic algorithm (GA) is used to find the best hyperparameters so as to obtain the optimal hyperparameters of support vector regression (SVR) and multilayer perceptron (MLP) under different data partitions.

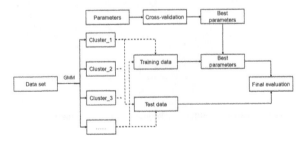

Fig. 2. Schematic diagram of modeling process.

2.4. *Evaluation*

R^2, RMSE and MAPE are used to evaluate the performance of the proposed model. They are defined as follows:

$$R^2 = 1 - \frac{\sum_{i=1}^{n} (y_i - \hat{y}_i)^2}{\sum_{i=1}^{n} (y_i - \bar{y})^2}, \tag{1}$$

$$RMSE = \sqrt{\frac{1}{n} \cdot \sum_{i=1}^{n} (y_i - \hat{y}_i)^2}, \tag{2}$$

$$MAPE = \frac{\sum_{i=1}^{n} |(y_i - \hat{y}_i)/y_i|}{n} \cdot 100\%, \tag{3}$$

where n is number of test samples, y_i indicates the value of real tested sample i, $\hat{y}_i$ and $\bar{y}$ are the predicted value and the corresponding average value respectively.

2.5. *Results and discussion*

The premise of using GMM in this paper is that there may be potentially multiple working conditions in the original data. The purpose of GMM is to ensure that the data distribution of the training data and test data can be more comprehensive. In this way, the irrationality of the data partitioning that may exist in the traditional modeling process is avoided. On the one hand, this approach ensures that the model is a global one that considers all data distributions. On the other hand, the comprehensiveness of the test data is ensured. It can be considered that with the gradual increase of cluster numbers, the trained model is more inclined to the global model, because it contains as much data distribution as possible and avoids falling into local optimum. At the same time, more comprehensive test data makes the performance of the model more reliable.

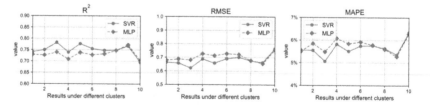

Fig. 3. Comparison of model effects under different partitioning strategies.

Figure 3 shows the R^2, RMSE and MAPE of the models constructed with different partitioning strategies on the corresponding test sets. It can be found that different partitioning strategies do affect the prediction performance of the model. Of course, this difference is jointly determined by training data and test data. This is because using GMM to partition the original dataset into multiple sub-datasets affects the distribution of the final training and test data. Therefore, when researchers build global models, the performance of their models will be largely influenced by the data partitioning.

In addition, it can be found that whether SVR or MLP, the evaluation results show a similar trend with the increase of the cluster numbers. However, their performance varies with a specific cluster number indicating that model's type are also matters. When the number of clusters is 3, the R^2 of the SVR model is taken to the maximum, and the RMSE and MAPE are taken to the minimum at the same time. When the number of clusters is 9, the R^2 of the MLP model is taken to be the maximum, and the RMSE and MAPE are taken to be the minimum. So as far as these three metrics are concerned, SVR and MLP achieve the best performance when the cluster number is 3 and 9, respectively.

The prediction error distribution of SVR and MLP under different cluster numbers is shown in Fig. 4. The dotted lines are gaussian fitting curves of the

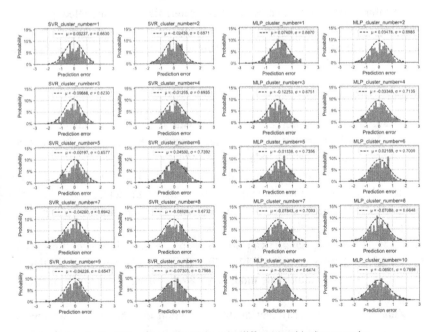

Fig. 4. Prediction errors of models under different partitioning strategies.

prediction error. It can be seen from Fig. 4 that when the number of clusters is 3, the standard deviation of SVR is the smallest, and when the number of clusters is 9, the mean and standard deviation of MLP are both the smallest. This also shows that data partitioning affects the performance of the model.

3. Conclusion

In this paper, a large amount of process data and quality data were collected, and the data set for modeling was constructed by processing the fine-grained data into usable coarse-grained data through the interval meaning method. In the data partitioning stage, GMM is introduced to divide the original data set into multiple sub-data sets. Then, each sub-data set is divided into sub-training data and sub-test data proportionally. Finally, they are integrated into the final training and test data. It is found that the best performance of SVR and MLP is achieved when the number of clusters is 3 and 9 respectively. The results show that both the model's type and the division of training and test data can affect the model's performance. Therefore, researchers should not only focus on the model itself when building a global one, but also on the local characteristics of the data. In order to obtain a robust model that truly reflects objective facts requires a reasonable division between training and test data.

In future work, we will analyze the characteristics of the modeled data more from the perspective of mechanistic knowledge and discuss the specific reasons for the improved or decreased performance of the models under specific partitioning strategies.

References

1. Yuan, Xiaofeng, et al. "Deep learning with spatiotemporal attention-based LSTM for industrial soft sensor model development." *IEEE Transactions on Industrial Electronics* 68.5 (2020): 4404-4414.
2. Geng, Zhiqiang, et al. "Novel transformer based on gated convolutional neural network for dynamic soft sensor modeling of industrial processes." *IEEE Transactions on Industrial Informatics* 18.3 (2021): 1521-1529.
3. Choi, Hyun-Kyu, Sang-Hwan Son, and Joseph Sang-Il Kwon. "Inferential model predictive control of blow-line fiber morphology in a continuous pulp digester via multiscale modeling." *2021 American Control Conference (ACC)*. IEEE, 2021.
4. Zhang, Hao, et al. "Effluent quality prediction in papermaking wastewater treatment processes using dynamic Bayesian networks." *Journal of Cleaner*

Production 282 (2021): 125396.

5. Fang, Yijing, et al. "Soft sensors based on adaptive stacked polymorphic model for silicon content prediction in ironmaking process." *IEEE Transactions on Instrumentation and Measurement* 70 (2020): 1-12.

6. Yuri, et al. "Modelling the strip thickness in hot steel rolling mills using least-squares support vector machines." *The Canadian Journal of Chemical Engineering* 96 (2018): 171-178.

7. Kadlec, Petr, Bogdan Gabrys, and Sibylle Strandt. "Data-driven soft sensors in the process industry." *Computers & Chemical Engineering* 33.4 (2009): 795-814.

8. Ferreira, Jimena, Martín Pedemonte, and Ana Inés Torres. "Development of a machine learning-based soft sensor for an oil refinery's distillation column." *Computers & Chemical Engineering* 161 (2022): 107756.

9. Guido, Rosita, Maria Carmela Groccia, and Domenico Conforti. "A hyperparameter tuning approach for cost-sensitive support vector machine classifiers." *Soft Computing* (2022): 1-19.

10. Guo, Yu, Jian-Yu Li, and Zhi-Hui Zhan. "Efficient hyperparameter optimization for convolution neural networks in deep learning: A distributed particle swarm optimization approach." *Cybernetics and Systems* 52.1 (2020): 36-57.

11. Gao, Yikai, et al. "Twin support vector machine based on improved artificial fish swarm algorithm with application to flame recognition." *Applied Intelligence* 50.8 (2020): 2312-2327.

A new Fuzzy Trapezoidal Naive Bayes Network as basis for assessment in training based on virtual reality

Arthur R. R. Lopes* and Jodavid A. Ferreira[†]

Lab. of Technologies for Virtual Teaching and Statistics, Federal University of Paraíba
João Pessoa, Paraíba, Brazil
* arthurlopes@mat.ci.ufpb.br
[†] jodavid@protonmail.com

Liliane S. Machado[‡] and Ronei M. Moraes[§]

Graduate Program in Decision Models and Health, Federal University of Paraíba
João Pessoa, Paraíba, Brazil
[‡] liliane@di.ufpb.br
[§] ronei@de.ufpb.br

Previous assessment models based on computational intelligence for virtual reality simulators did not consider intervalar-valued data, which can be modelled by trapezoidal distribution. This work presents the proposal of a new Fuzzy Trapezoidal Naive Bayes Network as basis for a single user assessment system (SUAS) to be used in virtual reality simulation for training purposes. The results showed that the assessment system based on the trapezoidal distribution was able to achieve better results when compared to other SUAS based on different Naive Bayes Networks.

Keywords: Fuzzy Trapezoidal Naive Bayes; trapezoidal distribution; user's assessment; virtual reality.

1. Introduction

Assessment models based on computational intelligence have been proposed for use in virtual reality (VR) simulators[2] aimed at training technical skills in safe environments. An important advantage of these simulators is their possibility to collect user's interactions in real time and use this data to assess user's performance. For this reason, the feedback must also occur in real time and can be used to provide a report on the user's skills or to modify the difficulty level of the simulation. Previous works proposed single (SUAS) and multiple (MUAS) users assessment systems to be coupled to virtual reality simulators for training of procedures.[4]

Assessing a procedure demands the modelling of metrics parameters and the monitoring of users' interactions. It is know that VR simulators present reality approximations[2] and, consequently, the use of fuzzy modelling of events is suitable for assessing purpose. Considering that each procedure has particularities due to the assessment metrics, the data follows specific distributions. Then, as better is the fit of the statistical distribution as better could be the assessment results.

SITEG 2.0 is a virtual reality simulator that features realistic graphics and interactive tasks aimed at gynecological examination training.[3] This simulator allows the practice of cases of healthy patients and patients with Herpes, HPV (Human Papiloma Virus) and cervical cancer in different degrees of disease severity. Considering the different levels of severity of the diseases, SITEG 2.0 integrates an assessment system, capable of monitoring user's interaction in the anamnesis and physical examination stages of the simulation. For this reason, it uses a haptic devide assuming the role of a spatula or cotton swab in order to allow the interaction with virtual models. The SUAS presented in SITEG 2.0 is responsible for assess user's simulation. According to medical protocol, the collection of material in the gynecological examination must be performed with a spatula[3] in a specific area of the cervix, defining a three-dimensional interval with fuzzy limits, which can be modelled by a three-dimensional trapezoid. However, assessment methods based on trapezoidal distribution were not found in scientific literature. The proposition and testing of a SUAS based on a new Fuzzy Trapezoidal Naive Bayes Network using trapezoidal distribution is presented in this paper. The following sections describe the theoretical basis for this SUAS and the results obtained by simulation data of SITEG 2.0, as well as a comparison with three other assessment methods.

2. Statistical Modeling

2.1. Trapezoidal distribution

A random variable X follows a trapezoidal distribution if its probability density function (pdf) $f(X)$ has the shape of a trapezoid.[1] This distribution is provided by four parameters, defined as a, b, c, d, where a and b are the lateral points of the trapezoid and c and d define the flat part of the trapezoid. This distribution requires that $a \leq c$, $c \leq d$ and $d \leq b$. Thus, it is possible to define that, let $X \sim Trapezoidal(a, c, d, b)$, its pdf is given by Eq. (1), where $h = 2/((c - a) + 2(d - c) + (b - d))$.

$$f(x; a, c, d, b) = \begin{cases} 0, & \text{if } x \leq a, \text{ or } x \geq b \\ \frac{(x-a)}{(c-a)} h, & \text{if } a \leq x \leq c, \\ h, & \text{if } c \leq x \leq d, \\ \frac{(b-x)}{(b-d)} h, & \text{if } d \leq x \leq b. \end{cases} \tag{1}$$

2.2. Mathematical properties

In this subsection, important results for the trapezoidal distribution are presented, such as the expectation and variance of the distribution. Thus, let $X \sim Trapezoidal(a, c, d, b)$, its expectation is given by

$$E(X) = \frac{h}{6} \left(\frac{b^3 - d^3}{b - d} - \frac{c^3 - a^3}{c - a} \right) = \frac{(b^2 - a^2) + (d^2 - c^2) - ac + bd}{3[(b - a) + (d - c)]} \tag{2}$$

and the variance of trapezoidal distribution is given by

$$\begin{aligned} V(X) &= E(X^2) - (E(X))^2 \\ &= \frac{6s^4 + 12(r + t)s^3 + [12(r + t)^2 - 6rt]s^2}{18(r + 2s + t)^2} \\ &+ \frac{6(r + t)(r^2 + rt + t^2)s + (r + t)^2(r^2 + rt + t^2)}{18(r + 2s + t)^2}, \end{aligned} \tag{3}$$

where $h = 2/(r + 2s + t)$, $r = (c - a)$, $s = (d - c)$ and $t = (b - d)$.

2.3. Parameters estimation

Let $X_1, \ldots, X_n$ a random sample i.i.d. of a random variable $X \sim Trapezoidal(\theta)$, such that $\theta = [a, c, d, b]^\top$ is a trapezoidal distribution parameter vector, with the restriction $a \leq c \leq d \leq b$. Thus, we have that $\hat{\theta} = [\hat{a}, \hat{c}, \hat{d}, \hat{b}]^\top$ is obtained by

$$\hat{a} = \min_{\{i=i,\ldots,n\}} (X_i), \qquad \hat{b} = \max_{\{i=i,\ldots,n\}} (X_i), \tag{4}$$

the parameters c and d are obtained finding the roots from a system of equations non-linear using the Newton-Raphson method[5] from Eqs. (2) and (3) on the equations in the following:

$$\overline{X} = \frac{-\hat{a}\hat{\theta}_0 - \hat{\theta}_0^2 + \hat{b}\hat{\theta}_1 + \hat{\theta}_1^2 + \hat{b}^2 - \hat{a}^2}{3\hat{\theta}_1 - 3\hat{\theta}_0 + 3\hat{b} - 3\hat{a}}, \tag{5}$$

$$S^2 = \frac{\left\{6(\hat{\theta}_1 - \hat{\theta}_0)^4 + 12\left[(\hat{\theta}_0 - \hat{a}) + (\hat{b} - \hat{\theta}_1)\right](\hat{\theta}_1 - \hat{\theta}_0)^3 + \right.}{18[(\hat{\theta}_0 - \hat{a}) + 2(\hat{\theta}_1 - \hat{\theta}_0) + (\hat{b} - \hat{\theta}_1)]^2}$$

$$\frac{\left\{12\left[(\hat{\theta}_0 - \hat{a}) + (\hat{b} - \hat{\theta}_1)\right]^2 - 6(\hat{\theta}_0 - \hat{a})(\hat{b} - \hat{\theta}_1)\right\}(\hat{\theta}_1 - \hat{\theta}_0)^2\right\}}{18[(\hat{\theta}_0 - \hat{a}) + 2(\hat{\theta}_1 - \hat{\theta}_0) + (\hat{b} - \hat{\theta}_1)]^2}$$

$$+ \frac{\left\{6(\hat{\theta}_1 - \hat{\theta}_0)\left[(\hat{\theta}_0 - \hat{a}) + (\hat{b} - \hat{\theta}_1)\right]\left[(\hat{\theta}_0 - \hat{a})^2 + \right.}{18[(\hat{\theta}_0 - \hat{a}) + 2(\hat{\theta}_1 - \hat{\theta}_0) + (\hat{b} - \hat{\theta}_1)]^2}$$

$$\frac{(\hat{\theta}_0 - \hat{a})(\hat{b} - \hat{\theta}_1) + (\hat{b} - \hat{\theta}_1)^2\right] + }{18[(\hat{\theta}_0 - \hat{a}) + 2(\hat{\theta}_1 - \hat{\theta}_0) + (\hat{b} - \hat{\theta}_1)]^2}$$

$$\frac{\left\{\left[(\hat{\theta}_0 - \hat{a}) + (\hat{b} - \hat{\theta}_1)\right]^2\right\}\left[(\hat{\theta}_0 - \hat{a})^2 + (\hat{\theta}_0 - \hat{a})(\hat{b} - \hat{\theta}_1) + (\hat{b} - \hat{\theta}_1)^2\right]\right\}}{18[(\hat{\theta}_0 - \hat{a}) + 2(\hat{\theta}_1 - \hat{\theta}_0) + (\hat{b} - \hat{\theta}_1)]^2},$$

$$\tag{6}$$

where $\overline{X} = \sum_{i=1}^{n} X_i / n$, $S^2 = \sum_{i=1}^{n}(X_i - \overline{X})^2/(n-1)$, $\hat{c} = min(\hat{\theta}_0, \hat{\theta}_1)$ and $\hat{d} = max(\hat{\theta}_0, \hat{\theta}_1)$.

3. A New Naive Bayes Network-based Assessment Method

A Naive Bayes network assumes that the variables are conditionally independent, i.e., the information about an event is not dependent on that of other events. Additionally, we assume trapezoidal distribution for variables present in the training simulation. So, we developed a new SUAS based on Naive Bayes Network with trapezoidal distribution.

Thus, let $\mathbf{x}_i = \{X_{i1}, X_{i2}, \ldots, X_{ik}\}$ a random vector of data in the i-th sample with k-information (dimension/variables) obtained when training is performed and $w_j, j \in \Omega$ the performance class most likely to be chosen, since the set $\Omega = 1, \ldots, M$ where M is the total number of performance classes for the assessment of a user in the simulator. The probability of the class w_j assuming that each variable X_{it} is conditionally independent of any other variable X_{il} for all $t \neq l \leq k$, is:

$$P(w_j|X_{i1}, X_{i2}, \ldots, X_{ik}) = \frac{1}{S}P(w_j)\prod_{t=1}^{k} P(X_{it}|w_j) \tag{7}$$

3.1. *The Trapezoidal Naive Bayes Network*

For better understanding, we present first the classical Trapezoidal Naive Bayes Network. In this case, it is assumed for $P(X_{it}|w_j)$ in Eq. (7) the conditional probability using Trapezoidal distribution. Thus, after mathematical manipulations, the Eq. (7) can be rewritten as a discriminating function g, as follows:

$$g(w_j|\mathbf{x}_i) = \log P(w_j|\mathbf{x}_i) \tag{8}$$

$$
= \begin{cases}
\log P(w_j) + \sum_{t=1}^{k} \log\left(\frac{X_{it}-a_j}{c_j-a_j}\right) + \sum_{t=1}^{k} \log A_t, & a_j \leq X_{it} \leq c_j \\[2mm]
\log P(w_j) + \sum_{t=1}^{k} A_t, & c_j \leq X_{it} \leq d_j \\[2mm]
\log P(w_j) + \sum_{t=1}^{k} \log\left(\frac{b_j-X_{it}}{b_j-d_j}\right) + \sum_{t=1}^{k} \log A_t, & d_j \leq X_{it} \leq b_j
\end{cases}
$$

where $A_t = \left[\frac{2}{(b_j-a_j)+(d_j-c_j)}\right]$, a_j, b_j, c_j and d_j are estimated using the training data of for each class $w_j, j \in \Omega$ and Newton-Raphson method.

The decision rule for the vector $\mathbf{x}_i$ is given by

$$\hat{w}_j = \arg\max_{j \in \Omega} g(w_j|\mathbf{x}_i).$$

3.2. *The Fuzzy Trapezoidal Naive Bayes Network*

A new SUAS named Fuzzy Trapezoidal Naive Bayes Network is proposed from union of the Zadeh's definition of probability of fuzzy events[6] and trapezoidal distribution. Formally, let $(\mathbb{R}^k, B, P)$ a probability space, where B is σ-field of Borel subsets in $\mathbb{R}^k$ and P is probability measure of $\mathbb{R}^k$. Let F in B a fuzzy event with membership function $\mu_F : \mathbb{R}^k \to [0,1]$, then the probability of a fuzzy event F is defined by the Lebesgue-Stieltjes integral presented in the Eq. (9).

$$P(F) = \int_{F \subseteq \mathbb{R}^n} \mu_F(x)dP = E(\mu_F) = \int_{F \subseteq \mathbb{R}^n} \mu_F(x)f(x)dP \tag{9}$$

where $f(x)$ is a density function of a random variable X.[6] Thus, let a random vector $\mathbf{x}_i = \{X_{i1}, X_{i2}, \ldots, X_{ik}\}$, such that each $X_{it}, t = 1, \ldots, k$ is a fuzzy random variable with membership function $\mu_j(X_{it}), j = 1, \ldots, M$, so we have

$$P(w_j|X_{i1}, X_{i2}, \ldots, X_{ik}) = \frac{1}{S}P(w_j)\prod_{t=1}^{k} P(X_{it}|w_j)\mu_j(X_{it}). \tag{10}$$

As in the case of the Trapezoid Naive Bayes Network, assuming that $P(X_{it}|w_j)$ follows a Trapezoidal distribution, and applying some mathematical manipulations, the Fuzzy Naive Bayes Trapezoid Network can be described as a discriminating function g_f:

$$g_f(w_j|\mathbf{x}_i) = \log P(w_j|\mathbf{x}_i)$$

$$= \begin{cases} \log P(w_j) + \sum_{t=1}^{k} \left(\frac{X_{it} - a_j}{c_j - a_j} \right) + \\ \sum_{t=1}^{k} A_t + \log \mu_j(X_{it}), \qquad a_j \leq X_{it} \leq c_j \\ \\ \log P(w_j) + \sum_{t=1}^{k} A_t + \log \mu_j(X_{it}), \quad c_j \leq X \leq d_j \qquad (11) \\ \\ \log P(w_j) + \sum_{t=1}^{k} \left(\frac{b_j - X_{it}}{b_j - d_j} \right) + \\ \log A_t + \log \mu_j(X_{it}), \qquad d_j \leq X \leq b_j \end{cases}$$

where $A_t = \left[\frac{2}{(b_j - a_j) + (d_j - c_j)} \right]$, a_j, b_j, c_j and d_j are estimated using the training data of for each class $w_j, j \in \Omega$ and Newton-Raphson method. When compared to Eq. (8) it is possible to see the membership function added on it.

The vector $\mathbf{x_i}$ will be assigned to the class that

$$\hat{w}_j = \arg \max_{j \in \Omega} g_f(w_j|\mathbf{x}_i).$$

4. Results

The evaluation of the proposed new Fuzzy Naive Bayes Trapezoid Network in a SUAS was performed in a Monte Carlo simulation with 1.000 replications. In each replica, two samples were generated with 600 observations each and 200 observations per class (3 classes of performance, representing three possible assessments of the procedure: Class 1: "the procedure was performed well", Class 2: "the user needs more training" or Class 3: "the user needs much more training"). The first sample was used for training and the second one for testing of the new SUAS based on Fuzzy Trapezoidal Naive Bayes Network. The samples were generated with the estimated parameters presented in the Table 1 and densities with parameters can be observed in the Fig. 1, according to trapezoidal distribution defined in Eq. (1).

For each Monte Carlo replica, the metrics of accuracy (A), kappa coefficient (κ) and kappa variance (σ_κ^2) were calculated, as well as the average of CPU time. The results were obtained for the thousand samples. It was

Table 1. Parameters used in the simulation by Monte Carlo.

Parameters	Class 1 $[a, c, d, b]^\top$	Class 2 $[a, c, d, b]^\top$	Class 3 $[a, c, d, b]^\top$
Dimension 1	[0.5, 0.6, 2.4, 8.1]	[4.1, 6.6, 13.2, 15.5]	[8.1, 12.0, 19.7, 21.7]
Dimension 2	[1.6, 5.4, 9.3, 9.8]	[4.2, 6.9, 10.7, 11.7]	[6.2, 8.5, 10.3, 13.5]
Dimension 3	[4.2, 4.2, 9.4, 16.9]	[6.5, 9.3, 14.1, 17.9]	[9.8, 11.9, 16.7, 19.9]

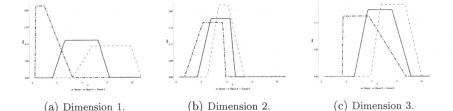

(a) Dimension 1.   (b) Dimension 2.   (c) Dimension 3.

Fig. 1. Trapezoidal distribution by dimension (variable) distinct by classes.

Table 2. Simulation results by Monte Carlo, where A is accuracy, κ is kappa coefficient, σ_κ^2 is kappa coefficient variance and CPU time.

Methods	$\overline{A}$ (%)	$\overline{\kappa}$ (%)	$\overline{\sigma_\kappa^2}$	CPU time
Naive Bayes	78.00	67.00	6.4×10^{-4}	0.55 s
Fuzzy Naive Bayes	78.05	67.07	6.4×10^{-4}	0.56 s
Trape. Naive Bayes	85.12	77.67	4.7×10^{-4}	2.56 s
Fuzzy Trape. Naive Bayes	85.76	78.65	4.6×10^{-4}	4.56 s

used a Intel Core i7-1165G7, 2.80GHz with 8 cores, with 16GB of RAM, running Ubuntu Linux. The code was parallelized among the CPU cores, using 5 of the 8 available. In the Table 2 are presented the results of assessments. The SUAS based on Fuzzy Trapezoidal Naive Bayes method was superior to the other SUAS in accuracy (85.76%), kappa (78.65%) and lower in kappa variance (4.6×10^{-4}). However, its average of CPU time was higher than others with 4.56 seconds for the 600 assessment discrimination. The Trapezoidal Naive Bayes was the second most accurate SUAS (85.12%) and demanded approximately 56% less CPU time. Both SUAS achieved superior results with accuracy and kappa when compared to the Fuzzy Naive Bayes and Naive Bayes SUAS. A higher accuracy is important when considering the assessment of future professionals for health area in training simulators as SITEG.

5. Conclusion

In this paper was proposed a new naive bayes network, named Fuzzy Trapezoidal Naive Bayes Network, which is able to treat multidimensional intervals modelling them using trapezoidal distributions. This network was used as basis for a SUAS for VR simulators as, for instance, SITEG 2.0.

Simulations were performed using data that followed a trapezoidal distribution, and compared with Naive Bayes and Fuzzy Naive Bayes SUAS. The simulation results showed that the SUAS based on the trapezoidal distribution were able to discriminate the assessments, surpassing the classic Naive Bayes and Fuzzy Naive Bayes.

The Fuzzy Trapezoidal Naive Bayes Network proposed in this paper can also be used for data and image classification when data can be assumed as trapezoidal distribution or considered as intervalar-valued data.

Acknowledgments

This project is partially supported by grants 315278/2018-8 and 465586/2014-4 received from the National Council for Scientific and Technological Development and by Fundação de Apoio à Pesquisa do Estado da Paraíba (FAPESQ).

References

1. R.N. Kacker and J.F. Lawrence, Trapezoidal and Triangular Distributions for Type B Evaluation of Standard Uncertainty, Metrologia **44**, p. 117 (2007).
2. R.M. Moraes, J.A. Ferreira and L.S. Machado, in *International Journal of Fuzzy Systems*, **23**, 849 (2021).
3. R.M. Moraes, I.L.A. Silva and L.S. Machado, Online Skills Assessment in Training Based on Virtual Reality Using a Novel Fuzzy Triangular Naive Bayes Network, in *Proc. FLINS*, (2020).
4. R.M. Moraes, L.S. Machado, A New Architecture for Assessment of Multiple Users in Collaborative Medical Training Environments Based on Virtual Reality, in *Proc. FLINS*, (2012).
5. K. Soetaert and P.M. Herman, *A Practical Guide to Ecological Modelling. Using R as a Simulation Platform* (Springer, 2009).
6. L.A. Zadeh, in *Journal of mathematical analysis and applications*, **23**, 421 (1968).

A linguistic ELECTRE III method for heterogeneous multicriteria ranking problems

Juan Carlos Leyva López[*], Jesús Jaime Solano Noriega[†] and
Jorge Anselmo Rodríguez Castro[‡]

Universidad Autónoma de Occidente
Culiacán, México
[*]juan.leyva@uadeo.mx
[†]jaime.solano@uadeo.mx
[‡]jorge.rodriguez@uadeo.mx
www.uadeo.mx

Luis Martínez López

Universidad de Jaen
Jaen, España
martin@ujaen.es

This paper proposes a new approach for the ELECTRE III method based on the linguistic 2-tuple fusion model for dealing with heterogeneous information. It provides a flexible evaluation framework in which decision-makers can supply their preferences using different information domains conform to the nature and uncertainty of criteria and their level of knowledge and experience. The new method uses a linguistic-based distance measure appropriate for multicriteria ranking problems. The feasibility and applicability of linguistic ELECTRE III are illustrated in an example for selecting a green supplier.

Keywords: Multicriteria decision analysis; ELECTRE III; 2-tuple linguistic representation model; heterogeneous information; linguistic preferences.

1. Introduction

Multicriteria Decision Analysis (MCDA) supplies a methodological structure for handling complex decision-making problems with multiple criteria in conflict. In MCDA, given a set of decision alternatives and based on their preferences, a decision-maker (DM) can make a description, a selection, a classification (sorting), or a ranking of the alternatives.[7] In the outranking approach of MCDA for the multicriteria ranking problem, the DM can rank the alternatives in decreasing order of preference, with the possibility of ties and incomparabilities between them.[2]

The ELECTRE III[7] is a representative method of MCDA that constructs and exploits a fuzzy outranking relation. However, ELECTRE III is limited regarding dealing with heterogeneous information and uncertainty.

This paper proposes a new approach for the ELECTRE III method to overcome such limitations, which provides a flexible heterogeneous evaluation framework. The heterogeneous information will be managed by a fusion linguistic approach[4] that transforms the heterogeneous information into a linguistic one. To construct the fuzzy outranking relation that allows linguistic modeling, we use the fuzzy linguistic approach based on the 2-tuple linguistic representation model.[3] The application of the proposed approach is demonstrated in the context of a case study where a set of green suppliers must be ranked.

The rest of the paper is organized as follows. First, fundamental concepts about the ELECTRE III method are introduced in Section 2. Then, a brief heterogeneous information background is presented in Section 3. Next, the linguistic ELECTRE III is proposed in Section 4, and Section 5 is shown an illustrative example. Finally, the conclusions are pointed out in Section 6.

2. The ELECTRE III Method

The ELECTRE III method is a multicriteria ranking method relatively simple in conception and application compared to other MCDA methods. It encompasses two phases. (i) the outranking relation between pairs of alternatives is formed. This results in a fuzzy outranking relation. (ii) the second phase consists of exploiting this relation, producing a partial preorder.[8] Let have the following notations: $A = \{a_1, a_2, ..., a_m\}$ is the set of alternatives, $G = \{g_1, g_2, ..., g_n\}$ is the set or family of criteria, and J denotes the set of criteria indices and $W = \{w_1, w_2, ..., w_n\}$ is the weight vector. Let us assume that $\sum_{i=1}^{n} w_i = 1$. $g_j(a_i)$ is the evaluation of criterion g_j for alternative a_i.

The ELECTRE III method establishes concordance and discordance measures for each ordered pair $(a_i, a_j) \in A \times A$. It combines these two measures to produce a credibility index $\sigma(a_i, a_j)$ $(0 \leq \sigma(a_i, a_j) \leq 1)$ that evaluate the intensity of the assertion that "a_i is at least as good as a_j, $a_i S a_j$." Therefore, ELECTRE III constructs a fuzzy outranking relation S_A^σ defined on $A \times A$. The next step carried out by ELECTRE III is to exploit S_A^σ to derive a ranking of alternatives using the distillation procedure.[7]

3. Heterogeneous Information in MCDA

3.1. *The heterogeneous framework*

The DM might express their preferences in the numerical, interval, or linguistic information domains, generating a heterogeneous framework[5] used in the proposed linguistic ELECTRE III.

3.2. The 2-tuple linguistic representation model

The proposed linguistic ELECTRE III method utilizes the 2-tuple linguistic representation model.[3] This model is based on a concept of symbolic translation used to represent heterogeneous information through a pair of values named 2-tuple (s,α), where s is a linguistic term and α is a numeric value representing the symbolic translation.

Definition 3.1 [3]. *Let* $S = \{s_0,...,s_h\}$ *be a linguistic term set. The symbolic translation of a linguistic term* $s_i \in S = \{s_0,...,s_h\}$ *is a numerical value assessed in* $[-0.5,0.5)$ *that supports the "difference of information" between an amount of information* $\beta \in [0,h]$ *and the closest value in* $\{0,...,h\}$ *that indicates the index of the closest linguistic term in* $S(s_i)$ *being* $[0,h]$ *the interval of granularity of S.*

Definition 3.2 [3]. *Let* $S = \{s_0,...,s_h\}$ *a linguistic term set and* $\beta \in [0,h]$ *a value supporting the result of a symbolic aggregation operation, then the 2-tuple that expresses the equivalent information to* β *is obtained with the following function:*

$$\Delta_S : [0,h] \to S \times (-0.5,.0.5) \tag{1}$$

$$\Delta_S(\beta) = (s_i,\alpha), \text{ with } \quad \begin{cases} s_i & i = round(\beta) \\ \alpha = \beta - i & \alpha \in [-0.5,0,5) \end{cases} \tag{2}$$

where round (·) is the usual round operation, s_i *has the closest index label to* "β" *and* "α" *is the value of the symbolic translation.*

Let $S = \{s_0,...,s_h\}$ be a linguistic term set and (s_i,α_i) be a linguistic 2-tuple. From this definition, a Δ_S^{-1} function can be defined, such that, from a 2-tuple (s_i,α_i) it returns its equivalent numerical value $\beta \in [0,h]$ in the interval of granularity of S in the following way:

$$\Delta_S^{-1} : S \times [-0,5,0.5) \to [0,h] \tag{3}$$

$$\Delta_S^{-1}(s_i,\alpha) = i + \alpha = \beta . \tag{4}$$

3.3. The linguistic fusion approach for heterogeneous information

The resolution process for the fusion of the information in Ref. 6 is organized into the following steps:

1. *Choosing the basic linguistic term set (BLTS)* $S_{BLTS} = \{s_0, s_1, ..., s_h\}$
2. *Transformation of the heterogeneous information into fuzzy sets in a linguistic domain*
3. *Transformation of fuzzy sets into linguistic 2-tuples values*

4. The Linguistic ELECTRE III Method

The methodology for modeling the linguistic outranking index is organized into three phases.

4.1. Fusion of heterogeneous information

The fused assessment for each criterion g_k, concerning each alternative a_i, is represented in a 2-tuple linguistic value $\overline{g}_k(a_i) = (s_i, \alpha_i) \in S_{BLTS}$.

4.2. Linguistic difference function between 2-tuple linguistic values

Definition 4.1. *Let* $S_{BLTS} = \{s_0, ..., s_h\}$ *and* $S^C = \{l_0^C, ..., l_{\hat{h}}^C\}$ *be the set of linguistic terms for preference values and the set of linguistic terms to express the linguistic difference value between two terms in* S_{BLTS}, *respectively. Let* (s_i, α_i) *and* (s_j, α_j) *be two 2-tuple linguistic values expressed in* S_{BLTS}. *The linguistic difference value between* (s_i, α_i) *and* (s_j, α_j) *expressed in* $\overline{S}^C$ *is computed by:*

$$D_S : \overline{S}_{BLTS} \times \overline{S}_{BLTS} \rightarrow \overline{S}^C \tag{5}$$

$$D_S((s_i, \alpha_i), (s_j, \alpha_j)) = \Delta_{S^C}\left(\frac{((\Delta_{S_{BLTS}}^{-1}(s_j, \alpha_j) - \Delta_{S_{BLTS}}^{-1}(s_i, \alpha_i)) + h)}{2.h} \cdot \hat{h}\right). \tag{6}$$

4.3. Linguistic concordance and discordance indices

4.3.1. The linguistic concordance indices

Let $(l_{t_{q_k}}, \alpha_{q_k})_q$ and $(l_{t_{p_k}}, \alpha_{p_k})_p$ be the indifference and preference thresholds, respectively.

Definition 4.2. *The linguistic concordance index concerning a criterion* g_k, $\overline{C}_k(a_i, a_j)$, *that denotes the linguistic concordance value expressed in 2-tuple linguistic values in* $S^P = \{s_0^P, ..., s_{h_p}^P\}$ *of the linguistic difference value between the alternative* a_j *over the alternative* a_i, *regarding criterion k,* $\overline{D}_S(a_i, a_j)_k = D_S(\overline{g}_k(a_i), \overline{g}_k(a_j)) \in \overline{S}^C$ *is defined as:*

$$\bar{C}_k(a_i,a_j):A_n\ A\dagger\ \bar{S}^P \tag{7}$$

$$\bar{C}_k(a_i,a_j)=\begin{cases}(s_0^P,0), & if & \bar{D}_S(a_i,a_j)_k>(l_{t_{p_k}},\alpha_{p_k})_p \\[2ex] \Delta_{S^P}\left(\dfrac{\Delta_{S_C}^{-1}(l_{t_{p_k}},\alpha_{p_k})_p-\dfrac{\hat{h}}{2}-[\Delta_{S_C}^{-1}(\bar{D}_S(a_i,a_j)_k)-\dfrac{\hat{h}}{2}]}{\Delta_{S_C}^{-1}(l_{t_{p_k}},\alpha_{p_k})_p-\dfrac{\hat{h}}{2}-\left(\Delta_{S_C}^{-1}(l_{t_{q_k}},\alpha_{q_k})_q-\dfrac{\hat{h}}{2}\right)}.h_p\right), \\[2ex] \qquad if\quad (l_{t_{q_k}},\alpha_{q_k})_q<\bar{D}_S(a_i,a_j)_k\le(l_{t_{p_k}},\alpha_{p_k})_p \\[2ex] (s_{h_p}^P,0), & if & \bar{D}_S(a_i,a_j)_k\le(l_{t_{q_k}},\alpha_{q_k})_q\end{cases},\ k=1,...,n \tag{8}$$

4.3.2. The comprehensive linguistic concordance index

Let w_k be the importance coefficient or the weight for criterion k, with $\sum_{i=1}^{n}w_i=1$. Then, the comprehensive linguistic concordance index $\bar{C}(a_i,a_j)$ is defined as follows:

$$\bar{C}:A\times A\to\bar{S}^P \tag{9}$$

$$\bar{C}(a_i,a_j)=\Delta_{S^P}\left(\sum_{k=1}^{n}w_k\left(\Delta_{S^P}^{-1}\left(\bar{C}_k(a_i,a_j)\right)\right)\right) \tag{10}$$

4.3.3. The linguistic discordance indices

Let $(l_{t_{v_k}},\alpha_{v_k})_v$ be the linguistic veto threshold.

Definition 4.3. *The linguistic discordance index for a criterion* g_k, $\bar{d}_k(a_i,a_j)$, *that denotes the linguistic discordance value expressed in 2-tuple linguistic values in* $S^P=\{s_0^P,...,s_{h_p}^P\}$ *of the linguistic difference value between the alternative* a_j *over the alternative* a_i, *regarding criterion* k, $\bar{D}_S(a_i,a_j)_k=D_S(\bar{g}_k(a_i),\bar{g}_k(a_j))\in\bar{S}^C$ *is defined as:*

$$\bar{d}_k(a_i,a_j):A\times A\to\bar{S}^P \tag{11}$$

$$\bar{d}_k(a_i,a_j)=\begin{cases}(s_0^P,0), & if\quad \bar{D}_S(a_i,a_j)_k\le(l_{t_{p_k}},\alpha_{p_k})_p \\[2ex] \Delta_{S^P}\left(\dfrac{\Delta_{S^C}^{-1}(\bar{D}_S(a_i,a_j)_k)-\dfrac{\hat{h}}{2}-\left(\Delta_{S^C}^{-1}(l_{t_{p_k}},\alpha_{p_k})_p-\dfrac{\hat{h}}{2}\right)}{\Delta_{S^C}^{-1}(l_{t_{v_k}},\alpha_{v_k})_v-\dfrac{\hat{h}}{2}-\left(\Delta_{S^C}^{-1}(l_{t_{p_k}},\alpha_{p_k})_p-\dfrac{\hat{h}}{2}\right)}.h_p\right), \\[2ex] \qquad if(l_{t_{p_k}},\alpha_{p_k})_p<\bar{D}_S(a_i,a_j)_k<(l_{t_{v_k}},\alpha_{v_k})_v \\[2ex] (s_{h_p}^P,0), & if\quad \bar{D}_S(a_i,a_j)_k\ge(l_{t_{v_k}},\alpha_{v_k})_v\end{cases}\quad k=1,2,...,n \tag{12}$$

4.4. The linguistic outranking relation in the linguistic ELECTRE III

The linguistic credibility index $\bar{\sigma}(a_i, a_j)$ is defined as follows:

$$\bar{\sigma}(a_i, a_j) = \begin{cases} \bar{C}(a_i, a_j), & if \quad \bar{K}(a_i, a_j) = \phi \\ \Delta_{S^P}(\Delta_{S^P}^{-1}(\bar{C}(a_i, a_j))) \bullet \prod_{k \in \bar{K}(a_i, a_j)} \dfrac{\Delta_{S_p}^{-1}(s_{h_p}^P, 0) - \Delta_{S_p}^{-1}(\bar{d}_k(a_i, a_j))}{\Delta_{S_p}^{-1}(s_{h_p}^P, 0) - \Delta_{S_p}^{-1}(\bar{C}(a_i, a_j))}) & if \ \bar{K}(a_i, a_j) \neq \phi \end{cases} \quad (13)$$

where $\bar{K}(a_i, a_j) = \left\{ g_k \in G \middle| \bar{d}_k(a_i, a_j) > \bar{C}(a_i, a_j) \right\}$ (14)

4.5. The ranking algorithm in the linguistic ELECTRE III

The next step in the linguistic outranking approach is to exploit the model and produce a ranking of alternatives from the linguistic outranking relation $S_A^{\bar{\sigma}}$. The final partial preorder of alternatives produced by the linguistic ELECTRE III method is obtained as the "intersection" of two complete preorders resulting from the so-called descending and ascending distillations. In the descending distillation, one orders the alternatives from the best to the worst. In contrast, in the ascending distillation, one ranks the alternatives oppositely, starting from the worst and finishing with the best.

5. An Illustrative Example

The application of the proposed approach is demonstrated in the context of a case study taken from Ref. 1 where a set of green suppliers must be ranked. It consists of three green suppliers that must be ranked according to their assessments on seven criteria. Each step of the linguistic ELECTRE III method is described below.

Step 1. Formulation of the multicriteria ranking problem

This case study was conducted in a company in which a DM with specific knowledge background evaluates a set of green suppliers $A @ \{a_1, a_2, a_3\}$, by using different expression domains: Numerical(N), Interval-valued(I), or Linguistic (L). A group of seven criteria $G @ \{g_1, g_2, g_3, g_4, g_5, g_6, g_7\}$ assesses the set of suppliers. Criteria $\{g_1, g_2, g_3, g_4\}$ are linguistic valued, g_5 is interval-valued, and $\{g_6, g_7\}$ are numerical valued. The DM expresses his linguistic assessments in a linguistic domain with nine linguistic terms, denoted by S^9.

$S^9 = \{ s_0$:Null (N), s_1 :AlmostNull (AN), s_2 : VeryLow (VL), s_3 :Low (L), s_4 : Medium (M), s_5 :High (H), s_6 :SlightlyHigh (SH), s_7 : VeryHigh (VH), s_8 : Perfect (P)$\}$

Step 2. Collecting the heterogeneous information

Table 1. Information provided by the DM expressed in S^0.

	g_1	g_2	g_3	g_4	g_5	g_6	g_7
a_1	M	VL	M	M	59-69	0.61	0.77
a_2	SH	SH	M	SH	66-83	0.79	0.88
a_3	VH	SH	SH	VH	80-91	0.87	0.97

Step 3. Fusion of the heterogeneous information

Table 2. Fused information provided by the DM.

	g_1	g_2	g_3	g_4	g_5	g_6	g_7
a_1	(M,0)	(VL,0)	(M,0)	(M,0)	(H,0.13)	(H, -0.12)	(SH,0.16)
a_2	(SH,0)	(SH,0)	(M,0)	(SH,0)	(SH, -0.03)	(SH,0.32)	(VH, 0.04)
a_3	(VH,0)	(SH,0)	(SH,0)	(VH,0)	(VH, -0.17)	(VH, -0.04)	(P, -0.24)

Step 4. Computing linguistic difference values between unified assessments

The linguistic difference value between a pair of 2-tuple linguistic values is expressed in the linguistic comparison scale $S^C = \{l_0^C, ..., l_h^C\}$.

Step 5. Computing linguistic concordance values

linguistic concordance index concerning a criterion g_k, $\bar{C}_k(a_i, a_j)$

The computation of the linguistic outranking value for each criterion is expressed in a linguistic preference scale $S^P = \{s_0^P, ..., s_8^P\}$ with nine linguistic terms. For each criterion g_k, its indifference $((l_{t_{q_k}}^C, \alpha_{q_k})_q)$, preference $((l_{t_{p_k}}^C, \alpha_{p_k})_p)$, and veto $((l_{t_{v_k}}^C, \alpha_{v_k})_v)$ threshold values are $(l_5^C, 0)_q$, $(l_6^C, 0)_p$, and $(l_7^C, 0)_v$ respectively.

For instance, on criterion g_4, the concordance matrix is defined in Table 3.

Table 3. Concordance matrix on a criterion g_4.

$\bar{C}_4(a_1, a_2)$	a_1	a_2	a_3
a_1	$(s_8^P, 0)$	$(s_8^P, 0)$	$(s_4^P, 0)$
a_2	$(s_8^P, 0)$	$(s_8^P, 0)$	$(s_8^P, 0)$
a_3	$(s_8^P, 0)$	$(s_8^P, 0)$	$(s_8^P, 0)$

The comprehensive linguistic concordance index $\overline{C}(a_i, a_j)$

Let $W = (0.1, 0.2, 0.1.0.2, 0.15, 0.1, 0.15)$ be the weight vector for the set of criteria. The value of $\overline{C}(a_1, a_2) = (s_6^p, 0.4)$.

The comprehensive linguistic concordance matrix is obtained (Table 4).

Table 4. Comprehensive linguistic concordance matrix.

$\overline{C}(a_i, a_j)$	a_1	a_2	a_3
a_1	$(s_8^p, 0)$	$(s_6^p, 0.4)$	$(s_5^p, 0.168)$
a_2	$(s_8^p, 0)$	$(s_8^p, 0)$	$(s_8^p, 0)$
a_3	$(s_8^p, 0)$	$(s_8^p, 0)$	$(s_8^p, 0)$

Step 6. Computing linguistic discordance values $\overline{d}_k(a_i, a_j)$

For instance, on criterion g_4, the discordance matrix is defined in Table 5.

Table 5. Discordance matrix on a criterion g_4.

$\overline{d}_4(a_i, a_j)$	a_1	a_2	a_3
a_1	$(s_0^p, 0)$	$(s_0^p, 0)$	$(s_0^p, 0)$
a_2	$(s_0^p, 0)$	$(s_0^p, 0)$	$(s_0^p, 0)$
a_3	$(s_0^p, 0)$	$(s_0^p, 0)$	$(s_0^p, 0)$

Step 7. Computing the linguistic outranking relation

Table 6. Linguistic credibility matrix in the linguistic ELECTRE III.

$\overline{\sigma}(a_i, a_j)$	a_1	a_2	a_3
a_1	$(s_8^p, 0)$	$(s_6^p, 0.4)$	$(s_5^p, 0.168)$
a_2	$(s_8^p, 0)$	$(s_8^p, 0)$	$(s_8^p, 0)$
a_3	$(s_8^p, 0)$	$(s_8^p, 0)$	$(s_8^p, 0)$

Step 8. Ranking of alternatives from the linguistic outranking relation $S_A^{\overline{\sigma}}$

The ranking algorithm can be applied according to the linguistic credibility matrix obtained by the linguistic ELECTRE III (Table 6). After completing the descending and ascending distillations, we got two complete preorders whose intersection creates the final ranking of the alternatives. The final ranking is: $[a_2, a_3]$ is in the first position in the rank, and then a_1 is in the second position.

6. Conclusions

A linguistic ELECTRE III method has been proposed to solve multicriteria ranking problems defined in heterogeneous contexts. The method fuses the heterogeneous information into 2-tuple linguistic values, enabling the decision-maker can provide their preferences using different expression domains, such as numerical domain, interval-valued domain, and linguistic domain

Acknowledgments

This work was partially supported by the Spanish Ministry of Economy and Competitiveness through the Spanish National Research Project PGC2018-099402-B-I00.

References

1. Espinilla, M., Halouani, N., and Chabchoub, H. (2015) Pure linguistic PROMETHEE I and II methods for heterogeneous MCGDM problems, *International Journal of Computational Intelligence Systems*, 8:2, 250-264.
2. Figueira J., Greco, S., Roy, B. and Slowinski, R. (2010). ELECTRE Methods: Main Features and Recent Developments. En Constantin Zopounidis y Pardalos Panos (Eds.). *Handbook in Multicriteria Analysis*. Berlin, Germany. Springer-Verlag.
3. Herrera, F. and Martinez, L. (2000). A 2-tuple fuzzy linguistic representation model for computing with words. *IEEE Transactions on fuzzy Systems.* **8**, 746–752.
4. Herrera, F, Martínez, L., and Sánchez, P.J. (2005) Managing non-homogeneous information in group decision making, *European Journal of Operational Research* 166, 115–132.
5. Martínez, L., Liu, J., and Yang, J.B. (2006). A fuzzy model for design evaluation based on multiple-criteria analysis in engineering systems, *International Journal of Uncertainty, Fuzziness and Knowledge-Based Systems* 14 (3), 317–336.
6. Martinez, L. and Herrera, F. (2012). An overview on the 2-tuple linguistic model for computing with words in decision making: extensions, applications, and challenges. *Information Sciences.* **207**, 1–18.
7. Roy, B. (1996). *Multicriteria Methodology for Decision Aiding*. Dordrecht, Holland: Kluwer.
8. Roy, B. (1991). The outranking approach and the foundations of ELECTRE methods. *Theory and Decision.* **31**, 49–73.

A named entity recognition model based on context and multi-granularity feature fusion for Chinese medical text

Xiong Liao, Zhen Jia, Fan Zhang and Tianrui Li*

School of Computing and Artificial Intelligence, Southwest Jiaotong University
Chengdu, Sichuan, China
*trli@swjtu.edu.cn

Medical named entity recognition (NER) is the pivotal pre-technology of medical knowledge graph (MKG) construction, but the existing methods are difficult to take into account the contextual information and the terms with different granularities in Chinese medical texts (CMT). Based on this, a NER model CMG-CRF for CMT is proposed, which extracts features with different granularities through StackCNN, and recognizes entities in combination with the contextual features obtained by BiGRU. The experimental results show that the proposed model has an average F1-score of 92.54% on the Chinese medical dataset, which performs better than the benchmark models.

Keywords: Named entity recognition; medical entity; feature fusion.

1. Introduction

Medical knowledge graph (MKG) is widely used in intelligent medicine. One of the basic tasks of constructing MKG is medical named entity recognition (NER). It requires to recognize medical entities from medical texts, e.g. `diseases, drugs, microorganisms, examinations`. Chinese medical texts (CMT) contain a large number of professional terms with high correlation and uneven granularity. These terms have different medical meanings in different contexts. For example, the `disease` has completely opposite significance in indications and contraindications. To recognize entities accurately, the model needs to extract contextual information and capture features with different granularities. The existing medical NRE methods are difficult to integrate these two types of information, such as LSTM-based,[1,2] attention-based,[3] and fusion-model based.[4]

To solve these problems, we propose a Context and Multi-Granularity CRF model (CMG-CRF) for recognizing Chinese medical entities, which utilizes BiGRU and StackCNN to capture contextual information and the terms with different granularities respectively. BiGRU is simpler in structure and easier to train than BiLSTM,[5] while using StackCNN can process coarse-grained information that cannot be extracted by ordinary CNN. Finally, we decode features by CRF to obtain entity labels. In order to verify the performance of our model, we perform a comparative experiment with some baseline models on the Chinese medical dataset. All resources from this project are available at `https://github.com/zhenjia2017/RDUKG`.

2. Related Work

Now the mainstream NER method is based on the architecture of **deep learning model + multiple classifier**. Different deep learning models and strategies will be used according to the different tasks. Due to the forward and backward dependence of tags in sequence labeling, CRF[6] is usually used as a classifier in this task.

Huang et al.[7] applied BiLSTM-CRF to the sequence labeling task in natural language processing (NLP) for the first time. And then Ma et al.[8] and Chiu et al.[9] captured character level features by combining CNN with BiLSTM-CRF. Attention based[10,11] models were also applied to NER task. Jia et al.[10] combined features of character and font, while Deng et al.[11] adopted capsule network rather than CRF. Lattice LSTM[12] has a unique structure, which can introduce external vocabulary in NER, but the model with this structure is hard to train. After that, the Soft Lexicon[13] strategy was proposed, which only modifies the word vector by weighting, so that the model is simple and efficient.

NER in the medical field needs to consider the domain characteristics of data. Chalaparty et al.[1] proposed a word based BiLSTM-CRF model for clinical concept extraction. Some researches[2,14] have shown that the character based model performs better than the word based model. Dong et al.[15] divided Chinese Electronic Medical Records (CEMR) into multiple subsets, and then classified each subset by CNN-based model. Similar to the general field, attention was also adopted for medical NER.[3,4,16] Zeng et al.[17] achieved good results in DDIExtraction2013 challenge through joint embedding of characters and words. Lexical information was also used for medical NER,[18] which improved the performance of rare entities in CEMR.

3. Approach

3.1. *Problem description*

Chinese medical NER task can be formulated as a token-level sequence labeling problem. Assuming the input $S = (x_1, x_2, \ldots, x_m)$ is a sequence of Chinese character, where m indicates the length of this sequence. We should predict a label sequence $L = (y_1, y_2, \ldots, y_m)$, where each y_i comes from a finite label set and corresponds to each x_i.

3.2. Model

As shown in Fig. 1, our model contains two key components, BiGRU and StackCNN.

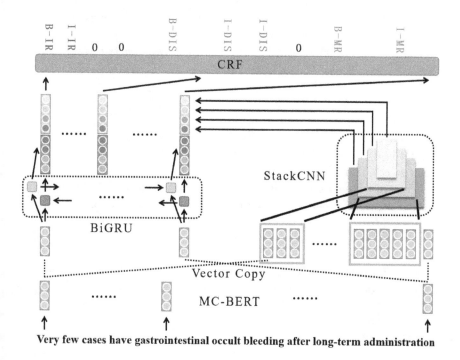

Fig. 1. The structure of CMG-CRF.

Firstly, the text feature X is obtained from MC-BERT,[19] which will be input into BiGRU and StackCNN, respectively. BiGRU is used to capture the contextual information of CMT. The hidden layer output H of BiGRU can be represented by Formula 1. The dimension of H is $m \times d_{GRU}$, and d_{GRU} is the hidden layer dimension of BiGRU.

$$H = BiGRU(X) = [\overrightarrow{GRU}; \overleftarrow{GRU}] = (h_1, h_2, \ldots, h_m) \tag{1}$$

StackCNN is a stack of one-dimensional CNNs, which contains p categories with different sizes, and each category has q CNNs of the same size. The CNNs with different category are used to extract information of different granularities, while the CNNs with the same size extract multiple information of the same granularity. The size of CNN gradually increases between categories. The initial size of CNN is k_b and the incremental size is k_s. When the hyperparameter k_s is determined, the other three parameters $p = \lfloor \frac{m}{k_s} \rfloor$, $q = \lfloor \frac{d_{SCNN}}{p} \rfloor$ and $k_b = k_s - 1$ are also determined, where $\lfloor \rfloor$ indicates round down. In order to maintain the dimension of X along the sequence direction, it is necessary to pad X before convolution, and the padding length is $l = \lfloor \frac{k_i}{2} \rfloor$, where $i \in [1, p]$.

The feature C with multiple granularities can be extracted by StackCNN from X, which is shown in Formula 2.

$$C = Tanh(Cat_{i=1}^{p}(Cat_{j=1}^{q}(CNN_{i,j}(X)))), \tag{2}$$

where $CNN_{i,j}$ refers to the j-th CNN of category i, $Cat()$ represents concatenating vectors and $Tanh()$ is a nonlinear activation function. The dimension of C is $m \times d_{SCNN}$.

After concatenation and dimension reduction of the two features H and C, CRF is used for entity recognition, as shown in Formula 3.

$$L = CRF([H; C] \cdot W + B) \tag{3}$$

The dimension of W is $(d_{GRU} + d_{SCNN}) \times d_L$, and B is the bias vector with dimension d_L. d_L indicates the number of entity labels.

4. Experimental Setup

4.1. Dataset

We use the Chinese medical dataset for the experiment, which is derived from the drug instructions. It contains nine independent sub datasets: ingredient (IGD), indication (IDC), adverse drug reactions (ADR), drug interaction (DI), precaution (PCT), medication during pregnancy and lactation (MPL), medication for children (MC), medication for the elderly (ME) and Dosage and Administration (DA). There are 28 entity categories in the dataset, such as disease, medicine, child and dosage. Each sub dataset contains 1,000 samples, and we divide the dataset into 4:1 for training and testing.

4.2. *Baseline*

- **CRF:**[2] The feature X of CMT is directly input into a linear layer, and then CRF is used for sequence labeling.
- **BiLSTM-CRF:**[20] The classic baseline model of sequence labeling task in NLP. We also replace BiLSTM with BiGRU for experiments.
- **Att-BiLSTM-CRF:**[16] After the BiLSTM model, attention is adopted to screen out the important information by weighting different features.
- **Lexicon Augmented NER:**[13] The lexical information is fused into the standard NER model by soft weighting to determine the entity boundary.

4.3. *Hyperparameter*

The number of hidden layer neurons of all RNNs is set to 128, and the incremental size k_s in CMG-CRF is taken as 2. The dropout of all models is 0.7 and the learning rate is 0.001. We train 100 turns with a mini-batch of size 64.

5. Results and Insights

F1-score is adopted as the evaluating indicator in the experiment, and results of NER are shown in Table 1.

CRF utilizes the text feature X directly rather than using the deep neural network for further processing, which leads to unsatisfactory results. Although BiLSTM-CRF and BIGRU-CRF can capture the contextual features, they cannot model the local information of the text. In contrast, StackCNN can effectively extract knowledge with different granularities from text. Attention can acquire multiple granularity features of text by adjusting the weights of different information, but this adjustment is not controllable. Lexicon Augmented NER combines lexical information in a soft weighted way to help determine the entity boundary. However, the granularity of words in the lexicon is generally small. CMG-CRF is more

Table 1.   Named entity recognition results.

Model	IGD	IDC	ADR	DI	Sub Datasets PCT	MPL	MC	ME	DA
CRF	93.61	87.29	88.74	84.56	88.24	89.36	91.67	84.85	83.79
BiLSTM-CRF	96.41	88.58	92.14	87.73	89.44	93.67	**95.61**	89.68	85.14
BiGRU-CRF	**97.10**	87.43	91.24	88.58	90.51	93.80	95.23	88.84	84.51
Att-BiLSTM-CRF	95.21	86.36	89.22	87.50	85.77	88.65	92.71	84.01	80.58
Lexicon Augmented NER	96.28	88.81	92.09	89.83	86.33	92.78	95.09	88.06	83.77
CMG-CRF	96.29	**90.33**	**94.34**	**92.02**	**91.22**	**94.37**	95.21	**91.05**	**88.00**

effective for CMT with large-grained entities such as `transient elevation of serum alkaline phosphatase`. From the results in Table 1, our model has the best performance on the seven sub datasets, with an average F1-score of 92.54%.

In order to compare the recognition effects of our model on different entity categories, we conduct experiments with entity level, and some results are shown in Table 2.

Table 2. Recognition results of various entities.

Model	Medicine	Elderly	Child	Gravida	Disease	Incidence	Dosage	Frequency	Treatment Course
					Entity Categories				
CRF	89.96	91.53	94.63	95.59	90.42	87.62	80.55	84.75	66.67
BiLSTM-CRF	91.01	97.20	96.59	96.32	93.28	90.00	81.48	**90.80**	70.59
BiGRU-CRF	91.88	96.50	96.35	**97.42**	92.61	89.50	78.15	87.50	76.00
Att-BiLSTM-CRF	90.18	95.47	93.33	95.59	92.18	83.05	76.34	84.92	69.09
Lexicon Augmented NER	92.75	96.86	**97.31**	96.73	93.42	90.67	83.33	88.00	66.67
CMG-CRF	**94.53**	**97.90**	96.59	96.32	**95.06**	**94.55**	**85.14**	90.29	**82.35**

Entities related to people (`Child` and `Gravida`) generally have relatively fixed expressions (`People:  Usage and Dosage`). Using simple models (BiLSTM-CRF) or combining word features (Lexicon Augmented NER) can improve the effect of entity recognition. Because of the similar expressions, the `Frequency` of medication is easy to be confused with the `Dosage` in Chinese drug instructions. For example, `three tablets at a time` is the entity of `Dosage`, while `three times a day` is the entity of `Frequency`. For other entities, our model has achieved the best performance, and the extraction results of the above three types of entities are not far from the optimal results.

6. Conclusions

In order to adapt to the information with high correlation and uneven granularity in CMT, we proposed a NER model, CMG-CRF, for CMT, which integrates the context and multi-granularity of text. The proposed model fuses features with context and multi-granularity to recognize medical entities in CMT. Through the comparison with various baseline models at the overall and entity levels, the effectiveness and rationality of the proposed model were verified. From the results, the difference between the results of each model is not significant in some cases, which indicates that single model for NER in CMT may not be greatly improved. Due to the preciseness of medical text, the NER method combined with external knowledge needs to be studied, which will be our follow-up work.

References

1. R. Chalapathy, E. Zare Borzeshi, and M. Piccardi, "Bidirectional LSTM-CRF for Clinical Concept Extraction," in *Proceedings of the Clinical Natural Language Processing Workshop*, 2016, pp. 7–12.
2. K. Xu, Z. F. Zhou, T. Y. Hao, and W. Y. Liu, "A Bidirectional LSTM and Conditional Random Fields Approach to Medical Named Entity Recognition," in *Proceedings of the International Conference on Advanced Intelligent Systems and Informatics*, 2017, pp. 355–365.
3. X. Y. Song, A. Feng, W. K. Wang, and Z. J. Gao, "Multidimensional Self-Attention for Aspect Term Extraction and Biomedical Named Entity Recognition," *Mathematical Problems in Engineering*, vol. 2020, pp. 1–6, 2020.
4. Z. J. Liu, X. L. Wang, Q. C. Chen, and B. Z. Tang, "Chinese clinical entity recognition via attention-based CNN-LSTM-CRF," in *2018 IEEE International Conference on Healthcare Informatics Workshop*, 2018, pp. 68–69.
5. K. Cho, B. Van Merriënboer, C. Gulcehre, D. Bahdanau, F. Bougares, H. Schwenk, and Y. Bengio, "Learning phrase representations using RNN encoder-decoder for statistical machine translation," *arXiv preprint arXiv:1406.1078*, 2014.
6. J. D. Lafferty, A. McCallum, and F. C. N. Pereira, "Conditional Random Fields: Probabilistic Models for Segmenting and Labeling Sequence Data," in *Proceedings of the Eighteenth International Conference on Machine Learning*, 2001, pp. 282–289.
7. Z. H. Huang, W. Xu, and K. Yu, "Bidirectional LSTM-CRF models for sequence tagging," *arXiv preprint arXiv:1508.01991*, 2015.
8. X. Ma and E. Hovy, "End-to-end Sequence Labeling via Bi-directional LSTM-CNNs-CRF," in *Proceedings of the 54th Annual Meeting of the Association for Computational Linguistics*, 2016, pp. 1064–1074.
9. J. P. Chiu and E. Nichols, "Named Entity Recognition with Bidirectional LSTM-CNNs," *Transactions of the Association for Computational Linguistics*, vol. 4, pp. 357–370, 2016.
10. Y. Jia and X. Ma, "Attention in Character-Based BiLSTM-CRF for Chinese Named Entity Recognition," in *Proceedings of the 2019 4th International Conference on Mathematics and Artificial Intelligence*, 2019, p. 1–4.
11. J. F. Deng, L. L. Cheng, and Z. W. Wang, "Self-attention-based BiGRU and capsule network for named entity recognition," *arXiv preprint*

624

arXiv:2002.00735, 2020.

12. Y. Zhang and J. Yang, "Chinese NER Using Lattice LSTM," in *Proceedings of the 56th Annual Meeting of the Association for Computational Linguistics*, 2018, pp. 1554–1564.

13. R. T. Ma, M. L. Peng, Q. Zhang, Z. Y. Wei, and X. J. Huang, "Simplify the Usage of Lexicon in Chinese NER," in *Proceedings of the 58th Annual Meeting of the Association for Computational Linguistics*, 2020, pp. 5951–5960.

14. C. Lyu, B. Chen, Y. Ren, and D. H. Ji, "Long short-term memory RNN for biomedical named entity recognition," *BMC Bioinformatics*, vol. 18, no. 1, pp. 462–472, 2017.

15. X. Dong, L. Qian, Y. Guan, L. Huang, Q. Yu, and J. Yang, "A multiclass classification method based on deep learning for named entity recognition in electronic medical records," in *2016 New York Scientific Data Summit*, 2016, pp. 1–10.

16. L. Luo, Z. H. Yang, P. Yang, Y. Zhang, L. Wang, H. F. Lin, and J. Wang, "An attention-based BiLSTM-CRF approach to document-level chemical named entity recognition," *Bioinformatics*, vol. 34, no. 8, pp. 1381–1388, 2017.

17. D. H. Zeng, C. J. Sun, L. Lin, and B. Q. Liu, "LSTM-CRF for Drug-Named Entity Recognition," *Entropy*, vol. 19, no. 6, pp. 283–294, 2017.

18. Q. Wang, Y. M. Zhou, T. Ruan, D. Gao, Y. H. Xia, and P. He, "Incorporating dictionaries into deep neural networks for the Chinese clinical named entity recognition," *Journal of Biomedical Informatics*, vol. 92, p. 103133, 2019.

19. N. Y. Zhang, Q. H. Jia, K. P. Yin, L. Dong, F. Gao, and N. W. Hua, "Conceptualized representation learning for chinese biomedical text mining," *arXiv preprint arXiv:2008.10813*, 2020.

20. Z. J. Dai, X. T. Wang, P. Ni, Y. M. Li, G. M. Li, and X. M. Bai, "Named Entity Recognition Using BERT BiLSTM CRF for Chinese Electronic Health Records," in *2019 12th International Congress on Image and Signal Processing, BioMedical Engineering and Informatics*, 2019, pp. 1–5.

Dynamic document clustering method based on neighborhood system and text connotation

Ling Yan[1], Hailiang Zhao[2] and Jie Xian[3]

School of Mathematics, Southwest Jiaotong University
Chengdu, 610031, China
[1]1021495347@qq.com
[2]hailiang@swjtu.edu.cn
[3]1482160005@qq.com

In the text clustering algorithm, the correlation between words which are extracted by the TFIDF is ignored, resulting in unclear geometric meaning of text vectorization and poor interpretability of clustering algorithms. In this paper, an improved clustering algorithm is proposed. According to the co-occurrence fuzzy relationship between words, the algorithm obtains co-occurrence keywords through the neighborhood systems of words, so as to enhance the relevance between words. Then, the text vectorization is performed using the word frequency which implies the importance of the word in the text. Each word is used as a feature axis in the feature space, and the frequency of the word is used as the size of the corresponding component of the vector which enables text vectorization to have a definite size and direction. Finally, the weighted combination of cosine distance and Euclidean distance is used to construct the clustering objective function. Compared with similar references, experimental results show that the algorithm can significantly improve the accuracy and recall of clustering.

Keywords: Dynamic text clustering; k-means; neighborhood systems; vector space models; co-occurring keywords.

1. Introduction

At present, the number of scientific research papers in various fields is increasing explosively. Clustering algorithm is an effective means to efficiently analyze these huge text data. However, the research technology of text clustering is not mature enough, and there is still a lot of work to be done.

Text clustering techniques are roughly divided into three categories, one is text feature-based clustering, the other is latent semantic analysis clustering, and the third is deep learning clustering. As a typical distance-based clustering algorithm proposed earlier, K-means clustering algorithm is also a commonly used clustering algorithm today. In response to the problems existing in the k-means algorithm, many researchers have also made many improvements. Such as Chen Baolou, Li Min [1, 2] and others proposed an improved clustering algorithm for the problem that the original k-means is significantly affected by outliers and initial cluster centers. Zhang Qun et al. [3, 4] proposed improved clustering algorithms for semantic problems. Wang Chen et al. [5] propose a text clustering that combines both algorithms. However, the obtained accuracy is low. S. Zhou, P. Srikanth et al. [6, 7] proposed a new similarity measurement method. In addition, latent semantic analysis [8, 9] and deep learning clustering [10, 11] are also widely used today. However, although topic models and deep learning clustering have enriched text clustering techniques to a certain extent, their interpretability is also problematic.

Based on the above considerations, this paper proposes an improved k-means algorithm to achieve dynamic document clustering. This paper is mainly divided into 4 sections. The first two parts briefly introduce the main techniques of text clustering and the theory of neighborhood systems. The third part gives the specific operation of dynamic text clustering. Firstly, the extended keyword set is obtained through the word co-occurrence neighborhood, and then the text vectorization is carried out using the word frequency representing the importance of the word in the text. Finally, the clustering objective function is constructed by the combination of Euclidean and cosine distances weighting. The last part gives the experimental results, which show that the accuracy is 83.57%, and the recall is 84.28%. It can be seen that the algorithm can effectively improve the effect of clustering.

2. Neighborhood System Related Theory

Obviously, everything has its own neighborhoods. Considering the problem within the scope of some neighborhoods of it and ignoring irrelevant factors will greatly improve the efficiency. From the perspective of neighborhood system, this paper constructs the neighborhood of co-occurring keywords and strengthens the connection between words, so as to solve the problem of excessive differences in text topics due to different expression methods of text.

The concepts of neighborhood and neighborhood system are as follows.

Definition 1 (*Neighborhood and Neighborhood System* [12]) *Let X be a universe of discourse, and x be an object in X, call a certain subset of X as the neighborhood of x, denoted as N(x). The set composed of all the neighborhoods of x is called a neighborhood system of x, denoted as NS(x). The union of the neighborhood systems of all objects in the universe X is called the neighborhood system of the universe X, denoted as NS(X).*

According to the definition, we have

$$NS(x) = \{A \mid A \subseteq X \text{ and } A \text{ is a neighborhood of } x\}$$

$$NS(X) = \bigcup_{x \in X} NS(x)$$

Notice that the form of the neighborhood may be different for different problems, and the same is true for the neighborhood system.

3. A Time-varying Dynamic Document Clustering Method

3.1. Extended keywords set

How to use a keywords set to describe text information is a key step in text clustering, which will directly affect the quality of the clustering results. The term frequency-inverse document frequency (TF-IDF) algorithm [13] is a statistical method commonly used in text processing. However, using TFIDF to extract keywords for clustering has a low accuracy, because each word is regarded as an independent individual, so the correlation between words is ignored.

Based on the theoretical basis of the neighborhood system, this paper constructs word co-occurrence neighborhood, so as to enrich the original text information. The detailed process of this method is as follows.

Let $D = \{d_1, d_2, \ldots, d_n\}$, where d_i is the ith text, the word $w \in d_i$, and $K(d_i)$ be the keywords set of d_i. The feature importance of word w in d_i is calculated according to the TF-IDF algorithm [13].

$$TFIDF\ (w, d_i) = TF\ (w, d_i) \times IDF\ (w) = \frac{freq\ (w, d_i)}{\max\ (freq\ (d_i))} \times \log\left(\frac{n}{n(w)}\right) \quad (1)$$

In expression (1), $freq(w, d_i)$ is the frequency of the word w appears in the text d_i, and $\max(freq(d_i))$ is the highest frequency of the words in d_i. n is the number of all texts, and $n(w)$ represents the number of texts where the word w appears. The use of $n(w)$ can reduce the weight of keywords that appear in almost all texts.

Let $K_\sigma(d_i) = \{w \mid TFIDF(w, d_i) \geq \sigma\}$, where σ is the appropriate threshold for cutting keywords. On the standard sample set, the σ that makes the best clustering effect can be selected through the training parameter σ. Using TFIDF combined with threshold, the keyword set of each text is obtained. Then let

$$K = \bigcup_{i=1}^{n} K_\sigma(d_i) \tag{2}$$

To enhance the relevance between words, co-occurring keyword neighborhoods are considered. First we need to introduce some concepts as follows.

Definition 2 (*α-cut set* [14]) *Let* $\mathcal{F}(X)=\{A|A$ *is a fuzzy set in the universe set X*}, $A \in \mathcal{F}(X)$, *and* $\alpha \in [0,1]$. *Let*

$$A_\alpha = \{x \in X \mid A(x) \geq \alpha\} \tag{3}$$

Call A_α *the α-cut set of Fuzzy set A, or the α-level set of A.*

It can be seen from the above definition that K is the keyword set of all texts, then the fuzzy set on the universe $X=K \times K$ is the fuzzy relation on K. Therefore, this paper defines the co-occurrence fuzzy relationship of keywords as follows.

Definition 3 (*word co-occurrence fuzzy relationship*) *Let* K *is the keyword set of all texts, n is the total number of texts, and* $X=K \times K$ *be the universe of discourse. For words* $w_i, w_j \in K, i \neq j$, *let* $N(w_i, w_j)$ *represent the number of texts in which* w_i *and* w_j *co-occur. Let*

$$\tilde{A}(w_i, w_j) = \frac{N(w_i, w_j)}{n} \tag{4}$$

Obviously, $\tilde{A}$ *is a fuzzy set on X, and is called a fuzzy co-occurrence relation.* $\tilde{A}(w_i, w_j)$ *is called the degree of co-occurrence of the words* w_i *and* w_j.

Definition 4 *Let the universe of discourse* $X=K \times K$, *A is a word co-occurrence fuzzy relation on K, and* $\alpha \in [0,1]$. *Let*

$$A_\alpha = \{(w_i, w_j) \in X \mid A(w_i, w_j) \geq \alpha\} \tag{5}$$

A_α *is called the α-level co-occurrence relation, and the word* w_i *and* w_j *are co-occurring at the α level.*

So the co-occurrence keyword neighborhood of $w_i(w_i \in K)$ at the α level can be obtained as $S_\alpha(w_i) = \{w_{i_1}, w_{i_2}, \ldots, w_{i_s}\}, w_{i_j} \in K, j = 1,2,\ldots,s$. The selection of the threshold α is the same as the parameter σ above. Then, the α-level extended keyword set $E_\alpha(d_i)$ of the text d_i can be expressed by

$$E_\alpha(d_i) = K_\sigma(d_i) \cup \bigcup_{w_i \in K_\sigma(d_i)} S_\alpha(w_i) \tag{6}$$

where $K_\sigma(d_i)$ is the keyword set of d_i, and $S_\alpha(w_i)$ is the co-occurrence keyword neighborhood of w_i. Therefore, this paper compresses the text into an extended keyword set to describe. Then, the equivalence relation of the $D = \{d_1, d_2, \ldots, d_n\}$ can be transformed into the equivalence relation of the extended keywords sets $H = \{E_\alpha(d_1), E_\alpha(d_2), \ldots, E_\alpha(d_n)\}$. The definition of the quotient of the set H is shown in formula (7).

Definition 5 (α-level quotient) Let H be the extended keywords sets of all texts, $H \neq \emptyset, R_\alpha = \left\{ \left(E_\alpha(d_i), E_\alpha(d_j) \right) | E_\alpha(d_i) = E_\alpha(d_j) \right\}$, here $E_\alpha(d_i), E_\alpha(d_j) \in H$. Let

$$H / R_\alpha = \left\{ \left[R_\alpha(d_i) \right]_{R_\alpha} \mid E_\alpha(d_i) \in H \right\} \tag{7}$$

Call H/R_α the quotient of the relation of H set with respect to R_α.

The definition means that if extended keywords sets of two texts d_i and d_j are same, then the two texts are equivalent, that is, they are regarded as the same texts.

3.2. Text vectorization

The vectorization of text is a very critical step in clustering, which will directly affect the measurement of text similarity. The most commonly used model is the vector space model. The model is intuitive and easy to understand. But many texts don't give a clear explanation of its geometric meaning. They just form a large amount of data into a list or matrix and read them one by one, that is, they do not give the text a real vector meaning. Based on the above considerations, this paper uses word frequency to represent the weight of feature words, thereby mapping each text to a point in a high-dimensional space, and each keyword represents a feature axis. The frequency of the word is used as the size of the corresponding component of the vector which enables text vectorization to have

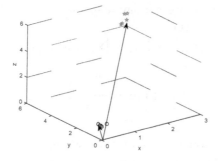

Fig. 1. Text distribution in three-dimensional space.

a definite size and direction. If the word frequency is larger, the vector modulus length is larger, and the importance contribution to the direction is larger. For example, as shown in Fig. 1.

Each point in the three-dimensional space represents a text, then we can intuitively imagine the distribution of texts. If the points in a certain area are dense, it is likely to belong to the same research direction of the text; if the frequency of a certain keyword is larger, the point on the corresponding feature axis should be farther away from the origin; The origin represents the position of empty texts, that is, contains no keywords. For ease of analysis, assuming that all keywords in $D = \{d_1, d_2, \ldots, d_n\}$ are $H = \bigcup_{i=1}^{n} E(d_i) = \{w_1, w_2, \ldots, w_p\}$. In order to perform vector operations in high-dimensional space, it is necessary to unify the vector dimensions of each text. The vectorization of d_i is denoted as $V_{d_i} = \{v_{ij} \mid j = 1, 2, \ldots, p\}$, where

$$v_{ij} = \begin{cases} 0, & w_i \notin d_i \\ c_i, & w_i \in d_i \end{cases} \tag{8}$$

and p is the number of all keywords in H, c_i is the frequency that the keyword w_i appears in the text d_i. Expression (8) means that if the keyword w_i appears in this text, the weight is set to the frequency of w_i, and 0 if w_i doesn't appear.

3.3. Clustering objective function

In this paper, the weighted combination of cosine distance and Euclidean distance is used to construct the clustering objective function. Because Euclidean distance describes the length of the vector and the cosine distance describes the consistency of the directions of two vectors. The larger the distance between the two points, the lower the similarity between the two texts; conversely, the smaller the distance, the higher the similarity. In addition, if some texts belong to a research direction, they should roughly appear in the nearby direction in the feature space.

Suppose $V_{d_i} = \{v_{i1}, v_{i2}, \ldots, v_{ip}\}$, $V_{d_j} = \{v_{j1}, v_{j2}, \ldots, v_{jp}\}$, let

$$\cos(d_i, d_j) = \frac{\sum_{k=1}^{p}(v_{ik} \cdot v_{jk})}{|V_{d_i}| \cdot |V_{d_j}|} \tag{9}$$

Call $\cos(d_i, d_j)$ the vector cosine of text d_i and d_j. The larger the $\cos(d_i, d_j)$, the smaller the angle, and the more consistent the research directions of the two texts. According to the vectorization of the two texts, this paper uses the Euclidean distance to describe the distance between the two points, as shown in expression (10).

$$d(i,j) = \sqrt{\left(v_{i1} - v_{j1}\right)^2 + \cdots + \left(v_{ip} - v_{jp}\right)^2} \tag{10}$$

Where $d(i,j)$ is the distance between d_i and d_j. If $d(i,j)$ is smaller, the similarity is higher.

Notice that if the extended keyword sets of the two texts are the same, this paper directly treats them as the same texts and does not distinguish.

Based on the above analysis, the clustering objective function is shown in expression (11). Let

$$Sim\left(d_i, d_j\right) = \lambda \cos\left(d_i, d_j\right) + \mu\left(1 - \frac{d(i,j)}{\max d}\right) \tag{11}$$

Call $Sim\left(d_i, d_j\right)$ the similarity between two texts d_i and d_j, where max d is the maximum Euclidean distance in the D which is the same as Section 3.1. λ and μ are the weights given to the cosine distance and the Euclidean distance respectively, such that $\lambda + \mu = 1$. In addition, because the cosine distance may be much smaller than the Euclidean distance, them are not on the same rank of magnitude which results in the occurrence of Large numbers eat small numbers. To avoid this, the Euclidean distance needs to be normalized.

4. Experimental Results and Analysis

In order to verify the effectiveness of the proposed clustering algorithm, 499 texts are randomly selected in CNKI, including three topics of face recognition, unmanned driving and text classification. Two performance evaluation indicators which are accuracy and recall are used in this paper. Accuracy means the proportion of correctly classified samples. Recall means the proportion of correctly identified samples in all true classification results. The classified results are compared with traditional k-means and existing methods, as shown in Table 1.

Table 1. Experimental results and their comparison.

Experimental program	Accuracy	Average Recall
Traditional k-means	0.6653	0.7127
Improved clustering	**0.8357**	**0.8428**
Reference [4]	0.8300	0.8900
Reference [5]	0.5728	0.5624

It can be seen from Table 1 that the accuracy of the improved clustering algorithm in this paper is 83.57%, and the recall is about 84.28%. Compared with traditional k-means, the algorithm proposed is effective, and the accuracy and recall have been significantly improved. What's more, this paper makes a comparison with similar references [4, 5]. The results of the reference [4] are almost the same as the results of this paper. However, the method of reference [4] requires clustering twice, first clustering to form semantic clusters, and then perform k-means clustering again according to the semantic cluster centers, which requires more computation, but this paper only needs to cluster once. The accuracy and recall of the reference [5] are much lower than the results of this paper.

5. Conclusions

Based on the idea of neighborhood system, a text vectorization method using word frequency is given according to the word co-occurrence neighborhood. Experimental results show that the accuracy reaches 83.57%, and the recall reaches about 84.28%. Compared with the existing methods, the improved clustering algorithm proposed is simpler, and can significantly improve the accuracy and recall of clustering.

References

1. Chen Baolou. Research on K-Means algorithm and its application in text clustering[D]. Anhui University, 2013(in Chinese).
2. Li Min. Improvement of K-means algorithm and its application in text clustering[D]. Jiangnan University, 2018(in Chinese).
3. Zhang Qun, Wang Hongjun, Wang Lunwen. A Short Text Clustering Algorithm Combining Context Semantics[J]. Computer Science, 2016, 43(S2): 443-446+450(in Chinese).
4. Qi Xiangming, Sun Xujiao. Chinese Text Clustering Algorithm Based on Semantic Clusters[J]. Journal of Jilin University (Science Edition), 2019, 57(05):1193-1199(in Chinese).
5. Wang Chen, Dong Yongquan. Integrating chemical reaction optimization and K-means text data clustering[J].Computer Engineering and Design, 2021, 42(08): 2248-2256(in Chinese).
6. S. Zhou, X. Xu, Y. Liu, R. Chang and Y. Xiao, "Text Similarity Measurement of Semantic Cognition Based on Word Vector Distance Decentralization With Clustering Analysis," in IEEE Access, vol. 7, pp. 107247-107258, 2019.

7. P. Srikanth and D. Deverapalli, "CFTDISM:Clustering Financial Text Documents Using Improved Similarity Measure," 2017 IEEE International Conference on Computational Intelligence and Computing Research (ICCIC), Coimbatore, India, 2017, pp. 1-4.
8. Zou Xiaohui. Application of LDA topic model in text clustering[J]. Digital Technology and Application, 2017(12):76-77(in Chinese).
9. J. Rashid et al., "Topic Modeling Technique for Text Mining Over Biomedical Text Corpora Through Hybrid Inverse Documents Frequency and Fuzzy K-Means Clustering," in IEEE Access, vol. 7, pp. 146070-146080, 2019.
10. Lu Ling, Yang Wu, Yang Youjun, Chen Menghan. Chinese short text classification method combining semantic expansion and convolutional neural network[J]. Computer Applications, 2017, 37(12): 3498-3503(in Chinese).
11. Sun Zhaoying, Liu Gongshen. Research on short text-oriented neural network clustering algorithm[J]. Computer Science, 2018, 45(S1): 392-395(in Chinese).
12. Zhao H L. A dynamic optimization decision and control model based on neighborhood systems[C]// Proceedings of 2013 6rd International Congress on Image and Signal Processing, Dec 16-18 2013:1329-1334.
13. Jiang Wei. Text Analysis and Text Mining[M]. Beijing: Science Press, 2018.11(in Chinese).
14. Hu Baoqing. Fuzzy Theory Foundation (Second Edition)[M]. Wuhan: Wuhan University Press, 2010.6(in Chinese).

A principle of clause elimination: Multi-literal implication modulo resolution

Xinran Ning* and Ying Xie

School of Computer Science and Engineering, Southwest Minzu University
Chengdu, Sichuan, China
* ningxinran99@foxmail.com

Guanfeng Wu†, Yang Xu and Peiyao Liu

National-Local Joint Engineering Laboratory of
System Credibility Automatic Verification
Southwest Jiaotong University, Chengdu 610031, China
† wgf1024@swjtu.edu.cn

Preprocessing techniques play a great role in efficient propositional solving and clause elimination methods are significant parts of them, which speed up SAT solvers' solving process by deleting redundant clauses in CNF formulas without influencing the satisfiability or unsatisfiability of the original formulas. In this paper, a novel theoretical principle of clause elimination *multi-literal implication modulo resolution* (MIMR) is put forward. Its soundness proof is also given, to prove any clause satisfying the principle of MIMR is redundant. Besides, effectiveness of MIMR is discussed compared with that of implication modulo resolution (IMR), which is higher than that of IMR.

Keywords: Redundancy; clause simplification; multi-literal implication modulo resolution.

1. Introduction

Clause-elimination techniques that simplify formulas by removing redundant clauses play an important role in modern SAT solving. In the beginning, simple clause elimination methods were used in SAT solvers, like pure literal elimination,[1] tautology elimination and subsumption elimination.[2] After that, more complicated clause elimination methods were proposed, like *blocked clause elimination* (BCE),[3] *hidden tautology elimination* (HTE),[4] *asymmetric tautology elimination* (ATE),[4] *hidden subsumption elimination* (HSE),[4] *asymmetric subsumption elimination* (ASE)[4] and so on, which can eliminate more clauses and improve the efficiency of SAT solvers significantly. In 2012, Heule et al.[5] combined resolution with clause elimination methods HTE, ATE, HSE, ASE and so on and developed novel clause elimination methods RHTE, RATE, RHSE, RASE and so on. No exception, clauses deleted by all the clause elimination methods are redundant clauses in corresponding CNF formulas, which means satisfiability or unsatisfiability of those formulas will not be changed without those clauses. Research on redundancy property of clauses is crucial, which is the base of clause elimination methods and novel clause elimination methods can be developed according to those found redundancy properties. In 2016, Kiesl et al.[6] came up with the conception of super-blocked clause which is redundant clause, which could be seen the extension of blocked clause. Whether a clause C is a super-blocked clause is determined by the literal set of C, while the estimation of a blocked clause C' is up to one literal of C'. Ning et al.[7] created the conception of set-blocked clauses and extended set-blocked clauses in first-order logic without equality and with equality, which can be seen as mirgation and improvement of super-blocked clause in propositional logic.[6] Kiesl et al.[8] proposed a unifying principle implication modulo resolution for clause elimination in first-order logic CNF formulas without equality in 2017. After that, Ning et al.[9] developed a variant of implication modulo resolution (IMR) which can be lowered into proposition logic, developing several new clause elimination methods and yielding their soundness proofs.

A novel principle of clause elimination, called as multi-literal implication modulo resolution (MIMR), is introduced in this paper, which learn from the view of super-blocked clause and implication modulo resolution to generate a more extensive principle of clause elimination.

The main contribution of this paper are as follows: (1) Develop the principle of multi-literal implication modulo resolution in propositional logic (2) Prove the soundness of multi-literal implication modulo resolution. (3) Analyze and compare the effectiveness of multi-literal implication modulo resolution with that of implication modulo resolution.

2. Preliminaries

In this section, some symbols, terms and definitions used in the paper are introduced.[4,5]

A *clause* is a disjunction of literals and a CNF *formula* is a conjunction of clauses. A *literal* l is a variable x or the negation of variable $\neg x$. A truth assignment is a function τ that maps literals to $\{0,1\}$ under the assumption $\tau(x) = v$ if and only if $\tau(\neg x) = 1 - v$. A clause C is satisfied by τ if $\tau(l) = 1$ for some literal $l \in C$. If the assignment τ satisfies a formula F, it means it satisfies every clause in F, τ is called as a model of F. If a formula F implies a clause C, every model of F is also a model of C, that is, $F \models C$. A formula F is called satisfiable if there exists an assignment α satisfies F, while it is called unsatisfiable if there exists no assignment satisfies F. A clause is a *tautology* if it contains both x and $\neg x$ for some variable. A clause C_1 *subsumes* clause C_2 if $C_1 \subseteq C_2$. A CNF formula F is *equisatisfiable* with the other formula F', if they are satisfiable or unsatisfiable consistently. A clause is *redundant* in a CNF formula F, if F and $F\backslash\{C\}$ are equisatisfiable. The definitions of implication modulo resolution and effectiveness are shown as below.[4,9]

Definition 2.1. A clause C is *implied modulo resolution* upon the literal $l \in C$ by the formula F, if all the resolvents of C with any clause D containing the literal $\neg l$ in $F\backslash\{C\}$ are implied by $F\backslash\{C\}$.[9]

Definition 2.2. Assumed that two clause elimination procedures CE_1 and CE_2, $CE_1(F)$ and $CE_2(F)$ is the new gotten equisatisfiable CNF formulas for any CNF formula F, separatively after F handled by CE_1 and CE_2. CE_1 is *at least as effective as* CE_2, if $CE_1(F) \subseteq CE_2(F)$. CE_1 is *more effective* than CE_2, if CE_1 is at least as effective as CE_2 and there exists at least one formula F', $CE_1(F') \subset CE_2(F')$.[4]

3. Multi-literal Implication Modulo Resolution

Multi-literal implication modulo resolution is an extension of implication modulo resolution in propositional logic, which breaks through the limitation of one-literal base. In this section, the definition of multi-literal implication modulo resolution is introduced firstly. Subsequently, its soundness proof is given, to illuminate that any clause that satisfies the conditions of multi-literal implication modulo resolution is redundant in its corresponding formula. Finally the comparison of its effectiveness with implication modulo resolution's effectiveness is written.

3.1. *Definition and soundness proof of multi-literal implication modulo resolution*

First of all, it is given that the definition of $\hat{S}^{l_i}$ and S^{l_i} of clause C and clause D before the definition of multi-literal implication modulo resolution, in which, S is a literal set of C , l_i is a literal in the set S, $\neg l_i$ is a literal of D.

Definition 3.1. Consider that the clause $C = l_1 \vee l_2 \vee \cdots \vee l_n \vee C'$ ($S = \{l_1, l_2, \ldots, l_n\}(n \geq 1)$) and the clause $D = \neg l_{i_0} \vee D'(1 \leq i_0 \leq n)$, it is claimed that $\bar{S} \vee D'$ is the $S^{\hat{l}_{i_0}}$-resolvent of C and D, as well as, it is claimed that $C' \vee (D' \backslash (\bar{S} \backslash \{\neg l_{i_0}\}))$ is the $S^{l_{i_0}}$-resolvent of C and D, with $S = \{l_1, l_2, \ldots, l_n\}$ and $\bar{S} = \{\neg l_1, \neg l_2, \ldots, \neg l_n\}$.

In Definition 3.1, C' and D' represent empty clauses or disjunction of literals. Besides, $D' \backslash (\bar{S} \backslash \{\neg l_{i_0}\}$ is a new clause in which all the literal are from D' but not from $\bar{S} \backslash \{\neg l_{i_0}\}$. An example is written below to make Definition 3.1 more understandable.

Example 3.1. Given two clauses $C = a \vee b \vee c \vee d$ and $D = \neg a \vee \neg c \vee d \vee e$, a literal set in clause C is chosen as $S = \{a, c, d\}$, then the $\hat{S}^a$-resolvent of C and D is $\neg a \vee \neg c \vee \neg d \vee d \vee e$, while the S^a-resolvent of C and D is $b \vee d \vee e$.

From the example, it can be seen that the $\hat{S}^a$-resolvent and S^a-resolvent of C and D are closely related to the choice of S and a in C. Supposed that the literal set S in C is chosen as $S' = \{a, b\}$, then the $S'^{\hat{a}}$-resolvent and S'^a are $\neg a \vee \neg b \vee \neg c \vee d \vee e$ and $c \vee d \vee \neg c \vee d \vee e$ separately, which are quite diverse from $\hat{S}^a$-resolvent and S^a-resolvent of C and D.

Based on the definition of $S^{\hat{l}_i}$ and S^{l_i}, following is given the definition of multi-literal implication modulo resolution in propositional logic.

Definition 3.2. Supposed a clause C based on a literal set $S = \{l_1, l_2, \ldots, l_n\}(n \geq 1, S \subseteq C)$ in a CNF formula F, it is called that the clause C is multi-literal implied modulo resolution (MIMR) upon $S = \{l_1, l_2, \ldots, l_n\}$ by F, if the condition below is satisfied:

- the $S^{\hat{l}_i}$-resolvent of C and D is a tautology or the S^{l_i}-resolvent is implied by $F \backslash \{C\}$, for any clause D containing the literal $\neg l_i (1 \leq i \leq n)$ in the CNF formula $F \backslash \{C\}$.

For Definition 3.2, it should be emphasized that all the $S^{\hat{l}_j}$-resolvent and the S^{l_j}-resolvent should be gotten, based on l_j from $j = 1$ to $j = n$. A example is as below.

Example 3.2. Consider the clause $C = a \vee b \vee c \vee d$ and the formula $F = \{a \vee b \vee c \vee d, \neg a \vee b \vee \neg e, \neg b \vee a \vee \neg d, \neg b \vee e \vee d, e \vee d, \neg e \vee \neg c, \neg d \vee a \vee e\}$. If the literal set in C is chosen as $S = \{a, b\}$:

(1) based on a, the clause C can only be resolved with the clause $\neg a \vee b \vee \neg e$ in formula F, and the $\hat{S}^a$-resolvent of C and $\neg a \vee b \vee \neg e$ upon S is $\neg a \vee \neg b \vee b \vee \neg e$, which is a tautology.

(2) based on b, the clause C can only be resolved with the clauses $\neg b \vee a \vee \neg d$ and $\neg b \vee e \vee c$. The $\hat{S}^b$-resolvent of C and $\neg b \vee a \vee \neg d$ is $\neg a \vee \neg b \vee a \vee \neg d$, which is a tautology. While the S^b-resolvent of C and $\neg b \vee e \vee c$ is $c \vee d \vee e \vee c$, which is subsumed by the clause $e \vee d$ in formula $F\backslash\{C\}$. It can be inferred that $c \vee d \vee e \vee c$ is implied by $e \vee d$, which means $c \vee d \vee e \vee c$ is implied by $F\backslash\{C\}$.

According to Definition 3.2, it is known that the clause C is multi-literal implied modulo resolution upon S by F. From the example, the literal a and the literal b, both of them, should be considered. If there exists no literal set in C satisfying the condition of Definition 3.2, then C is not a MIMR clause.

Supposed that a clause C is multi-literal implied modulo resolution in a formula F, it is redundant in the formula F. Subsequently, the soundness proof of MIMR clause will be given. Before that, a lemma is introduced below.

Lemma 3.1. *In a formula F, a clause C is a MIMR clause upon a literal set S ($S = \{l_1, l_2, \ldots, l_n\}$). If an assignment α satisfies $F\backslash\{C\}$ but falsies C, then the new assignment α' is obtained by flipping the truth values of literals in $S = \{l_1, l_2, \ldots, l_n\}$ assigned by α, satisfies C, as well as satisfies $F\backslash\{C\}$.*

Proof. Assumed that the new assignment α' obtained by flipping the truth values of all the literals in the literal set S ($S = \{l_1, l_2, \ldots, l_n\}$) from α, falsies the clause D in the formula $F\backslash\{C\}$, then there is at least one literal $\neg l_k$ ($\neg l_k \in \bar{S} = \{\neg l_1, \neg l_2, \ldots, \neg l_n\}$) in D. Without loss of generality, assume that clause D contains the literal $\neg l_1$ (if D contains several literals in $\bar{S}$, the proof is similar). Since C is multi-literal implied modulo resolution upon S by F, it has that the $\hat{S}^{l_1}$-resolvent of C and D is a tautology or the S^{l_1}-resolvent $(C\backslash\{l_1, l_2, \ldots, l_n\}) \vee (D\backslash\{\neg l_2, \ldots, \neg l_n\})$ is implied by $F\backslash\{C\}$. According to the condition, it is discussed as below:

(1) If the $\hat{S}^{l_1}$-resolvent $\bar{S} \vee (D\backslash\{\neg l_1\})$ of C and D is a tautology and as $\bar{S} \vee (D\backslash\{\neg l_1\})$ is a tautology, the assignment α' satisfies $\bar{S} \vee (D\backslash\{\neg l_1\})$. Besides, the assignment α' is generated by flipping the truth values of all the literals in $S = \{l_1, l_2, \ldots, l_n\}$ assigned by α from 0 to 1,

therefore α' falsies all the literals in $\bar{S}$ and it can be concluded that α' satisfies $D\backslash\{\neg l_1\}$. Hence it can be inferred that α' satisfies D, which is contradictory with the conjecture.

(2) If the S^{l_1}-resolvent $(C\backslash\{l_1, l_2, \ldots, l_n\}) \vee (D\backslash\{\neg l_2, \ldots, \neg l_n\})$ of C and D is implied by $F\backslash\{C\}$, α satisfies $(C\backslash\{l_1, l_2, \ldots, l_n\}) \vee (D\backslash\{\neg l_1, \neg l_2, \ldots, \neg l_n\})$ since α satisfies $F\backslash\{C\}$. Moreover, α falsies $C\backslash\{l_1, l_2, \ldots, l_n\}$, as a result, α satisfies $D\backslash\{\neg l_2, \ldots, \neg l_n\}$. Since α' is given by flipping the truth values of all the literals in S assigned by α, α' also satisfies $D\backslash\{\neg l_2, \ldots, \neg l_n\}$. It can be inferred further that α' satisfies D, contradictory with the conjecture.

In general, by flipping the truth value of all the literals in S assigned by α, the obtained assignment α' can not only satisfies C but also satisfies $F\backslash\{C\}$, therefore the lemma is true. □

According to the lemma, the soundness of MIMR clauses can be inferred. The theorem is given as following.

Theorem 3.1. *In a formula F, if a clause C is a MIMR clause upon a literal set S ($S = \{l_1, l_2, \ldots, l_n\} \subseteq C$) by F, C is redundant in F.*

Proof. It can be divided into two conditions to discuss:

(1) When the clause set $F\backslash\{C\}$ is unsatisfiable, then F is also unsatisfiable. Hence C is redundant in F.

(2) When $F\backslash\{C\}$ is satisfiable, then there exists an assignment β satisfying $F\backslash\{C\}$. Further more, a new assignment β' obtained by flipping the truth value of all the literals in S given by β, not only satisfies $F\backslash\{C\}$, but also satisfies C. Therefore β' satisfies F, which means F is satisfiable, as a result, C can be inferred that it is redundant in F.

In summary, if a clause is MIMR upon S ($S = \{l_1, l_2, \ldots, l_n\} \subseteq C$) by F, it being added or it being removed does not change the satisfiability or unsatisfiability of F. Hence it can be concluded that it is redundant in F. □

3.2. *Effectiveness comparison with implication modulo resolution*

MIMR can be considered as the extension of IMR. While IMR clause C is determined based on one literal in C, MIMR clause C' is determined based on one literal set in C'. Therefore, the effectiveness of multi-literal implication modulo resolution is higher than implication modulo resolution.

Proposition 3.1. *The principle MIMR in propositional logic is more effective than the principle IMR in propositional logic.*

Proof. Firstly, it should be proved that if a clause C is IMR based on literal $l(l \in C)$ in a formula F, then it is also MIMR based on the literal set $S(S = \{l\})$. Assumed that clause D is a clause in $F \backslash \{C\}$ with the literal $\neg l$, then l-resolvent of C and D is $(C \backslash \{l\}) \cup (D \backslash \{\neg l\})$. According to the definition of IMR, $(C \backslash \{l\}) \cup (D \backslash \{\neg l\})$ is implied by $F \backslash \{C\}$. Besides, the $\{l\}^l$-resolvent of C and D is

$$(C \backslash \{l\}) \vee ((D \backslash \{\neg l\}) \backslash (\bar{S} \backslash \{\neg l\})) = (C \backslash \{l\}) \vee (D \backslash \{\neg l\}),$$

it can be seen that the $\{l\}^l$-resolvent is the same as the l-resolvent. Therefore the $\{l\}^l$-resolvent of C and D is also implied by $F \backslash \{C\}$. This situation can be extended to all the $\{l\}^l$-resolvents of C and any clause containing the literal $\neg l$, then it can be inferred that C is MIMR upon $S = \{l\}$ by F according to the definition of MIMR. On the contrary, if a clause C' is MIMR upon a literal set $S'(S' = \{l_1, l_2, \ldots, l_n\}(n > 1))$by a formula F', the clause C' may not be IMR. For example, in Example 3.2, the clause C is not IMR no matter based on any literal in C while it is MIMR based on the literal set $S = \{a, b\}$. Hence, MIMR is more effective than IMR. $\square$

From the proposition, it can be seen that IMR is a particular case of MIMR. Clause elimination according to the principle of MIMR can eliminate more redundant clauses than or the same redundant clauses as clause elimination according to the principle IMR.

4. Conclusion

In this paper, we generalized IMR in propositional logic further and got a new redundancy property known as MIMR, which breaked through the limination of one-literal base for IMR. And also, the soundness proof of MIMR is given, illuminating the removal or deletion of MIMR clauses in a CNF formula has no influence the satisfiability or unsatisfiability of the original CNF formula. Finally, the effectiveness of MIMR and IMR was compared, getting the conclusion that MIMR is more effective than IMR.

Theoretical work is mainly focused on in this paper. In the future, new clause elimination methods under the principle of MIMR will be considered to develop and corresponding algorithms of clause elimination will be designed, expecting to become the preprocessing techniques of SAT solvers and improve the efficiency of problem solving.

Acknowledgments

This work is supported by the Research Start-up Fund for introducing talents of Southwest Minzu University, China (No. RQD2021089), the Fundamental Research Funds for the Central Universities of Southwest Minzu University, China (No. 2020NQN40), the National Natural Science Foundation of China (Grant No. 62106206) and by the National Natural Science Foundation of China under Grant No. 61902326.

References

1. M. Davis, G. Logemann and D. W. Loveland, A machine program for theorem-proving, *Communications of the ACM* **5**, 394 (1962).
2. G. Gottlob and A. Leitsch, On the efficiency of subsumption algorithms, *Journal of the ACM* **32**, 280 (1985).
3. M. Javisalo, A. BIiere and M. Heule, Blocked clause elimination, *16th International Conference on Tools and Algorithms for the Construction and Analysis of Systems* **6015**, 129 (2010).
4. M. Heule, M. Javisalo and A. Biere, Clause elimination procedures for cnf formulas, *Proceedings of the 17th International Conference on Logic for Programming, Artificial Intelligence, and Reasoning* **6397**, 357 (2010).
5. M.Javisalo, M.Heule and A. Biere, Inprocessing rules, *The 6th International Joint Conference on Automated Reasoning* **6364**, 355 (2012).
6. B.Kiesl, M. Seidl, H. Tompits and A. Biere, Super-blocked clauses, *Proc. of the 8th Int. Joint Conference on Automated Reasoning* **970**, 45 (2016).
7. X. Ning, Y. Xu, G. Wu and H. Fu, set-blocked clause and extended set-blocked clause in first-order logic, *Symmetry* **10**, p. 553 (2016).
8. B. Kiesl and M. Suda, A unifying principle for clause elimination in first-order logic, *Conference on Automated Deduction,* **10395**, 274 (2017).
9. X. Ning, Y. Xu and Z. Chen, Mingti luoji kemanzuxing wenti qiujieqi de xinxing yuchuli ziju xiaoqu fangfa [novel preprocessing clause elimination methods for sat solvers], *Jisuanji jicheng zhizao xitong* **26**, 2133 (2020).

Component preserving and adaptive Laplacian Eigenmaps for data reconstruction and dimensionality reduction

Hanlin Zhang, Yu Ding, Hua Meng and Shuxia Ma*

School of Mathematics, Southwest Jiaotong University
Chengdu, Sichuan 611756, China
*masuxia@swjtu.edu.cn (Corresponding author)

Zhiguo Long

School of Computing, Southwest Jiaotong University
Chengdu, Sichuan 611756, China

Laplacian Eigenmaps (LE) is a widely used dimensionality reduction and data reconstruction method. When the data has multiple connected components, the LE method has two obvious deficiencies. First, it might reconstruct each component as a single point, resulting in loss of information within the component. Second, it only focuses on local features but ignores the location information between components, which might cause the reconstructed components to overlap or to completely change their relative positions. To solve these two problems, this paper first modifies the optimization objective of the LE method, proposes to describe the relative position between different components of data by using the similarity between high-density core points, and solves optimization problem by using gradient descent method to avoid the over-compression of data points in the same connected component. A series of experiments on synthetic data and real-world data verify the effectiveness of the proposed method.

Keywords: Dimensionality reduction; cluster analysis; Laplacian Eigenmaps; spectral methods.

1. Introduction

Dimensionality reduction and reconstruction of data are important to research in data mining.[1] This kind of methods can avoid the curse of dimensionality and improve the accuracy of classification and clustering algorithms. It can also reconstruct data with manifold or graph structure in low-dimensional Euclidean space for data visualization.

Data reconstruction methods represent another direction of dimensionality reduction, including Laplacian Eigenmaps (LE),[2] Locally Linear Embedding (LLE),[3] Isometric Mapping (Isomap),[4] and their variants are also

widely used in manifold learning.[5] LE is an outstanding representative of
the data reconstruction methods, which has been widely used[6] and has
many variants, e.g., LPP,[7] SLE,[8] and SSLE.[9] These methods attempt to
maintain the local similarity between sample points during the reconstruction process.

Although various improvements have been made in the literature[10] to
address different shortcomings of LE and its variants, few have considered
the performance of LE on multi-component data.

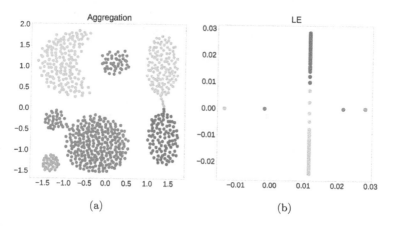

Fig. 1.   Dataset with multiple connected components and LE reconstruction results.

As shown in Fig. 1, (a) is the original multi-component data and (b) is
the data after LE dimensionality reduction. In this figure, the data of reconstructed multi-component data are often compressed into a single point and
the relative position between components is destroyed. The main reason
is that for multi-component data, the Laplacian matrix of LE method will
have multiple zero eigenvalues, and zero eigenvalues will make the projection result of the same component be the same point in the new subspace.
Moreover, LE only cares about local similarities of nearest neighbors, which
might not include information about components, because components are
relatively far away from each other. The latter problem exists not only in
the original LE but also in many of its variants. Therefore, in this paper,
we focus on the above two problems of LE and model the overall structure
of the data by finding the core points of the data, to maintain the structure
within the connected components of the dataset and the relative positions
between the components.

The rest of the paper is organized as follows: Section 2 proposes an improved model; Section 3 evaluates the performance of the new method on synthetic and real-world datasets; Section 4 concludes the paper.

2. The CPALE Algorithm

Suppose the dataset contains n samples and each sample has m features and is represented as a matrix $X_{m \times n} = (x_1, x_2, \ldots, x_n)$, where each $x_i \in R^m$ is an m-dimensional column vector. To characterize the component structure of the data, inspired by the Density Peaks Clustering (DPC[11]) method, this paper introduces the concept of core points, which, roughly speaking, are the local density peak points.

2.1. *Density and core points*

Let r be the maximum distance between any two points in the data.

Definition 2.1. For any $x_i \in X$, and a given number of nearest neighbors k, define the density of the point as:

$$\rho_i = kr - \sum_{j=1}^{n} dist_{ij} \tag{1}$$

where $dist_{ij} = \begin{cases} \|x_i - x_j\|_2 & x_j \in N_k(x_i) \\ 0 & \text{otherwise} \end{cases}$.

Definition 2.2. For any $x_i \in X$, define its leader point $Lead(x_i)$ as follows.

- If $N_k(x_i)$ contains points with higher density than x_i, the point x_j with higher density than x_i and closest to x_i is selected from $N_k(x_i)$ and $Lead(x_i) = x_j$ is defined.
- If the density of x_i is higher than the density of the other points in $N_k(x_i)$, then x_i is said to be a *core point*, and $Lead(x_i) = \{x_i\}$ is defined.

We denote by $Core(X)$ all the core points of X. By the definition, one can identify a core point simply by checking if a point has higher density than its neighbors. For any x_i, by using the $Lead$ operator repeatedly, x_i will be moved to a unique *core point*, which is called the *core leader* of x_i and is denoted as $core(x_i)$.

2.2. Construct the similarity matrix

2.2.1. Similarity within a component

Similar to the LE method, the similarity matrix W^{TT} of points and neighboring points is constructed.

$$W_{ij}^{TT} = \begin{cases} \exp\left(-\dfrac{\|x_i - x_j\|_2^2}{\sigma_1^2}\right) & x_j \in N_k(x_i) \vee x_i \in N_k(x_j) \\ 0 & \text{otherwise} \end{cases} \tag{2}$$

where $\sigma_1 \in R$.

The similarity matrix W^{TC} between the sample point to the core point it belongs to is constructed to bring the sample point closer to the core point it belongs to, and W^{TC} is defined as follows.

$$W_{ij}^{TC} = \begin{cases} \exp\left(-\dfrac{\|x_i - x_j\|_2^2}{\sigma_1^2}\right) & x_j = core_i \\ 0 & \text{otherwise} \end{cases} \tag{3}$$

The local and intra-component similarity matrices are obtained by weighted merging W^{TT} with W^{TC}.

$$W^{component} = W^{TT} + \alpha * W^{TC} \tag{4}$$

where $\alpha \in R$ is a hyperparameter.

2.2.2. Similarity between core points

We want core points to maintain relative positions in data reconstruction, so we need to define the similarity matrix W^{CC_1} between core points:

$$W_{ij}^{CC_1} = \begin{cases} \exp\left(-\dfrac{\|x_i - x_j\|_2^2}{\sigma_2^2}\right) & x_i, x_j \in Core \wedge x_i \neq x_j \\ 0 & \text{otherwise} \end{cases} \tag{5}$$

where $\sigma_2 \in R$ is a hyperparameter.

It is noted that the points in the same connected component should be more similar, so we introduce the graph distance between core points and according to Floyd-Warshall algorithm,[12,13] use the adjacency matrix $dist$ to calculate the shortest path distance between two points on the adjacency graph, namely the geodesic distance, denoted as $dist\_G_{ij}$.

$$W_{ij}^{CC_2} = \begin{cases} \exp(-dist\_G_{ij}{}^2) & x_i, x_j \in Core \wedge x_i \neq x_j \\ 0 & \text{otherwise} \end{cases} \tag{6}$$

Combining W^{CC_1} and W^{CC_2}, we get the matrix of position relations between core points:

$$W^{core} = W^{CC_1} + \beta * W^{CC_2} \tag{7}$$

where $\beta \in R$ is a hyperparameter.

2.3. Optimization of the objective function

We hope that after reconstruction, similar points are still similar, and the distance between common points and core points is as close as possible. We also want the reconstructed data to maintain the mutual position of the core points, i.e., the close core points are also relatively close after reconstructing. In summary, we need to optimize the following objectives.

$$\arg\min_{Y} tr(Y^T L_b Y) + tr(Y^T L_c Y) \text{ s.t. } Y^T D^{core} Y = I \tag{8}$$

where $Y = (Y_{ij})_{n \times d}$ is the result after data reconstruction; I is a unit matrix; D^{core} is the diagonal matrix with diagonal element values: $D_{ii}^{core} = \sum_{j=1}^n W_{ij}^{CC_1}$. The constraint is added to remove the effect of scaling on the model, borrowing from the LE approach.

In order to solve model (8) and prevent the data from being over-compressed, the gradient descent method is used in this paper for solving the model.

3. Experimental Analysis

To illustrate the effectiveness of the CPALE method, experiments are conducted on the synthetic datasets with multi-connected component structures and real-world datasets, respectively, and the comparison algorithms involved are: LE, LLE, Isomap and LPP, where LLE and Isomap are from scikit-learn library and the default parameters are used. For the sake of fairness, the parameters k involved in the experimental part of this paper are fixed as 10. CPALE algorithm parameters are set as follows: $\sigma_1 = \sigma_2 = \max(dist) \times 20\%$, $\epsilon = 1 \times 10^{-7}$.

The results on the synthetic dataset Aggregation is shown in Fig. 2. We can find that, as the number of iterations increases, the same-component data become more and more compact and the relative positions between different core points can be well maintained. Moreover, after a certain number of iterations, the data can maintain as much intra-cluster similarity structure as possible, while keeping the relative position relationship between clusters.

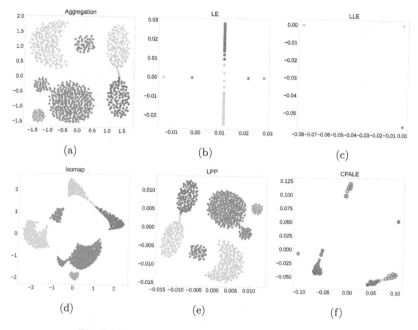

Fig. 2.   Data reconstruction results for Aggregation.

We also conducted experiments on ten real-world datasets, and the final results $Y_{n \times d}$ obtained from CPALE were subjected to traditional $Kmeans$ clustering to obtain the corresponding clustering metrics. Three metrics are used, i.e., NMI (Normalized Mutual Info citeNMI), ACC (Accuracy[14]) and ARI (Adjusted Rand Index[15]). The dimension of data reconstruction is set to the number (n_class) of classes of the dataset; the number of classes of Kmeans clustering is also set to n_class; however, the dimension of data reconstruction selected by CPALE is set to $n\_class+1$. The two parameters α and β of CPALE are both set as 5. The results are all averaged over 10 repeated tests.

Table 1 shows the three clustering metrics (NMI,[16] ACC,[14] ARI[15]) obtained from the experiments of CPALE+Kmeans with LE+Kmeans, LLE+Kmeans, LPP+Kmeans and Isomap+Kmeans algorithms on 10 real-world datasets, respectively. In the tables, N/A means that the output dimension of LLE method should not be larger than the input dimension during data reconstruction, otherwise it is invalid. Bold data is the best result. From the NMI metrics in Table 1, we can see that the CPALE+Kmeans method performs better on most of the datasets, and CPALE can gener-

Table 1. Comparison of NMI/ACC/ARI on the ten real-world datasets.

	LE+Kmeans	LLE+Kmeans	LPP+Kmeans	Isomap+Kmeans	CPALE+Kmeans
abta	7.66/35.78/6.44	7.78/32.86/4.92	8.17/37.48/5.01	9.54/35.93/6.85	**11.01/40.92/8.40**
alphabet	5.75/**49.30**/6.53	1.33/46.93/-0.28	0.56/47.17/0.13	5.34/41.78/2.31	**6.79**/47.29/**7.51**
breastEW	63.47/91.92/69.91	14.74/65.13/8.47	4.85/66.43/6.52	61.99/**92.27/71.16**	**64.73**/91.97/70.08
isolet2	2.06/58.14/2.59	1.88/57.43/2.21	0.13/50.06/0.00	1.85/57.76/2.35	**2.44/58.87/3.09**
mfeat-mor	62.67/58.32/46.41	NA/NA/NA	40.83/45.25/27.88	68.40/64.13/54.86	**68.85/64.56/54.98**
psis	28.03/53.13/21.67	44.81/64.06/34.31	20.17/50.00/3.15	52.71/**71.88**/45.70	**56.27/71.88/47.09**
segmentation	53.46/46.67/31.32	41.59/41.02/22.39	52.87/52.29/40.10	54.03/49.90/37.43	**60.79/62.97/50.69**
spliceEW	1.46/52.19/0.55	1.69/48.54/0.64	0.91/39.84/1.16	5.08/48.43/7.39	**6.02/55.65/8.99**
ver2	31.71/48.06/23.08	16.55/52.55/10.95	32.86/54.97/**27.08**	32.26/48.71/24.78	**36.05/55.00**/23.86
wdbc	**66.27/93.67/76.08**	23.66/76.63/26.16	38.95/82.00/39.46	63.86/92.97/73.61	64.00/ 93.32/74.87

ally improve by more than four or five percentage points compared to the traditional LE+Kmeans method, indicating that our improved method is effective.

4. Conclusion

In this paper, we propose the LE dimensionality reduction and reconstruction method for multi-component data based on data core points (CPALE), which solves the problem that the traditional LE method will overly "compress" the dataset with multiple connected components. It has achieved good results in both synthetic data visualization and real-world data clustering analysis. In the future, we would like to take more topological structures into consideration.

Acknowledgments

This work was supported by the National Key Research and Development Program of China (2019YFB1706104).

References

1. R. Houari, A. Bounceur, M.-T. Kechadi, A.-K. Tari and R. Euler, Dimensionality reduction in data mining: A copula approach, *Expert Systems with Applications* **64**, 247 (2016).

2. M. Belkin and P. Niyogi, Laplacian eigenmaps for dimensionality reduction and data representation, *Neural Computation* **15**, 1373 (2003).

3. S. T. Roweis and L. K. Saul, Nonlinear dimensionality reduction by locally linear embedding, *Science* **290**, 2323 (2000).

4. J. B. Tenenbaum, V. d. Silva and J. C. Langford, A global geometric framework for nonlinear dimensionality reduction, *Science* **290**, 2319 (2000).

5. D. Lunga, S. Prasad, M. M. Crawford and O. Ersoy, Manifold-learning-based feature extraction for classification of hyperspectral data: A review of advances in manifold learning, *IEEE Signal Processing Magazine* **31**, 55 (2013).

6. X. Ye, H. Li, A. Imakura and T. Sakurai, An oversampling framework for imbalanced classification based on laplacian eigenmaps, *Neurocomputing* **399**, 107 (2020).

7. X. He and P. Niyogi, Locality preserving projections, *Advances in Neural Information Processing Systems* **16** (2003).

8. Q. Jiang, M. Jia, J. Hu and F. Xu, Machinery fault diagnosis using supervised manifold learning, *Mechanical Systems and Signal Processing* **23**, 2301 (2009).

9. K. Kim and J. Lee, Sentiment visualization and classification via semi-supervised nonlinear dimensionality reduction, *Pattern Recognition* **47**, 758 (2014).

10. A. Jansen, G. Sell and V. Lyzinski, Scalable out-of-sample extension of graph embeddings using deep neural networks, *Pattern Recognition Letters* **94**, 1 (2017).

11. A. Rodriguez and A. Laio, Clustering by fast search and find of density peaks, *Science* **344**, 1492 (2014).

12. R. W. Floyd, Algorithm 97: shortest path, *Communications of the ACM* **5**, p. 345 (1962).

13. S. Warshall, A theorem on boolean matrices, *Journal of the ACM* **9**, 11 (1962).

14. Y. Yang, D. Xu, F. Nie, S. Yan and Y. Zhuang, Image clustering using local discriminant models and global integration, *IEEE Transactions on Image Processing* **19**, 2761 (2010).

15. D. Steinley, Properties of the Hubert-Arable Adjusted Rand Index, *Psychological Methods* **9**, 386 (2004).

16. W. Xu, X. Liu and Y. Gong, Document clustering based on non-negative matrix factorization, in *Annual International ACM SIGIR Conference on Research and Development in Information Retrieval*, (ACM, 2003).

650

Some discussions of Yager preference aggregation with uncertainty[*]

LeSheng Jin

Business School, Nanjing Normal University
Nanjing, China
jls1980@163.com

Ronald R. Yager

Machine Intelligence Institute, Iona College
New Rochelle, NY 10801, USA
yager@panix.com

Zhen-Song Chen[†]

Department of Engineering Management, School of Civil Engineering
Wuhan University, Wuhan 430072, China
zschen@whu.edu.cn

Luis Martínez

Department of Computer Science, University of Jaén
23071 Jaén, Spain
martin@ujaen.es

Yager-preference-involved decision making and aggregation methods proved to be quite flexible and are widely applied in numerous areas. This work discusses the preference involved evaluation in some detailed scenarios of large-scale group decision making. In the proposed evaluation frame, we separately consider the evaluation information provided by consultants and the preference information offered by respondents. The real value and probability information for the frame are both analyzed.

Keywords: Uncertain decision making; aggregation operators; ordered weighted averaging operators; preference involved decision making.

1. Introduction

Aggregation theory and information fusion [1, 2] are with significance in almost all of the decision making problems, including preference and uncertain decision

[*]This work was supported by the National Natural Science Foundation of China (Grant No. 71801175).
[†]Corresponding author.

making. Most of mean type aggregation operators require some pre-determined weights vectors (or weights functions). Two types of weights vectors are usually applied: one corresponding to relative importance of evaluation criteria, and the other corresponding to bi-polar preferences (e.g., optimism-pessimism preference).

To determine the relative importance of a given set of evaluation criteria $\{C_i\}_{i=1}^n$ or a collection of experts $\{E_i\}_{i=1}^n$, decision makers can use some methods like subjective determination method and the analytic hierarchy process (AHP) method [3]. To determine the weight vectors with a given bi-polar preferences, a very powerful, flexible and convenient method is to use Yager's preference aggregation and related weights allocation methods such as by the ordered weighted averaging (OWA) weight vectors [4] and regular increasing monotone (RIM) quantifiers [5].

In large scale group decision making problems, the total number of included experts n is usual quite large, and the involved computation complexity usually make some weights allocation methods like subjective method and AHP method impractical. Nevertheless, due to the particular flexibility and special properties, Yager's preference aggregation and related weights allocation methods can still work well. The reasons majorly lie in that many parameterized of families of OWA weight vectors can be automatically generated for all the dimensions, and that the method for generating discrete weight vectors from RIM quantifiers also has no bearing to the dimensions.

Therefore, under Yager's preference decision theories [6], this work will discuss some detailed preference involved decision making problems in problems with uncertainty, which may provide more decision choices and methodologies for related practitioners and theorists. The remainder of this work is organized as follows. Section 2 reviews ordered weighted averaging operators and some related weights allocation methods. In Section 3 we discuss a preference involved decision scheme for large scale group decision making. Section 4 presents a numerical example of preference aggregation with probability forms. Section 5 concludes and remarks this work.

2. Ordered Weighted Averaging Operators and Some Weights Allocation

Aggregation operators [1, 2] are powerful and systematical tools in numerous decision making and evaluation problems. Without loss of generality, an aggregation operator (of dimension n) is a function $A:[0,1]^n \to [0,1]$ such that

(i) $A(0,...,0) = 0$ and $A(1,...,1) = 1$; and

(ii) $A(\mathbf{x}) \leq A(\mathbf{y})$ whenever $x_i \leq y_i$ for all $i \in \{1,...,n\}$.

A weighted arithmetic mean (WAM) with weight vector $\mathbf{w} = (w_i)_{i=1}^{n} \in [0,1]^n$ ($w_i \geq 0$) is an aggregation operator $WA_{\mathbf{w}} : [0,1]^n \to [0,1]$ such that

$$WA_{\mathbf{w}}(\mathbf{x}) = \sum_{i=1}^{n} w_i x_i \tag{1}$$

An OWA operator with weight vector $\mathbf{w} = (w_i)_{i=1}^{n}$ is also an aggregation operator $OWA_{\mathbf{w}} : [0,1]^n \to [0,1]$ such that

$$OWA_{\mathbf{w}}(\mathbf{x}) = \sum_{i=1}^{n} w_i x_{\sigma(i)} \tag{2}$$

where $\sigma : \{1,...,n\} \to \{1,...,n\}$ is any suitable permutation satisfying $x_{\sigma(i)} \geq x_{\sigma(j)}$ whenever $i < j$.

The orness/andness degrees of OWA weight vectors reflect their respectively involved optimism and pessimism. Yager defined orness/andness of OWA weight vector $\mathbf{w}$ in what follows [4]:

$$orness(\mathbf{w}) = \sum_{i=1}^{n} \frac{n-i}{n-1} w_i \quad \text{(with } andness(\mathbf{w}) = 1 - orness(\mathbf{w})) \tag{3}$$

A RIM quantifier $Q : [0,1] \to [0,1]$ is a non-decreasing function with $Q(0) = 0$ and $Q(1) = 1$. In general, a larger quantifier can generate discrete OWA weight vectors with larger orness degrees, and vice versa.

Yager ingeniously proposed a method [5] to generate any OWA weight vector $\mathbf{w}$ from given RIM quantifier Q such that

$$w_i = Q(i/n) - Q\big((i-1)/n\big) \, (i = 1,...,n) \tag{4}$$

3. A Preference Involved Decision Scheme with Uncertainty in Group Decision Making

For a large number of decision makers who form the decision making body, we consider the decisional situation in which all the experts can be classified into two parts. The first one part usually includes more experts who in general are *respondents* and can only offer their respective quantifiable bipolar optimism-pessimism preference. The second one part includes fewer experts $\{E_i\}_{i=1}^{n}$ who in general are *consultants* and can provide more detailed evaluation information.

We consider two evaluation scenarios.

In the first scenario, consultants are requested to respectively evaluate a possible value for a certain object under evaluation. That is, a vector of real values $\mathbf{x} = (x_i)_{i=1}^{n} \in [0,1]^n$ should be obtained in which x_i is given by consultant E_i accordingly.

In the second scenario, we need to evaluate the probability distribution on a set of m different outcomes $\{\omega_j\}_{j=1}^m$. In addition, we suppose a linearly ordered set $(\{\omega_j\}_{j=1}^m, <)$ is formed such that $\omega_j < \omega_{j+1}$ for all $j \in \{1,...,m-1\}$. That is, n probability vectors $\mathbf{p}_i = (p_{ij})_{j=1}^m$ ($i \in \{1,...,n\}$) on $(\{\omega_j\}_{j=1}^m, <)$ should be obtained by each consultant in $\{E_i\}_{i=1}^n$, respectively, in ordered to be further aggregated into a resulting probability vector as the plausible prediction.

As for the role of respondents, they are assumed to be not willing or not able to provide detailed individual evaluation such as the preceding mentioned real value x_i and probability vector $\mathbf{p}_i$. Instead, each of the respondents $y \in [0,1]$ is only required to provide a numerical bipolar optimism-pessimism preference $\alpha_y \in [0,1]$ over the evaluations of the set of n consultants. For all the respondents, we order their optimism-pessimism preferences α_y from smallest to the highest in a non-decreasing order. Since the respondents are in large scale, then by approximation we can form a RIM quantifier $Q:[0,1] \to [0,1]$ (with $Q(0) \overset{\Delta}{=} 0$ and $Q(1) \overset{\Delta}{=} 1$) such that $Q(y)$ indicates that there exists some respondent whose preference $\alpha_y = Q(y)$. Hence, if more of the respondents are with more optimism, then we may obtain a larger RIM quantifier Q; and vice versa. Note that as an alternative reasonable understanding, we can also use a quantifier Q' that is further derived from the obtained Q and satisfies $Q'(z) = 1 - \inf\{y : \alpha_y \geq 1-z\}$ when $z \in (0,1)$. Then an OWA weight vector $\mathbf{w}$ can be derived from Q using Yager's method.

Next, we discuss the preference aggregation to the information provided by consultants ($\mathbf{x} = (x_i)_{i=1}^n$ and $\mathbf{p}_i = (p_{ij})_{j=1}^m$, respectively) with the derived OWA weight vector $\mathbf{w}$ from respondents.

The real value type aggregation involves a real vector $\mathbf{x} = (x_i)_{i=1}^n$ and OWA weight vector $\mathbf{w}$ and can be easily performed by using OWA operator $OWA_{\mathbf{w}}(\mathbf{x})$ by (2).

For the probability forms, we consider using the aggregation techniques discussed in [7]. For aggregating n probability vectors $\mathbf{p}_i = (p_{ij})_{j=1}^m$ ($i \in \{1,...,n\}$), we firstly transform each vector into a new non-decreasing cumulative vector $\mathbf{p}_i' = (p_{ij}')_{j=1}^m$ such that $p_{ij}' = \sum_{k=1}^j p_{ik}$ ($j = 1,...,m$). Then, for each $j = 1,...,m$, aggregating the vector $\mathbf{y}_j = (p_{ij}')_{i=1}^n$ using OWA aggregation $OWA_{\mathbf{w}}(\mathbf{y}_j)$. Next, with the obtained new cumulative vector $\mathbf{q}' = (q_j')_{j=1}^m = (OWA_{\mathbf{w}}(\mathbf{y}_j))_{j=1}^m$, transform it back into a new probability vector $\mathbf{q} = (q_j)_{j=1}^m$ (such that $q_j = q_j' - q_{j-1}'$ for $j = 1,...,m$ with $q_0' \overset{\Delta}{=} 0$) as the final resulting one to help make further decision making.

4. A Numerical Example of Preference Aggregation with Probability Forms

In what follows we consider the discussed method in uncertain decision-making environment. Suppose an important project involves making some predictions about the probability of the possible market share outcomes of a certain product, with outcome set $(\{\omega_j\}_{j=1}^4, <)$ such that

$\omega_1 =$ "low market share",

$\omega_2 =$ "medium market share",

$\omega_3 =$ "high market share",

and $\omega_4 =$ "dominant market share".

Assume the optimism-pessimism preferences from all the invited respondents approximately construct a RIM quantifier Q with $Q(y) = y^2$ (indicating a moderate pessimism atmosphere between those respondents). Suppose we also have three consultants who have made detailed predication with probability information of $(\{\omega_j\}_{j=1}^4, <)$ with $\mathbf{p}_1 = (0.2, 0.3, 0.4, 0.1)$, $\mathbf{p}_2 = (0.4, 0.3, 0.2, 0.1)$, and $\mathbf{p}_3 = (0.3, 0.5, 0.2, 0)$. Therefore, an OWA weight vector with dimension 3 should be derived using (4) with $\mathbf{w} = (w_i)_{i=1}^3 = (1/9, 1/3, 5/9) = (0.11, 0.33, 0.56)$.

Next, form the three corresponding cumulative vector $\mathbf{p}_1' = (0.2, 0.5, 0.9, 1)$, $\mathbf{p}_2' = (0.4, 0.7, 0.9, 1)$, and $\mathbf{p}_3' = (0.3, 0.8, 1, 1)$. Then, we accordingly obtain the four vectors $\mathbf{y}_1 = (0.2, 0.4, 0.3)$, $\mathbf{y}_2 = (0.5, 0.7, 0.8)$ and $\mathbf{y}_3 = (0.9, 0.9, 1)$ and $\mathbf{y}_4 = (1, 1, 1)$. Perform four times of OWA aggregation for $\mathbf{y}_j$ we obtain

$OWA_\mathbf{w}(\mathbf{y}_1) = 0.322$, $OWA_\mathbf{w}(\mathbf{y}_2) = 0.734$,

$OWA_\mathbf{w}(\mathbf{y}_3) = 0.956$, $OWA_\mathbf{w}(\mathbf{y}_4) = 1$.

Consequently, from the intermediately obtained accumulative vector $\mathbf{q}' = (q_j')_{j=1}^4 = (OWA_\mathbf{w}(\mathbf{y}_j))_{j=1}^4 = (0.322, 0.734, 0.956, 1)$ we finally obtain a probability vector $\mathbf{q} = (0.322, 0.412, 0.222, 0.044)$ as the plausible prediction, which can be used to help make further decision making, for example, by being multiplied by a vector of possible payoffs corresponding to outcomes. Note that the above simple example is only for illustration, and in practice the involved number n can be in any large scale.

5. Conclusions

In large scale group decision making problems, many weights allocation methods such as subjectivity weight allocation and AHP method are difficult to apply. However, the weights allocation methods based on Yager's preference aggregation still work well. This work discussed the preference involved evaluation in some detailed scenarios. We considered the large scale group decision making situation in which all involved experts can be classified into two large groups, consultants and respondents, who play different roles in the frame and offer data information and preference information, respectively. The detailed models of real value and probability information for the frame were also analyzed, and more models based on different data types [8-11] other than the two discussed types can be also developed in future studies.

References

1. M. Grabisch, J.L. Marichal, R. Mesiar, E. Pap, Aggregation Functions, Cambridge University Press (2009), Cambridge, ISBN:1107013429.
2. T. Calvo, R. Mesiar, R.R. Yager, Quantitative weights and aggregation, IEEE Trans. Fuzzy Syst. 12(1) (2004) 62–69.
3. T.L. Saaty, Axiomatic foundation of the analytic hierarchy process, Manage. Sci. 32(7) (1986) 841–855.
4. R.R. Yager, On ordered weighted averaging aggregation operators in multicriteria decision making, IEEE Trans. Syst. Man Cybern. 18(1) (1988) 183–190.
5. R.R. Yager, Quantifier guided aggregation using OWA operators, Int. J. Intell. Syst. 11 (1996) 49–73.
6. W. Xiong, H. Liu, An Axiomatic Foundation for Yager's Decision Theory, Int. J. Intell. Syst. 29 (2014) 365–387.
7. R. Mesiar, L. Sipeky, P. Gupta, L. Jin, Aggregation of OWA operators, IEEE Trans. Fuzzy Syst. 26 (1) (2018) 284–291.
8. G. Muhiuddin, D. Al-Kadi, M. Balamurugan, Anti-Intuitionistic Fuzzy Soft a-Ideals Applied to BCI-Algebras, Axioms, 9(3) (2020) 79. doi: 10.3390/axioms9030079
9. P. Tiwari, Generalized Entropy and Similarity Measure for Interval-Valued Intuitionistic Fuzzy Sets With Application in Decision Making. International Journal of Fuzzy System Applications (IJFSA), 10(1) (2021) 64–93. doi:10.4018/IJFSA.2021010104
10. M. Boczek, A. Hovana, O. Hutník, M. Kaluszka, New monotone measure-based integrals inspired by scientific impact problem, European Journal of Operational Research 290 (2021) 346–357.

Research on the restoration of costumes in the paintings of ladies in the Ming Dynasty

Xiaoning Li, Kaixuan Liu and Fei Gao

College of Apparel and Art Design, Xi'an Polytechnic University
Xi'an, 710048, China
1481378612@qq.com

Ancient painting is a precious cultural heritage. Unfortunately, these paintings may fade, darken and crack due to natural or human factors. Therefore, it is urgent to protect painting. In this paper, virtual fitting technology and reverse engineering technology were used to restore the three-dimensional virtual clothing in the paintings of ladies of the Ming Dynasty. 2D paintings were converted into 3D models, which creatively show the costumes in the paintings. Based on the structural characteristics of clothing, we used reverse engineering technology to obtain the two-dimensional patterns of the clothing top, and used the method of flat pattern-making to obtain the two-dimensional patterns of the clothing bottom. We completed the structural restoration and fabric restoration of the garment. Based on the research on color, pattern, and fabric physical properties, we have completed the fabric restoration of clothing. On this basis, the Analytic Hierarchy Process-fuzzy comprehensive evaluation model was used to analyze and evaluate the modeling effect. Research shows that it is feasible to develop the patterns of garments by combining reverse engineering technology and flat pattern-making technology. This method provides a new idea for the protection and development of paintings, and can be used for three-dimensional restoration and display of ancient clothing-type paintings.

Keywords: Ancient painting; virtual clothing; Ming Dynasty clothing; virtual fitting technology; reverse engineering technology.

1. Introduction

With the increasingly prominent problems of contemporary resources and ecological environment, human beings need to coordinate and integrate the relationship between science and technology, economy and natural resources. In the 1980s, the strategy of sustainable development was put forward to solve this problem. All industries actively respond to the strategy and adopt strategies such as saving resources, adjusting industrial structure and improving resource utilization.[1] The protection, development and display of traditional cultural relics often require a lot of energy, while virtual reality technology provides technical means for digital cultural relics, breaking the barriers of large space and high maintenance cost of traditional display, so as to save resources and spread culture.

Ancient painting is an important cultural heritage with artistic, historical and cultural values.[2] These cultural relics reflect the ancient people's way of life, economic situation, and aesthetic taste and so on. Unfortunately, over time, these paintings have been damaged to varying degrees due to natural or human factors. The protection of painting can only slow down its degradation, and cannot completely stop the process of degradation. The emergence of digital technology provides a new means for the protection and display of painting. It can transform cultural relics into renewable and shareable digital forms.[3,4] Kuzmichev V et al.[5] studied the clothes in the photos. They reconstructed three-dimensional copies of historical clothing with the help of virtual fitting technology.[6] This is the virtual model of clothing obtained by two-dimensional to three-dimensional design method in the virtual environment. However, this method requires high professional knowledge of fashion designers. Kaixuan Liu et al.[7] Proposed a new method of garment design from three-dimensional to two-dimensional to obtain garment patterns. This method is suitable for obtaining patterns of loose clothing and tight clothing. The reverse engineering technology from three-dimensional to two-dimensional flattening is less used in the display of cultural relics.

Tang Yin was a painter in the Ming Dynasty. His paintings are most representative of ladies' paintings. From the perspective of garment engineering, this study studies the three-dimensional restoration of women's clothing in the Ming Dynasty by using digital technology and reverse engineering technology. The three-dimensional display is not only conducive to the protection of painting and improve the interest of visitors, but also conducive to the dissemination of clothing culture.

2. Method

The pictures of ladies in the Ming Dynasty are important image materials for studying the costumes of the Ming Dynasty. Referring to the unearthed objects, we determined that the ladies in the picture are wearing *Shan* for their tops and horse-faced skirts for their bottoms. Based on the structural characteristics of Ming Dynasty clothing, we used reverse engineering technology to obtain the two-dimensional patterns of the clothing top, and used the method of flat pattern-making to obtain the two-dimensional patterns of the clothing bottom.

2.1. Analysis of lady figures

Tang Yin, a painter in the Ming Dynasty, is good at landscape and figure painting. Most of his figure paintings take historical stories as the content and contemporary figure images as the material. This study collected Tang Yin's pictures of ladies, namely *Chang'e Holding the Osmanthus*, as shown in Fig. 1.

Fig. 1. Lady Figure (Quoted from the book *High Definition Pictures of Tang Yin's Works*).

2.2. Drawing clothing from painting

The regular clothes of Han women in the Ming Dynasty can be divided into "tops" and "bottoms". Based on the study of Ming Dynasty historical materials and the existing physical materials of Ming Dynasty women's clothing, we inferred that the women in the painting wear a *Shan* on the top and a horse-face skirt on the bottom.

Shan is the most common type of women's regular clothes in the Ming Dynasty. The style features of *Shan* in Fig. 1 are cross collar, right lapel and short style. Referring to the data of unearthed clothing, we determined that the sleeve length of the restored costume is 208cm, the length of the garment is 58cm, the width of the sleeve is 33cm, the width of the cuff is 15cm, the width of the hem is 58cm, the width of the collar is 70cm, and the height of the slit is 16cm. The restored style of the *Shan* is shown in Fig. 2.

Fig. 2. Style pattern of *Shan*.

The horse-face skirt of the Ming Dynasty is usually composed of 7 pieces of cloth, with each 3.5 pieces forming a skirt. The two skirts are symmetrical in structure, and "horse faces" are set at both ends of the skirt. The width of "horse face" is generally 20 to 24cm. The style of horse face skirt is shown in Fig. 3. Referring to the data of unearthed clothes, we set the length of the skirt of the restored skirt as 86cm, the waist inlaid height as 11.5cm, the waist circumference as 115cm and the horse face width as 21cm.

Fig. 3. Style pattern of horse-face skirt.

The textile industry of the Ming Dynasty was very prosperous, and the quantity and quality of textiles exceeded that of the previous dynasty.[8] During this period, cotton was widely planted in the Central Plains and the Yangtze River Basin, so cotton cloth became the main fabric used by the people. As for the fabric color, most of the noblewomen in the Ming Dynasty wore full red robes with large sleeves. The ordinary women in this study can only wear pink, blue, purple, green and light colors.

Decorative patterns require the unity of beauty and auspicious content, which is the characteristic of Chinese clothing art. We divided the patterns in the pictures of ladies into three types: plant patterns, geometric patterns, and animal patterns.

2.3. Construction of 3D garment model

2.3.1. Construction of the initial 3D model of the Shan

The lady wears light-colored cross-collar *Shan* with animal patterns on the collar and cuffs of the *Shan*. The lower body wears a horse-faced skirt with geometric patterns on the skirt. Based on the structural characteristics of clothing, we used reverse engineering technology to obtain the two-dimensional patterns of *Shan*, and used the method of flat pattern-making to obtain the two-dimensional patterns of the horse-face skirt.

We extracted the contour lines of the style map as clothing patterns, and performed initial clothing modeling. To avoid inaccuracy, we stretched the surface of the garment to be flat while ensuring that the area of the garment triangle mesh is not changed.

2.3.2. 3D to 2D flattening of Shan

The structure of ancient Chinese traditional costumes has always followed the cross-shaped flat structure, with the length of the sleeves as the horizontal direction, the front and rear center lines as the vertical direction, and there is no dart. Following this principle, we draw structural curves on the smooth garment surface. These curves divided the garment into many small surfaces. The 3D surfaces were developed into 2D patterns using the geometric unfolding method.

2.3.3. The establishment of 3D model of the whole suit

We used reverse engineering to obtain the *Shan* patterns. The patterns of the horse-face skirt were obtained by the method of flat pattern-making. We simulated the entire suit and reduced the triangle mesh size to optimize the simulation.

The restoration of the fabric is another focus of the 3D model establishment. Based on the above analysis, the type of clothing fabric is set to cotton. Adjust the parameters of the fabric until the appearance of the fabric achieves the desired effect. The patterns of *Shan* are cranes. The patterns of the skirt are geometric patterns with a continuous pattern of squares. Finally, the 3D model of the entire suit is displayed.

2.4. Evaluation

There is currently no unified evaluation method for the effect of virtual modeling of ancient costumes. Analytic Hierarchy Process-fuzzy comprehensive evaluation method can solve problems that are difficult to quantify. Therefore, we used this method to evaluate the modeling effect of this ancient costume.

The first step is to determine the evaluation project indicators. According to the characteristics of ancient costumes and virtual modeling, the four project indicators of virtual modeling effect evaluation were determined as clothing style, clothing pattern, clothing color, and fabric material.

The second step is to determine the weight of the evaluation items. Each indicator has a different degree of influence on the modeling effect. So AHP is used to determine the weight of each indicator.

The third step is to construct an evaluation matrix. A questionnaire survey was used to investigate the effect of 3D modeling.

Finally, the evaluation results are calculated. According to the principle of maximum membership, the modeling effect is "very good".

It shows that it is feasible to obtain the three-dimensional model of ancient costumes by combining reverse engineering technology with flat pattern-making technology.

3. Result

Based on the structural characteristics of *Shan* and horse-faced skirt in Ming Dynasty costumes, this study adopted different methods for patterns development and 3D modeling. We used reverse engineering technology to obtain the two-dimensional patterns of *Shan*, and used the method of flat pattern-making to obtain the two-dimensional patterns of horse-face skirts. After finishing the structural modeling of the garments, the modeling of the fabrics was completed. Finally, the three-dimensional modeling and display of the three sets of clothing were carried out, as shown in Fig. 4.

Fig. 4. Display of 3D models.

4. Discussion

This study takes the pictures of ladies in the Ming Dynasty as the research object, and uses virtual fitting technology to virtual restore the ancient costumes in the pictures.

At present, scholars' research on the protection of ancient paintings mainly focuses on detection and restoration, and lacks three-dimensional exploration of paintings. The author tries to convert two-dimensional images into three-dimensional models using digital technology. Digital technology has changed the way of protection of traditional cultural relics, allowing people to enjoy human culture more widely. Digitization of cultural relics is an inevitable trend.[9] In order to innovatively protect and rationally develop these precious cultural relics, the author uses digital technology to perform three-dimensional virtual restoration of the costumes in the paintings. This method not only provides a new means for the display of paintings, which can be used for interactive display of clothing-type paintings, but also provides a foundation for the establishment of ancient clothing museums.

For the 3D modeling of clothing-type paintings, this research is only a preliminary exploration. The modeling of the model's head, the modeling of the makeup, the modeling of the hairstyle, and even the modeling of the environment all need to be considered. Only when these are completed can the effect of immersive viewing be achieved. 3D displays can increase visitor interaction and even foster public interest in art.[10]

5. Conclusion

This study used digital technology to transform two-dimensional images of ladies' paintings of the Ming Dynasty into three-dimensional models. Compared with traditional image restoration methods, this method achieved the purpose of saving resources and spreading culture. This method innovatively transformed precious traditional cultural relics into sustainable resources, and provided new ideas for the protection of traditional cultural relics. And we draw the following conclusions: 1) The uniforms of Han women in the Ming Dynasty can be divided into tops and bottoms. The woman in the painting wears a Shan on her top and a horse-face skirt on her lower body. 2) Digitizing cultural relics is an inevitable trend. The method of obtaining clothing samples using 3D fitting technology modeling and reverse engineering technology is suitable for the digitization of clothing type paintings.

Acknowledgments

The work was financially supported by Social Science Fund Project of Shaanxi Province, China (No. 2018K32), Natural Science Basic Research Program of Shaanxi Province, China (No. 2019JQ-848), Innovation ability support plan of Shaanxi Province-young science and Technology Star Project, China (No. 2020KJXX-083), and The Youth Innovation Team of Shaanxi Universities, China (No. 21JP048).

References

1. Da Giau, A., Foss, N. J., Furlan, A. and Vinelli, A, Sustainable development and dynamic capabilities in the fashion industry: A multi-case study, *Corporate Social Responsibility and Environmental Management* **27**, 1509 (2020).

2. Wang, J., Hu, D., Xing, H., Qi, Y. and Li, Y, Facile and Scalable Conservation of Chinese Ancient Paintings Using Water-Borne Fluoropolymer, *ACS omega* **5**, 33162 (2020).

3. Kioussi, A. et al, A computationally assisted cultural heritage conservation method, *Journal of Cultural Heritage* **48**, 119 (2021).

4. Fusco Girard, L. and Vecco, M, The "Intrinsic Value" of Cultural Heritage as Driver for Circular Human-Centered Adaptive Reuse, *Sustainability* **13**, 1 (2021).

5. Kuzmichev, V., Moskvin, A., Moskvina, M. and Pryor, J, Research on 3D reconstruction of late Victorian riding skirts, *International Journal of Clothing Science & Technology* **30**, 790 (2018).

6. Volino, P., Cordier, F. and Magnenat-Thalmann, N, From early virtual garment simulation to interactive fashion design, *Computer-aided design* **37**, 593 (2005).

7. Liu, K. et al, 3D interactive garment pattern-making technology, *Computer-Aided Design* **104**, 113 (2018).

8. Chen, K., Lu, D., Jin, Z., Su, M. and Jin, J, Song Brocade in the Ming and Qing Dynasties, *Clothing and Textiles Research Journal* **38**, 285 (2020).

9. Moskvin, A., Kuzmichev, V. and Moskvina, M, Digital replicas of historical skirts, *The Journal of The Textile Institute* **110**, 1810 (2019).

10. Raya, L., García-Rueda, J. J., López-Fernández, D. and Mayor, J, Virtual Reality Application for Fostering Interest in Art, *IEEE Computer Graphics and Applications* **41**, 106 (2021).

Author Index

CPSIA information can be obtained
at www.ICGtesting.com
Printed in the USA
JSHW040005110123
36110JS00001B/31

9 789811 269257